SIX-GUN LAW
Volume 3

Westerns of the 1950s:
The Classic Years

Wild Bill Elliot

SIX-GUN LAW
Volume 3

Westerns of the 1950s: The Classic Years

by Barry Atkinson

Midnight Marquee Press, Inc.
Baltimore, Maryland, USA

Copyright © 2021
Interior Layout: Gary J. Svehla
Cover Design: A. Susan Svehla
Copy Editors: Dan Leissner; Janet Atkinson

Without limiting the rights under copyright reserved above, no part of this publication may be reproduced, stored in or introduced into a retrieval system, or transmitted, in any form, or by any means (electronic, mechanical, photocopying, recording or otherwise), without the prior written permission of the copyright owner or the publishers of the book.

Paperback ISBN 978-1-64430-117-3
Casebound ISBN 978-1-64430-123-4
Library of Congress Catalog Card Number: 2021934478
Manufactured in the United States of America

First Printing by Midnight Marquee Press, Inc., April 2021

DEDICATION

As usual, to my wife Janet
whose dedication and perseverance in tracking down
many Western rarities and then negotiating on price
has lifted the burden of doing so off my shoulders.
And to Gary Svehla (horror and Western buff!)
for his support and enthusiasm for the project,
unwavering at every bend of the trail!

Rio Bravo **French Grande poster**

Contents

8	Foreword
11	Chapter 1: 1950
51	Chapter 2: Johnny Mack Brown at Monogram
65	Chapter 3: 1951
102	Chapter 4: 1952
136	Chapter 5: Wild Bill Elliott at Republic, Monogram and Allied Artists
149	Chapter 6: 1953
186	Chapter 7: Tim Holt at RKO-Radio
200	Chapter 8: 1954
229	Chapter 9: 1955
264	Chapter 10: Allan "Rocky" Lane at Republic
282	Chapter 11: 1956
331	Chapter 12: The James Stewart/Anthony Mann Westerns
341	Chapter 13: 1957
382	Chapter 14: 1958
420	Chapter 15: Hope Out West: *Fancy Pants*, *Son of Paleface* and *Alias Jesse James*
428	Chapter 16: 1959
451	Chapter 17: Whip Wilson at Monogram
466	Chapter 18: The Classics: *High Noon*, *Shane*, *The Searchers* and *Rio Bravo*
478	Film Titles

Foreword

Listed in the "What's on TV section" in an English Saturday newspaper supplement for Tuesday, December 12, 2017 was George Stevens' *Shane* with the following comment: "In a decade full of forgettable Westerns, Alan Ladd is the nowhere man riding into town to make a difference." Forgettable Westerns? Either "forgettable" should have read "unforgettable" or the writer was of an age where, cinematically (and historically) speaking, he simply had no idea what he was talking about. There are no two ways about it—the 1950s was the decade in which the American Western flourished and attained an absolute peak of perfection. Over 600 were churned out by major and minor studios; in addition, you had the numerous television Western series adding greatly to the mix. Universal-International's output came out tops, Columbia and Warner Bros. a close second; the standard 70-to-85-minute Universal Western was high in production values, brash, hard hitting, fast-moving, gritty and exciting, very difficult for the opposition to beat. Before, in the 1940s, the Western had been guilty of being occasionally blighted by too much talk and too many peripheral individuals, comedy elements and hayseed humor spoiling the broth; from mid-1960 onwards, the genre was in definite decline as audience interest waned. The 1950s was *the* heyday, Hollywood's top actors boosting rugged, involving, incisively directed (and scripted) big-budget and low-budget productions steeped in vivid colors, rousing soundtracks and stunning locations, with tough, complex and much darker characters to match. The psychological Western was born, focusing on the damaged mental state of many a villain, culminating in Fox's 1958 horror Western *The Fiend Who Walked the West*, handed an "X" Adults Only rating in Britain and banned outright in some areas of Europe.

In compiling this volume on the 1950s Western, I have omitted, through fear of repetition, the 141 features made during this period starring Randolph Scott, Audie Murphy, Joel McCrea, George Montgomery, Richard Widmark, Rory Calhoun, Rod Cameron and Sterling Hayden, the subjects of *Six-Gun Law 1* and *2*. More family-oriented fare, such as Disney's *Davy Crockett* movies and *The Light in the Forest*, haven't been included. Likewise, Roy Rogers' (and others) singing/musical cowboys flicks, comedy Westerns (with the exception of three out-and-out Bob Hope classics), modern-day Westerns and social drama containing a faint Western slant; these are not mentioned. But that leaves more than enough material to dig one's spurs into and 446 titles from the great Western canon are covered, including chapters on Johnny Mack Brown, Wild Bill Elliott, Tim Holt, Allan "Rocky" Lane and Whip Wilson, five of the principal cowboy stars who specialized in the hour-long serial/series-type oater. Reviews are followed by highlights, a snippet of dialogue and trivia facts; highlights and trivia are not included if they don't really exist. Chapters dealing with Westerns released in a particular year are preceded by poster blurbs, and I have used IMDb and Wikipedia as the main source of reference.

As far as the once-mighty Western motion picture goes, where do we stand today? "Isn't it curious that the film genre that defined the mythology of America, the Western, the genre that ruled the movie screens during the 1950s and 1960s and the television airwaves during this same period, is mostly forgotten today, or at least has become irrelevant, with a few Westerns released each year to lack-luster reviews and box-office muscle." So wrote Gary Svehla in his foreword to *Midnight Marquee #80* (April 2018). And Gary hit the nail right on the head—as a form of cinematic entertainment, the

American horse opera, guaranteed to fill an auditorium to capacity 50-to-60 years ago, is now dead in the water, but if it is *ever* to be resurrected, it will never be in the same vital form that it took during those halcyon years all those decades go.

So saddle up, strap on your single or double holster gun belt, grab your rifle, check your weapons are loaded and get ready to ride into a hot, dusty and highly dangerous universe populated by not-so-good guys bent on vengeance, cowardly townsfolk, bad hombres, rampaging Redskins, glamorous dames in distress, evil land-grabbers, corrupt saloon owners, masked raiders, outlaw gangs, rustlers, psychotic villains, bank and stage holdups, train robberies, wagon trains under attack, cattle barons feuding with sheep farmers, ghost towns, gripping gunfights, bruising fistfights, crooked town officials, stand-alone lawmen, gun-toting ladies, cold-hearted killers, stampeding cattle and horses, comical sidekicks, cavalry versus Indian battles, engaging 10-year-olds as tough as the adults, lone, trigger-happy strangers met with slit-eyed suspicion and towns where trouble lurks on every street corner, all set against America's striking natural scenery and mostly shot with an expertise unknown to a generation of 21st-century moviegoers fed on a never-ending diet of CGI-dominated movies with nary a Stetson or horse in sight. As stated, the 1950s was the decade in which Western movies thrived and reigned supreme; this volume hopefully, and conclusively, sets out to prove it.

Film Ratings

Dead Shot *****
Hits the target ****
Finger on the trigger ***
Half-cocked **
Firing blanks *

Italian poster for *Broken Arrow*

Chapter 1
1950

SHE SOUGHT REVENGE WITH A WHIP ...A GUN ... AND A KISS!
Bandit Queen

YOU CAN'T KILL A PHANTOM WITH BULLETS!
Border Outlaws

TAKE YOUR FILTHY HANDS OFF HIM!
The Daltons' Women

THERE'S ALWAYS ANOTHER TOO QUICK ON THE DRAW!
Firing Blanks

HIS ONLY FRIEND WAS HIS GUN ... HIS ONLY REFUGE—A WOMAN'S HEART!
The Gunfighter

HUNTED! HAUNTED HOUNDED!
High Lonesome

DESPERADOES CRINGED WHEN THE BULLWHIP CRACKED!
King of the Bullwhip

THEY'RE OUT TO LOOK FOR THE U.S. MAIL WITH DYNAMITE, BULLETS OR A WOMAN'S WILES!
Wyoming Mail

Ambush

MGM; 90 minutes; Producer: Armand Deutsch; Director: Sam Wood; Cast: Robert Taylor; Arlene Dahl; John Hodiak; John McIntire; Don Taylor; Jean Hagen; Bruce Cowling; Leon Ames *****

Sam Wood's final film (he died of a heart attack on September 22, 1949 aged 66 before post-production work had been finalized) is a tough account of U.S. cavalry life in Arizona, 1878. Robert Taylor (his second Western), an ex-army scout/Indian guide/prospector hired to locate a general's daughter, abducted by Apache chief Diablito. Shot at a cost of $1,700,000 amid the towering rock formations at Lupton, Arizona, containing vivid black-and-white photography from Harold Lipstein, Marguerite Roberts' pithy screenplay (from Luke Short's story) centers on fort gossip and intrigues in addition to outstanding action sequences. Taylor falls for the kidnapped woman's sister, Arlene Dahl, who's being romanced by Captain John Hodiak; Lieutenant Don Taylor cares for Jean Hagen, the physically abused wife of alcoholic trooper Bruce Cowling; and when, in the movie's final section, Major Leon Ames gets a pitchfork in the guts from Cowling after he's busted jail, high and mighty Hodiak takes command, clashing with Taylor over tactics to bring in Diablito, the missing woman *and* the scout's interest in Dahl. There are two ambushes for your ticket, the first being when Taylor runs off the Apache ponies and Diablito's 200-strong savages are caught in troop crossfire. The second where Hodiak's detail is wiped out bar one man by the Redskins who conceal themselves in the scrub; Taylor, with reinforcements, comes across the massacre and shoots Diablito dead. Taylor and Dahl stand side-by-side in the closing minutes as Fort Gamble raises a flag to honor its dead, while Hagen stares at Taylor and runs off, her husband having been killed by the Apaches. A fine-looking, sweaty, hard-edged Western that packs a real punch, Rudolph G. Kopp's rousing score keeping things on the move.

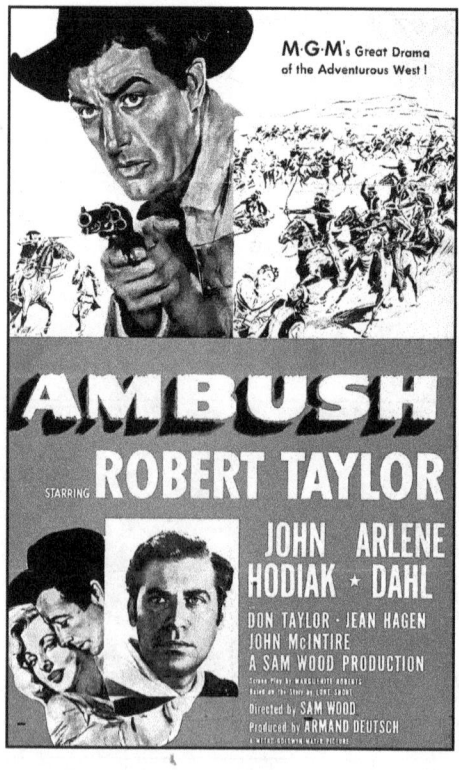

Highlights:
Lupton's spectacular rocky scenery, splendid cavalry-Redskin clashes, Taylor on top form and Dahl living up to her reputation as one of Hollywood's most beautiful actresses.

Dialogue:
Taylor to Ames and Hodiak on what will happen to Dahl's sister at the hands of Diablito: "If he finds out she's army and that you want her, he'll send her head back in a sack."

Bandit Queen

Lippert Pictures; 70 minutes; Produced and Directed by William Berke; Cast: Barbara Britton; Phillip Reed; Willard Parker; Martin Garralaga; Barton MacLane; Angelo Rossitto; Mikel Conrad; Anna Demetrio ****

In Old California during the gold rush of 1846, the native Spanish population is under persecution from the white Americans. Lawyer Willard Parker and Sheriff Barton MacLane arrange for the murder of the Montalvo family in order to lay their hands on the family's property and its five gold mines, but there's a witness to the killing—daughter Barbara Britton. Donning a Zorro-type mask and wielding a bullwhip, Britton, as Zara the Bandit (the "Angel of the Sierras"), hits the vengeance trail with her band of vigilantes, strangling all those who attended the slaughter of her parents and robbing gold shipments, handing back the loot to the locals from whom it was stolen. Padre Martin Garralaga of the San Sebastian mission knows the female terror's true identity and, eventually, so does fellow bandit Phillip Reed, the pair falling in love. A superior low-budgeter that moves like an express locomotive, driven by Albert Glasser's pounding score (his title music is memorable), *Bandit Queen* packs more into its 70 minutes than many movies twice the length; Ernest Miller's deep black-and-white nighttime photography is also a bonus. The picture climaxes in a furious shoot-out among California's towering Vasquez Rocks (how many hooves thundered past these striking rock formations over the following decade?), Parker and MacLane biting the dust. Britton and Reed get hitched, both are promised a pardon by the new governor and diminutive troublemaker Angelo Rossitto helps himself to a large slice of wedding cake. Tremendous B-Western thrills, directed with verve by William Berke.

Dialogue:
Garralaga to Britton and Reed, engaged in learning the finer arts of using a bullwhip: "Forgive me for saying it, but you two seem to be whipping up a friendship."

Barricade

Warner Bros.; Technicolor; 77 minutes; Producer: Saul Elkins; Director: Peter Godfrey; Cast: Dane Clark; Raymond Massey; Ruth Roman; Robert Douglas; Walter Coy; George Stern; Robert Griffin; Morgan Farley ***

Fugitive Dane Clark, wounded lawyer Robert Douglas and girl-on-the-run Ruth Roman find themselves, through circumstances, in a mining camp run by despot Raymond Massey and his thuggish assistant Robert Griffin; the workforce (lawless outcasts to a man) hate their boss, conniving to get rid of him at the earliest opportunity. A sweaty remake of Jack London's novel *The Sea Wolf*, filmed in 1941, *Barricade*, after a storming start shot around the Vasquez Rocks (William Lava's rousing music comes into its own), settles into a wordy, heated melodrama, each desperate character playing off the other, all plotting for Massey's downfall, including limping Robert Douglas, the voice of reason in this hellhole. Massey killed his brother to lay his hands on the mine and knows that nephew Clay is out there in the wastes, looking for revenge. Massey (in snarling, leering form) scowls and bashes anyone who gets on his wrong side while drunken judge Morgan Farley rants and raves about the Almighty and, as expected, Clark and Roman fall in love. It's an uneven mix that just about holds the attention, Massey's outfit and his nephew's boys wiping each other out in the end. Clark and Massey fight inside the workings, the bogus mine owner perishing under a roof collapse, allowing Clark and Roman to leave the accursed place in a wagon.

Dialogue:
Massey to Clark: "You over there, that new man. Come here. What's your name?"
Clark: "Peters."
Massey: "Benson must have looked under a rock to come up with you." Clark goes to walk off. "I haven't finished yet."
Clark: "Then change your brand of talk. I don't like it."
Massey, sarcastically: "Oh, he's tough, too."

Border Outlaws aka Border Raiders

Jack Schwarz Prods./United Intl. Pictures; 57 minutes; Producers: Jack Seaman and Richard Talmadge; Director: Richard Talmadge; Cast: Spade Cooley; Maria Hart; Bill Edwards; Bill Kennedy; George Slocum; John Laurenz; Douglas Wood; The Six Metzetti Boys *

Like an artifact from a distant age, singing star Spade "The King of Western Swing" Cooley's third 1950 Western (*The Silver Bandit* and *The Kid from Gower Gulch* were the other two) is disjointed, haphazard, poorly acted and, to be frank, tedious. Cooley, owner of the Dungaree Ranch, becomes involved in the shady activities of The Phantom Raider, a black-clad Zorro-type figure tearing across the countryside, up to his neck in smuggling contraband across the Mexican border. Bill Edwards arrives at Cooley's ranch, a lawman out to nail the gang, while taciturn Bill Kennedy pretends he can't ride a horse, even though he's The Phantom. At the Cross Bar Ranch, Maria Hart's cowhands, led by George Slocum and John Laurenz, are in on the deal without her knowing; back at the Dungaree, gymnast group The Six Metzetti Boys perform back flips, somersaults and other crazy stunts as though they were starring in a Marx Brothers movie. Cooley's double gun and holster appears, disappears and appears again from one scene to the next; he gets to sing a song with Hart; and the comical (was it meant to be?) finale has the acrobatic troupe joining in on the roundup of Kennedy and his mob. A bow to composer Darrell Calker who put as much energy into his bombastic score as the Metzetti Boys did with their continuous vaudevillian antics, but after struggling through *Border Outlaws*, you will be asking yourself the important question: Did they *really* make Western films like *this* all those years ago?

Dialogue:
Cooley to Hart and Edwards, watching five of the Metzetti's jump on a horse: "I can see I'm gonna have a sway-backed horse by the time those guys get to the ranch."

Trivia:
Cooley's turbulent life (he was sentenced to life imprisonment for the murder of his second wife in April 1961) ended when he collapsed dead from a heart attack during a concert in November 1969; he was 58 years old.

Border Rangers

Lippert Pictures; 58 minutes; Produced and Directed by William Berke; Cast: Don "Red" Barry; Robert Lowery; Wally Vernon; Pamela Blake; Ezelle Poule; Paul Jordan; Lyle Talbot; Claude Stroud ****

Young Paul Jordan sees his Texas Ranger father and mother killed by outlaws; grabbing a six-gun, he vows revenge. The Ranger's brother, Don "Red" Barry, is also thirsting for blood, joining the Rangers and posing as outlaw The Rio Kid, infiltrating Robert Lowery's gang who were responsible for the death of his brother. Barry persuades Lowery, at first suspicious of the new recruit's outlaw credentials, to participate in robbing the El Paso Bank of $200,000, setting up an ambush with Captain Lyle Talbot which leads to a blazing shoot-out. Barry (aided by Jordan) puts two slugs into Lowery as he attempts escape and marries local beauty Pamela Blake, comic element Wally Vernon getting hitched to Blake's matronly aunt, Ezelle Poule. William Berke's low-budget oater is fast and furious, Barry handy with fists, twin Colts and pithy one-liners; whatever he may have been like on set, he carries the action in a great little B-Western propelled by Albert Glasser's thumping soundtrack.

Dialogue:
Lowery to Barry: "You talk mighty big."
Barry: "I'm the Rio Kid."
Lowery: "Whadd'ya want? Three cheers?"

Trivia:
Five-foot-four and a half Barry, once proclaimed "the new James Cagney," made his name in the Republic *Red Ryder* serials of 1940 and had a reputation for being troublesome on a shoot, his oversized ego and bad manners upsetting both fellow cast members and directors; at least two directors said they would never work with "the midget" ever again.

Branded

Paramount; Technicolor; 104 minutes; Producer: Mel Epstein; Director: Rudolph Maté; Cast: Alan Ladd; Mona Freeman; Charles Bickford; Robert Keith; Joseph Calleia; Peter Hansen; John Berkes; Tom Tully ****

Itinerant gunman Alan Ladd (as Choya) dodges a fusillade of bullets, escaping from a town's wrathful citizens and followed by varmints Robert Keith and John Berkes who have a plan. Ladd is to have a tattoo etched on his left shoulder corresponding with the identical birthmark on the son and heir to Charles Bickford's Bar M Ranch, worth a million dollars. The boy was abducted when he was five and has been missing 25 years. $100,000 reward money to whoever locates him; the scheme is to have Ladd hired as a hand, let slip about the mark, be welcomed as the long-lost son and then finish Bickford off, splitting the million three ways. Keith gets greedy, shoots Berkes in the back and is hired himself to ensure Ladd goes through with the deal. But the lone gunfighter has other ideas. Accepted as the missing son with open arms, he falls in love with Mona Freeman, Bickford and Selena Royle's daughter and, feeling uncomfortable, decides to steal the takings from the sale of the herd instead, totaling $183,000. In a game of Russian roulette, Keith admits, at gunpoint, kidnapping the boy and letting priests care for him; Ladd, his conscience in overdrive, tells Freeman he isn't her sibling and the mark is a fake, going to Mexico to find the real brother. Peter Hansen is the man, adopted by Mexican bandit Joseph Calleia as a baby and brought up as his own flesh and blood. When Ladd and Hansen make a dash across the Texas border to Bickford's ranch, Calleia and his posse are in hot pursuit, Keith intent on killing Ladd. He doesn't, pushed off a cliff edge by stampeding horses. At the ranch, everything is resolved after some heated exchanges; Hansen will inherit the Bar M and see his adoptive father on a regular basis. Ladd, now a more honest, calmer individual, rides away, Freeman declaring her love and departing with him. "A personal identity lost and found" sums up one of Ladd's best Westerns outside of his classic *Shane*, the charismatic actor one mighty tough hombre who finally discovers the true meaning of life and love.

Highlights:

Arizona's canyon country forms a craggy backdrop to a Western focusing more on emotional drama than gunplay.

Dialogue:

Calleia to Hansen, bowing to the inevitable: "Life is not by the blood but by the brand, eh, Tonio?"

Broken Arrow

20th Century Fox; Technicolor; 93 minutes; Producer: Julian Blaustein; Director: Delmer Daves; Cast: James Stewart; Jeff Chandler; Debra Paget; Basil Ruysdael; Will Geer; Arthur Hunnicutt; Jay Silverheels; Raymond Bramley ****

One of the earliest '50s Westerns to focus attention on the inhumane plight suffered by the Native American Indian, *Broken Arrow* was a wordy drama (script: Albert Maltz) set in 1870, relating how ex-army man-turned-gold prospector James Stewart set about learning the ways of the Apaches after treating a young Indian boy for battle wounds. Stewart, fighting prejudice on all sides, arranges a peace meeting with Cochise (Jeff Chandler) and General Basil Ruysdael after Chandler's warriors have annihilated a troop detachment and stolen several wagons (ironically, the young lad Stewart helped lies dead in the dust)—but the Apache chief, as promised to Stewart, has allowed the mail riders to go through his territory unmolested. Geronimo (Jay Silverheels) forms his own band of renegades, having no taste for peace treaties, while Stewart marries delectable squaw Debra Paget. The tragic climax sees Paget killed in a shoot-out with Redskin-hating Will Geer and his boys; hostilities over (for the time being) Cochise and his followers are given their own slice of Arizona real estate, Stewart riding off into the wilderness, content to be alone with his memories. Magnificent Arizona canyon scenery (photographer: Ernest Palmer), a thoughtful, sharp screenplay and a rousing action centerpiece is complemented by Chandler's dominating performance; Stewart may have been the bankable box-office star, but his awkward, somewhat fumbling turn is overshadowed by Chandler's stoical Cochise, eager to put in place a peace agreement but not trusting the whites an inch.

"Richly colorful and romantic," said the *New York Times*, *Variety* adding: "moving and well-staged." Kevin Costner's *Dances With Wolves* (1990) owes a lot to the themes contained within this film.

Dialogue:
Hunnicutt's words of warning to Stewart after learning of his intentions to infiltrate Cochise's camp: "Don't try it, Tom. The ants will be feedin' off your eyes."

Trivia:
Chandler (Cochise) and Silverheels (Geronimo) reprised their roles two years later in Universal's *The Battle at Apache Pass*.

California Passage

Republic; 90 minutes; Produced and Directed by Joseph Kane; Cast: Forrest Tucker; Adele Mara; Jim Davis; Peter Miles; Bill Williams; Charles Kemper; Rhys Williams; Estelita Rodriguez ***

In 1850, on the plains west of Missouri, Forrest Tucker saves settler Adele Mara and her son Peter Miles from a scalping after their wagon becomes separated from the train. Tucker turns out to be the boss of a saloon in Coarse Gold, California, where resident gambler Jim Davis falls for Mara when she arrives in town (the gal part-owns the Opal Mine), as does Tucker. Davis is behind a series of gold shipment and express box holdups and does his best to sabotage Mara's growing feeling towards his old friend Tucker by letting slip to the lady that it was Tucker who gunned down her hot-headed brother (Bill Williams) in a saloon standoff, even though Williams had it coming to him. He also pins the murder of a wealthy stage passenger on his pal by giving him a jeweled tie pin stolen off the man's body; Mara and Miles, on the stagecoach at the time, recognize it on Tucker's jacket and think he's the killer. Joseph Kane's standard Republic oater races through a familiar plot, culminating in Tucker shooting it out with Davis in the rocky hills, the two-timing rat falling to his death. Tucker then decides to hitch up with the woman he once called "My cold beauty." Mara is indeed a beauty, big guys Tucker and Davis strike sparks off each other and the result is undemanding fare that plays along the lines of an extended Allan "Rocky" Lane Western (see Chapter 10), also produced by Republic.

Dialogue:

Davis to Tucker: "I *was* right. This is one dame that Prescott (Tucker) feels different about. Watch out. She might draw a bead on you, right between the eyes."

Colorado Ranger

Lippert/Exclusive; 59 minutes; Producer: Ron Ormond; Director: Thomas Carr; Cast: Jimmie "Shamrock" Ellison; Russ "Lucky" Hayden; Raymond Hatton; Julie Adams (Betty Adams); Fuzzy Knight; Tom Tyler; John L. Cason; George J. Lewis *

Colorado Ranger was one of six low-budget Westerns directed by Thomas Carr over a 29-day period in January/February 1950 for Lippert writer/producer Ron Ormond, all featuring the same cast, locations and technicians. Carr, an old hand at knocking out serial-type, hour-long oaters, stated that at any given time, he was working on three to four different storylines in one day, so all credit to the continuity and editing team who, by and large, got it just about right on all six. All were remakes of 1930s Westerns, six-foot-two Ellison and six-foot-three Hayden former sidekicks to Hopalong Cassidy in the 1940s. *Colorado Ranger*, the fourth in the series, is a chaotic muddle, the worst of the six, concerning Ellison, Hayden and Hatton enlisted by crooked sheriff Stephen Carr (the director's brother) to run off ranchers from land in the vicinity of Cactus Junction, one thousand bucks each for the job. But Carr doesn't realize that all three are Colorado Rangers, the trio now focusing their efforts on getting rid of the gang, led by John L. Cason, busy terrorizing Fuzzy Knight and his homesteaders. The continuity is all over the place (not surprising, given the director's remit), with plenty of ridin' and shootin'

plus Hatton trapped in a cellar and stock footage inserted from the other entrants in the series, backed by Walter Greene's cacophonous, undisciplined score. An interlude with a baby providing a little light relief—Ellison gets to kiss Julie Adams as the curtain comes down. And I doubt that the British censor would condone the sight of a baby teething on the barrel of a six-gun, even today!

Dialogue:
Hatton to Ellison on the wailing baby: "Sounds like a sick cat … what ails that critter, anyway?"

Comanche Territory

Universal; Technicolor; 76 minutes; Producer: Leonard Goldstein; Director: George Sherman; Cast: Maureen O'Hara; Macdonald Carey; Will Geer; Charles Drake; Pedro de Cordoba; Ian MacDonald; Rick Vallin; Parley Baer **

Arizona's Sedona area of rugged red cliffs and mighty canyons is perfectly captured in Maury Gertsman's rich photography, one of the few points of interest in George Sherman's sluggish actioner concerning the greedy townsfolk of Crooked Tongue, led by Charles Drake, dying to get their hands on silver lying beneath sacred Comanche land. Drake's sister, fiery Maureen O'Hara, wants the staking of claims carried out legally, without upsetting Chief Quisima (Pedro de Cordoba) and his tribes, a new peace treaty deal in the offing. She eventually calls on scout James Bowie (Macdonald Carey) to come to the rescue when Drake and his hyenas attack the Comanche camp, the Indians armed only with bows and Bowie knives. O'Hara charges in with a wagonload of muskets, Drake's men are defeated, the leader arrested, Carey heading off in the direction of the Alamo, leaving O'Hara to hope for a new romance which, of course, never happened.

Will Geer, playing Carey's grizzled sidekick, turns in a lively performance, as does flame-haired O'Hara, but Carey is too laid-back in his role of the infamous knifeman and this, in tandem with the slight plot, drags the movie down.

Highlights:
Sedona's magnificent scenery which featured in umpteen Westerns during the '50s.

Dialogue:
O'Hara to Carey, on their first stormy meeting: "I said draw!"
Carey: "Sorry, Ma'am. Back in Louisiana when we meet any pretty ladies, we make love to them, we kiss 'em, spank 'em on occasions but we never go around shooting them."

Trivia:
This was O'Hara's second Western, as it was Carey's.

Copper Canyon

Paramount; Technicolor; 84 minutes; Producer: Mel Epstein; Director: John Farrow; Cast: Ray Milland; Hedy Lamarr; Macdonald Carey; Harry Carey, Jr.; Mona Freeman; James Burke; Taylor Holmes; Francis Pierlot **

Despite the enticing casting of Ray Milland and Hedy "The World's Most Beautiful Woman in Films" Lamarr, *Copper Canyon*, in the words of one critic, trots out the clichés in a top-heavy plot containing far too many peripheral characters—and the mock-up studio town, unusual in a Western of this period, virtually kills it. Vaudeville sharpshooter performer Milland is, in fact, an ex-Confederate colonel wanted by the Union for the theft of $20,000. He's also wanted by Taylor Holmes to protect miners and their ore shipments to Mesa City being preyed upon by corrupt lawman Macdonald Carey and his coyotes, acting under orders from Union sympathizers Ian Wolfe and Francis Pierlot, who want the Southerners out of the territory, ready to commit murder if anyone stands in their path. Lamarr (looking ill at ease) is in on the deal purely for financial reasons but changes her allegiance once Milland's charm offensive breaks down her barriers, leaving Carey, who loves her, fuming on the sidelines. After three miners are shot in the back in a saloon ambush, Milland straps on a gun and helps the Rebs overthrow Carey's mob in a blazing shoot-out at Pierlot's ranch house, Carey shot to death by both Milland and Lieutenant Harry Carey, Jr. Milland and Lamarr take the stage to 'Frisco, that $20,000, which Milland claims is his by right, to be used to finance the couple's marriage and Lamarr's proposed new theater. Attractive location work at Vasquez Rocks National Park and a solid score from Daniele Amfitheatrof compensate for a talky exercise in Western dramatics, where one is left waiting for some much-needed action between the lulls.

Highlights:
John Farrow focuses his camera a little too much on screen goddess Lamarr but with those dazzling, green-eyed features, who could blame him?

Dialogue:
Carey to Milland: "You're as full of tricks as a tame crow."

Crooked River

Lippert/Exclusive; 56 minutes; Producer: Ron Ormond; Director: Thomas Carr; Cast: Jimmie "Shamrock" Ellison; Russ "Lucky" Hayden; Raymond Hatton; Fuzzy Knight; Julie Adams; Stanley Price; John L. Cason; George J. Lewis ***

In this energetic third outing from the Thomas Carr/Lippert "six," taking place in the 1860s, Ellison is on the trail of the gang who murdered his parents in a wagon holdup. As headlines scream "Reign of Terror Continues," "Robbers Rule Range," and "Outlaws Hit Valley," baddies John L. Cason and his jackals split from nice outlaw Hayden and join the Gentry outfit, led by George J. Lewis who owns a Gatling gun, a $5,000 reward on his head. Ellison twirls his twin revolvers in front of pretty Julie Adams, Hayden's sister, trying to impress the dame and a storming finale sees Stanley Price's posse, all wearing white headbands, rounding up Lewis' gang in a canyon with help from Ellison wielding that deadly weapon. Fast-moving with attractive Lone Pine scenery as the backdrop, *Crooked River* is enjoyable Saturday Morning Pictures cheapo fun for the undiscerning cowboy buff.

Dialogue:
Hatton to Ellison: "Kent (Cason) would kill a man for a horse."
Ellison: "That's all he killed my folks for."

Trivia:
Stanley Price not only appeared in numerous low-budget oaters but was employed by Lippert and Monogram as a dialogue coach, notably on Whip Wilson's flicks.

Dallas

Warner Bros.; Technicolor; 94 minutes; Producer: Anthony Veiller; Director: Stuart Heisler; Cast: Gary Cooper; Raymond Massey; Ruth Roman; Steve Cochran; Barbara Payton; Leif Erickson; Antonio Moreno; Reed Hadley ***

More '40s than '50s in conception, John Twist's convoluted screenplay had Gary Cooper playing an ex-Reb officer, now a wanted criminal, bent on killing Steve Cochran, the loose cannon member of the Marlow clan. During the war, Cochran burned his ranch in Georgia and murdered his family; now, the Marlows, headed by carpetbagger Raymond Massey, are buying up property illegally under the guise of a real estate company, making life tough for local hacienda owners, in particular, the Robles family governed by Antonio Moreno. Cooper changes identity with prissy law officer Leif Erickson, dressed like a dandy, the bogus marshal winning the heart of Erickson's decorative intended, Ruth Roman, before putting paid to the Marlows in a furious nighttime shoot-out. Bags of hard ridin', Cooper escaping from jail (the film's best sequence), gunfights and a semi-humorous appearance by Reed Hadley, as Wild Bill Hickok in the opening 15 minutes, make for a hit-or-miss horse opera that, at times, is too mixed up for its own good. Worth watching for Cooper's customary laconic performance, sexpot Barbara Payton as the wife of one of the bad guys, Hollywood ladies' man Cochran, almost unrecognizable in bandit getup and a typical Warner Bros. Max Steiner stock score.

Highlights:
Cooper being Cooper (Robert Ryan, Robert Mitchum and Errol Flynn were considered for the role); and the Iverson Ranch setting in Los Angeles was used in literally hundreds of Westerns made up to 1960.

Dialogue:
Hadley to Erickson, sneering at his incompetent gun skills: "So long, marshal. The law is in your pretty hands."

Trivia:
Peroxide blonde Payton led a tragic life, even by Tinseltown's own hedonistic standards: The actress made only 14 movies, was married four times and had a number

of violent relationships before falling into drug abuse, alcoholism and prostitution, dying from heart and liver failure at the age of 39 in 1967.

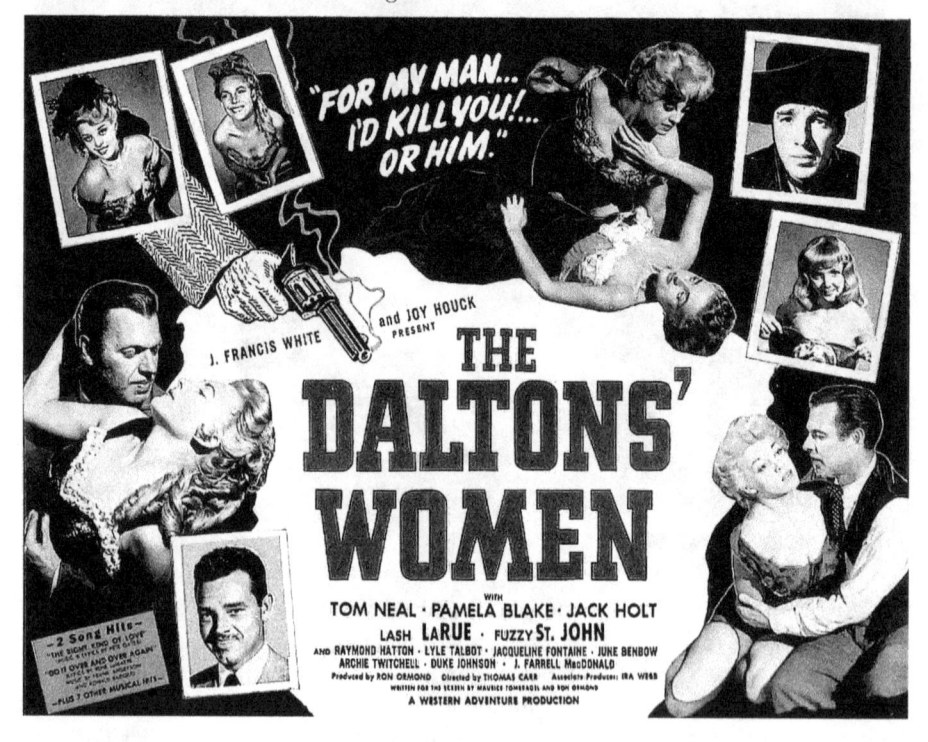

The Daltons' Women

Western Adventure Prods./Realart; 70 minutes; Producer: Ron Ormond; Director: Thomas Carr; Cast: Lash LaRue; Al "Fuzzy" St. John; Jack Holt; Pamela Blake; Lyle Talbot; Jacqueline Fontaine; Raymond Hatton; June Benbow ***

The first of six serial-type oaters '40s Western star Alfred Wilson "Lash" LaRue made in the 1950s, budgets not exceeding $40,000 per picture. The six-foot-one Humphrey Bogart look-alike, dressed from head to toe in black and sporting silver-studded twin holsters, his big horse Black Diamond completing the picture, was a throwback to the previous decade; this particular offering contained moments of moderate excitement amid moments of corn, including around 20 minutes of singing, dancing girls and comedy sketches—and there were *no* Daltons' women! LaRue played a marshal posing as a gambler ("I can handle a gun *and* a whip.") sent to Navajo to flush out the Dalton gang, led by Jack Holt masquerading as a saloon boss. Pamela Blake was an undercover Pinkerton agent, while ginger beer-guzzling Al "Fuzzy" St. John, resembling Popeye's grandpappy, aided (or hindered) LaRue, acting like a bewhiskered clown most of the time. A couple of saloon fistfights, two bank holdups, protracted horse chases in the hills and LaRue skulking in the alleys wearing a mask are enlivened by songstress Jacqueline Fontaine and saloon gal June Benbow engaging in a hilarious three-minute catfight over the dubious charms of client Archie Twitchell, both ladies ending up in their torn undergarments. Screen heavies Tom Tyler, Lyle Talbot, Stanley Price and Terry Frost back up Holt in the snarling stakes; it's all a bit haphazard, neither one thing nor the other, but entertaining enough, occasionally falling flat on its face, as does Fuzzy at the end after being kissed by Blake.

Dialogue:
Benbow to Twitchell who's eyeing up Fontaine: "She might have been fresh in Tombstone, but she's sure stale in Navajo."

Trivia:
Twitchell, an experienced pilot, was killed in a mid-air collision over Pacoima, California, in January 1957, aged 50. Singer Ritchie Valens was one of 74 students injured from plane debris falling on his school; ironically, two years later, in February 1959, he died in a plane crash with Buddy Holly and The Big Bopper.

Devil's Doorway

MGM; 84 minutes; Producer: Nicholas Nayfack; Director: Anthony Mann; Cast: Robert Taylor; Paula Raymond; Louis Calhern; Marshall Thompson; James Mitchell; Edgar Buchanan; Chief John Big Tree; James Millican ****

Anthony Mann's grim, almost *noir*, $1,300,000 Western (filmed in Aspen, Colorado) highlighted the persecution of the Native American Indian, in this case Shoshone Lance Poole, admirably played by Robert Taylor. Taylor has returned from the Civil War a Union hero, sporting the Congressional Medal of Honor, and all he wants to do is live the peaceful life of a cattle rancher on 50,000 acres of prime land known as Sweet Meadow, accessed through the Devil's Doorway gap. "Our people are doomed," intones his dying father. "We cannot live with the white man," and to prove his point, troublemaking, Indian-hating lawyer Louis Calhern is doing his best to get Marshall Thompson's sheep farmers onto land he reckons doesn't belong to any Redskin. Hero or not, Taylor is cold shouldered, even by friendly sheriff Edgar Buchanan; rival lawyer Paula Raymond tries to assist, but the word comes back that Taylor and his tribe must return to a reservation to avoid confrontation. The impasse leads to a prolonged assault on Taylor's homestead; Calhern and Buchanan are killed, the cavalry arrive to stop further bloodshed and Taylor, fatally wounded, drops dead, having realized he was fighting a losing battle. Once you get used to one of Hollywood's foremost leading men sporting slick long black hair and bottled tan (Taylor's next, MGM's $7,000,000 *Quo Vadis*, had him starring as Roman tribune Marcus Vinicius, demonstrating the actor's versatility), you have a downbeat Western complemented by Daniele Amfitheatrof's dramatic score that pulls no punches in the "all Indians are trash" stakes, Calhern a particularly revolting specimen of the kind that detests even breathing the very air in the presence of a non-white.

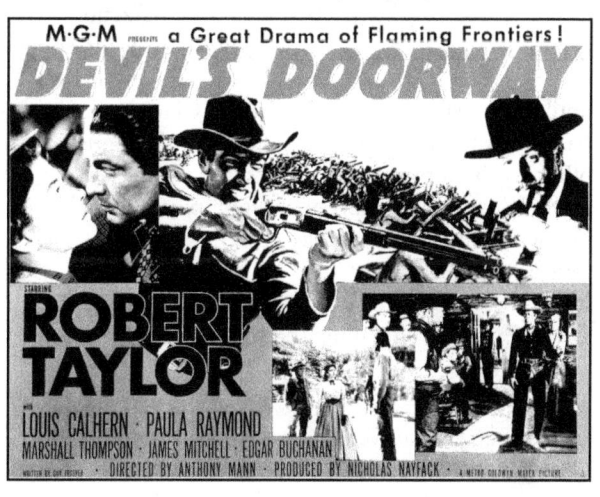

Highlights:
A terrific white sheep farmers versus Indian cattlemen clash featuring the throwing of dynamite amid the smoking guns.
Dialogue:
Taylor to barkeep Tom Fadden, after being refused liquor: "We'll take soda water."
Fadden: "Huh?"
Taylor: "No law against an Indian drinking water, is there? We can still breathe."
Trivia:
MGM almost pulled the plug on the movie, deeming it too gritty and dark, but the success of Fox's *Broken Arrow*, which ran on similar themes, forced them into a U-turn and the film made a profit, mainly due to Taylor's box-office muscle.

The Eagle and the Hawk

Paramount; Technicolor; 104 minutes; Producers: William H. Pine and William C. Thomas; Director: Lewis R. Foster; Cast: John Payne; Rhonda Fleming; Dennis O'Keefe; Thomas Gomez; Fred Clark; Frank Faylen; Eduardo Noriega; Grandon Rhodes **

1863, across the Mexican border in Corales, ammunition, arms, gunpowder and cash, financed by the French, are being made ready for Emperor Maximilian's proposed conquest of Texas; French agent Fred Clark and decorative mistress Rhonda Fleming are the go-betweens, stirring up trouble with General Thomas Gomez and his Juarez supporters. Texas Ranger John Payne and Yankee spy Dennis O'Keefe head south to sort out the trouble before a full-scale war develops, Payne coming under the spell of Fleming who he thinks is Clark's sister. Falling between too many stools, *The Eagle and the Hawk* is plot-heavy and talkative, endless scenes of dialogue replacing action, of which there is little apart from one harrowing sequence where Payne is tied to a pair of galloping horses and threatened with quartering until saved by O'Keefe. A fiery climax, Clark chased by Gomez up a blazing peak (Payne has set fire to the brushwood) and both men perishing, adds a spot of excitement, but otherwise it's a routine, overlong affair (Payne *does* get Fleming in the closing seconds); James Wong Howe's vibrant photography and solid star turns from Payne and O'Keefe just about make it watchable.

Dialogue:
Payne to O'Keefe: "Spying business. Wouldn't be dangerous, would it?"
O'Keefe: "The worst thing that can happen to you is to get killed."

Fast on the Draw

Lippert/Exclusive; 55 minutes; Producer: Ron Ormond; Director: Thomas Carr; Cast: Jimmie "Shamrock" Ellison; Russ "Lucky" Hayden; Raymond Hatton; Fuzzy Knight; Julie Adams; Tom Tyler; John L. Cason; Stanley Price **

"Marauding Gang Sweeps Territory" yell newspaper headlines, followed by three minutes of stock footage from old Lippert oaters and the "wagon holdup/parents killed" segment from *Crooked River*, a six-year-old boy wandering off grasping his dead father's notched gun. Years later, at the Larabie Town Fair, Ellison (who was the lad) is afraid, through the traumatic events of his parents' murder, to pull the trigger of Dad's pistol. Those pesky outlaws, led by The Cat, are still causing trouble, so Ellison and Hayden are appointed lawmen, Hayden covering for his pal's not-so-itchy trigger finger. Fuzzy Knight turns out to be The Cat after much riding, shooting and posse chasing, Ellison mooning over Julie Adams' charms and regaining the use of his will to use a six-gun following the return of his memory. The last entry in the now long-forgotten Carr/Lippert series doesn't quite go out with a bang but remains an entertaining-enough 55 minutes for the kids to enjoy all the same.

Dialogue:
Adams to Ellison who's gone all gooey-eyed at the sight of her: "What's the matter? Didn't you ever see a girl before?"
Ellison: "Ah, y-yes Ma'am, m-many times."

The Furies

Paramount; 109 minutes; Producer: Hal B. Wallis; Director: Anthony Mann; Cast: Barbara Stanwyck; Walter Huston; Wendell Corey; Gilbert Roland; Judith Anderson; Thomas Gomez; John Bromfield; Beulah Bondi ****

Set in New Mexico Territory, 1870, Grand Opera met the Western genre in Anthony Mann's highly melodramatic tale of the Jeffords family, ruled by tyrannical Walter Huston, a bully who does everything his way, regardless. Headstrong daughter Barbara Stanwyck is in line to inherit the Furies Ranch over ineffectual sibling John Bromfield, but when Huston, up to his eyes in IOUs (or TCs, named after his initials) brings manipulative widow Judith Anderson into the fold, partly for financial stability, Stanwyck is rudely shunted to one side and doesn't like it, not one bit. To the deafening sound of Franz Waxman's hyped-up score, Stanwyck has an on/off romance with devious Wendell Corey whose strip of land was taken by Huston, sees Huston order the hanging of childhood friend Gilbert Roland and burn down squatters' homes on his land, and hurls a pair of scissors into Anderson's fine-boned face when she learns that the haughty dame is to be the new mistress on the block. Stanwyck, brimming with hatred, vows revenge, siding with Corey (who she weds) and the Anaheim Bank by purchasing all 20,000 of her father's head of cattle under an assumed title—owing to her machinations, he can't pay the bank the $145,000 due; all he has to his name is a trunk full of worthless TCs. He's broke and the extensive Furies spread is now hers. Out in the street, Huston, a chastened man, expresses his desire to go into partnership but is shot in the back by Roland's mother, dying in his daughter's arms. "Our son will bear his name," says Corey to Stanwyck as they take Huston's body away to be buried on his beloved ranch. "A capably mounted immoral saga with psychological trimmings," commented Britain's *MFB* (*Monthly Film Bulletin*) on a gloriously over-the-top Western drama of the old school, crammed with Freudian excesses and blessed with a pair of scenery-chewing star turns from Stanwyck and Huston, two unquestionable movie greats in full flow.

Highlights:
Stanwyck had brains, beauty and acting talent to spare, a true Hollywood legend as *The Furies* demonstrates.

Dialogue:
Corey to Stanwyck, arriving for a date, referring to Huston: "Where's the king?"
Stanwyck: "In his counting house, waiting."

Trivia:
Walter Huston's last picture; he died on April 7, 1950, three months before the movie's premiere.

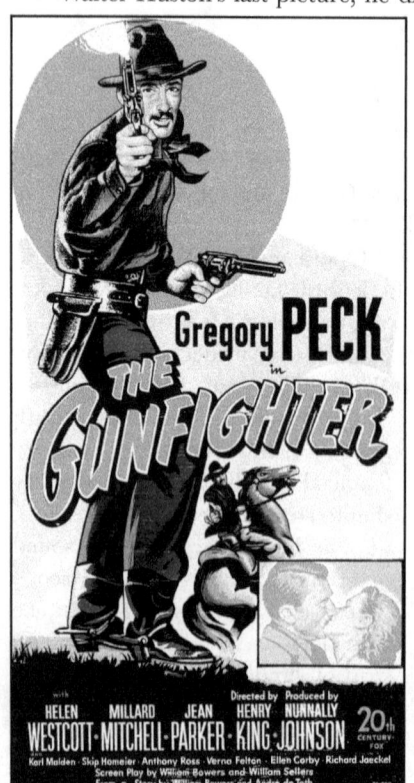

The Gunfighter

20th Century Fox; 85 minutes; Producer: Nunnally Johnson; Director: Henry King; Cast: Gregory Peck; Helen Westcott; Karl Malden; Millard Mitchell; Jean Parker; Skip Homeier; Anthony Ross; Richard Jaeckel *****

In the 1880s, retired professional gunman Gregory Peck (as Jimmy Ringo) walks into a saloon, minding his own business, and puts a bullet into young hothead Richard Jaeckel who's challenged him to the draw. Advised to leave town, Peck rides off to Cayenne to reunite with his schoolteacher wife Helen Westcott and son, ex-partner Millard Mitchell now the town marshal. But trouble isn't far behind; Jaeckel's three brothers are on Peck's trail while cocksure punk Skip Homeier is on the prod, itching to outdraw the taciturn killer. An edgy *noir* Western featuring one of Peck's most memorable star turns, *The Gunfighter* proves that, wherever you go, you cannot escape your reputation (15 men dead); it will always catch up with you, one way or the other. Here, Peck is shot in the back by Homeier after a fruitful meeting with Westcott and his boy to discuss their future but, dying, claims he drew first. This lets Homeier off the hook for murder, but the coward is now cursed as the man who gunned down Jimmy Ringo; every would-be gunslinger in the territory will be after him to prove that they're quicker than he is, a point made more forcibly by Mitchell who plants his boot firmly in Homeier's startled face ("They'll all be gunnin' for the man who killed Jimmy Ringo," the marshal growls). The *New York Times* commented on Peck's fine performance in "the tautest, most stimulating Western of the year," blessed with Alfred Newman's pulsating, exciting title score.

Highlights:
Peck, proving he was one of Hollywood's all-time greats, although by all accounts, not an easy man to work with.

Dialogue:
Jaeckel at the card table, staring at Peck: "He don't look so tough to me."
Friend: "Oh, if he ain't so tough, there's been an awful lot of sudden natural deaths in his vicinity."

Gunfire

Lippert Pictures; 59 minutes; Produced and Directed by William Berke; Cast: Don "Red" Barry; Robert Lowery; Wally Vernon; Pamela Blake; Leonard Penn; Steve Conte; Claude Stroud; Steve Pendleton ****

Following the murder of his brother Jesse at the hands of Bob Ford, Frank James (Don "Red" Barry) has retired from the outlaw life. Bandit Steve Conte can't persuade him to rob nearby Creede of its riches, so hits upon the idea of henchman Fenton (also played by Barry), a dead ringer for Frank, impersonating the notorious lawbreaker and thereby pin the robberies on him. In Creede, Marshal Robert Lowery has gunned down Ford in the street, but Frank still wants to take care of his brother, Charlie (Steve Pendleton), also mixed up with the Conte outfit; Lowery and new deputy Wally Vernon reckon Frank is innocent of a string of daring robberies committed by "the new James gang." Pamela Blake, Lowery's girl, is taken hostage by Conte's bunch after they've robbed the town bank, Frank eventually shooting his impersonator at the gang's hideout, the rest of the sidewinders arrested. Barry does exceptionally well in his dual roles, the tempo never lets up and Albert Glasser's noisy title score is a winner. Enjoyably tough B-action thrills.

Dialogue:
Pendleton: "I got no reason to be afraid of Frank. He, he's gone straight, got himself religion."

Conte: "I saw Frank today and when he heard your name, he wasn't thinking holy thoughts."

High Lonesome

Eagle-Lion Films; Technicolor; 81 minutes; Producer: George Templeton; Director: Alan Le May; Cast: John Drew Barrymore; Chill Wills; John Archer; Lois Butler; Kristine Miller; Basil Ruysdael; Jack Elam; Dave Kashner **

Utilizing the same crew that were behind Eagle-Lion's *The Sundowners*, Alan Le May's strange, little-seen Western filmed in Texas had abused youngster John Drew Barrymore (as Cooncat) playing a wild kid on the run, trying to convince rancher Basil Ruysdael, who accuses him of horse theft, that two malevolent, shadowy men on his tail killed a local trading post manager, not himself. Trouble is, no one but Barrymore can see these hombres, or "darned spooks," as Chill Wills calls them, and there's no body at the post, so the hot-tempered kid becomes a murder suspect. Le May (he also scripted) brewed up a confusing broth centered on a range war that once occurred between Ruysdael's outfit and the nearby Jessups who erected a "death fence," so-named because the bones of hundreds of steers that met their end on the line still lie on the ground. Could these two phantom cowpokes be connected to all of this? One of them, Jack Elam, turns out to be a Jessup, released from prison, and he's out to shoot Ruysdael in revenge. The whole shebang ends in a showdown at the post: Dave Kashner, Elam's partner, gets a bullet, so does Barrymore, and John Archer, romancing Kristine Miller, Ruysdael's feisty daughter, finishes off Elam. Barrymore, comforted by lass Lois Butler, now has a home for life if he wants it. Moments of mild humor and violence (Barrymore, roped to a horse by Archer and dragged over rough ground to make him talk) are offset by dim nighttime photography and a convoluted narrative that becomes tiresome after an hour. A real Western oddity.

Dialogue:
Miller to Archer, getting a little too frisky for her liking: "Pa said all along you were nothing but a loud yell with hands."
Trivia:
Barrymore's edgy, wild-eyed technique served him well in nine Italian peplum features, most notably as Aderbad, the mad warlock in Giuseppe Vari's *Rome Against Rome* (1964).

Hostile Country

Lippert/Exclusive; 59 minutes; Producer: Ron Ormond; Director: Thomas Carr; Cast: Jimmie "Shamrock" Ellison; Russ "Lucky" Hayden; George J. Lewis; Julie Adams; Fuzzy Knight; Tom Tyler; John L. Cason; Raymond Hatton ★★★★

The first of the Carr/Lippert Westerns and the best: Julie Adams is unable to lead her horses through a pass blocked by Oliver, a devious rancher who happens to be Ellison's stepfather—or is he? Ellison, with buddy Hayden, has ridden in to see him to claim half-ownership of the ranch but never met the man. Adams hires the duo, even though foreman Fuzzy Knight doesn't trust them. During a saloon poker game, Oliver (George J. Lewis) cheats and is shot by Hayden; it turns out that Lewis was an imposter, the real stepdad (George Chesebro) held prisoner by bad 'uns John L. Cason (who possesses a forged will) and Tom Tyler, the defile blocked to prevent Adams from selling her horses and going broke as a result, thus leaving her land open for the grabbers to move in. There's a wealth of horse chases, fistfights and gunfights, Hayden saving Ellison and Chesebro from being gunned down into their own graves, before Shamrock and Lucky blow the barricade to bits using dynamite from a mine; the horses gallop through, Adams sells her herd, Tyler is shot dead, Cason is slugged senseless, Ellison makes ranching plans with Chesebro and flirtatious Adams winds up getting a peck on both cheeks from our two heroes. Leisurely paced by Carr but, by these B-movie standards, top-notch fare.

Highlights:

For soundtrack buffs, take time out to listen to Walter Greene's elaborate soundtrack. Apart from a two-minute pause on the 50th minute, it plays virtually nonstop throughout, a veritable cascade of varying musical tones utilizing an entire orchestra that underlines every single second of action and nuance to perfection but never becoming intrusive, a symphonic form of cinematic art altogether lost from modern-day moviemaking. Greene scored 258 movies in his long career, plus being musical director on an additional 63, a prodigious output that should be recognized by all students of cinema.

Dialogue:

Raymond Hatton to Ellison: "Can you handle them six-guns or do you just wear 'em to keep your balance?"

I Killed Geronimo

Jack Schwarz Prods./Eagle Lion; 62 minutes; Producer: Jack Rabin; Director: John Hoffman; Cast: James Ellison; Virginia Herrick; Chief Thundercloud; Smith Ballew; Luther Crockett; Jean Andren; Myron Healey; Ted Adams **

Apache chief Geronimo died of pneumonia in 1909; in John Hoffman's cheapo version, relying on extensive stock footage from John Ford's *Stagecoach* to boost the action sequences, he died in 1882, falling on an upturned blade during a tussle with James Ellison. The ex-cavalry officer (his parents were killed by Redskins) is tasked by the Secretary of War at the White House to bring in Geronimo's head before he grabs a supply of repeating rifles and ammo and embarks on a reign of terror. In Lordsburg, Ellison infiltrates Ted Adams' gang, gets friendly with Virginia Herrick, demonstrates his skill with a pistol by shooting holes through the center of five coins and sets up a meeting with the Apache renegade (played by Chief Thundercloud) who demands weapons in return for keeping the peace. Some rifles are handed over but the firing pins are missing, the remainder secreted in another wagon bound for Fort Broken Bow. Enraged at the deception, Geronimo hits the warpath trail, cue for that *Stagecoach* footage, before fighting Ellison and toppling backwards onto his knife. Peace restored, Ellison cuddles up to Queen of the cut-price Western Herrick, the end to a minor Western offering that doesn't offer much except for Chief Thundercloud's scowling performance and Darrell Calker's noisy score.

Dialogue:
Herrick to stage passenger: "The mesa gets into your blood."
Passenger: "If the Indian arrow don't get into it first."

I Shot Billy the Kid

Lippert Pictures; 57 minutes; Produced and Directed by William Berke; Cast: Don "Red" Barry; Robert Lowery; Wally Vernon; Tom Neal; Wendie Lee; Claude Stroud; John Merton; Henry Marco **

Galloping past the Vasquez Rocks in umpteen repeated shots, 38-year-old Don "Red" Barry played 21-year-old Billy the Kid, the thickset actor putting in one of the most bizarre interpretations of "The Kid" ever to be captured on celluloid. Over a running time of less than an hour, Barry and his gang commit a string of robberies (horses and stages) and murders; in between, the notorious outlaw romances Wendie Lee, is seen as a heroic figure by her baby brother, Henry Marco, constantly busts Wally Vernon out of jail, befriends Robert Lowery (Pat Garrett) and refuses to hang up his guns on General Claude Stroud's promise of an amnesty. It all ends with Barry shot by Lowery in 1881. Made by the star's own production company, *I Shot Billy the Kid* has pace and plenty of gunfire plus a thumping Albert Glasser score, but the odd sight of grinning Barry, cigarette clenched in his teeth and strutting down the street, trying to behave like a young cowboy hoodlum, is too risible for words. OK fare for 10-year-olds.

Dialogue:
Marco in court, defending Barry's actions: "He was very kind. He didn't mean to kill anybody. Maybe they wanted to kill him first, so he had to shoot 'em."

King of the Bullwhip

Western Adventure Prods./Realart; 58 minutes; Produced and Directed by Ron Ormond; Cast: Lash LaRue; Al "Fuzzy" St. John; Anne Gwynne; Tom Neal; Jack Holt; George J. Lewis; Michael Whalen; Dennis Moore **

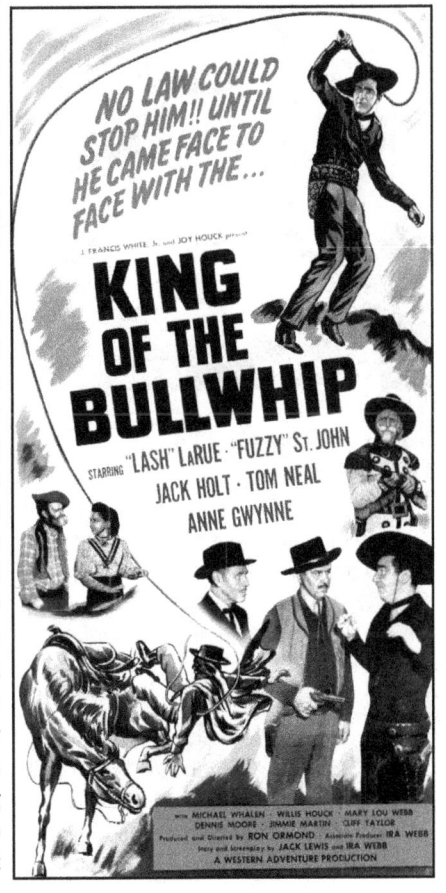

Shot in five days, *King of the Bullwhip*'s opening credits has Lash LaRue engaged in deadly whip combat with a lash-wielding desperado in a black mask; this sequence, padded out to five minutes, is repeated at the end of the movie. Further padding comes in the form of an overlong "masked bandits chasing stagecoach" scene, a protracted "masked riders chasing LaRue and Fuzzy" interval and a drawn-out saloon brawl. In Tioga, Marshal LaRue takes on the guise of El Azote, a masked, caped outlaw who is holding up banks and stages; hopefully, this will flush out the varmint and reveal his true identity. Following that climactic stinging lash contest, El Azote turns out to be bank official Dennis Moore, bent on building his own banking empire with stolen loot; possible candidates Tom Neal, George J. Lewis and Michael Whalen are quickly forgotten. Fuzzy uses a catapult to great effect, LaRue talks as though he's in a gangster movie and cowgirl Anne Gwynne flits in and out of the scenario when required. Full marks to composer Walter Greene whose cacophonous music keeps the narrative (and the interest) going when everything threatens to gallop into a blind alley with nowhere to go. A guest appearance by Buffalo Bill in the closing seconds, torpedoing Fuzzy's boasts that he's encountered every notorious character out West (Billy the Kid and Belle Starr among them) is relatively amusing.

Dialogue:
Fuzzy to LaRue, watching El Azote ride out of town: "Hey, uh, for a minute I thought you was him, but he's he and you's you so you can't be him!"

Trivia:
During the sequence when the outlaws are chasing LaRue and Fuzzy, one of the horses loses its shoe, the object flying right over the camera.

Marshal of Heldorado

Lippert/Exclusive; 63 minutes; Producer: Ron Ormond; Director: Thomas Carr; Cast: Jimmie "Shamrock" Ellison; Russ "Lucky" Hayden; John L. Cason; Tom Tyler; Fuzzy Knight; Raymond Hatton; Julie Adams; George J. Lewis ***

Heldorado, 1880: "Lucky" Hayden, looking for work, is handed the marshal's badge at $200 a month plus free drinks and a cabin in the hills. In rides foppish dude "Shamrock" Ellison on a donkey, needing a job, so he's quickly deputized. The pair are up against the Tulliver gang, terrorizing the territory and robbing banks, using Hayden's cabin as a hideout—Ellison, in fact, is a special investigator, sent to snoop on Raymond Hatton's corrupt bank dealings. The usual bout of frenetic horse chasing is topped off with a thrilling four-minute shoot-out in town, the remaining members of the Tulliver mob rounded up, Ellison making eyes at Julie Adams. Number two in the Carr/Lippert series moves like an express train, Ellison demonstrating a natural ability at self-deprecating humor.

Dialogue:
Ellison to Hayden, on swapping his fancy hat for Hayden's battered Stetson: "Oh, I wouldn't think of depriving you of your own hat. I can see that it's been a close part of you for a long, long time."
Hayden: "How do you know?"
Ellison: "I can smell, uh, I mean I can tell."

The Missourians

Republic; 60 minutes; Producer: Melville Tucker; Director: George Blair; Cast: Monte Hale; Paul Hurst; Roy Barcroft; Scott Elliott (Robert Neil); Lyn Thomas; Howard J. Negley; Lane Bradford; John Hamilton ***

Roy Barcroft's Missourians, a bunch of rampaging raiders, are causing havoc across the Texas border, prompting Marshal Monte Hale and sidekick Paul Hurst, a washed-up lawyer, to become involved when Barcroft turns up at the peaceful, crime-free town of Dorado; he's taking refuge in the family home, against Polish-born brother Scott Elliott's wishes. Barcroft and his boys want to grab the town's $10,000 church fund and as there's no bank in Dorado, the job appears to be a simple one. Into town waltzes Shakespearean actor Howard J. Negley, actually the front man behind the Missourians, determined to find out where that money is stashed (it's in the post office), Elliott blamed by the townsfolk when an outbreak of violent incidents threatens to disturb the tranquility. Negley shoots Mayor John Hamilton, Elliott festers behind bars but joins Hale in foiling a $50,000 gold bullion robbery at Cactus Point; Barcroft and Negley's gang smashed, Elliott marries Lyn Thomas and Dorado gets a new church. A fast-moving Republic oater, Roy Barcroft's snarling, unkempt villain (always stuffing his face with bread) stealing the acting honors.

Dialogue:
Lane Bradford's views on Dorado, to Barcroft: "No self-respecting crook would set foot in the place anyway. It's got no bank."

Montana

Warner Bros.; Technicolor; 76 minutes; Producer: Willam Jacobs; Director: Ray Enright; Cast: Errol Flynn; Alexis Smith; S.Z. Sakall; James Brown; Douglas Kennedy; Ian MacDonald; Paul E. Burns; Lester Matthews ***

In 1871, Australian sheep farmer Errol Flynn (as Morgan Lane) arrives in Montana after the Civil War with his flocks and creates his own war with cattle owners Douglas Kennedy and his fiancée, flame-haired Alexis Smith, in Warner Bros.' $2,000,000 "let's throw everything into the pot" Western which, at 76 minutes, was their shortest cowboy movie on record. Flynn (a real Australian) and his men set up camp on the cattle grazing border; during the night, their young guard is shot dead by cattlemen. To find out who the culprits are, Flynn, posing as a merchant, pretends to be a partner of traveling peddler S.Z. Sakall, enters town and finds himself up against Smith and Kennedy, owners of the Singleton spread. Going to the ranch to buy up land for his sheep (he doesn't let on about the sheep), he romances Smith with a guitar and song and inadvertently kicks off a sheep versus cattle dispute, determined to herd his flocks across the border. When Smith learns about his deception, Flynn rips up the land lease papers, Smith putting a temporary stop to their growing mutual attraction. Her brother later organizes a cattle stampede to trample Flynn's sheep to death but the scheme backfires, Kennedy killed in the fracas. Parading his sheep through town, Flynn has a showdown with Smith in the street; outdrawn by the lass, he collapses from a shoulder wound but she rushes over to him, displaying her love and affection. It's colorful (photographer: Karl Freund), contains a rowdy David Buttolph score, has plenty of rumbustious action and made the company a healthy profit. But it's not one of Flynn's better forays out West; sick of starring in Westerns, he didn't want to do the film (the picture was more or less completed in 1948 but left on the shelf) and the semi-comical elements let it down (as do the numerous clumsy back-projected sequences); neither does the short running time do *Montana* any favors, lending the production a rushed feel. But Flynn's renowned devil-may-care charm is evident, despite his misgivings at being handed the part, and Smith is splendidly decorative!

Dialogue:
Smith, addressing party goers: "Now it's war again. And whatever it costs in lives and property, you can blame it on one man. Morgan Lane."

Trivia:
Raoul Walsh directed a couple of scenes but pulled out of the project, disliking the material.

The Old Frontier

Republic; 60 minutes; Producer: Melville Tucker; Director: Philip Ford; Cast: Monte Hale; Paul Hurst; Claudia Barrett; William Henry; William Haade; Tristram Coffin; Lane Bradford; Victor Kilian **

Monte Hale is sworn in as marshal of Centerville, old sea dog Paul Hurst (speaking constantly in nautical terms) his deputy. When the bank is robbed within minutes of his appointment, Hale is up to his eyes in murder and mischief as crooked lawyer Tristram Coffin and henchman William Haade collude to murder the two men who know about Coffin's involvement in the holdup—Denver Pyle (stabbed) and Judge Victor Kilian (shot). Hale believes Doc William Henry, framed for the killings, to be innocent, arranging for him to escape from jail and help him round up Coffin and his men when they waylay a freight wagon carrying a valuable cashbox; Coffin is plugged during a shoot-out and Henry receives a microscope from the town for his endeavors. A standard hour-long Republic time-filler that runs out of steam midway through before ending in a fairly exciting gunfight.

Dialogue:
Hale to Almira Sessions who's complaining about backache to Henry, behind bars: "Might be the doc's worried more about his neck than he is about your back."

Rio Grande

Republic; 105 minutes; Producers: Merian C. Cooper and John Ford (both uncredited); Director: John Ford; Cast: John Wayne; Maureen O'Hara; Claude Jarman, Jr.; Victor McLaglen; Ben Johnson; Harry Carey, Jr.; J. Carrol Naish; Chill Wills *****

The final instalment of John Ford's cavalry trilogy (*Fort Apache*, 1948; *She Wore a Yellow Ribbon*, 1949), *Rio Grande*, budgeted at $1,200,000, was a sentimental, nostalgic tribute to the U.S. cavalry punctuated by moments of rousing action, comedy, songs (sung by the Sons of the Pioneers) and family drama. Stunningly shot in gleaming black-and-white by Bert Glennon, Utah's magnificent scenery formed a bleak, monolithic backdrop to life at Fort Starke in 1879, situated on the Mexican border and continually raided by Apaches. Among 18 new recruits being paraded before rascally Victor McLaglen (as Sgt. Major Quincannon, a memorable performance) is Lieutenant Colonel John Wayne's son, Claude Jarman, Jr., who's enlisted after failing at West Point. Hot on the lad's heels comes Maureen O'Hara, Wayne's estranged wife, wanting to take Jarman away from Fort Starke, even though he's determined to stay ("He shouldn't have enlisted. I've come to take him home."). Wayne and O'Hara slowly rekindle their relationship, McLaglen tries to keep control of his unruly greenhorn troopers (especially Ben Johnson and straw-chewing Harry Carey, Jr., an amusing double-act) and Wayne is given permission by General J. Carrol Naish to cross the Rio Grande and rescue the outpost's children, abducted by the Indians. In a thrilling climax, Johnson, Carey and Jarman are tasked with infiltrating the church where the kids are held captive (Jarman to Carey: "Sandy. Are you scared?" Carey: "Me? Yo!"), leading to a blazing skirmish. Devotees of *The Searchers* will spot many locations used in Ford's 1956 classic while, as in *The Searchers*, Wayne dominates the proceedings, a hard, stubborn man gradually thawing under

the gaze of O'Hara's beautiful eyes. Victor Young's melodic music tops off one of the genre's finest of all cavalry pictures that looks as great now as it did over 60 years ago.
Highlights:
Ford carefully placing his troop detachments amid those towering rock formations to create visuals of everlasting power.
Dialogue:
McLaglen to his fresh young recruits at horse-jumping practice: "When I was a young man like yourselves, I could jump nine feet tall, with an Indian under each arm!"
Pause, then Carey, straw in mouth, eyeing McLaglen: "What tribe?"
Trivia:
Filming took place around Utah's Moab region during the summer, the cast, in heavy costumes, wilting under the intense heat; O'Hara stated in her autobiography that several stuntmen died in the "muddy river" sequence, their bodies never recovered.

Rock Island Trail aka Transcontinent Express

Republic; Trucolor; 90 minutes; Producer: Paul Malvern; Director: Joseph Kane; Cast: Forrest Tucker; Bruce Cabot; Chill Wills; Adele Mara; Barbara Fuller; Lorna Gray (Adrian Booth); Grant Withers; Jeff Corey ***

A noisy, rowdy railroad concoction set in the 1850s that has chief engineer and president of the Chicago and Rock Island Rail Lines, Forrest Tucker, constructing rail tracks across the West to grab a lucrative mail contract, encountering one setback after another: dwindling finances, falling share prices, rampaging Indians and steamboat tycoon Bruce Cabot trying to put him out of business. Tucker's also in competition with Cabot over the hand of Adele Mara, while educated Indian princess Lorna Gray practically launches an all-out assault to coax the six-foot-four hunk into her wigwam ("I like men who build things."). Chill Wills, as usual, supplies the comic element as Tucker's whiskey-lovin' foreman, a bridge burns down, Tucker and Cabot engage in a duel, both wielding mops, Abe Lincoln (Jeff Corey) turns up as a rookie lawyer hired to sue Cabot for arson and there's a race between a locomotive and a stagecoach, not to mention a few shoot-outs, the whole colorful romp ending in a mass Indian attack; Gray is slain by an arrow, as is Cabot after he refuses to be spread-eagled over an anthill, and Tucker weds Mara. R. Dale Butts' music hammers away in a lively picture that entertains but falls a tad short of the "classic railroad Western" mark.
Highlights:
Those mighty impressive steam locomotives brought out of mothballs to star in the movie.

Dialogue:
Wills to Tucker: "Hey! You tryin' to insult me? I'm thin-skinned, y'know!"
Tucker: "Haha. Yeah—like an elephant!"

Rocky Mountain

Warner Bros.; 83 minutes; Producer: William Jacobs; Director: William Keighley; Cast: Errol Flynn; Patrice Wymore; Scott Forbes; Guinn "Big Boy" Willams; Dickie Jones; Howard Petrie; Sheb Wooley; Chubby Johnson *****

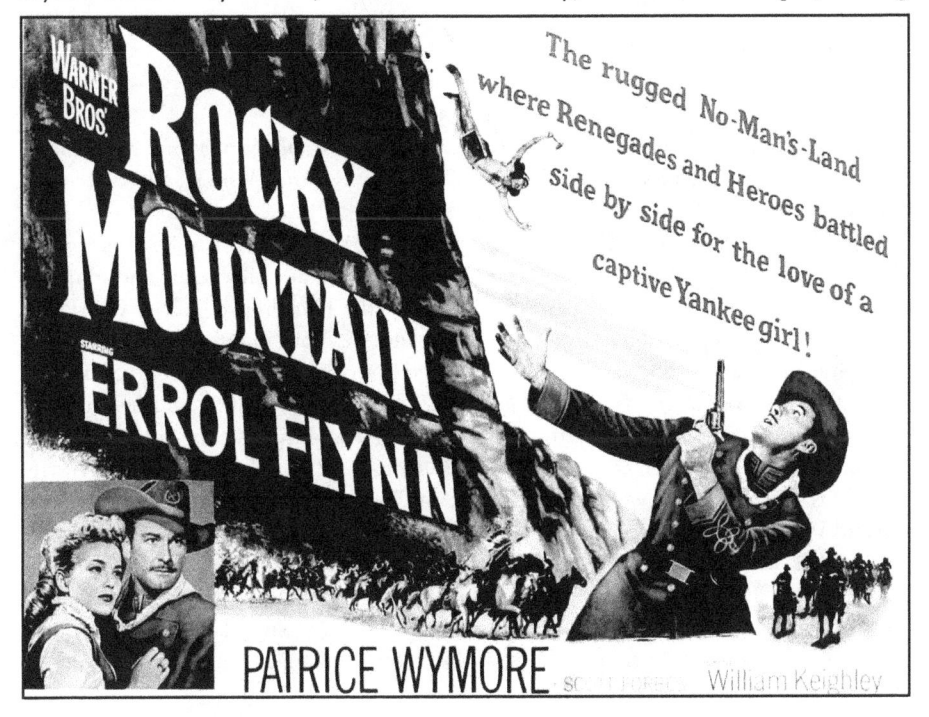

New Mexico's Gallup region would become a familiar sight to Western lovers throughout the decade, as well known for location filming as California's Lone Pine Alabama Hills. Three-times Oscar-nominee Ted D. McCord's hard-edged black-and-white photography brought the area's outstanding monumental rock formations to vivid life in a terrific outdoor actioner containing not a single interior/back-projected scene, much to its credit. The perfect background, then, to highlight Errol Flynn's last Western (out of eight); he's a Confederate captain leading seven hardened men across Shoshone territory in March 1865, hoping to rendezvous with Howard Petrie atop Ghost Mountain; their plan is to recruit a thousand Southern sympathizers and overrun California. Patrice Wymore and stage driver Chubby Johnson are rescued from a Redskin attack, Petrie leaves, vowing to return with those promised fighters (he doesn't; the Indians finish him off) and Lieutenant Scott Forbes' seven-strong Union platoon is held prisoner; they've come looking for Wymore, Forbes' fiancée. Writers Winston Miller and Alan Le May (from his story) flesh out each and every character to impart interest and to deflect the viewer's gaze from that magnificent scenery while Max Steiner, as usual, provides the perfect Western score. Needless to say, Wymore gets sucked into Flynn's world-weary charms, much to Forbes' dismay; the lieutenant escapes, heading for garrison reinforcements because of a possible Indian attack brewing and this is where *Rocky Mountain* pulls out the emotional stops. In allowing Wymore, Johnson and a single trooper to evade the Shoshone, Flynn, Wooley, Slim Pickens, Guinn "Big Boy" Williams, Jones, Robert "Buzz" Henry, Peter Coe and Rush Williams ride out to create a diversion (Flynn admirably demonstrates his horsemanship in this sequence). Pursued by the braves, they're cornered in a huge box canyon; turning round to face their foe, they wade into the savages, perishing to the last man in a brutally realistic skirmish, a moving, tragic climax mirroring the Custer massacre in *They Died With Their Boots On*, probably Flynn's finest hour in the saddle. And when Forbes, Wymore and the Union soldiers survey the carnage, who but the hardest among us will not shed a tear as Jones' pet dog Spot, in Wymore's arms, looks forlornly at his young master's broken body. In memory of their valiant last stand, Forbes orders the Confederate flag to be hoisted on Ghost (Rocky) Mountain in tribute to those eight brave souls. "Square-jawed and efficient," commented the *New York Times* on Flynn's engaging star turn; and the rest of the cast was just as good, natural and effortless in their portrayals.

Highlights:
Gallup's eye-boggling natural wonders and that final battle, bloody and vicious.

Dialogue:
Forbes to Flynn: "Miss Carter is my fiancée."
Flynn: "I know. That's the only reason you're alive. Don't force your luck."

Trivia:
John Wayne turned down a $200,000 salary to appear as the leading man, while Ronald Reagan complained that he should have been offered Flynn's role. Away from the cameras, director Keighley tried to prevent Wymore from associating with Flynn, Hollywood's most notorious womanizer, but failed miserably; the pair respectively packed in their partners and married soon after the film's completion, Wymore becoming Flynn's third wife. The film marked the debuts of Pickens and Wooley.

Sierra Passage

Monogram; 81 minutes; Producer: Lindsley Parsons; Director: Frank McDonald; Cast: Wayne Morris; Lola Albright; Lloyd Corrigan; Roland Winters; Alan Hale, Jr.; Billy Gray; Paul McGuire; Richard Karlan *****

Possibly ex-World War II decorated fighter ace Wayne Morris' most memorable Western? It's certainly one of Monogram's, a multi-layered tale of revenge and romance (with a few musical numbers tossed in) set against the backdrop of Lloyd Corrigan's traveling minstrel show. Corrigan, on a train, relates his story in flashback: 13-year-old Billy Gray's father is murdered for cash he received from the sale of a parcel of land. Gray rides after the three varmints (crooked gambler/killer Alan Hale, Jr., Paul McGuire and Richard Karlan) and is creased in the chest, tumbling from his horse; the lad is picked up by Corrigan and adopted by the kind-hearted showman. 12 years later, Gray (now Wayne Morris) is a sharpshooter wearing twin pistols in Corrigan's show, working with mentor Roland Winters. Saloon lass Lola Albright is recruited as a singer and stooge in the stage act and falls for Morris, but the big hunk ("He's sick inside.") has only one thing on his mind—to get even for his dad's murder. He remembers two things about the killer—a stubbed finger sporting a fancy ring and a maniacal laugh. Going from town to town, he spends nights questioning saloon barkeeps, his foe tantalizingly always one step ahead.

Albright desperately wants him to drop the quest and settle down, but Morris, a victim to his inner demons, just has to carry on ("Your mind is getting warped."). Finally, at a theater show, he recognizes that laugh in the audience; tracking Hale and his cohorts to a saloon where a poker game is in progress. Morris sits in, loses on purpose, reveals his identity ("That's the kid been huntin' you."), wounds McGuire and Karlan and fires eight shots at Hale, one smashing the glass he's holding, the other seven into his hands, ensuring that the thug will never cheat at cards again. Back in the present, Corrigan reunites with Winters and married couple Morris and Albright on their ranch, a touching closer to a minor Western gem that wears a lot of heart on its highly polished sleeve.

Dialogue:
Hale to Morris in the saloon showdown: "Where you headin' from here?"
Morris: "The end of a mighty long trail, mister."

Singing Guns

Republic; Trucolor; 91 minutes; Producers: Abe Lyman and Melville Tucker; Director: R.G. Springsteen; Cast: Vaughn Monroe; Ella Raines; Ward Bond; Walter Brennan; Jeff Corey; Barry Kelley; Harry Shannon; Tom Fadden ***

Republic boss Herbert J. Yates looked around for another cowboy star to boost box-office takings and hired popular '40s orchestra leader/singer Vaughn Monroe to play Rhiannon, an outlaw with a $5,000 price on his head, his hideout near Hangman's Mountain worth a $50,000 reward as it reputedly contains over a million in stolen gold. When Monroe wounds Sheriff Ward Bond, he takes him into Coldville, where doctor-cum-preacher Walter Brennan knocks Monroe out with a potion, shaves him and dresses him in new duds—while Bond recuperates, Monroe is now Coldville's new deputy, and only Brennan knows his true identity, hoping to save his soul. Soon, Monroe is smooching with sexy saloon owner Ella Raines (Bond's girl), singing three songs, reaching for his Colt, saving two men from a mine inferno and squaring off with slippery boss of the Great Western Gold Company, Jeff Corey; Corey was the man who claim-jumped him years back, and Monroe is stockpiling the stolen gold in revenge, his eyes set on a massive gold shipment due to take place on September 24. Monroe's pretence is unearthed in the final reel but not before he and Bond have gunned down Corey and his boys, Raines discovering the loot in the outlaw's lair and crossing Monroe in the name of good by handing it over to the state governor. Monroe is now up for a pardon and gets the hand of Raines into the bargain, Bond heading for the saloon with Brennan to drown his sorrows in whiskey. Good-looking Monroe acquits himself well in his first starring role, the rugged Sedona wilderness forms a fine backdrop and Nathan Scott conjures up a barnstorming score to add spice to the action.

Dialogue:
Raines to Monroe as he slobbers all over her: "Wait a minute, honey. I'm not broke yet. You'll have to spend at least as much time on me as you would a horse."

Trivia:
Monroe starred in a second Western for Republic, *Toughest Man in Arizona* (1952), followed by one episode in TV's *Bonanza* (1962), and then called time on his short screen career.

Streets of Ghost Town

Columbia; 54 minutes; Producer: Colbert Clark; Director: Ray Nazarro; Cast: Charles Starrett; Smiley Burnette; George Chesebro; Mary Ellen Kay; Stanley Andrews; Frank Fenton; Don Reynolds; Ozie Waters ***

Like the Lash LaRue Westerns of the '50s, Charles Starrett's *Durango Kid* oaters utilized a great deal of stock footage from the actor's previous films in the form of flashbacks to save on production costs, leading to a marked sameness in material. Here, Starrett (as Steve Woods and the Kid), Smiley Burnette, Mary Ellen Kay, Don Reynolds and Frank Fenton's gang are searching for a million dollars in stolen gold secreted in an old Spanish mine called Devil's Cave near a ghost town. In a series of those oft-used flashbacks (footage from 1946's *Landrush* and *Gunning for Vengeance* was used), we are informed that Kay's uncle, George Chesebro, double-crossed partner Fenton and hid the treasure in the abandoned mine behind a big steel door. He was then apprehended by The Durango Kid and put behind bars. Now blind and out of his mind, Chesebro, having escaped from prison, returns to locate the gold (Reynolds, his nephew, knows its whereabouts) but is shot dead by Fenton who's gunned down by The Durango Kid in a climactic chase; the riches are handed over to the government. Creepy atmospheric photography in the deserted town by Fayte M. Browne is a definite bonus in a Durango Kid feature that still has a '40s feel to it, the slightly macabre atmosphere ruined (some might say) by Burnett acting like a real scaredy-cat, looking over his shoulder for non-existent spooks hiding in every darkened corner.

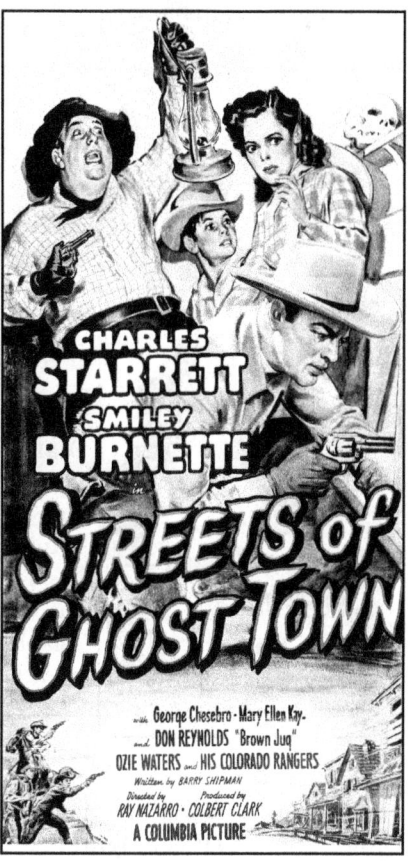

Dialogue:
Starrett to Burnett, alarmed at being told to turn on the lights inside the wrecked saloon: "Ghosts don't pull guns. Do as I say!"

The Sundowners aka Thunder in the Dust

Eagle-Lion Films; Technicolor; 83 minutes; Producer: Alan Le May; Director: George Templeton; Cast: Robert Sterling; Robert Preston; Chill Wills; Cathy Downs; John Litel; Jack Elam; Don Haggerty; John Drew Barrymore ***

Cattle rancher Robert Sterling is besieged on all sides, by cattle king John Litel, by crooked sheriff Don Haggerty (Litel's son), by unstable Jack Elam and his put-upon wife, Cathy Downs, and by the black sheep of the family, lead-slinger Robert Preston; only fellow rancher Chill Wills appears to be on his wavelength. When one of his boys is found dead by youngster John Drew Barrymore and some of his cattle are stolen, Sterling, furious, demands answers, fighting fire with fire, Preston (forever singing "There's a Girl in the Life of O'Reilly") gunning down anyone who stands in his and his brother's way, rustling other herds, selling the beef and handing the proceeds to Sterling. Alan Le May's ambiguous screenplay was adult-themed for its day, focusing on fractious relationships, a multitude of characters caught up in a very wordy narrative to the extent that it is difficult to figure out their precise motives; Preston drills Elam and Haggerty, leaving, in the end, Sterling with no other option but to challenge his troublesome psycho brother to a gunfight, Wills blasting the killer with a shotgun. There's a splendid nine-minute shoot-out between Preston, Wills, Sterling, Barrymore and a bunch of heavies in a deeply wooded canyon (Mexico's Palo Duro Canyon) which more or less irons out all the plot imperfections, and Leonid Raab and Rudy Schrager's dramatic music is a definite bonus. But it's not an easy ride, and cowboy-mad kids will find a lot of what's on offer just plain baffling.

Highlights:

The lengthy canyon shoot-out, highlighting Winton C. Hoch's pristine Technicolor photography.

Dialogue:

Preston, taunting Elam: "Sweet dreams, bub. Ain't nobody lives forever."

Trivia:

The film debut of Barrymore, credited as John Barrymore, Jr.; and the directorial debut of George Templeton, following a run of seven 20-minute shorts made between 1944/1946.

Trail of the Rustlers

Columbia; 55 minutes; Producer: Colbert Clark; Director: Ray Nazarro; Cast: Charles Starrett; Gail Davis; Tommy Ivo; Mira McKinney; Don C. Harvey; Smiley Burnette; Myron Healey; Boyd "Red" Morgan **

The first of Charles Starrett's 22 *Durango Kid* B-Westerns produced in the 1950s (as of 2018, four were unavailable and another four were online, in Portuguese only) is an amiable affair, not overly exciting, suitable for the kiddies; hardly any gunfights or bruising fistfights, 13-year-old Tommy Ivo hero-worshipping The Durango Kid to the point that he dresses like him and rides a white steed, Raider Junior. Mira McKinney plays the villain of the piece, sending out her boys to murder ranchers in the Rio Perdido Valley, thus enabling her to buy up all their land at a low price. Son Don C. Harvey impersonates The Durango Kid in a series of holdups and settler raids to tarnish his reputation; when friendly Starrett (as Steve Armitage;

he was always Steve in his features, from 1945 onwards), arrives in town, no one suspects him of being the masked crusader on the big white horse called Raider; Steve rides a big brown horse called Bullet. Bumbling buddy blacksmith Smiley Burnette warbles three songs (two with The Roundup Boys) and a lost river is located to cure the valley's drought problem. A couple of harmless punch-ups and mild shoot-outs culminate in Ma McKinney arrested with her outlaw offspring, Burnette, cozying up to Gail Davis (not a romance, surely!) and bidding farewell to Starrett who rides away to new adventures on the open range.

Dialogue:
Awestruck Ivo: "Gee! Durango called me partner!"

Two Flags West

20th Century Fox; 92 minutes; Producer: Casey Robinson; Director: Robert Wise; Cast: Joseph Cotten; Linda Darnell; Jeff Chandler; Cornel Wilde; Dale Robertson; Arthur Hunnicutt; Jay C. Flippen; Noah Beery, Jr. ****

1864, Major Jeff Chandler, commanding Fort Thorn, resents Confederate prisoners of war, led by Colonel Joseph Cotten, donning Yankee cavalry uniforms as a government pardon and taking up residence in his fort to fight the Indians. The embittered martinet also loves his dead brother's wife, Linda Darnell ("You make me feel unclean," she storms at him), as does Captain Cornel Wilde and Cotten. The Southerners plot to escape and rejoin the Southern army, rampaging Apaches and Kiowas are on the warpath, massacring a family of settlers, and Chandler's mental illness results in him killing the Kiowa chief's son, paving the way for an all-out war. Robert Wise's densely plotted John Ford-type cavalry saga, shot in New Mexico and boosted by Hugo Friedhofer's strident score and Leon Shamroy's gleaming black-and-white photography, just misses out on being a classic, maybe because of Chandler's unsympathetic performance as the unhinged officer who, after a bloody Redskins versus bluecoats skirmish, hands the command over to Cotten (the Confederate has ridden to the Fort's rescue with his men) and sacrifices himself to the Indians. And Cotten gets the girl, Wilde having succumbed to an Indian bullet. "Good rousing cavalry film," said the *New York Times*.

Highlights:
The six-minute climactic Alamo-type battle at Fort Thorn, violent, harrowing and brilliantly staged by Wise.

Dialogue:
Reb sergeant Arthur Hunnicutt to Union sergeant Jay C. Flippen: "If you Yanks could fight like you could lie…"

Trivia:
Chandler, a sufferer of chronic fatigue, found it tough commuting to Hollywood between shooting, mirrored in his testy portrayal of the bad-tempered major; the part was originally offered to Lee J. Cobb.

The Vanishing Westerner

Republic; 60 minutes; Producer: Melville Tucker; Director: Philip Ford; Cast: Monte Hale; Paul Hirst; Aline Towne; Roy Barcroft; Arthur Space; Richard Anderson; William Phipps; Dick Curtis *

Rancher Roy Barcroft organizes stage holdups, pinches the cash, bumps off his partners in crime and arranges the fake murder of Arthur Space, the sheriff of Broken Bow; Space disguises himself as his bewhiskered brother, Sir Cedric, from Sussex, England, to enable him and Barcroft to steal a $30,000 payroll from the sheriff's safe. In the meantime, young deputy Richard Anderson moons over fiancée Aline Towne while special investigators Monte Hale and his forever-hungry sidekick Paul Hirst, posing as wanted murderers, become involved in a few punch-ups and shooting matches before Barcroft and his gang are jailed and Space, false beard removed, shot dead in a cemetery, falling into his own open grave. A chaotic screenplay (Robert Creighton Williams) will leave you wondering what the hell Barcroft is up to during the first 30 minutes, such is the disjointed narrative; the final few minutes livens up, with a wagon chase through California's Red Rock Canyon cliffs and a different kind of cat-and-mouse shoot-up amid shadowy graves, cinematographer Ellis W. Carter's expertise showing itself in these two sequences. But apart from this, *The Vanishing Westerner* is a shambles, knocked out by Republic on the lowest of budgets, and seems to drag the action out, even at an hour-long running time.

Dialogue:
Hirst to an owl, as him and Hale snoop around the cemetery: "Shoo, you mangy feather duster."

Trivia:
Richard Anderson's first credited film role.

Wagon Master

RKO-Radio; 86 minutes; Producers: Lowell J. Farrell, Merian C. Cooper and John Ford; Director: John Ford; Cast: Ben Johnson; Harry Carey, Jr.; Ward Bond; Joanne Dru; Charles Kemper; Alan Mowbray; Jane Darwell; Kathleen O'Malley *****

One of John Ford's personal favorites, *Wagon Master* commences in brutal fashion, a pre-credits bank holdup carried out by Charles Kemper and his sons, before settling down. Two roaming cowpokes (Ben Johnson and Harry Carey, Jr.) ride into Crystal City with ponies for sale. Ward Bond, leader of a Mormon wagon train, buys the horses and offers $100 each to Johnson and Carey if they act as wagon masters and guide his people to the San Juan Valley in Utah. The pair agree and to the sound of the Sons of the Pioneers, who make up the bulk of the soundtrack, the train sets off into the wilderness. Shooting took place in Utah's Moab region, the magnificent Fisher Towers pinnacles featuring prominently in the film's second half, and in this respect, Ford's mini-epic (a lot briefer than most of his pictures) scored highly, Bert Glennon's superb photography bringing those towering rock walls to almost stereoscopic life. Doctor Alan Mowbray's traveling medicine wagon joins the settlers, Johnson courting two-bit actress Joanne Dru while Carey romances shy Kathleen O'Malley. Then Kemper's gang make their presence felt, forcing themselves on Bond's group, taking their weapons and living off their supplies. A meeting with friendly Navajo Indians results in gang member Fred Libby flogged for molesting a squaw; there's a nerve-racking ascent up a sheer-sided cliff face and, nearing the San Juan River, Kemper demands the grain wagon before departing. But Carey carries a smuggled pistol and in a superbly staged shoot-out, the two wagonmasters gun down Kemper and his clan. As the Sons of the Pioneers sing the stirring "Wagons West," Johnson cozies up to Dru and Carey plants a kiss on O'Malley, the wagons rolling towards their Promised Land. Short on action, maybe, but *Wagon Master* is almost poetic in its depiction of a wagon train out West, akin to a documentary in parts, a perennial classic still broadcast frequently on British television today. "A good outdoor action film," commented *Variety*.

Highlights:

Utah's spectacular rocky vistas and Johnson and Carey, two members of Ford's repertory company, proving a likeable, memorable double-act of sorts, as they were in *Rio Grande*.

Dialogue:

Johnson to Carey, seeing his pal tuck a six-shooter in the back of his pants, barrel down: "Careful that gun don't go off and blow yer brains out."

Trivia:

Johnson, a real-life ex-cowboy, performed all his own stunts; and the scene where a dog ripped Ward Bond's pants happened by accident, Ford, delighted, keeping it in the finished print.

West of the Brazos

Lippert/Exclusive; 58 minutes; Producer: Ron Ormond; Director: Thomas Carr; Cast: Jimmie "Shamrock" Ellison; Russ "Lucky" Hayden; Julie Adams; John L. Cason; Tom Tyler; Raymond Hatton; Fuzzy Knight; Stanley Price ***

Hard-of-hearing Hayden and pal Ellison come up against The Cyclone Kid and his gang in Brazos where Ellison is out to prove he's who he says he is, John L. Cason claiming *he's* Ellison to take possession of his victim's oil-rich Lazy Dollar Ranch worth $75,000. When Sheriff Stanley Price is wounded in a gunfight, Ellison takes on *his* identity in order to bring Cason and his bunch to justice. A letter proving Ellison to be the true heir is lost and retrieved by Cason, the dispute culminating in a farcical (and comical) courthouse hearing, presided over by Judge Fuzzy Knight. Cason (The Cyclone Kid) is awarded the ranch as legal claimant and Ellison accused of impersonating Price, but Hayden reads Cason's lips as the crook plans, alongside Tom Tyler, to dispose of wounded Price. At a shack, Ellison, after shooting snake-eyed Tyler, engages in a particularly vicious fistfight with Cason which would have had kids in the audience flinching in terror, and is established as the ranch's rightful owner. "Boys, there's gonna be a wedding," grins Hayden as Julie Adams and Ellison smooch on a fence, the end to number five in the Carr/Lippert Westerns and the most amusing.

Dialogue:

Hayden to Ellison in the courtroom, looking at Knight: "That old rooster doesn't treat you right, I'll shoot off his tail feathers."

Wyoming Mail

Universal; Technicolor; 87 minutes; Producer: Aubrey Schenck; Director: Reginald LeBorg; Cast: Stephen McNally; Alexis Smith; Dan Riss; Roy Roberts; Howard Da Silva; Whit Bissell; Armando Silvestre; Ed Begley ****

In 1869, mail-carrying locomotives en route to the west coast (the post office on wheels) are being sabotaged in Wyoming for their post and cash; Washington, worried about the expense, is threatening to pull the plug on the whole operation in 30 days if the gang responsible isn't brought to justice. Enter ex-army secret service agent-turned-boxer Stephen McNally, tasked by old boss Dan Riss with infiltrating the train robbing group under the guise of a wanted outlaw and nailing the entire bunch (James Arness and Richard Jaeckel are among their number). Harry Essex and Leonard Lee's involving screenplay sees McNally teaming up with Indian assistant Armando Silvestre, discovering that prison warden Ed Begley is using stolen loot, being incarcerated in a rough territorial prison to gain information from convict Whit Bissell, who teaches him the art of Morse code, escaping, romancing music hall singer Alexis Smith, being hired by gang chief Howard Da Silva in Crystal City because of his telegrapher skills and discovering the outlaws' hideout in ancient inaccessible cliff workings, accessed by two rickety ladders. Diehard movie buffs will quickly latch on to the fact that Roy Roberts, spotted in reel two, is the brains behind the robberies; the actor specialized in playing devious crooks so no surprise that he turns out to be the chief villain, falling to his death from the hideout after a fight with McNally. The robbers are arrested following attempts to relieve a train of $200,000 and Smith, who was in on the crimes but having second thoughts, marries McNally, the pair off on a loco to start a new life in San Francisco, McNally promoted to Rail Supervisor District 7. "A notch above the run-of-the-average sagebrush saga," commented the *New York Times*, for once praising a Western that deserved it: Reginald LeBorg's taut direction, Harry Lubin's resonant score plus Russell Metty's rich photography add to an exciting outdoor oater that delivers on all counts.

Highlights:

Alexis Smith, her radiant beauty lighting up the screen.

Dialogue:

McNally to Smith, trying to find out the brains behind the operation: "Who is Mister Big?" Smith, looking adoringly at McNally: "You are!"

Young Daniel Boone

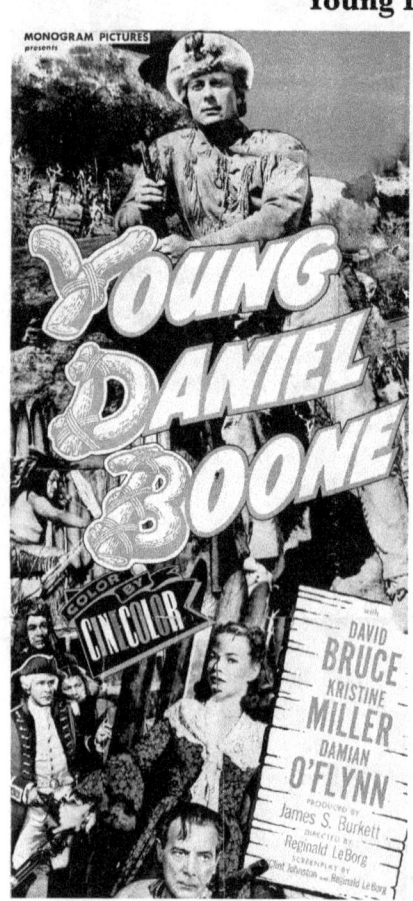

Monogram; Cinecolor; 71 minutes; Producer: James S. Burkett; Director: Reginald LeBorg; Cast: David Bruce; Kristine Miller; Damian O'Flynn; Don Beddoe; John Mylong; Mary Teen; William Roy; Stanley Logan **

In 1755, Daniel Boone (David Bruce) and his Redskin companion Little Hawk (William Roy) meet up with Colonel John Mylong and merchant Don Beddoe, on the run following an Indian massacre of colonial troops in the woods. Bruce has been tasked with gaining information about the enemy's movements, saving Beddoe's two captive daughters (Kristine Miller and Mary Teen) from a life of squawdom en route to Fort Harrison. At the deserted fort, Damian O'Flynn, who has joined the group, turns out to be a French traitor but joins forces with Bruce and company when the stockade is attacked by a bunch of Shawnee braves. The Shawnee are sent packing by homemade bombs and salvos from rigged muskets; O'Flynn falls on his own knife during a tussle with Bruce to the sound of Miller cooing "Daniel, darling!" and the frontiersman gallops off on a loaded wagon with Miller at the end, promising her a life of plenty ("A wonderful home!") in the North American backwoods; thus begins (states the narrator) the legend of Daniel Boone. A stodgy colonial yarn, suffering from murky cinematography (Gilbert Warrington) and disjointed continuity in the first half; Bruce (forever remembered for his zombie role in Universal's *The Mad Ghoul*) makes a personable Daniel Boone, but the picture is ragged around the edges, leaving you to struggle through its 71-minute running time.

Dialogue:

Bruce to Mylong: "If the Indians get ya, Colonel, they'll hang that white wig along with your natural hair as a pair of prize scalps."

Chapter 2
Johnny Mack Brown at Monogram

Johnny Brown was born in Dothan, Alabama on September 1, 1904, one of eight children. He became the star player of the college football team and went on to attend the University of Alabama where he shone as the university's halfback. A career in insurance beckoned but the powerfully built six-foot-one's handsome face appearing on cereal boxes saw him signed to MGM in 1927, his first screen appearance in the baseball movie *Slide, Kelly, Slide*. Brown starred in Mary Pickford's first talkie, *Coquette* (1929), but by 1931 things didn't look too promising, Clark Gable replacing him on the set of *Laughing Sinners*; he was also turned down for the lead role in *Tarzan the Ape Man*. But taking on the title role in King Vidor's *Billy the Kid* (1930) had been a success, so Johnny Mack Brown, as he was then known, gravitated into B-Westerns with Universal-International and Poverty Row outfits Mascot and Supreme Pictures; *Lasca of the Rio Grande* was his first Universal oater, released in 1931. In 1943, he joined Monogram as the company's answer to Buck Jones and his *Rough Riders* serials, starring in *Ghost Rider* as Nevada Jack McKenzie, a character he would play on numerous occasions; from 1943 to 1952, Brown appeared in 73 Westerns and was a recognizable name to millions of American cowboy-mad kids. His low-budget Monogram sagebrush sagas, like those of his fellow actors in this field, ended in 1952; he then appeared in a few television serials and had cameo roles in a further three Westerns in 1965 (*Requiem for a Gunfighter*, *The Bounty Killer*, *Apache Uprising*) before quitting the business. Johnny Mack Brown died on November 14, 1974, aged 70, having starred in over 170 pictures. Overweight and in his mid-'40s, Brown put the required amount of energy into his 1950s efforts but quite often appeared labored against his younger co-stars, Myron Healey figuring prominently among them; he was also one of the few B-stars not to be lumbered with a semi-comical sidekick. However, experienced B-movie directors Lewis D. Collins, Wallace W. Fox and Thomas Carr brought out the best in him and many of his Monogram efforts were surprisingly well constructed; on the whole, they remain entertaining to this day. All films are listed in order of release.

1950
West of Wyoming

Monogram; 57 minutes; Producer: Vincent M. Fennelly; Director: Wallace W. Fox; Cast: Johnny Mack Brown; Myron Healey; Milburn Morante; Stanley Andrews; Mary Gordon; Gail Davis; Paul Cramer; Milburn Morante ***

The first of 16 hour-long Johnny Mack Brown B-Westerns made in the 1950s saw bad guy Myron Healey making plans to steal Stanley Andrews' ranch from under his feet because of gold deposits discovered on the property near Mesa City; the crook has already bumped off another rancher's son who found his men looking for nuggets. Trouble is, fist-happy Brown from the Department of the Interior is pinning up notices stating that the Mesa City territory is open to settlers and homesteaders under a new government act, and there's nothing that Healey and his jackals can do about it. As Healey has already drawn up claims for the gold mines, he instructs two of his men to bushwhack a wagon train of settlers, resulting in the murder of Paul Cramer, Andrews' grandson. Aided by horse trader Milburn Morante, Brown brings the gang to justice at the Mesa City Relay Post; Morante's talkative other half, Mary Gordon, starts knitting baby socks for Gail Davis, Cramer's pregnant wife, who, judging by her beatific expression, seems oblivious to the fact that her new husband bit the dust a couple of days back.

Dialogue:
Morante: "Hey, Johnny, wait a minute. Look (holds up a baby sock), Nora was knitting this. I'm gonna be a poppa after all these years."
Brown: "Fine, Panhandle, just fine. Congratulations!"
Morante hears it's for Davis, and turns to Gordon: "You mean that you ain't, that I ain't, that we, we ain't, er ..."
Gordon: "'Course not, you old fool!"

Over the Border

Monogram; 58 minutes; Produced and Directed by Wallace W. Fox; Cast: Johnny Mack Brown; Myron Healey; Wendy Waldron; Marshall Reed; Milburn Morante; Hank Bell; Pierre Watkin; House Peters, Jr. **

Wells Fargo agent Johnny Mack Brown foils an attempt by crook Myron Healey and his outlaws in Pecostown to steal $30,000 from the company, buy silver bullion in Mexico and resell the bars at a profit over the border. Shooting Wells Fargo man Pierre Watkin when Mike Ragan pinches the loot, alcoholic Marshall Reed hides out in Milburn Morante's cabin, the back of which opens onto a tunnel which Healey's boys use for smuggling the silver bars. Rancher Wendy Waldron, Watkin's daughter, and her admirer House Peters, Jr. assist Brown in curtailing Healey's activities; Reed is killed by Morante, his body hidden in the hills, and in the climax, henchman Ragan is brought down by Sheriff Hank Bell's posse, Healey arrested following a two-second fistfight with Brown. Job wrapped up, our rather thickset hero rides away after promising to attend Waldron and Peters' wedding. A dull entry in the series. Edward J. Kay's music is curiously dated, the action at times threatening to grind to a halt, although cinematographer Harry Neumann brings some finesse to the proceedings.

Highlights:
Bell's vast, bushy whiskers; not for nothing did he earn the sobriquet of "Handlebar" in Hollywood.

Dialogue:
Reed to Morante on being offered a coffee: "What I need is a drink, not hogwash."
Morante: "Sorry, Bart, I ain't got a drop. I stopped drinkin' when I started to see pink elephants. Heh, heh, heh, I'll never forget the last time I got crocked. That elephant chased me …"
Reed: "Oh shut up, will yer?"

Six Gun Mesa

Monogram; 56 minutes; Produced and Directed by Wallace W. Fox; Cast: Johnny Mack Brown; Gail Davis; Riley Hill; Leonard Penn; Marshall Reed; Milburn Morante; Carl Mathews; Frank Jaquet ***

Oily town-grabber Leonard Penn arranges for four wranglers on a cattle drive to be poisoned at Six Gun Mesa, then orders his men to finish off the rest of the crew and steal the steers. Drover Riley Hill, in Redblade relaxing, is targeted by Penn's bullyboys, led by Marshall Reed and Carl Mathews, as he's the sole survivor of the massacre. Penn is also after laying his hands on the town's hotel managed by Milburn Morante so that he can run Redblade unhindered and set up a saloon and casino; the original owner was done away with on Penn's instructions. Hill is framed for the murder of local drunk Mike Ragan but saved from a hanging by Johnny Mack

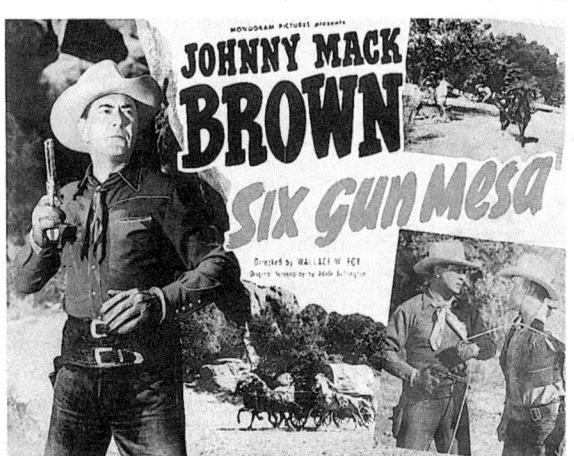

Brown, who appears on the scene after 14 minutes have gone by. Brown has inherited the hotel and sets about proving that Hill didn't shoot Ragan; he possessed a .44 gun, but Ragan was killed with a .45 bullet, Doc Frank Jaquet bribed by Penn to falsify the death certificate. Brown and Reed come to blows in a savage brawl, Brown eventually worming the truth out of Jaquet after pouring copious amounts of whiskey down his fat throat. At Penn's hangout, he defeats the crook in a bruising slugging match after Reed and his cronies have bitten the dust, Hill's reputation left intact. Signing the hotel over to Morante, Brown rides away to pastures new, leaving Hill to take up with pert saloon singer Gail Davis. A more inventive oater from the star, even though Edward J. Kay's score burbles in the background instead of nailing the action as it should have done.

Dialogue:

Jaquet to Reed: "Look me up, Bradley, the next time you tangle with that new hotel owner. From what I've heard about him, you're liable to wind up with something worse than a headache!"

Law of the Panhandle

Monogram; 55 minutes; Producer: Jerry Thomas; Director: Lewis D. Collins; Cast: Johnny Mack Brown; Jane Adams; Riley Hill; Myron Healey; Marshall Reed; Ted Adams; Lee Roberts; Carol Henry ***

Outlaws grabbing wealth by force; horses and cattle stolen; stagecoaches held up; street gunfights; and life savings wiped out in bank robberies. Yes, terror rules the Panhandle, and only Marshal Johnny Mack Brown astride his big Palomino steed Rebel can sort it out, Sheriff Riley Hill failing to nail the outlaw gangs responsible. Is the brains behind the mayhem crusty old rancher Ted Adams? Could it be stage line owner Myron Healey? Or is it persons unknown that have inside knowledge of post and freight movements, the information conveyed in unsigned letters, and arranging for lines of communication to be cut? Brown gallops into Green River, the center of all this lawlessness, to assist Hill in bringing in the desperados responsible and make the lawman appear bigger in Adams' eyes; after all, the guy wants to marry his daughter, Jane Adams. The required quota of gunfights, fisticuffs and chases (plus a stampede) ends with Healey revealed as the main culprit; he's bent on buying up every land deed in the area to sell to the new railhead at a healthy profit. Healey fires three slugs into Brown, thinking him dead, but those bullets were blanks, Brown having cottoned onto Healey in the final reel. Henchman Marshall Reed is punched and tied up, accomplice Milburn Morante gets shot in the back and Healey is arrested; Adams plans to sell his ranch to the rail bosses and finance Hill and Adams' wedding. *Law of the Panhandle* is fast-moving Western antics with much-underrated Healey, in particular, demonstrating a good line in two-faced villainy.

Dialogue:
Reed to Lee Roberts and Carol Henry: "We'll keep two jumps ahead of that marshal all the time."
Henry: "It'll take some doing. I've heard of this Johnny Mack Brown. He's no pushover."
Roberts: "Yeah. They say he's a tough man to tangle with."

Outlaw Gold

Monogram; 56 minutes; Producer: Vincent M. Fennelly; Director: Wallace W. Fox; Cast: Johnny Mack Brown; Jane Adams; Milburn Morante; Hugh Prosser; Myron Healey; Marshall Reed; Carol Henry; Bud Osborne *

"$100,000 seized by masked bandits" scream the headlines, Marshal Johnny Mack Brown, after saving Jane Adams and her father from bandits, going undercover in Latigo City to bring the villains to heel, aided by doddery deputy Milburn Morante, posing as a newspaperman. Hugh Prosser is the crook, melting the government gold into type print and ferreting the stuff out east in crates. When Brown gets the better of henchman Marshall Reed, Prosser hires gunfighter Myron Healey, released after a five-year-prison spell, to gun down Brown, the lawman who put him behind bars. In a street showdown, the marshal fires two slugs into Healey's shoulder instead of killing him; as a token of gratitude, Healey helps Brown round up Prosser's gang, gaining the admiring glances of Adams, Latigo's newspaper heiress. The only highlight in a dull JMB oater is the street stand-off between our hero and Healey; otherwise, the pace drags, even at 56 minutes, a decidedly amateurish air hanging over the whole tedious production.

Dialogue:
Morante: "A great headline! Sonny Lang (Healey) hangs up his gun! How about it?"
Brown: "You're gonna hang up this apron and get outta here! You don't know anymore about newspapers than I do."

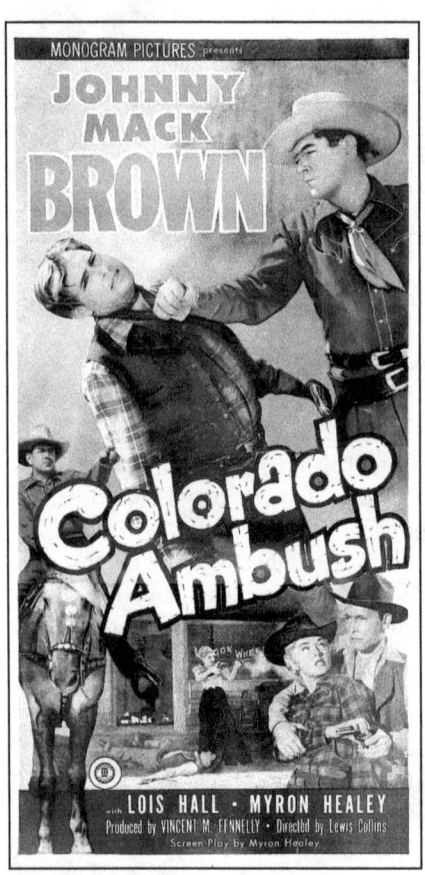

1951
Colorado Ambush

Monogram; 52 minutes; Producer: Vincent M. Fennelly; Director: Lewis D. Collins; Cast: Johnny Mack Brown; Myron Healey; Lois Hall; Tommy Farrell; Christine McIntyre; Lee Roberts; Marshall Bradford; Lyle Talbot ****

Myron Healey scripted a nicely constructed Johnny Mack Brown oater, one of the better entrants in the series. Healey and his boys, operating out of Booneville, are knocking off Wells Fargo cashboxes in stage holdups; young Tommy Farrell is in with the gang, his sister (Lois Hall) running a nearby horse ranch. Farrell is smitten with saloon hussy Christine McIntyre, but she's Healey's squeeze, the duplicitous pair planning to sneak into the Wells Fargo office and pinch the next mine payroll—and Farrell's father, Marshall Bradford, runs the office. Agent Brown canters in on Rebel, posing as a company horse trader, and soon he's firing hot lead, henchman Lee Roberts the first to bite the dust. During the robbery, Bradford removes Healey's mask and gets two slugs for his pains. Farrell, drunk, is jailed on suspicion of being in on the robbery but McIntyre hands him a gun through the bars and he busts out, only for Healey, as planned, to drop him in the saloon. Director Collins fashions a decent shoot-out finale for this type of low-budget fare: Healey pushes McIntyre, who's clutching the stolen cash, into the street where she pretends to be injured. Brown rushes over to her, Healey fires and wings Brown but falls to the agent's two bullets and Farrell, on the point of death, puts paid to McIntyre. Brown and Hall are last seen taking the stage to Denver.

Dialogue:
McIntyre to Healey: "Chet. Where's Gus?"
Healey: "Last time I saw him, he was stretched out waitin' for a tombstone."

Man from Sonora

Monogram; 54 minutes; Producer: Vincent M. Fennelly; Director: Lewis D. Collins; Cast: Johnny Mack Brown; Phyllis Coates; House Peters, Jr.; Lyle Talbot; Lee Roberts; Dennis Moore; John Merton; Pierce Lyden ***

The seventh of JMB's 1950s cheapo Monogram potboilers saw our brawny hero's beloved horse Rebel stolen by stagecoach robber Lee Roberts, right after he and his gang have held up the stage to Silver Springs. Ex-lawman Johnny hitches a ride into town, is assumed to be the new marshal and arrested by old chum Lyle Talbot for fighting Roberts in a saloon. But who's the brains behind the robberies? The guilty party is suave House Peters, Jr., romancing Phyllis Coates; the *real* marshal, Pierce Lyden, has been murdered, lowlife Dennis Moore taking his place and falling in with Peters and his gang. It's all good primitive fun (bereft of a score), resembling a late 1930s Western but with one or two moments of '50s violence added for good measure; Johnny Mack takes care of Peters after the louse has gunned down his compatriots to grab the stolen cash for himself, gets his horse back and rides off for further adventures on the Monogram backlot, Coates looking at his retreating back, all misty-eyed.

Dialogue:
Brown to Roberts: "What's on your mind?"
Roberts: "Your horse."
Brown: "My horse?"
Roberts: "I know just how you feel. But I gotta have your horse"
Brown: "Wouldn't you settle for my bankroll?"
Roberts: "I can't ride a bankroll across the desert."

Blazing Bullets

Monogram; 51 minutes; Producer: Vincent M. Fennelly; Director: Wallace W. Fox; Cast: Johnny Mack Brown; Lois Hall; House Peters, Jr.; Edmund Cobb; Milburn Morante; Forrest Taylor; Stanley Price; Dennis Moore ***

Outlaws are on the rampage and lawlessness rules the territory, a U.S. treasury cashbox full of stamped gold bars stolen and hidden away. Forrest Taylor ("Nothing but crime in the papers.") refuses to acknowledge unemployed House Peters, Jr. as his daughter's (Lois Hall) intended and when Taylor vanishes, slugged by a masked man, the finger of suspicion points to Peters. Marshal Johnny Mack Brown arrives on the scene after being winged by a gold rifle bullet, shot by crusty old miner Milburn Morante. Rumors of a ghost surround Hall's empty ranch, leading Brown and Peters, now deputized, to investigate the place, Taylor found trussed up in the cellar, some of the gold bullion being turned into jewelry. Sheriff Edmund Cobb and his henchmen, aided by Morante, are behind it all; in a climactic set-to, Morante is tied up, Cobb slugged and the baddies gunned down, the cash returned to town. Taylor now views Peters in a much different light, bestowing his blessing on their forthcoming nuptials.

Dialogue:
Taylor, ranting to Hall: "There are entirely too many hot-tempered, gun-crazy kids in this territory. When I was a boy back in Boston, you didn't see every young loafer walking around the streets with a gun on his hip."

Montana Desperado

Monogram; 51 minutes; Producer: Vincent M. Fennelly; Director: Wallace W. Fox; Cast: Johnny Mack Brown; Myron Healey; Virginia Herrick; Lee Roberts; Edmund Cobb; Marshall Reed; Steve Clark; Carl Mathews ****

Johnny Mack Brown, away for a few years, returns to his ranch, the Double B, to discover that the previous four tenants have been murdered by persons unknown. Who is the mysterious masked man in black, lining up ranchers in his rifle sight, picking them off and then disappearing? The Double B controls half of the water rights in the valley and someone wants to own the entire area, including every homestead on it, resorting to criminal activity and written warnings. Mine engineer Myron Healey, ranch girl Virginia Herrick's fiancé, reckons there's copper on Johnny Mack's property and offers to buy his spread for $5,000, paid for by his mining company. Brown agrees to the sale just as another local rancher is murdered but has no intention of leaving, setting a trap involving the use of a mirror. Overlooking the ranch, the masked killer shoots Brown's image and is then pursued through the hills by his very-much-alive victim and Sheriff Steve Clark's posse. Giving them the slip through that oft-used Monogram tunnel, he changes garb, revealing himself to be Healey, backtracking to the ranch where he finds Herrick alone with wounded foreman Lee Roberts. In a quick shoot-out, Brown plugs Healey through an open window, explaining to everyone that Healey was the masked man all along, sole owner and shareholder of his company and wanting to own the valley for its water and possible mineral wealth. Her fiancé out of the way, pert Herrick homes in on Roberts as possible husband material, Brown grinning his head off. Experienced Western writer Daniel B. Ullman scripted and it showed, a far more inventive JMB oater than usual, like a snapshot of the distant Western past played out amid the sunlit hills surrounding Los Angeles' Iverson Ranch and, of its type, highly enjoyable.

Dialogue:
Herrick, on realizing what a rat Healey had been, to Brown: "Oh Johnny! He was going to kill all of us."
Brown: "I know, Sally."
Herrick: "And to think I was going to marry him."

Oklahoma Justice

Monogram; 56 minutes; Producer: Vincent M. Fennelly; Director: Lewis D. Collins; Cast: Johnny Mack Brown; James Ellison; Lane Bradford; Phyllis Coates; I. Stanford Jolley; Marshall Reed; Barbara Woodell; Kenne Duncan ****

Joseph O'Donnell scripted a sparkling Johnny Mack Brown outing in which our hero (displaying a noticeable paunch) turned up on the ninth minute wearing a white shirt, black hat and black mask and proceeded to rob the Coldwater Bank, shooting dead bank teller Bruce Edwards, engaged to saloon gal Phyllis Coates. But the whole charade is a fake. Brown happens to be a U.S. marshal posing as an outlaw, hoping to bring to justice a gang who have been robbing banks and holding up stages for mine payrolls in the area. Naïve sheriff Kenne Duncan is unwittingly passing on information to widowed Barbara Woodell (as Ma), boss of the Bar X Ranch and head of the bunch that includes crack gunshot Lane Bradford, saloon boss Marshall Reed and the real brains behind it all, bank examiner I. Stanford Jolley. Brown attempts to infiltrate the outfit by sweet-talking Woodell into taking him on; she's interested but hulking Bradford is suspicious, even though Brown and pal James Ellison have recently robbed the stage in Walker's Pass of $50,000, takings from the Wild Oaks Mine—so he must be a bona fide outlaw, mustn't he? The money is stashed away in the hills; Brown offers to cut Woodell's gang in but is trussed up in the ranch house instead. In a frenetic closing reel, outlaws and posse clash in the hills, Bradford is arrested, Reed puts a bullet in Woodell, Brown plugs Jolley during a struggle and, in a final shoot-out, Reed is brought down by Brown, the gang surrendering. Coates gets wed to Edwards, Ellison, promoted to deputy marshal, waving to Brown as he rides away on Rebel's broad back. Composer Raoul Kraushaar and cinematographer Ernest Miller demonstrate conclusively that, even within the realm of the B-Western, their services did matter; both score and photography are exemplary considering the movie's low finances.

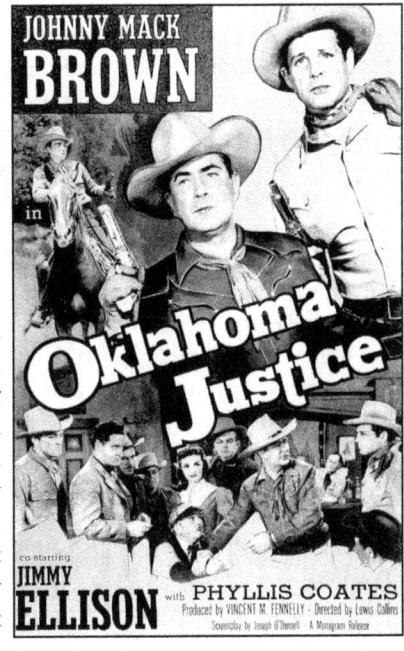

Highlights:
A great example of how to produce a cracking hour-long Western on a budget of $50,000; and the fistfight between Brown and Bradford in a saloon ruckus is a real bruiser.

Dialogue:
Woodell, sneering, to Brown: "Rate yourself pretty high."
Brown: "If I don't, who will?"

Whistling Hills

Monogram; 58 minutes; Producer: Vincent M. Fennelly; Director: Derwin Abrahams; Cast: Johnny Mack Brown; James Ellison; Noel Neill; I. Stanford Jolley; Marshall Reed; Lee Roberts; Pierce Lyden; Pamela Duncan ****

A mystifying bandit in black hat and cape is galloping like the wind up in the Whistling Hills, directing outlaws to rob I. Stanford Jolley's gold shipments; in town, Johnny Mack Brown reclaims his stolen Palomino, Rebel, from crook Pierce Lyden and, following a saloon fracas, is hired by Jolley to bring the miscreants to heel. Johnny Mack has to work with Sheriff James Ellison who has been unable to corner the gang and the so-called Whistling Ghost of Spanish legend ("It's like tryin' to round up a handful of smoke."); the lawman seethes with jealousy as our hero slowly but surely uncovers the outfit's secrets and finds time to take Ellison's squeeze, Noel Neill, for a ride in the country. Marshall Reed and henchman Lee Roberts are the villains, gaining information about what exactly Jolley's stages are carrying through none other than Neill, the stage line owner's niece. She's the whistling black-clad figure, aggrieved that when her father died, he handed the business to Jolley, not to her. In a climactic skirmish in Coyote Pass, Ellison's posse wipes out the outlaws as they converge on the stage and Neill expires in the dust, admitting "I was trying to get what was mine." The movie ends on a downbeat note (for a Johnny Mack Brown Western), Ellison breaking the news to Jolley that Neill is dead, Brown riding away on Rebel. The Zorro-type character that Neill played also figured in *Montana Desperado* and *Canyon Ambush*; *Whistling Hills* is a fast-moving 11th entry, orchestrated with pace by TV director Derwin Abrahams, Brown in bruising form.

Dialogue:
Jolley to onlookers: "You mark my words. That Johnny Mack Brown is dynamite. That Whistling Ghost outfit's in for an unpleasant surprise."

Texas Lawmen

Monogram; 54 minutes; Producer: Vincent M. Fennelly; Director: Lewis D. Collins; Cast: Johnny Mack Brown; James Ellison; I. Stanford Jolley; Lee Roberts; Terry Frost; Marshall Reed; John Hart; Pierce Lyden ****

Three masked bandits rob a stage, murdering both driver and guard. In an ensuing chase, the sheriff of King City is killed, James Ellison handed the job. But Ellison is the son of grizzled I. Stanford Jolley, murderous leader of the Morrow gang who have been terrorizing the territory for months. Moreover, Jolley won't touch King City because he relies on information given to him by his law-abiding offspring, planted there for this specific purpose. In rides Marshal Johnny Mack Brown to wipe out Jolley's viper's nest, eventually assisted by Ellison, the lawman realizing what a snake his old feller is. At the Blue Girl Mine, Brown ambushes the bunch as they're in the act of rifling the contents of the safe and in a chase guns down Lee Roberts; Jolley pretends to give up his shooter, goes to fire and is dispatched by beefy Johnny Mack. Ellison is allowed to keep his badge in a well-formulated, female-free Johnny Mack Brown oater boosted by Jolley's venomous performance, Ernest Miller's sparkling photography and Raoul Kraushaar's lively score.

Dialogue:
Ellison, pointing his gun at Jolley, Roberts and Terry Frost: "I'm arresting you. All of you." Roberts: "Why, you phoney sheriff!"

1952
Texas City

Monogram; 54 minutes; Producer: Vincent M. Fennelly; Director: Lewis D. Collins; Cast: Johnny Mack Brown; James Ellison; Lane Bradford; Lois Hall; Lorna Thayer; Lyle Talbot; Marshall Reed; Terry Frost ****

Actually, it's Dawson City, a ghost town where corrupt army officer Lyle Talbot and his varmits are operating from, robbing U.S. army gold shipments and leaving no one alive at the scene; the opening seven minutes is given over to a mildly violent (by JMB standards) holdup. The outlaws' hideout is an abandoned mine connected to the Old Grand Western Hotel via a secret tunnel; blonde Lois Hall has recently inherited the joint, arriving with Lorna Thayer and handyman Lane Bradford to tidy up the place. Johnny Mack doesn't appear until the 14th minute, a marshal assigned to crack the case, disgraced officer James Ellison infiltrating the gang to clear his name and assist Brown en route. Scriptwriter Joseph F. Poland cooks up a decent-enough storyline with some witty banter (Thayer: "Oh, why didn't I stay in Connecticut?" Bradford: "Well, didn't they have any shootings back there?" Thayer: "Ah, not since 1776.")—there's plenty of lively action and loud gunplay in and around the derelict town and Bradford (for a change, playing a good guy) winds up marrying Thayer after Talbot and his bunch are arrested; Ellison is restored to the army ranks, much to Hall's delight.

Dialogue:
Ellison to Hall: "You run a hotel in a ghost town?"

Man from the Black Hills

Monogram; 58 minutes; Producer: Vincent M. Fennelly; Director: Thomas Carr; Cast: Johnny Mack Brown; James Ellison; Rand Brooks; Lane Bradford; I. Stanford Jolley; Stanley Andrews; Florence Lake; Denver Pyle ****

Writer Joseph O'Donnell concocted an intriguing screenplay for this superior, tightly constructed Johnny Mack Brown horse opera in which James Ellison attempts to prove to blind father Stanley Andrews that he's his real long-lost son, not Rand Brooks, who's an imposter. Brooks and his storekeeper father, I. Stanford Jolley, plan to lay their hands on Andrews' Gold Girl Mine but, in a twist of events, Andrews' gold shipments have been waylaid by law officers and secreted in the Railhead Bank because of crooked parties interested in the blind man's fortune; and, against type, screen bruiser Lane Bradford plays a sheriff! Ellison has been summoned to Rimrock by his uncle, Ray Bennett, to meet Andrews; Bennett gets fatally injured in a stage holdup, Denver Pyle helping himself to the gold but not letting on to his fellow lawmen. Pyle also wants a third of the cut when Jolley and Brooks eventually take over the mine. A trap is set by Johnny Mack Brown and Bradford at Bennett's shack; Brooks and Jolley are both arrested after a chase and a fistfight. Ellison is reunited with his dad, promising to pay for an operation to restore his sight, housekeeper Florence Lake making plans to marry him as soon as possible.

Dialogue:
Brown to Lake: "When is this wedding going to take place? Before or after the operation?"
Lake: "Before. I'm not taking any chances with him changing his mind when he gets to look at me!"

Trivia:
Note the opening, and particularly the final, sequences, filmed in a howling gale that sprung up during shooting; finances dictated that there was no time for a re-shoot under more favorable conditions.

Dead Man's Trail

Monogram; 59 minutes; Producer: Vincent M. Fennelly; Director: Lewis D. Collins; Cast: Johnny Mack Brown; James Ellison; Barbara Woodell (Barbara Allen); Lane Bradford; Terry Frost; Dale Van Sickel; I. Stanford Jolley; Stanley Price ***

Bank robber Dale Van Sickel escapes from prison. Texas Ranger Johnny Mack Brown is tasked with bringing him to justice, retrieving the $100,000 the outlaw secreted away and nailing his old gang, the Black Hills outfit, also after the loot. In a shoot-out near Lobo City, Sickel, who has been grabbed by Lane Bradford and his boys, is shot dead; Bradford and company ride to Silvertown where Sickel's brother, James Ellison, works as a bank teller. At his house, Mum Barbara Woodell has taken up residence, Ellison is confronted by Bradford and, during a meal of coffee and donuts, is given a few days to let on where the stolen cash is—or else he gets a bullet. But Ellison doesn't know where that money lies hidden, joining forces with Brown and ransacking Sickel's old cabin, to no avail. Scriptwriter Joseph F. Poland piles on the incident over the space of an hour. Bradford forces Ellison to give him the combination to the bank's safe but is prevented from stealing the takings by Brown's timely intervention; Deputy Sheriff Terry Frost falls in with Bradford's mob, shooting Sheriff I. Stanford Jolley in the back and blaming the murder on Ellison; a map behind a painting pinpoints where the cash is hidden, beside a certain tree in Dark Canyon; and after getting their grubby paws on the dollars, the outlaws are caught by Brown and Ellison. Frost is shot dead, along with Bradford's two henchmen, the leader arrested after a slugging match with Brown. The ending is a bit abrupt, but Raoul Kraushaar's full-blast score and Ernest Miller's deep monochrome photography add spice to the penultimate Johnny Mack Brown Western, even though the leading man's thickening waistline makes him appear a tad uncomfortable at times.

Dialogue:
Bradford to Ellison: "Have you any idea where Walt hid that money?"
Ellison: "No."
Gregg Barton, going for his gun: "He's lyin'."
Bradford: "I know it, but shootin' won't do any good, we're here to open his mouth, not to close it."

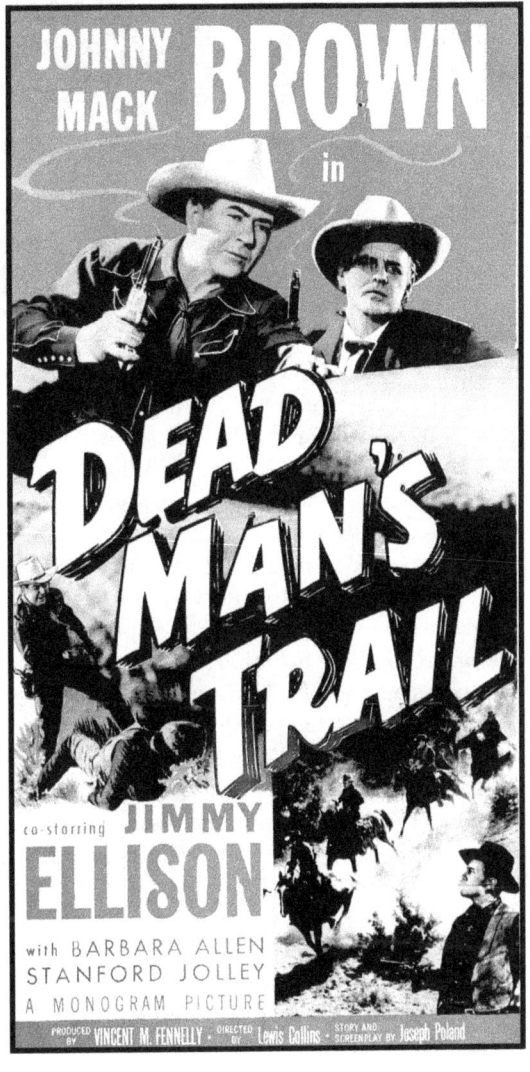

Westerns of the 1950s: The Classic Years

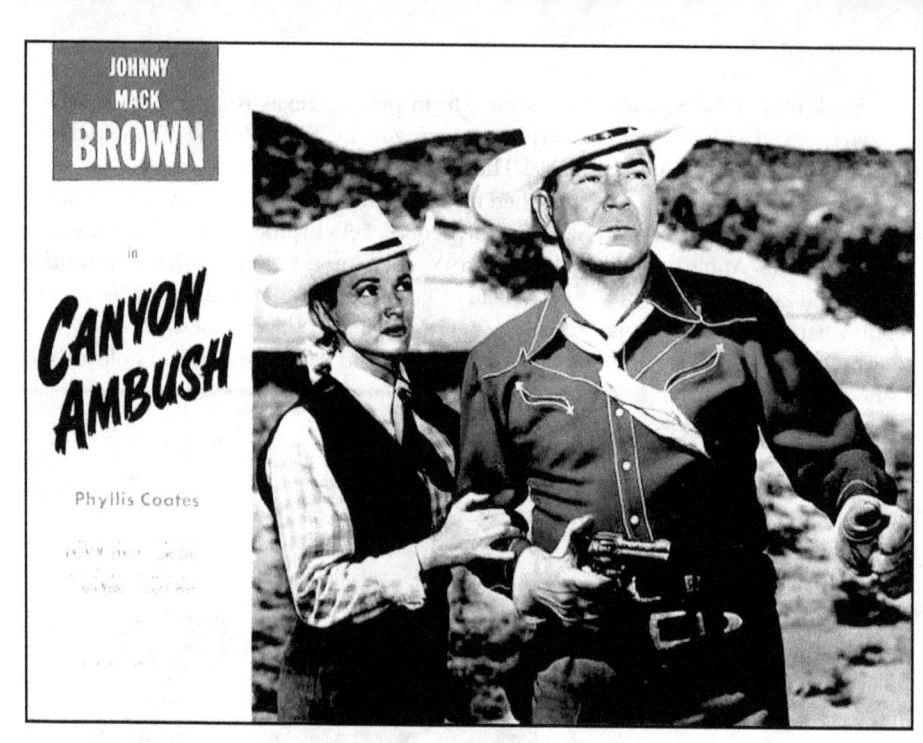

Canyon Ambush

Monogram; 53 minutes; Producer: Vincent M. Fennelly; Director: Lewis D. Collins; Cast: Johnny Mack Brown; Phyllis Coates; Hugh Prosser; Lee Roberts; Dennis Moore; Pierce Lyden; Marshall Reed; Russ Whiteman **

The Johnny Mack Brown serial-type oaters ended on a flat note: As in *Montana Desperado* and *Whistling Hills*, an unknown gunman in black hat, cape and mask is terrorizing the Wyoming border territory and Border City's residents are placing the blame on Sheriff Lee Roberts; why, they ask, hasn't he caught this desperado and the gang who are robbing Wells Fargo shipments? In canters Johnny Mack Brown to assist beleaguered Roberts in flushing out the outlaws and rescuing the guy's faltering romance with newspaper gal Phyllis Coates, resulting in umpteen chases, a few gunfights and a very familiar plotline. Crooked lawyer Dennis Moore and rancher Russ Whiteman are behind the crimes, Wells Fargo agent Hugh Prosser the mastermind (and the man in black); he picks up coded messages to Brown on his own telegraph machine, giving him inside information as to the lawman's movements. After disposing of Moore and Whiteman, Prosser is apprehended by Johnny Mack following a daring escape on a runaway stagecoach; his honor restored, Roberts makes plans to marry Coates. An outdated final entry in a series that, by 1952, bore little relevance to what was occurring elsewhere in the Western movie sphere.

Dialogue:
Brown to Coates, on meeting her for the first time: "If your paper looks as good as you, it should have a large circulation."
Coates, smiling: "Why, thank you."

Trivia:
Denver Pyle is listed in the credits but didn't appear in the film; Russ Whiteman took over his role and never received a credit.

Chapter 3
1951

A MARSHAL WHOSE HIDE NO BULLET COULD TOUCH ... AND THE GIRL THAT GOT UNDER HIS SKIN!
Along the Great Divide

THE APACHES ARE OVER THE BORDER ... TO BURN ... TO LOOT ... TO KILL!
Apache Drums

TOUCH WHAT'S MINE AND YOU WON'T LIVE TO TELL THE TALE!
Border Fence

GUNS SHOT FASTER, MEN DIED QUICKER ... UNDER THE ICE-COLD GAZE OF A WESTERN BEAUTY!
Cattle Queen

WHERE "KILL OR DIE" WAS THE INDIAN CRY!
Fort Defiance

LONELY WOMEN AT THE MERCY OF THE WEST'S MOST HUNTED MEN!
The Secret of Convict Lake

THEY KNEW BUT ONE LAW ... THE LAW OF VENGEANCE!
Three Desperate Men

Across the Wide Missouri

MGM; Technicolor; 78 minutes; Producer: Robert Sisk; Director: William A. Wellman; Cast: Clark Gable; Maria Elena Marqués; Ricardo Montalban; Adolphe Menjou; J. Carrol Naish; John Hodiak; Alan Napier; Jack Holt *******

Undeniably, MGM's $2,000,000 frontier saga, set in the 1830s, is a feast for the eyes, Colorado's mountains, plains, rivers and forests brought to vivid life by cameraman William C. Mellor. But against this picturesque canvas, you had, at times, a rather plodding yarn concerning, at first, beaver trapper Clark Gable's marriage to Blackfoot squaw Maria Elena Marqués; following a long opening 20 minutes, Gable and his new woman head off into the wilds with his unruly pals, planning to hunt off the land. Trouble comes in the shape of Redskin Ironshirt (Ricardo Montalban), who wants to prevent

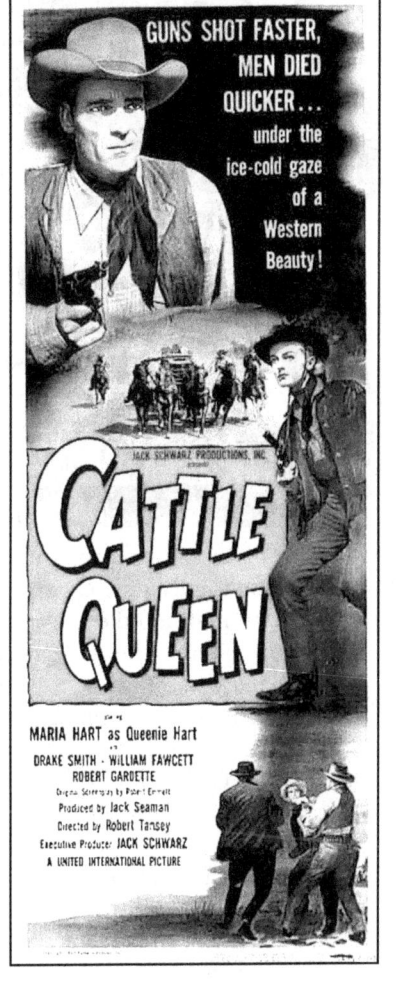

Gable and his mountain men from poaching on his territory, culminating in a number of brutal deaths, including Gable's delightful wife. In revenge, Gable kills Montalban by firing a ramrod into the savage's chest; after Marqués' moving burial, he rides off on his own with his baby son, teaching the lad how to handle a horse and allowing the boy to be educated so that he can cope with an ever-expanding America. The movie, an authentic snapshot of frontier life of that period, is too short and should have been a good 10 minutes longer to expand on the many different characters involved; however, King Gable is Gable and Mexican actress Marqués is not only a stunner but a delight playing the Indian lass falling for Gable's manly charms.

Highlights:
Colorado's magnificent scenery and a captivating performance from sexy Marqués.
Dialogue:
Gable, looking out over the endless valleys: "I never saw anything like it. The best beaver country in the world."
Trivia:
Howard Keel narrated throughout; during filming, Montalban was knocked off his horse and trodden on by another, resulting in a spinal injury that he never fully recovered from.

Al Jennings of Oklahoma

Columbia; Technicolor; 79 minutes; Producer: Rudolph C. Flothow; Director: Ray Nazarro; Cast: Dan Duryea; Gale Storm; Dick Foran; Guinn "Big Boy" Williams; James Millican; John Dehner; Raymond Greenleaf; Louis Jean Heydt ***

Al Jennings (1863-1961) was a real-life lawyer who turned to a life of crime following the unjust killing of one of his brothers. Dan Duryea played Jennings as a lovable, quick-tempered rogue who packs in his job as a barrister, shoots his brother's murderer, devious lawyer John Dehner (released on bail), and joins Guinn "Big Boy" Williams' Long Riders bunch with brother Dick Foran, the outfit busy working out of Harry Shannon's Diamond B Ranch; he ends up the scourge of the territory, a $20,000 price on his head. A stodgy first half bursts into life once Duryea and his gang embark on a reign of terror, Duryea deciding to quit and set up home in New Orleans with Gale Storm (decorative but vacant). On his final job, a $200,000 haul from a train robbery, he's badly wounded in the leg, arrested illegally over the Arkansas state line by agent John Ridgely and given a life sentence for manslaughter; five years later, his term quashed due to irregularities, he's set free and resumes his career as a lawyer. "He Abandoned the Practice of Law to Break the Law," proclaimed the posters of a formulaic Western given weight by personable Duryea's solid performance and a gritty Mischa Bakaleinikoff soundtrack.

Dialogue:
Duryea to Louis Jean Heydt about Dehner, who's just killed his brother: "They tell me he's quite a political figure around here. Is that right, John?"
Heydt: "There's no doubt he carries some weight."
Duryea: "He'll be carrying a lot more weight if they turn him loose."

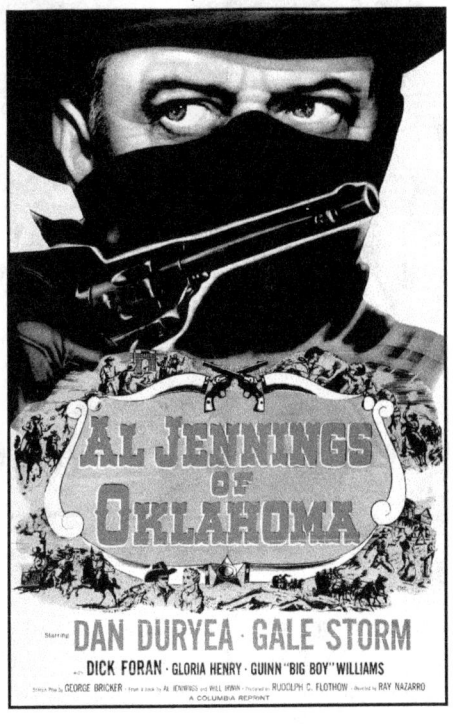

Along the Great Divide

Warner Bros.; 88 minutes; Producer: Anthony Veiller; Director: Raoul Walsh; Cast: Kirk Douglas; Virginia Mayo; Walter Brennan; John Agar; Ray Teal; Morris Ankrum; James Anderson; Hugh Sanders ***

Raoul Walsh followed two incisive 1949 features (*Colorado Territory* and *White Heat*) with the slower-paced *Along the Great Divide*, a showcase for up-and-coming star Kirk Douglas' talents. "Second-grade," carped the *New York Times*, adding, "Routine ... Douglas is a shade short of absurd." Harsh words, but with a ring of truth. In his first Western, Douglas did look a *tad* hesitant in the role and the movie verged on the routine, Douglas a marshal saving Walter Brennan from a lynch mob and escorting him across wild terrain to Santa Loma, to stand trial on a charge of cattle rustling and murder. Rancher Morris Ankrum claims Brennan shot his son in the back; Brennan denies it, and his tomboy daughter, Virginia Mayo (minus her usual glamorous make-up; one of the director's favorite actresses) does her darnedest to prevent her father from being strung up while falling in love with Douglas. Ankrum's other son, James Anderson, is the murderer; insanely jealous of his brother, he committed the dirty deed but accidentally dropped his engraved watch at the scene of the crime as incriminating evidence. All is made clear just as Brennan is found guilty, the noose placed around his neck; Anderson is revealed as the killer, shooting Ankrum, but Douglas gets the drop on him as he rides off. Released, Brennan has the prospect of Douglas as a son-in-law to look forward to. Cinematographer Sidney Hickox's deep-focus views of Lone Pine's Alabama Hills and the Mojave Desert, complemented by David Buttolph's noisy score, added to an interesting oater that concentrated more on Douglas' damaged psyche and his relationship with Mayo than all-out action. Douglas saw his lawman father hanged and has never got over it. Deputies Ray Teal and John Agar lend good support, Brennan is as impish as ever and Mayo is bewitching in her tousled-haired urchin getup. Although it lacks the full-blooded excitement of Walsh's two earlier efforts, the picture is still a solid-enough Western, Douglas (*not* absurd!) allowing his box-office charisma to shine through—and it made big money for Warners.

Dialogue:
Brennan, watching Douglas and Mayo kiss and cuddle: "A law officer in the family. I tell yer, it's downright terrifying!"

Apache Drums

Universal; Technicolor; 75 minutes; Producer: Val Lewton; Director: Hugo Fregonese; Cast: Stephen McNally; Coleen Gray; Willard Parker; Arthur Shields; James Griffith; Armando Silvestre; Ruthelma Stevens; Clarence Muse ****

Apache Drums was to be producer Val Lewton's final film; he died in March 1951 at the age of 46, a month before the movie was released. A Universal generic oater from this halcyon period is normally a cut above the rest, *Apache Drums* featuring splendid photography (Charles P. Boyle) shot amid California's Red Rock Canyon and Tucson's arid wastes, a great Hans J. Salter score and a bulldozing performance from burly Stephen McNally, playing a gambler going from zero to hero. Kicked out of the one-horse mining town of Spanish Boot for killing a man at a card table, he then comes to the townsfolk's aid when Mescalero Apaches threaten to annihilate the community, even though he's fallen foul of Mayor Willard Parker (a dead ringer for actor Peter Graves). Both are romancing Coleen Gray, and she can't make up her pretty little mind whether to go with dishonest McNally or self-righteous Parker. Apaches massacre a party of dancing girls on their way to Silver Springs and the body of a messenger is dumped in the town's well, forcing McNally, Reverend Arthur Shields and volunteers to obtain fresh water from the river. On their return, they're attacked by Indians and meet up with Lieutenant James Griffith and his troops, thus setting the scene for a nightmarish showdown in a high-walled adobe church. The Apaches, painted in various bright colors, leap from the high windows, cause mayhem and burn the door down before retreating when a platoon of soldiers arrive in the nick of time; McNally gets the girl, Parker having succumbed to a spear in the back. The movie ends on a cute note, a burro reunited with her youngster in the wreckage of the church.

Highlights:
McNally slowly making his way through hostile canyons and gulches, a reminder of America's natural wild scenery bought to vivid life in most '50s Westerns.

Dialogue:
McNally to Gray, explaining his no-nonsense stance on life: "This is a rough country. You gotta take care of yourself."

Trivia:
The marauding Apaches jumping from the church windows were lifeguards painted up, hired for their athleticism and a lot cheaper than employing Hollywood stuntmen.

Arizona Manhunt

Republic; 60 minutes; Producer: Rudy Ralston; Director: Fred C. Bannon; Cast: Michael Chapin; Eilene Janssen; James Bell; Lucille Barkley; Roy Barcroft; John Baer; Stuart Randall; Hazel Shaw ***

During the '50s, children everywhere loved to play cowboys. Child actor Michael Chapin did it for real in the movies, *Arizona Manhunt* the third of four "Rough-Riding Kids" features he starred in (as "Red" White) with Eilene "Little Miss America of 1944" Janssen and James Bell. *Buckaroo Sheriff of Texas* (1951), *The Dakota Kid* (1951) and *Wild Horse Ambush* (1952) were the other three. Fifteen at the time of shooting (Janssen was 13), Chapin helps Sheriff Bell, Deputy John Baer and Hazel Shaw locate a quantity of stolen gold hidden in a cave by the Willard gang whose surviving member, Roy Barcroft, is behind bars. The outlaw's boss, Lucille Barkley, poses as a welfare worker, threatening to place Janssen, Barcroft's orphaned niece who has lived with the bank robbers all her life, into a home for wayward juveniles; Baer and Shaw wish to adopt her. It's lively fare which might even now appeal to some members of the younger generation and, despite Chapin's presence, doesn't stint on the gunplay (the movie kicks off with an explosion and a bank robbery). Duplicitous Barkley and Barcroft (he's been sprung from jail) meet their Maker when, following the discovery of the cashbox, their runaway stage crashes over a broken bridge into a river; Janssen is adopted by Chapin and his family, the film ending on a happy note.

Dialogue:
Chapin to Bell in the cave: "Gramps, wait. There's a guard outside. Better take my gun."
Bell: "It's only a toy, a cap-buster."
Chapin: "He doesn't know it."

Trivia:
Chapins's younger brother, Billy, was also a child star; he can be seen in *Tension at Table Rock* (1956).

Badman's Gold

Jack Schwarz Productions/Eagle-Lion Classics; 56 minutes; Producers: Jack Schwarz and Robert Emmett Tansey; Director: Robert Emmett Tansey; Cast: Johnny Carpenter; Alyn Lockwood; Clarke Stevens; Kenne Duncan; Vern Teters; Jack Daly; Emmett Lyn; Bill Chaney *

In between Daisy the Dog performing various tricks and cavorting with a skunk, Johnny Carpenter (first seen in black hat, black duds, white neckerchief, fancy boots and even fancier gun belt) joins forces with brother and sister Clarke Stevens and Alyn Lockwood in Goldfield to nail a gang of stage robbers led by Kenne Duncan; inept sheriff Vern Teters can't handle the job on his own. The outlaws are waylaying gold shipments, storing the bars in an abandoned mine and planning, with the help of alcoholic professor Jack Daly, to melt the gold down, pour the metal over rock and mine it legitimately as gold ore. Daisy acts as watchdog ("Wherever we go, she goes.") as the trio skulks around town, spending a great deal of time in the telegraph office to determine that Daly is an escaped convict. Carpenter poses as notorious outlaw Red River Johnny to infiltrate the gang and in an unbelievable climax filmed in back-projected streets, Duncan's boys plus the Dylan gang are picked off by sharpshooter Lockwood, one man at a time; Duncan is wounded and arrested in one of the genre's worst-ever showdowns. Carpenter (he starred in a number of these low-cost oaters in the 1950s) is as stiff as a plank, matching the cardboard mine set; the fistfights are lame, Darrell Calker's muted score goes nowhere and the continuous shooting makes every weapon sound curiously like a kid's pop gun. "Well, guess that does it folks. The case is closed," grins Stevens at the end. Yep, this is one grade Z Western (budget: $20,000) that stinks as much as that pesky skunk that gets under Lockwood's delectable nose in reel three. The pooch is cute, though!

Dialogue:
Bill Chaney to Duncan: "Rance. We might be in trouble."
Duncan: "Whadd'ya mean, trouble?"
Chaney: "The old mine we were hiding the stuff has just been filed on."
Chaney: "That's ridiculous. There isn't any more gold in that mine than in your teeth."

Trivia:
　　Badman's Gold was one of the last movies made by writer/director Robert Emmett Tansey before he died from a sudden heart attack in June 1951, aged only 53.

Best of the Badmen

RKO-Radio; Technicolor; 84 minutes; Producer: Herman Schlom; Director: William D. Russell; Cast: Robert Ryan; Claire Trevor; Robert Preston; Jack Buetel; Walter Brennan; Bruce Cabot; John Archer; Barton MacLane *****

RKO's third in their *Bad Men* trilogy (*Badman's Territory*, 1946 and *Return of the Bad Men*, 1948, both starring Randolph Scott) took place immediately after the end of the Civil War. A group of ex-Rebs, the remnants of Quantrill's Raiders, are on the run with nowhere to go; Union officer Robert Ryan (Jeff Clanton) offers them immunity from the rope if they swear an oath of allegiance to the United States, much to carpetbagger Robert Preston's annoyance—he wants the whole lot turned over to the law and convicted, pocketing the reward money. During a fracas orchestrated by Preston, Jack Buetel (Bob Younger) is shot in the arm, one of Preston's men killed. Ryan, arrested on a trumped-up charge of murder, busts out of jail with the help of Preston's wife, the lovely Claire Trevor, teaming up with the Quantrill mob in crime-ridden Quinto and embarking on a series of bank and office stickups to put Preston's detective agency out of business, a $5,000 reward on his head. Trevor joins them, falling for Ryan, Buetel, his right arm useless, falling for *her*, as does John Archer (Curley Ringo). Archer, jealous of Ryan and incensed at being booted out of the gang by leader Bruce Cabot (Cole Younger), turns traitor, siding with Preston to wipe out the gang in a train robbery. A dynamite (in more ways than one) finale

***Best of the Badmen* Italian poster**

sees Ryan, Buetel and "Doc Butcher" Walter Brennan in Breckenridge, Missouri, using explosives to winkle Preston out of hiding. Preston is accidentally shot in the back by cohort/crooked sheriff Barton MacLane; Buetel and Brennan set off for the Californian goldfields, while Ryan is determined to clear his name and settle down with Trevor. A solid-as-a-rock, high-octane Western of the old school, featuring a memorable cast in top form, glowing photography from Edward Cronjager and a blistering score courtesy of Paul Sawtell.

Highlights:
Utah's rugged Kanab region plus Ryan, Preston, Brennan, Buetel, Trevor, Archer and Cabot acting as if they were born in their roles.
Dialogue:
Brennan, talking about Quinto: "Plenty fellers vacation there. Mostly bad gunhands who didn't like the smell of rope."
Trivia:
Keen-eared soundtrack buffs might detect snatches of Paul Sawtell's score from Toho's monster movie *Rodan*; RKO distributed the Japanese film in 1957, snippets of Sawtell's music supplementing Akira Ifukube's soundtrack in one or two places.

Bonanza Town

Columbia; 56 minutes; Producer: Colbert Clark; Director: Fred F. Sears; Cast: Charles Starrett; Fred F. Sears; Smiley Burnette; Myron Healey; Luther Crockett; Charles Horvath; Slim Duncan; Vernon Dent *

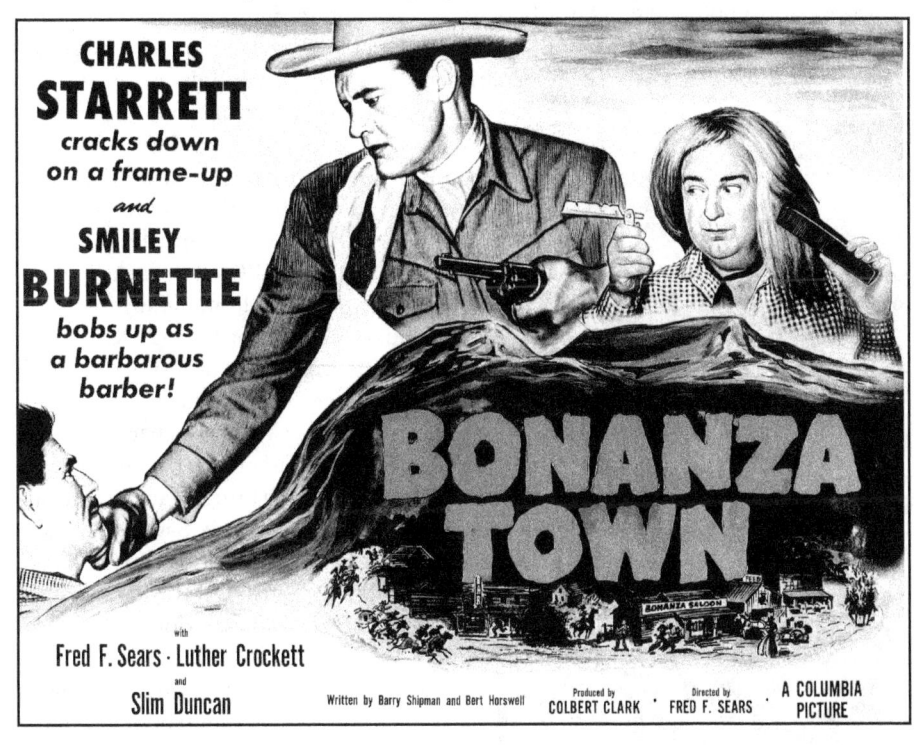

Too much stock footage from Starrett's previous *Durango Kid* Westerns contributes to a confusing muddle which will have diehards shouting midway through: "What the hell is *this* all about?" The rambling plot hinges around bigtime Bonanza Town crook Fred F. Sears (who directed as well as starred), corrupt lawyer Luther Crockett and ambitious town boss Myron Healey; law officer Charles Starrett (Steve Ramsey aka The Durango Kid) is seeking $30,000 in marked notes, stolen from Dodge City by Sears. One shoot-out and chase sequence follows another as we learn (or try to keep up with) the events surrounding Sears and his gang, the story veering off on a tangent with the murder of rancher Nolan Leary by Sears' varmints and futile attempts to keep Leary's mentally unbalanced son, Glen Stuart, under control; Stuart's sister, Nancy Saunders, is intimidated by Sears as he's after her ranch. Sears also apparently dies in a rockfall caused by an explosion of his own doing—or does he? Combined with Smiley Burnette using hair restorer after an irate customer has shaved his locks off, Crockett shot dead, Al Wyatt (who witnessed the killing of the town marshal) sprung from behind bars and The Durango Kid plugging Sears on a rooftop and you have a cobbled-together recipe for Western disaster, one of the worst in the series by far. Columbia should have kept it simple, as Poverty Row merchants Monogram and PRC would have done; less is more in this case.

Dialogue:
Burnette to Starrett, showing him his new mop of blond hair: "Ooh, Steve. Look at the hair I growed. Ain't that nice? I took a little bottle and a whole bunch of bottles and I mixed 'em together and I can grow hair. We're gonna make a million dollars, I'm gonna build a factory, then I can buy me a new team of horses ... oh, go on and laugh, I won't look so funny when I got a million dollars."

Border Fence aka Cactus Barrier

Gulf Coast Prods./Astor Pictures; 59 minutes; Producer: H.W. Kier; Directors: H.W. Kier and Norman Sheldon; Cast: Walt Wayne; Lee Morgan; Mary Nord; Steve Raines; Henry Garcia; LeRoy Fisher; Frank Savage; Charles Clark *

In 1950, writer/producer/director H.W. Kier formed his own production company, Gulf Coast Productions, and came up with this solitary effort, filmed in San Antonio, Texas on a $15,000 budget; Astor bought the distribution rights, but the movie sank without trace. Cited as the worst B-Western ever made (that should read Z-Western), *Border Fence* is inept in every single department: Acting from the unknown cast (most only appeared in this one film) is terrible, Walt Wayne, and especially Mary Nord (their features frozen in panic), pausing between exchanges of dialogue, no doubt trying to recall their lines; the script, by Norman Sheldon, is stilted ABC stuff; Jack Specht's cinematography veers from muddy to murky; the soundtrack consists of Jerry O'Dell's jaunty hillbilly tones and tagged-on semi-classical music; and Kier's camera, for the most part, remains static. Plot? Young rancher Wayne, his Uncle Bill (LeRoy Fisher) and pal Steve Raines (out on parole) help in bringing to justice cattle rustlers Lee Morgan, Frank Savage and their sidewinders, busy stealing steers and hiding out in Raines' homestead at Del Rio. Nonsensical interludes include Raines, seriously wounded, getting up from his deathbed and joining a ranchers versus rustlers shoot-out, Nord falling off her horse (was that unintentional?) and a prolonged showdown between Wayne and Morgan in which both their pistols each fire around 30 bullets without reloading, Morgan taking minutes to die in front of Kier's wobbly camera. Kier's last venture into filmmaking *could* be classed as an antique-looking guilty pleasure of sorts, appealing to fans of the awful; mercifully, the picture is difficult to lay hands on today, and perhaps that's just as well!

Dialogue:
Mexican Henry Garcia to Wayne as they look at a range bereft of cattle: "Si, si, those thieves with the cow, they make one big cleanup."

Buckaroo Sheriff of Texas

Republic; 60 minutes; Producer: Rudy Ralston; Director: Philip Ford; Cast: Michael Chapin; Eilene Janssen; James Bell; Hugh O'Brian; Steve Pendleton; Tristram Coffin; William Haade; Alice Kelley **

The first of the four "Red" White/"Rough-Riding Kids" Westerns starring Michael Chapin and Eilene Janssen had the youngsters foiling a plot by Tristram Coffin and William Haade to take over Steve Pendleton's Panhandle Ranch in Texas after the Civil War; bauxite has been discovered in soil samples, Pendleton signing a contract with the Ace Aluminium Company to work the ore, keeping the secret to himself—and Coffin is after that secret. Writer Hugh O'Brian and Sheriff James Bell are on hand to prevent Chapin and his toy pistol from getting into mischief in an oater that no doubt had the 10-year-olds stomping their feet and shouting their heads off during the Saturday Morning matinees; now, it's all rather tame, even though Bell is tied to a hitching post and given a mild whipping at the beginning, Pendleton, playing Chapin's father, killed during a tussle with Coffin after losing his memory and the baddies' mine hideout blown to kingdom come in a climactic shoot-out, annihilating Coffin and his gang. O'Brian has just enough time to put his arm around Alice Kelley's slim waist as Chapin and Janssen gallop off for more dangerous adventures, with or without adult supervision.

Dialogue:
Janssen to Kelley, told to do some housework: "Ah! Dustin's for girls!"

The Bushwhackers aka The Rebel

Jack Broder Prods./Realart Pictures; 70 minutes; Producer: Larry Finley; Director: Rod Amateau; Cast: John Ireland; Dorothy Malone; Wayne Morris; Lon Chaney, Jr.; Myrna Dell; Frank Marlowe; Charles Trowbridge; George Lynn ***

Confederate John Ireland lays down his gun after the Civil War, now a pacifist riding into the town of Independence and getting caught up in a land-grabbing war between evil arthritic rancher Lon Chaney, Jr. and his jackals, led by Lawrence Tierney (Jack

Elam among them), and squatters who, according to Chaney, "got no right bein' here. They're land thieves. Got to drive 'em out." The despot is also afraid that once settler George Lynn and his boys find out that the railroad is due, they'll sell their land for a small fortune. Marshal Wayne Morris is in Chaney's pocket, as is town banker Charles Trowbridge and what's more, the rancher's tomboy daughter, Myrna Dell, is just as cracked as he is. After honest newspaperman Frank Marlowe is brutally shot to death for exposing Chaney, Ireland straps on a gun belt and organizes an ambush on 20 of Chaney's hired gunslingers; they're wiped out in a fierce exchange of gunfire, Chaney, on hearing the news, dies from a heart attack. Crazy with revenge, Dell confronts Trowbridge, demanding $40,000; she shoots him but, dying, he guns her in the back as she leaves his offices. Peace restored to Independence, Morris hands in his badge and Ireland decides to take over Marlowe's business, doe-eyed Dorothy Malone (Marlowe's daughter) by his side. A gritty little B-Western containing a cacophonous score from Albert Glasser and Chaney, in a blond hairpiece, acting as though he's caught up in one of his old Universal-International horror outings.

Dialogue:
Ireland to Tierney, refusing a drink in the saloon: "I'll buy my own. It's plain enough. You cut 'em down and Franklin (the undertaker) there plants 'em."

Cattle Queen aka Queen of the West

Jack Schwarz Prods./Eagle-Lion Classics; Color tinted; 72 minutes; Producers: Johnny Carpenter and Jack Seaman; Director: Robert Emmett Tansey; Cast: Maria Hart; Drake Smith; William Fawcett; Robert Gardette; Johnny Carpenter; Emile Meyer; James Pierce; Joe Bailey ****

Peroxide blonde Maria Hart (Queenie Hart), kitted out in black hat, check shirt, jeans, boots and sporting hefty hardware, was one of a number of feisty female gals to boss the men around in 1950s Westerns. Okay, *Cattle Queen* had no pretensions of rising above its lowly status. Most of the supporting actors had brief film careers (Drake Smith's tally was three Westerns), the budget was around $30,000 and Robert Emmett Tansey (this was his final film) contributed to a screenplay that skewed off-track around the half-hour mark. But it entertained, thanks to Hart's delicious over-the-top performance and a trio of rascally heavies led by Emile Meyer. Cattle boss Hart and her sidekick William Fawcett (Alkali) clash with lawless Big Bend's corrupt rancher Robert Gardette over cattle rights; her herd is falsely accused of contracting Blackleg disease and evicted from their pens, a nearby waterhole dynamited, depriving the steers of water. Hart hires drovers Drake Smith and Johnny Carpenter (the Tucson Kid) to back her up and, as Big Bend's new marshal, Smith arranges for hard men Meyer (Shotgun Thompson), James Pierce (Bad Bill Smith) and Joe Bailey (Blackie Malone) to be paroled and sort out Gardette's mob; if they succeed, they'll get a pardon. "The only law in this town is written by the six-gun in lead," states crooked doc Edward Clark while Hart ("I haven't got time for men.") eyes up Smith, dressing for camp dinner in what appears to be a shimmering ball gown ("It's not customary to whistle at the boss," she coos). Prayers are said for rain which arrives in the form of divine providence and Bailey, in collusion with saloon lass Alyn Lockwood, is pumped full of slugs by Meyer and Pierce for doing the dirty on Hart. With Smith on trial for a trumped-up robbery/murder charge, Hart leads Big Bend's womenfolk on a crusading march (they've been given the right to vote by congress) and the movie climaxes in a mass shoot-out among stampeding cattle between Gardette's boys and Hart's gunmen, the latter triumphing at the expense of Carpenter (he's an orphan) who dies in Hart's arms (she's also an orphan). "After all, I'm just a woman," sighs the smitten cattle queen, kissing Smith passionately at the end, marriage now on her mind, while Meyer and Pierce receive their pardons. Enjoyable, fast-paced tosh, quite amusing in parts, Hart striding purposefully through the action with determination written all over her pretty face.

Dialogue:
Hart, gun strapped on her trim waist, barging her way through two of Gardette's toughs: "Get outta my way. Don't you know a lady when you see one?"

Cave of Outlaws

Universal; Technicolor; 75 minutes; Producer: Leonard Goldstein; Director: William Castle; Cast: Macdonald Carey; Alexis Smith; Edgar Buchanan; Victor Jory; Houseley Stevenson; Hugh O'Brian; Russ Tamblyn; Hugh Sanders ***

The cave is the star of this particular horse opera, New Mexico's Carlsbad Caverns used for location shooting to imaginative effect, William Castle concocting a lively oater with a difference. In 1880, outlaws relieve a train of a rich consignment of gold bullion, hiding the loot in a vast cave system, teenager Pete Carver (Russ Tamblyn) the only survivor left from a shoot-out with a posse. Fifteen years later, Carver (now Macdonald Carey), released from Kansas State Prison, canters into Copper Bend, tailed by Wells Fargo agent Edgar Buchanan. The man is allowed unlimited credit; after all, he's the one person who knows where that gold is and once he lays his hands on it, he'll be very rich indeed ("The cave's been a nice safe bank for 15 years."). Well-upholstered Alexis Smith, resplendent in green, gets Carey (resembling Gregory Peck in some scenes) interested in reviving her missing husband's newspaper business, as well as in herself, much to town boss/copper mine owner Victor Jory's chagrin: He wants to wed Smith, and shot her husband dead in the cave years back when they were looking for the gold. Much coming and going in the picturesque underground passages, plus a duel between Carey and Jory, results in the discovery of the dead man's corpse alongside the cash; in a cave showdown, Jory's two henchmen are dispatched, Buchanan putting a slug into Jory and promising Carey a reward for handing the gold back over to Wells Fargo. This will enable him to keep the *The New Clarion* going *and* marry Smith into the bargain.

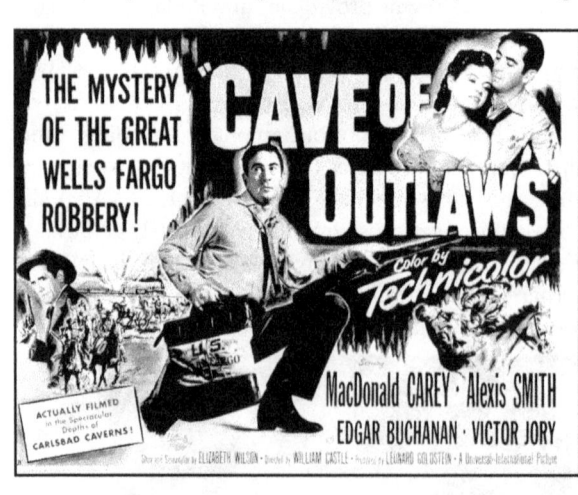

Highlights:
A Western with an unusual setting, the Carlsbad Caverns used to great effect, photographed brightly by Irving Glassberg. Eagle-eyed fans will note that many of the striking cave sequences cropped up eight years later in Fox's *Journey to the Center of the Earth*, also filmed at Carlsbad.

Dialogue:
Deputy to Sheriff Hugh Sanders at the cave entrance: "Hey, wait a minute."
Sanders: "What?"
Deputy: "You're not goin' in there?"

Sanders: "What's the matter?"
Deputy: "I don't like caves. Indians tell stories about 'em. They won't go near them. They say you *never* come out."

Trivia:

Universal's musical director, Joseph Gershenson, compiled a soundtrack from the works of 11 composers: Keen-eared music buffs will detect William Lava's title score to *House of Dracula*, used incongruously during the posse/bandits chase in the first 10 minutes.

Distant Drums

Warner Bros.; Technicolor; 101 minutes; Producer: Milton Sperling; Director: Raoul Walsh; Cast: Gary Cooper; Mari Aldon; Richard Webb; Ray Teal; Arthur Hunnicutt; Robert Barrat; Raymond Kentro; Sidney Capo *****

Gary Cooper's star clout plus unusual Florida Everglades location shooting meant a $3,000,000 profit for Warner Bros. in a rousing tale set during the Seminole Indian wars of 1835-1842. Naval officer Richard Webb and 40 soldiers are charged with hauling a large boat across the Florida bush and, using Cooper and Arthur Hunnicutt as guides, infiltrate a fortress used by the Indians and gun runners, spike the cannons, blow the place to smithereens and head back to the boat and safer waters. Everything goes well until the Seminoles, led by Chief Oscala (Raymond Kentro), are alerted to their presence; the boat ambushed, Cooper, Hunnicutt, Webb and a party of captives rescued from the fort plunge into the swamps in a desperate bid for survival, splitting into two groups to outfox the pursuing Indians. What ensues is a gripping chase movie filmed in striking locales (oddly reminiscent in some scenes of Mel Gibson's *Apocalypto*, made 55 years later), the delightful, busty Aldon falling for Cooper's masculine, rugged charms. Sidney Hickox's superb color photography brings to vivid life the mysterious, jungle-type Everglades, weed-choked water courses shimmering under a hot sun; there are tense, bloody encounters with both Seminoles (resembling Mayan warriors) and alligators, Coop finally killing the chief in a hand-to-hand knife struggle in a turquoise lagoon situated beside the island he lives on. After Oscala's death, the Seminoles retreat, Aldon electing to stay behind with Coop and his six-year-old half-Indian son on the island. Action maestro Raoul Walsh piles on the exciting incident in an actioner that looks gorgeously different from anything else produced in this period, and it goes without saying that Cooper, who *never* made a bad Western in his career, is at the top of his game in this one.

Highlights:

Filmed in the dazzling green and blue Everglades, *Distant Drums* is a unique Western in looks and feel, almost like a travelogue in some instances.

Dialogue:

Aldon to Cooper, about his lifestyle: "What's so good about it?"

Cooper: "At night, you sleep like a king."

Aldon: "Yes. Cold and alone."

Cooper, moving closer for a kiss: "I guess you wouldn't like that kind of livin', would you ... would you?"

Aldon, getting up: "Goodnight, your majesty!"

Trivia:

Hollywood didn't make enough of Aldon, a real beauty who spent most of her career in television. And note Max Steiner's music when Webb's boat makes shore; it's the same leitmotif used when Robert Armstrong and company land on Skull Island in the original *King Kong*.

Drums in the Deep South

RKO-Radio; SuperCinecolor; 87 minutes; Producers: Frank and Maurice King; Director: William Cameron Menzies; Cast: James Craig; Barbara Payton; Guy Madison; Craig Stevens; Barton MacLane; Robert Easton; Taylor Holmes; Tom Fadden ****

William Cameron Menzies, who won an Oscar for his production design on *Gone With the Wind*, seemed to be back on similar territory during the first 20 minutes of this Civil War saga, what with James Craig doing a so-so impersonation of Clark Gable's Rhett Butler, sultry Barbara Payton playing a glamorous Southern belle living in an ornate mansion on a plantation in Atlanta and some splendid pictorial composition by the director, enhanced by thunder and lightning effects. On the outbreak of hostilities between North and South, Payton and her husband, Craig Stevens, reunite with friends Guy Madison and Craig. Craig is Payton's ex-beau and still loves her; he goes off to fight with the Confederates, Stevens and Madison with the Union. Stevens, in fact, disappears from the picture at this point, Menzies discarding the romantic angle and going for all-out action, forwarding to 1864 after a montage of battle scenes. Craig and his Johnny Rebs cart four 12-pounder cannons up through a system of caves riddling the impregnable Devil's Mountain where, from the summit, they can blast the enemy trains using the rail lines hundreds of feet below. Following a bombardment in which 30 Bluecoats are killed, Major Madison arrives on the scene with orders from high command to eliminate the Rebs; after his 15-inch naval gun is blown to bits, he decides to shift the Graycoats by dynamiting the entire mountain, even though the resulting cataclysm will bury the vital

Snake Gap rail link under tons of rock. Madison delays the inevitable when he learns that Craig is on the mountain, rekindling his romance with Payton, but the gal dies from a bullet wound and Craig, refusing to surrender, decides to join her in the hereafter ("I'll never leave you again."), the huge explosion reducing Devil's Mountain to smoking rubble. Vivid photography from Lionel Lindon (lost on current DVD issues) and a pulsating Dimitri Tiomkin score make for a highly unusual Civil War drama strong on visuals, as one would expect from a director of Menzies' caliber.

Highlights:
Most of the events are cave-based, a novel setting for a picture of this type.

Dialogue:
Officer to Madison: "We got enough powder stacked up there to erupt a volcano."

Trivia:
The King Brothers sued RKO for what they viewed as poor distribution of their $300,000 film, blaming the company for not making enough profit; most copied prints these days are of poor quality, the original version very hard to track down.

Fort Defiance

Ventura/United Artists; Cinecolor; 82 minutes; Producer: Frank Melford; Director: John Rawlins; Cast: Ben Johnson; Peter Graves; Dane Clark; Tracey Roberts; George Cleveland; Craig Woods; Ralph Sanford; Bryan "Slim" Hightower *****

Not seen for years, *Fort Defiance* is a gem of a B-Western concerning two feuding brothers, quick-on-the-draw Dane Clark (presumed dead but very much alive) and blind rancher Peter Graves, both coming under the influence of taciturn Ben Johnson. Johnson is out to kill Clark as a result of him causing the death of *his* brother during the final stages of the Civil War but has befriended Graves to the extent that he's been offered a partnership in the Triple T spread. When fellow cattle owner Craig Woods, who nurses a grievance against Graves, shoots Graves' uncle dead in a showdown and Brave Bear's warriors start causing a nuisance by rustling cattle, Clark, Graves and Johnson head off into the Redskin-infested Navajo Canyons pursued by Woods and his coyotes, arguing among themselves and attacked by an Indian raiding party when they come to the assistance of a stricken stagecoach (director Rawlins dispenses with

Westerns of the 1950s: The Classic Years 81

music at this point, content to let the action speak for itself). The cavalry intervenes and, in Fort Defiance, Clark forces Woods' operative at gunpoint to buy Graves' ranch for $2,500. Handing the cash to his brother to start a new life, he sacrifices himself, walking out into the street, twin revolvers at the ready, shooting down Woods' men in a blaze of gunfire and expiring on the sidewalk; Johnson puts several bullets into Woods, the street littered with bodies. Graves now plans to set up house with saloon gal Tracey Roberts who he encountered on the stage, while Johnson's wife arrives in town, the pair reunited after several years apart. Louis Lantz's sparky script breathes life into a group of well-rounded characters, Stanley Cortez's photography highlights the towering rock formations in Gallup's Red Rock Park, while Paul Sawtell proves once again that in the realm of the low-to medium-budget Western, his scores remained a vital ingredient, one of the best composers of his type in this setup. A picturesque, finely acted, exciting winner.

Highlights:
The pithy interplay between Clark, Johnson and Graves, plus Red Rock Park's magnificent cliffs and canyons.

Dialogue:
Clark to Johnson: "Why don't you come to San Francisco with Ned (Graves) and me? In a little while, I'll be running that town."
Johnson: "How many people d'ya figure to kill runnin' it?"
Clark: "As many as I have to."
Johnson: "You're crazy."
Clark: "You're a mush head."

The Great Missouri Raid

Paramount; Technicolor; 84 minutes; Producer: Nat Holt; Director: Gordon Douglas; Cast: Macdonald Carey; Wendell Corey; Ward Bond; Ellen Drew; Bruce Bennett; Bill Williams; Anne Revere; Edgar Buchanan ****

A potted history of the James and Younger gangs' trail of terror and robbery, culminating in the death of Jesse James at the hands of Bob Ford. Gordon Douglas goes for the throat in a series of gunsmoke-filled shoot-outs, bank raids and train holdups, major-turned-detective Ward Bond (whose brother was killed by Jesse) bent on exacting revenge. The pace slows in the final few minutes, Frank James realizing the outlaw life is no longer for him and Jesse shot in the back by cowardly Ford (played by sweaty, nervous Whit Bissell). Exciting stuff all round. Macdonald Carey makes a good fist of Jesse, as does Wendell Corey of Frank, while Bond roars, glowers and chews the scenery. Great color photography (Ray Rennahan) and pulsating score (Paul Sawtell) makes for a lively horse opera of the type they just don't come up with any more, a solid example of the '50s Western in full, gun-blazing, fast-ridin' glory.

Dialogue:
Bissell to Carey: "You're kidding, Jesse. Why, everyone's scared of you. Mention your name to someone and they go white in the face."

The Last Outpost aka Cavalry Charge

Paramount; Technicolor; 89 minutes; Producers: William H. Pine and William C. Thomas; Director: Lewis R. Foster; Cast: Ronald Reagan; Rhonda Fleming; Bruce Bennett; Bill Williams; Noah Beery, Jr.; Charles Evans; Ewing Mitchell; John Ridgely ***

On the dusty Santa Fe Trail in 1862, Ronald Reagan and Bruce Bennett play officers on opposing sides during the Civil War, Reagan a Rebel, Bennett a Bluecoat.

When Reagan discovers that the Union army plans to employ Apache warriors to fight the Confederates, he dons Yankee uniform, impersonates a Union general, has a powwow with ex-army officer-turned-Indian Charles Evans in the Apache camp and rides into Union-held San Gil with sidekicks Bill Williams and Noah Beery, Jr. to hopefully free imprisoned Geronimo and prevent a massacre. Problems of a romantic nature surface when Reagan meets lovely Rhonda Fleming, once his girl but now Bennett's. Lewis R. Foster's cavalry yarn sags in the middle (a case of how and when Reagan will be unmasked), but the final 10-minute battle, Bennett's soldiers almost cut to pieces but rescued by Reagan's forces, is a thriller, the director taking the audience right into the fierce heat of battle. Great photography of Old Tucson's arid, cactus-strewn landscape (Loyal Griggs) and Fleming's bright green dress showing off her red locks to perfection are reasons enough to catch one of the 40th President of the United States' better excursions out West.

Highlights:
The lengthy climactic cavalry versus Apaches clash, a real corker.

Dialogue:
Evans to Reagan, realizing he's a Reb under that blue uniform: "You might as well tell the truth. You're probably going to be spread-eagled over an anthill anyway."

Trivia:
Reagan insisted on riding his own steed during the shoot, ensuring, unlike the Hollywood horses, that the animal was fresh in every take; this was cheapo producers Pine and Thomas' biggest success, the two earning the nickname "The Dollar Bills" for bringing in movies in double-quick time on minimum finances.

Little Big Horn aka The Fighting Seventh

Lippert/Bali; 86 minutes; Producer: Carl K. Hittleman; Director: Charles Marquis Warren; Cast: Lloyd Bridges; John Ireland; Hugh O'Brian; Reed Hadley; Jim Davis; John Pickard; Marie Windsor; Rodd Redwing *****

The low-budget Western meets *film noir* in Charles Marquis Warren's riveting story of a small column of battle-weary soldiers led by Lloyd Bridges, who leave Fort Abraham Lincoln in June 1876, their mission to warn General Custer, stationed at Camp Yellowstone, of the build-up of Sioux around the Little Bighorn (Big Horn in this picture); they've got 250 miles to cover in three days, so rest is at a premium, basic bivouacs the order of the day. Second-in-command John Ireland is romancing Bridges' wife, Marie Windsor; she's sick of garrison life, hates her husband and wants to move back east, so there's a lot of friction between the two men. As one trooper after another on point duty is killed, the platoon sides with Ireland, Bridges viewed as hard and unreasonable,

Warren's acerbic screenplay focussing on their fears, complaints and mistrust as they near the Little Bighorn. During a fierce skirmish, Bridges receives three war arrows in the chest and it is left to Ireland and the seven remaining survivors to form a diversionary suicide squad ("Sacrifice a few to save many.") by charging into a pack of several hundred Indians on the banks of the river, dying to a man. Tough and violent (an arrow through the neck; a scout hung up in the heat; Hugh O'Brian virtually skinned alive), *Little Big Horn* faultlessly demonstrates what can be achieved on low funds (the budget came to $184,000) in the Western sphere; this is a mini-classic deserving of reappraisal.

Highlights:

The entire movie is a compact masterpiece, Paul Dunlap's fine score used sparingly to add to the suspense—and Ernest Miller's black-and-white photography is a delight.

Dialogue:

Bridges to his men: "Get your shelters up. Those are orders."

John Pickard: "We're not going to disobey those orders, Cap'n. It's just that we're not going to obey them."

Trivia:

Windsor stated that when the picture ran out of funds, several pages of the script were ripped up to reduce further costs.

My Outlaw Brother aka My Brother, the Outlaw

Eagle-Lion Classics; 82 minutes; Producer: Benedict Bogeaus; Director: Elliott Nugent; Cast: Mickey Rooney; Wanda Hendrix; Robert Preston; Robert Stack; Carlos Múzquiz; José Torvay; Fernando Wagner; Hilda Moreno **

After a run of over 150 family-type movies, including the *Mickey McGuire* shorts and the *Andy Hardy* series, five-foot-two Mickey Rooney was yearning for straighter roles, yet he still clowned around in *My Outlaw Brother*, a mediocre cut-price Western adapted from Max Brand's novel, shot in Mexico. He played an innocent from New York, traveling to the Mexican border town of San Clemente to meet his surly brother, Robert Stack, owner of a silver mine. Unbeknown to Rooney, Stack has taken on the guise of El Tigre, a fearsome "Indian" bandit chief who raids banks on both sides of the border. Accompanying Rooney is Texas Ranger Robert Preston, while secret service man Carlos Múzquiz has infiltrated the gang to bring Stack/El Tigre to justice. It's a rum mix, Rooney jumping on horses backwards, falling off horses, threatening to thump outlaws twice his size and eventually romancing Wanda Hendrix, the local haughty beauty who is spurning short-fuse Stack's clumsy overtures (well, Rooney *was* married eight times and produced eleven children!). It all climaxes in a shoot-out in which Stack expires, his bunch rounded up by the Mexican army; Rooney gallops off to play house with Hendrix, the unlikely hero of the hour. Mexican composer Manuel Esperón's title score is fantastic but the picture isn't, sagging in the middle like a half-risen soufflé, neither one thing nor another. Hyperactive Rooney is as watchable as always but you can't help wondering why he chose to star in this unsatisfactory Western vehicle that runs out of steam well before the hour is reached.

Dialogue:
Hendrix to Rooney: "But you're not much taller than I am."
Rooney: "I know, but I've been used to whoppers."
Hendrix: "Eh?"
Rooney: "Big girls. Big girls? Well, I've been out with some regular whales. Like I've never talked to a girl who's under six-feet tall."

Trivia:
   At one point, Rooney uses the term "cold-cock." This expression originated in the latter stages of World War I, not in the 1880s.

New Mexico

   United Artists; Anscocolor/Black-and-White; 76 minutes; Producers: Irving Allen and Joseph Justman; Director: Irving Reis; Cast: Lew Ayres; Marilyn Maxwell; Andy Devine; Robert Hutton; Ted de Corsia; Lloyd Corrigan; Raymond Burr; Jeff Corey ****
   New Mexico's Gallup region, with its towering weathered sandstone cliffs, deep canyons and monolithic rock faces, has very rarely been better presented than in

Irving Reis' pulsating actioner; terrific use of these sun-baked natural wonders is made throughout, imparting the movie with a rugged, almost prehistoric, aura. *New Mexico* was originally released in both color and black-and-white, current DVDs in the latter format, a shame as the cinematography (Jack Greenhalgh, William E. Snyder and Lester White) is superb, even in ragged prints. Chief Acoma (Ted de Corsia) is promised peace when Abe Lincoln visits New Mexico (he never did); when the President is assassinated a few days later, the treaty is torn up, Indian settlers evicted, supplies withheld, and Acoma jailed in Fort Union. The chief escapes, killing the tyrannical fort commander, followed across country by Captain Lew Ayres, an Indian sympathizer, and his detachment of dissenting troops. En route, blonde singer Marilyn Maxwell and her manager join them after their stagecoach is attacked, the narrative then concentrating on Ayres and his men fighting off Acoma's warriors by scaling a vertiginous rock face and using the old dwellings at the summit for cover. Two of Acoma's kids are hiding in the village; Raymond Burr callously shoots one dead, the other shows Maxwell where water can be found, in a secret underground cave next to a cache of ammunition and explosives. Conniving, Redskin-hating judge Lloyd Corrigan is led to safety by the boy, or so he thinks; seized by Acoma, the rat is buried up to his neck in sand and trampled to oblivion by horses. There's no happy ending in this picture: After pushing flaming brushwood and boulders onto the rampaging savages, the troops find themselves totally outnumbered; Ayres, fatally wounded, blows up the supply dump and the surrounding cliff, Maxwell and the young Indian boy the only survivors, galloping off into the distance. A little-seen low-budget winner from United Artists that looks fantastic and contains a vibrant score from French composers René Garriguenc and Lucien Moraweck.

Highlights:
 The wild, all-blazing climactic gun battle between Ayres' depleted troops and Acoma's hordes, filmed atop a gigantic mesa; intense and violent.

Dialogue:
Worried Andy Devine to scout Jeff Corey, watching in horror as Corrigan's head is ridden over: "I'm wonderin' how you get transferred out of this outfit."

Northwest Territory

Monogram; 61 minutes; Producer: Lindsley Parsons; Director: Frank McDonald; Cast: Kirby Grant; Chinook; Gloria Saunders; Warren Douglas; Pat Mitchell; John Crawford; Duke York; Sam Flint ***

The sixth entry in Monogram's Kirby Grant/Chinook the Wonder Dog's adventures had our beefy hero combating oil claim snatchers in the form of Warren Douglas, John Crawford, Duke York and a few others; old-timer Sam Flint is shot dead because he possesses a map showing the whereabouts of the "black gold" deposits near a rock formation called "Old Indian," and Douglas and his cronies are after laying their murderous hands on it. Mountie Grant changes into civilian garb and takes on the guise of a mineralogical surveyor to flush out the gang of crooks, aided by Gloria Saunders, nine-year-old Pat Mitchell (Flint's grandson) and Chinook, his energetic white-haired (and very fierce) buddy. Attractively shot around California's picturesque San Bernardino Forest by photographer William A. Sickner and bolstered by a decent score from Edward J. Kay, *Northwest Territory* will appeal to the kiddies, even though it contains a lot of shooting, bruising fistfights and a harrowing sequence where Crawford is mauled to death by Chinook's deadly fangs and claws.

Dialogue:

Grant to Saunders: "Say, I don't know if it's safe to leave Billy (Mitchell) with you now. After all, there's not that many girls you can trust with a young bachelor worth half a million dollars."

Only the Valiant

Warner Bros.; 105 minutes; Producer: William Cagney; Director: Gordon Douglas; Cast: Gregory Peck; Ward Bond; Barbara Payton; Lon Chaney, Jr.; Neville Brand; Gig Young; Jeff Corey; Steve Brodie **

Shunned by his fellow soldiers and girlfriend Barbara Payton by being blamed for the death of popular officer Gig Young, murdered by Apaches, Gregory Peck (he was only obeying orders in allowing Young to escort captured Apache chief Tucsos to Fort Grant) is told to defend Fort Invincible, a stronghold erected at the mouth of a deep pass to keep out the Indians. Along for the suicide mission is a motley gang of resentful troopers, malcontents every one of them, including a drunkard, a coward and a deserter. All would love to put a bullet in Peck, but against mounting odds, the fort is held after a number of bloody skirmishes, a relief column arriving on the scene to send the warriors packing with the help of a Gatling gun. Peck finishes off Tucsos (Michael Ansara) and redeems himself in the eyes of the military, regaining the love of Payton. Violent in parts, *Only the Valiant*'s lumpy narrative drags in places and is let down by the obvious sound stage setting of Fort Invincible. Peck looks stiff and unhappy, and it is left to Ward Bond, Neville Brand and horror stalwart Lon Chaney, Jr. to shine; Franz Waxman's music is also a bonus in a cavalry saga based on duty, honor and conscience that overstays its welcome by at least 10 minutes.

Highlights:
Bearded Chaney, proving he could be as menacing outside the horror milieu as he was inside it.

Dialogue:
Brand, peeling off his socks: "Ah! First time in four days these toes have seen daylight."

Trivia:
Peck denounced the movie (as he would with another of his Westerns, *Mackenna's Gold* [Columbia, 1969]) as one of the worst he had appeared in ("A step backwards in my career,"), even though, as compensation, he carried out an affair with Payton for the entire shoot and was paid $60,000 for his trouble.

Passage West aka High Venture

Paramount; Technicolor; 80 minutes; Producers: William H. Pine and William C. Thomas; Director: Lewis R. Foster; Cast: John Payne; Dennis O'Keefe; Arleen Whelan; Frank Faylen; Dooley Wilson; Arthur Hunnicutt; Mary Anderson; Richard Travis ***

1863: Six convicts led by John Payne break out of Salt Lake Prison and force themselves on Preacher Dennis O'Keefe's wagon train, traveling to Meadowlands in California. After a grueling trek, driven by rifle-wielding Payne, Angel's Creek is arrived at, O'Keefe's intended, redhead Arleen Whelan, having thrown herself at Payne. But Payne, busy drinking in a saloon, rebuffs her and, while blasting rock in a cave for a new church, discovers gold. In a shoot-out with his greedy cohorts, Payne, wounded, tosses a lantern into a powder keg, bringing the roof down in a landslide, leaving crestfallen Whelan to run after O'Keefe in the hope of a reconciliation. The opening 50 minutes, filmed partly in the arid Mojave Desert region, is tough and involving, both wagons and settlers succumbing to the harsh conditions; the picture then runs out of steam once the town is reached. It's almost a movie of two contrasting parts, seeming much longer than its running time, but Payne is excellent as the hardened convict with a heart of granite, refusing to be converted into the ways of God, and O'Keefe also shines as the preacher very handy with his fists.

Highlights:
Payne and O'Keefe's lengthy bruising fistfight, not for the squeamish.
Dialogue:
Black slave Dooley Wilson, collapsing in the dirt from exhaustion: "Please, Lord, hear my prayer. Save us. Save us, Lord. Save us."
Payne: "You're wastin' your breath. Ain't nothin' listenin' except lizards and snakes and buzzards."

Raton Pass

Warner Bros.; 84 minutes; Producer: Saul Elkins; Director: Edwin L. Marin; Cast: Dennis Morgan; Patricia Neal; Steve Cochran; Scott Forbes; Dorothy Hart; Basil Ruysdael; Louis Jean Heydt; Roland Winters ****

Virtually unrecognized among Warner Bros. Westerns of the early 1950s is *Raton Pass*, a highly melodramatic exercise in female go-getting courtesy of venomous Patricia Neal. She's the ambitious lady alighting in Raton Pass, New Mexico and making a beeline for rancher Dennis Morgan, son of Basil Ruysdael who is owner of the half-million-acre Challon Ranch. Before we know it, Neal and Morgan are wed but soon, she's objecting to being simply a wife; the vixen wants to run the spread *her* way and give her *own* orders. When Morgan goes on a trip to Kansas City, Scott Forbes from the Kansas and Western Railroad enters the frame; he looks upon the ranch as an investment and falls for Neal's predatory charms. On his return, Morgan catches them smooching; against Ruysdael's wishes, he sells the conniving pair the ranch, hoping that they'll fall on hard times. One heated incident after another sees rival rancher Louis Jean Heydt and his "Lava gang" joining forces with Morgan's men, Neal having employed smirking, unhinged gunslinger Steve Cochran and his gorillas to back her up in the range war. Morgan is accused of rustling while Heydt is imprisoned on trumped-up charges by ineffectual sheriff Roland Winters; Cochran shoots Morgan in the back, Heydt is murdered, Forbes walks out on Neal, Cochran means to take over the spread and in a well-orchestrated gun battle at the Challon house, Ruysdael meets his Maker, Morgan, having fully recovered (in record time, it must be said!), joining in the fray. Fatally wounded, Cochran has enough energy left to put paid to Neal with two slugs in her back, leaving Morgan to start a relationship with Spanish lass Dorothy Hart, which he should have done in reel one. The movie would have benefited from color photography; nevertheless, it possesses an in-your-face edge from two quarters: Neal's performance as the Western Queen Bitch to top 'em all, and

Max Steiner's powerhouse score. In his work on *The Searchers*, Steiner pulled out all the stops and he does so here, each scene considerably strengthened by his driving music, an absolute delight to aficionados of classic film soundtracks and which elevates *Raton Pass* to the status of "gone, but shouldn't be forgotten."

Highlights:

Neal in evil form, a complete contrast to her next role in *The Day the Earth Stood Still*, where she was sweetness itself; and Steiner's blistering score which acts like a double-edged sword. Magnificent music that alas has vanished altogether from today's cinematic culture.

Dialogue:

Neal to Cochran: "You stupid, swaggering fool. If anything happens to him …"
Cochran, slapping her hard: "Some kinda talk I just can't listen to—not even from a harpy like you."

Rawhide

20th Century Fox; 89 minutes; Producer: Samuel G. Engel; Director: Henry Hathaway; Cast: Tyrone Power; Susan Hayward; Hugh Marlowe; Jack Elam; Dean Jagger; Edgar Buchanan; George Tobias; Jeff Corey ****

Never has Jack Elam looked so malevolently ugly as in Henry Hathaway's enthralling hostage drama; the scene where he approaches Susan Hayward, the camera zooming in on his leering features, is enough to put anyone off their popcorn. Perhaps the director was trying to contrast Elam's less-than-pleasing physiognomy with that of Tyrone Power, undeniably one of Hollywood's most handsome of all leading men. Power, Hayward and Hayward's baby niece Calli are held captive in the Rawhide Pass relay station after escaped killer Hugh Marlowe's gang (Elam, George Tobias and Dean Jagger) have arrived on the scene, Elam callously gunning down station boss Edger Buchanan. The eastbound stage is due, carrying $100,000 in gold bars, and Power realizes that once Marlowe gets his hands on it, his life won't be worth a dime. It's a case of whether Power and Hayward can outwit their captors (and Hayward escape the clutches of Elam) before the stage arrives. Digging a hole through their room with a knife is one answer but, in the end, it's the gang's fragile nature that outwits Marlowe. On the morning of the stage's arrival, Elam, for a third time, assaults Hayward, shoots Marlowe twice and kills Tobias, Jagger fleeing in terror. Challenging Power to a draw, Elam hits the dust, Hayward pumping two rifle bullets into him. The Lone Pine backdrop is splendid (celebrating 31 years as a movie location), but this is a scenario set in isolated confined spaces, relying on the ramping up of suspense rather than outdoor gunplay, and in this respect, *Rawhide* delivers the Western goods; besides, how can you possibly ignore any movie that stars Power and Hayward? "Exciting sagebrush entertainment," said *The Hollywood Reporter*.

Movie theater banner for *Rawhide*

Highlights:
Power and Hayward, two of Hollywood's most attractive leads, on top form; unsurprisingly, the pair once had a brief fling in the late '40s.

Dialogue:
Power to Hayward as she tests the door lock to her room: "What are you afraid of? Coyotes?"
Hayward: "Yeah. The kind with boots on."

Trivia:
Alfred Newman's jaunty title theme to 1940's *Brigham Young: Frontiersman* was reprised here, as it was in *Yellow Sky* (1948) and *The Silver Whip* (1953); Hathaway labelled Hayward a "bitch to work with" but appreciated her professionalism, especially as the movie was shot in the dead of winter, the entire cast often blue with cold; and would any picture these days be allowed to show a toddler tottering among frisky horses' legs *and* being shot at?

Red Mountain

Paramount; Technicolor; 84 minutes; Producer: Hal B. Wallis; Director: William Dieterle; Cast: Alan Ladd; Lizabeth Scott; Arthur Kennedy; John Ireland; Jay Silverheels; Jeff Corey; Neville Brand; James Bell ***

Colorado territory, 1865. Confederate Alan Ladd puts a slug into a crooked assay officer in Broken Bow, who cheated him out of a gold claim; Arthur Kennedy is blamed, hiding from the posse in a cliff cave after Ladd has saved him from being lynched. Kennedy's gal, Lizabeth Scott, falls for Ladd's silent charms, the trio at the mercy of John Ireland (as Quantrill) and Ute war chief Jay Silverheels' men when Ladd double-crosses the guerrilla boss. A savage shoot-out among the lofty red cliffs sees Kennedy and Silverheels killed, Ireland escaping when Broken Bow's men arrive in force and Scott cozying up to Ladd. The real stars of this colorful actioner are the towering rock formations at Gallup, New Mexico which literally dwarf the characters (cinematography: Charles B. Lang, Jr.); Franz Waxman's flamboyant score also threatens to overwhelm what's taking place under those mighty sandstone walls. Ladd is dependable without displaying too much exertion (or emotion), Kennedy plays a rat to the hilt (as he often did) and Scott is alluring in a check shirt. Enjoyable but no classic—the magnificent scenery's the thing here.

Dialogue:
Ireland to Silverheels: "Do we not walk the same trail? Are we not brothers?"
Silverheels: "We are not brothers, white man. The deer travels with the coyote for fear of the snake. The coyote is not brother to the deer."

The Redhead and the Cowboy

Paramount; 82 minutes; Producer: Irving Asher; Director: Leslie Fenton; Cast: Glenn Ford; Rhonda Fleming; Edmond O'Brien; Alan Reed; Morris Ankrum; Ray Teal; Douglas Spencer; Ralph Byrd ***

In New Mexico, 1865, wandering cowpoke Glenn Ford gets mixed up in a Civil War espionage plot involving saloon beauty Rhonda Fleming, shady cattle buyer Edmond O'Brien, two-timing Confederate boss Alan Reed, dogged sheriff Morris Ankrum, two ornery mercenaries in the grizzled forms of Ray Teal and Douglas Spencer and a trail of corpses. Fleming is supposed to deliver a coded message to Reed regarding an impending Union gold shipment, unaware that Reed the Rebel wants the gold all for himself; anyone crossing his path is murdered. Played out against the tremendous cliff formations at Sedona's Red Rock Crossing, Arizona, *The Redhead and the Cowboy* is akin to a convoluted chase story, everybody double-crossing everybody until Reed is taken care of following an abortive raid on the Union wagons, leaving Ford to take care of Fleming. David Buttolph's pumping score and Daniel L. Frapp's pristine black-and-white photography are a bonus in a star Western that vaguely disappoints despite the presence of Ford and Fleming, a case of too many characters spoiling the broth.

Dialogue:
Ford to Fleming, gazing at her features: "Trying to figure out what makes your eyes snap the way they do. It's very pretty."
Fleming: "Can't we talk about something more important than my eyes?"
Ford: "Why sure, we'll talk about your nose. That's very pretty too."
Fleming: "Also very unimportant."

The Secret of Convict Lake

20th Century Fox; 83 minutes; Producer: Frank P. Rosenberg; Director: Michael Gordon; Cast: Glenn Ford; Gene Tierney; Ethel Barrymore; Zachary Scott; Ann Dvorak; Jack Lambert; Richard Hylton; Harry Carter ****

September 1871: Twenty-nine convicts escape from Carson City penitentiary, only five making it over the mountains to the village of Monte Diablo—but Glenn Ford has led them there on purpose. He's out to kill Harry Carter whose lies put Ford behind bars for a murder he didn't commit; he also stole the $40,000 that Ford's gang were imprisoned for, and Zachary Scott, Richard Hylton, Cyril Cusack and Jack Lambert want that money, regardless of who gets hurt in a place populated by women only, the menfolk having been away for three months looking for silver; bedridden grandma Ethel Barrymore presides over the unprotected girls, shotgun in hand ("You get ugly with the women, I'll kill you," spits Ford to Scott). Leon Klatzkin and Sol Kaplan's doom-laden soundtrack underlines an atmospheric *noir* Western where the accent is very much on repressed sexual desires. Spinster Ann Dvorak falls for the rough charms of Scott, even though the rat is only after a hidden stash of guns and that cash; Barbara Bates, a virgin, lusts after young Richard Hylton, a full-blown psychopathic killer; and the delicious Gene Tierney, due to marry Carter, throws herself at Ford up in the hills. In a climactic showdown, Ford shoots Carter when the men return, Hylton and Cusack hit the dirt and Scott tumbles from a mountain ledge, $40,000 in notes fluttering away in the breeze. On a posse's arrival, Tierney points to "five graves—five bodies," and the sheriff departs, convinced that all five men, including Ford (who gets Tierney), are dead. Supposedly based on a true story, *The Secret of Convict Lake* is tautly handled by Michael Gordon, with Ford and Tierney on mesmerizing form.

Dialogue:

Ford to Tierney, who, holding a rifle, wants him and his men to go: "You're taking a lot on yourself, aren't you Ma'am? Judge, jury and hangman all wrapped up in pretty skirts, having yourselves a ladies' lynching party."

Trivia:

Dana Andrews was originally earmarked for Glenn Ford's role.

Three Desperate Men

Lippert Pictures; 71 minutes; Producer: Sigmund Neufeld; Director: Sam Newfield; Cast: Preston Foster; Jim Davis; Kim Spalding (Ross Latimer); Virginia Grey; William Haade; Monte Blue; Rory Mallinson; Sid Melton ****

Jim Davis and Monte Blue track two outlaws to their hideout; in the ensuing gunfight, one is killed, the other (William Haade) jailed. When brothers Foster and Davis learn that their sibling, Kim Spalding, is due to be hanged in a small Californian town on trumped-up charges brought about by Rory Mallinson, they turn in their badges, ride to the town and free Spalding as he's about to be lynched. During the fray, Davis shoots a guard dead; the three brothers are now wanted men, hotly pursued by Mallinson and a posse, falsified charges bumping up a reward of $5,000 on their heads. Crossing the state border, the trio joins up with Haade, released from prison, and decide to become full-blown outlaws; after all, if they're wrongly accused of committing umpteen bank and train holdups, they might as well reap the rewards by carrying out the real thing. Boosted by three more men, the Denton gang embark on a trail of robbery, the reward escalating to $40,000 ("The Biggest Reward in History!"). Grey, suffering from ill health and ashamed of Preston's much-publicized deeds, leaves Fort Grant for New Mexico, Preston later informed by his mother that the lass died from her illness. In one final attempt to strike it rich, the gang decides to raid Fort Grant's bank and express office in a double-hit that could fetch them $100,000, but as the robberies get underway, Mallinson and his posse appear on the scene, resulting in a ferocious four-minute shoot-out in which the citizens join in with guns and rifles; Foster, Haade, Spalding and gang member Steve Belmont perish in a hail of lead,

Mallinson drilled by dying Spalding. Riddled with bullets, Davis is dumped on a wagon to be tended to. A superior oater from budget producer Robert L. Lippert, showing the plight of men on the run; thirst, poor rations ("Cold beans and water—not exactly a banquet," moans Davis), broken dreams and forever having to look over your shoulder for the approaching law. Orville H. Hampton's script is as sharp as Jack Greenhalgh's photography while composer Albert Glasser provides one of his customary bombastic soundtracks. All this plus mean performances from the three leads adds up to a B-Western packing one almighty wallop.

Dialogue:
Foster to Davis: "Fred. After today, they'll forget all about the Youngers and the James boys, it'll be us. None of them ever took two places at once."

The Thundering Trail

Western Adventure Prods./Realart; 55 minutes; Produced and Directed by Ron Ormond; Cast: Lash LaRue; Al "Fuzzy" St. John; Sally Anglim; Archie Twitchell; Ray Bennett; John Cason; Clarke Stevens; Terry Frost ***

For 15 years, outlaws have terrorized the country around Capitol City, forcing the town's citizens to appeal direct to the president for help. Governor Archie Twitchell is sent to sort things out, lawmen Lash LaRue and Al "Fuzzy" St. John to provide safe conduct, but crooked saloon owner Ray Bennett has other ideas; he wants the area to stay lawless, instructing his team of sidewinders headed by John Cason to waylay and murder Twitchell before his stage reaches town. Twitchell's staying at Sally Anglim's ranch where her supposedly deaf-mute servant, Clarke Stevens, isn't so deaf-mute, passing on information to Bennett concerning the governor's movements. Running a gauntlet of raiding bad guys, Twitchell's stage eventually makes it to town where he takes up his seat of office after LaRue, Fuzzy and a few armed townsfolk hiding in a covered wagon have ousted the outlaws, Terry Frost, Bennett's number two, falling backwards over a cliff. Bennett is arrested and LaRue gets to kiss Anglim, much to Fuzzy's amusement. Decent B-Western thrills if you ignore the fact that footage from half-a-dozen Lash movies is included, some newer sequences dragged out to interminable lengths for a picture five minutes short of an hour. Once again, Walter Greene's all-guns-blazing score keeps the momentum going when things threaten to peter out.

Dialogue:
Fuzzy to LaRue: "Hey, wait a minute."
LaRue: "What's the matter, Fuzzy? Your nose botherin' you again?"
Fuzzy: "Aw, it tickles. You know that means trouble."

Trivia:
Sally Anglim only starred in two feature films, both in 1951, before quitting the industry.

Tomahawk aka Battle of Powder River

Universal; Technicolor; 82 minutes; Producer: Leonard Goldstein; Director: George Sherman; Cast: Van Heflin; Preston Foster; Alex Nicol; Yvonne De Carlo; Susan Cabot; John War Eagle; Jack Oakie; Tom Tully *****

"Nothing exceptional" was the *New York Times*' unbalanced opinion of *Tomahawk* which just goes to prove how wrong some film critics can be. Over 82 minutes, George Sherman's pro-Indian outing delivers the goods: A fine Hans J. Salter score, gleaming color photography from Charles B. Boyle, filmed in South Dakota's Black Hills, and Silvia Richards and Maurice Geraghty's clever script bring this tale of scout Jim Bridger's attempts to prevent a war between the Sioux and the U.S. army to vivid life.

At a conference between Red Cloud's Sioux and whites in 1866, Indian sympathizer Van Heflin (Bridger) reckons the Redskins have had enough of being shoved from one piece of worthless property to another ("White men are liars; all treaties fake," states the chief); it's their land as well as ours, he tells the unreasoning military high command. Lieutenant Alex Nicol, a cold-eyed bigoted Indian-hater, partly responsible for the death of Heflin's Cheyenne wife and infant years back in an Indian massacre organized by the Colorado Volunteers, thinks all Native Americans are scum and should be treated as such. At Fort Phil Kearny deep inside Sioux territory, Colonel Preston Foster orders Nicol to keep his hatred in check; it doesn't work, the hothead shooting dead in cold blood a young Indian lad, one of two caught stealing a horse. Furious Red Cloud (John War Eagle) sets the war drums rolling while back at the fort, Cheyenne Susan Cabot (as Monahseetah) comes under Nicol's baleful glare, Yvonne De Carlo, part of Tom Tully's traveling sideshow, making her own eyes at Heflin after rejecting Nicol's clumsy advances. When Heflin's partner, Jack Oakie, heads off to bring in much-needed repeating rifles, Nicol and a detachment ride out to assist a wood cutting detail in trouble; against orders, the promotion-mad officer attacks a war party ("I want a scalp!"), falling straight into a trap. He escapes, his men slaughtered. Heflin catches up with the coward; after a fight in a river, Nicol gets a thoroughly deserved arrow in the back from the youngster whose pal he shot. A well-staged Sioux against Long Knives clash, soldiers hidden behind wagons with their new carbines, sees Red Cloud's braves cut to ribbons but victory is ultimately theirs: A Washington peace treaty hands them back their territory in 1868, Fort Phil Kearny abandoned and destroyed by fire. For lovers of cavalry/Redskin movies, Universal's highly polished offering to the genre is as good as it gets.

Highlights:

South Dakota's rolling Black Hills region, beautifully photographed by Boyle, forms a stunning backdrop to the all-guns-blazing climactic battle.

Dialogue:

Ann Doran to De Carlo after De Carlo has given Cabot a brooch: "Did you ever notice? Trouble seems to make us women forget differences. With men, it seems to turn them into snapping dogs."

Trivia:

Rock Hudson has a "blink and you'll miss me" part in the final reel; the film was unsuccessfully revamped by Columbia in 1955's inferior *The Gun that Won the West*.

The Vanishing Outpost

Western Adventure Prods./Realart; 56 minutes; Produced and Directed by Ron Ormond; Cast: Lash LaRue; Al "Fuzzy" St. John; Riley Hill; Sharon Hall; Clarke Stevens; Archie Twitchell; Cliff Taylor; Sue Hussey **

"The town needs a new sheriff" says Pinkerton agent Riley Hill to Lash LaRue and Fuzzy after they've dealt with troublesome bar saddle tramp Archie Twitchell in the opening five minutes; the crusading duo are hired to intercept a coded letter that will give law officers details of the next train robbery to be carried out by the Taggart and Jackson gang, holed up in the ghost town of Star City; it's here that they're all eventually wiped out. *The Vanishing Outpost* was made up of 26 minutes of new material and 30 minutes of footage cannibalized from *Mark of the Lash* (1948) and 1949's *Son of Billy the Kid*, *Son of a Badman* and *Outlaw Country*, those fresher sequences dragged out to boost the running time. We get to see plenty of LaRue's trademark vicious, two-fisted assault on the bad guys, a lot of riding around and very little else apart from a running gag concerning Fuzzy's aching tooth which is knocked out in a door collision at the end. A tired effort containing a recycled plot, notable for one thing—Walter Greene's stock score. In 21st-century filmmaking, music, by and large, doesn't figure in the majority of films on release. Sixty years ago, composers like Greene drummed up highly elaborate soundtracks that were as important to the finished product as the director's contribution (in this case, more important!). Greene utilizes every instrument and musical theme known to man to keep the narrative on the move. It's a sterling effort that should never go unrecognized.

Dialogue:
Fuzzy to LaRue: "Just because you're smarter than me, there's no reason why I'm dumber than you!"

Vengeance Valley

MGM; Technicolor; 83 minutes; Producer: Nicholas Nayfack; Director: Richard Thorpe; Cast: Burt Lancaster; Robert Walker; Joanne Dru; Sally Forrest; Ray Collins; John Ireland; Hugh O'Brian; Carleton Carpenter ***

In Irving Ravetch's screenplay (taken from a Luke Short story), there are a great deal of characters asking, "Whose is it?" "Who is he?" and "What," the reason being that, horror of horrors, Sally Forrest, has just given birth and no one knows who the father is. Burt Lancaster, adopted son of rancher Ray Collins, gives her $500 and is targeted by Forrest's two gun-happy brothers, John Ireland and Hugh O'Brian; the pair want to kill Lancaster as they reckon he's the guilty party. But Collins' real son, rotten apple Robert Walker, is the culprit, even though he's wed to Joanne Dru who, in turn, hates him and holds a candle for Lancaster. Walker and Lancaster just about manage to get on, although Walker makes it quite clear that he has his father's blood running through his veins and therefore half of the old man's spread is his by right. Richard Thorpe's wordy, adult-themed Western melodrama won't suit the kiddies; there's a minimum of gunplay, a couple of vicious fistfights and the plot becomes a tad murky at times, particularly in the first half. Fine use of the Colorado scenery during a cattle roundup of winter stock, boosted by Rudolph G. Kopp's score, and Walker betraying Lancaster by selling off most of the herd for his own profit and arranging for Ireland and O'Brian to ambush him up the excitement level. In the end, the violent waster hits the dust after being outdrawn by his half-sibling; Dru can now claim the hunk as her own, and lanky cowpoke Carleton Carpenter can wed Forrest to legitimize her baby. "Creditable entertainment," said the *New York Times*.

Highlights:

Lancaster is always worth the price of a ticket; and there are some fabulous shots of the Colorado Coal Creek and Oak Creek locations, the cattle being driven under an imposing line of huge white cliffs.

Dialogue:

Collins to Lancaster, about Walker: "You didn't kill him. I did. Long time ago. Day I looked away and hoped he'd change. Hoped he'd work out."

Trivia:

This was Lancaster's first Western; Dru disliked being around horses, even though she starred in plenty of Westerns in her time; and Walker, of whom great things were expected by the Hollywood chiefs, died in tragic circumstances a year later, aged only 32.

Westward the Women

MGM; 118 minutes; Producer: Dore Schary; Director: William A. Wellman; Cast: Robert Taylor; Denise Darcel; John McIntire; Hope Emerson; Julie Bishop; Henry Nakamura; Beverly Dennis; Pat Conway *****

In 1851, rancher John McIntire, owner of Whitman's Valley in California, recruits 140 women from Chicago to become spouses for his sex-starved workforce; Robert Taylor and 15 cowpokes are to guide them across 2,000 miles of wild territory to their new life. A recipe for over-sentimentality or even comedy? Not one bit of it. MGM, writer Charles Schnee and William A. Wellman's "women are *not* the weaker sex" saga strove for authenticity in every department, even eschewing a standard soundtrack (silence can sometimes work wonders) and portraying Taylor as a hard-bitten tough who thinks nothing of putting three slugs into one of the men for assaulting former prostitute Julie Bishop. At this point in the narrative, the cowboys quit with eight women, leaving Taylor, Japanese Henry Nakamura, Pat Conway and McIntire as the only males around for the next 1,000 miles. Hardship follows hardship—hauling wagons up and down precipitous slopes, the tragic death of a child, a hazardous desert crossing, a birth in a broken wagon, McIntire expiring after an Indian raid and sexy French dame Denise Darcel falling for Taylor (even though she states, "Don't you ever shave? You look so dirty!"). New clothes are ordered from town and the spruced-up ladies, led by matriarch Hope Emerson, get hitched to their new husbands, Taylor and Darcel going off to play house. Location shooting took place in Tucson, Utah's Kanab canyon country and California's Death Valley, harshly lit by William C. Mellor; superb performances all round and a commendable gritty approach make *Westward the Women* (budgeted at $2,200,000) an engrossing classic Western wagon train drama.

Dialogue:
Taylor to McIntire: "There's only two things that scares me and a good woman's both."

Chapter 4
1952

FLAMING ARROWS! SMOKING GUNS! *Apache War Smoke*

COCHISE! GERONIMO! ... BLOOD BROTHERS OF VENGEANCE AGAINST THE U.S. CAVALRY!
The Battle at Apache Pass

WAR DRUMS ROLL ... THE FRONTIER FLAMES ... AS BLOOD-MAD SIOUX TAKE THE TERROR TRAIL!
Buffalo Bill in Tomahawk Territory

THE PHANTOM MASQUERADE IS CLEARED WITH THE FLASH OF THE LASH!
The Frontier Phantom

WHERE ANYTHING GOES ... AT A PRICE!
Rancho Notorious

RANGE WAR SPLITS THE GREAT MONTANA DIVIDE!
Smoky Canyon

Apache War Smoke

MGM; 67 minutes; Producer: Hayes Goetz; Director: Harold F. Kress; Cast: Robert Horton; Gilbert Roland; Barbara Ruick; Patricia Tiernan; Gene Lockhart; Myron Healey; Harry Morgan; Glenda Farrell ***

In MGM's cut-price oater, a bunch of disparate people marooned at the Tonto Valley relay station find themselves at the mercy of Geronimo's Apaches, among them station boss Robert Horton; his father, bandit Gilbert Roland; Horton's ex-love Patricia Tiernan; former Hollywood sex bomb Glenda Farrell, lusting after Roland; Horton's new admirer Barbara Ruick; and bad guy Myron Healey. How they react to one another and their perilous situation forms the backbone to a no-frills Western filmed in Tucson, Arizona. Tiernan and Ruick both hanker after Horton who has his hands full with Roland; the outlaw wants to steal the Wells Fargo box and hightail out, drawing the Indians away from the station. But it's Healey the Redskins want to scalp; he killed several of them a while back and they're lusting for revenge. Healey is eventually forced out of the station wearing Roland's gaudy outfit; he's promptly shot to pieces and the Apaches ride off. As the stage takes its contingent of passengers on their journey, Ruick decides to stay and play pat-a-cake with Horton. An unpretentious little actioner, cheaply made by MGM's usual expensive standards, but containing a lively Alamo-type battle when the Redskins attack the station and a winning performance from Roland as the likeable rogue of the piece.

Dialogue:
Ruick to Roland, watching Tiernan forcing herself on Horton: "How do you fight a woman like her?"
Roland: "Same as you fight any other fight. Pick your position, keep the wind to your back and shoot to kill."
Ruick: "I'll remember that."

Trivia:
This was movie editor Kress' last of three full-length feature films where he directed; MGM's top man at his job went on to win Oscars for editing in *How the West Was Won* (1962) and *The Towering Inferno* (1974).

The Battle at Apache Pass

Universal; Technicolor; 85 minutes; Producer: Leonard Goldstein; Director: George Sherman; Cast: Jeff Chandler; John Lund; Susan Cabot; Jay Silverheels; Richard Egan; Beverly Tyler; Bruce Cowling; John Hudson ***

Major John Lund has his work cut out at Fort Buchanan. Cochise, chief of the Chiricahua Apaches, has more or less settled for peace but renegade Geronimo wants war with the white eyes ("Cochise talks with a woman's tongue!"); then government Indian advisor Bruce Cowling arrives on the scene, intent on engineering events to wipe out the various Apache tribes. A Western where scenery and sweeping vistas take precedence over action. Shot in glowing colors by Charles P. Boyle amid the magnificent red rock formations at Arches National Park, Moab, Utah, the cast are often in danger of being upstaged by those mighty canyons and ravines, and the movie would have worked better with a stronger lead, Lund adequate but not commanding enough. Disappointingly, Hans J. Salter's score is a bit *too* jaunty. There are wagon train massacres, skirmishes a-plenty and a parley under a flag of truce that turns sour before Jeff Chandler (Cochise) and Jay Silverheels (Geronimo) join forces, Cowling and sidekick Jack Elam lying about the Chiricahua having caused all the mayhem when Geronimo's warriors are the true culprits, the army hanging three of Cochise's family. The climactic battle at Apache Pass is brilliantly staged, the Indians fleeing before the devastating fire from two howitzer cannons, Geronimo taking to the hills after losing a tussle with Cochise. "Peace later. Warriors still angry," says Chandler to Lund as he rides off with his wife (Susan Cabot) and newborn son, Cowling and Elam having both perished Apache-style. "Magnificent Technicolored scenery reduces the participants to mere specks on the horizon," stated the *New York Times*. How right they were.

Highlights:
The battle of the title, an exciting set piece to climax a standard Universal B-Western.

Dialogue:
Chandler to Silverheels, after he's spared his rival's life in a fight: "Geronimo shall live but must for ever as an outcast who walks alone. And Apaches shall spit upon him for he's no longer a warrior."

Trivia:
This was the second of three appearances as Cochise for Chandler: Here, in Fox's *Broken Arrow* and in Universal's *Taza, Son of Cochise*. Ditto for Silverheels playing Geronimo: Here, in *Broken Arrow* and in Universal's *Walk the Proud Land*.

The Battles of Chief Pontiac

Jack Broder Prods./Realart Pictures; 72 minutes; Producers: Jack Broder and Irving Starr; Director: Felix E. Feist; Cast: Lex Barker; Helen Westcott; Lon Chaney, Jr.; Berry Kroeger; Roy Roberts; Larry Chance; Ramsay Hill; Katherine Warren ****

Lon Chaney, Jr. always made a believable Indian; here, he's Chief Pontiac, chief of the Ottawa tribe, longing for friendly relations with the colonials in the 1760s but driven to war by German colonel Berry Kroeger and his Hessian regiments who have needlessly slaughtered an entire Ottawa village. Kroeger (a performance steeped in undiluted evil) was once tortured by the Arapaho, so the sadist's main quest in life is to exterminate every Redskin in the territory, whether they desire peace or not. Ranger Lex Barker, a pal of Chaney's, clashes with Kroeger before traveling to Fort Detroit to deliver urgent documents to Major Roy Roberts. En route, he meets Helen Westcott, imprisoned in Chaney's camp, and she becomes his unofficial squaw to save her from Larry Chance's (Hawkbill) lustful overtures. Kroeger, spitting venom and malice, takes over command at Fort Detroit, snubs Chaney's peace mission ("A Redskin messiah," he sneers), sticks Barker in a cage for insubordination and, for good measure, sends smallpox-contaminated bedding and clothing to the Ottawa camp, resulting in an outbreak of the disease; he then plans to march his soldiers into the camp and eliminate the Indians—men, women and children. Barker escapes, kills Chance in a hand-to-hand fight and tends to the Ottawa sick with Westcott. Trooping out of the fort, Kroeger consigns himself and his men to death, unaware that the Ottawa and surrounding tribes are amassing in the forest; Barker, back at Fort Detroit, is ordered to inform the German of a trap being laid in the woods. Caught in an ambush, the Hessians are decimated, their leader captured after he's shot Barker. Tied to a tree, Kroeger's shirt is ripped open by Chaney, his arms slashed and his body wrapped in a contaminated blanket ("White man's torture!"); the man later dies in agony. Recovered from his wound, Barker embraces Westcott, Chaney and Roberts smoking the peace pipe, the movie ending on a sad note as Chaney looks around him, at the lakes and the forests, and reflects: "One day, the Indian will disappear from this, his beloved land." How prophetic those words were. *The Battles of Chief Pontiac* was noted

The Italian poster for *The Battles of Chief Pontiac*

composer Elmer Bernstein's second feature film, shooting taking place in Colorado. Largely overlooked today, it's an enjoyable, at times exciting, colonial actioner enlivened by two great pieces of acting: Chaney as the noble savage of the title, and Kroeger the not-so-noble colonel brimming with hatred towards his fellow man.
Dialogue:
Kroeger to General Ramsay Hill: "Pontiac is the Devil in war paint, sir. A treacherous beast with the brain of a fox and the fangs of a wolf."

The Big Sky

Winchester/RKO-Radio; 122 minutes; Produced and Directed by Howard Hawks; Cast: Kirk Douglas; Dewey Martin; Arthur Hunnicutt; Elizabeth Threatt; Steven Geray; Hank Worden; Buddy Baer; Jim Davis *****

In 1832, a keelboat heads north up the Missouri River from St. Louis, embarking on a 2,000 mile journey to trade with the Blackfoot tribes in uncharted Montana territory. On board among the French contingent are trapper Kirk Douglas, quick-tempered fugitive Dewey Martin, part-Indian frontiersman Arthur Hunnicutt and beautiful Blackfoot princess Elizabeth Threatt. Rapids, currents, river snags, haul ropes snapping, waterfalls, deadly encounters with warlike Crow Indians, Douglas losing a finger and confrontations with Jim Davis and his cronies, instructed by the Missouri Trading Company to stop the expedition in its tracks because of competition, end with Martin marrying Threatt, the chief's daughter, Douglas (who loves her) and company announcing that they will return in a year for more trading. Fresh from the success of *The Thing from Another World* (Christian Nyby, editor on *The Big Sky*, is credited with directing *The Thing* but Hawks was undoubtedly the man behind the camera), Hawks' much-loved $2,000,000 frontier adventure, boasting an evocative Dimitri Tiomkin score, originally came in at 140 minutes, thought too lengthy by RKO executives who trimmed the movie by 18 minutes. The director also cast around for names such as Charlton Heston, Gary Cooper, Marlon Brando and John Wayne for the lead before begrudgingly settling on Douglas. Yes, it moves at a leisurely clip (Douglas and Martin don't board Steven Geray's *Mandan* until the 20th minute) but drips in period atmosphere, more a series of vignettes narrated by Oscar-nominee Hunnicutt, Russell Harlan (the film's second Oscar-nominee) imbuing the rugged landscapes (Wyoming's Snake River and Grand Teton Range) in vivid black-and-white hues. Douglas, 35 at the time, displayed 100% red-blooded masculinity, Hank Worden was a hoot playing loony old gap-toothed Redskin Poor Devil while Threatt glowed as Teal Eye, choosing Martin over Douglas ("Why?" must have been the word on punters' lips at the time). A timeless saga of the American

A West German poster for *The Big Sky*

West before it opened up that, like a good wine, improves with age.

Highlights:

The overall look of the picture; A.B. Guthrie, Jr.'s lucid script containing many of Hawks' trademark overlapping dialogue exchanges; and Douglas at his sexually potent best.

Dialogue:
Martin, emerging from Threatt's wigwam and hearing the sound of drums, to Hunnicutt: "What's all the noise about?"
Hunnicutt: "They're celebratin' yer wedding."
Martin: "Wedding?"
Hunnicutt: "You mebe don't know it but you're married man now."
Martin: "Married? And I ain't got nothin' to say about it?"
Hunnicutt: "Wouldn't do you no good to say."

Trivia:

Doe-eyed Threatt (she had Cherokee blood) quit the movie business after completing the shoot, her one and only foray into Hollywood; *The Big Sky* has been the most-seen Western shown on British television, a regular fixture during the 1960s and 1970s and still broadcast frequently today.

The Big Trees

Warner Bros.; Technicolor; 89 minutes; Producer: Louis F. Edelman; Director: Felix E. Feist; Cast: Kirk Douglas; Eve Miller; Edgar Buchanan; John Archer; Patrice Wymore; Roy Roberts; Harry Cording; Alan Hale, Jr. **

"Plot and emoting as old as the Redwoods," complained the *New York Times* of a Western lumberjack feature that Kirk Douglas once named as his worst-ever picture. Douglas agreed to work for nothing to extricate himself out of his Warner Bros. contract; the company also saved money by including extensive footage from their 1938 production *Valley of the Giants*. Douglas played an unscrupulous timber baron from Wisconsin in 1900, always broke, always flashing that disarming grin, promising his crew a million dollars in riches if they go with him to Northern California and tackle those giant Sequoias just waiting to be cut down in the name of profit ("I'm the one that's gonna knock 'em down."). Once there, Douglas' problems mount up: A Quaker colony views the trees as sacred ("They are our place of worship.") and dig their pious heels in over land rights; quick-on-the-draw pal Edgar Buchanan turns against him, elected town marshal; partner John Archer sides with rival Harry Cording and tries to have Douglas bumped off by three gunman who end up shooting Buchanan instead; ex-flame dancer/singer Patrice Wymore arrives on the scene, only to find Douglas hankering after Quaker widow Eve Miller; and Judge Roy Roberts presides over which party owns what land, whether or not they have legal claims in felling the trees and which of all the numerous shady deals has been sanctioned by Washington, not only for the cast's benefit but for the audience watching this confusing tale. When Miller's father is flattened by a falling Redwood, Douglas, at first charged with his murder, changes from villain to hero, dispatching Archer, blowing up an obstructive dam and marrying Miller. The big bonus point is Bert Glennon's glowing photography, filming taking place in California's

Redwood Groves area; and there's a fairly exciting sequence when Douglas clambers over logs on a runaway train towards a caboose containing Miller that's heading for a demolished bridge. Otherwise, it's pretty to look at but dull, one of the few occasions (if not the *only* occasion) where Kirk Douglas starred in a very ordinary movie; now how many times can you say that?

Dialogue:
Douglas to Archer, after being invited out by Miller: "This must be good luck. I've known a lotta gals. It's the only time one of them ever asked me to come up to see her tree."

The Black Lash

Western Adventure Prods./Realart; 54 minutes; Produced and Directed by Ron Ormond; Cast: Lash LaRue; Al "Fuzzy" St. John; Peggy Stewart; Ray Bennett; Byron Keith; Kermit Maynard; John Cason; Clarke Stevens **

A rehash of 1948's *Frontier Revenge*, kicking off with six minutes of stock footage from other LaRue movies plus Lippert's *Crooked River* and *Fast on the Draw*, Lash not making an appearance until 17 ragged minutes has drifted by. He's a marshal posing as a member of the Dawson gang, inveigling himself and pal Fuzzy into Ray Bennett and Byron Keith's setup; the crooks are planning to rob the Silver Queen Mine of its bullion, Bennett set on taking moll Peggy Stewart to San Francisco to live the high life on the proceedings. Stewart sings a song, Bennett's gang is eliminated prior to the robbery and Fuzzy puts two slugs into Bennett after Keith gets plugged by his would-be partner. The bewhiskered chump is promptly handed the job of sheriff of Rhyolite, the mayor grinning at camera, stating "What a pair" when Lash and Fuzzy go out to clean up the town. The penultimate Lash LaRue adventure is a real cut-and-paste job if ever there was one, showing signs of "we've seen it all, many, many times before" in every department.

Dialogue:
Keith to Bennett on hearing that LaRue's not a bad guy: "LaRue? I thought he was…"
Bennett: "An outlaw? It's a ruse. He's still a marshal. The guy can't get it out of his system."

Buffalo Bill in Tomahawk Territory

Jack Schwarz Prods./United Artists; 66 minutes; Producers: Bernard B. Ray and Edward Finney; Director: Bernard B. Ray; Cast: Clayton Moore; Slim Andrews; Rodd Redwing; Chief Yowlachie; Sharon Dexter; Charlie Hughes; Charles Harvey; Helena Dare **

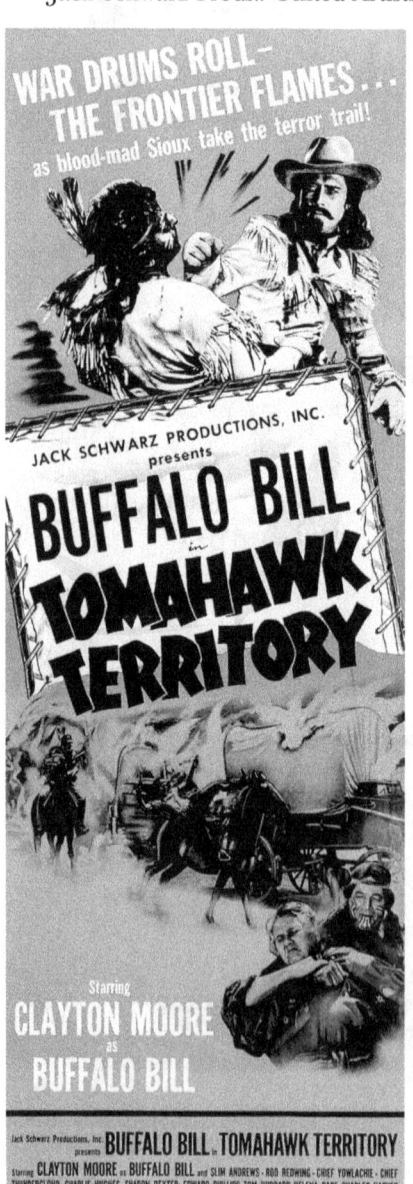

On a hiatus in 1952 from playing The Lone Ranger in the popular television series, due to a studio contract dispute, Clayton Moore starred as Buffalo Bill Cody in this cobbled-together oater that appeared to be 20 years out of date, even at the time of release. The answer as to why the film resembles a museum piece lies in the title theme and soundtrack: Frank Sanucci's score was lifted from some of the 140 plus B-Westerns he participated in from 1936 onwards, those distinctly non-'50s orchestral tones of the type that would back a '30s crooner like Rudy Vallee. Likewise, many of the action scenes were filched from any number of long-forgotten Westerns director Bernard B. Ray made during the same period, new footage added to bring it in line with 1950s values. The end result is a scratchy, creaky mishmash in which Moore (goatee beard and long hair), aided by cantankerous varmint Slim Andrews (Cactus), foils a scheme hatched by crook Edward Phillips: His gang, dressed as Redskins ("We're gonna play Indians again."), is attacking wagon trains and rustling cattle owed to the Indians under a peace deal, the idea being that the treaty between the whites and Chief White Cloud (Chief Yowlachie) is broken, allowing Phillips to move in on Sioux territory and lay his hands on the gold lying there (the first wagon train they raid has the defenders dressed as women). Running Deer (Rodd Redwing), firmly against any treaty, goes on the warpath, committing suicide after losing a knife tussle with Moore, and Yowlachie finally makes peace at Fort Randall when he and his braves charge into Phillips' "braves," unmasking them as the fakes they are. "My people starve. Must have cattle in three days or no peace," intones Yowlachie to Moore, one of several amusing deadpan exchanges between the two, followed by the threat of "Killer of buffalo not welcome in land of Sioux. Your hair will hang in my tepee" if the frontier legend can't produce more steers in the required time. Andrews is lustfully pursued throughout the movie by overweight Indian cook Helena Dare and The Broome Brothers play three songs, fronted by singer Sharon Dexter. An ancient-looking concoction crammed full of grainy stock footage, produced on a tiny budget and so clumsily executed that it definitely comes under the title of "Western guilty pleasure"; Chief Yowlachie's monosyllabic delivery just about makes this gimcrack cowboys-versus-Indians oddity watchable.

Dialogue:
Lieutenant Charles Harvey, on seeing white men kitted out as women: "This is the first time I've ever seen soldiers in skirts."

Trivia:
Dexter only made one movie after this fiasco; it was composer Sanucci's last outing, and the final throw of the dice (bar two further efforts) for director Ray and producer Finney.

Bugles in the Afternoon

Warner Bros.; Technicolor; 85 minutes; Producer: William Cagney; Director: Roy Rowland; Cast: Ray Milland; Helena Carter; Hugh Marlowe; Forrest Tucker; Barton MacLane; Sheb Wooley; James Millican; George Reeves ****

Drummed out of the army for assaulting fellow officer Hugh Marlowe (quite rightly as it turns out), Ray Milland enlists as a private at Fort Abraham Lincoln, Dakota where, by chance, Marlowe is running one of the regiments in preparation for a campaign against the Sioux. He's also romancing Helena Carter, the lass falling for Milland's more cultured charms. When General Custer (Sheb Wooley) heads for a showdown with the Sioux nations at Little Bighorn, Marlowe does his damnedest to make sure that his hated rival is bushwhacked by Indians and eliminated; the rat's plan backfires when he's shot in the back during a hillside fight with Milland who is then promoted to captain for his bravery and wins the hand of Carter. A large-scale battle in the movie's final third, bolstered by Dimitri Tiomkin's resonant music and Wilfrid (Wilfred) M. Cline's photography (Kanab, Utah was used as the location), makes for a rousing, fast-moving and extremely noisy cavalry yarn; Milland and Marlowe are a gutsy hero and

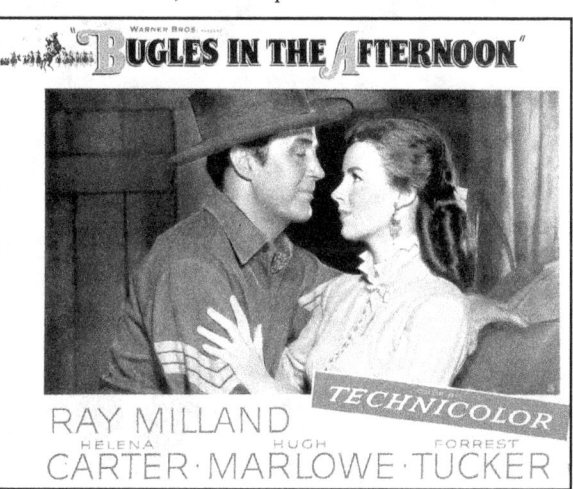

villain, dependable Forrest Tucker stands out as a fist-happy, rough 'n' ready trooper and Carter's clipped English vowels make her appear like a schoolmistress out West.
Highlights:
Milland forced by Marlowe to slowly canter through a pack of hostile Redskins and pick out the two responsible for having just massacred a party of prospectors.
Dialogue:
Tucker to Milland, both cornered in a box canyon, realizing that Marlowe has sent them to a probable death: "May the hounds of hell rest on his chest and howl for his soul."
Trivia:
The brief snippet of Custer's 7th Cavalry slaughtered at Little Bighorn is taken from 1941's *They Died With Their Boots On*, tinted to blend in with the color.

California Conquest

Columbia; Technicolor; 78 minutes; Producer: Sam Katzman; Director: Lew Landers; Cast: Cornel Wilde; Teresa Wright; Alfonso Bedoya; John Dehner; Lisa Faraday; Edward Colmans; George Eldredge; Eugene Iglesias **

In the early 1840s, Russia and France eye up Mexican-held California in order to gain a foothold on American soil while Cornel Wilde, part of a movement by the U.S. to annexe the state, dashes here, there and everywhere, trying to prevent the Russians from moving in. Tomboy Teresa Wright, a crack shot, is his partner, the lass bent on killing bandido captain Alfonso Bedoya who shot her father, a gunsmith, after his store was raided for weapons. Slippery customer John Dehner turns up in a role he could have sleepwalked through, that of a devious Don who is out to line his own pocket by becoming Governor of Monterey, whoever he crosses. Wilde (posing as a lowly peon) and Wright fall in lust, hatching a plan to join Bedoya's gang, busy terrorizing local farmers sympathetic to the U.S. cause, in order to gain inside information; when they're caught out, Wilde is whipped (his chest, not his back), Wright blasts the bandit chief and the pair escape to drum up support. Eventually, the Russians are brought to heel at Dehner's hacienda when Californian citizens overwhelm Bedoya's desperadoes and Russian soldiers with a little help from a wagon loaded with gunpowder; Dehner and Wilde fight to the death, the two-timing Don succumbing to a knife in the back. Wilde and Wright can now get married and start producing the first of those 14 children they have promised each other! Lew

Landers' vigorous actioner suffers from Wilde's erratic Spanish/American accent and Wright isn't all that convincing as a tough-shooting gal out for justice; the color photography (Ellis W. Carter) is nice and Bedoya chews the scenery, but then the Mexican-born actor practically played the same part in every film he appeared in.

Dialogue:
Tomboy Wright to Wilde. "Come on, amigo. I talk too much."
Wilde: "Good. It's the only way I can tell you're a woman."

Cattle Town

Warner Bros.; 71 minutes; Producer: Bryan Foy; Director: Noel M. Smith; Cast: Dennis Morgan; Ray Teal; Amanda Blake; Philip Carey; Robert J. Wilke; Rita Moreno; George O'Hanlon; Paul Picerni **

One minute, Robert J. Wilke is viciously clubbing to death Paul Picerni with his gun butt; the next minute, we have Dennis Morgan warbling a song while tending a herd of cattle. William Lava's semi-comical title theme segues into Morgan and pal George O'Hanlon singing a ditty, one of several scattered throughout the movie, leaving you to wonder whether *Cattle Town* was planned as a musical Western, a comedy or serious drama. Moments of brutality (Ray Teal stampeded to death at the end) are interlaced with musical interludes, making for a very lumpy ride that will turn most diehard Western aficionados off. In 1888, Morgan, on instructions from the governor, is sent to Questa, Texas, to mediate between Teal's Hastings Cattle Company and Philip Carey's settlers. They've set up home on Teal's land and he demands that they remove themselves pronto, also wishing to grab their valuable beef into the bargain. Amiable Morgan does his best to sort things out without resorting to gunplay, peace restored in the end when Teal, after shooting chief henchman Wilke, is flattened by those rampaging steers. Morgan takes off with haughty Amanda Blake, Teal's daughter (and not dark-haired sexpot Rita Moreno), the film (as it had started) ending on a song—but not on a high note! An unsatisfactory blend of forgettable tunes (there's even a barber-shop quartet) and roughhouse action that jars after the first few minutes; a real oddity, and not a very successful one.

Dialogue:
Wilke to Teal: "The bullets in my gun don't stop just because they see a badge."
Trivia:
Noel M. Smith returned after a 10-year hiatus (Universal's *Gang Busters*, 1942) and made this effort, his last picture.

Westerns of the 1950s: The Classic Years

Desert Pursuit

Monogram; 71 minutes; Producer: Lindsley Parsons; Director: George Blair; Cast: Wayne Morris; Virginia Grey; George Tobias; Anthony Caruso; John Doucette; Emmett Lynn; Robert Bice; Frank Lackteen
***

Panning for gold with grubby old talkative prospector Emmett Lynn, Wayne Morris realizes that his partner has drunkenly blabbed about the gold to three outlaw Arabs. Virginia Grey, from Carson City, turns up at their camp, accused of cheating at cards and on the run, and accompanies Morris on a perilous trip over the Death Valley wastes to San Bernardino, informing him that his fiancée has married someone else. The Arabs appear at the camp on camels (camels were part of the American Camel Corps of 1856 and, 10 years later, could still be found wandering in the desert), bludgeon Lynn to death (a vicious scene, out of keeping with the movie's tone) and pursue the couple across the wilderness (Lone Pine and California's Olanche Dunes were the locales used). An encounter with Frank Lackteen's Indians on Christmas Eve results in George Tobias, Anthony Caruso and John Doucette being mistaken for the Three Wise Men; the ruse uncovered, Morris and a brave hunt the outlaws among the rocks. Tobias and Caruso fall to their deaths, Doucette makes off on his unwieldy steed and Morris decides to settle down to the ranching life with "squaw" Grey; in blonde rinse, check shirt and jeans, she's a very attractive proposition indeed. A likeable low budgeter from Monogram shot in stark surroundings by William A. Sickner and featuring pleasing on-screen chemistry between Morris and Grey plus an evocative score from Edward J. Kay.

Dialogue:
Morris to Lackteen, trying to describe a camel: "Camels (stoops and makes grunting noises)."
Lackteen: "Loco."
Grey: "They think you're crazy."

The Frontier Phantom

Western Adventure Prods./Realart; 55 minutes; Produced and Directed by Ron Ormond; Cast: Lash LaRue; Al "Fuzzy" St. John; Archie Twitchell; Virginia Herrick; Kenne Duncan; Clarke Stevens; Bud Osborne; Sandy Sanders *

The final Lash LaRue Western was a retread of 1949's *Outlaw Country*, extensive footage of which was used in the flashback sequences where U.S. Marshal LaRue narrates to disbelieving sheriff Archie Twitchell how he came to be mixed up with his twin brother, The Frontier Phantom, a notorious outlaw. The Phantom is in hospital recovering from a gunshot wound but three of his gang are due in Sawyer's Creek at midnight, LaRue planning for a showdown in the Birdcage saloon; he hopes, with Twitchell's help, to bring the bunch to justice, which is accomplished in the final reel. Even if you haven't caught *Outlaw Country*, it's a confusing affair and not a very professional editing job of combining new footage with old, leaving many viewers scratching their heads over just what is going on. LaRue went into television after the movie was completed, old sparring partner Al "Fuzzy" St. John hanging up his well-worn boots at the age of 58, having starred in 337 pictures over a span of 40 years. 1952 was the year of *High Noon*—hour-long B-Westerns of the type represented by *The Frontier Phantom* no longer figured in the scheme of things and would die out altogether a year later.

Dialogue:
Dan White to his men, being hit from both sides by LaRue and The Phantom: "Fighting these two brothers is like tangling with the U.S. army."

Gold Fever

Monogram; 63 minutes; Producer: John Calvert; Director: Leslie Goodwins; Cast: John Calvert; Ralph Morgan; Ann Cornell; Eugene Roth; Tom Kennedy; Judd Holdren; Danny Rense; Robert Graham ****

A stranger (John Calvert who also produced) rides into the town of Yermo in 1893, sells his trick horse to Eugene Roth for $100 on condition he can buy it back for $125 and teams up with old-timer Ralph Morgan (as Nugget Jack); the prospector has a gold mine hidden somewhere in the hills and sees Calvert as his ideal partner. Also, after the gold is Roth, Indian Robert Graham instructed to tail the pair and report back where the mine is. Tomboy Ann Cornell gets in on the action as Roth, Tom Kennedy and Judd Holdren converge on the mine, all three crooks dynamited to bits at the end—and is Cornell, who has promised

Westerns of the 1950s: The Classic Years   115

to wed Calvert, really Morgan's long-lost daughter? Morgan hands the grubstake over to Calvert who gets his favorite steed back and wanders into the arid wastes in search of more discoveries. Johnny Richards' racket of a score, combined with Glen Gano and Clark Ramsey's pristine black-and-white photography (Lone Pine was used as the location) and Leslie Goodwins' fast-paced direction, makes this B-Western a cut above the average Monogram effort, even though Morgan's motor-mouthed delivery is occasionally as loud as the soundtrack!

Dialogue:
Calvert, treating a snakebite on Morgan's filthy leg: "You'll live, you scallywag, but the snake'll probably die."

Trivia:
Calvert's one and only Western virtually completed a career that amounted to 13 films; he was once a double for Clark Gable. And *Gold Fever* marked the final movie appearance of 69-year-old Morgan.

The Half-Breed

RKO-Radio; Technicolor; 81 minutes; Producer: Herman Schlom; Directors: Stuart Gilmore and Edward Ludwig (uncredited); Cast: Robert Young; Janis Carter; Jack Buetel; Barton MacLane; Reed Hadley; Tom Monroe; Judy Walsh; Damian O'Flynn ***

Filmed in rich Technicolor by Oscar-winner William V. Skall (*Joan of Arc*, 1948) and shot around Arizona's rocky Sedona region, *The Half-Breed* tells of traveling gambler Robert Young's friendship with half-Apache, Jack Buetel (as Charlie Wolf, the title character) and his attempts to prevent an Indian uprising. Town crook Reed Hadley is stirring up trouble, wanting the Redskins off their reservation so that he can lay his hands on the gold deposits buried underneath, and the only way he can do it is to provoke them into going on the warpath. Burly marshal Barton MacLane doesn't want Young hanging around his patch but mellows when it's apparent that the dude is about the only person who can put a stop to impending wholesale scalping, making him temporary Indian agent. Meanwhile, Young forms a relationship with singer Janis Carter, the well-built dame reptilian Hadley is after and who rouses the lust in Buetel when he's allowed into town to watch her act. When Hadley rapes and murders Buetel's sister (Judy Walsh), the war drums beat ever louder; Young hunts the killer down, tussling with him on a cliff, the rat tumbling to his death, and delivers his corpse to the Apaches just as they are about to attack Captain Damian O'Flynn's troop regiment. Hostilities over, Buetel and his warriors withdraw, Young galloping back to San Remo to begin a new life with Carter. Paul Sawtell provides a terrific score in an interesting if slightly dull pro-Indians oater, amiable Young (made up to look older than his 45 years) not really cutting it as a man not to be messed with.

Dialogue:
Buetel, in a saloon, to barkeep: "Whiskey."
Barkeep: "We don't serve whiskey to Indians."
Buetel: "Half white. Drink white man's half."

Trivia:
Carter, once destined for a career in opera, sang all her songs in the picture.

Hiawatha

Monogram; Cinecolor; 80 minutes; Producer: Walter Mirisch; Director: Kurt Neumann; Cast: Vince Edwards; Yvette Duguay (Dugay); Keith Larsen; Morris Ankrum; Stephen Chase; Katherine Emery; Eugene Iglesias; Ian MacDonald **

"Worthy but dull" sums up Monogram's low-budget attempt at bringing Henry Longfellow's 1855 poetic work *The Song of Hiawatha* to the big screen in Cinecolor. There's not a white man anywhere to be seen as our hero of the title, played by Vince Edwards (his third movie), tries to make peace between his own tribe, the Ojibway, and the neighboring Illinois and Dakotas, thwarted at every turn by psychotic Keith Larson (as Pau Pukkewis) who lusts for war at any price. Edwards meets Dakota maiden Yvette Duguay (Minnehaha), falls in love with her after one day in her company and they marry against his tribe's wishes. Larson bumps off two of Edwards' best friends, blames it on the Dakotas and slaughters an Illinois hunting party, precipitating an attack on his village in which Chief Morris Ankrum is killed. Edwards has a fight with his long-lost father who left him when he was an infant, and Larsen is unveiled as the troublemaker just before the Dakotas and the Ojibway clash, dispatched with Edwards' knife. Hostilities over, the three tribes can now begin to live a life of harmony together. Attractive wooded scenery around California's Bass Lake and a melodic Marlin Skiles' score compensate for a stodgy narrative and "Me Heap Big Indian" performances, Duguay's good looks overpowering the rest of the slightly wooden cast. On initial release, *Hiawatha* came in for a certain amount of old-style Hollywood Commie bashing from some quarters, due to the fact that the narrative centered solely on Indians—which, of course, given the material, it would do.

Dialogue:
Stephen Chase's words of wisdom to Edwards after Duguay has thrown a tantrum: "You will learn, if you haven't already, that women, even when they know they're wrong, seldom admit it. My daughter is no exception."

Horizons West

Universal; Technicolor; 81 minutes; Producer: Albert J. Cohen; Director: Budd Boetticher; Cast: Robert Ryan; Rock Hudson; James Arness; Julia (Julie) Adams; Raymond Burr; John McIntire; Judith Braun; Dennis Weaver ****

An iconic example of an early 1950s Universal-International Western: Incisive direction, bright color photography, intelligent script and a strong cast. Confederates Robert Ryan (six-foot-four), Rock Hudson (six-foot-five) and James Arness (six-foot-seven) return from the war. Hudson, Ryan's brother, and Arness plan to take up ranching where they left off, but Ryan has different ideas; he wants to get rich, quick, and will adopt ruthless tactics to achieve his goal, including crossing local magnate Raymond Burr, flirting with his unhappy wife, Julia Adams, gathering together a gang of desperadoes ("the dregs of war") to rustle other ranchers' cattle and falling out with his father, John McIntire, boss of the Circle H Ranch. As to be expected, it's a powerhouse performance from Ryan, one of Hollywood's most gifted actors, the man without a conscience leaving a trail of corpses in his climb to power ("A rule of terror grips Austin" scream the headlines): Burr, falling foul of Ryan's fists, is shot by Hudson, ravishing Adams throws herself at Ryan, homesteaders are forced out of their properties and gunned down, Ryan kills Arness and stolen cattle is sold across the Texas border to General Rodolfo Acosta, boss of Zona Libre. Sick and tired of Ryan's ambitions built on intimidation and violence, local ranchers club together with McIntire and Hudson to bring him to justice, his gang wiped out in a showdown. In a tense climax, Ryan is shot dead in Zona Libre after using his own father as a shield to escape being caught. Shortish and hard-hitting, *Horizons West* is another superb sagebrush saga from the Universal Western stable.

Highlights:
Budd Boetticher's tightly edited style of filmmaking, plus Ryan in blistering form and Adams flaunting her sexuality to perfection.

Dialogue:
Ryan to Adams on his personal vision: "Because when I started out, I had two ideas. To build a Western empire and to make you the greatest lady in Texas … I want the empire, honey."
Adams: "More than you want me?"
Ryan: "One doesn't go without the other."

Trivia:
Ryan (43) was only two years younger than McIntire (45) who played his father.

The Kid from Broken Gun

Columbia; 55 minutes; Producer: Colbert Clark; Director: Fred F. Sears; Cast: Charles Starrett; Jock (Jack) Mahoney; Angela Stevens; Tristram Coffin; Myron Healey; Smiley Burnette; Edgar Dearing; Chris Alcaide **

The final Charles Starrett *Durango Kid* Western was composed of around 35% new footage, taking place at Benton County Court House, and 65% footage from 1946's *The Fighting Frontiersman*. Jock Mahoney is on trial for murdering Chris Alcaide, Myron Healey the prosecuting counsel. Of course, he's innocent; how he got framed forms the background to the tale, told in convoluted flashback style. It turns out that defense counsel Angela Stevens pulled the trigger in a fracas; she was in cahoots with Tristram Coffin over stealing a hoard of Spanish gold coins once owned by Mexico's Santa Anna, destined to be used in the building of a new hospital. By blaming the murder of Alcaide on Mahoney and pretending the gold was stolen, she and Coffin reckoned they had provided the perfect cover to enable them to hightail it without anyone realizing they had committed a crime. The Durango Kid (aka Steve Reynolds) conducts the final session, Stevens unmasked as the killer, the deadly dame and Coffin arrested; Mahoney is a free man, free enough to doff his hat at the nearest passing filly in the street! Not quite a damp squib to bow out on, but certainly nothing outstanding; Burnette, dressed as a charlady in court and spitting sweets at the judge, provides mild amusement, Starrett content to sit on the benches and listen to the testimonies against Mahoney, retirement no doubt on his mind.

Dialogue:
Burnette to Starrett: "Oh, whoever heard of a lady lawyer defending a man. Jack don't stand a chance in here."

The Lawless Breed

Universal; Technicolor; 83 minutes; Producer: William Alland; Director: Raoul Walsh; Cast: Rock Hudson; Julia (Julie) Adams; John McIntire; Mary Castle; Hugh O'Brian; Lee Van Cleef; Race Gentry; Glenn Strange ***

"I only ever killed a man in self-defense," says Rock Hudson (as gunfighter John Wesley Hardin) to a judge and jury. Not true. Hardin was an unhinged sociopath who is said to have murdered over 40 men for simply rubbing him up the wrong way; in Raoul Walsh's watered-down version of the Hardin legend, he's a man on the run from a series of events whereby he has been forced into using his gun. Released from Huntsville Prison, Texas in 1894, Hudson hands his written life story to the editor of *The Texas Clarion* and we are in flashback territory, Hudson escaping the clutches of his sadistic preacher father and staying with his uncle (John McIntire plays both roles), promising to wed sweetheart Mary Castle; it all goes wrong when he outdraws Michael Ansara at the card table, Ansara's three brothers (Hugh O'Brian, Lee Van Cleef and Glenn Strange) hell-bent on revenge. One incident after another causes Hudson to become a wanted fugitive ("John Wesley Hardin has made the name of Texas stink in the nostrils of justice."), Castle dying in crossfire after the Texas Rangers storm McIntire's homestead; Hudson later marries showgirl Julia Adams who gives birth to their son at the same time her husband is arrested, spending 16 years in the state pen. On his release, Hardin senior finds that Hardin junior (Race Gentry) shows disturbing signs of following in his infamous father's footsteps, but the reformed gunman puts a stop to it after a saloon standoff. Hudson stands out in his first-ever leading role, Walsh orchestrates a few imaginative showdowns (Hudson versus Van Cleef in a windswept street is the best) and overall, *The Lawless Breed* is your archetypal Universal-International '50s B-Western, colorful, fast-moving, noisy and entertaining.

Highlights:
The lovely Julia Adams stripping down to her mauve lingerie and showing plenty of leg (and bosom) to boot.

Dialogue:
Adams to Hudson, explaining why she detests life on the farm: "If the weather doesn't get you, the grasshoppers do."

Trivia:
Henry Mancini and Herman Stein's strident title score was reused in Universal's classic monster yarn, *Tarantula* (1955), *and* in 1956's *Showdown at Abilene*.

Lone Star

MGM; 94 minutes; Producer: Z. Wayne Griffin; Director: Vincent Sherman; Cast: Clark Gable; Ava Gardner; Broderick Crawford; Lionel Barrymore; Beulah Bondi; James Burke; Moroni Olsen; William Farnum ***

In 1845, ex-president Andrew Jackson (Lionel Barrymore) and his senators discuss the annexation of Texas into the United States; in Texas, gun-toting senator Broderick Crawford and his cronies are sowing the seeds of unrest, wanting Texas to remain a Republic, even if it means a war with Mexico. Cattle baron Clark Gable is sent to Austin with partner James Burke, ostensibly to sell beef to the army; in reality, they're to meet up with General Sam Houston (Moroni Olsen) and persuade the renowned leader of men to convince the local populace that joining the Union is the way forward. In Austin, Gable and Crawford come to blows because of their differing political beliefs and the fact that Gable takes a fancy to his rival's intended, Ava Gardner, boss of the *Austin Blade* newspaper. The combined star power of Gable and Gardner, sparring and kissing in close-up, helped rake in a healthy $2,000,000 profit for MGM; those were the days when, like all major Hollywood players, Gable's box-office clout could produce bumper ticket sales, regardless of the material involved, and here, the material was very thin indeed. Following a turgid opening of political chitchat (non-Americans would find it all a puzzle), Gable and Burke journey to Austin where Crawford cuts up rough. Okay, matters improve when Gable is hunted in the wilds by Crawford and his hyenas, but the final skirmish between opposing factions in Austin falls flat, though Gable and Crawford's knife fight is a bruiser. Crawford actually smiles in the dying seconds as news arrives that Houston is all for annexation and that state troopers have been drafted in to deal with those pesky Mexicans. As for Gable, he, naturally, pinches Gardner ("A lot of woman!") from his foe. Color would have helped in a semi-historical romp that, if it wasn't for the leading man and lady (Gardner looks ravishing and gets to sing at one stage), wouldn't be worth all that much to diehard Western buffs.

Highlights:

David Buttolph's stirring title music; and Crawford's outlandish proposed map of the United States depicting Texas taking up half the continent!

Dialogue:

Gardner, inspecting a cut on Gable's neck: "You better have a doctor look at this."
Gable, closing in for the kill: "Is that an order? I don't want to make any more mistakes."
Gardner, fixing him with a frosty stare: "You're making one right now."

Trivia:

The final film of 73-year-old Barrymore (he guested as himself in 1953's *Main Street to Broadway*); and the debut of George Hamilton, aged 12.

Montana Belle

RKO-Radio; Trucolor; 82 minutes; Producer: Howard Welsch; Director: Allan Dwan; Cast: Jane Russell; George Brent; Scott Brady; Forrest Tucker; Andy Devine; Jack Lambert; Ray Teal; John Litel ***

Belle Starr (Jane Russell) teams up with the Dalton gang, falls out with them and forms her own bunch, Starr's outfit the scourge of the West; the two gangs then decide to rob George Brent's saloon, The Birdcage, *and* the bank in Guthrie, Oklahoma of a million dollars at the same time without each realizing it. Trouble is, Russell plans to marry Brent and live with him in Mexico, so her loyalties are divided. Allan Dwan's highly fictionalized account of the lady bandit's life was originally to have been released by Republic in 1948/1949, but the film rights were sold to RKO who issued it in late 1952. "A splendid strumpet" is the view of those watching Russell in a blonde rinse strutting her stuff through two lengthy song numbers while Forrest Tucker and Scott Brady fight for her affections in the street. Jack A. Marta's Trucolor photography sparkles (some prints are in black-and-white), the gunfights are spectacular (especially Brady and Tucker walking to their deaths in a hail of lead) and Russell gives the production her all in a flashy Western built solely around the lady's considerable twin assets!

Dialogue:
Brent: "It's quite an accomplishment to grow old in this country, especially with the Daltons around."

Montana Territory

Columbia; Technicolor; 64 minutes; Producer: Colbert Clark; Director: Ray Nazarro; Cast: Lon McCallister; Wanda Hendrix; Preston Foster; Clayton Moore; Hugh Sanders; Myron Healey; Jack Elam; Eddy Waller ***

1863: Gold has been discovered in Montana, leading to an influx of thieves and killers. Lon McCallister, son of a famous judge, witnesses the murder of a gold prospector and his son and reports the incident to Sheriff Preston Foster in Bannack. But Preston, along with corrupt deputy Clayton Moore, is in collusion with the outlaw gangs, the brains behind a string of stage holdups and bank robberies and to cover his tracks, he deputizes McCallister, giving the youngster his first tough job, hoping that he'll soon be dispatched: The deputy is to provide protection to Hugh Sanders on the stage to Montana City and guard the $10,000 that Sanders is carrying. McAllister covers himself in glory by defeating the two outlaw road agents on the stage plus Jack Elam's bandits; at the way station, the deputy attempts to romance tomboy Wanda Hendrix while her father, Eddy Waller, is suspicious of Preston and Moore, as is Sanders and right-hand man Myron Healey. When Waller is callously murdered by Foster for voicing his doubts, Sanders forms a vigilante group to rid Montana of all outlaws, hanging those caught alive. McCallister steadfastly refuses to accept that Foster is a bad 'un until he sees him take a shot at Hendrix. In a climactic showdown at the way station, Foster is wounded by McCallister, Elam plugged, Moore remanded in custody and Montana declared a state by Congress; McAllister and Hendrix cozy up in the closing seconds. It's short, bright and breezy and contains plenty of gunplay, but 28-year-old McCallister is simply too slight and boyish-looking to be taken seriously as a lawman facing up to heavyweight Preston and his hyenas; the role would have better suited Hendrix's ex, Audie Murphy (but he was on contract to Universal-International.)

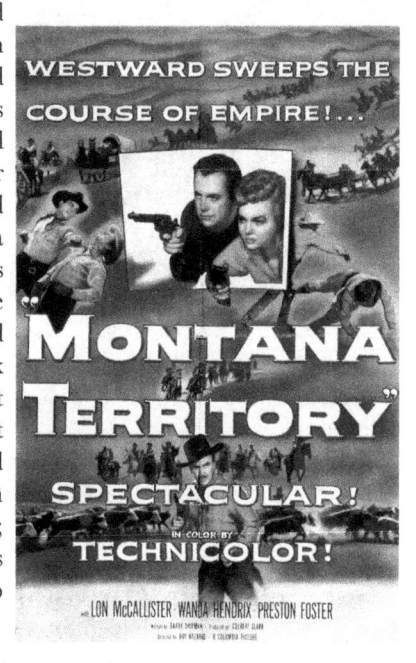

Dialogue:
Foster to Moore, watching McCallister walk off: "There goes a deputy whose career will probably be the shortest on record."

The Outcasts of Poker Flat

20th Century Fox; 81 minutes; Producer: Julian Blaustein; Director: Joseph M. Newman; Cast: Anne Baxter; Dale Robertson; Cameron Mitchell; Miriam Hopkins; Craig Hill; Barbara Bates; William H. Lynn; Dick Rich ****

Following Hugo Friedhofer's emotion-charged title score, Joseph M. Newman's atmospheric *noir* Western (based on Bret Harte's 1869 short story) opens in spellbinding style. Three prairie rats creep stealthily through Poker Flat's muddy streets after dark, the noise of bawdy saloon laughter, a piano playing and shouts breaking the night air; this is what the hubbub of a Wild West town during the 1860s probably sounded like, a highly dangerous place to be, and it's an eerie evocation of a long-vanished time and place the director expertly conjures up. The three no-goods blow a safe; two are shot dead, the third (Cameron Mitchell) escaping into the snowbound wastes. The next morning, Dale Robertson, Anne Baxter, Miriam Hopkins and William H. Lynn are thrown out of town for being a bad influence; all four plus Mitchell, Craig Hill and wife Barbara Bates find themselves sheltering in a mountain cabin, at the mercy of a blizzard and each other's fragile temperaments. Mitchell is married to Baxter who loathes him ("You and I are finished. I hate your guts."); he's the one packing a gun (Robertson's is hidden up the chimney) so *he* calls the shots, Robertson, a gambler by trade, waiting for the right opportunity to outwit him. Baxter falls for the good-looking card sharp, Mitchell, fuming, realizes what's going on and Hill goes into town with $500 of the crook's stolen bankroll to purchase much-needed supplies. Tensions rise, Mitchell begins to sweat, plugs whiskey-sodden Lynn in the back and, in a struggle outside in the snow, is throttled to death by Robertson, a grim ending. At the conclusion to a gripping, claustrophobic little drama, Robertson and Baxter elect to ride off together to start a new life well away from Poker Flat.

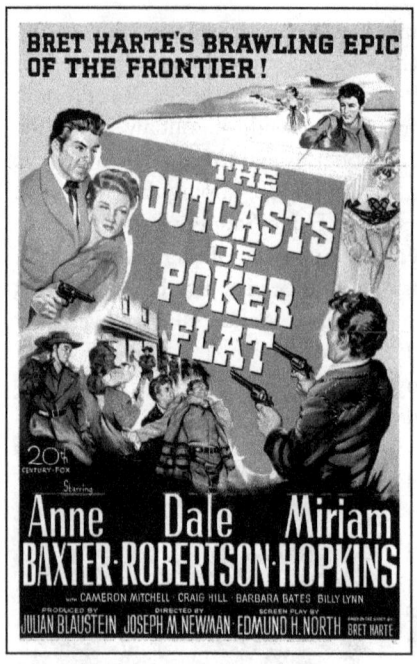

Dialogue:
Hopkins, after Poker Flat's righteous citizens have booted her out of town: "If there's one thing that turns my stomach, it's responsibility."

Outlaw Women

Lippert/Howco; Cinecolor; 75 minutes; Producer: Ron Ormond; Directors: Sam Newfield and Ron Ormond; Cast: Marie Windsor; Richard Rober; Carla Balenda; Allan Nixon; Richard Avonde; Jackie Coogan; Jacqueline Fontaine; Leonard Penn ***

"Six Gun Sirens Who Shoot to Thrill." Thus proclaimed the posters to indie outfits Lippert and Howco's kitsch-laden frolic in which the town of Las Mujeres is run by the female of the species, saloon boss/gambler Marie Windsor (Iron Mae) ruling the roost. An assortment of characters enter the town, most from nearby Silver Creek. Doc Allan Nixon, forced there at gunpoint by tomcat Carla Balenda; Richard Rober and past-his-prime gunman Jackie Coogan, intent on taking over the joint. Quack medic Billy House and his useless remedies; and outlaw Richard Avonde who, with Leonard Penn (as Sam Bass), wants Windsor to help him knock off a quarter of a million dollars, a massive payroll on its way from the Silver Creek Bank to Utah City. Add to this a couple of tuneful songs (one by The Four Dandies), a few bouts of gunplay, dancing gals flashing their pins and pistol-toting butch dame Marcia Hart lighting matches on her teeth and you have a guilty pleasure presented in flashy Cinecolor that, given the hokey material on hand, could have been a *little* more over-the-top than it actually turned out to be. But Queen of the Bs Windsor, looking gorgeous in crimson, was always worth any fan's attention and writer Orville H. Hampton conjures up some glorious deadpan lines ("How do you fight a woman?" "The only town in the West where girls get an even break" and "Anybody wearing trousers doesn't stand a chance in Las Mujeres."). The whole gaudy shebang ends in happily-ever-after fashion, Rober elected marshal and marrying Windsor while Nixon cozies up to Balenda, now attired in a dress instead of cowboy gear. The movie closes on Hart firing up another match on her teeth and winking at the camera. Great stuff!

Dialogue:
Nixon to Windsor, alarmed at Balenda being told to contact Avonde's bunch about the forthcoming robbery: "She's not leaving."
Windsor: "Who said so?"
Nixon: "A mere man."

Pony Soldier aka MacDonald of the Canadian Mounties

20th Century Fox; Technicolor; 82 minutes; Producer: Samuel G. Engel; Director: Joseph M. Newman; Cast: Tyrone Power; Cameron Mitchell; Thomas Gomez; Penny Edwards; Robert Horton; Anthony Numkena; Stuart Randall; Howard Petrie **

Canadian Mountie Tyrone Power departs from Fort Walsh in 1876 to track down a bunch of renegade Cree who have taken two white captives, using them as an insurance policy for the tribe to move north to their reservation in Canada unmolested; Montana, to the south, has the required buffalo meat but by going there, the Cree are in serious breach of a peace treaty. Assisting Power is half-Blackfeet Thomas Gomez, trembling at the sight of a mirage of a lake on the horizon. Commencing with a furious cavalry versus Indians clash (footage from 1944's *Buffalo Bill* was used), the plot gets bogged down once Power and his overweight scout are escorted to the vast Cree camp, director Newman focusing on the animosity between Power and Cameron Mitchell (Konah), Stuart Randall (Standing Bear) trying to calm things down. Captive Robert Horton turns out to be not only an Indian-hating rat but an escaped bank robber, Penny Edwards earmarked as Mitchell's next wife. It is left to charming 10-year-old Anthony Numkena to bring some life into the narrative, a Cree orphan who adopts Power as his father. After much discussion regarding the release of the prisoners, Power uses the image of a ship, seen as a mirage, to scare the superstitious

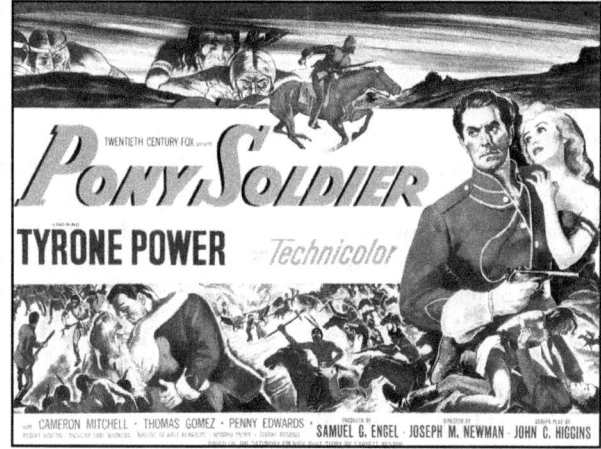

Indians into letting Edwards and Horton go; Edwards is almost burned to death but freed, Horton (he slays Mitchell's brother, burying a hatchet in the brave's face) is wounded trying to escape and after a fairly edgy cat-and-mouse hunt among rocks, young Numkena fires an arrow into Mitchell as he's about to kill Power. The Cree then prepare to depart for their reservation, Power, his new adopted son Numkena (now named Duncan), Gomez, Edwards and trussed-up Horton returning to Fort Walsh. A bread-and-butter offering from Fox, produced on medium finances. Power is sturdy enough, Harry Jackson does a good job in highlighting Sedona's red rock formations but the lack of action makes for fidgety viewing.

Dialogue:
Horton to Power: "Talk with an Indian? Take it from me, Jess Calhoun. The only talkin' Indian understands is hot lead in his belly."

Rancho Notorious

Fidelity Pictures/RKO-Radio; Technicolor; 89 minutes; Producer: Howard Welsch; Director: Fritz Lang; Cast: Marlene Dietrich; Arthur Kennedy; Mel Ferrer; Gloria Henry; Lloyd Gough; John Doucette; Jack Elam; William Frawley ****

"Run of the mill," stated the *New York Times*; "Corny plot … Marlene Dietrich is sultry and alluring," commented *Variety*; "A different kind of Western," said *The Hollywood Reporter*. Yes, the critics were divided over what some termed as Fritz Lang's $900,000 oddball remake of Universal's 1939 classic *Destry Rides Again*, which also featured Dietrich. Here, she was owner of the Chuck-a-Luck Ranch, a remote outpost harboring the territory's worst outlaws; in return for shelter from the law, she gets 10% of their "earnings." In gallops Wyoming ranch hand Arthur Kennedy; he's been tracking the decorative dame for months (her story is told in a series of flashbacks) following the violation and murder of fiancée Gloria Henry. Kennedy is certain that the killer is hiding out at Dietrich's spread and when he sees her sporting the very same brooch he bought for his intended, he's certain of it. Much to charismatic gunman Mel Ferrer's annoyance, Dietrich ("A pipe dream in blue jeans.") falls for Kennedy's charms; she's Ferrer's girl, and he doesn't like the attention his rival's receiving. Eventually, Kennedy unmasks the killer who gave Dietrich the brooch; it's Lloyd Gough and he's arrested after backing down to Kennedy's quick draw in a saloon standoff. Gough is sprung from jail and in a final showdown at Chuck-a-Luck, Gough and several of the gang are blasted by Kennedy and Ferrer; Dietrich expires in her ornate boudoir, blood seeping from her chest, leaving Kennedy and Ferrer to ride off together, the pair having formed an unlikely bond of sorts. Lang orchestrates a particularly vicious fistfight between Kennedy and Fred Graham in a barber's shop, and a taut bank raid plus the climactic shoot-out go for the throat. Perhaps William Lee warbling "The Legend of Chuck-a-Luck" at sporadic intervals lessens the tough mood and the interior stage sets appear artificial under photographer Hal Mohr's bright lighting but, overall, *Rancho Notorious* is a hammy and flamboyant Western presented in a hard-edged style by Lang, the third and last of his three forays out West.

Dialogue:
Dietrich to Kennedy who's moving in for a smooch: "Vern. When you come to a fenced range, do you always try to climb over?"
Kennedy: "I always see if the gate's open first."

Trivia:

Cinematographer Mohr (two Oscars: 1943's *Phantom of the Opera*; 1935's *A Midsummer Night's Dream*) nearly walked off set due to the leading lady's tantrums; Dietrich had worked with him on *Destry Rides Again* and insisted he shot her face in soft focus to make her appear younger than her 50 years.

Riders of Vengeance
aka The Raiders

Universal; Technicolor; 80 minutes; Producer: William Alland; Director: Lesley Selander; Cast: Richard Conte; Viveca Lindfors; Morris Ankrum; Richard Martin; Barbara Britton; William Bishop; John Kellogg; Hugh O'Brian ***

During the California gold rush of 1849, corrupt official Morris Ankrum uses a gang of toughs to steal miners' claims, thus enabling him to gain financially and bribe officials not to vote for the state becoming a member of the Union. If California remains independent, Ankrum will have free rein to ride roughshod over all and sundry without undue interference. When Richard Conte's wife is brutally murdered and his gold stolen, his brother killed in a shoot-out,

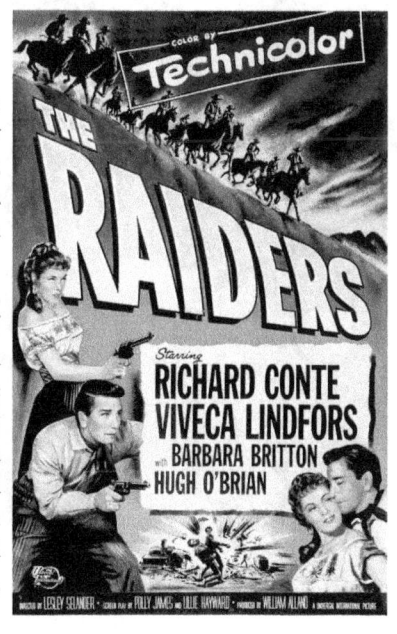

Conte, burning with revenge, joins forces with Richard Martin and his vigilantes, all of who have suffered at the hand of Ankrum's unscrupulous dealings; the group forms the Sunset Land Company in order to outfox Ankrum's Sierra Land Company. Several showdowns and set-tos later, Conte (a wanted man) puts a bullet in Ankrum and is subsequently arrested for murder; California is rubber-stamped as a Union member, Conte released under a new amnesty deal, now free to ride off with Martin's sister, Viveca Lindfors, and not, as the audience expected, Ankrum's delectable daughter Barbara Britton (she gets handsome marshal William Bishop). Lesley Selander's rough and rowdy oater contains a couple of blazing set pieces and a tense opening 20 minutes where Conte and brother William Reynolds stalk the four lowlifes who have killed Conte's wife; it gets a tad wordy after that, although Selander's forceful direction, backed by Henry Mancini's strident score, keeps things moving at a fair old speed.

Highlights:
Hugh O'Brian's black-clad rattlesnake of a killer; and the much-used Iverson Ranch location, brightly photographed by Carl E. Guthrie.

Dialogue:
Conte to one of Ankrum's guards after looking at his own wanted poster stuck on the wall: "They must want that outlaw pretty bad."
Guard: "Yeah. $10,000 worth. If I ever get within seeing distance of Morrell (Conte), he sure won't get away from me."
Conte: "I guess you don't see so good. Take a look at that poster!"

Trivia:
Dennis Weaver made his uncredited movie debut in the film.

Rose of Cimarron

20th Century Fox/Johnar Film Productions; Cinecolor; 72 minutes; Producer: Edward L. Alperson; Director: Harry Keller; Cast: Mala Powers; Jack Buetel; Bill Williams; Jim Davis; Art Smith; Irving Bacon; Dick Curtis; Bob Steele ***

Comanches wipe out a party of mule skinners, a baby surviving the massacre. Brought up by a family of friendly Cherokees, Mala Powers hits the vengeance trail when her adoptive parents are gunned down by a trio of outlaws who have just robbed a bank. With "brother" Jim Davis in tow, the lass straps on a double-holstered gun belt (most cowboys in the movie sport double holsters) and heads out to Dodge City, bent on retribution ("If the law fails, I won't."). Siding with Marshal Jack Buetel, she blasts two of her quarry in the street and becomes involved in a train holdup with outlaw boss Bill Williams, Bob Steele and Art Smith, Buetel trying to rein in her murderous desires while falling for the feisty dame; her and Davis are arrested for taking the law into their own hands, but the marshal doesn't want to see "Rose of Cimarron" behind bars. Steele and Smith both dead, black-clad Williams attempts to hightail it with the gold bullion and is wounded in a climactic shoot-out, tumbling from a huge rock to his death. Harry Keller's enjoyably noisy actioner (music: Raoul Kraushaar, Edward L. Alperson, Jr.) moves like a rocket, shot in garish Natural Color (or Cinecolor), Powers a bewitching gun-toting femme fatale with attitude, her snap response to a request being, "Oblige!"

Highlights:
Powers in a figure-hugging corset, trying to prove she is more feminine than Buetel believes she is.

Dialogue:
Powers to Buetel: "I want you to hang three men."
Buetel: "Hang three men?"
Powers: "As quick as possible."

Trivia:
Good-looker Buetel was famous for playing Billy the Kid opposite Jane Russell in Howard Hughes' notorious *The Outlaw* (RKO, 1943) but failed to make any kind of impact after that.

The Rough, Tough West

Columbia; 54 minutes; Producer: Colbert Clark; Director: Ray Nazarro; Cast: Charles Starrett; Jock Mahoney; Carolina Cotton; Smiley Burnette; Marshall Reed; Tommy Ivo; Valerie Fisher; Bert Arnold ****

Ex-Texas Ranger Jock Mahoney (as Big Jack Mahoney) is ambitious, wanting to rule the town of Hard Rock and the surrounding mines, henchman Marshall Reed at his side. When former partner Charles Starrett (Steve Holden) rides in, Mahoney quickly offers him a job but Starrett turns it down, dismayed at his friend's ruthless streak. Songstress Carolina Cotton, Mahoney's intended, also worries over her boyfriend's far-from-honest tactics in bringing the miners to heel by erecting a toll road, charging 10% of their load value if they wish to proceed. But Mahoney, under attack from Valerie Fisher's paper, has a soft side, taking lame Tommy Ivo on horse runs and promising to pay for a doctor to attend to the boy's crippled leg. Starrett's secret other self, The Durango Kid, comes to Fisher's rescue when Reed and two thugs threaten her, leaping from roof to roof (as he does in all his movies) to avoid capture; fireman Smiley Burnette, warbling with Pee Wee

King and His Band, performs a couple of comedy routines, while charming onetime radio singing star Cotton, "The Yodeling Blonde Bombshell," bounces her pretty way through a tuneful ditty containing the great line of "You got to get a gun to go after your guy if you want a wedding ring." When Ivo is badly wounded in a shoot-out after warning miners that Reed and his heavies are going to steal their gold, The Durango Kid joining in on the action, Mahoney has a fit of conscience, attempting to rescue the sick lad from his bed when the newspaper office is burned to the ground. Starrett saves Mahoney and Ivo in a fiery scene, Reed and his mob are rounded up following a street gunfight and Burnette tries to put out the fire with a leaky bucket. Surveying the charred ruins of Hard Rock, Mahoney promises to put all his wealth and energy into rebuilding the town; Ivo yells "Buck-high, Ranger!" and Burnette closes the highly enjoyable proceedings with another song.

Dialogue:
Starrett to Burnette: "Water my horse, will you Smiley."
Burnette: "Will he drink out of a hose?"
Starrett: "Yes, but don't expect him to turn it on."

The Savage

Paramount; Technicolor; 95 minutes; Producer: Mel Epstein; Director: George Marshall; Cast: Charlton Heston; Susan Morrow; Peter Hansen; Ian MacDonald; Joan Taylor; Don Porter; Richard Rober; Milburn Stone ****

1868: An 11-year-old boy from Virginia, the sole survivor of a wagon train massacre by Crow Indians, is raised by the Miniconjou Sioux, Chief Yellow Eagle (Ian MacDonald) his surrogate father. As War Bonnet (Charlton Heston), he learns the ways of the Indian, dark-haired Joan Taylor (Luta: the first of four '50s Westerns in which the actress played a squaw) loving him from afar, thus invoking the wrath of bitter rival Running Dog (Don

Porter). Chief White Thunder (John Miljan) advocates war with the whites; Heston has two moons in which to travel to Fort Duane and return with concrete evidence that the peace treaty will not be broken. Saving a platoon from a Crow attack, Heston is hailed as a hero at the fort and comes under the gaze of Susan Morrow, the sister of easygoing lieutenant Peter Hansen. But prejudice against the Sioux remains in the form of Captain Richard Rober, an uncouth brute who would like nothing better than to wipe out every red face in the territory. When Taylor is shot dead by Rober's troops in an unprovoked ambush, Heston vows revenge ("Let no man call me white!") but, on seeing wagons full of women and children, has a fit of conscience, recalling his past life; ignoring MacDonald's plans, he prevents a mass assault on the fort after Rober and most of his detachment have been decimated by Crows. Clashing with MacDonald over his confused loyalties, Heston, wounded in the chest by MacDonald's lance, is taken to the fort on a litter, hundreds of Sioux departing in peace. A pre-*Ten Commandments* Heston holds up well in an articulate pro-Indian Western filmed in South Dakota's Black Hills (photographer: John F. Seitz); the movie contains splendid action sequences orchestrated with zeal by George Marshall and an excellent Paul Sawtell score.

Highlights:
Cracking cavalry versus hostiles sequences taking place in dense wooded locales instead of out in the open, a refreshing change.

Dialogue:
Hansen, seeing Heston leaning over a dead Crow, knife in hand: "Wait a minute. White men don't take scalps."
Heston: "I do. I take Crow scalps."

Trivia:
Richard Rober's final film (RKO's *Jet Pilot*, released in 1957), was made in 1949/1950; the tough-guy actor was tragically killed in a car crash in May 1952, aged only 42.

Smoky Canyon

Columbia; 55 minutes; Producer: Colbert Clark; Director: Fred F. Sears; Cast: Charles Starrett; Jock Mahoney; Danni Sue Nolan; Smiley Burnett; Tristram Coffin; Guy Madison; Sandy Sanders; Leroy Johnson ****

Montana, 1880: A range war rages, cattlemen versus sheep men, tomboy Danni Sue Nolan (swell in a check shirt) instructing her heavy brigade to terrorize the sheep farmers; the gal's got an almighty chip on her shoulder following the death of her father by outlaw Jock Mahoney (playing Jack Mahoney!). Mahoney, a $2,500 reward on his head, was her boyfriend but he's innocent, Tristram Coffin behind the deed. Coffin's determined to cause trouble between the two factions and, in doing so, pushes up the price of beef to feather his own nest. Enter tough hombre

Charles Starrett (as Steve Brent), rejecting Nolan's offer of a job by telling everyone he's gonna nail Mahoney to collect the reward; actually, he's out to nail Coffin's mob and the syndicate behind them to hopefully restore peace to the territory with a little help from his black-clad alter-ego, The Durango Kid. Starrett comes up against Mahoney's bunch who are unaware that Sandy Sanders is relaying information back to Coffin, busy planning to burn hundreds of head of cattle in Smoky Canyon. In an explosion, the cattle stampede, killing henchman Guy Madison. The Durango Kid rescues Mahoney and Nolan, and, in a landslide, corrupt sheriff Larry Hudson and Coffin are buried alive; Smiley Burnette, meanwhile, beats up Sanders. Mahoney, back in Nolan's arms, is made sheriff of Timber Rock but still determined to catch Steve Brent; The Durango Kid lets his mask slip to Nolan, revealing his true identity—she says she will ensure her new husband won't pursue his quest! A fast-moving entry in the series, containing a rousing Mischa Bakaleinikoff stock score, plenty of action and six-foot-four ex-stuntman Mahoney on engaging form; the requisite musical numbers are also reduced to one only, making the narrative flow more smoothly.

Dialogue:
Burnette to traitor Sanders: "You killer in sheep's clothing!"

Springfield Rifle

Warner Bros.; Warnercolor; 93 minutes; Producer: Louis F. Edelman; Director: André De Toth; Cast: Gary Cooper; Phyllis Thaxter; David Brian; Paul Kelly; Lon Chaney, Jr.; Philip Carey; Guinn "Big Boy" Williams; James Millican ****

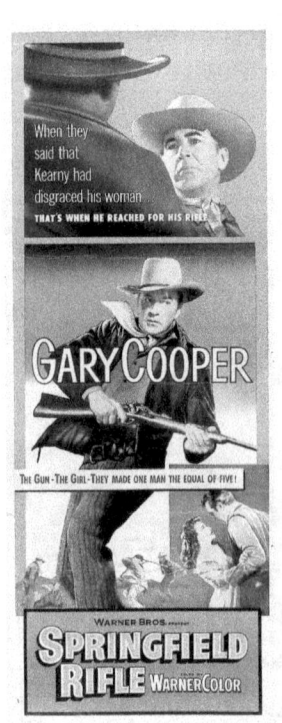

During the Civil War, the U.S. war office is concerned over the repeated loss of horses meant for the Union army; raiders are attacking troop detachments and stealing the animals for the Confederate cause. Gary Cooper (Major Alex Kearney) arranges, in a series of staged incidents designed to fool the enemy, to be cashiered out of the army at Fort Headley on a charge of dereliction of duty, thus enabling the "disgraced" officer to join up with horse traders David Brian and Lon Chaney, Jr. and discover the identity of the spy supplying information to the renegades on troop/horse movements. It happens to be his own commanding officer, Paul Kelly. Following the critical and commercial success of *High Noon*, Cooper was back in the saddle in a grand-scale, colorful Western, featured as perplexed as ever, the North's first counterespionage agent, but it was bullish Chaney who stole Coop's thunder on this occasion; the star showed he could produce the goods outside of his favored horror genre, turning in a rascally, lip-smacking performance, one of his best during the 1950s. Visually arresting, Edwin B. DuPar's deep-focus photography of (first) California's Mount Whitney region and then Lone Pine's Alabama Hills a pleasure to behold, *Springfield Rifle*'s tortuous narrative was pushed along splendidly by Max Steiner's stomping score. Packed full of treacherous dealings, gunfights, fistfights, ambushes, rampaging horses and an exhilarating 15-minute climax, you couldn't go far wrong in finding exciting Western entertainment other than with this film, even though one fervently wished that, just for once, the leading man's pained expression might break into a grin—after all, he had the arms of the lovely Phyllis Thaxter to fall into at sporadic intervals! And yes, those famous fast-action carbines don't really enter the equation until the 73rd minute.

Dialogue:
Chaney, growling to Kelly: "You shoulda let me finish Kearney when we had him."
Kelly: "I can't say I disagree with you, Pete. Your hindsight is great!"

Trivia:
The film debut of Fess Parker.

Untamed Frontier

Universal; Technicolor; 78 minutes; Producer: Leonard Goldstein; Director: Hugo Fregonese; Cast: Joseph Cotten; Shelley Winters; Scott Brady; Minor Watson; Lee Van Cleef; Suzan Ball; Douglas Spencer; Robert Anderson ***

"Jazzed-up melodrama," was the *New York Times*' opinion, unfairly comparing *Untamed Frontier* to King Vidor's $8,000,000 *Duel in the Sun* (1946), itself a masterpiece of overblown melodramatics. The Denbow Ranch in Texas, presided over by crippled tyrant Minor Watson and warring cousins Scott Brady and Joseph Cotten, refuses to allow settlers across its land, even though the government has declared the property open range. Bored waitress Shelley Winters, fending off Richard Garland's overtures, makes a beeline for bad-boy Brady at a local shindig; Garland sees them smooching and goes for his gun, which has been removed from its holster by saloon girl Suzan Ball, who has the hots for Brady. Brady shoots Garland and is arrested for murder, Winters the only witness. Let out on bail, he decides first to bribe Winters to leave town: She rejects the $10,000 offer, so he proposes marriage as, in law, wives cannot testify against their husbands. But on their wedding day in San Antone, Douglas Spencer's newspaper headlines spell it out. Their wedding will mean Brady escaping the noose. Winters feels betrayed and fumes, the sham marriage isn't consummated, Brady treats his new wife like dirt and hitches up with Ball while Cotten and Winters develop mutual feelings. Egged on by ambitious Ball (who threatens blackmail by spilling the beans about Garland's "missing" gun), Brady decides, with Lee Van Cleef's help, to rustle some of his father's cattle over the Texas/Mexican border at the Rio Grande River and split the takings three ways: himself, Van Cleef and Ball. Then settlers arrive, led by Robert Anderson, demanding that the Denbows tear down their fences—or else. Hugo Fregonese's involving, slightly muddled, horse opera climaxes in Brady being plugged by Van Cleef and Van Cleef being plugged by Cotten during a cattle stampede. Watson and his vaqueros face Anderson and his homesteaders across the fence; in a set-to, Watson is shot dead and Cotten, arriving on the scene, orders the fences to be pulled down. "Come on through," he tells the settlers as he prepares to play house with Winters. Hans J. Salter's score is a prime example of this underrated composer's work, California's Agoura landscapes are picturesque but the film sags in the middle and Cotten, a fine actor, never seemed quite at home in the Western milieu.

Dialogue:
Watson to Winters, perturbed by her hasty wedding plans to Brady: "It's been my experience, Miss Stevens, if you can never tell about cattle or women until they've been on your range for a while."
Trivia:
   Fess *Davy Crockett* Parker's first credited film role.

Wild Stallion

Monogram; Cinecolor; 70 minutes; Producer: Walter Mirisch; Director: Lewis D. Collins; Cast: Ben Johnson; Edgar Buchanan; Martha Hyer; Hayden Rourke; Don Haggerty; Orley Lindgren; Hugh Beaumont; I. Stanford Jolley ***

1851: Orley Lindgren's parents are murdered by Indians, his home burned to the ground, his young colt Top Kick galloping off into the wilds. Taken in by horse trader Edgar Buchanan, Lindgren vows to capture Top Kick when he's older. Flash forward a few years. Ben Johnson (Lindgren as an adult) resides on an army post with Major Hayden Rourke and his daughter, Martha Hyer, assisting Buchanan in rounding up wild horses to sell to the army—but he's still determined to rope frisky Top Kick, the magnificent white stallion now leading the herds, and have him as his own, despite army opposition. Family entertainment of a kind, *Wild Stallion* steers clear of Disney cuteness by the inclusion of a renegade Indian attack and Sergeant Don Haggerty's brutal methods of horse-taming which result in the oaf being flattened by Johnson in two bruising fistfights. Although Top Kick is classed as army property when he's eventually brought to heel, Johnson is allowed to keep his beloved steed in the end ("I want to ride him in the cavalry.") and winds up marrying Hyer; the narrative is told in flashback, the elderly couple heading off to San Francisco with 32-year-old Top Kick and Buchanan to live a more peaceful life away from the West and its rigors. Pleasantly shot around the Simi Hills in bright Cinecolor by Harry Neumann, Monogram's long-forgotten horse opera will appeal to both kids *and* adults, the movie containing a decent performance from John Wayne's old buddy, ex-rodeo star Johnson, who had a real affinity with horses, as the film so ably demonstrates. Marlin Skiles' lush score is also an added plus.

Dialogue:
Buchanan to Lindgren: "Say, you got a nice touch with horses. You ain't afraid of 'em, are you?"
Lindgren: "No. I like 'em."
Buchanan: "I like 'em too. Always have. Some of 'em are a lot nicer than the people who ride 'em."

Chapter 5

Wild Bill Elliott at Republic, Monogram and Allied Artists

Born Gordon Ami Nance on a farm in Pattonsburg, Missouri on October 16, 1904, William "Bill" Elliott (he adopted the name in 1938) grew up around horses and steers on a ranch near King City, Missouri, catching the movie bug by taking lessons at the Pasadena Playhouse (also attended by future cowboy star Randolph Scott), gaining an uncredited slot in Warner Bros. 1925 comedy, *The Plastic Age*. His first Western was Fox's 1927 production *The Arizona Wildcat*. Gordon Elliott, as he was then known, remained uncredited throughout dozens of movies right up to 1938 when Columbia thrust him into the limelight in their 15-chapter serial *The Great Adventures of Wild Bill Hickok*; it was an instant hit, Bill Elliott becoming one of the B-Western's favorite stars, his trademark double revolvers worn butt-forward for fancy, instant action. Elliott went on to feature in 16 of Republic's popular *Red Ryder* series of Westerns from 1944 to 1946, continuing to make low-budget oaters up to 1954, retiring from the business in 1957 after appearing in five modern police dramas, a total of 275 productions under his belt. Settling down on a ranch near Las Vegas (he was a breeder of Appaloosa horses), Elliott died on November 26, 1965, aged only 61. Elliott's B-Westerns are a little more polished and lengthier than the opposition, more like A-Westerns in parts, the plots inventive, his brusque acting style tough and mean (very much like Western star George Montgomery), the man rarely smiling or loosening up, spitting out acid one-liners between gritted teeth; he also played a different-named character in each production and didn't encumber himself with a sidekick. That's just what his legion of admirers liked in those far-off days and his stern-faced, terse demeanor brings a sense of gravitas to many of his cowboy pictures, giving them a harder edge and covering up the cheapness of what he was appearing in. Elliott's horse operas still have the capacity to entertain after all these years, and that's due to the actor's downbeat, gritty screen persona. The films are listed in order of release.

1950
The Savage Horde

Republic; 90 minutes; Produced and Directed by Joseph Kane; Cast: William Elliott; Lorna Gray; Grant Withers; Jim Davis; Noah Beery, Jr.; Barbara Fuller; Bob Steele; Will Wright ****

Utah, 1881: Cavalryman Jim Davis is on the trail of John Baker aka The Ringo Kid (William Elliott), wanted for the murder of an army officer—but the outlaw ("The fastest gun in the country.") happens to be Davis' brother, claiming he shot in self-defense. A manhunt sees Elliott firing at Davis and grazing his head, the action (filmed in California's Red Rock Canyon) switching to Gunlock where Elliott rolls into town minus his quick gun and becomes embroiled in a range war, Grant Withers, owner of the Bar K, clashing with Noah Beery, Jr., boss of a much smaller spread. Withers and his cronies, headed by gunmen Bob Steele and Roy Barcroft, want to run the independent ranchers off their land and own the territory; the heavyweight thug is also romancing Lorna Gray, at one time Elliott's gal. Elliott, as handy with his fists as he is with a Colt, goes into partnership with Beery, leading to an all-out range war, Steele gunning down warbling cowhand Stuart Hamblen while Withers forces Judge Will Wright to pin up illegal notices claiming the Bar K Ranch to be the owner of the entire range. When the army enters Gunlock, Elliott's true identity comes to light; handcuffed, he's led away by Davis but returns with his gun to sort out a major fracas between ranchers and Withers' boys ("Get Ringo. He's gun-mad!") who have taken over the town. Elliott drops Steele and Barcroft and Withers collapses in the street, dead from a gunshot wound. "I'll be back," says Elliott to Gray as he goes off to clear his name, Beery back with fiancée Barbara Fuller. A densely plotted Republic oater, given a bigger budget than normal, Elliott in commanding, stern-faced form, the picture directed with purpose by Joseph Kane.

Dialogue:
Steele to Barcroft, watching the ranchers ride into town en masse for the final four-minute showdown: "They're makin' it easy for us. Puttin' all their eggs in one basket." Barcroft: "For us to scramble, hahaha!"

The Showdown

Republic; 86 minutes; Producer: William J. O'Sullivan; Directors: Dorrell McGowan and Stuart E. McGowan; Cast: William Elliott; Walter Brennan; Marie Windsor; Harry Morgan; Jim Davis; Rhys Williams; William Ching; Nacho Galindo ****

His face set grimmer than usual, William Elliott (Shadrach Jones) joins Walter Brennan's Circle K cattle drive to Montana as foreman, determined to find out who shot his brother in the back with a derringer pistol. *The Showdown* commences in a graveyard during a violent thunderstorm, Elliott digging up his brother's body, Brennan and gun-happy Harry Morgan looking on. It's a bleak, gloomy opener, like a scene from a 1930s horror flick, and that bleakness doesn't really let up. Under Brennan's watchful gaze, Elliott drives the surly cowhands hard, almost to the point of mutiny; the ex-State Police Officer trusts no one, not even saloon lass Marie Windsor, along for the ride and taking a shine to the tough guy who shoots off blunt one-liners with the speed of a rifle bullet. Brennan is the culprit—he murdered Elliott's brother after losing heavily at cards, a fact he confesses after a steer's horns have punctured his lungs in a death charge. "I'm gonna leave you with the buzzards," spits Elliott but, holding a crucifix, realizes what an inhuman specimen he has become, asking William Ching to stay with the dying man, Windsor gratified at seeing a fleeting smile crease those set-in-stone features. Deep black-and-white imagery from Reggie Lanning and a forceful Stanley Wilson score, plus Elliott's solid performance, make for a dark, moody Republic Western that has a great deal more bite than most.

Dialogue:
Windsor to Elliott, catching him staring at her shapely legs: "See anything interestin' mister?"
Elliott: "Yeah. Quite a bit."
Windsor: "I was talkin' of the register."
Elliott: "So was I—partly."

1951

The Longhorn

Monogram; Orig. in Sepiatone; 70 minutes; Producer: Vincent M. Fennelly; Director: Lewis D. Collins; Cast: Wild Bill Elliott; Myron Healey; Phyllis Coates; I. Stanford Jolley; Lane Bradford; John Hart; Marshall Reed; Lee Roberts ****

William Elliott now became Wild Bill Elliott, taken from his credited name in the *Red Ryder* serials, in the first of four oaters made for Monogram. Cattle rancher Elliott (Jim Kirk) has a lucrative plan, to breed Longhorns with Hertfords (or Herefords), producing a new breed of steer that will contain twice as much beef as the average cow. He sets off for Oregon to purchase a herd, unaware that devious partner Myron Healey has fallen in with crook John Hart; the saloon boss wants to stampede the cattle on the return trip, kill Elliott and sell the Hertfords at a healthy price. On the dusty journey out, Healey is seriously wounded in a skirmish with Indians, recuperating at I. Stanford Jolley and Phyllis Coates' ranch, leaving Elliott to buy 1,000 head of Hertfords and recruit a gang of ex-convicts and gunslingers at the Star saloon to act as trail hands on the promise of regular wages and a job at his ranch. A superior low-budget effort from Monogram, Daniel B. Ullman's screenplay taking in treachery, romance and disenchantment among the rough 'n' ready crew led by hulking Lane Bradford. Healey loves Coates, but she fancies Elliott; the men grumble because Elliott refuses to sacrifice a single steer to supplement their potato-based diet (he eventually slaughters a deer); and Healey has an attack of conscience over his friendship with Elliott, thwarting Hart's surprise attack in Sweetwater Canyon but paying with his life. Back at his ranch, mission successfully accomplished, Elliott looks forward to claiming Coates as his wife and to producing a profitable crossbreed.

Highlights:
   The Longhorn is a prime example, in looks and execution, of a modest '50s B-Western that still shines over 60 years later.

Dialogue:
Elliott to Coates: "On a cattle drive, there are two nos. No whiskey, and no women."

Trivia:
   The film was remade by Allied Artists in 1956 as *Canyon River*, George Montgomery in the main role, Ullman rehashing his *Longhorn* script.

1952
Waco aka The Outlaw and the Lady

Monogram; 68 minutes; Producer: Vincent M. Fennelly; Director: Lewis D. Collins; Cast: Wild Bill Elliott; I. Stanford Jolley; Pamela Blake; Paul Fierro; Rand Brooks; Lane Bradford; Richard Avonde; Ray Bennett *****

The degree of excellence prevalent in Wild Bill Elliott's oaters showed no signs of letting up in a splendid example of his work from this period, Daniel B. Ullman's intricate script containing more twists and turns than a corkscrew. You needed to concentrate fully as Elliott (Matt Boone) turned up in Waco, Texas, hired as a stage driver and given an advance of $40 on his wages. In a card game, he shoots cheating Ray Bennett in self-defense but is quickly accused of murder; fleeing Waco and the law, he falls in with I. Stanford Jolley, elderly boss of the Ivers gang, the two forming a bond. Several holdups later in Limestone County, Elliott gets badly wounded in the leg during a bank raid. Recovered, he's acquitted on a charge of homicide relating to Bennett's killing and given the job of Waco's sheriff, even though he states, "You know, I have a lot of friends who are outlaws." Ejecting noisy cowpokes from the saloon, plus Bennett's daughter, Pamela Blake, Elliott (who up until now hasn't smiled once) meets with Jolley, the outlaw chief promising to keep his nefarious activities away from Waco. "They made you a sheriff," Jolley says. "I can't be on both sides of the law," is the terse reply. Proving that "being a lawman is a lonely job," Elliott arrests another card sharp (Rory Mallinson) on a murder charge, beating his accomplice, Richard Paxton, to the draw with his butt-forward pistol; Mallinson is later hanged. When the Ivers outfit holds up a stage, trigger-happy Paul Fierro, attired in black, guns down the guard in cold blood and abducts Blake; Elliott visits the gang's hideout, Blake is released and Fierro kicked out of the bunch. To keep things on the boil, Ullman and Lewis D. Collins then have Texas Rangers delivering Jolley into Elliott's custody, young outlaw Rand Brooks slumped dead over a horse; Fierro lurks in the hills, waiting to force Elliott out into the open. Elliott releases Jolley, throws in his badge and, in a tense showdown, pumps three bullets into the black-clad killer after Jolley has caught a bullet himself, telling Elliott to put the badge back on. Waco is now a peaceful community, kids playing in the streets; Blake is last seen heading for the sheriff's office with one thought on her mind—marriage!

Highlights:

Waco crams more incident into its 68 minutes than many larger scale Westerns manage to accomplish in twice the length, a tribute to the professionalism of all concerned; in many ways, a mini-classic of B-movie enterprise.

Dialogue:

Blake, spitting at Elliott: "They needed a sheriff and they got a dirty rotten killer!"

Kansas Territory

Monogram; 65 minutes; Producer: Vincent M. Fennelly; Director: Lewis D. Collins; Cast: Wild Bill Elliott; House Peters, Jr.; Peggy Stewart; Lane Bradford; I. Stanford Jolley; Fuzzy Knight; Marshall Reed; Lyle Talbot ****

One more entry in a continuous run of "I'm gonna get the man who killed my brother" scenarios, Wild Bill Elliott (as Joe Daniels) bulldozing his no-nonsense way through a plot concerning his dead sibling; was he a doggone, nasty critter, a fast-drawing card cheat who deserved a bullet in the back, or wasn't he? Elliott refuses to believe the stories emanating from the town of Redding, riding over there and coming up with a wagonload of grief in the form of saloon boss I. Stanford Jolley, henchmen Lane Bradford and Marshall Reed, his brother's fiancée, Peggy Stuart, her crippled father, Lyle Talbot and shady lawyer House Peters, Jr. Elliott now owns half of Jolley's saloon but won't rest until his brother's killer is unearthed, turning down the job of sheriff which is passed onto Peters. Elliott also learns that Talbot was crippled by a bullet from his not-so-saintly brother. Peters turns out to be the culprit, running a gang of outlaws behind the town's back and stealing Elliott's will; he's after running the saloon himself. In a street showdown, Bradford shoots the corrupt attorney and Elliott, at last realizing his brother was a no-good outlaw, leaves his half of the saloon to Stewart and Talbot. Another rock-solid turn from the leading man ensures a good time to be had by all; the story may be slight, but Elliott's machismo presence carries the day. And Fuzzy Knight, playing Cap, kept it straight, as he would do in his other Wild Bill Elliott roles, as opposed to his frequent clowning in the Whip Wilson programmers.

Dialogue:
Elliott, in a saloon full of onlookers, lays it straight on the line: "In case there's anybody who doesn't know why I'm here, I'll tell yer. I'm going to find the man who killed my brother. And when I do, I'll kill him."

Fargo

Monogram; Orig. in Sepiatone; 69 minutes; Producer: Vincent M. Fennelly; Director: Lewis D. Collins; Cast: Wild Bill Elliott; Myron Healey; Phyllis Coates; Jack Ingram; Fuzzy Knight; Arthur Space; Robert J. Wilke; Terry Frost ****

In Fargo, Texas, Wild Bill Elliott (Bill Martin) comes to the aid of farmers who are entrenched in a range war with cattlemen, his brother trampled to death in a cattle stampede ("Joe never did know how to fight. I do."). Fences are being pulled down, homesteads burned, crops ruined. Arthur Space, estate manager of the Austin Land Company, is the sidewinder behind the raids, instructing henchman Myron Healey (a great performance) to hire a bunch of coyotes and cause maximum damage to nesters' properties ("We need real rough boys who will strike hard and fast."). Elliott, Fuzzy Knight and the settlers retaliate by fixing barbed wire fences; cows are injured on the barbs, so a new type of less-harmful wire is produced, but not before Healey and his bunch have destroyed the workshop and trussed up Elliott in his own wire. Cattleman Jack Ingram is on Elliott's side and against all the violence, realizing that the range can't be open to steers forever, recognizing the need for change; besides, daughter Phyllis Coates is making eyes at Elliott big time. *Fargo* climaxes in a terrific four-minute smoke-filled shoot-out at Rock Canyon, Healey falling to Elliott's bullet as his men are rounded up by the town posse. And the main man comes up with a gem of a line that sums up the attitude of every Western hard guy ever to appear on the silver screen: "Emotion gets in the way of action."

Dialogue:
Elliott to Healey, throwing down the gauntlet: "How about it, Red? Man to man."
Healey: "I'm doing this my way."
Elliott: "Yeah, your way. Like a rat."

The Maverick

Allied Artists; Orig. in Sepiatone; 71 minutes; Producer: Vincent M. Fennelly; Director: Thomas Carr; Cast: Wild Bill Elliott; Myron Healey; Phyllis Coates; Richard Reeves; Florence Lake; Robert J. Wilke; Eugene Roth; Terry Frost **

1892: Following a cattlemen versus settlers range war, the territory is under martial law. Lieutenant Wild Bill Elliott (Pete Devlin) leads a detail over rough terrain to Fort Jeffrey, tailed by Robert J. Wilke and his pack of hyenas. They're keen on springing loose the four important prisoners ("A likely kettle of prima donnas!") being escorted; Elliott's orders are to bring these jaspers in alive, despite Sergeant Myron Healey's wishes that they be taken care of with a bullet. Elliott, barking out orders, driving the men on without rest and displaying as much warmth as a block of ice, argues incessantly with Healey, demoting him to private; he's just as rude to Phyllis Coates ("You enjoy being a bully," she levels at him) and her grandma, Florence Lake, the ladies having joined the nightmare trek in their wagon. Needless to say, disgruntled Healey, who hates discipline and fancies Coates, throws in his lot with the three criminals on the promise of $500; the fourth miscreant, Richard Reeves, is in the wagon, recovering from a knife wound caused by Healey. A grand shooting match at the end sees Wilke plugging Healey in the back; Elliott shoots Wilke, the gang surrenders and the troop continues on to the fort, Elliott's severe countenance cracking into a smile in the dying seconds, returning Coates' winning smile. Minus his trademark reverse-draw guns, Elliott is a thoroughly dislikeable character in a rough and ready production that's almost drowned out by Raoul Kraushaar's nonstop raucous soundtrack; your ears will be ringing by the end of it.

Dialogue:
Eugene Roth, trussed up on his horse, to Healey: "I got an itch."
Healey: "Scratch it."
Roth: "I can't."
Healey: "Tough."

1953
The Homesteaders

Allied Artists; 62 minutes; Producer: Vincent M. Fennelly; Director: Lewis D. Collins; Cast: Wild Bill Elliott; Robert Lowery; Emmett Lynn; George Wallace; Rick Vallin; James Seay; Tom Monroe; Ray Walker ****

In 1870, rancher Wild Bill Elliott (as Mace Corbin) purchases five wagonloads of dynamite from the army, planning to blast flat the boulder-ridden country around Rock Hill, Oregon, thus creating a level pass for homesteaders to graze their cattle in a fertile valley. But Wild Bill has the odds stacked against him. Debt-ridden partner Robert Lowery (resembling, at times, Clark Gable) has fallen in with crooked mine boss James Seay, who is willing to pay a lot of cash for the explosives; Elliott is forced to recruit 18 ex-prisoners as trail crew, all itching to cut loose and cause trouble; and the dynamite is unstable, its content of nitroglycerin at a highly volatile level. Old-timer Emmett Lynn acts as supervisor as the wagons set off, George Wallace stirring up trouble en route, the men having to ward off an Indian attack. Wallace is shot dead by Elliott after stoking the fires of mutiny and conscience-stricken Lowery confesses his double-cross to Elliott, shooting down Seay when his gang attempt a raid on the wagons. Elliott and Lowery bury their differences, the team carrying on to Rock Hill to complete their mission. A slow-paced but well-constructed oater from Elliott, concentrating more on characterization than action, with the usual team of director Collins, composer Raoul Kraushaar and cinematographer Ernest Miller in fine fettle.

Dialogue:
Lynn to Elliott, worried about Wallace's complaining: "I sure got an itchy feeling up and down my spine."
Elliott: "We're getting to a creek. Try washin' your shirt."

Rebel City

Allied Artists; Orig. in Sepiatone; 52 minutes; Producer: Vincent M. Fennelly; Director: Thomas Carr; Cast: Wild Bill Elliott; Marjorie Lord; Robert Kent; Keith Richards; Denver Pyle; Ray Walker; Otto Waldis; John Crawford ***

In 1864, Kansas is overrun by Confederate sympathizers calling themselves The Copperheads, a secret group dedicated to the downfall of the Union. Wild Bill Elliott (Frank Graham) gallops into Junction City to unravel the circumstances surrounding the death of his father, whose freight business in nearby Belfry was bought with $2,000 worth of counterfeit notes. Who are the forgers, how are they tied up with The Copperheads and who plunged a knife in his father's back? Flitting between Junction City and Belfry, it's not until half an hour has gone by that Wild Bill dispenses with his derringer and straps on those lethal double pistols, hired as teamster in Marjorie Lord's freight company and poking his nose into Keith Richards' Acme Trading Company and a suspicious printing shop; he gets severely beaten by four hombres for his troubles. Richards, in fact, is smuggling rifles through the U.S. Army Inspection Station in order to arm the rebel group, Copperhead leader Captain Robert Kent in on the deal, the counterfeit money being used for the Confederate cause. After Elliott is falsely accused of Denver Pyle's murder, Colonel Ray Walker assists in clearing his name and unmasking Ramsey who is eventually shot dead, Richards arrested; there's a hint of a partnership in the air as Elliott, his father's company and wagons returned to him, and Lord get cozy. Full marks to composer Raoul Kraushaar for his stirring title score in a Wild Bill Western that is a tad slower paced compared to his previous efforts.

Dialogue:
Elliott to Lord: "I've been slugged, robbed, used as a knife target and jailed for murder."
Lord: "Frank. Please. Leave it to the authorities."
Elliott: "No thanks. This is my affair and I'm going to see it through."

Topeka

Allied Artists; Orig. in Sepiatone; 69 minutes; Producer: Vincent M. Fennelly; Director: Thomas Carr; Cast: Wild Bill Elliott; Rick Vallin; Phyllis Coates; Fuzzy Knight; Harry Lauter; Denver Pyle; Dick Crockett; John James *****

Bank robber Wild Bill Elliott (Jim Levering), leader of the Levering gang, carries out a string of holdups: The Rock City Bank, the Cattle Bend Bank and, in a lengthy sequence staged with artistic flair by Thomas Carr, the Guthrie Bank. Reaching Topeka in Kansas after months on the run, the five weary outlaws hit upon a plan. Oust town crime boss Harry Lauter and his thugs, get enlisted as lawmen and butter up the citizens, then, when things have quietened down, rob the bank and stores and take over Lauter's protection racket which rakes in $8,000 a week. But Elliott and Rick Vallin are sick of being hunted men; the pair are conscience-stricken, wanting to settle down and commit themselves to Topeka—in Elliott's case, Fuzzy Knight's attractive daughter, Phyllis Coates, has a lot to do with it. Restless gang members Denver Pyle, Dick Crockett and John James have other ideas, falling in with Lauter and double-crossing Elliott and Vallin. James bushwhacks a punter who was handed back his money by Elliott after being swindled at cards and is kicked out of the bunch, joining the others and Lauter's varmints in robbing the bank and stores. They hightail out to Lauter's hideout where, in a shoot-out, three are killed (including Lauter) and one wounded. Back in Topeka, Knight and Coates admit that they were fully aware of Elliott's past all along ("We knew all about you boys but kept quiet."), giving him a chance to redeem himself by becoming sheriff. With the offer of a pardon in the air, Elliott resumes his role as town peace officer, Vallin his deputy, grinning as Coates pins on his tin star with loving eyes. The quintessential Wild Bill Elliott Western: terse script (Milton R. Raison), deep monochrome photography (Ernest Miller), a careful spread of music (Raoul Kraushaar) and clever use of the camera by director Carr (close-ups, tracking and crane shots, tilted angles) make for a riveting minor oater that, if given a bigger budget and an A-list star, could have given Universal, Columbia and the rest of the big boys a run for their money. The fistfights are tough, the cranked-up action knife-edged, the

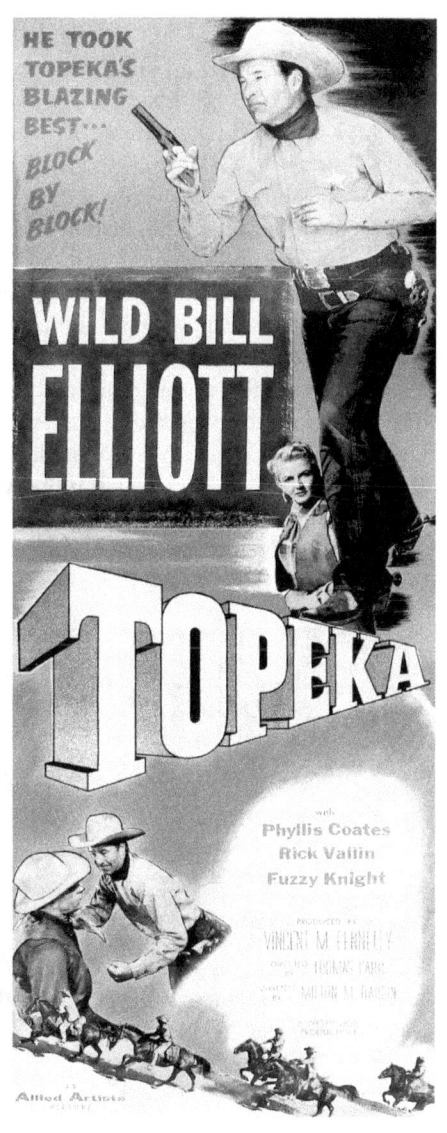

entire cast on sparkling form with the leading man exuding meaner-than-mean attitude throughout. A highly entertaining B-Western classic!
Highlights:
The sheer expertise in producing a Western as brilliant as this over 69 minutes on a low budget is, in this day and age, almost beyond belief.
Dialogue:
Lauter to Elliott after his men have been pulverized by Elliott and his buddies in a punishing saloon brawl: "I'm giving you fair warning. Get out of town. All of you." Elliott: "Who's goin' to throw us out? You and that bunch pickin' themselves up off of the floor? Listen Mister Wilson, the next time you want to try any strong-arm tactics with us, bring men, not boys."

Vigilante Terror

Allied Artists; 70 minutes; Producer: Vincent M. Fennelly; Director: Lewis D. Collins; Cast: Wild Bill Elliott; Mary Ellen Kay; Myron Healey; Robert Bray; Fuzzy Knight; I. Stanford Jolley; Henry Rowland; George Wallace ****

Following the California gold rush, the lawless mining town of Pine Top is run by masked vigilantes ("A bunch of hotheads who'd jump anybody."), the gang in cahoots with George Wallace's outlaws, plundering gold shipments, planting false evidence on innocent people and stringing them up. Preventing storekeeper I. Stanford Jolley from being hanged for a robbery he didn't commit, Wild Bill Elliott (Tack Hamlin) is rendered unconscious by a scalp wound; coming to, he finds that his outlaw brother, John James, has been hanged in Jolley's place. Now on a mission of revenge, Wild Bill enters Pine Top, roughs up a few saloon troublemakers, suspects mine manager Robert Bray of being the criminal mastermind and is handed the role of sheriff by Mayor Henry Rowland, Fuzzy Knight deputized. Very soon, Elliott's jail is full to capacity, forcing Myron Healey and his vigilantes to pin the latest robbery on the new sheriff. Elliott, Jolley and Knight are saved from the noose by Jolley's rifle-toting daughter, Mary Ellen Kay (a nervy, uneasy sequence), the inmates of Pine Top's jail then sprung loose. In a frenetic finale, Wild Bill, Jolley, Knight and Kay pursue Wallace's outlaws while Healey's mob pursues *them*, ending in a six-minute shoot-out in which practically every villain of the piece bites the dust. Bray, who knew nothing of Healey's involvement with Wallace, thanks Elliott for recovering the mine's gold and Pine Top is now free of vigilantes for good, all down to our "don't mess with me" peacemaker. Another hard-driving Elliott programmer, decently scripted by Sidney Theil, director Lewis D. Collins keeping the action flowing smoothly, the picture featuring a great lineup of Monogram/Allied Artists scowling, unkempt heavies; Lee Roberts, Denver Pyle, Michael Colgan, Zon Murray, Richard Avonde and Frank Ellis. Needless to say, the main man is in top, grim-faced, no-nonsense form.

Dialogue:
Healey's threat of recriminations to Elliott if he continues to lay down the law: "You'll learn different."
Elliott's blunt response: "Who's gonna teach me? Scared little men who wear masks, or you?"

1954
Bitter Creek

Allied Artists; 74 minutes; Producer: Vincent M. Fennelly; Director: Thomas Carr; Cast: Wild Bill Elliott; Carleton Young; Beverly Garland; Claude Akins; Jim Hayward; John Harmon; Veda Ann Borg; John Pickard ***

The penultimate Wild Bill Elliott oater trod familiar territory, our tight-lipped hero trotting into town to find out who has put a bullet in his rancher brother's back and why a big cattle outfit has moved in on the dead man's spread. Crooked cattleman Carleton Young, owner of the Lazy Q, is the suave villain, employing a crew of gun toughs to ensure that the town and its citizens are firmly under his corrupt thumb. In standard no-nonsense fashion, Wild Bill (as Clay Tyndall) bulldozes his unsmiling self through the narrative, alcoholic doctor Jim Hayward and veteran stage driver John Harmon the only two citizens who will help him in his mission of revenge, resulting in extremely noisy gunfights and bruising brawls. Elliott also finds himself increasingly attracted to Beverly Garland, who's traveled all the way from St. Louis to marry Young. Among the cast, chief bad guy Claude Akins (his first credited movie role) stands out while Garland and blonde Veda Ann Borg are decorative fluff; Raoul Kraushaar's rattling good score is a real bonus, as is George Waggner's witty script. Young gets his comeuppance in the final reel, leaving glum-faced Elliott to carry on with Garland. Run-of-the-mill stuff from the star with nothing new on offer, but at this late stage in his Western career, what could you really expect?

Dialogue:
Akins to Elliott, on being challenged to a fight: "Don't tempt me. The boss says no trouble. He's in a romantic fog. But you know how fogs are. They blow away."

The Forty-Niners

Allied Artists; 71 minutes; Producer: Vincent M. Fennelly; Director: Thomas Carr; Cast: Wild Bill Elliott; Harry Morgan; John Doucette; Lane Bradford; Virginia Grey; I. Stanford Jolley; Dean Cromer; Harry Lauter ****

Wild Bill Elliott's final Western saw him going out with a bang, narrated *Dragnet*-style by the man himself, playing Marshal Sam Nelson, on the hunt for a couple of killers in the Californian gold rush days of 1849. A marshal has been shot dead over a claim dispute, mine operator I. Stanford Jolley arrested for complicity in the crime and stating that Harry Morgan, a traveling gambler, knows who the two men are. After combing every backwater in Northern California, Elliot, masquerading as a gunman, finds his quarry, as usual cheating in a saloon. Rescuing him from being lynched, he forms an odd bond of sorts with Morgan, at first to get the card sharp to tell him who the killers are but secondly to give the gambler a second chance in life; Morgan is a waster, tired of what he has become, wishing to settle down and go straight by hitching up with old flame Virginia Grey, married to John Doucette, one of the men on Elliott's wanted list (the other is Cold Water's corrupt sheriff, Lane Bradford). Morgan has blackmailed Doucette and Bradford by writing an incriminating letter, naming them as the murderers of the marshal; if they don't play ball by allowing him to become a business partner in their Ace High saloon, the letter will be released to the authorities—and he has backup in Elliott ("A big dumb gunslinger.") and his twin fast-shooting irons. Thomas Carr's taut direction navigates itself through the intricacies of Daniel B. Ullman's pithy screenplay, aided by Raoul Kraushaar's noisy score and pristine monochrome photography of the Ray Corrigan Ranch in California's Simi Valley (a popular location for Western filmmakers) courtesy of Ernest Miller—Bradford shoots Morgan in the end but, in a showdown that Bradford's been itching for, Elliott plugs the sheriff three times; Doucette, wounded in both hands, is arrested and has the hangman's noose to look forward to.

Dialogue:
Morgan to Elliott: "With my brains and your guns, we can go far. Very far."

Trivia:
Ironically, Elliott was 49 when shooting *The Forty-Niners*; after completing the picture, the actor starred in five detective thrillers up to 1957 and then quit the movie world; his part as Sam Nelson is taken from the director's name who started his career rolling in 1938's *The Great Adventures of Wild Bill Hickok*.

Chapter 6
1953

OUT OF THE WEST'S INDIAN COUNTRY OF 1869 ... AND RIGHT TO YOU ... THROUGH THE MIRACLE OF 3 DIMENSION!
The Charge at Feather River

RED SAVAGE AND SCARLET TROOPER. SETTING THE CANADIAN FRONTIER ABLAZE!
Fort Vengeance

TERROR! TENSION! SUSPENSE ... IN 3 DIMENSIONS!
Gun Fury

TEN AGAINST TEN THOUSAND!
Last of the Comanches

MAN-OH-MAN! WHAT A WOMAN! SHE'S A ROOTIN' TOOTIN' STRAIGHT SHOOTIN' BUNDLE OF CURVES!
The Marshal's Daughter

THEY EAT 'EM ALIVE!
Shark River

Westerns of the 1950s: The Classic Years

Ambush at Tomahawk Gap

Columbia; Technicolor; 73 minutes; Producer: Wallace MacDonald; Director: Fred F. Sears; Cast: John Hodiak; John Derek; David Brian; Ray Teal; John Qualen; Otto Hulett; Maria Elena Marqués; Percy Helton ★★★★

Following a five-year stretch in Yuma Territorial Prison, four disparate outlaws (John Hodiak, David Brian, John Derek and Ray Teal) head for the ghost town of Tomahawk Gap to retrieve $10,000 stolen cash left there by Brian's brother, encountering Navajo lass Maria Elena Marqués en route. The windswept town is occupied by "crazy old coot" John Qualen, tending the local graveyard; government agent Otto Hulett turns up, taking the ex-convicts captive and tasked with returning the cash to the army. But the money can't be located, even though part of the town is ransacked, and all thoughts of locating it are dashed when marauding Apaches have everyone fighting for their lives.

In a series of violent encounters, the men are stabbed, speared, arrowed and shot to death, Hodiak sacrificing himself by igniting a gunpowder keg under his body, blowing the Indians to bits in a gully. As survivors Derek and Marqués leave Tomahawk Gap, the stolen bank notes, caught in a blaze, flutter away unnoticed in the wind. A tough, gritty programmer from Columbia, shot in California's Simi Valley (photography: Henry Freulich), epitomizing the low-budget B-Western of the early '50s at its gutsy best.

Dialogue:
Qualen to Hulett: "I don't know who you are, mister, but you can't be no crazier than these rascals, comin' into my town, diggin' up my graves."

Trivia:
The "outlaws look for hidden loot in a ghost town besieged by Indians" scenario probably attained its peak in MGM's *The Law and Jake Wade* (1958), starring Robert Taylor and Richard Widmark; great things were expected of Hodiak but tragically, the actor died from a heart attack on October 19, 1955, aged only 41.

Arrowhead

Paramount; Technicolor; 105 minutes; Producer: Nat Holt; Director: Charles Marquis Warren; Cast: Charlton Heston; Jack Palance; Brian Keith; Katy Jurado; Mary Sinclair; Milburn Stone; Robert J. Wilke; Pat Hogan ****

The early '50s Western theme of compassion towards Native Americans was thrown out of the window by producer Nat Holt and writer/director Charles Marquis Warren, presenting us with Apache-hating scout Charlton Heston doing his utmost to convince the army at Fort Clark that all Apaches were evil, murderous scum, and that Jack Palance (Toriano), educated out East, was arriving at the fort with only one thing on his mind—war. Heston has spent time with the Apaches himself, while on/off mistress Katy Jurado is part Apache, part Mexican. *Arrowhead* is a violent, downbeat Western in an attractive setting, the Texas plains around Brackettville shot in bright colors by double Oscar-winner Ray Rennahan; Paul Sawtell's score pumps up the action scenes, Palance and his hordes embarking on a bloodthirsty rampage. Brawny Heston (who doesn't smile once) is fired from his position as chief scout by new commander Brian Keith, both men vying for the attention of widow Mary Sinclair; Heston and pal Milburn Stone shot three Apaches whom Keith reckons were go-betweens, not bent on mischief, so Heston is blamed for the problems now occurring. When Palance turns up at Fort Clark, proudly displaying his long hair, it only needs one look at those grinning features to know that soon, he's going to strip down to Redskin garb, paint himself and start yelling "Death to the whites." Heston is reinstated because of his knowledge of Indians, Jurado knifes herself after Heston (who treats her like dirt) has drowned her scheming half-Indian brother in a creek and, in a climactic hand-to-hand combat, the big scout breaks Palance's neck. Their "invincible" leader dead, the Chiricahua Apaches depart in peace, destined to live on a reservation in Florida ("Go back to your homes. This was a false dream."). Without doubt one of director Warren's crowning achievements, *Arrowhead* looks the business, is well-acted by all concerned but, in some instances, makes for unsettling viewing (Stone's arrow-riddled corpse and the sounds of torture). The *New York Times* commented: "Heston is dark and sour ... Palance dour ... Jurado slinky and sultry ... the scenery pretty."

Highlights:

Splendid panoramic shots of the wide, flat Texas scenery and plenty of cavalry/Indian skirmishes to appease all action fans.

Dialogue:

Heston to a guard, staring at Jurado's body with a complete lack of compassion: "There's a dead Apache in here. Get it out."

Trivia:

The first credited movie role for Brian Keith.

Born to the Saddle

Astor; Cinecolor/Black-and-White; 77 minutes; Producer: Hall Shelton; Director: William Beaudine; Cast: Chuck Courtney; Leif Erickson; Donald Woods; Rand Brooks; Karen Morley; Bob Anderson; Glenn Strange; Dolores Prest ***

Vengeful orphan Chuck Courtney gallops into town searching for his uncle and takes a bullet intended for gambler/outlaw Donald Woods, who shoots the gunman—none other than Courtney's uncle! Fussed over by Woods' radiant wife, Karen Morley, who's physically abused by her husband, Courtney recovers, looked after by Rand Brooks and then Leif Erickson (Morley's former beau) whose tomboy niece, Dolores Prest, switches her affections from ranch hand Bob Anderson to the troubled blond newcomer. Woods has Courtney down to ride Blue Chip in a July 4 horse race, but the card sharp who, it turns out, killed the youngster's father and is the brains behind a stage robbery (Brooks and henchman Glenn Strange are involved) has other ideas, fixing the event to line his own pocket by inserting wire into Blue Chip's front fetlock to prevent him from winning the big race; it doesn't, the steed limping past the winning post. Strange goes mad, his reputation in tatters because he backed down to Courtney who had him covered with an empty Colt; he's later hanged, Brooks throttled but surviving the noose. In a climactic saloon shoot-out, Brooks, hit twice, puts a slug into Woods, saving Courtney the trouble, and the last we see of the "kid" is him riding off with Prest to play teenage house. Current prints of Astor's erratic low-grade oater are in black-and-white, so the Lone Pine photography

is lost; it's rather old-fashioned fare, Woods' stiff turn contrasting starkly with excitable Courtney who snorts "I'm gonna kill ya" every time someone rubs him up the wrong way.
Dialogue:
Erickson to Courtney: "Oh, ah, Bill, I apologise for my niece," after Prest has given the kid a piece of her mind, calling him a "nester brat."
Courtney: "It's alright—she's just a *girl*."

The Charge at Feather River

Warner Bros.; Warnercolor; Orig. in 3-D; 92 minutes; Producer: David Weisbart; Director: Gordon Douglas; Cast: Guy Madison; Frank Lovejoy; Helen Westcott; Vera Miles; Dick Wesson; Neville Brand; Steve Brodie; Ron Hagerthy ****

1869: Ex-captain/rancher/surveyor Guy Madison is asked to head a motley troop of ne'er-do-wells, the "Guardhouse Brigade," out from Fort Bellows on an eight-day twin assignment: to prevent the Cheyenne, led by Chief Thundercloud, from disrupting a new railhead, and rescue two white women abducted by the tribe five years ago. But when the girls are rescued, one, Vera Miles, objects; she likes the Indian way of life and is due to marry the chief, planning to do her utmost to sabotage the mission. Several exciting skirmishes down the line, Fort Bellows is reached, its inhabitants massacred, meaning a four-day trek to Fort Darby via Feather River; here, Gordon Douglas treats the audience to a series of thrilling Redskin attacks before Madison sends Thundercloud to the happy hunting grounds with a knife in his belly and treacherous Miles falls over a precipice to her death. Their chief gone, the Cheyenne pull back, just as the cavalry arrive from Fort Darby, Helen Westcott grinning from ear to ear; not only has she escaped life as a Redskin squaw, she's bagged good-looking Madison into the bargain. A big hit in Britain when released in September 1953, *The Charge at Feather River* is a rugged 3-D Western featuring loads of outdoor action sequences (some of them quite violent) and a plethora of objects (arrows, lances, bodies) flung at camera for the (then) novel three-dimensional effect. One minor quibble; although Max Steiner's title music is a cracker, his use of a semi-comical leitmotif when dopey Dick Wesson is on screen occasionally spoils the mood. "Exciting … not a trick missed," commented the U.K.'s *MFB*.
Highlights:
After seeing the film, thousands of British kids (including the author) recreated the Feather River assaults in their own backyards; the sequences are that memorable.
Dialogue:
Wesson: "Of all the women west of the Mississippi and we gotta end up with the war chief's bride."

City of Bad Men

20th Century Fox; Technicolor; 81 minutes; Producer: Leonard Goldstein; Director: Harmon Jones; Cast: Dale Robertson; Jeanne Crain; Lloyd Bridges; Richard Boone; Carole Mathews; Whitfield Connor; Hugh Sanders; Don Haggerty ****

Carson City, Nevada, 1897: The Stanton gang, led by Dale Robertson, away fighting in Mexico for six years, rides into town, ostensibly to watch a world heavyweight championship fight between James J. Corbett and Bob Fitzsimmons; in reality, they plan to steal the fight's receipts, around $100,000. Harmon Jones' tightly directed Western heist offering may be on the talky side (script by writing partners George W. George and George F. Slavin) but there's a lot of incident and intrigue taking place to maintain the interest, Robertson one smartly attired cool dude in a town seething with gun-happy miscreants, Richard Boone (Johnny Ringo) and Don Haggerty (Bob Thrailkill) among them. Robertson has to contend not only with troublesome Boone and Haggerty but brother Lloyd Bridges, a weakling hungering to take command as gang boss, ex-love Jeanne Crain, now betrothed to smooth promoter Whitfield Connor, and Connor's sister, man-eater Carole Mathews. The lengthy buildup to the fight and robbery is staged with a fair degree of suspense, Boone galloping off with the takings to the Fitzsimmons training camp, shooting Bridges and expiring in a hail of gunfire from Robertson who has previously been deputized by Hugh Sanders to keep the peace! The money returned to Carson City, Crain gets back her tall, taciturn (now reformed) man in the end, Connor bowing to the inevitable. A thumping score from Cyril J. Mockridge keeps the momentum going in a spiffy medium-budget oater (cost: $750,000) that hustles and bustles its way through a complex plot with brio.

Dialogue:
John Doucette to Bridges, as Mexican partner Pascual García Peña, mouths words of delight on seeing three scantily dressed dancing girls: "What's he sayin'?"
Bridges: "Same as you're thinkin'."

Trivia:
The debut of screen heavy Leo Gordon.

Conquest of Cochise

Columbia; Technicolor; 70 minutes; Producer: Sam Katzman; Director: William Castle; Cast: John Hodiak; Robert Stack; Joy Page; Rico Alaniz; Edward Colmans; Robert Griffin; Steven Ritch; Rodd Redwing ***

In 1853, The Gadsden Purchase of land in Southern Arizona will hopefully ensure that Mexicans can live in peace from both Indians and Tucson's rowdier elements, led by agitator Robert Griffin—but only if Apache chief Cochise (John Hodiak) can keep the peace with the whites, his renegade braves *and* warmongering Comanche chief Red Knife

(Rodd Redwing). Cavalry officer Robert Stack, in between eyeing up every pretty filly in sight, acts as peacemaker, siding with Hodiak and getting rebuffed by Joy Page, the sister of Rico Alaniz, a hothead out to kill the Apache boss, his wife having been slain by an Apache arrow in the opening minutes. William Castle's low-budget horse opera is an entertaining mix, shot around the red sandstone buttes of California's Santa Clarita region, stern-faced Hodiak a noble savage, his wife (Carol Thurston) murdered by Alaniz who in turn receives an arrow in the back; Hodiak then turns down the advances of Page who wants to share his tepee, and does his best to prevent Redwing going on the warpath by issuing a series of ultimatums. Hodiak's suffering of the Three Deaths (hung over a boiling spring; slashed by knives; burned alive) is interrupted when Redwing is shot dead, and in the end, Cochise's braves see off the Comanches during a barnstorming raid, the Apache chief once more vowing to keep the lid on any further trouble—and Stack *doesn't* get the girl!

Dialogue:
Hodiak to Page, after receiving a kiss on the lips: "I think perhaps there are customs of yours superior to ours."

Trivia:
Full marks to Mischa Bakaleinikoff for utilizing the works of seven composers (including his own) to create a stirring stock soundtrack, an art that has altogether disappeared from modern-day cinema.

Cow Country

Allied Artists; 82 minutes; Producer: Scott R. Dunlap; Director: Lesley Selander; Cast: Edmond O'Brien; Helen Westcott; Robert J. Wilke; Robert Lowery; Barton MacLane; Peggie Castle; James Millican; Robert Barrat **

Texas, 1875: Due to the collapse of the meat market, land-grabbers led by corrupt banker Barton MacLane are moving in on ranchers and nesters (homesteaders), foreclosing on property, withdrawing credit and using Robert J. Wilkes' rendering company to turn steers into tallow and hides. Edmond O'Brien's freight company is shifting the hides, coming up against boss of the Circle G Ranch, Robert Barrat, who wants cattlemen to reclaim their rights. Barrat also happens to be the father of Helen Westcott,

Westerns of the 1950s: The Classic Years 155

O'Brien's ex-flame, now betrothed to slimeball Robert Lowery, who in turn has promised to wed nester Peggie Castle. Not one of Lesley Selander's better Westerns. Everyone outsmarts everyone else in a talkative, convoluted plot and there's hardly any action to speak of until the last few minutes when O'Brien finally puts on a gun belt and faces up to Wilke and MacLane, shooting the pair of polecats in a street standoff (Millican has already blasted Lowery with four rifle bullets, getting Castle into the bargain). Wilke, as usual, is eminently watchable, giving a masterclass in sneering Western villainy, Castle outshines Westcott in the beauty stakes, California's Vasquez Rocks location work is striking but overall, it's a dull affair that seems a lot longer than its 82-minute running time.

Highlights:
Castle, enraged at finding out that Lowery is marrying Westcott, laying into the rat with a whip, "You dirty lyin' pig."

Dialogue:
Wilke, spotting O'Brien walking towards him wearing an iron, "So that's the way he wants it."
MacLane: "Don't be crazy. Wait'll he gets here and let him have it."
Wilke: "If I ain't faster on the draw than he is, he deserves to win."

Trivia:
O'Brien didn't think much of Adele Buffington's screenplay but agreed to star as he rated Lesley Selander's work on low-budget Westerns.

Devil's Canyon

RKO-Radio; Technicolor; Orig. in 3-D; 92 minutes; Producer: Edmund Grainger; Director: Alfred L. Werker; Cast: Virginia Mayo; Dale Robertson; Stephen McNally; Robert Keith; Jay C. Flippen; Arthur Hunnicutt; Whit Bissell; George J. Lewis ****

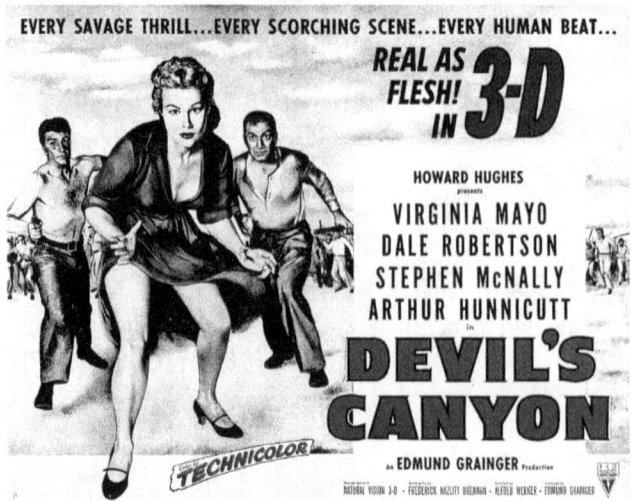

1897: The grim Territorial Prison of Arizona, whose walls are eight-foot thick, houses 500 tough male inmates—and Virginia Mayo in a pink dress! Mayo is there on a two-year sentence for armed robbery, although her real motive is to spring her pair of admirers out from behind bars. Psycho gunman Stephen McNally and ex-marshal Dale Robertson, serving 10 years for strapping on his pistols and killing McNally's two brothers in a "No Guns" zone ("People like you and me just ain't gonna know how to live in a place where killing's illegal," says Tom Powers to Robertson). McNally's after Robertson's hide; Mayo is aware of this, using her feminine wiles to smuggle shooting irons into the infirmary under the noses of warden Robert Keith and sadistic guard Jay C. Flippen. RKO's brutal, in-your-face prison drama (you half expect to see James Cagney walk out on set) mirrored changing attitudes in the Western format, cold-blooded action laced with psychological overtones taking over from 1940s homespun whimsy. Filmed in pastel shades by Nicholas Musuraca, Daniele Amfitheatrof's loud score assaulting the eardrums, Alfred L. Werker's taut bruiser of a picture moves towards a splendid climax when the prisoners, led by snarling McNally, break out, the unhinged outlaw spitting at Robertson, "I'm gonna splatter your brains all over that wall," only to be mowed down by his nemesis wielding a Gatling gun. Ordering the inmates to return to their cells, Robertson is promised a pardon along with Mayo, the two kissing as the picture ends.

Highlights:
Robertson belting on a double holster and stalking McNally's two brothers in a highly charged opening cat-and-mouse sequence.

Dialogue:
Bewhiskered Arthur Hunnicutt, on seeing Mayo stepping out into the prison yard: "She's real! If I had a razor, I'd shave."

Trivia:
Mayo, once voted "The Most Beautiful Blonde in the World," said her two favorite leading men were James Cagney and Alan Ladd, both just over five-foot-six inches tall.

Escape from Fort Bravo

MGM; Anscocolor; 99 minutes; Producer: Nicholas Nayfack; Director: John Sturges; Cast: William Holden; Eleanor Parker; John Forsythe; Richard Anderson; William Campbell; William Demarest; John Lupton; Polly Bergen *****

High on excitement, high on relationships, MGM's $1,500,000 *Escape from Fort Bravo* is an overlooked classic from 1953 concocted with guts and pace by action director John Sturges. At Fort Bravo in 1863, Confederates are held hostage in a stockade, tough Union officer William Holden first seen dragging an escapee back on the end of a rope. In the surrounding rocky heights, Mescalero Redskins keep a watchful eye, as does Rebel captain John Forsythe, waiting for a chance to escape. Enter Eleanor Parker, ostensibly to attend Polly Bergen's marriage to Richard Anderson; in fact, she's there to assist Forsythe, her lover, to break out. But what the fancy dame hasn't reckoned on is falling hook, line and sinker for Holden's masculine charms (and his beefed-up hairy chest!), throwing herself at him in wanton lust. When Forsythe, John Lupton, William Demarest and William Campbell sneak out in a wagon, accompanied by Parker, Holden scrapes together a detail and goes on the chase, the detachment reduced to just Holden, Anderson and an Indian scout when the soldiers are needed to boost the ranks of another regiment who are going to the rescue of a wagon train under attack from the Mescaleros. The climactic thrilling 25 minutes has the whites pinned down in a hollow, fending off one assault after another until Lupton, who has ridden off on the one horse available, brings in the cavalry. Holden and Anderson, both wounded, plus Parker (everyone else lies dead in the dust) return to the fort, grateful to be alive. Tremendous New Mexico scenery bathed in Robert Surtees' brash colors, a raucous Jeff Alexander score and hard-bitten Holden commanding the attention (the whole cast is on top form), combined with Sturges' incisive direction, add up to the kind of outdoor horse opera they simply don't make anymore. "Colorful and packed with action," said *Variety*.

Highlights:
The exciting final sequence, Holden and company crouching in their hollow, bullets whining and ricocheting, arrows raining down on their heads.

Dialogue:
Parker to Holden: "I've never been in a fort before. Is it safe to walk around at night?"
Holden: "No."
Parker: "I mean with you."
Holden, blowing out her match: "You'll get burned."

Trivia:
The movie was originally earmarked as a 3-D production.

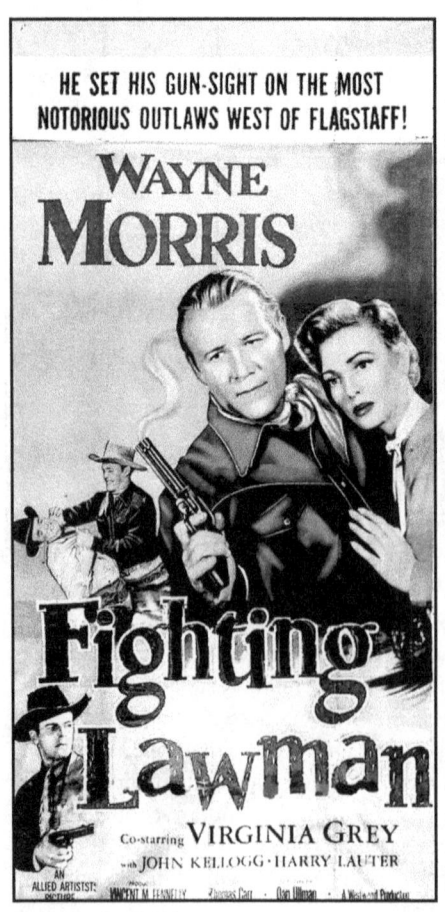

The Fighting Lawman

Allied Artists; 71 minutes; Producer: Vincent M. Fennelly; Director: Thomas Carr; Cast: Wayne Morris; Virginia Grey; John Kellogg; Harry Lauter; John Pickard; Rick Vallin; Myron Healey; Dick Rich ***

1886: Marshal Wayne Morris apprehends outlaw Rick Vallin, part of a four-man gang who have just robbed Flagstaff's bank; sentenced to 10 years, Vallin breaks out after three years and is shot by Morris, revealing the names of his three compatriots and sister before expiring. In Prescott, Vallin's devious sister, Virginia Grey, has Harry Lauter pining for her hand in marriage while gang boss John Kellogg, once her beau, has to fend off Morris and Sheriff Myron Healey when they come snooping around. A brisk, rather convoluted, little B-oater featuring Grey as the real villain on the range. The devious hussy wants all the cash from the robbery, coercing Lauter into killing fellow outlaw John Pickard and grabbing the loot from Kellogg's safe. In a shoot-out at Grey's home, Healey is wounded in the leg, Grey is killed attempting to escape and in a fight, Kellogg is plugged by Morris. Raoul Kraushaar's lively music pushes the

narrative along nicely, Morris proving that he was one of the better of the legion of minor stars who populated these low-budget Westerns during the early '50s.
Highlights:
Healey playing a good guy; the star of over 300 movies was usually cast on the side of bad, a dependable face in countless '50s Westerns.
Dialogue:
Opening narrative by Morris: "The date was August the 10th, 1886. It was a hot, dry dusty day. It seems like it always is when you're chasin' bank robbers."
Trivia:
Grey replaced Beverly Garland who had her nose broken when a horse swung its head into her face.

Fort Vengeance

Allied Artists; Cinecolor; 75 minutes; Producer: Walter Wanger; Director: Lesley Selander; Cast: James Craig; Keith Larsen; Morris Ankrum; Reginald Denny; Michael Granger; Paul Marion; Peter Camlin; Rita Moreno **

Director Lesley Selander, composer Paul Dunlap and photographer Harry Neumann must have had an off day, judging by this routine actioner set in Canada, 1877. James Craig and Keith Larsen played outlaw brothers from Montana who join the North West Mounted Police at Fort Vengeance, just across the U.S./Canadian border; Craig is the sensible one, Larsen his opposite, having already killed a Blackfoot warrior en route. Sioux supremo Sitting Bull (Michael Granger), following his triumph at Little Bighorn, is trying to recruit Morris Ankrum's peaceful Blackfoot tribe to wage a war on the white dogs south of the border. Larson aggravates the building tension by stealing furs from the Indians with trapper Peter Camlin, then murdering the man to cover his tracks. Ankrum's son, Paul Marion, is blamed for the killing but as he faces a firing squad, Craig brings in Larsen's body. In a fight between the siblings, Peter Coe dispatches Larsen with an arrow; he's the brother of the Blackfoot Larsen shot out of hand at the beginning. Marion is released while Ankrum, outside the fort with his warriors, shouts, "No war!" and withdraws, justice seen to be done. Rita Moreno briefly appears, singing, dancing and flirting, completely superfluous to plot requirements, and the picture doesn't even bow out with a much-needed climactic clash; and B-movie stalwart Ankrum (star of over 270 features) looks uneasy wearing a full-feathered headdress. This conventional material was handled much better a year later in Universal's *Saskatchewan* and represents a rare misfire for the usually reliable Selander.

Dialogue:
Larsen, staring at a wagonload of furs: "Valuable stuff."
Craig, staring at Moreno's curves: "Yeah. Dangerous, too."

The Great Jesse James Raid

Lippert Pictures; Anscocolor; 73 minutes; Producer: Robert L. Lippert, Jr.; Director: Reginald LeBorg; Cast: Willard Parker; Barbara Payton; Tom Neal; Wallace Ford; Jim Bannon; James Anderson; Richard H. Cutting; Barbara Woodell **

Jim Bannon (Bob Ford) and Richard H. Cutting enlist the aid of Willard Parker (Jesse James), Wallace Ford, Tom Neal and James Anderson to dynamite their way into the Big Bob Mine and steal $300,000 worth of gold; Parker gets 25% share, the others divide the rest among themselves. An uninspired effort from Reginald LeBorg, despite a graphic opening whipping scene. A long 20 minutes go by before Parker, reluctant at first, recruits three miscreants for the job, a further 16 minutes spent in Neal and Anderson brawling in a saloon over the delights of Barbara Payton; the mine isn't reached until the final third of the picture where the action picks up. Only Parker and Bannon make it out alive after a set-to involving men from the nearby town forces Ford into blasting a hole into flooded workings, killing him and the others. Payton, who was along for the ride, lies crushed to death under a broken wagon and, as Parker and Bannon depart their separate ways, Bannon eyes the $10,000 reward on his friend's head and licks his lips in anticipation; Western buffs all know what will happen next.

Dialogue:
Neal in the mine, surveying the gloomy rock walls: "I've seen caves at home in Kentucky like this. They make good tombs."

Trivia:
The film is made that much more interesting by the inclusion of ex-boxer Neal and buxom Payton. In 1951, the two carried out a torrid affair that hit the gossip columns; when Payton decided to marry actor Franchot Tone, Neal gave him a savage beating, resulting in serious injury to Tone. Payton married Tone but, 53 days after the wedding, returned to Neal who, because of the incident, was blackballed by Hollywood; Neal and Payton split soon after. As a side note, Neal was charged with the manslaughter of his wife in 1965 and served six years of a 10-year prison sentence.

The Great Sioux Uprising

Universal; Technicolor; 81 minutes; Producer: Albert J. Cohen; Director: Lloyd Bacon; Cast: Jeff Chandler; Faith Domergue; Lyle Bettger; Peter Whitney; John War Eagle; Stacy Harris; Walter Sande; Glenn Strange ***

During the Civil War, rival horse traders Faith Domergue and Lyle Bettger are supplying much-needed mounts to the Union army, but Bettger, romancing Domergue, wants to run the whole show himself, his men rustling the extensive Sioux herds at the risk of war. Chief Red Cloud (John War Eagle), furious at the loss of his "sacred horses," is on the verge of breaking the peace treaty with the whites when, on the 18th minute, Doctor/Surgeon/Veterinary Jeff Chandler canters into the Sioux camp, tending to the chief's horse and promising to straighten things out. Right away, he becomes the town's new medical practitioner and the subject of Domergue's attentions ("Thinking gives a woman wrinkles," is his first chat-up line). Bettger, aided by eye-patched killer Stacy Harris, gets jealous, frames Chandler for the murder, by stabbing, of Walter Sande (one of the townsfolk seething over Bettger's monopoly of selling horses to the army) and almost starts an Indian uprising by cheating everyone in sight before his outfit and Harris are wiped out by the Sioux in the frenetic climax; Bettger is taken into custody. Peace is finally restored with the Sioux chief and Chandler takes on the position of army surgeon, promising besotted Domergue he'll be back in her loving arms before too long. A slightly below-their-normal excellence Universal horse opera (with the accent firmly on the horse) containing no real Great Sioux Uprising as such and a great deal of talk. Chandler is stoically wooden, Domergue flashes her gorgeous eyelashes, burly Peter Whitney puts in an enjoyable performance as an Old Testament-spouting blacksmith and Bettger is his usual slimy, conniving self. And would Bettger *really* be able to throw his weight around only days after having his appendix removed by Chandler, using Harris' knife! A rousing Universal stock score plus Maury Gertsman's bright photography hoist Lloyd Bacon's standard oater into the realms of the acceptable rather than the tedious. "Strictly minor league … routine," stated the *New York Times*.

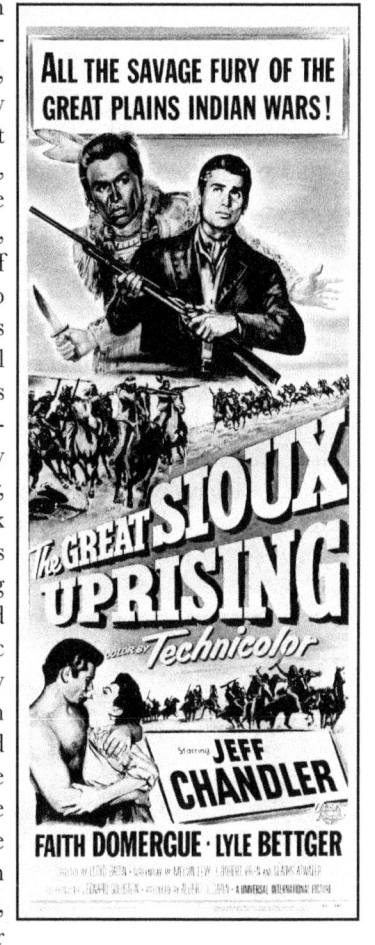

Highlights:
Not that many, but the numerous shots of horses charging across the grasslands should appeal to all horse lovers.

Dialogue:
Chandler to Domergue: "This territory needs a good veterinary. And you need a good husband."

Trivia:
Between 1865-1867, Chief Red Cloud conducted a two-year campaign against army construction troops on his land; he eventually ended his days on the Red Cloud Agency in Nebraska, dying in 1909 at the age of 87.

Gun Fury

Columbia; Technicolor; Orig. in 3-D; 83 minutes; Producer: Lewis J. Rachmil; Director: Raoul Walsh; Cast: Rock Hudson; Philip Carey; Donna Reed; Leo Gordon; Pat Hogan; Roberta Haynes; Lee Marvin; Neville Brand ***

Six-foot-five Rock Hudson meets six-foot-four Philip Carey and six-foot-two Leo Gordon in Raoul Walsh's standard Columbia oater originally shown in 3-D. Carey's an immoral ex-Confederate thief who, with Gordon and cohorts (heavies Lee Marvin and Neville Brand among their number), holds up a stage and falls in lust with Donna Reed, due to marry Hudson. Her fiancé is shot in the skirmish, believed dead, but he isn't, teaming up with Gordon after the burly outlaw has been tied to a fence and left for buzzard food by Carey, and Indian Pat Hogan, nursing a grievance against the narcissistic crook. *Gun Fury* develops into a chase movie, Hudson and company pursuing Carey's mob, hoping to catch them before they cross the border and Carey carts Reed off to Mexico to play house on his terms, and is fairly exciting at times, Arizona's rocky Sedona wilderness lending the picture a distinct red/green look. It's let down by muddy nighttime photography and too many scenes of objects being thrown straight at the camera for the required 3-D effect. A furious shoot-out at Mel Welles' rundown hacienda sees Carey disposing of jealous Mexican girlfriend Roberta Haynes; he then shoots Gordon during an exchange deal (Gordon for Reed), meeting his doom following a cliff-edge tussle with Hudson, Hogan's knife sunk squarely between his shoulder blades; Hudson is at last reunited with Reed.

Highlights:
As in so many Westerns made during this period, the scenery plays a major role, the red sandstone buffs and mesas of Sedona, Arizona a visual knockout.

Dialogue:
Gordon to Carey, failing to figure out why he's so hooked on Reed: "Far as I'm concerned, all women are alike. They just got different faces so you can tell 'em apart."

Trivia:
Like director André De Toth, Raoul Walsh had only one eye, so was unable to appreciate the 3-D format in the finished article.

Hondo

Warner Bros.; Warnercolor; Orig. in 3-D; 83 minutes; Producers: Robert Fellows and John Wayne; Director: John Farrow; Cast: John Wayne; Geraldine Page; Lee Aaker; Ward Bond; Michael Pate; Rodolfo Acosta; James Arness; Leo Gordon ****

Produced during the 3-D craze of 1953, *Hondo* comes across as a companion piece to *Shane*, John Wayne's Hondo Lane arriving horseless, his dog Sam in tow, at Geraldine Page's homestead where he quickly befriends the woman ("You remind me of my wife.") and her six-year-old son, Lee Aaker (famous for playing Rusty in TV's *The Adventures of Rin Tin Tin*). Wayne has Apache blood coursing through his veins and lived with the Indians for five years, handy when Page (her screen debut) is frequently visited by Chief Vittorio's (Michael Pate) Apache warriors who are curious rather than murderous. Where is her husband, Pate asks, when that "young warrior" urgently needs a father? Husband Leo Gordon is a drinking bully, spending months away from the family home and later shot by Wayne as he goes to drill the big scout in the back. Director John Farrow crams in an abundance of incident and excitement, foot pressed firmly on the throttle, effortlessly mixing the burgeoning Wayne/Page/Aaker relationship with the Indian way of life and their beliefs; the movie culminates in an exciting seven-minute pony soldiers/settlers versus Redskins confrontation, Wayne knifing renegade chief Rodolfo Acosta to death and riding off with Page and her cute little boy to set up house together. The only sour note in an otherwise colorful, scenically splendid production is the brutal death of Wayne's dog, skewered by an Apache war lance; was this *really* necessary?

Highlights:

Wayne in commanding form, plus wonderful Mexican scenery and Page's performance which earned her an Oscar nomination; 32 years later, she won the Oscar for her role in *The Trip to Bountiful*.

Dialogue:

Wayne to Page: "I'm part Indian and I can smell you when I'm downwind of you."
Page: "Impossible!"

Trivia:

In the 78th minute, *Star Trek*'s Leonard Nimmoy can be seen for around two seconds; he's the warrior to the right of Adolfo Acosta. John Ford directed the climactic battle scenes, John Farrow busy on other commitments, but didn't receive a credit.

Jack Slade aka Slade

Allied Artists; 90 minutes; Producer: Lindsley Parsons; Director: Harold D. Schuster; Cast: Mark Stevens; Dorothy Malone; Barton MacLane; Paul Langton; Harry Shannon; John Harmon; John Litel; Sammy Ogg *****

In the town of Carlysle, Illinois in 1841, 12-year-old Sammy Ogg hits a man with a stick and kills him while playing in the street; leaving the town by stage, his father is shot dead out of hand in a holdup, driver Harry Shannon caring for the boy. Seven years later, Mark Stevens (as Jack) has become a cold-blooded, quick-on-the-draw hombre nursing enough psychological problems to keep psychiatrists busy for months. If anyone challenges him or gets in his way, he doesn't talk, he shoots. Stevens gets a job as a guard on the Great Missouri Freight lines but drummed out of town for being *too* fast. In Julesburg, he's offered a similar position by Paul Langton because of his reputation, meeting and marrying half-Comanche Dorothy Malone, whom Langton has his eyes on; the gal is all over Stevens like a rash, lusting for excitement ("You're all I want. You belong to me. Marry me. Today."), even though he warns her the marriage will never last. Scripted by Warren Douglas, *Jack Slade* is an extremely violent, very dark *noir* Western containing enough shoot-outs, standoffs and gunplay (there's even a graphic hanging) over 90 minutes to satisfy all those with a bloodlust for such things, and Stevens' portrayal of a sick man whose broken soul gradually disintegrates is nothing short of brilliant. The scene where he rescues 13-year-old David May from a horse thieves' lair and promises to care for him, only for the lad to die from two bullets, is heartrending, showing the man's caring side; his *uncaring* side manifests itself when he pumps four slugs into arch-enemy Barton MacLane (another great performance), even though the gunman has begged to be given one more chance. But in a previous set-to involving an outlaw gang, Stevens has accidentally shot dead his old friend Shannon (the outfit's cook) and hits the whiskey bottle hard, the town's citizens wanting him out ("You're blind to everything but violence, drinking and murder."). Leaving Malone ("You belong here. I don't."), he's hunted down by Langton for the murder of Shannon and, in a hail of lead exchanged between the two, expires in Langton's arms, his body taken into town. William A. Sickner's needle-sharp black-

and-white photography and Paul Dunlap's vital score, combined with expert direction from Harold D. Schuster, make for a little-seen, pared-to-the-bone B-Western classic, tough, bullet-strewn, bleak and uncompromising; in Britain, it narrowly avoided an "X" certificate, rated "A" instead.

Highlights:
Stevens and MacLane's artfully orchestrated, tense street standoff, made years before Sergio Leone perfected it in his *Dollar* movies.

Dialogue:
Stevens: "I seem to draw trouble like a dead horse draws flies. Wonder who's got the bullet with my name on it?"

Last of the Comanches aka The Sabre and the Arrow

Columbia; Technicolor; 85 minutes; Producer: Buddy Adler; Director: André De Toth; Cast: Broderick Crawford; Barbara Hale; Lloyd Bridges; Johnny Stewart; Mickey Shaughnessy; Hugh Sanders; John War Eagle; Chubby Johnson ****

August 1876: In a blazing opening few minutes, the town of Dry Buttes is burned to the ground by renegade Comanche Indians, its citizens massacred, six surviving troopers led by gruff sergeant Broderick Crawford heading out into the desert towards Fort Macklin. En route, the stagecoach *Buttercup* is met, as well as Hugh Sanders, busy selling carbines to the hostiles, and young Johnny Stewart, a Kiowa educated by the white man. Lying low in a ruined mission and attempting to trade guns for water with Chief Black Cloud, the beleaguered bunch fight off repeated ferocious raids, suffering appalling casualties, until the cavalry arrives to send the Comanches packing. André De Toth's remake of 1943's *Sahara* (which Lloyd Bridges also starred in) is a vigorous "men against desperate odds" yarn, very violent for its time. Contorted bodies strewn in the dust, Bridges peppered with arrows and a startling shot of Dry Buttes as a blackened scene of devastation. Crawford bulldozes his way through the relentless action, firing off terse one-liners as though he was in a crime drama, Barbara Hale is on hand to provide feminine support (but no romance) and Ray Cory and Charles Lawton, Jr.'s photography bathes the arid Tucson scenery in bleached-out colors. Grim, gritty and underrated, even though it was rumored that Crawford was hitting the bottle heavily at the time.

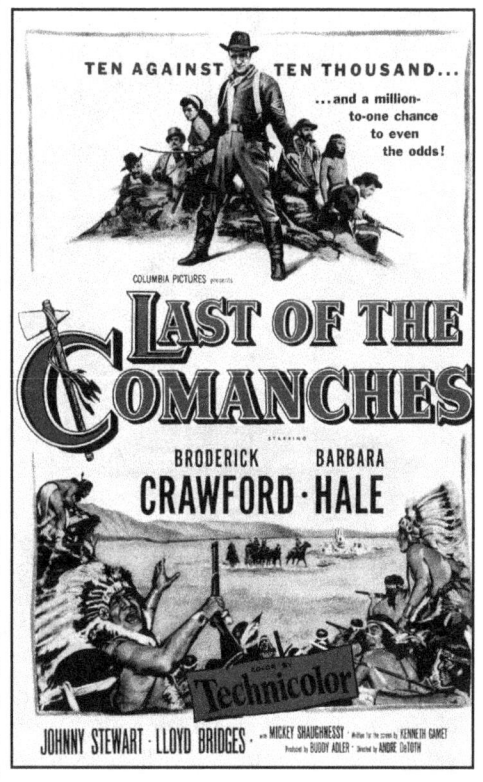

Highlights:
A riveting matte image of burned-out Dry Buttes, plus a telling shot of Crawford and Bridges conferring in silhouette against a blood-red setting sun.

Dialogue:
Hale to Crawford on why Stewart should receive a drink: "He's only a child."
Crawford: "Yeah, sure, a child today and a young buck tomorrow, with war paint on his face and a scalping knife in his hand."

Trivia:
The film debut of Mickey Shaughnessy.

The Last Posse

Columbia; 73 minutes; Producer: Harry Joe Brown; Director: Alfred L. Werker; Cast: Broderick Crawford; John Derek; Charles Bickford; Wanda Hendrix; Henry Hull; Skip Homeier; James Bell; Warner Anderson ****

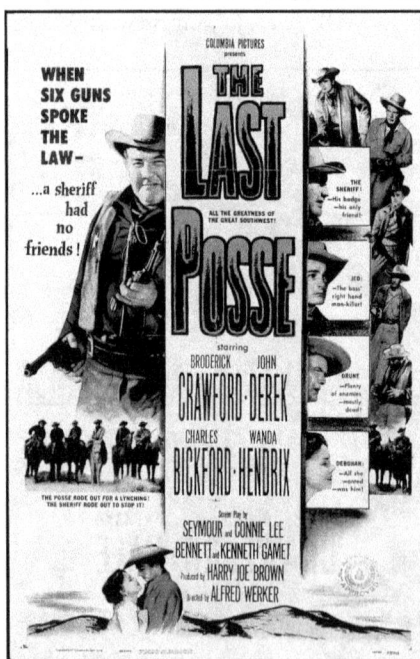

A posse slowly enters the town of Roswell, bedraggled, dirty and ill-tempered, Sheriff Broderick Crawford badly wounded. Questions are rebuffed in curt answers ("We've all changed."). Why? In three lengthy flashbacks, the tale unfolds: John Derek, alcoholic Crawford, Charles Bickford, Warner Anderson and company hunt down cattle farmer James Bell, his brother Guy Wilkerson and son Skip Homeier who have stolen $105,000 from Bickford; he bought their cattle for $5 a head, sold them at $35 a head and they feel cheated. Into the mix is the Derek/Bickford relationship: Derek is Bickford's ward, his father having been killed 15 years back. But Crawford knows that Bickford murdered him in a fight and that Bell witnessed the act, the main reason why Bickford wants Bell dead. For a B-movie, it's a complex storyline, shot in pristine monochrome by Burnett Guffey amid Lone Pine's towering hills (a favorite location of producer Harry Joe Brown), resulting in Derek finding out the truth and shooting Bickford, thus becoming the heir to his property; Anderson and three others decide to pocket the cash following the demise of Bell, Homeier and Wilkerson. In Roswell, they come clean about the missing money in front of Judge James Kirkwood; Crawford, who has been listening, slumps dead in a chair. Tautly directed by Alfred L. Werker, *The Last Posse* is intriguingly different and well-acted, Crawford's burly, growling presence mirroring the actor's own private battles with the bottle.

Dialogue:
Derek to Crawford: "How does it feel to track down your friends?"
Crawford: "Sheriff's got no friends, just a job."

Law and Order

Universal; Technicolor; 80 minutes; Producer: John W. Rogers; Director: Nathan Juran; Cast: Ronald Reagan; Dorothy Malone; Preston Foster; Chubby Johnson; Alex Nicol; Russell Johnson; Dennis Weaver; Barry Kelley ****

Probably Ronald Reagan's best Western: He plays a hard-bitten sheriff first seen delivering outlaw Wally Cassell to justice in Tombstone, fighting off a lynch mob and giving in his badge; he's bought a ranch in lawless Cottonwood and wants set to set up house there with saloon owner Dorothy Malone. Brothers Alex Nicol and Russell Johnson, plus undertaker Chubby Johnson, accompany him and soon the foursome are up to their necks in trouble: Cottonwood is run on the lines of intimidation by corrupt Preston Foster, his two troublesome brothers and inept sheriff Barry Kelley, and they object to Reagan (and his reputation) being there; they string troublemakers up, he wants to give everyone a fair trial. When Nicol, made marshal to keep the peace, is gunned down by Dennis Weaver in a saloon fracas, Reagan straps on his gun belt, takes his dead brother's place and attempts to clean up the town by enforcing a "No Guns" policy. Johnson, in love with Ruth Hampton, Weaver's sister, kills Weaver in self-defense, Reagan tasked with the job of hauling him in for trial, even though he's not a murderer. Foster, following a brutal fistfight with Reagan, is run over and killed by a runaway buckboard before the marshal confronts Johnson atop a huge cliff, bringing his hotheaded brother into town and throwing in his badge to work the cattle ranch with Malone; Kelley has had enough, riding away to California. A standout Universal oater packed with tense incident, ably demonstrating why, in this period, their Westerns seemed to pack more of a colorful punch than others.

Highlights:

The opening and closing scenes, set among the giant fluted rock columns at California's Red Rock Canyon.

Dialogue:

Cassell to Reagan, passing Tombstone's crowded cemetery: "You shoot 'em all?"

Reagan: "Only those that didn't get hung."

Trivia:

Reagan was known as the law and order president from his performance in this movie.

The Man from the Alamo

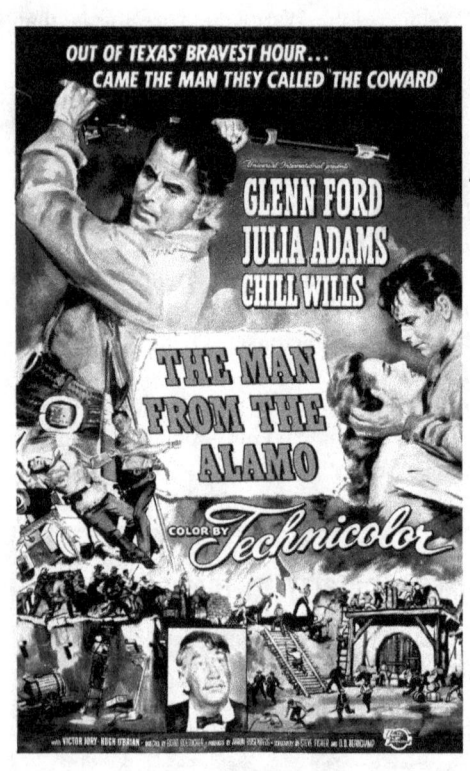

Universal; Technicolor; 79 minutes; Producer: Aaron Rosenberg; Director: Budd Boetticher; Cast: Glenn Ford; Julia (Julie) Adams; Hugh O'Brian; Chill Wills; Victor Jory; Marc Cavell; Neville Brand; John Daheim *****

Budd Boetticher is known for manufacturing seven superb Randolph Scott Westerns between 1956-1960; here, his taut, economical style highlights a fast-moving oater which kicks off with a potted, 16-minute version of the Alamo siege of March, 1836. Lots are drawn to enable one man to leave the mission and warn the homesteaders around the Texas Oxbow area of General Santa Anna's plans to sweep across the state; Glenn Ford is the man chosen. Finding his farm burned to the ground, his wife and child murdered by American land-grabbers posing as Mexicans, Ford gallops into the town of Franklin full of hate, youngster Marc Cavell by his side, and immediately gets tarnished with the brush of cowardice, under threat from a necktie party. How tight-lipped, mean-fisted Ford redeems himself makes for satisfying viewing: Saturnine Victor Jory, as expected, is the chief villain, unhinged outlaw Neville Brand one of his sneering henchmen; attractive, dark-haired Julia Adams believes Ford isn't the coward everyone thinks he is (and she's proved right in the end); one-armed Chill Wills eventually comes to Ford's aid when Jory decides to raid wagons loaded with the town's cash, headed for the Trinidad River; and aloof cavalry officer Hugh O'Brian also gets off his mighty high horse to shake Ford's hand. Jory falls to his death over a waterfall during a ferocious gun battle and the final evocative shot is of Ford riding off into the wide blue yonder, Adams praying that he'll return to play house with her.

Highlights:
A superior medium-budget Western from Universal, featuring "spacious Technicolor scenery" (the *New York Times* commenting on Russell Metty's cinematography), a fine Frank Skinner score and a solid central performance from Glenn Ford.

Dialogue:
Soldier to messenger O'Brian during the opening stages of the Alamo battle: "Worse that can happen to you is somebody will say you died a hero. There's a man (pointing at Ford) gonna be called a coward for the rest of his life."

Trivia:
O'Brian was awarded a Golden Globe for Most Promising Newcomer, even though Ford outshines him in every scene they're in together.

The Marksman

Allied Artists; 62 minutes; Producer: Vincent M. Fennelly; Director: Lewis D. Collins; Cast: Wayne Morris; Elena Verdugo; Frank Ferguson; Rick Vallin; I. Stanford Jolley; Tom Powers; Robert Bice; Stanley Price ***

Lawman Wayne Morris, a top sharpshooter with the single-loading rifle, poses as a prospector when Marshal I. Stanford Jolley is murdered by one of Frank Ferguson's boys in the Sangre De Cristo hills. Ferguson has been rustling cattle undetected for three years and local ranchers are demanding action. "I'm the government executioner," moans Morris as he departs on his mission, sick of all the killing, but he still manages to bump off Ferguson, Robert Bice, Rick Vallin and three others by the final reel, in addition to the six sidewinders he has dispatched in reel one, making for a B-Western with a very high body count. Blonde novelist Elena Verdugo, Ferguson's niece, thinks Morris' exploits make good copy and ends up marrying the big guy with a future writing project in mind, promising to read a cookbook on their honeymoon! Raoul Kraushaar's rowdy score and a plethora of roughhouse shenanigans ensure that Lewis D. Collins' "sniper with a conscience" effort maintains the interest on a basic cowboy movie level, Morris a tough but amiable hero.

Dialogue:

Verdugo, eyeing Morris across the dinner table: "Gee! A prospector who's young and handsome and went to college."

Ferguson: "Interesting character for your book, huh, Jane?"

Verdugo, licking her lips: "Very!"

The Marshal's Daughter

United Artists; 71 minutes; Producer: Ken Murray; Director: William Berke; Cast: Laurie Anders; Hoot Gibson; Harry Lauter; Bob Duncan; Robert Bray; Tom London; Ken Murray; B.G. Norman *****

"Oh, you been a heap of joy. How I wish you'd been a boy." So runs a line in Tex Ritter's catchy title song, and heroine Laurie Anders, sole survivor of an Indian massacre orchestrated by outlaw Bob Duncan (who wrote the script), wishes she *was* a male. Her father, Marshal Hoot Gibson (60 at the time), travels under the guise of a proprietor of a medicine sideshow, bent on tracking down Duncan who was responsible for his wife's death in the massacre *and* cleaning up lawless vermin in the towns they pass through. Anders assists where she can ("I tried to help Dad on his last job but he said it wasn't ladylike."), boyfriend Harry Lauter unaware that the attractive blonde, who can sing, dance, and ride horses standing up, is a ventriloquist and a martial arts/Japanese wrestling expert (she's also got a great pair of legs). She is none other than El Coyote, the "Mysterious Masked Rider in Black" who vanquishes the bad guys with her combat skills, howling like the mangy critter she's named after. Farce? Comedy? Parody? Satire? Anders was plucked out of producer Ken Murray's 1951 TV show and given a stab at stardom in a Western that's so utterly mad as to be a unique one-off, containing flashbacks within flashbacks, witty one-liners courtesy of Duncan, Murray playing stand-up comedian "Smiling" Billy Murray, a clutch of tuneful melodies, Anders and gunman Bob Gross performing a bizarre, acrobatic dance number, guest appearances from Johnny Mack Brown, Buddy Baer and Tex Ritter and, when the going gets serious, a pulsating Darrell Calker score. After Duncan is arrested, Robert Bray enters the scene, a corrupt banker staging train holdups and rustling herds in order to steal the ranchers' properties, shooting Anders' uncle dead and determined to steal $75,000, being money withdrawn from the bank by ranchers and given to Duncan for safekeeping. El Coyote takes care of Bray after Duncan, held captive, is freed, the rogue shot dead falling on his own rifle; dressed to the nines, she kisses Lauter at the end and he spots her El Coyote outfit, wondering what on earth he's let himself in for; a girl with one heck of a dual personality, that's what! Tremendous fun from start to finish; ridiculous, as crazy as they come but thoroughly entertaining.

Highlights:
Anders as El Coyote, riding over the hills howling, Calker's music an exciting, thunderous aural backdrop.

Dialogue:
Youngster B.G. Norman to Anders, thirsting for revenge after his grandpa has been murdered: "Gosh. I wish I was a big man."
Anders: "So do I!"

Trivia:
This was Anders' one and only feature film, the actress retiring after its release; on March 13, 1967, scriptwriter/actor Duncan (62) shot himself in the head after calling the police to say that he was going to commit suicide.

The Moonlighter

Warner Bros.; Orig. in 3-D; 77 minutes; Producer: Joseph Bernhard; Director: Roy Rowland; Cast: Fred MacMurray; Barbara Stanwyck; Ward Bond; William Ching; Morris Ankrum; Myra Marsh; Charles Halton; Norman Leavitt **

Cowpoke Fred MacMurray (he rustles cattle by moonlight) is flung into Yellowknife's jail and changes cells, the new occupant of his cell (Norman Leavitt) grabbed by a lynch mob and strung up. MacMurray breaks out, witnesses the hanging (which should have been his), terrorizes and hunts down a couple of the necktie party and, wounded, reunites with his brother, William Ching, a bank teller who's romancing MacMurray's old love, Barbara Stanwyck. Ex-partner Ward Bond turns up, planning to rob the Rio Hondo Bank with MacMurray's help—and Ching's. Ching is killed in the robbery, Bond double-crosses his former pal, riding off with the loot, and Stanwyck, deputized, hits the vengeance trail, shooting Bond and determined to turn MacMurray over to the law. But following a near-fatal incident under a raging waterfall, the pair rekindle their passion, MacMurray stating that he will turn himself in and start a new life with Stanwyck on his release. "A horrible mistake" was Stanwyck's acid opinion on a picture that perhaps Warner Bros. would have hoped for a better outcome. The actress and MacMurray were reunited after their pairing in Paramount's classic *film noir*, *Double Indemnity* (1944) but here, the sexual chemistry was missing; and why was the film presented in 3-D, not color (and why an intermission at 45 minutes?). The critics hated it, *The Hollywood Reporter* commenting "muddled," the *New York Times* calling the production "shapeless, dull low-budget ... a sow's ear." *The Moonlighter* wanders all over the place, a series of vignettes taking precedence over a cohesive plot, containing an unnecessary lengthy flashback (Stanwyck conversing with the coroner over Murray's "missing body") and a clumsy scene where MacMurray and Bond escape the bank holdup in a motor vehicle (although the narrative *is* set around 1900). Heinz Roemheld's full-blooded score tries to keep things on an even keel and the waterfall sequence is moderately exciting but, all in all, this bizarre peculiarity ranks as the worst of the four movies the two leading stars made together.

Dialogue:
MacMurray to Stanwyck: "I'm probably the only man alive that saw himself hang."

Trivia:
During the waterfall episode, shot at the Peppermint Falls in California's High Sierras, Stanwyck insisted on doing her own stunts, resulting in many cuts and bruises when she slipped and fell into the rapids; and this must be the only 3-D film where *nothing* is thrown at the camera.

The Nebraskan

Columbia; Technicolor; Orig. in 3-D; 68 minutes; Producer: Wallace MacDonald; Director: Fred F. Sears; Cast: Philip Carey; Roberta Haynes; Lee Van Cleef; Richard Webb; Wallace Ford; Jay Silverheels; Maurice Jara; Pat Hogan **

Aimed specifically at the new (and novel) 3-D market of the day, Columbia's contrived oater, set in Nebraska, 1867, had army scout Philip Carey, Wallace Ford, husband and wife Richard Webb and Roberta Haynes plus renegade trooper Lee Van Cleef and Indian Maurice Jara pinned down in Ford's way station, besieged by rampaging Redskins. Jay Silverheels (Spotted Bear) and his Sioux are on the warpath, claiming that Jara (Wing Foot) killed Chief Thundercloud, although he maintains he's innocent. Carey believes him, even when the warriors are raining down arrows, firing one volley after another and blowing up a station wall. Haynes (surprise! surprise!) just happens to be Carey's old flame, so when jealous Webb is stabbed to death with an arrow as he goes to kill Carey, the way is left open for the big scout to rekindle his relationship with the dame. Pat Hogan (Yellow Knife) unmasks his own father, Silverheels, as the murderer who did the deed to start a war; during a fight, Silverheels falls on his own knife and Hogan is proclaimed the new chief, desiring peace with the whites at Fort Kearny. Plenty of "knives, arrows and crashing ceiling timbers" pointed directly at camera for the 3-D effects, plus clumsily inserted stock footage of an Indian attack on a wagon, make for a humdrum, slightly tiresome effort that plays it strictly by numbers; not the worst 3-D Western ever made, but certainly not among the best.

Dialogue:

Ford, after firing at one Injun after another: "Couldn't ask for more if we was in darkest Africa."

Pony Express

Paramount; Technicolor; 101 minutes; Producer: Nat Holt; Director: Jerry Hopper; Cast: Charlton Heston; Forrest Tucker; Rhonda Fleming; Jan Sterling; Michael Moore; Henry Brandon; Stuart Randall; Porter Hall ***

A mostly fictitious account of how the Pony Express mail route was formed in 1860; Joseph, Missouri to Sacramento, California in 10 days, half the time it took the Overland stage to complete the run. It was battle of the giants time as buckskin-clad six-foot-two and a half Charlton Heston (as federal scout Buffalo Bill Cody) and smart dude six-foot-four Forrest Tucker (Wild Bill Hickok) thwarted a scheme by Henry Brandon, Michael

Moore and Stuart Randall to sabotage the route by blowing up relay stations *and* kick California out of the Union for financial gain. In between gunfights, raiding hostile Indians, fighting Chief Yellow Hand (Pat Hogan) to the death and preventing Brandon's jackals from selling rifles to the Redskins, Heston has to ward off the feminine advances of glamorous Rhonda Fleming and the tomboy advances of stick-thin Jan Sterling. Double Oscar-winner Ray Rennahan's fine photography (Utah's Kanab area), combined with Paul Sawtell's rousing score, contribute to a Western that's a tad heavy-footed in parts, hindered by Charles Marquis Warren's lukewarm script. There's plenty of action, gunplay and hard ridin' and Heston and Tucker make an engaging double-act, yet you get the distinct impression that the movie could have been a whole lot better than it turned out.

Highlights:
Heston and Tucker, both sporting double holsters, playing a game of "who's the best shot" in a crowded street.

Dialogue:
Tucker to Sterling, on how to trail Fleming's movements: "Listen, Shorty, you follow the redhead and *I'll* marry you."
Sterling: "Easy for you to say. You don't like women."
Tucker: "That's right. Maybe that's why I'm so fond of you."
Sterling: "Thanks! Go shoot yourself."

Trivia:
Buffalo Bill Cody would have only been 14 years old at the time of the events depicted in the picture!

The Redhead from Wyoming

Universal; Technicolor; 81 minutes; Producer: Leonard Goldstein; Director: Lee Sholem; Cast: Maureen O'Hara; Alex Nicol; William Bishop; Alexander Scourby; Robert Strauss; Gregg Palmer; Jack Kelly; Dennis Weaver *****

It's cattlemen versus settlers as ambitious William Bishop, visions of becoming Governor of Wyoming swimming in his devious head, takes on ex-flame/saloon mistress Maureen O'Hara as a partner in the cattle business, in direct opposition to rancher Alexander Scourby: He resents squatters taking maverick steers from what he classes as his land; Bishop states that settlers have the right to claim unbranded cattle unmolested. Bishop, in fact, is crossing everyone he comes into contact with, including

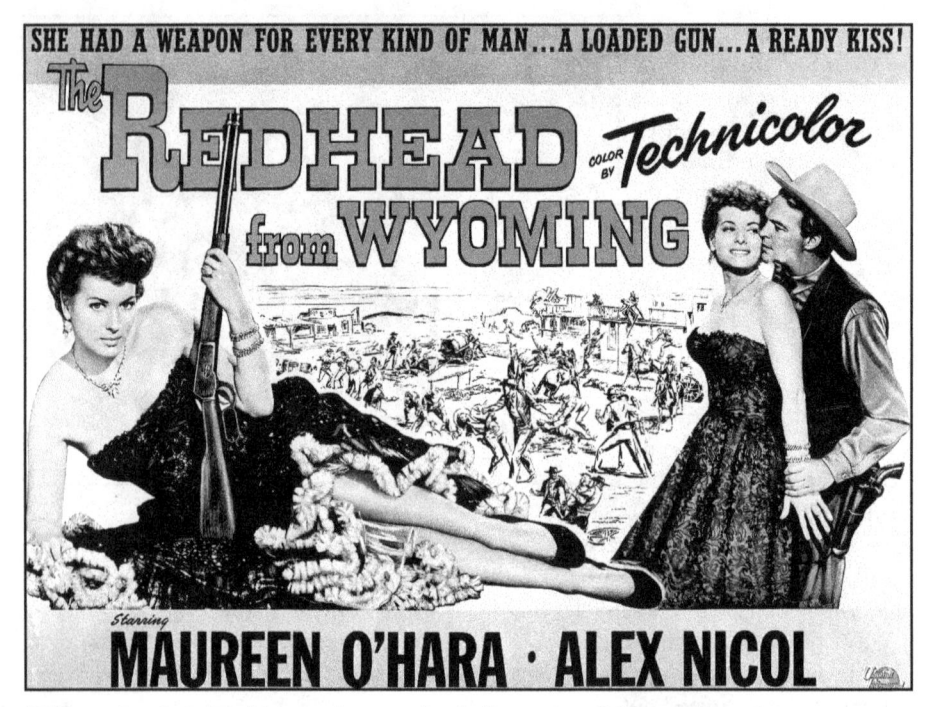

O'Hara, hoping that his connivances (including using O'Hara's brand to stamp over Scourby's) will result in a range war that will see him emerge as top dog. But the rat hasn't reckoned with the feminine wiles of his flame-haired, green-eyed partner, also boss of Kate's Place: She takes a shine to drifter-cum-sheriff of Sweetwater Alex Nicol, the pair (with a little help from her two-fisted minder, Robert Strauss) eventually foiling Bishops' murderous scheming when the smartly dressed dude brings in an army of gunslingers to wipe out Scourby's men, only to find the presumed "dead" settlers rising to their feet and covering every gunman in their rifle sights; following a furious shoot-out, Bishop and henchman Jack Kelly are shot dead and Nicol gallops off with O'Hara to play house on a piece of land he has his eyes on. Polly James and Herb Meadow's witty, complex script piles on the twists and turns, Herman Stein's music blasts forth, Winton C. Hoch's bright photography lights up the screen, Lee Sholem directs with purpose but above all else, O'Hara has a high old time of it. An absolute stunner in her prime, who else, in the words of the *New York Times*, could fight a range war wearing a strapless evening gown, just one of many gaudy outfits showcasing her curvaceous figure. The dame with attitude chews the scenery big time in a Western high on energy and action, a Universal-International winner that still makes for splendid rip-roaring entertainment over 60 years on.

Highlights:

O'Hara in full flow—where are the actresses of today who can claim to possess even one tenth of her glamor and charisma, not to mention her acting ability.

Dialogue:

Nicol to O'Hara, after she has been sprung from her cell: "You didn't spend much time in jail."

O'Hara, dressed to the nines: "Couldn't afford it, sheriff. Too many chores."

Ride, Vaquero!

MGM; Anscocolor; 90 minutes; Producer: Stephen Ames; Director: John Farrow; Cast: Robert Taylor; Anthony Quinn; Ava Gardner; Howard Keel; Kurt Kasznar; Ted de Corsia; Jack Elam; Charlita ****

"The Anthony Quinn show" said one critic of the hyperactive star's virtuoso performance as Mexican bandido boss José Constantino Esqueda; a wine bottle glued to his lips, Quinn bullies, shouts and wenches his way through an underrated Western, silent gunslinger Robert Taylor (Rio) his right-hand man. Quinn's script must have been 10 times the length of Taylor's: Clad in black, his gun belt, wrist cuffs and saddle embossed in silver studs, cold-as-ice Taylor doesn't say a great deal, a mysterious figure whose inner demons and motives are never fully revealed to anyone, including Ava Gardner, wife of rancher Howard Keel. When the black-haired beauty plants a kiss on those impassive features, he retreats into a shell, going it alone (Taylor's already quit Quinn's mob and joined up with Keel on a campaign to rope wild horses). The Civil War over, Quinn is afraid that law and order will make its way south to Texas, so the brigand plays rough, burning Keel's homestead to the ground, carrying out a similar action when Keel rebuilds his ranch (the attempt fails) and taking command of Brownsville ("I am the law!"), the sheriff and its citizens powerless to act, although Keel does try ("Murderer, thief, coward, scum!" he levels at grinning Quinn). The expected saloon showdown between Keel, Taylor and Quinn results in the bandit chief firing three slugs into Keel, seriously wounding him; Taylor calls Quinn out, the pair shooting each other dead. Keel forgives Gardner for having some feelings towards Taylor and, his wounds needing tending to, takes her home, just as the U.S. cavalry arrives to restore peace. A colorful, noisy picture (Bronislau Kaper's busy, evocative score is a delight), vividly filmed in Kanab, Utah (photographer: Robert Surtees), *Ride, Vaquero!* is as hot, greasy and sweaty as Quinn's unkempt, *almost* unlovable, Esqueda, dripping in period atmosphere; MGM made a decent profit, Taylor, Quinn and Gardner all big box-office draws at the time.

Highlights:

Quinn at his roisterous best; his wild performance contrasts sharply with taciturn Taylor's, a darker role for the popular Hollywood star.

Dialogue:

Taylor to Quinn: "What kind of miracle is this? You spittin' out wine."

Trivia:

Although married to Frank Sinatra, Gardner had an affair with director Farrow during filming; in 1966, Farrow's daughter, Mia, married the crooner, proving that in Hollywood, what goes around comes around!

Seminole

Universal; Technicolor; 87 minutes; Producer: Howard Christie; Director: Budd Boetticher; Cast: Rock Hudson; Barbara Hale; Richard Carlson; Anthony Quinn; Hugh O'Brian; Ralph Moody; Russell Johnson; James Best ***

In the Florida Everglades of 1835, Major Richard Carlson, commanding Fort King, plans to wipe out the Seminole tribes, even though Chief Osceola (Anthony Quinn) desires peace. Fresh from West Point, Lieutenant Rock Hudson fiercely opposes the martinet's actions, eventually leading to his court martial; Hudson relates his story to the judges, the events told in flashback. Quinn is half-Indian and a former friend of Hudson; when the dragoons enter the swamps to attack the Seminole village, hauling a cannon, Hudson is determined that it doesn't all end in bloodshed, even though Carlson, a Captain Bligh-like figure in a perpetual state of frenzy, drives his men to the brink of exhaustion, losing the cannon in a quicksand. Barbara Hale, sharing her affections between Hudson and Quinn (what a choice for a gal to have!) acts as a go-between and shaven-headed renegade Hugh O'Brian, fearsome in red and yellow war paint, organizes a surprise ambush behind Quinn's back, Hudson and Carlson both wounded, the men massacred; Hudson is carted off by the Indians for treatment and later accused of being a traitor. Quinn, flung into a pit on Carlson's orders when attempting to make peace, drowns in a cloudburst, Hudson charged with his murder after tussling with O'Brian in the flooded cage. On the day of Hudson's execution by firing squad, O'Brian and his braves surround the fort and take Quinn's body back for burial, the new Seminole chief telling the military hierarchy that he was responsible for Quinn's death and now wishes peace; Hudson is exonerated, a commission set up to investigate Carlson and his stricter-than-strict command methods. Russell Metty's vivid photography (the movie was shot in Florida's Everglades National Park) and an atmospheric soundtrack (during the middle section) composed of the din created by monkeys, birds and cicadas compensate for Quinn, resembling an Arabian prince, appearing slightly uncomfortable in his role, as does Hale and, occasionally, Hudson. Carlson, usually cast as a good guy, comes out on top as a man playing everything by the book, one step away from total madness.

Highlights:

The grueling struggle through the swamps, every actor looking the worse for wear.

Dialogue:

Carlson to Hudson: "Indians in the swamps are no different from Indians in the woods. And I'm an old hand at killing them."

Shark River

United Artists; Cinecolor; 80 minutes; Produced and Directed by John Rawlins; Cast: Steve Cochran; Carole Mathews; Warren Stevens; Robert Cunninghan; Spencer Fox; Ruth Foreman; Bill Piper ****

Filmed entirely in Florida's Everglades, *Shark River* had outlaw brothers Steve Cochran and Warren Stevens taking to dugout canoes and trekking through the creeks and swamps in the year 1869, hoping to get to the Gulf and build their own plantation in Cuba. With them is wounded Robert Cunningham who claims to possess the deeds to their new property. The trouble is, Cunningham has no deeds, and Cochran doesn't want to go, especially when they encounter Carole Mathews, a widow living in the bush with her son (Spencer Fox) and mother-in-law (Ruth Foreman). Mathews hungers for Cochran's manly embrace, Stevens fumes at the delays and Cunningham expires from his wound, Seminole Indians making life tough for all concerned. Foreman is killed, the remaining four heading east; in a fight, Stevens is brought down by an Indian bullet and dies in Cochran's arms, leaving Mathews, Fox and Cochran to walk off along a beach to start a new life together. A plethora of wildlife footage showing alligators, snakes and screeching birds make for an unusual, claustrophobic setting, photographed in dark color schemes by Stanley Cortez—one half expects Universal's gill-man to leap up from the silent waters at any given moment. Together with Irving Gertz's melodious, atmospheric score, *Shark River* is a refreshingly different rarity that warrants praise and is well worth seeking out.

Dialogue:
Cochran, wondering where their next meal is coming from: "Let us eat 'gator."
Stevens: "'Gator tail is full of solid meat."
Cochran: "'Gator's not gonna like it. I'll expect he'll object. The question is how?"

Son of Belle Starr

Allied Artists; Cinecolor; 70 minutes; Producer: Peter Scully; Director: Frank McDonald; Cast: Keith Larsen; Peggie Castle; Myron Healey; Dona Drake; James Seay; Lane Bradford; Robert Keys; Regis Toomey ***

Troubled Keith Larsen, half-Cherokee son of the West's most infamous female outlaw, was framed for a gold shipment robbery from the Griswald Mine 12 months ago. Now crooked Sheriff Myron Healey wants him in on an identical heist, $100,000 to be split five ways; "The Kid" agrees, hoping to flush out the fifth partner who appears

Westerns of the 1950s: The Classic Years 177

to be the connection behind the robberies. Is it either one of newspaper girl Peggie Castle's brothers, Regis Toomey and Robert Keys, or mine owner James Seay? Larsen participates in the holdup but, suspicious of a possible double-cross by Healey, Lane Bradford and Paul McGuire, hides some of the gold bars in an old mine tunnel, the remainder dumped over the side of a small ravine. With hot-blooded Mexican lass Dona Drake clinging to his shirt tails, Larsen, using the backwater of Florris Flats as a base, then sets out to find the identity of Mister Big and deal with him, outlaw style. Shot in shiny Cinecolor, Frank McDonald's "fugitive on the run" feature allows good-looking Larsen plenty of screen time and he makes the most of it, but it's the underrated Healey who steals the show, as he did in so many of the decade's minor Westerns. The mine entrance is dynamited with all of the gold inside and, back in town, Seay, who guns down Healey, turns out to be the chief baddie, knifed to death by Larsen in a livery stable tussle; fatally wounded, Belle Starr's son collapses in the street, letting the townsfolk know where the gold is before dying.

Dialogue:
Seay to worried Healey who's concerned that Larsen is on their tails: "You're not getting scared, are you?"
Healey: "No. But I don't like knives, especially when the kid's throwing 'em."

Son of the Renegade

United Artists; 58 minutes; Producer: Johnny Carpenter; Director: Reg Browne; Cast: Johnny Carpenter; Lori Irving; Joan McKellen; Valley Keene; Jack Ingram; Vern Teters; Bill Chaney; Ted Smile *

Was the contender for title of worst B-Western of the 1950s actually written by the King of the Awful, Edward D. Wood, Jr.? Some say so, although Johnny Carpenter is credited for the screenplay. Substitute 1933 for 1953 as a very wooden Carpenter ("Look, fella, why you wanna have trouble with me?"), son of the notorious Red River Johnny (we see his exploits in the first 15 minutes) attempts to regain his father's property with the oddest assemblage of characters ever to hit the Old West, harassed on all sides by one Bat Masters (Vern Teters) and Three-Fingers Jack (Jack Ingram): Wild Bill Coontz; Cherokee; Baby Face Bill; Canada; The Long-Haired Kid; Big Fred; The Australian Kid; The Texas Kid; even Wild Bill Hickok; and two gals, Dusty (white) and Valley (Indian):

everyone involved in clumsily choreographed fights, corny dialogue, erratic continuity and situations, riding over the same old ramp-like trail time and time again and, when it comes to biting the dust (as most do), overacting like crazy (as opposed to all the bad acting that has gone before), not to mention irrelevant shots of cowboys breaking in buckin' broncos. The mass shoot-out at the end has to be seen to be believed, the whole cockamamie enterprise rounded off by Pat McGeehan's monosyllabic narration and Darrell Calker's "let's chuck everything into the mix" score. In a year that produced *Shane*, *Hondo*, *The Naked Spur* and a clutch of Randolph Scott/Audie Murphy/George Montgomery classics, *Son of the Renegade* is to Westerns what Howco's *Mesa of Lost Women* was to horror cinema, only worth seeing for its novelty value and nothing else.

Dialogue:
Bill Chaney to Teters: "Bat. The more I hear the sicker I get. An' Bat. If you don't holster that gun, I'm gonna put a hole in you that you could ride a stagecoach through."

Trivia:
Reg Browne's one and only feature film, produced on a budget of $17,500.

The Stand at Apache River

Universal; Technicolor; 77 minutes; Producer: William Alland; Director: Lee Sholem; Cast: Stephen McNally; Julia Adams; Hugh Marlowe; Jaclynne Greene; Russell Johnson; Jack Kelly; Edgar Barrier; Hugh O'Brian ***

Take a tough, no-nonsense sheriff (Stephen McNally) and his captive (Russell Johnson); a martinet, Indian-hating army colonel (Hugh Marlowe); two women dissatisfied with their partners (Julia Adams and Jaclynne Greene); and an Apache chief (Edgar Barrier) who refuses to keep the peace, and what you get is a bog-standard Universal oater that rattles through its 77 minutes in entertaining, if not memorable, fashion. This quarrelsome, disparate bunch are snared like rabbits in the remote Apache River Station by 50 Redskins who have broken out of the San Carlos reservation, murdered three settlers and have come looking for food; the place is reached by a barge, and it's a case of who makes it and who doesn't when the hostiles attack. Everyone has his/her personal hang-ups, not helped when Barrier, wounded, is brought in as prisoner; Greene's husband, Hugh O'Brian, appears, torpedoing her plans to run off with station manager Jack Kelly, the pair reuniting but perishing when the blazing roof of a barn falls in on them. Marlowe is killed in a skirmish and the Redskins exterminated in a series of shoot-outs except for Barrier who wanders off, the stage arriving just as Adams decides to make a new life for herself with McNally. Focusing more on human drama than straightforward cowboys versus Indians action, Lee Sholem's brisk little feature highlights the fact that, while not being up there with the greats, McNally was perfectly capable of carrying a Western on his broad shoulders, even though his repertoire fluctuated between a scowl and a half-grin most of the time.

Highlights:
   A striking shot of the station overshadowed by a vast wall of red rock.

Dialogue:
McNally to Marlowe: "I think killing Apaches is something you like to do."

Trivia:
   Douglas Sirk assisted with the direction but didn't receive a credit.

The Tall Texan

Lippert Pictures; 84 minutes; Producers: Robert L. Lippert, Jr. and T.F. Woods; Director: Elmo Williams; Cast: Lloyd Bridges; Marie Windsor; Lee J. Cobb; Luther Adler; Syd Saylor; Samuel Herrick; George Steele; Dean Train ****

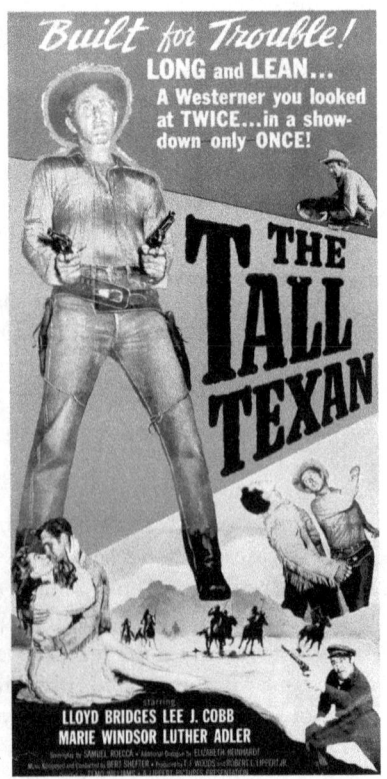

"Long, Lean and Lethal" Lloyd Bridges boards a wagon bound for El Paso in handcuffs. The wagon picks up wounded Indian George Steele and is attacked by Steele's tribe; the wagon overturns, Marie Windsor's beau Dean Train suffers a broken neck and Steele promises to lead them on foot to gold deposits in a river if he can keep an Indian pony. Once at the rock-strewn site, *The Tall Texan* turns into a tale about the lust for gold. Bridges' cuffs come off, allowing him to pan on his own; Windsor attracts the attention of Captain Lee J. Cobb, but she falls for Bridges; Sheriff Samuel Herrick is determined to bring his prisoner in to stand trial for a murder he says he never committed; immoral trader Luther Adler wants to hunt for gold in a nearby Indian burial ground; and Syd Saylor has no luck in his fruitless search for the yellow dust. Filmed around New Mexico's arid City of Rocks State Park (stark photography from Joseph F. Biroc), Lippert's pared-to-the-bone Western, produced on a $102,000 budget, is a tightly constructed yarn that mirrors the harshness of the surroundings these disparate characters find themselves caught up in, Bert Shefter's menacing score adding to the tension. As expected, Bridges gallops off to El Paso after Windsor in the final reel, Indians having picked off the rest of the party (Adler has murdered Saylor for his gold watch), enraged at Sadler encroaching on sacred ground for nuggets—and Cobb sacrifices himself by allowing Bridges to reunite with Windsor. An engrossing B-oater handled admirably by the small cast that, if made by a bigger company with more resources, might have become a classic of its kind.

Dialogue:
Adler to Saylor, both busy panning: "What'ya gettin', Carney?"
Saylor: "Sand fleas and sore knees."

The Vanquished

Paramount; Technicolor; 84 minutes; Producers: William H. Pine and William C. Thomas; Director: Edward Ludwig; Cast: John Payne; Jan Sterling; Coleen Gray; Lyle Bettger; Willard Parker; Roy Gordon; Charles Evans; John Dierkes **

It's "battle of the decorative sexy dames" time as doctor's daughter Coleen Gray clashes with ambitious white trash Jan Sterling over the masculine charms of Southerner John Payne. Payne has returned to Galeston after serving 18 months in a Union prison hospital to find the town under martial law, his family mansion taken over by civil administrator Lyle Bettger. Noose-happy Bettger (when did the actor play anything else *but* a rat?) rules Galeston with an iron fist, Sterling his mistress who's not afraid to flaunt her wares in front of Payne. Payne adopts secret tactics to bring about Bettger's downfall, falling in with the crook and making himself unpopular with Galeston's downtrodden citizens by becoming a tax collector, evicting those from their properties who can't or won't pay; it's the only way, he reckons, to unmask Bettger as the unscrupulous louse he is. A convoluted screenplay plus Lucien Cailliet's over-busy score thundering away in the background add up to a pretty-to-look-at but contrived mess, shades of *Gone With the Wind* creeping into the plot as Sterling overacts like a second-rate Scarlett O'Hara, two-timing Bettger and draping her luscious body all over Payne, much to Gray's annoyance (she's Payne's childhood sweetheart). Payne is framed for the murder of General Charles Evans, an investigative inspector from the main tax office who has arrived in town to "clean out the scum," and that includes Bettger; Gray and Sterling engage in a catfight with scissors and Sterling shoots Bettger in the back in a rowdy climax, claiming all his worldly goods which now amount to nothing. Payne is cleared of Evans' murder, kissing Gray in the closing seconds. All rather flashy and a bit stodgy, the lovely Jan Sterling about the only thing to keep audiences (the male contingent!) watching.

Dialogue:
Sterling to Payne, dropping her off in the street: "I can't come upstairs with you. It wouldn't be proper."
Payne: "Not only that. I haven't asked you."
Sterling: "You might. Some day."

War Arrow

Universal; Technicolor; 78 minutes; Producer: John W. Rogers; Director: George Sherman; Cast: Jeff Chandler; Maureen O'Hara; John McIntire; Henry Brandon; Noah Beery, Jr.; Charles Drake; Suzan Ball; Jay Silverheels ****

The Kiowas are on the warpath in Texas and Major Jeff Chandler's solution to the problem is to enlist Henry Brandon's Seminoles ("Four tribes of vagabonds."), at present peaceful but wandering aimlessly and, deep down, thirsting for some good old action, train them in the use of repeating rifles and trench warfare and use them to put an end to the Kiowa menace; their reward will be bountiful supplies and a new hunting ground. Martinet John McIntire, commander of Fort Clark, only partly agrees, mistrusting the Indians and thinking the plan a failure; besides, he's jealous of the attention given to Chandler by Maureen O'Hara (never looking lovelier) whose husband went missing some time ago. A big success for Universal at the time, *War Arrow* never lets up on the intrigue and set pieces, Chandler and his two sergeant buddies (Noah Beery, Jr. and Charles Drake) an engaging trio, Arizona's Nogales region an eye-catching backdrop to the numerous skirmishes which result in an Alamo-type mass attack on the fort by Jay Silverheels' Kiowa warriors led by O'Hara's missing husband, Jim Bannon. A Confederate, he resents the Union army and this is his way of getting back at the Bluecoats. McIntire, treating the Seminoles' like scum, is forced to eat humble pie at the end ("Never have I been so wrong.") when Silverheels and his tribe are defeated, Chandler riding off with O'Hara, her husband having succumbed to a Kiowa bullet.

Highlights:
The prolonged assault on Fort Clark, a real barnstormer; and O'Hara's radiant, green-eyed features.

Dialogue:
McIntire, scoffing at Chandler's suggestion to utilize the Seminoles inbuilt fighting qualities: "You couldn't get a Seminole Indian to fight for his sister's virtue."

Trivia:
Suzan Ball, who played Indian lass Avis, was Lucille Ball's second cousin, and only made one feature film after *War Arrow* (Universal's *Chief Crazy Horse*); suffering tumors on her right leg which had to be amputated, she died of lung cancer on August 5, 1955, aged only 21.

War Paint

Bel-Air/United Artists; Pathécolor; 89 minutes; Producer: Howard W. Koch; Director: Lesley Selander; Cast: Robert Stack; Joan Taylor; Charles McGraw; Peter Graves; Robert J. Wilke; Keith Larsen; Walter Reed; Douglas Kennedy *****

Lieutenant Robert Stack heads a detail of bedraggled troops over arid Death Valley, determined to deliver a peace treaty to Chief Gray Cloud in six days. Trouble comes in the form of the chief's son, Taslig (Keith Larsen) who, thirsting for war, takes them on a merry dance while adorned in war paint. Larsen's sister Wanima (Joan Taylor in fetching buckskins, looking highly desirable) tails them, sabotaging their water supply and running off their horses; and disgruntled foot soldier Peter Graves nurses a grudge against Stack's strict military stance when the odds are stacked against the patrol delivering the treaty, the going more hostile and tougher by the hour. One trooper dies in agony after drinking poisoned water and Douglas Kennedy is killed by Taylor who in turn is captured; Graves then callously shoots Larsen in the back and an old Spanish gold mine is reached, leading to a climactic showdown between Graves' supporters (greedy for gold) and Stack and McGraw. Following a savage fistfight, Graves lies sprawled in the dust, a knife in his back; Stack and Taylor, the two survivors, get to the Indian camp to deliver the precious treaty. Whether the stern-faced officer will head back to his fort (his wife apparently hates the West) or into the arms of seductive Taylor is anyone's guess. Lesley Selander's grim, unsentimental "men on a mission" feature is a masterpiece of Western minimalism, with outstanding Death Valley scenery harshly lit by Gordon Avil (you can feel the heat burning through the screen), Arthur Lange and Emil Newman's thumping marching score moving the action along nicely. And Taylor, without doubt, is the sexiest-looking squaw in B-Western history—or in *any* Western!

Highlights:
Stack and Graves' ferocious set-to at the movie's end, plus vivid location work in California's Death Valley; Joan Taylor's charms are an added bonus.

Dialogue:
Robert J. Wilke, gulping back water after days of not tasting a drop: "Ah! I never thought I'd find anything I like better than a woman!"

Trivia:
Most of the crew fell victim to mild sunstroke during the two-week shoot.

Woman They Almost Lynched

Republic; 90 minutes; Produced and Directed by Allan Dwan; Cast: John Lund; Audrey Trotter; Brian Donlevy; Joan Leslie; Ben Cooper; Jim Davis; Nina Varela; Reed Hadley ****

Two rootin' tootin' ladies for the price of one as blonde Audrey Trotter (Kate Quantrill) goes head-to-head with brunette saloon owner Joan Leslie, not quite the demure-looking lass she appears to be. In 1865, the Civil War rages on but Border City, positioned across the North-South state line, remains neutral, a crime-ridden town populated by renegades and murderers ("A sanctuary for the flotsam and jetsam of humanity."), a place "too tough for lace petticoats and pink ribbons" where stern-faced spinster Nina Varela dishes out hangings at the swish of her black dress. "Ma. I wanna see the hangin'. I ain't ever see a man hung," pesters a kid to his mother, showing the huge change in society over the intervening century and just one example of Steve Fisher's witty script. Outraged at seeing a nice young lieutenant gunned down by Quantrill's Raiders during a stage holdup, Leslie makes it to town, meeting her debt-ridden brother (Reed Hadley) in his saloon. In a fracas, Hadley, on the prod, is shot dead by Confederate sympathizer John Lund, Leslie forced into taking up the ownership reins, reopening the joint and falling for Lund in the process ("I'm now the honky-tonk queen!"). In rides Quantrill (Brian Donlevy) and his outfit, demanding that Lund hands over the lease to a lead mine he owns in exchange for Yankee gold; Jim Davis (Cole Younger) sets his sights on Leslie ("I bet a kiss from you would be like a kick from a mule.") while young Ben Cooper (Jesse James) struts around sporting double guns, putting the fear of God into everyone. But it's in the various overwrought confrontations between fiery Trotter and just-as-fiery Leslie that the movie rises to delicious heights in female jealousy ("You vile murderess!" Leslie spits at her); the two have a saloon catfight ("This is a better fight than the North and the South."), Leslie pummeling her rival senseless and later outdrawing her in a street showdown. When Union soldiers arrive in Border City, the narrative descends into bedlam at times; Trotter and Leslie make up, there's a furious shoot-out between the troops and Donlevy's boys, Lund is badly wounded and Leslie arrested as a spy, earmarked for a lynching by Varela. Leslie is freed from the rope on Trotter's evidence; the Quantrill lady then gallops away to start a new life (she's last heard of singing in New Orleans), leaving Border City to celebrate the end of the war and for Leslie and Lund to tie the knot. Hugely enjoyable nonsense!

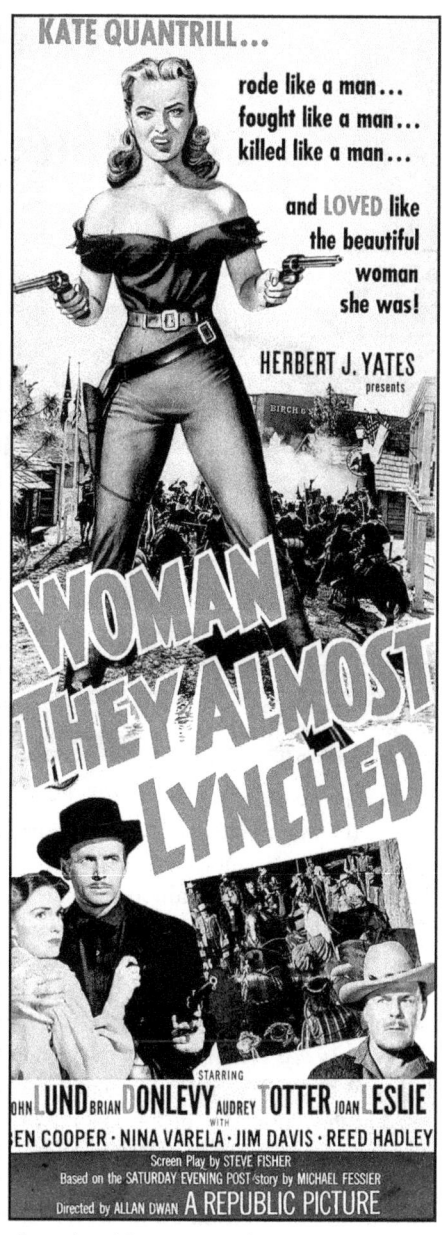

Dialogue:
Donlevy to Trotter who's been wounded in a gunfight with Leslie: "Why don't you give up? She fights better than you, she shoots better than you, she talks better than you." Davis: "Yeah, I bet she even cooks better than you!"

Trivia:
Donlevy had played Quantrill once before, in the Audie Murphy Western *Kansas Raiders* (Universal, 1950).

Chapter 7

Tim Holt at RKO-Radio

Son of famous silent cowboy star Jack Holt, Tim was born Charles John Holt on February 5, 1919 in Beverly Hills, Los Angeles, making his film debut at the age of nine in Paramount's 1928 production *The Vanishing Pioneer* alongside father Jack. Holt, Jr. always bragged to his classmates that one day, he would be as famous as his dad, practicing hard with toy revolvers to perfect his drawing technique. Holt kicked off his career as a Westerner in 1938, starring in RKO-Radio's *The Renegade Ranger*. He made a name for himself in RKO's *The Law West of Tombstone* in the same year, and the company signed him in 1939, the versatile, youthful-looking actor appearing in big prestige pictures such as *The Magnificent Ambersons* (1942), *My Darling Clementine* (1946) and *The Treasure of the Sierra Madre* (1948). Holt also achieved a distinguished military career during the war, flying as a B-29 bombardier and wounded on the last day of the Pacific conflict while on a mission over Tokyo; he was decorated several times and awarded the Purple Heart. But his main forte still remained the B-Western, in which he continually starred right up to 1952 when, disillusioned with the low-budget Western format (most of his films from 1950 onwards lost money) and suffering health-wise through having experienced a catalogue of serious movie-related injuries during his stint in the saddle, he quit the industry, returning from semi-retirement in 1957 to star in United Artists' *The Monster that Challenged the World*, one of the '50s finest of all creature-features. Very little was heard from him after that date, Holt dying from bone cancer on February 15, 1973 at the tender age of 54. His RKO B-oaters are standard matinée-morning stuff, all produced on budgets of around $90,000 but given extra bite by having directors in the driving seat who were expert at pulling it off in 60 minutes, with the added bonus of a decent score from Paul Sawtell and attractive location work boasting excellent cinematography. They make for entertaining, thick-ear trail bustin' action, ideal cowboy fodder for a good night in. All films are listed in order of release.

1950
Riders of the Range

RKO-Radio; 60 minutes; Producer: Herman Schlom; Director: Lesley Selander; Cast: Tim Holt; Richard Martin; Jacqueline White; Reed Hadley; Robert Barrat; Robert Clarke; Tom Tyler; William Tannen ***

The first of 16 low-budget RKO Westerns Tim Holt (packing two six-guns but always running out of cartridges) made in the 1950s, all featuring Richard Martin as his Mexican/Irish/Spanish lady-killing saddle pal Chito Jose Gonzales Bustamonte Rafferty (they first met in 1947's *Thunder Mountain*), we see him pitting his wits against saloon owner Reed Hadley in Cedar Hill, Arizona. Jacqueline White's brother, Robert Clarke, has IOU's amounting to $3,000 and Hadley suggests he rustles some of his sister's cattle to pay off the debt. The Ringo Kid (veteran movie heavy Tom Tyler) is hired at a cost of $1,000, the rustlers, led by henchman William Tannen, are foiled, Tyler grabs another $3,000 from Hadley and loses it in a tussle with Holt (playing Kansas Jones) and Martin, the duo taken on as cow punchers by White. When Sheriff Robert Barrat finds Tyler's cash, in Hadley's wallet, on Martin, the fast-talking dude and Holt are blamed for Hadley's death at the hands of Tyler who (yep!) had stolen *another* $3,000, the money that White paid for her brother's IOU's. Sixty minutes rattle by in this fast-paced programmer shot around California's attractive San Bernardino Forest, the action propelled by Paul Sawtell's lively score, a mass shoot-out at Tyler's bolthole wrapping things up nicely, Martin reunited with his lucky peso.

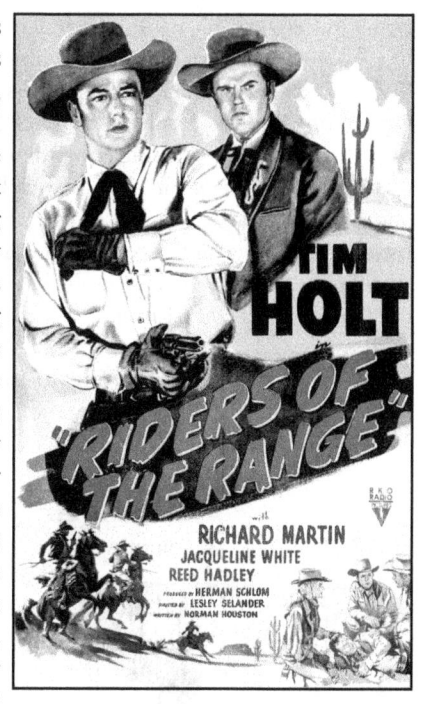

Dialogue:
Martin to Barrat. "My amigo and me, we are always together, side by each."

Trivia:
Holt and Tyler both appeared in *Stagecoach* (UA, 1939) in which John Wayne found stardom playing the Ringo Kid; Martin starred as his Chito Rafferty character in 33 movies, 29 of them with Tim Holt.

Dynamite Pass

RKO-Radio; 61 minutes; Producer: Herman Schlom; Director: Lew Landers; Cast: Tim Holt; Richard Martin; Lynne Roberts; Regis Toomey; John Dehner; Robert Shayne; Don C. Harvey; Ross Elliott
***

In Mesa City, New Mexico, Regis Toomey's attempts at constructing a serviceable, toll-free road to neighboring Clifton are thwarted by greedy rancher John Dehner. The rogue has erected his own toll barrier, charging those who pass through extortionate fees, Toomey's corrupt boss, Robert Shayne, in on the deal; Dehner's bent on sabotaging Toomey's efforts to line his own pockets. Frustrated Toomey hits the whiskey bottle, his wife (Lynne Roberts) hiring Tim Holt (Ross Taylor) and Richard Martin to act as guards to protect precious surveying equipment needed for the job. Filmed among Lone Pine's rocky terrain, *Dynamite Pass* moves, well, like dynamite, baddies Ross Elliott, Denver Pyle and Don C. Harvey coming up against Holt and Martin's six-guns and Holt's handy fists. It ends in one almighty shoot-out, Dehner's skunks against our two heroes and the sheriff's posse after Toomey's wagon has avoided being blown to bits. The plot is simplicity itself, but you still get 61 minutes-worth of rollicking cowboy action for your money.

Dialogue:
Sheriff Don Haggerty, refusing to believe that Dehner is planning to dynamite Toomey's wagon: "Dynamite my eye."
Martin: "I'd like to!"

Storm Over Wyoming

RKO-Radio; 61 minutes; Producer: Herman Schlom; Director: Lesley Selander; Cast: Tim Holt; Richard Martin; Bill Kennedy; Kenneth MacDonald; Tom Keene; Noreen Nash; Betty Underwood; Mike Ragan ****

In a twist on the old storyline, that of cattle versus sheep, the sheepmen are the baddies in Lesley Selander's action-filled oater, trying to force cattle rancher Kenneth MacDonald off his land; Bill Kennedy, foreman of the Big M sheep ranch, is the villain, causing mayhem with both guns and lynching ropes behind his boss' back, planning to sell the flocks across the Colorado border to feather his own nest—and his boss (Noreen Nash) happens to be a very good-looking dame. Tim Holt (Dave Saunders) and Richard "Chito" Martin are hired by MacDonald to protect his interests in Sundown Valley and to prevent him being labeled a rustler, womanizing Martin pursued by man-hungry dancer/singer Betty Underwood throughout the entire length of the picture. The more modern world of ballistics enters the frame, Holt determined to prove that the slug that killed herder Mike Ragan came from Kennedy's rifle, not his six-gun; there's a blazing shoot-out in the final reel when Nash and Holt are cornered in dense brushwood by Kennedy's boys, Chito bringing in MacDonald's cattle hands to mop things up. Kennedy is jailed and we last see Martin being chased by Underwood who has marriage on her mind—he doesn't! A polished effort from Selander, with J. Roy Hunt's sharp black-and-white photography and Paul Sawtell's thundering score adding to an

exciting hour-long B-feature, one of Holt's best from this period.
Dialogue:
Holt to MacDonald, watching Underwood chase after Martin into the distance: "Looks like Chito's got a tiger by the tail and can't let go of it."

Rider from Tucson

RKO-Radio; 60 minutes; Producer: Herman Schlom; Director: Lesley Selander; Cast: Tim Holt; Richard Martin; Elaine Riley; Douglas Fowley; Veda Ann Borg; Robert Shayne; Marshall Reed; William Phipps ****

Commencing with Tim Holt (Dave Saunders again!) and "Chito" Martin displaying their skills (or lack of them in Martin's case) at the Tucson Rodeo Fair, the two saddle pals travel to Oro Grande, Colorado, where acquaintance William Phipps is in fear of his life. He's due to marry Elaine Riley but worried about her safety as claim jumpers are after his hidden diggings and will do anything to lay their hands on the site. Hard-faced blonde Veda Ann Borg, weak hubbie Robert Shayne, cohort Marshall Reed and no-good Douglas Fowley—all cross each other in an attempt to possess the whereabouts of that reputedly rich mine. Riley is abducted by Fowley on Borg's orders but freed by Holt and Martin, Borg drills Fowley through a window at her Sycamore Canyon Ranch, Holt is blamed for the killing and Phipps is forced at gunpoint to ride out to Chimney Rock and disclose the whereabouts of his working to the lady and her scallywags; following a shoot-out among rocks, crusty old gold miner Harry Tyler joining in on the action, Borg and Shayne are arrested by the sheriff and Phipps gets to marry his sweetheart. An industrous 60 minutes, notable for cinematographer Nicholas Musuraca's wonderful deep-focus pictorial views of Lone Pine's lofty Alabama Hills region and Paul Sawtell's standard but right-on-the-button Western soundtrack.

Dialogue:
Confirmed bachelor Martin to Phipps and Holt at the wedding reception: "I don't understand you Americanos. You get married and you call that lucky!"

Border Treasure

RKO-Radio; 60 minutes; Producer: Herman Schlom; Director: George Archainbaud; Cast: Tim Holt; Richard Martin; John Doucette; Jane Nigh; House Peters, Jr.; Inez Cooper; Julian Rivero; Kenneth MacDonald ****

Azteca, Mexico is hit by an earthquake. Mexican lady Inez Cooper organizes a relief fund for victims of the catastrophe; House Peters, Jr. casts his greedy eyes over the treasure being amassed and gallops back to Los Alamos to inform crooked saloon owner John Doucette, the pair planning to steal the hoard when it enters Spanish Pass.

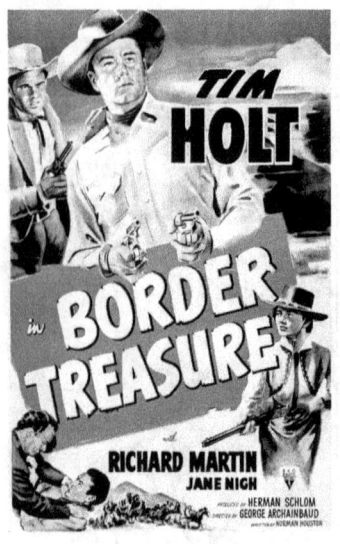

The customary seven-minute opener done and dusted, wranglers Tim Holt (Ed Porter) and Richard Martin ride into Los Alamos where Lothario Martin is rebuffed by ex-flame singer Jane Nigh, also in on Doucette's deal. Doucette is arrested by Sheriff Kenneth MacDonald after a bruising fight with Holt, leaving it clear for Peters to take command of the gang and grab those golden goodies, hiding them in a ranch house. But self-preening Nigh cannot help flaunting a stolen necklace, alerting Holt as to who is behind the robbery. Doucette busts out of jail and turns up at the ranch, reinstating himself as leader; in a furious shoot-out with Holt, Martin and a posse, Doucette shoots Peters in the back and is then slugged unconscious by Holt, Nigh and the gang arrested; the treasure is finally on its way for a more deserving cause. Less paint-by-numbers than others in the series, *Border Treasure* is directed with vim and features, as usual, pristine photography of the Lone Pine Hills from J. Roy Hunt, a rousing Paul Sawtell score and solid performances from the cast, although "Chito" Martin's nonstop flirting with anyone wearing a skirt does get a bit tiresome at times.

Dialogue:
Doucette, pointing a gun at Martin: "We're looking for mules."
Martin: "Mules? Are my ears that long?"

Rio Grande Patrol

RKO-Radio; 60 minutes; Producer: Herman Schlom; Director: Lesley Selander; Cast: Tim Holt; Richard Martin; Jane Nigh; Douglas Fowley; John Holland; Cleo Moore; Rick Vallin; Larry Johns ****

Laredo's saloon owner John Holland is smuggling machine guns over the Mexican border, the weapons capable of firing off 400 shots a minute. Scarred bad guy Douglas Fowley offers to buy them for $3,000 each, not the $5,000 asking price, but on the condition he arranges to bump off snooping border patrol hombres, Tim Holt and Richard "Chito" Martin. Holland hides the guns under the floor of his office, singer Jane Nigh, busy putting her four new dancing gals through their paces, gets suspicious, dancer Cleo Moore sees a marriage prospect in Chito (he doesn't!) and slit-eyed Tom Tyler is handed the job of eliminating Holt (Kansas Jones) and Martin, which he bungles. Filmed around the Ray Corrigan Ranch in California's Simi Valley, *Rio Grande Patrol* looks great and is expertly handled by Lesley Selander, containing amusing lines courtesy of Norman Houston (Moore to Martin after he's given her his full name: "What a mouthful." Martin, taking in her blonde features: "What an eyeful!"), attractive song and dance numbers from lovely Nigh and her leggy, bottom-wiggling troupe and several blazing shoot-outs, Holt's horse Lightning (which he used throughout the series) stealing the show at one point. An excellent Tim Holt oater with one gaping plot hole. Towards the end, Holt, on Lightning, tails Holland in his rig and is captured by Fowley's jackals. In the last few seconds, he mentions taking Holland, who's apparently in jail, to Texas. What happened to the villain in the interim period?

Dialogue:
Martin to Doc Larry Johns who reckons wounded Rick Vallin will pull through from his gunshot wound: "Oh, I've been paralyzed sometimes and the next morning, I wish I was dead."
Holt: "Sometimes you act like you are!"

Trivia:
"The Queen of the B-Movie Bad Girls," Moore tragically died from a heart attack a week before her 49th birthday, on October 25, 1973.

1951
Law of the Badlands

RKO-Radio; 59 minutes; Producer: Herman Schlom; Director: Lesley Selander; Cast: Tim Holt; Richard Martin; Joan Dixon; Robert Livingston; Leonard Penn; Harry Woods; Larry Johns; Kenneth MacDonald ***

In Washington, 1890, state officials are concerned over the amount of counterfeit notes flooding the country. The source seems to come from Texas, so Texas Rangers Tim Holt (Dave Saunders) and "Chito" Martin are ordered to go to the town of Willcox, rendezvous with undercover agent Harry Woods, who is relaying messages to his boss via carrier pigeon, and unearth the crooks responsible ("It's like looking for a haystack in a needle," complains work-shy Martin). In Badland, a town bereft of any law, rancher Leonard Penn is using the talents of forger Larry Johns to smuggle out the notes in sacks of grain, $60,000 worth of cash stacked in his barn. Penn hires Holt and Martin, posing as wanted outlaws, much to the anger of heavies Robert Livingston and Robert Bray who reckon the two newcomers ain't who they're supposed to be. A planned robbery on Willcox's newspaper office for supplies of ink and paper is scuppered by our two heroes, Joan Dixon (the new "fluff" in town) appears as a saloon singer, intent on getting Martin to settle down (a lost cause!). Woods is shot dead after being found out, the forgery plates are discovered in Johns' store and Lesley Selander tops off the proceedings with a noisy, smoke-filled shoot-out between Penn's buzzards, Holt and Martin and Captain Kenneth MacDonald's troopers. "I am through with women," says Martin as Dixon prepares to dig her claws into him; no chance of that happening!

Dialogue:
Dixon to Martin: "You have more girls than a dog has fleas."

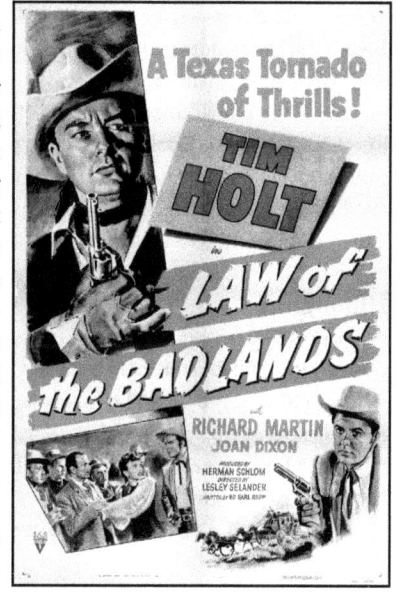

Saddle Legion

RKO-Radio; 60 minutes; Producer: Herman Schlom; Director: Lesley Selander; Cast: Tim Holt; Richard Martin; Dorothy Malone; Cliff Clark; Robert Livingston; Mauritz Hugo; James Bush; Robert J. Wilke *****

Tim Holt (Dave Saunders) and Richard Martin, looking for work, prevent cattle rancher Cliff Clark's herd from stampeding over a cliff, the result of obstreperous, drunken cow puncher James Bush (a marvelous performance) shooting at an empty whiskey bottle *and* his boss. The pair hired for their efforts, Clark is taken to Doctor Dorothy Malone for treatment—and Romeo Martin, spotting decorative Malone alight from her buggy, likes what he sees! Troublemaker Bush, meanwhile, crosses the border into San Lenore, where corrupt saloon owner Mauritz Hugo is planning to steal Clark's beef by murdering a cattle inspector due on Clark's spread and getting Robert Livingston to impersonate him; Livingston will then lie about the cattle being infected by Blackleg, the steers will be taken to Box Canyon and eventually herded across the border into Mexico, to be sold at profit. The ruse works at first, the cattle falsely classed as condemned, but Holt becomes suspicious, leading to several brawls with Bush and fellow henchman Robert J. Wilke. Malone proves to be Livingston's undoing after swotting up on the Blackleg disease, the chief inspector arriving on the scene to back Holt's claim that Livingston is a fraud. In a blazing showdown in the canyon, Hugo shoots Bush, Holt takes care of Wilke and ranchers headed by Clark force Hugo and his men to surrender, just as Holt runs out of bullets (which he was always doing). Probably the finest of all Tim Holt's '50s oaters, *Saddle Legion* is a blueprint of how a B-Western should be made. Director Lesley Selander doesn't waste a single second of celluloid, expertly composing his actors and views in carefully framed shots while ensuring the pace flows, as if he was working on much higher finances than $80,000. It's a joy for all cinemagoers of a certain age to watch, a masterclass in low-budget filming, J. Roy Hunt's glistening monochrome photography highlighting the rugged wooded scenery around California's Garner Ranch, Paul Sawtell's score nailing the proceedings beautifully and Ed Earl Repp providing a witty script (Holt to Martin: "Your guitar playing's improving, Chito. Even the cows are liking it!"). All this *and* Dorothy Malone—what more can a B-Western movie buff ask for?

Highlights:

Frame by frame, *Saddle Legion* looks the business, an archetypal example of the 1950s 60-minute trail buster *and* of Lesley Selander's overlooked talent; if made in color, it would have been a classic of its type.

Dialogue:

Holt to Martin, seeing Malone for the first time: "Thought I sent you for the doctor."
Martin: "She *is* the doctor."
Holt to Malone: "I'm sorry. I thought Chito had gone on the prowl again."

Gunplay

RKO-Radio; 61 minutes; Producer: Herman Schlom; Director: Lesley Selander; Cast: Tim Holt; Richard Martin; Joan Dixon; Harper Carter; Mauritz Hugo; Robert Bice; Robert J. Wilke; Marshall Reed ****

Hired as hands by Joan Dixon, Tim Holt (as Tim Holt this time around, and for the remainder of the series) and "Chito" Martin come to the aid of young Chip (played by 11-year-old Harper Carter) after his father (Robert Bice) has been found hanging from a tree. Bice went into Orodale to confront bigwig Mauritz Hugo, a crook who swindled him out of a fortune 12 years back. Bice demanded everything Hugo had amassed over the years; Hugo gave him $2,000 on account, then ordered Robert J. Wilke and two heavies to string him up. Dixon takes the lad into her care, but Hugo, on learning that Bice had a son, drums up papers enabling him to adopt the boy to keep his past, and Bice's murder, a secret. However, Carter, handy with a firearm and detesting his new father (and especially his striped pyjamas!), sides with Holt and Martin in bringing the rat to justice, an incriminating photograph found in Hugo's room showing him to be the elusive "Matt Potter" that Bice rode into town to meet. Carter springs his two buddies from behind bars after they're jailed for disorderly conduct by prizing open the floor to their cell; Hugo shoots Wilke and boards the stage to Arizona City where Dixon is taking that picture for verification of his true identity. Holt and Chito hold up the stage, Hugo is slugged, arrested and forced to walk back into town while Carter, reunited with Dixon, is packed off to military school—Holt doesn't want him turning out to be like Chito, Carter's idol! Number nine in the Holt/Martin series showed no signs of flagging or loss of quality, an entertaining package boosted by a charming performance from child actor Carter and the continuing buddy-buddy chemistry existing between the two leads.

Dialogue:
Carter, armed with a shotgun, to Dixon, told to lay his blond mop low as Hugo's jackals blaze away at the ranch: "How'm I gonna pick off those buzzards if I get my head down?"
Trivia:
Carter made three films as a child actor, three more as an adult, then quit the industry for the world of big business and high finance.

Pistol Harvest

RKO-Radio; 60 minutes; Producer: Herman Schlom; Director: Lesley Selander; Cast: Tim Holt; Richard Martin; Joan Dixon; Robert Clarke; Robert J. Wilke; Mauritz Hugo; Edward Hearn; Harper Carter ***

Richard "Chito Jose Gonzales Bustamonte Rafferty" Martin doesn't chase a single female; Tim Holt is getting married, giving up a life on the trail with his pal; Holt and Martin don't appear until the ninth minute; and arch Western villain Robert J. Wilke is *almost* (but not quite) a good guy! Yes, it was all change of a sort in *Pistol Harvest*, perhaps an attempt to try something different for a change. Stranded from their wagon train in the windswept wilds, young brother and sister Harper Carter and Joan Freeman become separated, Freeman rescued by a stranger. Fifteen years later, Freeman (now Joan Dixon) lives with her rescuer, rancher Edward Hearn, who has just sold cattle for $30,000, the money to be used in buying a ranch for Dixon and Tim Holt, engaged to be married. Shipping company owner Mauritz Hugo, his eyes on a steamboat, wants that 30 grand, instructing penniless drifters Robert Clarke and Wilke to grab the cash from Holt and Martin; the attempt fails, Clarke and Wilke demanding another $100 from Hugo for their troubles *and* a free passage out of the country. Not to be put off, Hugo shoots Hearn dead at his ranch and hightails it with the money, Clarke later wounded in a gunfight. Dixon then discovers Clarke is her long-lost brother, Wilke going into town to force Hugo to get a doctor for Clarke and is killed. Realizing his game is up, Hugo sets fire to his office and is arrested with partner-in-crime Billy Griffith, just as he plans to set off on his new boat. Not one of the best in the series but still entertaining cowboy fodder and, like all of Holt's oaters from this period, good to look at, featuring attractive Santa Clarita location work.

Dialogue:
Martin to Dixon after uttering a Spanish oath: "If you knew what I was thinking in Spanish, you would plug up your fingers with your ears."
Trivia:
This was actress Joan Freeman's first feature film.

Hot Lead

RKO-Radio; 60 minutes; Producer: Herman Schlom; Director: Stuart Gilmore; Cast: Tim Holt; Richard Martin; Joan Dixon; Ross Elliott; John Dehner; Robert J. Wilke; Paul Marion; Kenneth MacDonald ****

Joan Dixon, boss of the Circle Bar Ranch, is on the point of firing womanizer Richard Martin, busy flirting with a saloon lass in Trail Head instead of herding her cattle. The locomotive pulls in, three masked bandits come away empty-handed, one of Dixon's cowpokes is killed in the crossfire and Martin moans "It's all my fault." Meanwhile, bad guy turned good guy Ross Elliott is released from the state pen but pounced upon by John Dehner and his cohorts, Robert J. Wilke and Paul Marion; they try to coerce him into using his telegrapher skills in finding out when gold shipments are due in Trail Head and then passing on the information. Elliott doesn't want to know; he's just been hired by Dixon and the two have quickly fallen for each other. Dehner, intent on forcing Elliott to side with him, kills the town telegraph operator, the crime pinned on Elliott, and has Marion hold Dixon hostage. Tim Holt, after knocking Marion senseless, hatches a plan with doubtful sheriff Kenneth MacDonald to lure the outlaws to the station with Elliott's assistance, where a train will pull in containing no gold; Dehner has his suspicions when the ex-con offers him the bait and in the ensuing holdup, Dehner and Wilke are slugged and arrested. Elliott and Dixon then make their own plans for an early wedding, Holt and Martin riding off, arguing with each other in a friendly kinda manner! Not a great deal of action in *Hot Lead*, writer Willian Lively focusing on Martin's mangling of the English language—and any film featuring snarling baddies John Dehner and Robert J. Wilke in their prime simply cannot be ignored!

Dialogue:
Martin, referring to Elliott's newfound skills as a cow puncher: "Si, Dave is still a tenderhorn."
Holt: "It's tenderfoot, Chito. Greenhorn."
Martin: "Well, it's the same difference. That's what I say. Greenfoot."

Overland Telegraph

RKO-Radio; 60 minutes; Producer: Herman Schlom; Director: Lesley Selander; Cast: Tim Holt; Richard Martin; Gail Davis; Mari Blanchard; Hugh Beaumont; George Nader; Robert J. Wilke; Cliff Clark ****

Two cow punchers looking for work (Tim Holt and Richard Martin) become embroiled in a plot hatched by trader George Nader and Mesa City's wealthy saloon owner, Hugh Beaumont, to disrupt the transcontinental telegraph network which is causing the closure of forts and outposts along the route, a lucrative source of income for both men. Nader, engaged to dance hall lovely Mari Blanchard, is against the idea but happens to be in debt to Beaumont to the tune of $20,000 and feels he owes him a favor; he urgently needs the cash as well. Meanwhile, masked saboteurs are blowing up telegraph poles and workers' camps, causing delays and netting Beaumont and Nader $50,000 in revenue, so Gail Davis, tomboy daughter of Cliff Clark, boss of the Arizona Overland Telegraph outfit, employs Holt and Martin to find out who's behind the disruptions. When Clark is killed in a stage holdup, suspicion falls on Nader who gets ready to talk; Beaumont, aware that he's about to be crossed, pays villainous gunman Robert J. Wilke $10,000 to finish him off. A blazing shoot-out at Beaumont's ranch, two wagonloads of Davis' men coming to our heroes' aid, puts paid to Beaumont and company, Nader now free to marry Blanchard. A fast-moving enjoyable entry in the Tim Holt series, even though the leading man is unusually tetchy with his skirt-chasing co-star whose mindset appears to be "Ladies first, the job in hand second."

Dialogue:
Martin to Holt: "Every time I meet a pretty girl, you have to go along and spoil it by thinking about work."

1952
Trail Guide

RKO-Radio; 60 minutes; Producer: Herman Schlom; Director: Lesley Selander; Cast: Tim Holt; Richard Martin; Linda Douglas; Robert Sherwood; John Pickard; Kenneth MacDonald; Frank Wilcox; Wendy Waldron ***

Trail guides Tim Holt and Richard Martin are escorting homesteaders to the Promised Land of Silver Springs, but saloon owner Frank Wilcox doesn't want them around, even though the country is classed as open range. He employs young Robert Sherwood and sister Linda Douglas to scare off the settlers, fooling the pair into thinking that the newcomers will tear up the land and destroy property; gunman John Pickard is also in on the act. Wagonmaster Kenneth MacDonald is wounded in a holdup, masked riders pinching the homesteaders' land claims, Martin flirts with saloon lass Wendy Waldron, Wilcox is after oil on Sherwood's ranch and threatens to harm Douglas, Martin gets accused of the murder of Sherwood and Paul Sawtell's music pumps away merrily in the background. The tried and trusted homesteaders versus ranchers/cattlemen scenario is trotted out for the umpteenth time, but Lesley Selander, an old pro at this kind of stuff, keeps it on the boil, and Holt is as sturdy as ever, sturdier than his skirt-chasing pal, last seen dodging a lass who has marriage on her mind after Wilcox and his boys are arrested, Douglas seeing the error of her ways.

Dialogue:
Douglas to Holt, wielding a six-gun: "Let go of my brother."
Holt, turning to Sherwood: "Does jumpin' people with guns run in this family?"

Road Agent

RKO-Radio; 60 minutes; Producer: Herman Schlom; Director: Lesley Selander; Cast: Tim Holt; Richard Martin; Noreen Nash; Mauritz Hugo; Dorothy Patrick; Robert J. Wilke; Tom Tyler; Edward Hearn
****

"Tim's A Two-Gun Robin Hood!" screamed the posters and they're right; clad in black capes and masks, Holt and "Chito" Martin rob the rich (in particular land owner/cattle buyer Mauritz Hugo) to pay the not-so-poor cattlemen of Trail City, Arizona who are being charged extortionate prices for passing their herds through Hugo's toll roads. They want a fair price, but he's not interested ("$20 a head or you don't move a single steer."). Feisty Noreen Nash, owner of the Big D Ranch, sets her pretty blue eyes on Holt (*not* Chito!) and wonders if *he's* Robin Hood ("Who is our unknown benefactor?") while gunman Robert J. Wilke, fired by Hugo for ineptitude, kills his ex-boss' clerk, robs the safe and starts to live life high on the hog. Thanks to Holt and Martin's not-so-legal handouts, the cattlemen get their toll road permits, paid for by Hugo's own money, and the customary climactic showdown takes place at Wilke's ranch, Hugo shooting the gun tough and then arrested by Sheriff Edward Hearn. Bags of action, mistaken identities, Martin pretending to have smallpox, blonde saloon gal Dorothy Patrick a sexy delight and the amusing sight of our two heroes charging around the countryside like caped crusaders make for an invigorating 60 minutes of Holt/Martin mayhem.

Dialogue:
Martin to Wilke: "Excuse me, Senor Slob."
Wilke: "Slab's the name."
Martin: "Slab. Slob. What's the difference?"

Westerns of the 1950s: The Classic Years   197

Target

RKO-Radio; 61 minutes; Producer: Herman Schlom; Director: Stuart Gilmore; Cast: Tim Holt; Richard Martin; Linda Douglas; Walter Reed; Harry Harvey; John Hamilton; Lane Bradford; Riley Hill ***

The penultimate Holt/Martin horse opera showed a slight fall in quality, both in script and plot—the movies weren't making money and, by 1952, were viewed as old-hat by RKO executives. In Pecos, Texas, 1893, railroad land-grabber Walter Reed orders his hoodlums, led by hulking Lane Bradford, to rough up newspaperman Harry Harvey for daring to print inflammatory remarks about his underhand tactics; Reed is bullying ranchers into selling their land at a loss to enable the new railhead to proceed through the county at a profit—his profit. In steps Holt and Martin to break up the fight (a violent scene, this), the pair then hired by rancher John Hamilton to act as his personal bodyguard. A tough new law officer is required in Pecos—Linda Douglas arrives on the stage, daughter of a feared lawman ("A fancy Dan with a gun!"), to take up the position (he's in hospital) as she needs the money; sure, she can shoot, but is a "petticoat marshal" what the town really needs? Hamilton decides to sell up but only receives $1,500 instead of $15,000, beaten to the ground by Bradford. Holt and Martin aim to get back Hamilton's ranch for him and explain to the railroad supremo just what is taking place in Pecos; Bradford is put behind bars but refuses to spill the beans on his boss. He's sprung from jail, there's a shoot-out among rocks, Holt drops Reed and slugs Bradford with a single punch; Martin, who's missed out on most of the action, sprawled unconscious on the jail floor, wonders what has happened at the end when Holt and Douglas, who has nabbed Reed's illegal land deals, turn up and revive him.

Dialogue:
Holt to Martin after Bradford has hit him in the eye, in retaliation for him being struck in the eye: "Now I know what they mean by that old saying, "An eye for an eye.""

Trivia:
One of the few Tim Holt B-Westerns where he wears a gun belt sporting a full complement of bullets.

Desert Passage

RKO-Radio; 62 minutes; Producer: Herman Schlom; Director: Lesley Selander; Cast: Tim Holt; Richard Martin; Joan Dixon; Walter Reed; John Dehner; Lane Bradford; Denver Pyle; Dorothy Patrick ***

After spending three years in Yuma prison, parolee Walter Reed makes his way on foot to Lavic, Arizona to retrieve the $100,000 he embezzled from Joan Dixon's father who committed suicide as a result of the loss. Also, after laying their hands on the loot are Reed's lawyer, John Dehner, ex-cons Lane Bradford and Denver Pyle and Dorothy Patrick and her boyfriend, gambler Clayton Moore. Meanwhile, Tim Holt and Richard Martin have put their stage line business up for sale; they're losing money, but if they insist on charging passengers a measly dollar for transporting their wares, that's not surprising. *Desert Passage* marked the end of the trail for our chunky hero and his womanizing sidekick, the movie climaxing the series not quite with a bang but certainly not with a whimper. After Reed has paid Holt $1,000 to take him to the Mexican border, the entire cast finds itself embroiled in a search for the hidden cash at Michael Mark's relay station, much talking and skulking around replacing all-out gun action; after several standoffs, Dehner is shot, Bradford wounded and the remainder arrested by the sheriff's posse. The money is recovered, Holt and Martin receiving a substantial reward, enough to continue the running of their stage operation, either at a loss or a profit! The two actors went their own separate ways after this; what they left behind were perhaps some of the finest examples of the one-hour B-Western to have been produced in the early 1950s. Tim Holt's oaters possessed an extra sheen and a touch more professionalism than most of the competition and were terrific to look at. All of them, without exception, are worth an hour of any fan's time.

Dialogue:

The last word, naturally, has to go to the garrulous Martin in response to Dixon stating: "I know all about Chito's shenanigans."

Martin: "There's nobody in my family by that name. I got Gonzales Bustamonte Rafferty. But no shenanigans."

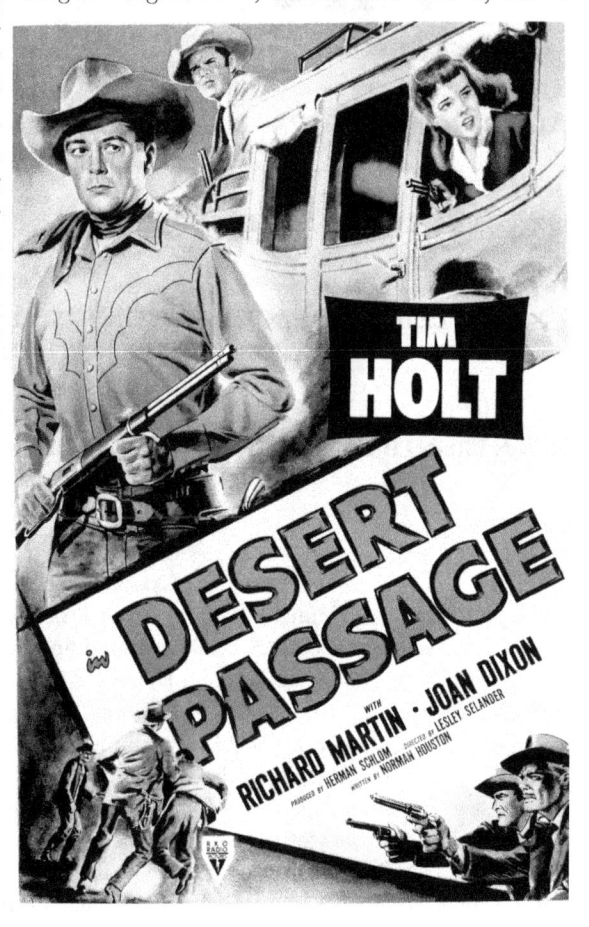

Chapter 8
1954

SHE STRIPS OFF HER PETTICOAT ... AND STRAPS ON HER GUNS!
Cattle Queen of Montana

THE BATTLE OF THE SEXES AND SIXES RAGES ACROSS THE LUSTY WEST!
Jesse James' Women

HARD-AS-SPIKES MEN AND SOFT-AS-SILK WOMEN ... THEY RAN INTO TOWERING CANYON AND COMANCHE TERROR WHEN THEY RAN THE RAILROAD TO THE GOLD COAST! *Overland Pacific*

THE MIGHTY SAGA OF THE NORTHWEST MOUNTED POLICE! *Saskatchewan*

THE BIGGEST BATTLE THAT EVER SHOOK THE WEST!
Sitting Bull

HE LED THE APACHE NATION'S WILD REVOLT AGAINST GERONIMO'S PILLAGING HORDES!
Taza, Son of Cochise

WHEN FRONTIER FLAMED WITH THE LURE OF GOLD ... AND A WOMAN'S UNCLAIMED LIPS!
Yellow Mountain

Apache

United Artists; Technicolor; 91 minutes; Producers: Burt Lancaster and Harold Hecht; Director: Robert Aldrich; Cast: Burt Lancaster; Jean Peters; John McIntire; Charles Bronson; Walter Sande; John Dehner; Morris Ankrum; Monte Blue ***

The second Hecht-Lancaster production (1952's *The Crimson Pirate* was the first) saw Burt playing Apache warrior Massai at the time of Geronimo's surrender in 1886. Escaping from captivity and going on the run with squaw Jean Peters, he's hunted remorselessly by crooked reporter John Dehner, benevolent John McIntire and Indian scout Charles Bronson, who desires Peters as his wife. A pro-Indian effort directed with flair by Robert Aldrich, Lancaster and Peters make two fine blue-eyed Apache specimens but the actor, despite his commanding physique, doesn't seem quite right for the part, and we get to see practically nothing of the famous Lancaster flashing grin, although perhaps here, it wasn't called for. There's plenty of rough stuff in the middle section when Lancaster embarks on a one-man war against authority and Walter Sande's cavalry, but during the final 30 minutes, the action slows. Lancaster, resigned to being a simple farmer and going to ground in a mountain shack with heavily pregnant Peters, is trapped by McIntire's boys in a cornfield; hearing his new baby crying, he walks away towards his home, McIntire reluctantly allowing him to go on his way, the last of his kind, the war with the Apaches finally at an end—and no more fighting for men of McIntire's breed.

Highlights:
Sedona's majestic Red Rock Crossing scenery, a typically muscular performance from the leading man and Massai, on the loose in St. Louis, totally bewildered by the white man's trappings.

Dialogue:
McIntire, cuffing Lancaster: "You're just a whipped Indian. And nobody sings about handcuffs."

Trivia:
Robert Aldrich (this was his first Western) disliked the optimistic ending, wanting Lancaster to go out in a blaze of glory instead.

The Black Dakotas

Columbia; Technicolor; 65 minutes; Producer: Wallace MacDonald; Director: Ray Nazarro; Cast: Gary Merrill; Wanda Hendrix; John Bromfield; Noah Beery, Jr.; James Griffith; Jay Silverheels; John War Eagle; Fay Roope ****

Short and violent sums up Ray Nazarro's Civil War tale concerning Southerner Gary Merrill taking on a murdered man's identity in order to deliver a Union peace deal, signed by Abe Lincoln, plus $100,000 in gold, to the Sioux and then break it; the aim is to create an Indian uprising against the Northerners, the Confederacy benefiting from the ensuing massacre and the gold which will boost their war fund. Merrill plays an out-and-out bad 'un verging on the psychopathic, shooting everyone he thinks will prevent him from nabbing the gold for himself, racking up a pretty high body count. Even town outcast Wanda Hendrix is a target, saved by Noah Beery, Jr. who himself is shot dead by Merrill. With Merrill's Southerner gang wiped out to a man (most by Merrill) and a stagecoach crew slaughtered, the killer attempts to escape with the $100,000 but is slugged senseless in a pool by Hendrix's lover, John Bromfield. In Dakota, Chief Thundercloud (John War Eagle) puts his mark on the treaty, saying he now yearns for peace; judging by the scowl on Black Buffalo's face (Jay Silverheels), that peace ain't gonna last very long! An energetic oater from Nazarro who knew how to frame his protagonists in his customary "in-your-face" close-up shots; the familiar storyline cropped up in many a '50s Western, United Artists' *Revolt at Fort Laramie* being one example.

Dialogue:
Fay Roope to Merrill, regarding Merrill's false identity: "You better remember your new name."
Merrill: "Zachary Paige. It's my neck in a rope if I don't."

Cattle Queen of Montana

RKO-Radio; Technicolor; 88 minutes; Producer: Benedict Bogeaus; Director: Allan Dwan; Cast: Barbara Stanwyck; Ronald Reagan; Lance Fuller; Gene Evans; Anthony Caruso; Yvette Duguay (Dugay); Jack Elam; Morris Ankrum ***

"She strips off her petticoats ... and straps on her guns!" So proclaimed the posters to Allan Dwan's over-plotted oater concerning Barbara Stanwyck (as Sierra Nevada Jones) determined against the odds to claim her rights to Buffalo Valley in Montana, stolen by land-grabber Gene Evans; the crook is bribing Blackfoot renegade Anthony Caruso (Natchakoa) to run off (and massacre) new settlers migrating into the area by offering the savage rifles and whiskey. Educated, peaceful Indian Lance Fuller (Colorados) befriends Stanwyck after her $20,000 herd is rustled and her father killed in the raid, his intended, Yvette Duguay (Starfire), jealous of the Stetson-wearing dame, eventually siding with Caruso when the tribe splits; she pays with an arrow in the chest. Add to this Ronald Reagan as an undercover agent out to expose Evans and his gang and Jack Elam skulking in the background and you have a flashy Western that lurches from one sequence of events to another without pausing for breath, attractively shot in Montana's Glacier National Park. There's too much going on, Stanwyck switching outfits at an alarming rate, leaving you admiring the scenery rather than the action, which comes in fits and starts. But Stanwyck was always worth watching, even though her chemistry with Reagan misfires (and Fuller is as wooden as a fence post); she puts in a rootin' tootin' performance that holds the whole narrative together when it threatens at times to drift off into the wilderness.

Dialogue:
Fuller to Duguay, over her concern for his feelings for the more mature Stanwyck: "You are a lovely young girl. Act like one."

Trivia:
Robert Mitchum was offered the Reagan role but turned it down, saying he disliked Robert Blees and Howard Estabrook's script.

The Command

Warner Bros.; CinemaScope/Warnercolor; 94 minutes; Producer: David Weisbart; Director: David Butler; Cast: Guy Madison; Joan Weldon; James Whitmore; Carl Benton Reid; Harvey Lembeck; Ray Teal; Don Shelton; Robert Nichols ****

The first Western released in CinemaScope was set in Wyoming, 1878 and had army doctor Guy Madison placed in command of a battle-weary cavalry troop detail after his commanding officer dies in an Indian attack. In a nearby town, he's then ordered by excitable General Carl Benton Reid (forever on the verge of a heart attack) to act as a rearguard backup to his infantrymen, who are escorting a wagon train of migrating settlers to Fort Stark via Paradise River. As soon as they hit the trail, trouble starts. Reid raves at Madison, dictating how *he* thinks the troop formation should be deployed; disease breaks out, attributed to smallpox; the men mistrust Madison's leadership; infantry surgeon Ray Teal is next to useless; and Joan Weldon tries hard not to fall for Madison's good looks. But Madison redeems himself in the end, successfully planning unorthodox methods in which to defeat the Redskins before the wagons arrive at Paradise River, including infecting them with chickenpox, not smallpox as thought; in reward for getting the wagons and soldiers through, he cozies up to Weldon on a wagon. A wordy initial 20 minutes picks up when the wagons are on the move, events culminating in a climactic, and bloody, 14-minute clash with Indians, a stupendous action set piece underlined by Dimitri Tiomkin's thumping score (not only was the noted Russian one of Hollywood's greatest composers, winning four Oscars, he was also one of the genre's greatest). James Whitmore adds solid support as the hardened sergeant on Madison's side, Weldon is the picture of loveliness and California's rolling Agoura plains sparkle under Wilfrid M. Cline's photography. Definitely one for cavalry versus Injuns fans.

Highlights:
That 14-minute battle, thrillingly orchestrated by David Butler, one of the very best of its kind from the 1950s.

Dialogue:
Whitmore to Madison, describing Indian battle tactics: "If they're runnin' against a big outfit like we're tied up with now, they keep hackin' and choppin' away at your weak spots till they wear you down. Then they go ring-o-round and once they get you in a circle, they know you're finished."

Trivia:
Warner Bros. planned to issue a 3-D version in normal screen ratio but scrapped the idea in favor of CinemaScope; and several stuntmen were badly injured during the lengthy battle sequences.

The Desperado

Allied Artists; 80 minutes; Producer: Vincent M. Fennelly; Director: Thomas Carr; Cast: Wayne Morris; Jimmy Lydon; Beverly Garland; Rayford Barnes; Dabbs Greer; Lee Van Cleef; Nestor Paiva; Roy Barcroft *****

In 1873, Texas carpetbaggers are trampling over the peoples' rights, vigilante gangs causing havoc ("Blue Bellies Go Home!"). Fresh-faced Jimmy Lydon and pal Rayford Barnes, blamed as troublemakers after a saloon is blown sky-high, are roughed up by Captain Nestor Paiva in a sequence of prolonged brutality; the pair break out of custody, Lydon meeting wanted gunman Wayne Morris (20 notches on his belt) on the trail, Daniel Mainwaring's script piling on the incident. Lydon's girl, Beverly Garland, is also coveted by deeply jealous Barnes, the weasel turning traitor in order to claim the reward money on his friend's head *and* grab the lass for his own; horse thief Lee Van Cleef is gunned down by Lydon, who also shoots his twin brother; Morris teaches the youngster how to handle those double shooters to deadlier effect; Lydon is framed for the murder of Paiva, killed in cold blood by the cowardly Barnes; and at Lydon's trial, Dabbs Greer, Abilene's marshal, latches on to Barnes' deceit, Lydon freed to wed Garland, Morris allowed to go on his way, still carrying a $10,000 bounty on his head. A smart little oater well worth any fan's time: The Morris/Lydon relationship is based on a mutual understanding of each other's needs and makes for interesting viewing, while Carr's direction is bang on target, bolstered by Raoul Kraushaar's noisy soundtrack and Joseph M. Novak's sharp photography—a classy B-Western of its type from the '50s, cramming everything into the 80-minute running length, Morris' tough but affable Sam Garrett one of the genre's most likeable gunslingers.

Highlights:
Morris instructing tenderfoot Lydon how to draw accurately with twin Colts.
Dialogue:
Morris to Lydon: "Bad guns are like bad friends. They let you down when you need them the most."
Trivia:
Mainwaring's screenplay (from a Clifton Adams story) was reused in Allied Artists' 1958 *Cole Younger, Gunfighter*; and war-hero Morris was only 45 when he died in September 1959 from a heart attack.

Drum Beat

Warner Bros.; CinemaScope/Warnercolor; 111 minutes; Producers: Alan Ladd and Delmer Daves; Director: Delmer Daves; Cast: Alan Ladd; Audrey Dalton; Charles Bronson; Marisa Pavan; Robert Keith; Warner Anderson; Anthony Caruso; Frank DeKova ****

In Washington, 1872, President Ulysses S. Grant (Hayden Rorke) asks renowned Indian fighter Johnny MacKay (Alan Ladd) to travel to the California-Oregon border and negotiate, without resorting to the use of firearms, a peace treaty with Modoc chief Kintpuash, also known as Captain Jack (Charles Bronson). Demure Audrey Dalton accompanies Ladd on the journey, the new peace commissioner having his hands full with both Indian hating Robert Keith and scowling Bronson. The volatile Modoc boss wants the coveted Lost River territory all for himself, refusing to listen to reason ("You're a two-bit tyrant, Jack," Ladd says to his face). Friendly Modoc Anthony Caruso and his sister, Marisa Pavan, try to pacify Bronson, but warmonger Modoc Frank DeKova fans the flames of Bronson's hatred for whites, leading to 18 settlers massacred when the Indians embark on a rampage. Bronson sets up a stronghold atop a mesa overlooking Fort Klamath and callously shoots a peace envoy sent to placate him. Ladd, wounded, recovers to head an all-out assault on the mesa, all thoughts of peace now out of the question. A fierce barrage of gunfire and arrows has the cavalry retreating, Ladd organizing a volunteer party to pursue Bronson and his warriors across country, the Modocs splitting into three groups. Sick of the fighting, the hostiles surrender, except for Bronson; captured after a bruising fight with Ladd, the chief is hanged by the military, Ladd planning to settle down with Dalton after Indian maiden Pavan, who loved him, loses her life in a skirmish. Beautiful Arizona scenery and Victor Young's pounding score add up to what many regard as Ladd's second-best Western after *Shane*, a big hit for Warner Bros. and a colorful reminder of just how good the genre could be in this decade.

Highlights:
Arizona's Red Rock Crossing and Coconino National Forest lovingly photographed by J. Peverell Marley.

Dialogue:
Ladd, receiving an offer from Pavan which any red-blooded male would find impossible to refuse: "Take me for your woman tonight and I will swear with all my heart that I will make you very happy. I will do all those things you would wish me to do as your woman."

Trivia:
Drum Beat was the first film in which Charles Buchinsky changed his name to Charles Bronson. It was also the first picture made under Ladd's production company, Jaguar.

Jesse James vs. the Daltons

Columbia; Technicolor; Orig. in 3-D; 65 minutes; Producer: Sam Katzman; Director: William Castle; Cast: Brett King; Barbara Lawrence; James Griffith; John Cliff; Rory Mallinson; Nelson Leigh; Richard Garland; William Tannen ****

According to William Castle's unsubtle but lively oater, Jesse James may not have died; he's out there somewhere and knows the whereabouts of a stolen $100,000 hidden in a suitcase. Young punk gunman Brett King, who reckons to one and all that he's James' long-lost son, hitches up with tomboy Barbara Lawrence at Coffeyville after saving her from a lynch mob, commits a daring train robbery and worms himself into the rampaging Dalton gang, promising them a cut of that cash if it's located. None other than Bob Ford (Rory Mallinson, resembling Randolph Scott) turns up at James' former hideout, the money is discovered under a bunk and turns out to be Confederate notes, not worth a dime, Mallinson infers that he didn't shoot James and King turns out to be a baby the notorious outlaw picked up in his time spent with Quantrill's Raiders. The whole historically inaccurate shebang climaxes in the Coffeyville twin banks holdups, the street full of gun smoke and whizzing bullets as the Daltons bite the dust in a hailstorm of lead; King and Lawrence then decide to get married. Okay, numerous objects are hurled at the camera in the name of 3-D effects but there's no getting away from the fact that, at just over an hour long, Castle's colorful effort is pure Western shoot-'em-up entertainment, featuring a particularly strong performance from James Griffith as the no-nonsense leader of the Dalton boys.

Highlights:
The Coffeyville raid, three minutes of bullet-ridden mayhem marvelously conjured up by Castle.

Dialogue:
Train guard to King: "You're crossin' the sheriff, the railroad, the Daltons. You're gonna be right popular, Mister Davis."

Jesse James' Women

Panorama/United Artists; Technicolor; 83 minutes; Producers: T.V. Garraway and Lloyd Royal; Director: Don "Red" Barry (Donald Barry); Cast: Don "Red" Barry; Jack Buetel; Sam Keller; Peggie Castle; Lita Baron; Joyce Barrett; Betty Brueck; Laura Lea **

With the amount of skirt-chasing Jesse James (Don "Red" Barry) does in this movie, it's surprising he found the time to commit bank robberies, let alone keep his disgruntled, restless gang in check. "How does he do it?" must have been on the lips of many in the audience as five-foot-four and a half, barrel-chested Barry, 42 at the time, gets to kiss a bevy of lovelies all vying for his affections, each unaware that he's using them to feather his own nest ("Women are tools to be used."): Tyrone Power (who starred in Fox's 1939 *Jesse James*) he ain't! Perhaps it would have been more appropriate to cast good-looking Jack Buetel in the role of the cowboy Casanova, instead of him playing James' brother Frank—or was that Barry's perverse intention? Peggie Castle (Waco), Lita Baron (Delta), Joyce Barrett (Caprice) and Betty Brueck (Cattle Kate) all fall under his "spell," even teenager Laura Lea (Angel, the sheriff's daughter), eying up the legendary outlaw's portly figure and panting that he's her hero. Apart from all the lustful shenanigans, groping and bitchiness, there's a bank holdup, trouble at the card table, rows with Michael Carr (Bob Ford), a $1,000 encounter with a prizefighter, a catfight and a money belt containing $10,000 stolen cash that passes from one female to the next; it's eventually shared between Lea (to buy a new horse) and a poor dirt farmer. Barry (as director) conjures up a Spaghetti Western-type standoff between Brueck and Castle in Silver Creek and the film ends with newspaper headlines announcing the killing of James by Ford on April 3, 1882, Lea, grown up with two sons (surely not Barry's!), on her way to church. Scripted by Barry, Garraway and D.D. Beauchamp, *Jesse James' Women* has "spoof" written all over it, whether that was the idea or not. Either way, it's very hard for more serious Western fans to accept Barry as a womanizing, iconic bad/good guy, or as someone who has such a devastating effect on the opposite sex, the *New York Times* particularly acerbic, hoping that this "cheap caricature of a picture will become aware of its grubbiness and go away."

Dialogue:
Castle to Barry after he's bragged about his appeal to the ladies: "Did you say red-blooded American man?"
Barry: "Yeah."
Castle: "Well, I have some advice for you. You better change your nationality or the color of your blood or you won't have any manhood left."

Jubilee Trail

Republic; Trucolor; 103 minutes; Produced and Directed by Joseph Kane; Cast: Vera Ralston; Joan Leslie; Forrest Tucker; John Russell; Ray Middleton; Pat O'Brien; Buddy Baer; Jim Davis ****

Maybe not "The Greatest American Drama since Gone With the Wind," but the highly colorful *Jubilee Trail* certainly packs in the flashy drama, seemingly much longer than its 103-minute running time. Republic boss Herbert J. Yates' wife, Vera Ralston (once named the worst actress of all time), is a dance hall songstress in New Orleans, 1845, on the run from the police for a murder she claimed she didn't commit, joining settlers on the long trip to California. Passengers include husband and wife John Russell and Joan Leslie, guide Forrest Tucker, man-mountain Buddy Baer (playing a Siberian) and Doc Pat O'Brien. En route, Leslie is wounded in a Redskin attack and Russell crosses swords with arrogant brother Ray Middleton at Middleton's hacienda; the man turns out to be an emotionless bully. A year or so back, Russell made Spanish girl Pilar Del Rey pregnant and Middleton wanted him to marry the lass in order to bring in her father's lands to his property. He blames Leslie and later tries to steal *her* baby when Del Rey commits suicide, riding over a cliff with her infant. Russell is killed in a fracas with the girl's father and in Los Angeles, Ralston sings, rolls her eyes, shows plenty of shapely leg and flashes her mile-wide smile. Middleton is shot dead by O'Brien, gold is discovered in California and Tucker decides to settle down with Leslie and her baby boy, leaving the fiery Ralston to (maybe) take up with "handsome brute" Baer. Bags of incident and romance, sexy Ralston doing her hardest to dispel that "worse actress"

tag, plus lavish interior design work and scenic shots of California's Red Rock Canyon, are boosted by Jack A. Marta's vivid photography and a truly memorable title theme score from Victor Young; it's reprised at intervals throughout the narrative and quite rightly so. The *New York Times* liked the picture, calling it "handsome mounted" and singling out Tucker's performance as the best in the film; the public also liked it, the movie raking in a gross of nearly $1,500,000.

Dialogue:
Ralston to Baer who's grabbed her arm: "Customers can look but mustn't touch. Rule of the house."

The Law vs. Billy the Kid

Columbia; Technicolor; 72 minutes; Producer: Sam Katzman; Director: William Castle; Cast: Scott Brady; Betta St. John; James Griffith; Alan Hale, Jr.; Paul Cavanagh; Steve Darrell; Richard Cutting; Otis Garth **

A drab re-telling of the Billy the Kid legend, from his days working on a ranch to his fateful meeting with Pat Garrett, his romance with Nita Maxwell, his turning to a life of crime and his subsequent death at the hands of Garrett. The main problem with the movie is Scott Brady in the title role: At 29, he's too old (William Bonney was 21 when he died), too tall (six-foot-two), too beefy-looking and too bland. James Griffith's Pat Garrett, on the other hand, works because of the actor's understated playing, while Betta St. John (as Nita) is simply ravishing. Hulking bully Alan Hale, Jr. is the chief villain, jealous of St. John's association with the wanted outlaw and enlisting the aid of corrupt sheriff Steve Darrell to track him down; Darrell meets his end in a saloon shoot-out, Hale blasted to death on an hotel stairway. Promising a fresh life for St. John in New Mexico, Brady is shot twice in the chest by his onetime friend Griffith in the closing stages, the lass weeping over his body. Apart from a lengthy blazing showdown between Griffith's posse and Brady's bunch in a shack, there isn't a great deal of action and Scott is as wooden as a hitching post; not one of William Castle's better Westerns of the 1950s.

Dialogue:
Brady to St. John: "What you said about being fancy free? Well, I'm glad you're free. And I'm sure glad you're fancy."

Belgian poster for *The Law vs. Billy the Kid*

Massacre Canyon

Columbia; 66 minutes; Producer: Wallace MacDonald; Director: Fred F. Sears; Cast: Douglas Kennedy; Philip Carey; Audrey Totter; Jeff (Jean) Donnell; Guinn "Big Boy" Williams; Charlita; Ross Elliott; Steven Ritch **

Three hundred Henry repeating carbines loaded on two wagons led by Sergeant Douglas Kennedy, soon to be lieutenant, are needed urgently at Fort Collier. At the relay station of Spanish Bit, whiskey-sodden Philip Carey turns out to be the lieutenant the fort is waiting for, stalling Kennedy's promotion dreams, while traveling trader Ralph Dumke, discovering the wagons are carrying rifles, strikes a deal with Indian tease Charlita to sell the weapons to Black Eagle (Steven Ritch) and his Apaches; she stabs him in the back and disappears, the wagons setting off with driver Guinn "Big Boy" Williams, two women looking for husbands (one is Williams' ex-love; the other goes sweet on Carey), Carey, now sober, and Ross Elliott, a demoted major. Fred F. Sears' oater appears cheap and under-developed, the best scenes those of the wagons thundering through the dust and a fracas set during a fierce sandstorm when Running Horse (Chris Alcaide), who has infiltrated the group, causes trouble and is killed by Carey. Their water barrels pierced by the Apache's knife, the wagons head through a tunnel in Massacre Canyon (California's Bronson Canyon) for water, the Apaches in pursuit; dynamite puts paid to the injuns, a lake is glimpsed and the film suddenly ends, as though funds had run dry which, judging by the brief running time, they had. A case of making the picture a lot more interesting and well-rounded if extra finances had been available.

Dialogue:
Kennedy, trying to calm down Williams who is spoiling for a fight: "Where did you ever get that name Peaceful?"
Williams: "It's better than some of the names they call you."

The Outcast aka The Fortune Hunter

Republic; Trucolor; 90 minutes; Producer: William J. O'Sullivan; Director: William Witney; Cast: John Derek; Jim Davis; Joan Evans; Catherine McLeod; Bob Steele; Frank Ferguson; Taylor Holmes; James Millican ****

John Derek returns to Colton, Colorado to claim his dead father's ranch, the Circle C: under a forged will concocted by lawyer/silent partner Taylor Holmes, the ranch was left to Derek's uncle, Jim Davis, and the cattle baron isn't too pleased at Derek taking over the adjacent Newmark Valley spread with the help of eight gunslingers; Derek's eventual aim is to claim back the Circle C as his rightful inheritance. A myriad of well-rounded characters populate Republic's classier-than-usual Western. Catherine McLeod, the smart dame from Virginia, due to wed Davis without realizing what a tyrant he is; Joan Evans, the daughter of rancher Frank Ferguson, dying to marry Derek after he's kissed her ("I don't suppose I'm the first girl you've kissed. But I don't care as long as I'm the last.") and ostracized by her puritanical father; James Millican, one of Davis' henchmen, always on the prod; murderous Bob Steele, Derek's head gunmen, also suffering from an itchy trigger finger; Ben Cooper, a young hothead out to carve himself a reputation; hotelier Nan Bryant, caring for Evans after her father whips her for being "wanton"; and Bill Walker, an ex-prizefighter blacksmith and friend of Derek. Several gunfights spread over 85 minutes, Derek attempting to snatch McLeod from under Davis' nose or ruin their nuptials ("After the wedding, don't throw the flowers away. You may need them for a funeral.") results in a four-way shoot-out, Millican, Derek, Davis and Holmes blazing away at each other in the street; Evans' brother, Slim Pickens, shoots Millican in the back, Holmes is plugged by Davis after letting on about the fake will and Derek drops his uncle; the Circle C is now his by right. Evans back in Derek's arms, a preacher is called for, McLeod riding off, her fiancé's body lying in the dust. A plaintive score from R. Dale Butts, picturesque Colorado location work and pacey direction from William Witney add up to a solid Western, the entire cast in fine fettle.

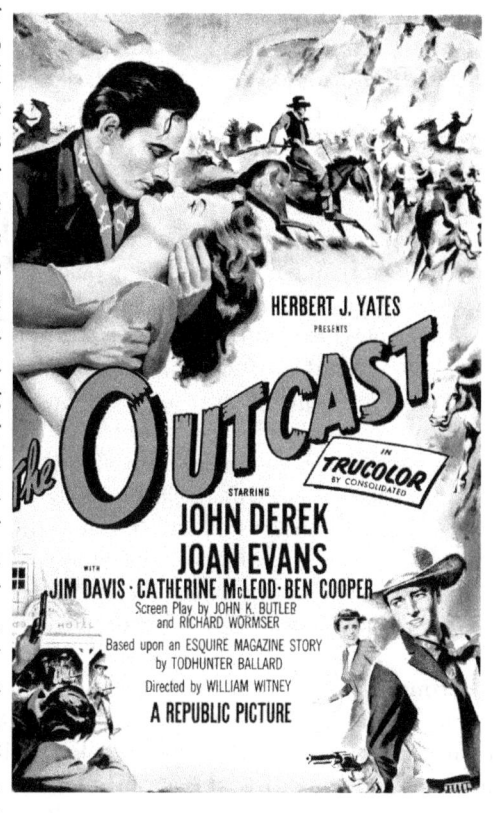

Dialogue:
Davis to Holmes, who's threating to spill the beans: "It takes a man to cross me, not a rabbit. If I didn't need you, I'd kill you."

The Outlaw's Daughter

Edward L. Alperson Prods./20th Century Fox; Eastmancolor; 76 minutes; Produced and Directed by Wesley Barry; Cast: Jim Davis; Bill Williams; Sheila Connolly (Kelly Ryan); Guinn "Big Boy" Williams; Elisha Cook, Jr.; George Barrows; George Cleveland; Nelson Leigh ***

"Dames into outlaws" was a popular theme in 1950s Western movies, and *The Outlaw's Daughter* is a nifty addition to the sub-genre—unfortunately, DVD prints today [2018] are of ragged quality, Gordon Avil's Eastmancolor hues reduced to a bleached-out mauve. Convinced that Marshal Jim Davis and Deputy Guinn "Big Boy" Williams shot dead her father, the ex-outlaw boss of the Dalton Ranch, feisty tomboy Sheila Connolly embarks on a criminal rampage with no-goods Bill Williams, Elisha Cook, Jr.

and George Barrows after spurning Davis' romantic overtures; banks and mine offices are robbed in an orgy of violence. Two-faced Williams, in fact, killed the rancher and murders Connolly's elderly uncle (George Cleveland) to prevent him blabbing to Davis; Williams also wants to marry Connolly, but she remains undecided. The movie develops into a fairly exciting manhunt, taking place in Utah's picturesque Kanab region and Arizona's mesa-ridden Sedona area, Williams, the reward mounting on his head, turning against Connolly after one rejection too many. Callously allowing Cook to take a bullet during a shoot-out, he rides off into the wilderness; Cook, dying, tells Connolly that Williams was the louse behind her father and uncle's deaths, leading to a showdown atop a gigantic cliff between Davis and Williams; Williams drops his guns but draws a derringer, winging the lawman and receiving a derringer bullet himself, his lifeless body sliding over the cliff edge. Connolly is back with the man she fancied all along, even though Davis tells her that she faces a long prison sentence for her misdeeds. A bow must go to composer Raoul Kraushaar for providing another terrific score to keep the action flowing, as he did so often in these B-Westerns.

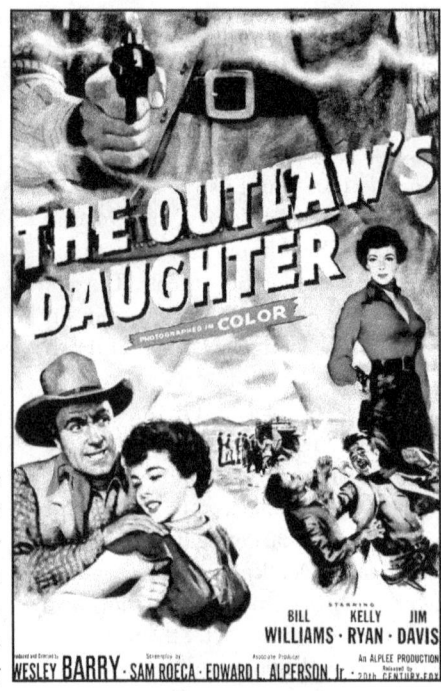

Dialogue:
Davis to Connolly: "You know, you interest me. An Irish tongue like a bullwhip but pretty as a picture."

Overland Pacific

United Artists; Cinecolor; 73 minutes; Producer: Edward Small; Director: Fred F. Sears; Cast: Jock Mahoney; Peggie Castle; William Bishop; Adele Jergens; Chubby Johnson; Walter Sande; Pat Hogan; Chris Alcaide ***

In the guise of a telegrapher, railroad agent Jock Mahoney turns up in Oaktown to find out who's supplying repeating rifles to Pat Hogan's Comanches, the Redskins causing so much disruption to the new railway that construction crews are on the verge of quitting. Silver

Dollar saloon owner William Bishop, an old wartime buddy of Mahoney's, is behind it all, smuggling the weapons into town in whiskey barrels, trusting that Hogan's tribe will force the rail bosses to divert the tracks away from the mountains and straight through Oaktown, where it will benefit his business. The smooth rat murders girlfriend Peggie Castle's father Walter Sande, who disliked him, lies his head off to Mahoney and then puts a bullet in devoted ex-gal Adele Jergens. In three climactic Indian attacks on the railhead, Mahoney and the crew toss dynamite into the warriors, forcing them to retreat, while Bishop stabs Hogan to death. Mahoney pursues Bishop into the rocks, shoots him and ambles off with Castle in the closing credits. A serviceable oater shot around California's Simi Hills region in over-bright Cinecolor, *Overland Pacific* moves quickly through its set pieces, Mahoney's left arm in a sling for half the picture, although this doesn't prevent the ex-stuntmen from roughing up gunslinger Chris Alcaide in a balletic fistfight; Irving Gertz's melodic score is an added treat.

Dialogue:
Jergens, slobbering all over Bishop in an attempt to rekindle their love: "Why don't you forget the little princess and come back to the common herd?"
Bishop, pushing her away: "The only thing you find in herds is cows."

The Raid

Panoramic Prods./20th Century Fox; Technicolor; 83 minutes; Producer: Robert L. Jacks; Director: Hugo Fregonese; Cast: Van Heflin; Anne Bancroft; Peter Graves; Richard Boone; Tommy Rettig; Lee Marvin; Claude Akins; John Dierkes ****

Based on a true-life incident, Hugo Fregonese's involving yarn tells of seven Confederate prisoners who escape from the Union stockade in Plattsburg in September 1864; six make it to St. Albans where they plan to link up with other escapees and sack the town, making their way to the Canadian border and freedom. Van Heflin plays the group's leader, Peter Graves his second-in-command, while Lee Marvin is a loose cannon thirsty for Yankee blood, be it man, woman or child. Posing as a property dealer and setting up base in widow Anne Bancroft's hotel, Heflin organizes his raid, bonding with Bancroft's young son, Tommy Rettig, and having to contend with anti-Rebel comments from one-armed officer Richard Boone. In a town seething with Confederate haters, can Heflin pull it off and, more importantly, should he? After all, these are real people whose lives he is toying with, regardless of whether they're Union sympathizers or not. Matters hit boiling point when Marvin, drunk, beats a soldier to death and staggers into a church congregation waving a pistol. To preserve anonymity, Heflin has no other option but to shoot him dead and is hailed a hero, the townsfolk even buying him a parcel of land in gratitude ("We're glad you're going to be one of us."). But despite his growing affection for Bancroft and Rettig, Heflin grits his teeth, pushes his conscience aside and proceeds with his mission. Dressed in Confederate uniforms, his men rob the town's two banks, burn shops to the ground with incendiaries, cause havoc and use the panicking citizens as a barricade in a final thrilling set piece. The cavalry arrives but too late—the Confederates light out to the border, setting a vital bridge on fire to prevent being followed. In a wrecked, smoking St. Albans, Bancroft reads a note from Heflin, saying that he had to carry out his duty, regardless of what he felt for her. A taut suspenser all round, Roy Webb's menacing score heightening the tension in a little-seen picture that grabs the attention and refuses to let go.

Dialogue:
Marvin in St. Albans, surveying the town: "Burn real pretty."

Rails into Laramie

Universal; Technicolor; 81 minutes; Producer: Ted Richmond; Director: Jesse Hibbs; Cast: John Payne; Dan Duryea; Mari Blanchard; Joyce Mackenzie; Myron Healey; Lee Van Cleef; Harry Shannon; James Griffith ***

Wyoming 1869: Tough army sergeant John Payne is sent to Laramie to find out why the railhead has stalled five miles out of town, the construction crew engaged in drinking, gambling and little else. As soon as you see Dan Duryea, Myron Healey and Lee Van Cleef eyeing Payne as he rides in, you know darned well who's behind the delays. But *why* is another matter, and therein lies the film's major flaw—there appears to be no logical reason in preventing the rail lines from reaching Laramie; Duryea and the town's tradesmen are already lining their pockets by supplying liquor and food on credit to the crews anyway. Payne, brought in to restore order, is an old pal of Duryea's but still lays down the law to him (and Laramie's critical town council), the hunk catching the eye of Duryea's mistress, fancy saloon dame Mari Blanchard. Eventually, Duryea is found guilty of participating in the murder of Sheriff James Griffith by America's first all-female jury; busted out of the jug by his wife, Joyce Mackenzie, he boards the work train with Healey (Van Cleef has been eliminated by Payne), the two crooks succumbing to Payne's fists. Payne gets Blanchard at the end, promising to marry her and jointly run the saloon. *Rails into Laramie* exhibits all the spit and polish of a typical 1950s Universal-International Western, the acting is solid throughout, but the puzzling plot and rushed climax leave a feeling of disappointment.

Dialogue:
John Payne to the doctor after bringing in Griffith's body: "Take him down to the undertakers. And Doc—tell 'em to stay open."

Saskatchewan aka O'Rourke of the Royal Mounted

Universal; Technicolor; 87 minutes; Producer: Aaron Rosenberg; Director: Raoul Walsh; Cast: Alan Ladd; Shelley Winters; Robert Douglas; J. Carrol Naish; Hugh O'Brian; Jay Silverheels; Richard Long; Antonio Moreno ****

The mountains, waterfalls, rivers, lakes and forests of Canada's Banff National Park, Alberta, lovingly photographed by seven-times Oscar-nominee John F. Seitz—these play just as important a role in *Saskatchewan* as do Alan Ladd and company, director Raoul Walsh ensuring that we are not allowed to forget it. It's spring, 1877. Ladd stars as a Royal Mounted Policeman who, alongside English commander Robert Douglas and scout J. Carrol Naish, escorts a troop detachment and wagons loaded with munitions across wild, Indian-infested country to Fort Walsh— Cock-a-hoop after their defeat of Custer at the Little Bighorn, the Sioux have crossed the Canadian border, wishing to join forces with the Cree and wipe out all white dogs, so the fort urgently requires those rifles and bullets. Also, on the trek, is Shelley Winters (sole survivor of a Sioux attack) and Marshal Hugh O'Brian; Winters is wanted in Montana for the murder of O'Brian's brother, but the surly lawman is the culprit, jealous of his sibling's affair with the frisky blonde and in love with her himself. It makes for an action-packed trip, the Cree willing to ignore Sitting Bull and Crazy Horse's overtures for war if they are allowed weapons and ammunition of their own, Cree Jay Silverheels (Ladd is his adopted brother) advocating hostilities but later changing his mind. O'Brian is shot after confessing that Winters is innocent and Douglas, as green as grass, threatens

Ladd with court martial when his orders are disobeyed in the name of safety ("If we lose, we get scalped. If we don't, we hang," says Ladd to the troopers); at Fort Walsh, Ladd and his men are stuck in a detention cell for their troubles. Released by Silverheels, Ladd and his squad leave the fort with the ammo and cause havoc among the Sioux, resulting in a new peace treaty with the Cree. Ladd heads off to Montana with buxom Winters at his side, leaving Naish (who turns in the film's best performance) to contemplate kiddie number seven, produced by his Indian wife of, yep, seven years!

Highlights:
The stunning Canadian mountain backdrops, a Western travelogue come to vivid life.

Dialogue:
Winters to Ladd on seeing him in his uniform: "A policeman! I should have known it. I've heard about you Redcoats, you always get your man. Tell me, am I the first woman to your credit?"
Ladd: "Yeah. And I hope you're the last."

Trivia:
Ladd, at five-foot-six and a quarter inches, had to stand on higher ground in his scenes with six-foot O'Brian, the actor notoriously touchy about his height; he also had to fight off an infection for most of the shoot, the reason why he appears uncomfortable at times. The scenario covered almost the same ground that featured in Fox's 1952 *Pony Soldier*.

Siege at Red River

Panoramic Prods./20th Century Fox; Technicolor; 86 minutes; Producer: Leonard Goldstein; Director: Rudolph Maté; Cast: Van Johnson; Joanne Dru; Richard Boone; Jeff Morrow; Milburn Stone; Craig Hill; Robert Burton; Rico Alaniz **

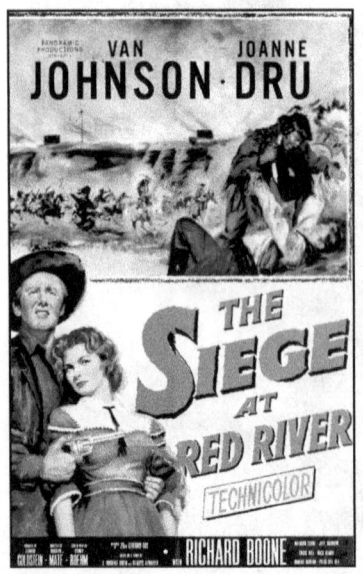

An invigorating finale more or less makes up for a "marking time" first hour in Rudolph Maté's unsatisfactory Rebs versus Bluecoats versus Injuns yarn, Sydney Boehm's dawdling script veering from bouts of limp action to comedic farce. It's November 1864: Confederates Van Johnson and Milburn Stone hijack a disassembled Gatling gun in a locomotive stickup and, under the guise of salesmen selling a potion that claims to promote muscle growth (Doc Sunderland's Muscle Builder), trundle their wagon across one Union state after another with the gun parts on board, receiving cryptic messages at each stopover. Loose cannon horse trader Richard Boone agrees to help them get to the Southern army, even though the war is almost lost, planning to sell the gun to Chief Yellow Hawk and his Sioux. There's a lengthy (and irrelevant) boring interlude where Milburn succeeds in getting nurse Joanne Dru drunk on herbal tea and his fake potion, bumbling Jeff Morrow and his Union troops tail Johnson and the narrative meanders like a desert river until that final 20 minutes. The Sioux attack Fort Smith, Boone manning the Gatling gun; the rat is knifed by Johnson who turns the weapon on the Indians, causing them to flee in terror from both gun and cavalry (footage of the Battle at War Bonnet Gorge from 1944's *Buffalo Bill* is included here). News that the war has ended means that Johnson is now free to romance Dru. Attractive location work (Moab, Utah and Durango, Colorado) and a rousing Lionel Newman stock score do little to compensate for a Western that drags its heels in the dust for much of its running time, with very little sparkle from the leading players.

Highlights:
The rugged, rocky Colorado wilderness, splendidly photographed by Edward Cronjager, and little else.

Dialogue:
Sergeant John Cliff to Milburn: "Muscle builder. Soon as the war's over, you oughta head south. The Rebs are gonna need a lot of muscle building when we get through with them."

Trivia:
Tyrone Power and Dale Robertson were both lined up for the principal male role, and Jean Peters for the female lead, but Maté and Goldstein insisted on drafting in Van Johnson from MGM, not, in this instance, a wise move ("Miscast," commented the *New York Times*.)

Silver Lode

RKO-Radio; Technicolor; 81 minutes; Producer: Benedict Bogeaus; Director: Allan Dwan; Cast: John Payne; Lizabeth Scott; Dan Duryea; Dolores Moran; Emile Meyer; Harry Carey, Jr.; Alan Hale, Jr.; Morris Ankrum ****

Filmed on *High Noon*-lines (the events take place over two hours) and anti-Joseph McCarthy (he of the 50s "Red Scare" movement) in concept, *Silver Lode* is a taut Western thriller featuring a terrific performance from Dan Duryea as Fred McCarty (another anti-commie dig). He's a killer posing as a marshal, riding into Silver Lode with three cohorts on John Payne's wedding day, determined to retrieve $20,000 Payne legitimately won from his brother in a poker game; Payne shot Duryea's sibling dead as he went for the draw, and Duryea is after that money *and* Payne's head, also accusing the rancher of cattle rustling and murder. Much like Gary Cooper in the Fred Zinnemann classic, Payne's up against the entire townsfolk, including bride-to-be Lizabeth Scott and Sheriff Emile Meyer; everyone refuses to be convinced by Payne's story, that's he's not a murderer and Duryea is an imposter holding a false warrant. Given two hours in which to prove that what he's saying is the truth, Payne gets into all kind of scrapes, gunning down two of Duryea's jackals (Stuart Whitman and Alan Hale, Jr.), Duryea shooting the third, Harry Carey, Jr., who was on the point of spilling the beans for $5,000. Dolores Moran, Payne's ex-love, a saloon tart with a heart of gold, is the only one to fully believe in him ("I'll take good care of you, honey."), forging, with Scott's assistance, a telegram message from the town of Discovery that proves Payne's innocence (the real message turns up minutes later); Duryea, unmasked at last, corners Payne in the church bell tower ("I want your land, your cattle and your money.") but gets a bullet in the heart, his slug ricocheting off the bell. A suspenseful oater set in a confined town setting, Duryea chewing the scenery with undisguised glee.

Highlights:
Dan Duryea, one of the screen's greatest exponents of the irrepressible, slightly psychotic, bad guy on blistering form.

Dialogue:
Duryea to Moran, irked at her meddling into his affairs: "Did you ever hear the fable of the interfering cat?"
Moran: "Yeah—she hated rats."

Trivia:
GI pinup favorite Moran's scandalous love life was far more interesting than her on/off movie career. The blonde temptress specialized in dating older married film executives (Howard Hawks among their number), had liaisons with a few of Hollywood's leading actors (including Mickey Rooney) and stole producer Benedict Bogeaus from his wife, who committed suicide two years after the pair married in 1946. *Silver Lode* was her final picture; she died of cancer in September 1982, aged 58.

Sitting Bull

United Artists; CinemaScope/Eastmancolor; 105 minutes; Producer: W. R. Frank; Director: Sidney Salkow; Cast: Dale Robertson; Mary Murphy; J. Carrol Naish; John Litel; Joel Fluellen; John Hamilton; Douglas Kennedy; William Hopper *****

Granted, Jack DeWitt and Sidney Salkow's screenplay doesn't exactly adhere to the true facts of events leading up to the Little Bighorn massacre of 1876, but *Sitting Bull* is one hell of an action-packed Long Knives versus Indians yarn, shot in Mexico and directed with zest by Sidney Salkow. Dale Robertson plays a conscientious army major who feels for the Redskins and their plight ("They're treated like dogs."), going against orders at every given opportunity. He refuses to take miners into the Black Hills for gold, allows captured Sioux to escape their appalling conditions at an agency run by ruthless Thomas Browne Henry, argues with General Custer (Douglas Kennedy) over military tactics and is demoted to captain. On top of that, love interest Mary Murphy, a perfidious go-getter, blows hot and cold by romancing reporter William Hopper, needing to move back East where she can shop to her heart's content. J. Carrol Naish is the noble Sioux chief of the title (tremendous in the role), holding on to peace, hoping for a powwow with President Ulysses S. Grant (John Hamilton) until, at the insistence of Crazy Horse (Iron Eyes Cody), rallying the various tribes for an all-out assault on Custer's 7th Cavalry at Little Bighorn, a spectacular, at times chaotic, 10-minute sequence that almost equals the same rousing set piece in Errol Flynn's 1941 classic *They Died With Their Boots On*. Robertson is sentenced to the firing squad for guiding the Sioux to pastures new, but Naish intervenes at the last minute ("You will be killing a patriot."), promising the President peace and friendship. Hopper killed at Little Bighorn, Murphy cuddles up to Robertson, although what the gal really needs is a hefty kick up her heavily skirted backside from her put-upon hero. An underrated pro-Indian movie of some merit.

Highlights:

A great operatic score from Raoul Kraushaar, a spellbinding climactic battle (one of the '50s finest) and "Stiff-backed pretty-boy" (Robertson, in the words of the *New York Times*) putting in a solid performance.

Dialogue:

Disgruntled gold miner William Tannen to Robertson, unhappy that Indians who have ransacked his wagons for food have been allowed to ride back to their camp. "Are you gonna let them go?"

Robertson: Yes."

Tannen: "I'll drive a hard case against you, soldier."

Robertson: "And I'll drive my fist down your throat if you open your mouth again."

Trivia:

Mary Murphy caught Montezuma's Revenge on the Mexican shoot, the reason why she looks so uncomfortable in her relatively short scenes.

Taza, Son of Cochise

Universal; Technicolor; Orig. in 3-D; 79 minutes; Producer: Ross Hunter; Director: Douglas Sirk; Cast: Rock Hudson; Barbara Rush; Rex Reason; Gregg Palmer; Morris Ankrum; Ian MacDonald; Eugene Iglesias; Robert Burton *****

Universal's follow-up to *The Battle at Apache Pass* (1952) had Cochise (a brief cameo from Jeff Chandler) dying in 1874, Taza (Rock Hudson) taking over as chief of the Chiricahua Apaches and determined to keep the peace by moving to the San Carlos reservation. His quarrelsome brother, Naiche (Rex Reason) doesn't believe in peace ("I will join Geronimo."); neither does Grey Eagle (Morris Ankrum), foul-tempered father of Oona (Barbara Rush) whom Hudson *and* Reason both hope to wed. Geronimo (Ian MacDonald), holed up in the mountains, under guard and lusting for blood. When Lieutenant Lance Fuller stupidly stabs an Apache prisoner to death, Taza forgets all about peace treaties, attacking Fort Apache in force and *then* deciding to start a new life at San Carlos; however, Naiche, Grey Eagle and Geronimo have other ideas, leading to a series of tribal in-fighting, culminating in a rip-roaring clash taking place in a deep canyon between Gregg Palmer and Robert Burton's regiments and Geronimo's warriors; Taza and his braves come to the rescue, Geronimo taken captive and carted off to a distant reservation. Peace restored, Taza, dressed in army uniform, makes plans to marry Oona now her sadistic father is dead. Russell Metty's vivid photography highlights the spectacular rock formations and scenery in Utah's Moab and Arches National Park areas, while Frank Skinner's score blasts away nonstop. As for six-foot-five Hudson, he's a magnificent example of '50s male beefcake, even though he makes absolutely no attempt to inflect just a modicum of broken American/Indian accent into his portrayal of Taza.

Highlights:

One of the best, most colorful, medium-budget cavalry versus Injuns yarns of the 1950s, containing breathtaking shots of Moab's awe-inspiring canyons and mesas.

Dialogue:

Scout Richard H. Cutting to Palmer, noticing what Taza has in his hair: "The chief's feather. It's being worn by Cochise's eldest son, Taza."

Palmer: "Oh. What's he like?"

Cutting: "Well, he's got it in him to be a greater chief than Cochise or a worse devil than Geronimo."

Trivia:

Douglas Sirk, who specialized in romantic melodramas, claimed that this, his one and only Western, was his favorite film.

They Rode West

Columbia; Technicolor; 84 minutes; Producer: Lewis J. Rachmil; Director: Phil Karlson; Cast: Robert Francis; Donna Reed; Philip Carey; May Wynn; Onslow Stevens; Roy Roberts; Jack Kelly; Stuart Randall ****

In Phil Karlson's solid Long Knives versus Injuns yarn, featuring a splendid Paul Sawtell score (and Roy Roberts as the obligatory whiskey-loving Irish sergeant), idealistic young medic Robert Francis arrives at Fort McCullough to find himself the center of open hostility, especially from six-foot-four Captain Philip Carey, an Indian/doctor-hating bigot. Francis wants to improve the lives of the nearby Kiowa tribe, stuck on a hated reservation and suffering from malaria, but Carey is having none of it ("It's not your job to wet nurse the enemy, mister."), convinced the Kiowa have stolen 10 carbines from his wagons, even though they're innocent. "Get that scared look off your face, mister, it's bad policy," snaps the officer to Francis as they enter the Kiowa camp to interrogate the braves, the doctor latching on to the fact that squaw May Wynn is a white woman living with the tribe and should be treated with dignity, despite Carey's roughhouse tactics. Back at the fort, Colonel Onslow Stevens' daughter, Donna Reed, flirts with all the officers but can't grab Francis' attention, the one man she's interested in. Branded a "Kiowa lover" and a "Woodhawk" (a bird that turns on its own kind), Francis sparks an Indian revolt through kindness and is confined to quarters when troops contract the disease; the Kiowas join forces with the Comanches, but after Francis successfully operates on the chief's son in the aftermath of a bloody skirmish, the two tribes leave in peace, to set up home in their beloved high country. Reed at last nabs Francis and Carey, who has sniped at the medic throughout the entire 84 minutes, is left speechless; what a pity he didn't receive a well-deserved war arrow between his brawny shoulder blades. *Variety* commented: "A cut above standard."

Highlights:

Several savage, hand-to-hand encounters between cavalry and hostiles, filmed in California's Simi Hills. And Carey has never been more of an unpleasant, pain-in-the-butt bully than in this picture.

Dialogue:

Francis to Carey: "You've got too much of a dislike for doctors."
Carey: "I guess I do, mister; you might as well know it. Your predecessor was a drunk, and before him a drug addict and before him a sadistic butcher who was never happy unless he had a knife in his hand. And now they send us schoolboys."

Trivia:

After appearing in only four pictures, Francis, one of *Screen World*'s Promising Personalities of 1954, was tragically killed when the private plane he was piloting crashed into a parking lot in July 1955; he was only 25.

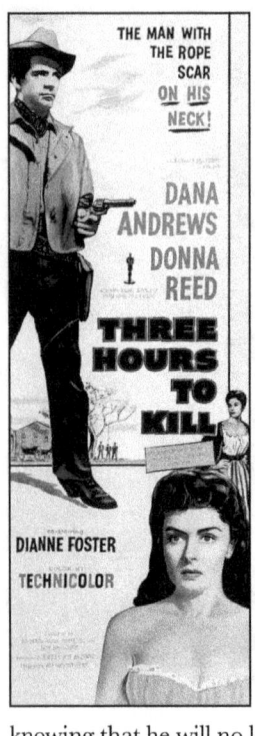

Three Hours to Kill

Columbia; Technicolor; 77 minutes; Producer: Harry Joe Brown; Director: Alfred L. Werker; Cast: Dana Andrews; Donna Reed; Stephen Elliott; Richard Coogan; Whit Bissell; Dianne Foster; Laurence Hugo; Richard Webb ***

Carrying the ragged mark of a rope branded across his neck, unshaven, unsmiling Dana Andrews returns to his hometown after a three-year absence to find out who killed Richard Webb, Donna Reed's over-protective brother; Andrews was blamed because Webb objected to his relationship with Reed but escaped the lynch mob ("They made a mistake. I wanna see them squirm."). Ex-fiancée Reed has married Richard Coogan, one of the suspects, the other three being saloon boss Laurence Hugo, barkeep James Westerfield and barbershop owner Whit Bissell. Sheriff Stephen Elliott turns out to be the murderer; he bumped off Webb at a dance because he owed him gambling debts, pinning the killing on Andrews. When Andrews shoots Elliott in a fight, he once again faces an angry necktie party, but Westerfield explains to the townsfolk that the sheriff shot Webb in the first place. His reputation restored, Andrews leaves Reed and Coogan alone, aware that their young lad is his son; as he gallops away, redhead saloon lass Dianne Foster goes after him, knowing that he will no longer yearn for Reed. A neat little Western whodunit, Andrews giving his usual excellent performance, something he was adept at doing whatever film role he was playing; Paul Sawtell also provides a fine score.

Dialogue:
Hugo to Bissell, Coogan and Westerfield: "Here we sit, the four of us, waiting for the executioner."

Thunder Pass

Lippert/Republic; 76 minutes; Producer: A. Robert Nunes; Director: Frank McDonald; Cast: Dane Clark; Dorothy Patrick; Andy Devine; John Carradine; Raymond Burr; Raymond Hatton; Mary Ellen Kay; Nestor Paiva ***

After having a powwow with Chiefs Growling Bear and Black Eagle of the Kiowa and Comanche tribes, Captain Dane Clark is granted two days to round up settlers, group them together at Chicataw Mesa Stage Stop and escort them through Thunder Pass to Fort Terrahawk. The Indians have been promised a new peace treaty, food and land; if they're not forthcoming, it will be war with the Long Knives. And what a bunch Clark has on his hands. Among others, gold miners Raymond Burr and Raymond Hatton grumble about leaving their grubstake behind, having just unearthed a nugget; Mary Ellen Kay flirts outrageously with the troopers; trader Nestor Paiva moans incessantly about his lot; blonde Dorothy Patrick spits out words of venom to Clark; scout Andy Devine backs up Clark's orders; and John Carradine rides in; a no-good supplying Winchesters to the Redskins (he was also once married to Patrick's sister). When a stranger is found seriously injured beside a runaway stage, Clark decides to take him with them, thinking (correctly) that he could be a government emissary from Washington on a peace mission; Burr, Paiva and Carradine reckon he's a gun runner, and object to hauling his litter over rough terrain. To the insidiously menacing drones of Edward J. Kay's music, the team treks through the pass and eventually, after much arguing and dealing with renegade Indians, reach a tunnel to safety, engaging in a three-minute shooting match with Black Eagle's war-hungry warriors before Growling Bear's braves break up the fight (Burr plugs Carradine in the back). At the fort, Kay weds trooper Rick Vallin and Clark gallops off to new adventures, taking Patrick with him. A routine actioner that moves briskly enough, the whole cast turning in believable performances, leaving the viewer with one question to contemplate; who had the bigger girth—Burr or Devine?

Dialogue:
Clark to reluctant travelers Burr and Hatton: "You can't spend yer money with an arrow in your back."

Trivia:
The Bronson Canyon setting, and that distinctive tunnel, cropped up in dozens of films made during the decade, both Western and horror.

Track of the Cat

Warner Bros.; CinemaScope/Warnercolor; 102 minutes; Producers: Robert Fellows and John Wayne (uncredited); Director: William A. Wellman; Cast: Robert Mitchum; Tab Hunter; William Hopper; Teresa Wright; Diana Lynn; Beulah Bondi; Philip Tonge; Carl "Alfalfa" Switzer ***

High up in the mountains, their homestead hemmed in by snow and blizzards, lives one of the West's most dysfunctional families, the Bridges: Egomaniac Robert Mitchum; innocent Tab Hunter; kindhearted, meek William Hopper; neurotic spinster Teresa Wright; matriarch Beulah Bondi; and Bondi's husband, Philip Tonge, a drunken lech. Carl "Alfalfa" Switzer plays a wizened old Indian servant, while pert Diana Lynn is Hunter's girlfriend. "Cold Comfort Farm in the mountains" is how one critic described William A. Wellman's over-talkative psychological Western drama, others calling it "heavy and clumsy" and "lacking in dramatic point," Britain's *MFB* stating that, "Despair hangs in the air like a curse." The cat of the title is simply a catalyst for the entire bunch of tortured souls to act out their personal grievances like a bunch of petulant children: Mitchum, a coward at heart but bossing his brothers about and vying for the attentions of Lynn, goes in search of the black panther with Hopper who's mauled to death. Pursuing the beast on his own after Hopper's body returns to the ranch on the back of a horse, Mitchum leaves the rest to squabble, argue and emote: Bible puncher Bondi doesn't

A LOVE STORY OF REAL, RAW, RUNAWAY EMOTIONS!
"Don't you want anything bad enough to fight for it?"
WARNER BROS.
ROBERT MITCHUM
TERESA WRIGHT
FROM THE PRODUCER-DIRECTOR OF THE HIGH AND THE MIGHTY
WILLIAM A. WELLMAN'S
Track of the Cat
CINEMASCOPE AND WARNERCOLOR
DIANA LYNN · TAB HUNTER
BEULAH BONDI
A. I. BEZZERIDES
A WAYNE-FELLOWS PRODUCTION
WILLIAM A. WELLMAN
WARNER BROS.

want Hunter marrying Lynn, Wright (dressed in black) anguishes over Bondi's religious zeal, Tonge, mentally abused for years by his wife, gets through around a dozen bottles of whiskey, Hunter tries hard to grow up and be his own man and Switzer (26 but made to look 126) scuttles around, no doubt wondering about his employers' unhinged state of mind. It's Hunter who disposes of the cat in the end (the animal is never seen, only heard), rescuing Mitchum who had fallen into a crevasse; he's then allowed to go and live with Lynn after his ma admits, "I done wrong," bringing a smile to his face—and boy, this is one picture that urgently needed a lot more smiles! The exterior shots, filmed in Arizona's White Mountains, are fantastic (photography: William H. Clothier), Roy Webb's music rings loud and clear but the interiors where most of the movie takes place impart the feeling of a stage play—the film wasn't a success at the time of release. For devotees of angst-ridden cinema (and Bob Mitchum) only.

Highlights:
The grandeur of Arizona's White Mountains and Mitchum, always worth a look.

Dialogue:
Tonge to Bondi: "Gotta keep drunk to forget I'm married to a clothespin."

Trivia:
Switzer, of Hal Roach's *Our Gang* fame, was shot dead at the age of 31 on January 21, 1959 over a dispute concerning $50 owed to him.

Two Guns and a Badge

Allied Artists; 69 minutes; Producer: Vincent M. Fennelly; Director: Lewis D. Collins; Cast: Wayne Morris; Morris Ankrum; Beverly Garland; Robert J. Wilke; William Phipps; Roy Barcroft; Chuck Courtney; I. Stanford Jolley ***

In the Arizona town of Outpost, the townsfolk are sick and tired of cowpokes causing violence and mayhem, particularly after two of Robert J. Wilke's rustlers kill each other in an argument. At a council meeting, Sheriff Morris Ankrum proposes they hire a fast gun as his deputy, a man whose reputation alone will scare off the gangs. Out on the trail, armed robber Wayne Morris, recently released from federal prison, stumbles across the body of the gunslinger Ankrum has hired; burying the corpse, Morris straps on the hombre's fancy double holster, trots into Outpost and is mistakenly identified as the new deputy. But Morris takes to the task; he's handy with his fists *and* can shoot, even though Ankrum and rancher Roy Barcroft know he's not the real article. If produced on a bigger budget, Morris' penultimate Western of the 1950s (he starred in 12, including one apiece with Randolph Scott and Rod Cameron) would have been a corker, given Daniel B. Ullman's sparkling script ("A fine night's rustling," bemoans rustler Mike Ragan. "Twenty cows!"). As it is, Morris rounds up Wilke's rustlers and uncovers the brains behind the operation

(Beverly Garland's boyfriend, William Phipps) with very little gunplay in evidence, the movie not really capitalizing on the fact that the guy is reputed to be a feared killer. He does, however, get to smooch with Garland and stays on as sheriff after Ankrum retires. Generally considered to be the last of the 1950s series-type B-Westerns and director Lewis D. Collins' final film (he died shortly after of a heart attack in August 1954, aged 55), *Two Guns and a Badge* adds up to an entertaining 69 minutes, likeable Morris, pert Garland and snarling Wilke making it all so watchable.

Dialogue:

Ankrum and Morris in the saloon, facing Wilke's mob: "His (Morris) first job is to get rid of you. Every one of you. And I don't care how he does it."

Vera Cruz

United Artists; SuperScope/Technicolor; 94 minutes; Producers: Burt Lancaster, Harold Hecht and James Hill; Director: Robert Aldrich; Cast: Gary Cooper; Burt Lancaster; Denise Darcel; Cesar Romero; Sara (Sarita) Montiel; Morris Ankrum; Henry Brandon; Ernest Borgnine *****

During the Mexican rebellion of 1866, two amoral, cynical adventurers and their motley gang of gunfighters join up with Emperor Maximilian's troops who are transporting $3,000,000 worth of gold hidden in a carriage to the port of Vera Cruz. Southerner Gary Cooper figures the loot should go toward helping Morris Ankrum's Juaristas; Denise Darcel desires the cash to "buy up Paris."; Marquis Cesar Romero needs the gold for the war effort; and Burt Lancaster wants it all for himself ("I'm a pig," he spits out). Filmed entirely on location in Mexico, Robert Aldrich's $3,500,000, slam-bang "soldiers/mercenaries of fortune down Mexico way" adventure is right up there with the best, never faltering for a second: Evocative score (Hugo Friedhofer), vivid photography (Ernest Laszlo), a witty script (Roland Kibbee and James R. Webb) and above all else, two screen icons acting their socks off. From the moment when taciturn Cooper meets all-grinning Lancaster, to the riotous sequence in Emperor George Macready's opulent ballroom with "little tin soldier" Henry Brandon, to the storming climactic rebels versus military showdown, this is incident-packed, timeless Western entertainment of the classic variety. What a pity that Coop (as expected) gets the drop on Burt in the closing minutes, tears visible in his eyes as he realizes that his reluctant friend/protagonist will be sorely missed.

"Colorful and actionful," said *Variety* of a picture that raked in takings of $11,000,000 when first released, proving that the Cooper/Lancaster edgy partnership was a sure-fire box-office winner.

Highlights:

Black-clad Lancaster's perpetual flashing grin, especially when he wipes his greasy mouth all over Brandon's pristine white gloves; the long caravan filing past monolithic Aztec ruins, the Pyramid of the Sun at Teotihuacán; and Cooper and Lancaster's interplay, top movie professionalism handled with consummate ease, as you would expect from actors of their caliber.

Dialogue:

Cooper, who needs a steed, to Lancaster after spotting a suitable mount: "How much?"
Lancaster: "$100. Gold."
Cooper: "That's mighty hard."
Lancaster: "So's walkin'."

Trivia:

Cooper, dosed up to the eyeballs on medication for recurring back trouble, disliked working with Sara Montiel, stating she was unhygienic; Borgnine and Charles Bronson, in town buying cigarettes, were arrested by federal police and held at gunpoint, mistaken for real bandidos as they were dressed in their Western gear; in her autobio, Mamie Van Doren said Lancaster attempted the seduce her for the lead female role, but she rebuffed him and didn't get the part; Cooper demanded changes in the script to portray him as being not *quite* as dark as his character turned out to be; and Lancaster and Jack Elam came to blows when Lancaster's children, on set, poked fun at one of the genre's all-time villain's less-than-pleasing features.

The Yellow Mountain

Universal; Technicolor; 77 minutes; Producer: Ross Hunter; Director: Jesse Hibbs; Cast: Lex Barker; Howard Duff; Mala Powers; William Demarest; John McIntire; Leo Gordon; Dayton Lummis; William Fawcett ****

It's the battle of the gold miners in Goldfield, Nevada as warring partners Lex Barker and Howard Duff face up to John McIntire and Leo Gordon, clashing over grubstakes on Columbia Mountain's southern slopes. Unknown to them, grizzled prospector William Demarest (Jackpot!) owns the defunct 50/50 mine on the north slope; because the southern lodes course in a northerly direction, the old gambling coot owns the whole mountain and his 50/50 prospect is, in fact, full of rich seams. Jesse Hibbs directed several Audie Murphy Westerns in his time; if Universal's number one cowboy star had appeared in *The Yellow Mountain*, it would have been labeled a near-classic instead of sinking into obscurity. It's that good. There's plenty of fistfighting between Barker and Duff, both vying for Mala Power's attention, and bruising Barker/Gordon encounters; Duff throws in his lot with McIntire in a sneaky effort to take over Demarest's claim and form a smelting company, Barker is bushwhacked and left to rot in the Mojave Desert and an explosion in the 50/50 exposes tons of high grade ore. In a street standoff, Barker shoots two of McIntire's heavies while Duff, wanting to put things right with Barker, guns down McIntire and Gordon, resigned to the fact that his partner is going to get hitched to the delightful Powers; as the gal is Demarest's daughter, Duff, Barker and Demarest are going to be very rich indeed. A solid, colorful Universal oater well presented and incisively acted by the entire cast.

Dialogue:
Powers to Demarest, watching Barker and Duff enter into a curtain-closing slugging match: "Dad! Stop them!"
Demarest: "What for. They're partners!"

Yukon Vengeance

Allied Artists; 68 minutes; Producer: William F. Broidy; Director: William Beaudine; Cast: Kirby Grant; Chinook; Monte Hale; Mary Ellen Kay; Henry Kulky; Carol Thurston; Park MacGregor; Billy Wilkerson ***

In the lumber outback town of Big Bear, the local payroll, delivered by canoe, is being robbed at the rate of $5,000 a week, the mail carrier slaughtered by a savage bear. In steps Corporal Rod Webb (Kirby Grant) and his big white dog Chinook (the Wonder Dog) to clear matters up. Monte Hale, in league with burly trapper Henry Kulky, who owns the bear, is the culprit, trying to pin the blame onto store keeper Park MacGregor and Mountie Grant while stirring up trouble with the Athapaskan Indians. Shot around California's San Bernardino National Forest area, *Yukon Vengeance* is great for kids as B-Western entertainment, the exception being the two ferocious fights between Chinook and the bear, far too realistic for today's sensitive souls. Kulky falls to his death from a waterwheel in the final reel, Grant undergoing a "trial by combat" with Hale in front of Chief Lone Eagle (Billy Wilkerson) and his tribe, Yellow Flower (Carol Thurston) throwing a well-aimed knife into Hale's retreating back. Last seen is Chinook playing with a bear skin; in the commissioner's words, "destroying the evidence."

Dialogue:
Hale to Grant, worried that Mary Ellen Kay has switched her affections: "I'm warning you Webb. If anything happens to that girl, you won't live long enough for an Athapaskan brave to shove a knife in your ribs."

Trivia:
This marked the tenth and final appearance of Grant and Chinook and the actor's last movie; he concentrated on the *Sky King* television series which ran from 1952 to 1959.

Chapter 9
1955

CALL HER HALF-BREED ... AND ALL HELL BREAKS LOOSE!
Apache Woman

THE SWEEP OF "RED RIVER" ... THE DRAMA OF "HIGH NOON" ...
AND NOW ... THE MIGHT OF KIRK DOUGLAS!
The Indian Fighter

HIS HOME WAS HIS SADDLE, HIS ONLY FRIEND A SIX-GUN
AND HIS COUNTRY THE WILD FREE RANGE!
Man Without a Star

SO CLOSE TOGETHER ... ONLY A BULLET CAN SEPARATE THEM! *The Naked Dawn*

THEY RISKED THEIR LUCK ON A TURN OF A CARD ... THEIR LIVES
ON THE DRAW OF A GUN!
The Rawhide Years

BROTHER AGAINST BROTHER ... BULLET FOR BULLET ... AND
THE HONEY-HAIRED BLONDE WAS THE PRIZE!
The Road to Denver

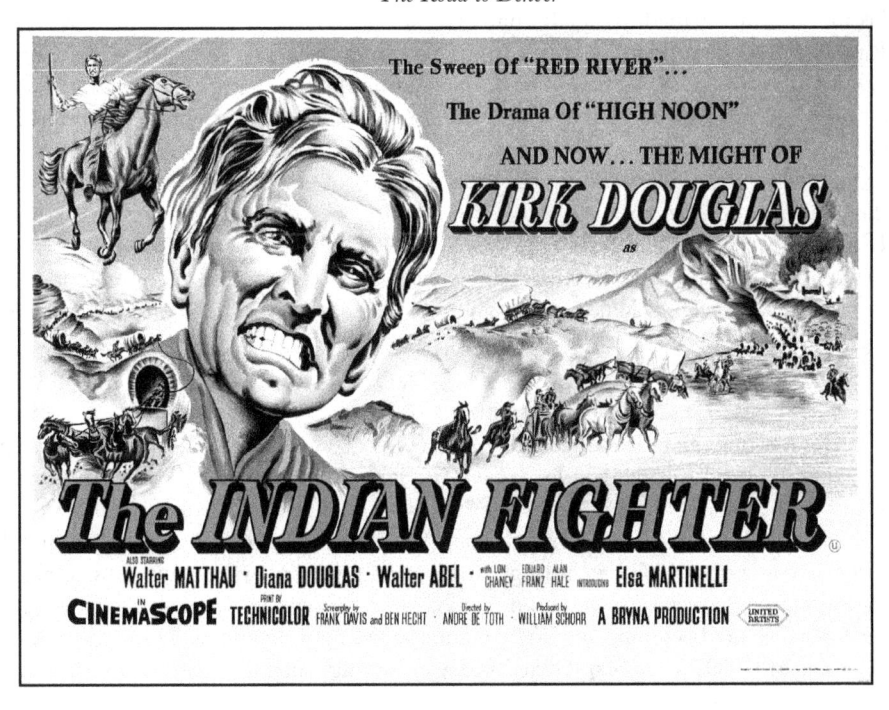

Apache Ambush

Columbia; 68 minutes; Producer: Wallace MacDonald; Director: Fred F. Sears; Cast: Bill Williams; Ray Teal; Alex Montoya; Movita; Adelle August; Richard Jaeckel; James Griffith; James Flavin ***

On the night of his assassination on April 14, 1865, President Abraham Lincoln (James Griffith) instructs former Union Indian scout Bill Williams and cavalry sergeant Ray Teal to move thousands of head of cattle from Texas to Kansas in order to replenish Union rations, depleted following the virtual end of the Civil War. In their path lie many disruptive elements: embittered Southern soldiers, Apaches and Alex Montoya's Mexican Jironza renegades, all wanting a slice of the beef for themselves. Padded out with footage from Columbia's 1940 $2,000,000 production *Arizona* (cattle drive; wagon trains; Indian attacks), *Apache Ambush* serves its purpose as a routine, no-nonsense second feature, most of the action set on the Texas/New Mexico border where Montoya's rowdy pistoleros and flighty mistress Movita are stirring up trouble, dying to get their hands on a shipment of 100 Henry repeating carbines. Colonel James Flavin can't give Williams the men he is after for his mission, one-armed soldier Richard Jaeckel causes unrest among the disgruntled Rebs, incensed that their cattle will feed Union mouths, while Apaches led by Chief Apaho (Iron Eyes Cody) are on the warpath. Dynamite wipes out Montoya's grinning coyotes and the Indians retreat under thousands of thundering hooves in the noisy climax. Adelle August supplies the female interest (albeit in small doses) and Williams, though solid enough, remains for the most part expressionless, old pro Teal turning in the film's best performance.

Dialogue:

Flavin, tired of all the fighting and changed orders: "Someday, it's gonna be wonderful to sit back in a rocking chair and not have to worry about Apaches, patrols, cattle and Jironzas."

Apache Woman

Golden State/ARC; Pathécolor; 69 minutes; Produced and Directed by Roger Corman; Cast: Lloyd Bridges; Joan Taylor; Lance Fuller; Paul Birch; Morgan Jones; Paul Dubov; Gene Marlowe; Lou Place ***

Joan Taylor stars as a half-French, half-Apache outcast whose brother, embittered failed lawyer Lance Fuller, is in league with a gang of outlaws; disguised as Indians, they're causing mischief to stir up a possible war between whites and Redskins, and the townsfolk are becoming edgy. Mean gunman Morgan Jones is assigned the task of disposing of Chief White Star (Gene Marlowe), forcing Fuller to confess to his sister that he's not the innocent she thinks; he's the brains behind all the attacks and he's also planning a bank robbery to feather his own nest. Taylor begs Fuller to stop and come away with her to start a new life, but her excitable brother's not interested. Commencing with a knife fight, Taylor (in white), who's been labeled a "dirty squaw," taking on Jonathan Haze (in black), broken up before someone gets killed by Indian agent Lloyd Bridges, and climaxing in a cliff top tussle, Fuller tumbling to his death following a fight with Bridges, Roger Corman's second Western feature is a shade above average, the director focusing much of his attention on Taylor's graceful features, if nothing else; a standard oater containing a few thrills and spills.

Highlights:

Taylor bathing naked in a pool, Bridges watching with lustful intent.

Dialogue:

Lou Place to Bridges: "Don't let that gal's beauty blind you."
Bridges: "Yeah, she sure is a pretty one, isn't she?"
Place: "So's a diamondbacked rattler."

At Gunpoint aka Gunpoint

Allied Artists; CinemaScope/Technicolor; 81 minutes; Producer: Vincent M. Fennelly; Director: Alfred L. Werker; Cast: Fred MacMurray; Dorothy Malone; Walter Brennan; Tommy Rettig; Skip Homeier; Frank Ferguson; John Qualen; Whit Bissell ****

The Dennis gang rides into the cozy little backwater of Plainview, robs the bank, kills the cashier and plugs the marshal; as they gallop off, Frank Ferguson wings the boss, John Pickard, and a second bullet from storekeeper Fred MacMurray makes him hit the dirt, his body lying next to the loot. MacMurray is proclaimed a hero, even though he insists it was a lucky shot, but turns down the offer to fill the marshal's vacancy ("I can't handle a gun."); Ferguson accepts the position but, minutes later, is pumped full of slugs by punk gunman Skip Homeier in revenge for his brother's killing. MacMurray claims the $2,500 reward on Pickard's head but finds himself a shunned man, a pariah in a town full of yellowbellies, the jittery citizens displaying their true colors by avoiding the man they know will be the Dennis gang's next target. Only Doc Walter Brennan has the guts to stick with MacMurray, his wife Dorothy Malone and their kid, Tommy Rettig. Matters reach crisis point when Malone's brother, James O'Hara, is shot dead, mistaken for MacMurray, worried bank manager John Qualen calling an urgent town council meeting and asking the storekeeper and his family to quit Plainview ("The gang might come back—after you."). But MacMurray's staying put in a place he now feels ashamed of, grabbing a revolver as Homeier and his three hombres enter a windswept town to finish him off, Qualen and company vanishing like scared rabbits.

Westerns of the 1950s: The Classic Years

However (for once), MacMurray's *not* a reformed gunman; he's every bit as bad as he says he is, his shots wide off the mark. Homeier, smiling, canters in for the kill but is blasted off his horse by Brennan wielding a shotgun, and those once-frightened menfolk appear from every town window, pointing rifles at the outlaws who surrender. Qualen admits that they were wrong and asks MacMurray for forgiveness; he elects to carry on as storekeeper, although why he should want to do so after the way he's been treated is anyone's guess. Disregard the *New York Times*' acidic comments of "a barefaced imitation of "High Noon," and "obvious and sluggish." Carmen Dragon's dramatic score hammers away as it did in *Invasion of the Body Snatchers*, director Werker organizes some stunning set pieces, Daniel B. Ullman delivers a pithy script and MacMurray, never a great fan of his own Westerns ("Me and horses never got along," he once said) turns in a solid performance, as do the rest of the cast; a slow-burner that never loses its grip.

Highlights:

Homeier and his boys riding into windy Plainview to get MacMurray; there's a lovely performance from 14-year-old Rettig as MacMurray's devoted son; and fan favorite Dabbs Greer makes a brief appearance as a preacher.

Dialogue:

MacMurray to drifter James Griffith after everyone deserts him in the saloon: "Haven't you heard? I'm the local hero."
Griffith: "You don't say."
MacMurray: "You're looking at the man who shot the notorious Alvin Dennis from a distance of half a mile—with a slingshot!"

Trivia:

Joel McCrea turned down the lead role because of other movie commitments.

Chief Crazy Horse

Universal; CinemaScope/Technicolor; 86 minutes; Producer: William Alland; Director: George Sherman; Cast: Victor Mature; John Lund; Suzan Ball; Ray Danton; Keith Larsen; James Millican; Dennis Weaver; Donald Randolph ***

The *New York Times* labeled George Sherman's sedate tale of Lakota Sioux Crazy Horse's life as "monotonous," which was unfair. Okay, there are only two action sequences (Custer's defeat at the Battle of Little Bighorn is mentioned but not shown); however, what you are presented with are lovely panoramic South Dakota landscapes beautifully photographed by Harold Lipstein, a lyrical Frank Skinner score and big Victor Mature commanding the attention in the title role. Mature is the "warrior of prophecy," leading his people into war with the white man when the Black Hills, the Sioux's sacred burial and hunting grounds, are invaded by gold-hungry prospectors, a provocative act instigated by brothers Robert F. Simon and James Westerfield. The noble chief, eventually forced to surrender because of his wife's (Suzan Ball) illness ("Hunger and cold have defeated Crazy Horse, not the army.") was murdered in 1877 at Fort Robinson by the thrust of a bayonet in the back, the culprit his treacherous cousin, Ray Danton (in this version), after he had begged General James Millican to allow the remnants of his tribe to buffalo hunt before winter arrived. It *is* rather slow-moving, the narrative told from both the Indian and trader John Lund's point of view, but there's no denying the film's pictorial impact, the production's one major saving grace. *Chief Crazy Horse* looks swell, despite lulls in the action department and was a sizeable hit at the time.

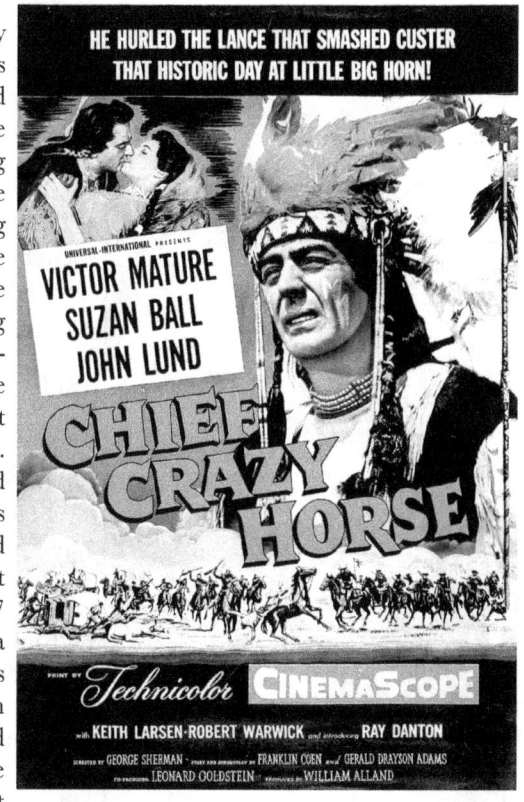

Highlights:
The rolling South Dakota scenery stretching as far as the eye can see.

Dialogue:
Keith Larsen to Mature, the pair viewing their warriors spying on an approaching troop detachment: "Lone Bear has no patience. He's itching to attack."
Mature: "If he doesn't wait for my signal, he'll itch no more."

Trivia:
Four months after the movie's release, radiant Ball tragically died from cancer at the age of 21.

The Far Horizons

Paramount; VistaVision/Technicolor; 108 minutes; Producers: William H. Pine and William C. Thomas; Director: Rudolph Maté; Cast: Fred MacMurray; Charlton Heston; Donna Reed; Barbara Hale; William Demarest; Ralph Moody; Alan Reed; Eduardo Noriega ****

Based on the Lewis/Clark expeditions of the early 1800s, which opened up vast areas of the Pacific northwest, *The Far Horizons* is stunning to watch: Cinematographer

Daniel L. Fapp, who would win an Oscar for *West Side Story*, bathes Wyoming's Grand Teton National Park's wild, rugged mountainous scenery in vivid colors, complemented by Hans J. Salter's bombastic score. Elsewhere, dour-faced Fred MacMurray (as Lewis) heads the expedition into deepest Louisiana (bought from the French for $15,000,000) with Charlton Heston (as Clark), the two at loggerheads over Barbara Hale; she's promised to marry Heston on his return to Washington, having rebuffed MacMurray's too-earnest overtures. Troublesome, two-timing Indians, a treacherous French trapper (Alan Reed), the navigation of raging, snag-filled rivers, waterfalls, wrong turnings, rapids, Redskin ambushes and the two stars glaring at each other—Rudolph Maté's outdoor opus packs it all in and then some, and, to Paramount's credit, not a single back-projected scene in sight which adds greatly to the realism. However, the focus switches attention from MacMurray to Heston in the middle section with the arrival of Shoshone maiden Donna Reed (as Sacajawea), held captive by the Minitari tribe. In the opening banquet sequence, MacMurray comes across as the good guy, Indian fighter Heston the bad; Reed changes all that, MacMurray shown to be a pompous boor while much-tougher Heston melts under those smoldering brown eyes. Reed, Shoshone chief Eduardo Noriega's sister, promises to guide the expedition across the mountains to "the great salt sea," even though she's been given to trapper Alan Reed *and* promised to renegade buck Larry Pennell (Wild Eagle). When Heston beats the Frenchman in a knife fight, Reed states that she's his for evermore ("I belong to you now. I am your woman."), MacMurray fuming that Heston, whom he perceived stole Hale from him, is now carrying on with a savage, albeit a highly desirable one, and even wishing to marry her. Heston is threatened with court martial by MacMurray for disobedience, the Pacific is arrived at and, back in Washington in 1807, President Thomas Jefferson peruses the charts and reports, MacMurray (the only part in the film where he actually smiles) having torn out the pages referring to Heston's court martial. Reed has accompanied her intended to Washington but after a meeting with Hale realizes that the Washington social scene, with all its fancy trappings, is not for her ("It is not my country, not my people."); on the President's request, she's last seen riding away in a coach, tears running down her radiant cheeks, sacrificing her love for Heston for a life among her own kind; Heston, in the White House, is left a broken man.

Highlights:

Grand Teton's spectacular scenery and ex-beauty queen Reed's exquisite role-playing of Sacajawea; many attractive Hollywood actresses starred as Indian squaws in the 1950s, but perhaps Reed, in this picture, topped the lot, and those final emotive moments will have the ladies reaching for their hankies.

Dialogue:

Reed, on why her potions made Heston recover from sickness: "I used another medicine." Heston: "Tasted like boiled gunpowder!"

Trivia:

Gary Cooper and John Wayne were originally considered for the leads; Cooper rejected the script while Wayne had other projects in the pipeline.

Five Guns West

ARC/Palo Alto Productions; Pathécolor; 78 minutes; Produced and Directed by Roger Corman; Cast: John Lund; Dorothy Malone; Mike (Touch) Connors; R. Wright Campbell; Jonathan Haze; Paul Birch; James Stone; Jack Ingram **

Five Union criminals, wanted for murder, are pardoned by the Confederates on condition they waylay a stage carrying a turncoat Southern official who is carrying $30,000 in gold and intelligence reports on the Confederate army's movements, and bring him (and the cash) back for interrogation. Roger Corman's "Dirty half-dozen out West" feature, after an intriguing start, betrays its $60,000 origins, the argumentative five entering a town bereft of citizens to wait for the stage, only tomcat Dorothy Malone and her uncle, James Stone, on the scene. And when the stage arrives, four Union troopers accompany it, not a full complement. John Lund turns out to be a rebel officer overseeing the operation, smooth-talking Mike Connors tries his charms on Malone, brothers R. Wright Campbell (he wrote the script) and Jonathan Haze are a crazy pair of polecats and old-timer Paul Birch rides away at the end, leaving them to it. After a shoot-out and fistfight, Connors, Campbell and Haze lie dead in the dust; Lund escorts Jack Ingram, the man they were after, back to camp, promising to return and begin a romance with Malone. An undistinguished low-budget time-passer; Corman did slightly better the following year with the camp *Gunslinger*.

Highlights:

A classy piece of devilry from Connors, plus Malone and her cleavage; that's just about it!

Dialogue:

Lund to the Confederate officer, after hearing about their mission: "Well, let's see now. All we have to do is to make a hard four-day ride in about three days, get through the state plains full of Indians looking for white scalps, cross over the Union lines, hold up a stage escorted by Yankee troops, then bring some traitor all the way back here for Southern justice. That is, uh, quite an order, captain."

Trivia:
Roger Corman's debut as a director; he was so nervous during the nine-day shoot that he had to pause to be sick on his way to the set.

Fort Yuma

Bel-Air/United Artists; Technicolor; 78 minutes; Producer: Howard W. Koch; Director: Lesley Selander; Cast: Peter Graves; Joan Vohs; Joan Taylor; John Hudson; William Phillips; James O'Hara; Abel Fernandez; Addison Richards ****

Lesley Selander's pro-Indian companion piece to 1953's *War Paint* came under criticism from the Production Code Administration for its overt violence and sadism; several scenes of torture and brutality were cut before the movie went on general release in October 1955. Quick-tempered Lieutenant Peter Graves is the main instigator, an Indian-hating officer guiding a supply column over desolate wastes (Arizona's Kayenta, Sonoita and Sedona areas were used for location filming; great photography from Gordon Avil) towards Fort Yuma and harassed on all sides by Abel Fernandez's Apaches; the young warrior's father was shot dead by a disgruntled settler and he desires revenge. Graves detests his Apache scout, John Hudson, but cannot hate the Redskins all that much; Indian lass Joan Taylor, Hudson's sister (ravishing as a squaw in *War Paint*; equally delectable here), loves him and shares his tent of a night ("He uses you like an animal," Hudson complains to Taylor). To add fuel to a simmering fire of racial tension, blonde missionary Joan Vohs has the hots for Hudson, but he warns her off ("I'm an Apache. We're different."). Paul Dunlap's powerful score switches from pounding drums in the action sequences to sorrowful leitmotifs during the romantic interludes as the Apaches pick off the troopers one by one, stripping the bodies of their uniforms to enable them to enter Fort Yuma in disguise and massacre everyone there. Grim-faced Graves hangs one captive after threatening to "roast his brains over a fire," soldier James O'Hara suffers a slow, agonizing death when a spear is embedded in his back and Taylor is fatally shot during a prolonged skirmish among rocks, Graves a grieving yet changed man. A savage tussle between Graves and Fernandez results in the young Apache expiring in the dust, his braves retreating before a cavalry attack. Leaving Hudson and Vohs standing beside Taylor's lonely burial mound, Graves rides off, perhaps not the Indian hater he once was.

Highlights:

The cavalry versus Indians attacks are uncompromisingly violent for a mid-'50s Western, orchestrated with bravado by Selander.

Dialogue:

An example of Danny Arnold's biting script, demonstrating Graves' abuse of a captive: "Now listen to me, animal. You and your red brothers have killed four of my men, so when I talk to you, you better answer me, or I'll tear out your insides and feed them to the wolves."

Trivia:

Joan Vohs was given a chance to show her acting mettle after complaining to producer Howard W. Koch that she was always being cast as a dumb blonde.

The Gun that Won the West

Clover/Columbia; Technicolor; 71 minutes; Producer: Sam Katzman; Director: William Castle; Cast: Richard Denning; Dennis Morgan; Paula Raymond; Chris O'Brien; Robert Bice; Michael Morgan; Roy Gordon; Howard Wright *

Cheapo producer Sam Katzman and director William Castle cobbled this lame yarn together (set in the 1880s, a mistake; the events depicted here dated from the 1860s) utilizing a great deal of footage from Fox's 1944 Western *Buffalo Bill*, the cast wasted on this occasion. Richard Denning, the alcoholic owner of the Jack Gaines Wild West Show; Dennis Morgan as frontier scout Jim Bridger, who covers for Denning when he's too drunk to perform; and Paula Raymond playing Denning's wife, decorative but wooden. All three are sent west to help in setting up a chain of forts from Fort Laramie, Wyoming that will cross Sioux and Cheyenne territory; the new, powerful Springfield rifle will hopefully scare the Injuns, eight thousand in number, off. But when Morgan raids a buffalo herd for much-needed meat (more inserted footage), Chief Red Cloud (a poker-faced Robert Bice) and hothead Afraid of Horses (excitable Michael Morgan) join forces with the Cheyenne, even after they've witnessed a demonstration of the Springfield's deadly accuracy from Denning, who, confined to barracks, convinces Colonel Roy Gordon that the weapon *will* frighten the Indians into submission. Morgan's overtures to make love to restless Raymond are turned down, the dame riding off with a reformed, sober Denning after we've been treated to several minutes of cavalry versus Redskins action filched from the Fox oater that starred Joel McCrea, Morgan drowning Afraid of Horses in a river. An inferior rehash of Universal's magnificent *Tomahawk*: Take away the extensive *Buffalo Bill* footage and you are left with a very drab, cheapskate production indeed, the normally reliable and personable Denning in particular looking bored to tears.

Dialogue:
Bice to Gordon at Fort Laramie, after being warned about the Springfield's potential: "If you had the guns now, I would know it. Perhaps by the time such guns are ready for you, there will be none of you left to use them."

The Indian Fighter

United Artists; CinemaScope/Technicolor; 88 minutes; Producers: Kirk Douglas and William Schorr; Director: André De Toth; Cast: Kirk Douglas; Elsa Martinelli; Walter Matthau; Lon Chaney, Jr.; Diane Douglas; Walter Abel; Eduard Franz; Alan Hale, Jr. *****

The first production by Kirk Douglas' own company, Bryna, *The Indian Fighter* may well be one-eyed director André De Toth's finest Western. Filmed on location in the Oregon woods and taking place after the Civil War in 1870, Douglas (on top virile form) plays a scout on the side of Eduard Franz's Sioux, falling in lust with the chief's daughter, Elsa Martinelli (the Italian actress' movie debut; she's first seen bathing nude in a river). The Indians are keeping to the peace treaty, making good powwow with Captain Walter Abel at the nearby fort. But when lowlifes Walter Matthau and Lon Chaney, Jr., greedy for gold, stir up trouble with the tribe and Franz's brother, Gray Wolf, is murdered, the bodies of three scalped soldiers, tied to their horses, trot into the compound and an outgoing wagon train bound for Oregon is under threat, leading to accusations that Douglas is a dirty, no-good Indian lover. The wagons retreat to the fort, widowed Diane Douglas chats up the cleft-chinned scout to no avail, there's a blazing finale but eventually, Douglas tells Franz that he plans to start a life with Martinelli and it would be best if peace was restored between whites and the Reds; agreeing to this, the Sioux ride away from the stockade, the final image showing Douglas romping in a river for the second time with his beautiful squaw. Colorful photography (Wilfrid M. Cline), a thumping score (Franz Waxman), spot-on direction from De Toth and iconic Douglas showing what screen masculinity was all about in those days (and these days!) make this a tremendous mid-'50s Western produced on a relatively low budget, a huge hit in England when released in June 1956. "Douglas looks great in buckskins ... sturdy entertainment," enthused the *New York Times*.

Highlights:
Douglas (38) and Martinelli (20) making love in a river à la *From Here to Eternity*. The grinning pair looked as though they were thoroughly enjoying themselves and they were; in his memoirs, Douglas claimed they had nonstop sex throughout the entire shoot.

Dialogue:
Douglas to Matthau, after agreeing to challenge Gray Wolf for the right to take him prisoner: "I gotta fight him for your hide."
Matthau: "What happens if you lose?"
Douglas: "My troubles will be over. Yours will just begin."

Trivia:
John Wayne turned down the lead role, and a whopping $400,000 salary to go with it; and Douglas collided with his steed's head early in the shoot, breaking his nose.

The Kentuckian

United Artists; CinemaScope/Technicolor; 104 minutes; Producer: Harold Hecht; Director: Burt Lancaster; Cast: Burt Lancaster; Dianne Foster; Diana Lyn; Walter Matthau; Donald MacDonald; John McIntire; John Carradine; Una Merkel ***

Escaping a feud between two families, backwoodsman Burt Lancaster, young son Donald MacDonald and their dog Faro set off for a new life in Texas, encountering one stumbling block after another until they finally embark on their quest with Dianne Foster, a "bond girl" who has captured Lancaster's eye. The Lancaster-Hecht production company came up with a rambling period piece set in Kentucky circa the 1820s, short on action, long on talk, Burt not really flexing his masculine muscles until the last third of the movie (the author caught it as a nine-year-old in 1956 and fidgeted the whole way through). Walter Matthau (his film debut) played a bullwhip-wielding baddie in the community of Humility, poking fun at Lancaster who thinks that the President of the United States will pay him a fortune for a worthless freshwater pearl, while schoolteacher Diana Lyn falls for the buckskin-clad hunk and tries to convince him, and MacDonald, that life in the town is better than chasing a dream in unknown Texas. Even brother John McIntire, a tobacco salesman, and his snooty wife Una Merkel attempt to change Lancaster into a law-abiding businessman, but to no avail. MacDonald hates the place and is picked on at school, pining for the wide-open spaces and freedom, Lancaster worrying over his son's future in Humility. In a lively finale, two of the Frome Brothers come gunning for Lancaster; Matthau is beaten to death, Foster shoots one and Lancaster batters the other, the trio plus Faro starting off for Texas as originally planned. *The Kentuckian* is atmospheric in its depiction of insular backwoods culture, enriched by Bernard Herrmann's telling score, while MacDonald is captivating as Lancaster's discontented son, but the big man playing what amounts to a simpleton is a bit hard to take; audiences were used to seeing the star throwing his weight around, not bumbling from one scene to the next, although this didn't prevent the film from being a sizeable hit for United Artists. "Hairy frontier fable," commented one critic.

Highlights:
Kentucky's Cumberland Falls State Park's lovely wooded scenery, photographed in bright colors by Ernest Laszio, plus a delightful performance from 14-year-old child actor MacDonald.

Dialogue:
Lancaster to Lyn, explaining MacDonald's unhappy state: "A town ain't easy for a hunter. And he's got hunter's blood in him."

Trivia:
Whip Wilson's last film; he was hired for instructions on how to use a whip.

Kentucky Rifle

Howco International Productions; Pathécolor; 84 minutes; Produced and Directed by Carl K. Hittleman; Cast: Chill Wills; Lance Fuller; Cathy Downs; Jess Barker; Jeanne Cagney; John Pickard; Rory Mallinson; Henry Hull *

Wrapped up and premiered in New Orleans in April 1955 but not given a general release until July 1956, *Kentucky Rifle* is unpalatable fodder, a lumpy confection firing on blanks that may well count as grumpy old rascal Chill Wills' worst-ever Western. But then, Howco International was responsible for 1953's legendary horror clunker *Mesa of Lost Women* and Ed Wood's *Jail Bait* (1954), so what can you expect? Wills and Kentucky scout Lance Fuller are transporting a wagon train through Comanche territory. One wagon hits a rock, breaking the axle and wheel. Wills, Fuller and a few others decide to stay and repair the damage while the rest of the wagons continue onwards. Jeanne Cagney (James Cagney's sister) is about to have a baby; worried husband John Pickard frets over her condition; Cathy Downs, betrothed to Jess Barker, fancies Fuller; Sterling Holloway acts like a complete, stuttering fool, which he is; preacher Henry Hull prays to the Lord; John Alvin rides off to warn the wagons of Indians on the prowl and is found butchered; and Wills, as garrulous as ever, keeps an eye open for whooping Redskins. Shot under the shadow of California's Vasquez Rocks and cursed with a curiously dated Irving Gertz score, Carl

K. Hittleman's badly scripted potboiler (he contributed towards the screenplay) had treacherous Barker threatening to hand over Fuller's entire stock of Kentucky rifles to Rory Mallinson's tribe in exchange for a safe passage; naturally, it doesn't work, the heathens (all 20 of them) attacking the whites and mown down by Kentucky's new super-weapon, Barker receiving a lance in the chest for his troubles. The chief finishes off one of his own warriors who has fired an arrow into Wills' back, Cagney gives birth, Downs falls into Fuller's arms and Wills dies from his wound, clutching his beloved rifle "Sweet Betsy," the wagon at last hitting the trail. Cheap, corny and ultimately tedious, *Kentucky Rifle* looks like something manufactured in the 1940s, not in the same year that the likes of *The Indian Fighter* and *White Feather* were produced; even at 84 minutes, it's a burden on the senses to sit through.

Dialogue:
Wills to anyone in earshot: "Rifles and women don't mix."

The Last Frontier

Columbia; CinemaScope/Technicolor; 98 minutes; Producer: William Fadiman; Director: Anthony Mann; Cast: Victor Mature; Robert Preston; Guy Madison; James Whitmore; Anne Bancroft; Pat Hogan; Peter Whitney; Russell Collins **

Fort Shallon is surrounded by two warring tribes and commanded by play-it-by-the-book officer Robert Preston who lost 1,500 men in a single Civil War battle at Shiloh. In ambles jovial fur trapper Victor Mature with buddies James Whitmore and Pat Hogan; the three are enlisted as scouts by Captain Guy Madison, Mature making a play for Preston's frigid wife (an unrecognizable Anne Bancroft), getting on the wrong side of sadistic sergeant Peter Whitney and eventually helping thwart a mass Redskin attack, stiff-collared Preston dying in the skirmish. Mature, eager to become a soldier, finally dons a sergeant's uniform and, spruced up, is free to focus his questionable charms on Bancroft, now free of her intolerable husband. Aficionados will recognize the wooded fort setting, overshadowed by a dormant Mexico volcano, as that used a year later in the Randolph Scott oater *7th Cavalry*. They might *not* recognize Mature's wildly over-the-top turn as rough-hewn trapper Jed Cooper, rolling drunk one minute (with an oddly irritating laugh) and slobbering all over Bancroft the next; it's a central performance that you'll either love or hate. Anthony Mann conjures up a thrilling Injuns versus cavalry finale in what one critic described as a "disordered movie" with "dim photography," the audience "not getting a decent deal." The picture isn't that bad, but Mature's bull-in-a-china shop performance is jarring to say the least and, in the scene where, full of whiskey, the big man staggers across a parade inspection shouting insults, clumsily put across. Not one of director Mann's greatest achievements.

Highlights:
The attractive Mexican scenery and the climactic battle at Fort Shallon.
Dialogue:
Whitmore, trying to knock some sense into Mature's thick head over his infatuation with Bancroft: "Stay away from her. She's a fancy lady and she needs a fancy gent. You can't even read or write."
Trivia:
Although Whitmore is supposed to be the father figure to Mature's "lad," he was in fact, at 34, eight years younger than Mature, 42.

Last of the Desperados

AFRC; 72 minutes; Producer: Sigmund Neufeld; Director: Sam Newfield; Cast: James Craig; Jim Davis; Margia Dean; Barton MacLane; Bob Steele; Stanley Clements; Dick Elliott; Mike Ragan ****

Sheriff Pat Garrett (James Craig) kills Billy the Kid but is forced into quitting his job as Lincoln County's top lawman, the cowardly citizens scared of reprisals from the Kid's old gang if he hangs around. Taking up the offer of running a store in the remote border town of Stone Center, Craig is hunted down by vicious outlaw Bob Steele; shots are exchanged, Craig, hit in the leg, riding after his wounded foe. In Tascosa, Craig stumbles into Margia Dean's saloon, his leg tended to. Dean employs Craig as resident barman/gunhand to sort out trouble and falls for him. But the dark-haired dame was once married to Billy the Kid; her brother, Stanley Clements, idolized the outlaw and when Craig's identity is revealed ("You murdered my husband!"), the youngster comes gunning for him. In a saloon shoot-out, Craig wounds the lad and then faces up to coyotes

Steele, Barton MacLane, Mike Ragan and Frank Sully in Tascosa's street ("Clear the decks for action," he tells the townsfolk), finishing off all four in a splendid showdown. His badge saving him from a bullet, Craig decides to return to Lincoln County with law officer Jim Davis, promising to take up with Dean, who had forgiven him, later—and Clements wants to become Craig's deputy; he's got a new idol to look up to. Proving you don't need a bank-busting budget to produce the goods, *Last of the Desperados* is a gritty, no-nonsense take on the Pat Garrett/Billy the Kid legend, quite violent at times, filmed in a bleak black-and-white wash by Edward Linden to mirror the times and containing yet another stirring Paul Dunlap score. As down-to-earth Westerns go, this is a long-forgotten beauty that is enjoyable in a grimy, authentic kinda way.

Dialogue:
Craig in bed, administered soup by Dean: "It's good. You make a practice of picking up drifters off the floor and putting them to bed?"

The Lonesome Trail

Lippert Pictures; 73 minutes; Producers: Earle Lyon and Richard H. Bartlett; Director: Richard H. Bartlett; Cast: John Agar; Wayne Morris; Margia Dean; Earle Lyon; Edgar Buchanan; Douglas Fowley; Ian MacDonald; Richard H. Bartlett **

John Agar stars as a half-breed Union soldier returning from the Civil War to find his homestead burned to the ground; land-grabbing baron Earle Lyon is buying up all the property in the territory, bribing wheelchair-bound rancher Edgar Buchanan into allowing him to marry his daughter (Margia Dean; she's Agar's sweetheart) on condition he leaves Buchanan alone. Agar stirs up trouble with fists and pistols in Wayne Morris' saloon, is badly wounded by one of Lyon's gun toughs and recuperates in "crazy old man" Douglas Fowley's cave hideout. The narrative crawls at a snail's pace throughout, the novel ending seeing Agar dispatching Lyon and his cohorts in the streets of Tyrone with a bow and arrow, not a six-gun, following the murder of Buchanan. Apache Ian MacDonald's repeated attempts at rolling a cigarette are mildly amusing, Agar is his usual dependable self but the director's deadly slow handling of the material (this was the second of three Westerns he made in 1955 with producer Earle Lyon) will lead to fidgeting in your seat.

Dialogue:
MacDonald to Fowley: "I go."
Fowley: "Where'ya goin'? You haven't even drunk your coffee yet."
MacDonald spits out a mouthful: "White poison!"

Trivia:
Morris' final '50s Western; he gravitated to TV oaters after this one.

Westerns of the 1950s: The Classic Years

A Man Alone

Republic; Trucolor; 96 minutes; Producer: Herbert J. Yates; Director: Ray Milland; Cast: Ray Milland; Mary Murphy; Ward Bond; Raymond Burr; Lee Van Cleef; Arthur Space; Alan Hale, Jr.; Kim Spalding ****

Ray Milland's directorial debut saw him playing a notorious outlaw who stumbles across a stagecoach massacre (three men, a woman and a child), then wanders into the windswept town of Mesa and witnesses a killing orchestrated by town official Raymond Burr. Milland becomes a wanted man for both sets of murders, taking refuge in Mary Murphy's home, her father (Ward Bond) recovering from yellow fever. In a *noir* Western dripping with tension, Milland doesn't utter a single word until 25 minutes have gone by; he eventually convinces Murphy that, despite his reputation, he's an innocent victim and the lass a victim herself, tied to the house by Bond who's a bully, not allowing his daughter to grow up and become a woman. Corrupt Burr is the man behind the massacre and a heap more robberies, Bond, Mesa's lawman, allowing it to happen to feather his own nest after failing as a dirt farmer. Murphy falls for Milland's tight-lipped, masculine charms and Bond, full of remorse for his past actions, spills the beans on Burr to the lynch-happy townsfolk after letting Milland loose in the desert. The gunfighter returns, nails sneering henchman Lee Van Cleef in a saloon shoot-out and Burr is arrested. Milland decides to stay put with Murphy and Bond in the "rotten town full of rotten people," determined to make it a better place to live. A lovely score from Victor Young, including a sweet, guitar-plucked leitmotif, plus assured direction from the main star, make this occasionally violent slow-burner an unmissable treat for lovers of the more adult-themed Western.

Highlights:
Milland, horseless, tramping over the desert wastes in the first 20 minutes, filmed in Utah's striking St. George area.
Dialogue:
Burr, backing away, to Milland: "You can't shoot an unarmed man."
Milland: "No, but I can sure beat you to death."
Trivia:
Milland had the reputation of being one of Hollywood's most accident-prone actors, suffering fractures, lacerations and severe cuts in several of his more energetic productions.

The Man from Bitter Ridge

Universal; Eastmancolor; 80 minutes; Producer: Howard Pine; Director: Jack Arnold; Cast: Lex Barker; Mara Corday; Stephen McNally; John Dehner; Trevor Bardette; Ray Teal; Myron Healey; Warren Stevens ****

Arrested for a robbery he didn't commit, Express Agent Lex Barker is escorted into Tomahawk where Sheriff Trevor Bardette is later forced to release him; Bardette has more than enough on his plate coping with John Dehner, who is after his job in the forthcoming town elections. Dehner's two venomous brothers (Myron Healey and Warren Stevens) are busy robbing stages to finance their boss' plans for town domination, $60,000 in gold stashed away, *and* causing trouble with Stephen McNally's sheep farmers, holed up in their own community of Crow's Nest. Barker meets McNally, makes an immediate play for Mara Corday, his girl ("She's open range!"), and then helps the sheep runners to overthrow Dehner's crooked tactics in a mass street shoot-up on Election Day. Universal B-Westerns nearly always rose above the rest of the pack, and Jack Arnold's lively outing was no exception: Glowing photography around California's Conejo Valley (Russell Metty); a raucous stock soundtrack drummed up by musical director Joseph Gershenson; bags of action; and pleasing performances throughout—Barker amiable and good-looking; Corday a dream in cowboy garb; McNally less ferocious than usual; and Dehner giving a masterclass in oily ambition, a speciality of his. As expected, Barker gets Corday, McNally resigned to losing the woman he was due to wed.

Highlights:
Barker, McNally, Dehner, Bardette, Healey and Teal demonstrate what male machismo in a generic '50s Western was all about.

Dialogue:
McNally, riding into Tomahawk and confronting Dehner: "Town hasn't changed much since I been here last. Same people, same houses (stares straight at Dehner), same rats."
Trivia:
Arnold and Corday were reunited a few months later in Universal's classic giant insect thriller, *Tarantula*.

Man with the Gun aka The Trouble Shooter

Formosa/United Artists; 83 minutes; Producer: Samuel Goldwyn, Jr.; Director: Richard Wilson; Cast: Robert Mitchum; Jan Sterling; Emile Meyer; Henry Hull; Karen Sharpe; John Lupton; Leo Gordon; Joe Barry ****

Lawless Sheridan City and its farmers are under the thumb of magnate Joe Barry and his jackals, Sheriff Henry Hull content to sit back and do nothing. The townsfolk, sick of all the trouble, hire town tamer Robert Mitchum to sort things out which he does, no-nonsense style. But soon the gunman is pushing things too far, causing loss of trade by imposing curfews and a "No Guns" policy, and those self-righteous citizens are regretting the day they ever employed him. Richard Wilson's taut Western throws in several gunfights, Mitchum trying to rekindle the flame of romance with icy ex-love Jan Sterling ("You'll never be human. You haven't any pity," she rants at him) while young Karen Sharpe forgets all about boyfriend John Lupton by setting her cap at the tall, tough stranger. When Mitchum burns down the Palace saloon in a fit of rage and drills the owner, Ted de Corsia, stone cold dead, a trap is set, corpulent Barry and sneering Leo Gordon arriving in town to finish the peacemaker off at a given time; Gordon receives two bullets from Mitchum (and fully deserves it after killing a boy's pet dog in the opening minutes), Barry five rifle slugs from Lupton and the wounded town peacemaker makes plans to quit, taking Sterling with him. The old "He's got too big for his boots" scenario is tightly shot in *noir*-fashion, the entire cast giving telling performances—and Mitchum, *the* expert in nonchalance and seeming disinterest, sleepwalks through the entire picture, as riveting to watch as always.

Highlights:
Mitchum, high up in the livery stable, shooting it out with Claude Akins and three gunslingers.

Dialogue:
Blacksmith Emile Meyer to Mitchum, explaining why the citizens want him out: "Town hires a man to fight its war. They find out he's fightin' because he's got an itchy trigger finger that ain't under control and never will be. They get scared. They gotta right to do something about it."

Trivia:
This was the screen debut of Wilson, who only directed 13 pictures in his short career, plus the

debut of producer Samuel Goldwyn, Jr. and, to some degree, actress Amzie Strickland who at long last received a named part credit (Mary Atkins) after appearing in 91 movies dating back to 1937, billed only as "woman in bar," "audience member," "harem girl" etc.

Man Without a Star

Universal; Technicolor; 89 minutes; Producer: Aaron Rosenberg; Director: King Vidor; Cast: Kirk Douglas; Jeanne Crain; William Campbell; Richard Boone; Claire Trevor; Jay C. Flippen; Eddy Waller; Myrna Hansen ****

Penniless drifter Kirk Douglas and youngster William Campbell get jobs as cattle hands on Jay C. Flippen's Triangle Ranch in Wyoming after running foul of the law in a train incident; Flippen is treading all over neighbor Eddy Waller's toes by increasing his herd from 10,000 to 15,000 and using up valuable grassland on Waller's ranch. Trouble brews when ambitious Easterner Jeanne Crain takes over the Triangle, demoting Flippen to foreman until she spots Douglas and his rugged grin; sexual sparks fly, Douglas views the dame in her fancy indoor bathtub, they start kissing and soon he's running the show, Campbell trying to live up to Douglas' reputation as a quick-draw. In from Texas rides grim-faced Richard Boone and his boys with the additional 5,000 head of steers, an old enemy of Douglas with ambitions of his own and intent on starting a range war with Waller. It turns out that Douglas has a phobia over barbed wire ("Wire means trouble.") and bears the scars on his chest to prove it; siding with Waller after rejecting Crain, he comes up against Boone's mob and Campbell who's anxious to prove himself, resulting in Boone receiving a well-earned thrashing and fences erected to separate the two ranches. Douglas rides away in the end, Campbell, his young hero-worshipper, cozying up to Myrna Hansen, Waller's daughter. Raking in a $2,000,000 profit for Universal, *Man Without a Star* appeared to be played for laughs during the first 20 minutes and then got serious, but one thing the picture ably demonstrated was Douglas' dynamic acting technique; from singing and clowning around to being tough, then romantic, then changing from friend to gun-wielding psycho in a flash (as when Campbell hits him in the Duck Bill saloon), this was a man whose name alone guaranteed box-office success. Douglas dominates throughout—there are very few today in the world of cinema possessing his kind of screen charisma. "A highly competent performance," commented the *New York Times*.

Highlights:

Douglas on full throttle, a pleasure to watch his terrific star turn from beginning to end.

Dialogue:
Sheb Wooley to Douglas after Crain has shown him the cold shoulder: "How does it feel to be put in your place?"
Douglas: "I wouldn't know. Why don't you try puttin' me there."

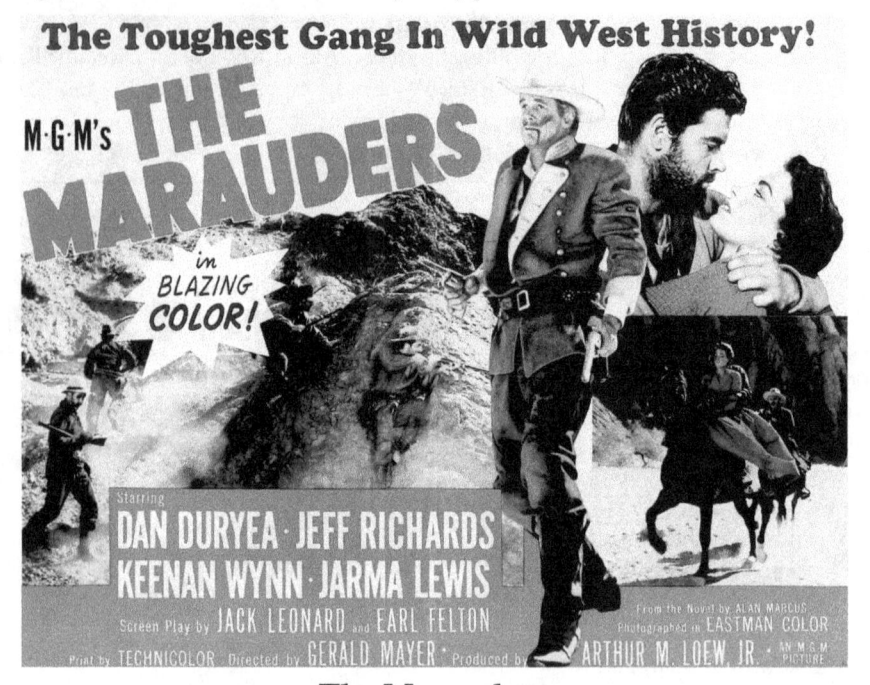

The Marauders

MGM; Eastmancolor; 81 minutes; Producer: Arthur M. Loew, Jr.; Director: Gerald Mayer; Cast: Dan Duryea; Jeff Richards; Keenan Wynn; Jarma Lewis; David Kasday; Harry Shannon; John Hudson; James Anderson ****

An unusual Western filmed entirely in the walled confines of California's towering Mecca Canyon. Squatter Jeff Richards is holed up in a box canyon near a well; Harry Shannon, who claims the land is his, wants that water badly, enlisting the aid of Dan Duryea and his army of ragbag mercenaries to flush Richards out. Settler James Anderson, wife Jarma Lewis and young son David Kasday get through to Richards' cabin, under bombardment from a barrage of whining, spitting bullets from Duryea's mob; Anderson then changes sides, leaving Richards, Lewis and Kasday to find a way of defeating the marauders. A tough, sweaty oater featuring Duryea in twitchy psycho mode; he just *has* to get Richards, even when Shannon and his son are shot dead, the conflict becoming a personal battle of wits. Anderson is killed and Richards constructs a bomb-throwing contraption that destroys the gunfighters, leaving Duryea, coughing up blood, collapsing dead in the dust from a chest complaint. Containing a great Paul Sawtell score and Keenan Wynn hamming it up as a hook-handed gunman, *The Marauders* is a terrific outdoor yarn set in a magnificent location—and Duryea is as watchable as ever.

Highlights:
Mecca Canyon serves as a reminder of how spectacular America's natural scenery is, and how often filmmakers utilized these rugged locales to their full advantage.

Dialogue:
Richards to Kasday: "You ever shoot a rifle, Albie?"
Kasday: "Sure. Hit a squirrel once. Never fired at a man, though."
Richards: "Let's hope you won't have to. If anything moves down there, just pretend it's a squirrel."

The Naked Dawn

Universal; Technicolor; 82 minutes; Producer: Josef Shaftel; Director: Edgar G. Ulmer; Cast: Arthur Kennedy; Betta St. John; Eugene Iglesias; Charlita; Roy Engel; Tony Martinez; Francis McDonald; Grady Sutton **

Hair dyed black, a handlebar mustache and a week's growth of stubble, Arthur Kennedy plays a charismatic philosophizing Mexican bandido who, following the robbery of a locomotive with accomplice Tony Martinez, wanders into the homestead of Eugene Iglesias; Martinez has died from a gunshot wound, and Kennedy wants to offload his stolen merchandise for cash in the nearest town. This is the dawn of the motor vehicle. Driving into Matamoras with Iglesias, he takes the money, spends time in a tavern and returns to the farmer's home where greed and lust raise their ugly heads; Iglesias eyes up the loot, wanting to better his lot, while his young wife, Betta St. John, eyes up Kennedy, sick of being abused by her immature husband. Don't expect any action in Edgar G. Ulmer's mood piece, just acres of talk, backed by Herschel Burke Gilbert's at times irritating flamenco guitar score. In the age of the motor car and telephone, Kennedy represents the last of a dying breed and expires lying against a tree, looking at his horse, after he's shot in the back by the shipping-agent he sold his watches to. A very slow-moving drama shot in Mexico, only held up by Kennedy's overripe turn as the bandit with nowhere to go and no one to share his bleak life with.

Highlights:
Kennedy's fine performance and Charlita flashing her shapely legs during a tavern dance.

Dialogue:
Kennedy to St. John: "Ah! The women of Vera Cruz. They're big and juicy but light as a feather—like you!"

Trivia:
Made over 10 days on a $200,000 budget; said to be the inspiration behind François Truffaut's *Jules and Jim*.

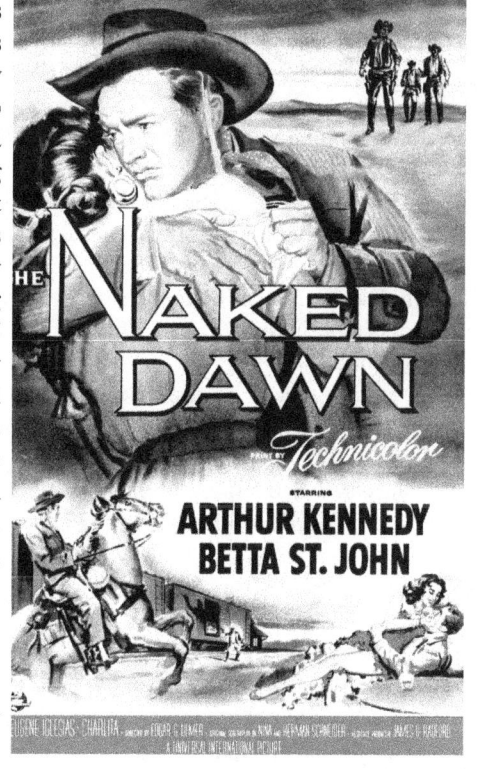

The Rawhide Years

Universal; Technicolor; 85 minutes; Producer: Stanley Rubin; Director: Rudolph Maté; Cast: Tony Curtis; Arthur Kennedy; Colleen Miller; Peter Van Eyck; William Demarest; William Gargan; Minor Watson; Robert J. Wilke **

Rudolph Maté's mishmash of a Western threw everything into the pot: Tony Curtis as a card sharp-turned-fugitive; lowlife Arthur Kennedy his rascally companion; showgirl Colleen Miller warbling three tunes; and Peter Van Eyck doing a bad impression of one of the genre's oiliest villains, John Dehner. Veering from one stock situation to the next, Curtis is blamed for the death of Minor Watson on board the riverboat Montana Queen, his partner at the gambling table, Donald Randolph, strung up for being in on the deed. Curtis, on the run, teams up with likeable, ever-smiling crook Kennedy and together, they somehow unmask William Demarest and Van Eyck as the figureheads of a gang of masked outlaws who have been robbing riverboats, the gold hidden in the wooden statue of an Indian. Miller plays Curtis' decorative girl, Kennedy bulldozes his way through Earl Felton's convoluted screenplay and Van Eyck confesses all to Galena's law-abiding folk before dropping dead from a gunshot wound to the chest. It seems to be a case of "chuck it all into the mix," with little cohesion, infrequent flashes of Lone Pine's scenery and the main star looking uncomfortable in cowboy gear. Not one of Universal's greatest efforts from the mid-'50s.

Highlights:
Arthur Kennedy's winning performance as a fast-drawing, no-good horse thief, always on the lookout to feather his own nest.

Dialogue:
Kennedy to Curtis, the pair fending off a posse attack: "This miserable country. Infested with decent citizens!"

The Return of Jack Slade

Allied Artists; SuperScope; 79 minutes; Producer: Lindsley Parsons; Director: Harold D. Schuster; Cast: John Ericson; Mari Blanchard; Neville Brand; Casey Adams; Jon Shepodd; Howard Petrie; Angie Dickinson; Mike Ross *****

Composer Paul Dunlap's inclusion in his score of "The Yellow Rose of Texas" song is put to effective use in this slick follow-up to 1953's *Jack Slade*, made by the same team. It's 1886: John Ericson (Jack Slade, Jr.) storms out of St. Joseph College of Law during a history class after waving a Colt .45 in his tutor's face, boards the train to Casper, Wyoming, befriends amicable, intoxicated cowpoke Jon Shepodd and gets offered a position as a Pinkerton detective by Howard Petrie; after all, fearsome lawman Jack Slade notched up 27 killings, so Slade junior must have inherited some of his gunfighting skills—and he has. Ericson's task is to infiltrate the stronghold of the Wild Bunch, or the

Hole-in-the-Wall gang (who robbed the train to Casper), and bring their leaders to justice. Shepodd yearns to tag along, but Ericson warns him off—it's far too dangerous for innocents like you, he states. At the hideout, pretty-boy Ericson attracts the women outlaws and impresses leader Casey Adams with his no-nonsense attitude and gun-twirling prowess but hothead killer Neville Brand itches to outdraw the youngster, especially when his shooting iron has been shot from his hand in a lightning display of fast firing. The taut narrative moves swiftly through its paces, featuring bright black-and-white photography courtesy of William A. Sickner (filming took place at Lone Pine) and a tough-as-they-come screenplay from Warren Douglas; Mari Blanchard (Texas Rose), sporting a peroxide blonde rinse (and highly manicured nails!), falls for Ericson, Shepodd worms his way into the stronghold, Angie Dickinson homing in on him, and Ericson reports back to Petrie in the Big Horn saloon on the gang's activities. Brand viciously puts two slugs into Shepodd's back, Blanchard throws herself at Ericson ("I'm your woman. Nobody touches me unless I give permission.") and a cunning trap is set by Petrie, who pretends to be drunk, letting on to Brand, Blanchard, Ericson and Mike Ross that the train from Cheyenne to Salt Lake City is carrying $100,000 in gold bullion. In fact, it's carrying a posse of Pinkerton armed guards and during the holdup, Blanchard is seriously wounded, and Adams killed, the outlaws scattering under a hail of rifle bullets. Up in the hills, Ericson drops Brand in a showdown and is last seen riding off with Blanchard to reach a doctor in Cheyenne. A shining example of a great low-budget Western that touches all bases throughout its running time, holding the attention from the very first minute; this was how it *used* to be done, everyone involved rolling up their sleeves and coming up with a product that still resonates over 60 years later.

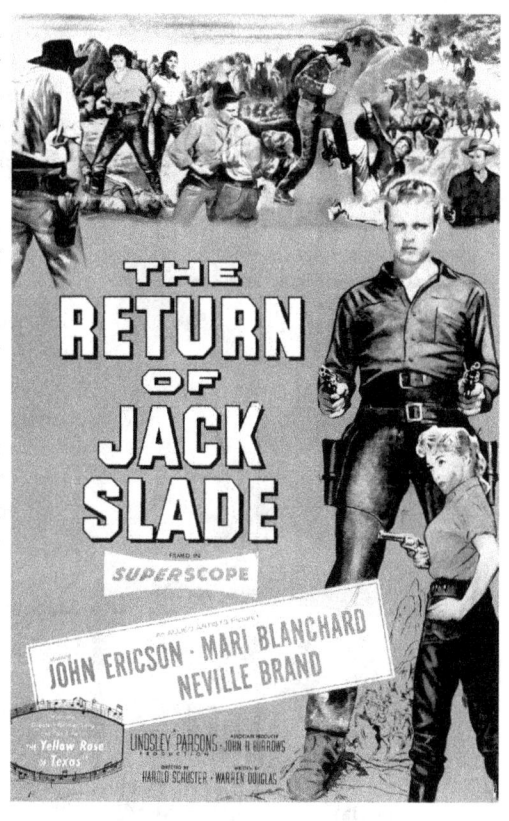

Highlights:

The Return of Jack Slade is almost a model of a five-star 1950s Western produced on minimal funds; everything works from start to finish.

Dialogue:

Adams to Brand, annoyed at the man's penchant for senseless shootings: "Someday, Harry, someone's gonna fill you so full of lead, they'll claim a stake on you."

Trivia:

Dickinson's first credited film role.

The Road to Denver

Republic; Trucolor; 90 minutes; Produced and Directed by Joseph Kane; Cast: John Payne; Skip Homeier; Lee J. Cobb; Mona Freeman; Ray Middleton; Lee Van Cleef; Andy Clyde; Glenn Strange ****

Texan siblings John Payne and Skip Homeier go their own separate ways ("Why don't you take that bull head of yours west and I'll take my future east."), older and wiser Payne sick of getting his hotheaded, neurotic sibling out of trouble, including springing him from jail. Payne rides into Central City and is offered a job by Ray Middleton, who plans to operate his own stage line to Denver. Town big shot Lee J. Cobb wants total control of Central City, aiming to put Middleton out of business with the help of a bunch of gunfighters, Lee Van Cleef, Glenn Strange and, lastly, Homeier (one of the actor's best roles) among them. Payne, showing interest in Middleton's pert daughter, Mona Freeman, enters into a partnership with his boss and in doing so comes up against Cobb's underhand methods *and* brother Homeier, a psycho in the making. Joseph Kane's medium-budget Western is a cracker, Payne's dour demeanor offset by Homeier's twitchy, motormouth punk gunslinger, Cobb's plan to steal $20,000 worth of gold dust on Middleton's inaugural run foiled by Payne who guns the corrupt saloon boss down in a great closing shoot-out. Filmed in Utah and Arizona, *The Road to Denver* looks good, even though, at 43, Payne was a tad too mature to romance 29-year-old Freeman. The ending, Homeier a reformed man, now turned stage driver, also seems a little rushed; surely, the cocky young snipe deserved a bullet for all the trouble he had caused? Composer R. Dale Butts creates a fine score to boost the action.

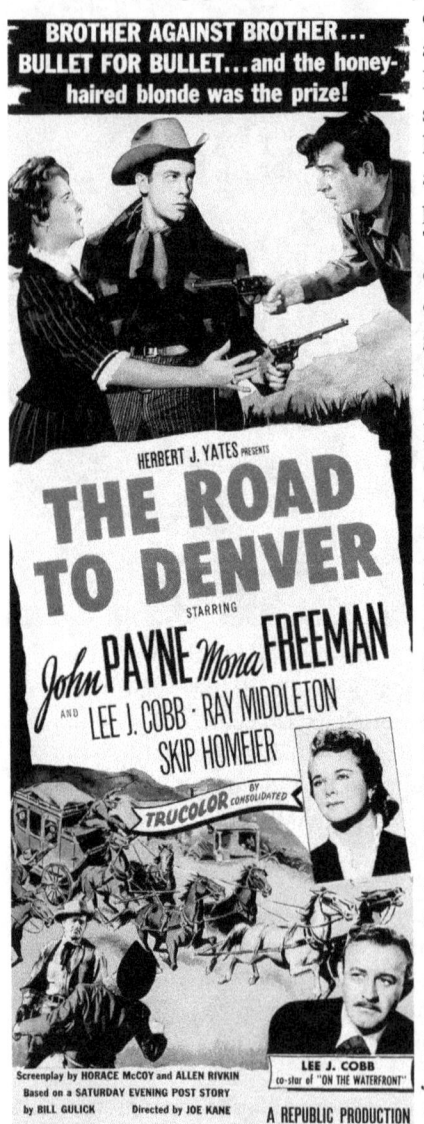

Dialogue:

John Payne to Homeier after one too many arguments: "An empty head and a loaded gun are bad partners."

Run for Cover

Paramount; VistaVision/Technicolor; 93 minutes; Producers: William H. Pine and William C. Thomas; Director: Nicholas Ray; Cast: James Cagney; John Derek; Viveca Lindfors; Jean Hersholt; Ernest Borgnine; Ray Teal; Grant Withers; Trevor Bardette ***

Ex-convict James Cagney and young sidekick John Derek are mistaken for robbers when the train to Madison is held up; Derek is badly injured in an ambush, Cagney hauled into town for an instant hanging. When Cagney convinces lawman Ray Teal that there's been a huge mistake, Teal is kicked out of office, Cagney gets the job of sheriff and Derek, after a lengthy recuperation at Viveca Lindfors' ranch, is made deputy. Cagney looks upon Derek as the son he once had, but the troubled youngster is determined to make himself richer by falling in with Grant Withers and his gang who relieve Madison's bank of $85,000 on Cagney and Lindfors' wedding day; Lindfors' father, dirt farmer Jean Hersholt, is killed during the robbery. The outlaws are tracked down, all slaughtered by Comanches; Derek throws in his lot with villainous Ernest Borgnine but during a standoff, he's shot dead by Cagney when he goes for his revolver and nails Borgnine. Back in town, Cagney hands over the money to the townsfolk and gallops off to take over Lindfors' ranch with his new wife. Shot in VistaVision, Nicholas Ray's picture is high, wide and handsome, filmed in Durango, Colorado, photographed in pristine Technicolor by Daniel L. Fapp and embellished by Howard Jackson's thunderous score. But Cagney, like his old sparring partner Humphrey Bogart, didn't really belong in the Western milieu, and therein lay the film's main handicap. His role would have better suited someone like Randolph Scott or Audie Murphy, stalwarts of the medium-budget Western; here, Cagney acted in some scenes as though he had just stepped out of one of his gangster features. Ray was no stranger to peculiar Westerns, having directed Republic's *Johnny Guitar, the* camp classic of 1954; in *Run for Cover* (poor title), he appeared to be making it up as he went along—let's have an Indian attack here, a bank robbery there, a hazardous desert crossing chucked in, a lot of it pure padding. A treat for Cagney fans, but distinctly odd fare for Western buffs.

Highlights:

Cagney, a Hollywood legend, going through the paces (he was 20 years older than love interest Lindfors); Aztec ruins standing in for the outlaws' hideout; and the picturesque mountain scenery around Durango, Colorado.

Dialogue:

Cagney to a bored, restless Derek: "Well, sometimes a deputy doesn't earn his pay for months on end. Comes trouble, you get caught up quick and fast, about the length of time it takes somebody to empty a gun at you."

Trivia:

Cagney, at five-foot-six and a half, was dwarfed by six-foot-one Derek which, to his credit, he felt quite amusing; this was the second of three Cagney Westerns, director Ray reported as saying he disliked the final product intensely.

The Silver Star

Lippert Pictures; 73 minutes; Producer: Earle Lyon; Director: Richard H. Bartlett; Cast: Earle Lyon; Edgar Buchanan; Marie Windsor; Richard H. Bartlett; Lon Chaney, Jr.; Barton MacLane; Morris Ankrum; Steve Rowland ****

"I don't like it, shootin' and killin' people. That's not my idea of a life." So says Earle Lyon on the first day of his job as Boyce's new sheriff. Lyon was voted in ahead of corrupt Lon Chaney, Jr., who sends three of his paid coyotes (Richard H. Bartlett, Earl Hansen and Bill Anders) into a town with a "No Guns" policy to finish off the rookie lawman. Former sheriff Edgar Buchanan sympathizes with Lyon but tells him he's gotta sort those hombres out pronto, while girlfriend Marie Windsor virtually accuses her man of cowardice in the face of the enemy ("It ain't no crime to wanna live," is his rejoinder). But Lyon happens to be very handy with a shooter and, on the point of retiring after just one day, goes after Bartlett and his gorillas when Buchanan buckles on a gun belt to do the job but is wounded in an ensuing shoot-out. Bartlett and Anders die in a hail of lead, young Steve Rowland puts a bullet in blacksmith Barton MacLane, another of Chaney's mob, and Chaney is arrested by Lyon who at last has found his feet (and won the admiration of Windsor). Written by Bartlett and produced by Lyon, *The Silver Star* is a low-budget minimalistic *noir* gem built on *High Noon* lines, Jimmy Wakely's singing of the memorable title track contrasting strongly with Leon Klatzkin's menacing score; Guy Roe's deep black-and-white photography is another reminder of how cinematographers of all shapes and sizes flourished in this heady moviemaking period.

Dialogue:
Lyon: "A man who carries a gun ain't got no future. Or the woman who marries him."
Edith Evanson (Buchanan's wife): "Amen!"

Trivia:
This was the fourth of B-producer Lyon's five films as an actor.

Smoke Signal

Universal; Technicolor; 88 minutes; Producer: Howard Christie; Director: Jerry Hopper; Cast: Dana Andrews; Piper Laurie; William Talman; Rex Reason; Douglas Spencer; Robert J. Wilke; Milburn Stone; William Schallert ****

A disparate bunch of troopers in a besieged fort, commanded by William Talman, entrust their lives to Captain Dana Andrews, on a charge of treason, desertion and murder by siding with Ute chief War Cloud; Andrews was only trying to make peace between the whites and Indians but the army, and Talman in particular, refuse to believe him. On Andrews' recommendation, they sneak out of the fort at night, taking to an uncharted river in two boats, fighting rapids and each other on their way to safety which is 300 miles distant; the Ute steer well clear of the river, saying that bad spirits lurk there. Strikingly filmed by Universal's special effects ace Clifford Stine in the Grand Canyon of Colorado, Utah and various Moab locations, *Smoke Signal* has a stronger than usual cast of players. Andrews is tough and surly as the group's savior; Piper Laurie enchants as the lass falling for him; Rex Reason attempts to kill Andrews, jealous of Laurie's growing feelings for the man; Douglas Spencer is terrific as the grizzled skin trader; and Talman excels as the ornery polecat determined to bring Andrews to a court martial and a firing squad, never mind the raging waters, Indians, shortage of food, partly submerged boulders and capsizing boats. The wild, rocky scenery is what makes the movie just that little bit more special, including a thrilling interlude when the team has to haul the one surviving boat up a precipitous cliff. And, in the last minute when the end of the journey is in sight, Talman, confronted by his mutinous troopers, has a change of heart and allows Andrews to swim off towards a bunch of friendly Apaches. "He'll be back," he tells Laurie, the distraught gal looking on with tears in her eyes.

Highlights:
The vivid rock formations hemming in the turbulent waters of the Colorado River form a surreal backdrop to a taut little gem from Universal.

Dialogue:
Reason to Laurie: "You're in love with a man who's gonna be shot. What a waste!"

Trivia:
Dana Andrews, who replaced Charlton Heston in the lead (Heston's wage demands were too much for Universal), was continually intoxicated during the shoot but didn't let it show on screen; and uranium fever was rife in the Moab district, making it difficult for Jerry Hopper to recruit locals as extras for the Indian roles.

The Tall Men

20th Century Fox; CinemaScope/DeLuxecolor; 122 minutes; Producers: William A. Bacher and William B. Hawks; Director: Raoul Walsh; Cast: Clark Gable; Jane Russell; Robert Ryan; Cameron Mitchell; Juan Garcia; Harry Shannon; Emile Meyer; Steve Darrell ***

A $3,000,000 budget; a lush score from Victor Young; and Leo Tover's breathtaking, panoramic cinematography, among the finest in any '50s Western. Yet *The Tall Men* (it made a healthy profit for Fox) is, in the words of the *New York Times*, "a mighty mild movie" and "ambling," focusing mainly on the Clark Gable/Robert Ryan/Jane Russell romantic triangle at the expense of all-out action, director Raoul Walsh's foot on the brakes for most of the picture's length. We all know that Gable is going to get Russell in the end—why spend so much time in protracted teasing spats (the first lasts 11 minutes) when it's such a foregone conclusion? In 1866, ex-Quantrill's Raiders Gable and younger brother Cameron Mitchell, in tandem with saloon owner Ryan, travel through Montana's snowy wastes to San Antone, Texas, buying up 5,000 head of cattle to sell at a healthy profit in Mineral City, Montana. En route, there's a violent set-to with Jayhawkers, Ryan and Mitchell constantly challenge each other to the draw, Russell flashes her legs and heaving bosom at Gable and, in the final reel, Walsh manufactures an exciting clash with Sioux Indians, shot around Mexico's striking Sierra de Organos area with its towering, jagged rock pinnacles. Mitchell's demise is gruesome, tied to a tree, five arrows sticking in his chest, and, in the last few minutes, Russell hitches her voluminous skirts to Gable, preferring to live life on a ranch rather than have Ryan wining and dining her every night, only to get nowhere ("My man is all man and the only one for me," she sings happily). A great-to-look-at Western that unfortunately lacks real dramatic thrust.

Highlights:

Viewing the movie in letterbox format is a must, to take in and fully appreciate Tover's stunning shots of Sun Valley, Idaho (for the snow sequences) and Mexico's arid Durango region.

Dialogue:
Russell to Ryan: "Oh, er, I guess we better get somethin' straight. When I take a bath, I surround myself with water and the tub, nothing and nobody else."
Trivia:
Critics generally thought that Gable (54), Ryan (46) and Russell (34) were too mature for their parts; and six-foot and a half Gable, in some scenes, had to stand on a higher level to match Ryan's six-foot-four. He also featured very rarely in the snow scenes, a double used instead.

Tennessee's Partner

RKO-Radio; Technicolor; 87 minutes; Producer: Benedict Bogeaus; Director: Allan Dwan; Cast: John Payne; Rhonda Fleming; Ronald Reagan; Coleen Gray; Leo Gordon; Anthony Caruso; Chubby Johnson; Myron Healey ***

In 1955, Benedict Bogeaus and Allan Dwan's chaotic feature (the two collaborated on a number of movies) would have been termed "a rip-roaring Western," full of dames in gaudy outfits, comedic elements, gunplay, bad guys and three likeable leads in John Payne, Rhonda Fleming and Ronald Reagan, all shot in flashy Technicolor. It now appears curiously dated, a '40s-style horse opera appearing a decade later. In the town of Sandy Bar, saloon gambler Payne (Tennessee) is carrying out an on/off affair with Fleming, duchess of a marriage parlor; when he's held up by a disgruntled loser, Reagan (Cowpoke), a gunslinger, comes to his rescue and the two wind up in Marshal Leo Gordon's jail. On release, they bond and embark on a series of adventures involving Chubby Johnson's gold mine, gold digger Coleen Gray, an ex-flame of Payne's who's arrived to marry Reagan but only to suit her own devious purposes, and villainous Anthony Caruso, after Johnson's mine and framing the murder of the prospector onto Payne. The narrative tears about here, there and everywhere, with shrieking girls, fistfights, lots of kissing and a few shootings all chucked into the mix. The final couple of reels sees Gray packed off to San Francisco by Payne, who reckons he's done Reagan a favor, and Reagan shot dead by Caruso, the crook arrested after the gambler slugs him senseless; Payne and Fleming then tie the knot, sailing off on a riverboat. Good old-fashioned noisy fun, but rather light in content for those requiring a bit more grit in their Western fare.

Highlights:
Gordon as a lawman—how often did *that* happen throughout the screen bruiser's long Western career?

Dialogue:
Reagan to Payne: "You oughta get married."
Payne: "Married!"
Reagan: "What's wrong with it?"
Payne: "You have to marry a woman."
Reagan: "Well, what's wrong with women?"
Payne: "They act like women!"

Treasure of Ruby Hills

Allied Artists; 71 minutes; Producer: William F. Broidy; Director: Frank McDonald; Cast: Zachary Scott; Carole Mathews; Barton MacLane; Charles Fredericks; Dick Foran; Lee Van Cleef; Lola Albright; Rick Vallin **

After his partner is shot in the back filing a claim for water rights at Thousand Springs in the Ruby Hills district, Zachary Scott rides to Soledad and finds himself in the middle of a range war between Barton MacLane and Charles Fredericks; both are itching to get hold of that land, each employing a gunslinger to take care of trouble—MacLane has Lee Van Cleef, Fredericks Gordon Jones. Rancher Carole Mathews and her brother, Rick Vallin, enter the equation, needing the vital water for their Double V Ranch, while Dick Foran lurks in the background, waiting for the opposing sides to wipe each other out so that *he* can claim those precious rights. Taken from a Louis L'Amour story, Tom Hubbard and Fred Egger's wordy screenplay baffles and confuses, not helped by too many characters coming and going, the baddies all looking similar to each other and a tad on the mature side (and everyone in the film bar Van Cleef sports a double holster), like extras from a 1940s oater. Scott wins the day (and the property titles) following a blazing showdown in the ghost town of Silvertown and grabs Mathews as a bonus; these two, plus a typical sneering performance from Van Cleef and Edward J. Kay's mournful music, make this somewhat drab horse opera just about watchable.

Dialogue:
Scott, entering the saloon by the side entrance and surprising Van Cleef, who's sipping whiskey: "Drink—then draw!"

Two-Gun Lady

L&B Prods./AFRC; 71 minutes; Produced and Directed by Richard H. Bartlett; Cast: Peggie Castle; William Talman; Marie Windsor; Earle Lyon; Ian MacDonald; Robert Lowery; Joe Besser; Barbara Turner ****

Peggie Castle starred as Annie Oakley look-alike Kate Masters, a trick-shot artist, arriving at Robert Lowery's saloon with roly-poly assistant Joe Besser to put on a show, the blonde nursing a hidden agenda. She's out to kill the three men who murdered her sheep-farming parents 15 years back, the burned remains of their homestead standing on cattle land belonging to town bigwig Ian MacDonald—and he was one of the sidewinders responsible, along with his two sons. Any cowpoke getting fresh with the female avenger quickly finds the barrel of her six-shooter stuck in his belly; soon, skeletons are falling out of closets. William Talman, hired by MacDonald as a gun hand (the rancher's right arm is paralyzed) happens to be a federal marshal, hoping to bring his new boss to justice; deposed gunman Norman Jolley wants to put a slug in rival Talman; and saloon dame Marie Windsor, fighting off Lowery's amorous advances, has hitched her skirts to outlaw Earle Lyon, MacDonald's psychotic son, who's just robbed a bank of $50,000. And why is Lyon terrified by the sound of sheep, especially tomboy Barbara Turner's pet lamb? Seems that Lyon, his brother (who Lyon also murdered) and MacDonald slaughtered Castle's family because of their contempt for sheep farmers, hence his hatred of the animals which leads to him getting rid of Turner's pet with a well-placed bullet. Talman reveals his true identity to Castle after he's planted a smacker on her lips; MacDonald is arrested following a showdown at his ranch, Lyon shooting Windsor dead and heading back to town. A tense, slow-burning finale in Lowery's saloon sees Castle, in fancy cowboy garb, facing up to Lyon; both reach for their pistols, both are wounded. As Lyon goes for the coup de grâce, he's blasted by Turner in revenge for killing her beloved lamb. Castle leaves on the next stage with Talman, the pair intending to tie the knot and care for Turner (now dressed in glad rags) when they return. Low on production values maybe, but *Two-Gun Lady* is a spiffy little B-oater, somewhat grim in mood, well-acted, intelligently scripted and given backbone by Leon Klatzkin's full-blooded score.

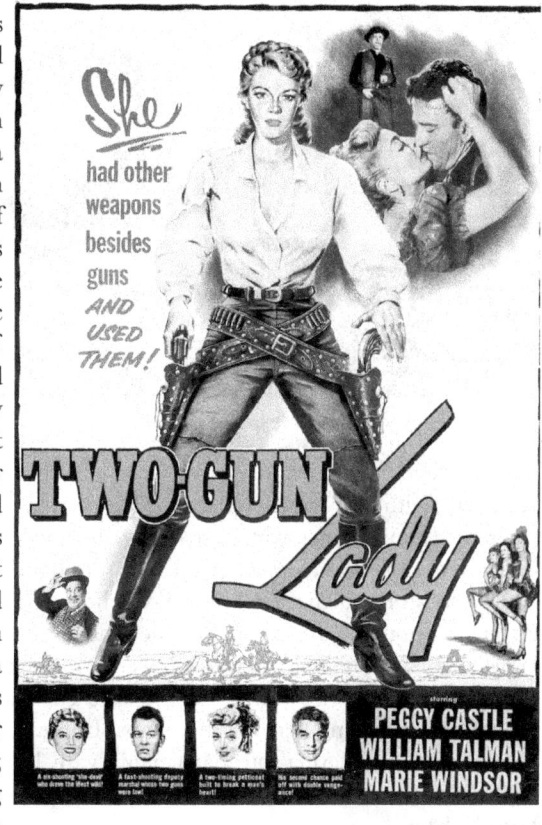

Dialogue:
Lowery to Lyon, about Castle: "She's got more guts than any man in this town."
Trivia:
Lyon, Jolley and MacDonald were all part of the film's production team.

The Violent Men

Columbia; CinemaScope/Technicolor; 96 minutes; Producer: Lewis J. Rachmil; Director: Rudolph Maté; Cast: Glenn Ford; Edward G. Robinson; Barbara Stanwyck; Brian Keith; Dianne Foster; Lita Milan; May Wynn; Warner Anderson ****

Ex-Union officer-cum-war hero Glenn Ford comes up against bullying crippled rancher Edward G. Robinson in Columbia's melodramatic range war horse opera, featuring a solid cast and superb location filming around Lone Pine's Alabama Hills region. Ford wants to sell up to Robinson's Anchor Ranch and move East with clinging fiancée May Wynn, but when Robinson only offers $15,000 and allows his men to ride roughshod over nesters' property, resulting in one innocent lad shot to death, Ford, up to then an advocate of peace, straps on the dead man's gun belt, rallies the farmers and all hell breaks loose. Power-mad Barbara Stanwyck, Robinson's wife, wants the "Big Valley" for herself, carrying on with her husband's brother (Brian Keith) behind his back; Keith also has a moll (Lita Milan) tucked away in town; Stanwyck's volatile daughter, Dianne Foster, is interested in Keith; and Wynn walks out on Ford, making him the most eligible bachelor around. To the sound of Max Steiner's pounding score, Ford and his crew dry-gulch the Anchor mob who have just burned his ranch; in retribution, Robinson's homestead is set on fire, the rancher presumed dead but returning from the grave to confront his wife, in widow's weeds, and Keith, the conniving pair planning to run the Anchor spread between them. Ford guns down Keith and Stanwyck bites the dust, Milan pumping her with two slugs. In the closing seconds, Foster eyes up Ford as he considers entering into partnership with Robinson, ending a thundering good Western of the old school, directed with zeal by Rudolph Maté.

Highlights:
The spectacular Lone Pine mountain backdrops and Ford's successful ambush of Robinson's men at night among rocks.

Dialogue:
Warner Anderson to Ford: "They're burnin' the ranch."
Ford: "Whadd'ya expect them to do? Give it a fresh coat of paint?"

Trivia:
Ford replaced Broderick Crawford who fell off a horse and injured a leg prior to filming; he was also known as being one of Hollywood's fastest-on-the-draw actors, on a level pegging with Audie Murphy and James Arness.

White Feather

Panoramic/20th Century Fox; CinemaScope/Technicolor; 102 minutes; Producer: Robert L. Jacks; Director: Robert Webb; Cast: Robert Wagner; Jeffrey Hunter; Debra Paget; Hugh O'Brian; John Lund; Eduard Franz; Virginia Leith; Milburn Stone ****

Surveyor Robert Wagner travels to Fort Laramie, Wyoming in 1877, becomes friendly with Cheyenne braves Little Dog (Jeffrey Hunter) and American Horse (Hugh O'Brian), falls for O'Brian's intended, Appearing Day (Debra Paget), and gets involved in a peace treaty with Chief Broken Hand (Eduard Franz). The Sioux, Blackfeet and Arapaho are moving off their lands and journeying south ("Heading for the Promised Land. I wonder how long they can live on promises?"), but the Cheyenne are stalling on the deal. A pro-Indian movie *par excellence*, thanks to a knowledgeable script (Delmer Daves and Leo Townsend), believable playing from the leads and wonderfully clear deep-focus panoramic views of the Durango plains in Mexico (photographer: Lucien Ballard). Young Wagner's loyalties are divided when Hunter and O'Brian, firmly against any peace deal, head for the hills, taking on the full strength of John Lund's troops who ride out alongside Franz's tribes, a fantastic sequence highlighted by Hugo Friedhofer's pounding score. O'Brian, wanting to kill Wagner for stealing his woman, is shot dead by Franz and Hunter meets his doom by charging into the mass ranks of cavalry. In a moving finale, Wagner arranges his friend's broken body in dignified repose, watched by the saddened chief, and rides away with Paget to a start a future together as man and wife. *White Feather* is slow and talky in parts, focusing on the Indian way of life as opposed to the white man's, but those fantastic widescreen vistas that fill the screen make the Western a must-see for any fan.

Highlights:

Cavalry and Indians converging on the sweeping plains in the climax, a magnificent Western spectacle.

Dialogue:

Paget to Wagner, after her first white man kiss: "I would like it again please—but longer."

Trivia:

In Indian terms, a white feather can mean cowardice, a sign of high respect, a challenge or a flag of truce.

Wyoming Renegades

Columbia; Technicolor; 73 minutes; Producer: Wallace MacDonald; Director: Fred F. Sears; Cast: Philip Carey; Gene Evans; Martha Hyer; William Bishop; Douglas Kennedy; Roy Roberts; George Keymas; Harry Harvey ****

Outlaw bank robber Butch Cassidy (Gene Evans) and his Hole-in-the-Wall bunch are causing havoc throughout America's Midwest territories; the Sundance Kid (William Bishop) rejoins them following a spell in the jug, but ex-gang member Philip Carey declines, wanting out. In Broken Bow, Carey is as welcome as a tick on a dog's rear end but takes up Douglas Kennedy's offer of a partnership in a blacksmith operation, much to girlfriend Martha Hyer's delight but not the town's ("I'm home and I mean to go straight."). Evans, though, plans to rob Broken Bow's bank and in doing so, Hyer's father is killed, Carey blamed for the holdup. Kennedy pulls a gun on the mob baying for Carey's blood, the pair joining up with Evans and Bishop, although viewed with a great deal of mistrust. Kennedy turns out to be a Pinkerton detective and has used Carey and his outlaw connections all along to infiltrate the gang and bring them to justice. A train holdup in Devil's Pass goes wrong, Kennedy is battered to death by Evans using a gun butt (a brutal scene) and, back in Broken Bow to regain the money dropped in the first robbery, the Hole-in-the-Wall outlaws are shot to ribbons by the town's women after the men have departed, a trap set by both Carey and Hyer who wind up in each other's arms. If you're looking for a standard, no-frills Technicolor '50s Western high on earthy excitement, tough performances and fetching locations (Bronson Canyon and Lone Pine), look no further; Fred F. Sears' high-spirited actioner epitomizes your basic oater produced in this decade, a thrill-a-minute ride made with a great deal of flair.

Highlights:
The well-orchestrated three-minute raid on Broken Bow, a flurry of bullets, smoke, terrified horses and bodies hitting the dust.

Dialogue:
Bishop to Evans regarding Kennedy's fate: "What are you gonna do with him?"
Evans: "Target practice. Start at his feet and work up. Drag it out real slow and make him pay for this."

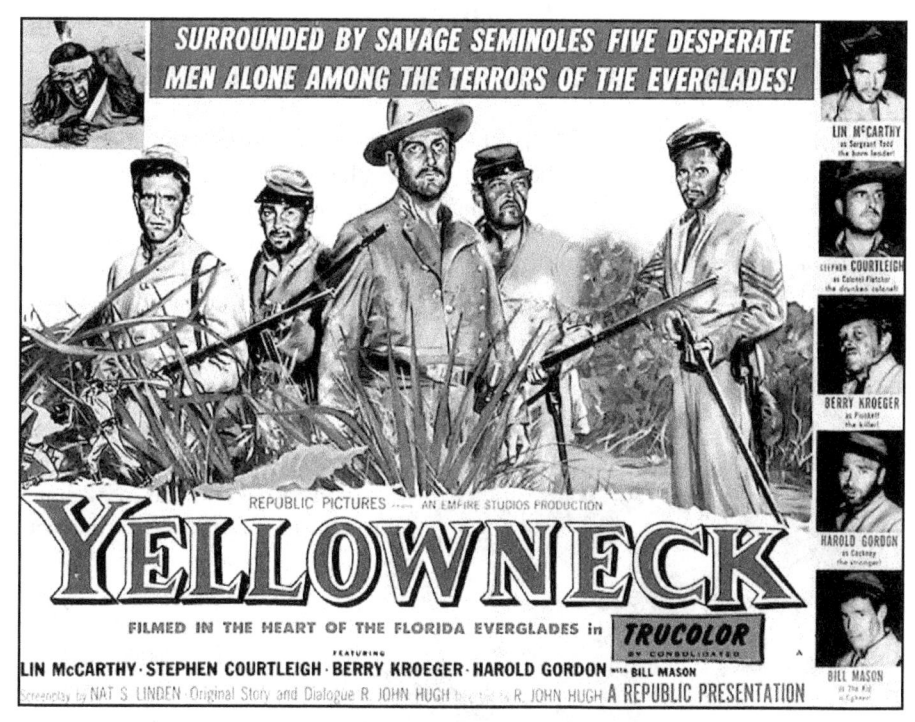

Yellowneck

Empire Studios/Republic; Trucolor; 83 minutes; Producer: Harlow G. Fredrick; Director: R. John Hugh; Cast: Lin McCarthy; Stephen Courtleigh; Harold Gordon; Berry Kroeger; Bill Mason; Al Tamez; Jose Billie; Roy Nash Osceola ***

Similar in theme to United Artists' *Shark River*, first-time director R. John Hugh's yarn told of four Confederate deserters trekking through the Florida Everglades in 1863 in an attempt to reach the coast, and then Cuba. Disgraced colonel Stephen Courtleigh joins them, making up a fifth member, the group encountering alligators in lagoons, Seminole Indians, a hurricane (a real one which sprung up during filming), fetid swamps and antagonism towards each other. Courtleigh dies from delirium and the effects of an arrow in the back; Cockney Harold Gordon (actually born in Brooklyn, an overripe peformance) expires from a rattlesnake bite; Berry Kroeger is eaten alive by alligators; Sergeant Lin McCarthy sinks in a bog (a harrowing scene, his bloody hand protruding above the mud); and only Bill Mason makes it to the coast, almost out of his senses in the blazing sun. Realistically shot in the hot, damp claustrophobic Everglades, *Yellowneck* is a little-known gem from Republic featuring a virtual cast of unknowns. It was composer Laurence Rosenthal's second score, cinematographer Charles T. O'Rork's first of four films, and the only movie produced by Harlow G. Fredrick; despite its low budget, the picture leaves a stark impression of men trapped in a hostile environment from which there is no escape.

Dialogue:
Courtleigh to McCarthy and company: "I don't want to be leader. If I was leader, I wouldn't want miserable, quavering, filth-infested scum like this in my command."

Chapter 10
Allan "Rocky" Lane at Republic

Allan "Rocky" Lane (Born Harry Leonard Albershart on September 22, 1909, Mishawaka, Indiana) was your archetypal B-Western hero of the 1930s/1940s; six-foot tall, athletic, matinée-idol good looks, smartly pressed shirt, black neckerchief, white hat and possessing a magnificent black steed in Black Jack. His first Western appearance was in RKO-Radio's 1938 production *The Law West of Tombstone*, taking over from Wild Bill Elliott in seven of Republic's *Red Ryder* movies (1946/1947) before becoming Allan "Rocky" Lane in 38 hour-long Republic oaters (starting with *The Wild Frontier*) up to 1953 (he guested as "Rocky Lane" in the Roy Rogers feature *Trail of Robin Hood* in 1950). He was also the voice of Mr. Ed, the popular TV series that ran from 1961-1966. A star of 128 films and television shows, Lane died of cancer, aged 64, on October 27, 1973. His "Rocky" Westerns, each produced on a $50,000 budget, are undemanding low-budget fun—don't expect anything of a cerebral nature as stern-faced, teetotal Rocky ("I never touch the stuff."), aided (and hindered) by ex-vaudeville star Eddy Waller's Nugget Clark, charges around sporting a double holster, vanquishes the bad guys (usually led by Roy Barcroft), never loses his hat in a fight (and the fistfights in Lane's movies are among the most bruising in any B-Western) and ends up riding into the dusty distance on his trusty stallion without so much as a backward glance, reinforcing the fact that on set, he could be demanding and throw his considerable weight around, both physically and verbally. The films are listed in order of release.

1950

Gunmen of Abilene

Republic; 61 minutes; Producer: Gordon Kay; Director: Fred C. Brannon; Cast: Allan "Rocky" Lane; Eddy Waller; Roy Barcroft; Donna Hamilton; Peter Brocco; Selmer Jackson; Duncan Richardson; Arthur Walsh ***

A rich vein of gold runs under the town of Blue Valley: Pharmacist Peter Brocco and gunslinger Roy Barcroft plan to bring the town to its knees by hiring gunfighters from Abilene to cause havoc, thus emptying the place of citizens, leaving them to mine the ore. Elderly, dithering sheriff Eddy Waller isn't up to the job of keeping the saddle trash at bay, so Marshal Allan "Rocky" Lane, on his steed Black Jack, is recruited to sort matters out. Lots of hard ridin' after the baddies, shoot-outs in darkened streets and Lane trussed up in mine workings leads to a literally explosive finale when the gunmen dynamite cliffs above retreating wagons full of Blue Valley's townsfolk; the wagons somehow escape serious damage and in retribution, Brocco, clasping a stick of explosive, is blown to bits, causing an avalanche that buries his cohorts in crime. Barcroft is taken into custody and Lane rides away for more Republic adventures, leaving forgetful Waller still in charge of Blue Valley, not a cause for celebration in view of his past record of incompetency!

Dialogue:
Lane to Waller, telling him to divert Brocco's attention: "Keep him busy."
Waller: "He'll be as busy as a rabbit in a lettuce patch."

Trivia:
The first of Lane's 21 Republic potboilers made between 1950-1953 (he also appeared in the Roy Rogers' singing Western, *Trail of Robin Hood*); he had starred in a further 17 from 1947 to 1949.

Code of the Silver Sage

Republic; 60 minutes; Producer: Gordon Kay; Director: Fred C. Brannon; Cast: Allan "Rocky" Lane; Eddy Waller; Roy Barcroft; Kay Christopher; Lane Bradford; William Ruhl; Richard Emory; John Butler ****

Arizona territory is being overrun by rampaging, plundering, looting, murdering skunks, the beleaguered citizens appealing direct to the President of the United States for assistance. "A strange, exciting story" promises the post-credit titles and by "Rocky" Lane standards, they're not far wrong. Megalomaniac gunsmith Roy Barcroft (looking cleaner and tidier than usual) has visions of grandeur, orchestrating the raids to enable him to rule the state like a Western emperor; in steps Cavalry Intelligence Lieutenant Allan Lane to upset his plans. Major William Ruhl turns up in Bolton City to organize a secret visit by the President, Lieutenant Richard Emory, romancing newspaperman Eddy Waller's niece, Kay Christopher, is accused of treachery and there's enough double-dealings, false identities, covert operations, fistfights, gunplay and intrigue afoot to fill a movie twice the length. A planned assassination attempt goes haywire when Lane and Waller outwit Barcroft's crackpot scheme to blow up the president, smoking "them ding dang sidewinders" out of a cabin at the East Bend relay station with gunpowder, the heavyweight villain falling on a regimental sword during a brawl with Rocky. One or two moments of artistic photography courtesy of John MacBurnie and nonstop action add up to an enjoyable hour spent in the company of Lane, Waller, Barcroft and, of course, that magnificent steed, Black Jack.

Dialogue:
Lane to Waller who's getting upset at being wrongly blamed for forging army identification papers: "Cut your suspenders and come down to earth."

Salt Lake Raiders

Republic; 60 minutes; Producer: Gordon Kay; Director: Fred C. Brannon; Cast: Allan "Rocky" Lane; Eddy Waller; Roy Barcroft; Martha Hyer; Myron Healey; Byron Foulger; Clifton Young; Rory Mallinson ***

Four riders dry-gulch a prison wagon, convict Myron Healey escaping the crash but apprehended by Marshal Allan Lane; Healey's served six years behind bars for the murder of Martha Hyer's father, a banker, and also (apparently) knows the whereabouts of $100,000 stolen from the bank heist. But is he innocent of all charges? Relay station manager Eddy Waller reckons so, teaming up with Rocky and Healey as they investigate the ghost town of Silver City, all three falling foul of Roy Barcroft, boss of the Condor gang, and his gun monkeys, looking for the loot believed buried there. Hyer appears on the scene, crooked lawyer Byron Foulger confesses to killing her father and after several shoot-outs and near escapes, the money is discovered hidden in saddlebags, Barcroft on the end of a particularly brutal, two-minute punch-up with Lane—Foulger is drilled full of lead, dying in the street, the outlaws rounded up by the sheriff's posse. As Rocky rides off, mission accomplished, Hyer has already planned to marry Healey, probably as recompense for those six wasted years spent in prison.

Dialogue:
Prisoner to Sheriff Rory Mallinson in the prison wagon: "Knockin' around like this. What'd they think we are? Cattle?"
Mallinson: "Look, we're movin' you to a nice new prison. Whadd'ya want, cushions too?"

Covered Wagon Raid

Republic; 60 minutes; Producer: Gordon Kay; Director: R.G. Springsteen; Cast: Allan "Rocky" Lane; Eddy Waller; Alex Gerry; Lyn Thomas; Byron Barr; Dick Curtis; Pierce Lyden; Rex Lease ****

Alex Gerry, West Bend's postmaster and boss of the Three Monkeys saloon, is hiring gunfighters to attack stagecoaches that contain mail and boxes of jewelry in the hope that his tactics will scare off potential settlers willing to purchase a parcel of land on the Chandler Ranch; he wants the whole spread for himself. Opening letters addressed to Eddy Waller, the ranch's foreman, he can gain inside information as to who is planning to visit the ranch and have them bumped off. Insurance

Westerns of the 1950s: The Classic Years   267

Special Investigator Allan Lane, after witnessing the murder of potential buyer Rex Lease and taking his young daughter into town, joins forces with Waller in an attempt to bring wily Gerry and his masked sidewinders to justice. Byron Barr, heir to the ranch and engaged to Lyn Thomas, is waylaid by Gerry's boys and the whole shebang climaxes in a shoot-out in Canyon Pass between the sheriff's posse, a wagon train and the outlaws. At the saloon, Lane engages in a terrific fistfight with heavy Dick Curtis, tables and chairs flying in all directions; Curtis knocked out, Lane dives over a table, reaches for his six-shooter and drops Gerry, a tremendous piece of action orchestrated by R.G. Springsteen who brings a bit more expertise to a very rewarding "Rocky" Lane feature.

Highlights:
Lane and Curtis' climactic punch-up, 'A' class and a little too realistic for comfort—but Rocky still doesn't lose his hat!

Dialogue:
Waller to Lane after the investigator has turned down an offer of a piece of the Chandler property as he's got to be on his way: "Hey. You gettin' itchy feet to go places and get yourself into heap more trouble?"

Trivia:
Actor Gig Young's real name was Byron Barr, the two men getting confused in some late 1940s productions; Barr, never achieving great things, died of unknown causes on November 3, 1966, aged only 49.

Vigilante Hideout

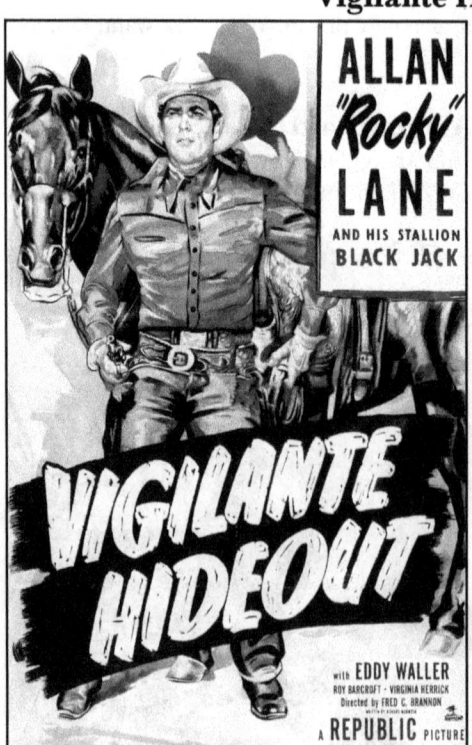

Republic; 60 minutes; Producer: Gordon Kay; Director: Fred C. Brannon; Cast: Allan "Rocky" Lane; Eddy Waller; Roy Barcroft; Don Haggerty; Virginia Herrick; Cliff Clark; Paul Campbell; Guy Teague ****

Range Detective Allan Lane assists Don Haggerty after he's caught in a landslide caused by Eddy Waller; the old coot, an amateur inventor, is trying to locate water to help the parched town of Cottonwood Springs by dynamiting the surrounding countryside. He's also called on Lane to help find his three prize steers, being nurtured on experimental feed and forever being rustled. Haggerty is in cahoots with bad 'un Roy Barcroft, whose gang is planning to extend the Blue Bonnet Copper Mine under the town's bank vault (and Waller's corral), blow it up and grab the $25,000 put by for an aqueduct. Richard Wormser won Western writing awards in 1960 and

1971 and brings a certain amount of freshness to his script, resulting in one of the more interesting and entertaining entrants in the "Rocky" Lane series; Waller's inventions include a talking tape machine, an automatic door opener and a primitive alarm device. The gang's activities are uncovered when Virginia Herrick's father, Cliff Clark, confesses all on Waller's recording machine and is then shot dead. Lane indulges in three bruising fistfights with Barcroft (hat *in situ* throughout!) and when the mine *is* dynamited (and Haggerty with it; Barcroft has surrendered), the explosion releases a flood of water to bone-dry Cottonwood; yep, Waller (as usual, Nugget Clark) has saved the day!

Dialogue:
Lane to Waller: "Wait'll the fellers in the Denver office hear this one. I come all the way down here to track down three cows!"

Frisco Tornado

Republic; 60 minutes; Producer: Gordon Kay; Director: R.G. Springsteen; Cast: Allan "Rocky" Lane; Eddy Waller; Martha Hyer; Stephen Chase; Ross Ford; Lane Bradford; Mauritz Hugo; Rex Lease ***

Corrupt insurance salesman Stephen Chase is running a protection racket out of Bold Bluff, hiking up his rates every time a stagecoach is attacked by outlaws—acting on his orders! Eddy Waller, boss of the Bold Bluff Stage Freight Lines outfit, refuses to pay any insurance to "that danged crook," and is getting fed up with his stages being hijacked and drivers and guards shot in the back by a killer posing as a passenger, so hires Marshal "Rocky" Lane to nail the culprits. Once again, there's a case of stolen/mistaken identity, Lane losing his papers during a shoot-out with Chase's prairie rats at a shack early in the proceedings and branded an imposter, while green young lawyer Ross Ford, acting for Chase, doesn't believe his boss is a swindler until the final reel. Martha Hyer flits around in the background looking pretty, and Chase comes on the receiving end of Lane's meaty fists in a ferocious climactic punch-up after his latest stage robbery goes horribly wrong, a sheriff's posse waiting in ambush. Good thick-ear stuff with all the usual "Rocky" Lane components firmly in place.

Dialogue:
Waller to Hyer, who asks him to try out her new typewriter: "Aha, not me. I wouldn't lay a finger on it. That durned thing ain't human."

Rustlers on Horseback

Republic; 60 minutes; Producer: Gordon Kay; Director: Fred C. Brannon; Cast: Allan "Rocky" Lane; Eddy Waller; Roy Barcroft; Claudia Barrett; John Eldredge; George Nader; Douglas Evans; Forrest Taylor ***

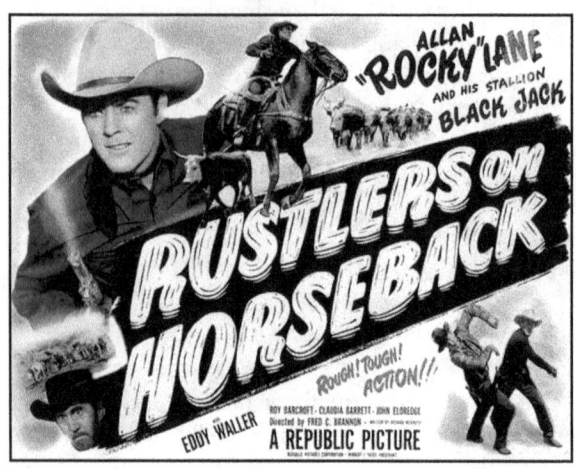

Pursued by Deputy Marshal Allan Lane on Black Jack, gunfighter Stuart Randall is felled by a tree branch, given a dose of Eddy Waller's old Indian remedy, recovers and then shot by gunman John L. Cason who thinks he's a lawman. Lane takes on Randall's identity, infiltrating Roy Barcroft's ranch with Waller to uncover Barcroft's scam. The crook has stolen the ranch from George Nader's family and plans to offer it to businessman Forrest Taylor for $125,000, kill Taylor, pocket the money and use the spread as a center for outlaw activity, hoping to run the territory. Randall was just one of many gunslingers ready to join up with Barcroft, so Lane is in a prime position to upset the rat's plans, which he does with a little help from Waller and Nader. John Eldredge is "Mister Big," working out of Sloan Junction; he tumbles into a river at the end when his buckboard crashes during a chase, Barcroft and his boys all biting the dust. Taylor buys part of the ranch from Nader and his wife, Claudia Barrett, planning to allow settlers to set up home there. An enjoyable 60 minutes of roughhouse action (particularly the bruising fistfights), smokin' guns and Waller, pretending to be a cook, a little less silly than normal.

Dialogue:
Barcroft to Taylor who doesn't believe Barcroft was shot at: "Yeah? Suppose a bumble bee put a hole in my hat!"

Trivia:
George Nader's film debut.

1951

Rough Riders of Durango

Republic; 60 minutes; Producer: Gordon Kay; Director: Fred C. Brannon; Cast: Allan "Rocky" Lane; Walter Baldwin; Aline Towne; Steve Darrell; Ross Ford; Denver Pyle; Stuart Randall; Hal Price ***

Grain shipments are being looted by masked outlaws, Durango's ineffectual "young pup" sheriff Ross Ford calling on Marshal Allan "Rocky" Lane for assistance before banker Hal Price forecloses on settlers' farms and ranches; saddle salesman Steve Darrell is behind the raids, hoping to get his hands on the expected cash that will pay the banker off. Forty thousand dollars sent from the council seat to satisfy Price is robbed and hidden in one of Walter Baldwin's grain sacks, but which one? Most of the film is spent in hunting down the relevant sack of grain containing the cashbox in the vicinity of Baldwin's ranch, an abundance of chases, fights and gunplay stirring up the action, Darrell eventually punched senseless by Lane in his office after Ford and his posse have rounded up the varmints. Sadly, there's no Nugget Clark to lighten the load (and wouldn't be for the next five Allan "Rocky" Lane features), motormouth Baldwin (as Cricket Adams) a poor and rather irritating substitute, forever berating his niece, Aline Towne, for falling for a no-hoper (in his eyes) like Ford, although the novice lawman is accepted by the talkative fool in the end

Dialogue:
Outlaw to Lane who surprises him in the dark: "Thought you was dead."
Lane: "Sorry to disappoint you. I'm alive and curious."

Night Riders of Montana

Republic; 60 minutes; Producer: Gordon Kay; Director: Fred C. Brannon; Cast: Allan "Rocky" Lane; Myron Healey; Roy Barcroft; Chubby Johnson; Claudia Barrett; Arthur Space; Morton C. Thompson; Marshall Bradford *

Number 26 in the series (counting those made in the 1940s) was a dull affair, scriptwriter M. Coates Webster trying to introduce too many twists and turns into a formulaic plot. State Ranger Allan "Rocky" Lane foils gunsmith Arthur Space's rustlers with the assistance of roly-poly sheriff Chubby Johnson, gullible Myron Healey the innocent accused of murdering Marshall Bradford, when Space's masked bandits, led by Roy Barcroft, are the no-gooders. Too much talk centering on the whereabouts of the meeting place in Rainbow Canyon, where worried ranchers are hiding their herds to prevent more being rustled, bogs down what little action there is; the gunfights and brawls look corny, Lane is as stiff as a buckboard and Claudia Barrett, the female interest, does nothing but drift around in the background. Perhaps everyone was missing the long-winded presence of ornery polecat Eddy Waller! One hour of Western tedium.

Dialogue:
Barcroft to Space: "I get it. You let the kid find out for us where them herds a meetin' and we fix 'em up, huh?"
Space: "That's right, Brink. Your brain's getting almost as big as your ears."

Wells Fargo Gunmaster

Republic; 60 minutes; Producer: Gordon Kay; Director: Philip Ford; Cast: Allan "Rocky" Lane; Chubby Johnson; Mary Ellen Kay; Michael Chapin; Roy Barcroft; Walter Reed; Stuart Randall; William Bakewell **

Kicking off with the obligatory "outlaws chasing stagecoach" scene, *Wells Fargo Gunmaster* is a heavy-going "Rocky" Lane outing, our beefy hero playing a Wells Fargo investigator on the trail of $20,000 in stolen bonds, hidden someplace around Cedarville, Arizona; saloon boss Stuart Randall wants to cash the lot in and retire ungracefully on the proceeds. No Eddy Waller again, just bumbling Chubby Johnson getting under Lane's boots as the investigator saves the life of young Michael Chapin in a horse-riding accident, thus prompting his brother, Walter Reed, who was in on the scam, to have a fit of conscience, telling Lane the whole deal; for blabbing, he gets a slug in the chest from Roy Barcroft. The bonds are hidden in Mary Ellen Kay's house (Chapin and Reed's sister); Randall grabs them, Lane is accused of murdering Reed and the final reel sees Randall falling off a buckboard to his death during a furious chase with Lane, Barcroft having been plugged in the bandits' silver mine hideout. Chapin receives a share of the Wells Fargo reward money and Lane rides off in the daylight, making up for a plethora of nighttime shots and too much coming and going in and around Kay's homestead.

Dialogue:
Lane to Barcroft and his boys, on seeing the stack of stolen goods in the cave: "Nice setup you got here. Looks like a Wells Fargo warehouse."

Fort Dodge Stampede

Republic; 60 minutes; Produced and Directed by Harry Keller; Cast: Allan "Rocky" Lane; Chubby Johnson; Roy Barcroft; Trevor Bardette; Mary Ellen Kay; Bruce Edwards; William Forest; Wes Hudman ***

Eddy "Nugget Clark" Waller still committed to star in other film consignments (he was much in demand as a minor character actor), Chubby Johnson stepped into his boots in a tale concerning $30,000 stolen from the Adams Bank and secreted somewhere in the derelict town of Fort Dodge, Nevada. Johnson owns the entire ghost town ("Kind of a king, huh?" says Lane), his barn a veritable Aladdin's cave of goodies; he's selling off parts of Fort Dodge to settlers who arrive looking for a new life. But jeweler Trevor Bardette wants to find out where that loot is, employing dimwitted leader of the Pike gang, Roy Barcroft, posing as a railroad surveyor, to create a series of diversionary tactics to get Johnson and Deputy Sheriff Allan Lane outta town so the barn can be ransacked. Bruce Edwards is also after the cash; his father owned the bank, and he wants to return the money. A coded map unearthed in a mailbox points to the cash being hidden under the floor of Bardette's jewelry store. Edwards' gal, Ellen Mary Kay, is held hostage as Barcroft and Bardette make their escape on a horse-driven cart with the dollars; during a fight on the speeding buckboard, Lane shoots Bardette and slugs Barcroft unconscious. Headlines announce the return of the $30,000 to the Adams Bank, and Johnson informs Rocky that Fort Dodge has a bright future as a new railroad is due to run through the town, our hero galloping away on Black Jack for pastures new.

Highlights:
Lane's vicious slugging match with Barcroft in reel two, the pair looking distinctly ragged after it's all over.

Dialogue:
Lane to his boss: "There's no more law in Fort Dodge than there is butter at the North Pole."

Trivia:
The oft-used scenario of "outlaws looking for stolen cash in a ghost town" was spruced up on a bigger budget in Columbia's 1953 outing *Ambush at Tomahawk Gap*.

Desert of Lost Men

Republic; 54 minutes; Produced and Directed by Harry Keller; Cast: Allan "Rocky" Lane; Irving Bacon; Mary Ellen Kay; Roy Barcroft; Ross Elliott; Cliff Clark; Boyd "Red" Morgan; Leo Cleary ***

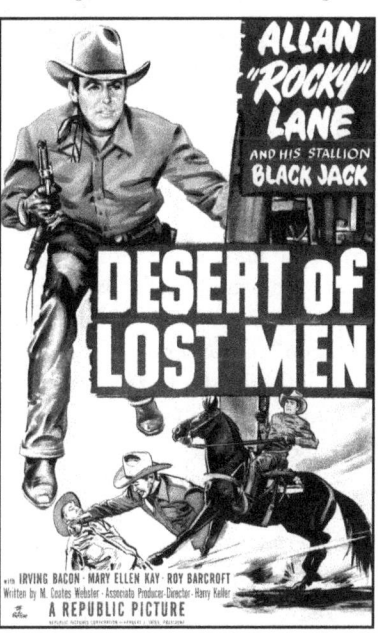

Forty thousand dollars earmarked for Bear Creek's new hospital has apparently been stolen by the mysterious band of outlaws known as the Lost Men, but in fact it hasn't—the cash is due to arrive on the next stage, the faked robbery a ruse set in motion by Deputy Marshal Allan Lane and Sheriff Irving Bacon to throw the gang, led by printing boss Cliff Clark and thug Roy Barcroft, off scent; Clark is after the money to line his own pockets. Ross Elliott, the town's medic, whose fellow doctor was killed in the opening minutes, wants to bring the coyotes to justice just as much as Lane does; Mary Ellen Kay supplies the love interest, playing Elliott's intended. To confuse Clark even further, Elliott's trumped-up wanted poster proclaims him to be the murderer of his partner, Barcroft the actual guilty party. The gang's hideout is *not* in the desert but in Republic's oft-used cave system, and Lane plus Bacon's posse eventually overturn the tables on the Lost Men as they're about to rob the stage, Clark shot in an out-of-control wagon tussle with Rocky, Barcroft punched senseless. That much-needed hospital can now be built. Too much dim photography in the movie's middle section is compensated by Elliott's professional performance; the popular support actor starred in over 250 features and always gave his role, however short, a smooth, classy sheen that added immeasurably to any picture he appeared in, as it did on this occasion.

Dialogue:
Bacon to Lane: "Why, we've had more killings than they had at Custer's Last Stand."

1952

Captive of Billy the Kid

Republic; 54 minutes; Producer: Harry Keller; Director: Fred C. Brannon; Cast: Allan "Rocky" Lane; Penny Edwards; Grant Withers; Clem Bevans; Roy Barcroft; Clayton Moore; Mauritz Hugo; Frank McCarroll ***

Five pieces of a map detailing the whereabouts of Billy the Kid's stolen loot—and five disparate people, each possessing one piece, all wanting to lay their hands on it: Penny Edwards, Grant Withers, Clem Bevans, Mauritz Hugo and Clayton *The Lone Ranger* Moore. Range Detective Allan Lane gallops into the town of Junction and becomes involved in trying to prevent the whole bunch from killing one another, Withers the villain of the piece who, abetted by surly henchman Roy Barcroft, is planning to eliminate the other four anyway, beginning with Hugo. Crusty old Bevans takes over from crusty old Eddy Waller, absent on this occasion, in a talkative "Rocky" Lane offering that features a better-than-usual Stanley Wilson stock score, sharp photography from John MacBurnie and a fast 'n' furious punch-up (not for the first time, and not for the last!) between Lane and Barcroft. In the final reel, Withers falls over a cliff, Barcroft bites the dust and Billy the Kid's fortune is found, Bevans sharing out the reward money with Edwards and Moore, Lane riding away on Black Jack for new adventures.

Dialogue:
Barcroft, moaning to Withers that he came off worse in his fistfight with Lane: "I couldn't help it. He keeps stickin' his face in."
Withers: "Looks like you stuck yours out."
Barcroft: "He's pretty handy with his fists."
Withers: "Maybe I should give you some lessons."

Leadville Gunslinger

Republic; 54 minutes; Produced and Directed by Harry Keller; Cast: Allan "Rocky" Lane; Eddy Waller; Roy Barcroft; Grant Withers; Elaine Riley; Richard Crane; Kenneth MacDonald; I. Stanford Jolley ****

Oil lies on Eddy "Nugget Clark" Waller's property (the old coot making a welcome return for the rest of the series) and Leadville's bigwig banker, Grant Withers, covets the black gold; he's in cahoots with Roy Barcroft and his gang who are holed up in a cave hideout in No Man's Land, an area without any law situated on the Leadville border. Marshal "Rocky" Lane rides in to investigate a series of armed stagecoach robberies that could put Waller out of business, has dinner at his ranch with Elaine Riley and boyfriend Richard Crane and decides to join in the hunt for the bandits when a geologist sent to determine whether or not oil exists on Waller's homestead, and the surrounding farms, is murdered; Withers sends an imposter in his place to state there is no oil, determined to oust Waller from his home by calling in his lease. Lane joins the gang, posing as a gunman, but is caught out in a climactic cave showdown, Withers receives a well-deserved slug and Barcroft, following a particularly punishing fistfight with Lane (did these two *ever* get hurt during these fights?), is arrested. "Best place to start drilling is right under your house," says Crane to a delighted Waller as the brawny hero of the piece gallops off into the distance, the end to a fast-moving Allan Lane feature that refuses to hang around for a single second.

Dialogue:
Waller: "Why Rocky, we ain't seen each other for a coon's age."
Lane: "Has been a long time, hasn't it."
Waller: "Yeah, too long. Lot of bridges gone under the water since then."

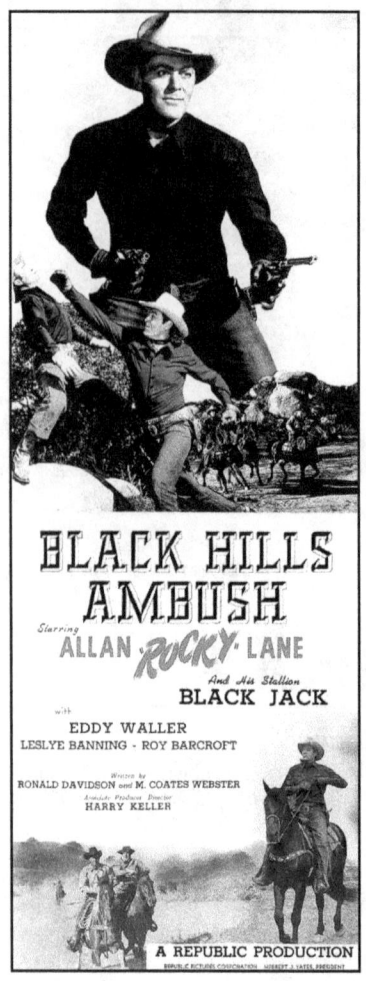

Black Hills Ambush

Republic; 53 minutes; Produced and Directed by Harry Keller; Cast: Allan "Rocky" Lane; Eddy Waller; Leslie Banning; Michael Hall; Roy Barcroft; John Vosper; Ed Cassidy; John L. Cason **

Marshal "Rocky" Lane infiltrates himself into Roy Barcroft and corrupt lawyer John Vosper's gang, who are stealing incoming crates from Eddy Waller's freight line, stacking them with gold bars and shipping them out in the same crates under Waller's unsuspecting nose. Youngster Michael Hall, whose outlaw brother was shot in the back by Barcroft, is cared for by Waller's niece, Leslie Banning, joining Lane in trying to bring the varmints to justice. Under his bandit guise, Lane holds up a freight wagon, takes it to Waller's barn, discovers the gold but is found out by Barcroft and company; it ends in the obligatory shoot-out, Hall deciding to attend law school and become a peace officer. Beginning (as most Allan Lane films do) with men chasing outlaws (or outlaws chasing a stage), *Black Hills Ambush* is ordinary fare for Lane aficionados, the big man simply going through the motions—even Waller is less garrulous and curmudgeonly than usual.

Dialogue:

Waller to Hall, tucking into Banning's pie: "That's the kind of vittles that stick to yer ribs. Why, in 30 days you'll be two inches taller and big and strong like me (hits his chest and explodes in a fit of coughing)."

Thundering Caravans

Republic; 54 minutes; Producer: Rudy Ralston; Director: Harry Keller; Cast: Allan "Rocky" Lane; Eddy Waller; Roy Barcroft; Mona Knox; Richard Crane; Isabel Randolph; William Henry; Stanley Andrews ***

Yep, *Thundering Caravans* is one of the few "Rocky" Lane movies that *doesn't* commence with bandits chasing a stage, or men, although this happens three minutes later! His need for a vacation turned down after dropping off a member of the Crowther gang, Marshal Lane is ordered to the town of Edgewater to assist harassed Sheriff Eddy Waller in bringing to heel an outfit who are stealing gold shipments from the local mine, furious mine owner Stanley Andrews labeling Waller incompetent. William Henry, whose witch-like mother, Isabel Randolph, runs the local newspaper, is the brains behind the robberies, escaped convict Roy Barcroft his chief henchman. Deputy Richard Crane, dating Andrews' daughter Mona Knox, knew Barcroft when he served a two-year stretch in the state pen; Barcroft, after unsuccessfully trying to blackmail Crane ("$1,000 or I talk.") lets on to Randolph who promises to expose Crane in her paper, hoping that Waller

Thundering CARAVANS

Starring ALLAN "ROCKY" LANE AND HIS STALLION BLACK JACK EDDY WALLER MONA KNOX ROY BARCROFT
Written by M. COATES WEBSTER Associate Producer RUDY RALSTON Directed by HARRY KELLER
A REPUBLIC PICTURE

will be ousted at the next elections and Henry made town sheriff. The gang's hideout is situated in a cavern beneath a house in the ghost town of Midas where most of the action takes place, Randolph planning to steal the mine's payroll and drive wagons loaded with gold worth $60,000 to another destination. Crane makes the damaging headlines, but Henry is apprehended by Rocky in a frenetic climax as he makes off with a wagonload of ore, and Randolph (62 at the time of filming) finds herself behind bars with her son, Waller re-elected as sheriff. M. Coates Webster's script provides crusty Waller with some amusing lines, Stanley Wilson's music and John MacBurnie's cinematography add flavor but, this late on in the series, staleness had understandably set in, Harry Keller using snippets from past "Rocky" Lane features to pad out the running time (the climactic wagon chase from *Wells Fargo Gunmaster* is shown in its entirety). The end of this type of '40s-style 60-minute matinée oater was just around the corner.

Dialogue:
Waller, on hearing that women could be allowed to vote in America: "Haha! Females a'votin'! Can you imagine what would happen to this country? Why, it wouldn't be a fit place for man or beast to live in. Huh, no siree, that's somethin' that ain't never gonna happen. And if'n it does, I'm movin' out!"

Desperadoes' Outpost

Republic; 54 minutes; Producer: Rudy Ralston; Director: Philip Ford; Cast: Allan "Rocky" Lane; Eddy Waller; Roy Barcroft; Myron Healey; Lyle Talbot; Claudia Barrett; Lane Bradford; Lee Roberts ****

In one of the best of the "Rocky" Lane adventures, set during the American/Spanish wars, masked bandits are holding up Eddy Waller's stagecoaches but, instead of robbing them, wrecking them. It's all part of a plan by Roy Barcroft and Lyle Talbot to bankrupt Waller and force him to sell his house, which lies adjacent to a lucrative mercury mine; the two villains, intent on making their fortune, are stealing 20 per cent of the ore and shipping it to Mexico, pocketing $40,000. In enters Federal Investigator Lane to clear matters up. Waller's niece, Claudia Barrett, is engaged to Lieutenant Myron Healey, the acting head of the mine's cavalry guard; he smells a rat when shifty Barcroft hints at the smelting equipment being faulty, while Waller becomes suspicious of "them ding dang bandits" when particles of quicksilver turn up in his water supply, a pipeline connecting his homestead to the mine's water reservoir. Plenty of chases, fistfights and shoot-outs over a 54-minute running time, plus a cunning trap set to unmask Fleming, Elmorado's financier, as the crook he is, ensure a rattling good Allan Lane oater that moves like wildfire.

Dialogue:
Lane to Waller, after seeing Barrett and Healey together: "He's a lucky lieutenant. She's pretty."
Waller: "You betcha. He didn't pick no lemon to mix with the orange blossom."

1953
The Marshal of Cedar Rock

Republic; 54 minutes; Producer: Rudy Ralston; Director: Harry Keller; Cast: Allan "Rocky" Lane; Eddy Waller; Phyllis Coates; Roy Barcroft; William Henry; Robert Shayne; Herbert Lytton; John Crawford ***

William Henry is allowed to escape from prison, Marshal Allan Lane tailing him on Black Jack in the hope that he'll lead him to the rest of his gang and $100,000 stolen cash. But Henry is an innocent man, caught up in a scam by corrupt banker Roy Barcroft to buy land owned by Eddy Waller's cattle ranchers at a rock-bottom price of $200 per acre, when the railroad arrives in Cedar Rock; the rail bosses will offer $600, and Barcroft wants to profit by selling the land on to them. Railroad official John Crawford is abducted by Barcroft's heavies and taken care of, imposter Robert Shayne taking his place, his mission to browbeat Waller into signing away his property for peanuts. Lane smells a rat and after several shoot-outs, Barcroft confesses all, Henry taking up with Waller's niece, Phyllis Coates. Punchy direction from Harry Keller and Stanley Wilson's rowdy score ensure a good time by all for fans of Lane's cheapo Republic oaters, but isn't it time he lost his swanky white hat in all those punchy fistfights?

Dialogue:
Waller, after a group of cowpokes has ridden into Cedar Rock, pistols blazing: "Bank robbers! Bandits! You gotta be a doggone outlaw to make a livin' round here!"

Savage Frontier

Republic; 54 minutes; Producer: Rudy Ralston; Director: Harry Keller; Cast: Allan "Rocky" Lane; Eddy Waller; Bob Steele; Dorothy Patrick; Roy Barcroft; Richard Avonde; William Phipps; Jimmy Hawkins *****

The end of the "Rocky" Lane series was in sight. Perhaps aware of this (the films were losing money and viewed as old-fashioned), Republic threw everything they had into *Savage Frontier*, a witty script from Dwight V. Babcock and Gerald Geraghty, pristine photography courtesy of Bud Thackery and a less derivative score from Stanley Wilson. Veteran Western heavy Bob Steele was drafted in to bring a touch of gravitas and polish, playing a reformed outlaw in Bitter Springs, under the thumb of ex-boss Roy Barcroft; Barcroft wants him in on a planned gold bullion robbery but Steele, now a farmer, will be breaking his parole conditions if he handles a six-shooter, so refuses the offer. Much of the excitement comes from Marshal Allan Lane's attempts to keep tabs on Richard Avonde (as Cherokee), a cold-blooded gunslinger who thinks nothing of pumping six bullets into a corpse, as witnessed in the film's opening sequence where he empties his revolver into a dead deputy marshal, strong stuff for this kind of fare; even Barcroft can't handle the killer. Steele packs a gun, wanting to turn Avonde over to the law, but he's shot in the back when Avonde breaks out of jail, Steele's brother, William Phipps, convinced that Lane did it. At a standoff in the gang's mine hideout, Phipps shoots Avonde dead while, back in town, Lane slugs Barcroft senseless. Steele recovers from his near-fatal wound and dentist-cum-barber-cum-lawman Eddy Waller is reinstated as sheriff. Dorothy Patrick supplies the female eye-candy, Lane shows off his equestrian skills to perfection, there's fisticuffs and gunfights a-plenty and Waller hustles and bustles as only he can. Tremendous B-movie entertainment.

Dialogue:
Young awestruck Jimmy Hawkins to Lane: "Gee, Rocky, I bet you and Nugget (Waller) are the greatest lawmen that ever lived."
Lane, grinning: "Well, sir, that's a fine compliment putting me in the same class as Nugget."

Bandits of the West

Republic; 54 minutes; Producer: Rudy Ralston; Director: Harry Keller; Cast: Allan "Rocky" Lane; Eddy Waller; Cathy Downs; Roy Barcroft; Trevor Bardette; Ray Montgomery; Harry Harvey; Robert Bice ***

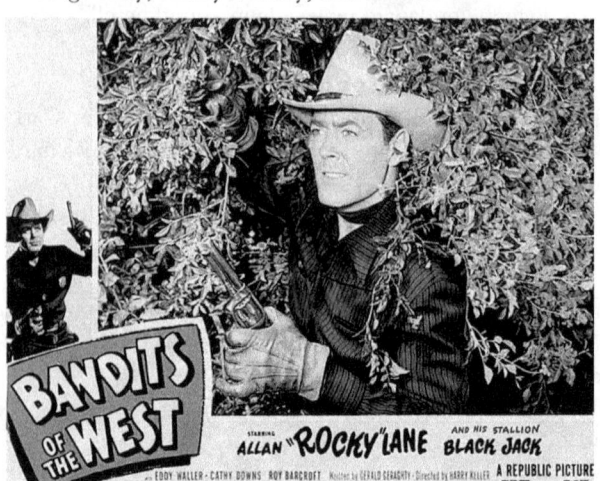

By 1953, the era of the hour-long, low-budget B-Western was fizzling out, looking decidedly old-hat. Nevertheless, Harry Keller manufactured a lively confection (boosted by a noisy Stanley Wilson score) to keep the momentum going, Allan Lane caught up in a war between rancher Trevor Bardette, just released from prison after serving a seven-year stretch for the murder of Cathy Downs' father, and Downs' Landale Gas Company who want to lay a gas pipe across his land. Judge Harry Harvey rules in Downs' favor, prompting henchman Roy Barcroft and his fellow partners in crime to sabotage the gas line *and* grab Bardette's ranch by selling off his entire herd of cattle and pocketing the cash; he was the man responsible for the murder, Bardette the innocent victim. Lane, deputized, and grizzled old sidekick Eddy Waller foil Barcroft's plans in a series of fistfights, gunfights and, last of all, an almighty gas explosion which finishes off the crooks. Lane hands in his badge, Bardette is cleared of all charges and Downs cozies up to Ray Montgomery as Lane gallops off on Black Jack for his final adventure in the series.

Dialogue:
Waller, watching Lane handcuff two of Bardette's rowdy ranch hands: "That'll fix them Chadwick hoodlums ... uh, uh, howdy Mr. Chadwick!" as Bardette enters the room.

El Paso Stampede

Republic; 53 minutes; Producer: Rudy Ralston; Director: Harry Keller; Cast: Allan "Rocky" Lane; Eddy Waller; Phyllis Coates; Stephen Chase; Roy Barcroft; Edward Clark; Tom Monroe; Stanley Andrews ****

America is at war with Spain. Clarksburg's burly dentist, Stephen Chase, aided by Roy Barcroft's jackals, is organizing gangs of rustlers to steal herds of beef due to the army, take them through a tunnel to a hidden valley and sell the steers to a Mexican dictator. Stanley Andrews, Clarksburg's new marshal, is gunned down on his way to take up the position, leaving U.S. Army Investigator "Rocky" Lane to join forces with storekeeper Eddy Waller in unmasking the brains behind the operation and ensuring the military receive that much-required beef. Chase longs for Waller's daughter, Phyllis Coates, but she's not interested, while Waller's timid assistant, Edward Clark, is tipping off Chase as to the movements of animal feed from his boss' store; the grain is urgently needed for those starving rustled cattle. Lane and Waller gather all the ranchers together, planning to ambush Chase's hombres at Canyon Pass when the outlaws home in on a fresh herd. Using their rigs and wagons as a barricade, the herd is turned back, the rustlers retreat and, back in town, Clark and Chase are uncovered as the villains. A surprise attack is coordinated, details of Waller's shipment of feed due at Mission Point at five o'clock leaked to Chase who has Coates captive, tied up in a cave. In an energetic finale, the ranchers' wagons form a circle, the outlaw rustlers surrender under intense gunfire and Lane pursues Chase through the cave, freeing Coates, knocking his enemy to the ground and discovering the valley full of grazing cattle, thus ending a run of 38 "Rocky" Lane Westerns stretching back to 1947, and the last B-Western Lane ever appeared in. Lane died on October 27, 1973, aged 64; Waller on August 20, 1977 aged 88; and Barcroft on November 28, 1969 aged 67. What they gave fans was 60 minutes of unsophisticated Western thrills of the cheap variety, but not without some merit. They entertained in a rough 'n' ready fashion and gave each production their all—what more could any cowboy-mad buff wish for?

Dialogue:
The final word, naturally, has to go to the incomparable Eddy "Nugget Clark" Waller in a classic example of his homespun vernacular: "God durned the ding dang luck."

Chapter 11
1956

APACHE BEND WAS A BLOOD-STAINED SPOT ON THE MAP ... UNTIL A TIN-STAR TORNADO WIPED IT CLEAN!
The Brass Legend

THEY'RE TOGETHER! SCREENDOM'S NEW TEENAGE SENSATIONS!
The Burning Hills

THIS WAS THE DAY OF THE ROPE AND THE RAVAGER!"
A Day of Fury

SPRAYING ITS STREETS WITH LEAD! LIGHTING ITS SKIES WITH GUNFIRE!
The Desperados Are in Town

BROTHER AGAINST BROTHER BLOOD-FEUD!
Gun Brothers

HIRED TO KILL THE WOMAN HE LOVED!
Gunslinger

SURGING ACROSS AMERICA'S VAST BADLAND IN THE MOST CHALLENGING MISSION OF HIS CAREER. HI-YO SILVER! TONTO, TOO! *The Lone Ranger*

Blackjack Ketchum, Desperado
Clover/Columbia; 76 minutes; Producer: Sam Katzman; Director: Earl Bellamy; Cast: Howard Duff; Victor Jory; Margaret Field (Maggie Mahoney); Angela Stevens; William Tannen; Martin Garralaga; Robert Roark; Ken Christy ****

There's plenty of hard-boiled action in TV director Earl Bellamy's take on, by now, a very familiar scenario, that of a ruthless cattle baron (Victor Jory at his reptilian best) trampling over ranchers' property because his steers need watering and feeding; all those opposing him and his brothers are murdered. What's more, Jory wants to own the town of Horseshoe lock, stock and barrel, hiring gunslinger William Tannen to impose *his* kind of law, not Sheriff Ken Christy's, the lawman shot by Tannen for getting in his way. In steps notorious ex-desperado Howard Duff (as Tom "Blackjack" Ketchum), dressed in black and sporting a silver-studded double holster, to organize a committee and eventually give Jory a taste of his own nasty medicine. Duff outdrew one of Jory's brothers a year back and the cattleman, thirsting for revenge, wants him dead, legal or not. There's a lengthy manhunt filmed at Lone Pine in which Duff whittles down Jory's six gunhands to two; Jory steals the town's ammunition and firearms, stampeding his steers through Margaret Field's Double R Ranch, resulting in the death of her father. In a showdown, Duff plugs Tannen, Jory is arrested, and younger brother Robert Roark promises to pay $10,000 to repair all the damage and call off the cattle war; Duff waltzes away with Field to begin life on his ranch. Blonde Angela Stevens is definitely superfluous to requirements (but looks nice), Mischa Bakaleinikoff's stock score (made up of seven composers' works) rings true and it's just a pity that, in the end, Jory didn't get a healthy dose of lead to wipe that evil smirk off his face.

Dialogue:
Jory to Tannen after the gunslinger has failed to nail Duff: "I reckon it's my fault. I thought I was hiring the best gun in the country. I got second best."

The Brass Legend

United Artists; 79 minutes; Producer: Herman Cohen; Director: Gerd Oswald; Cast: Hugh O'Brian; Nancy Gates; Raymond Burr; Donald MacDonald; Rebecca Welles; Robert Burton; Eddie Firestone; Willard Sage ****

Sheriff Hugh O'Brian has promised fiancée Nancy Gates that he'll throw in his badge when his term finishes in a year. Her father (Robert Burton) wants his prospective son-in-law to join him in the ranching business while Gate's 12-year-old brother (Donald MacDonald) hero-worships the double holster-wearing peacemaker of Apache Bend. But matters turn sour when, on MacDonald's tip-off, O'Brian arrests back-shooting killer Raymond Burr and incarcerates him in the town jail under heavy guard. Word leaks out via Willard Sage's paper that MacDonald tipped the sheriff off and the lad's life is now in danger, as is O'Brian's. MacDonald is seriously wounded while riding his new pony on the range, Burr's mistress (Rebecca Welles) rants and raves at O'Brian, her lapdog admirer (Eddie Firestone) is the coward behind MacDonald's shooting and the Barlow Brothers, wanted for murder in Lincoln County, hit town to break Burr out from behind bars. In a saloon shoot-out, O'Brian plugs two of the brothers, the third setting Burr free. O'Brian puts a slug into Firestone after Burr has shot dead Sage; out on the trail, O'Brian and Burr go head-to-head. In a flurry of gunfire, O'Brian is wounded twice but Burr expires in the dust, a smile on his face as he knows he has escaped the hangman's noose. Super Western fare from United Artists, a hard-boiled tale bolstered by Paul Dunlap's terrific score: O'Brian is solid and assured, Burr radiates pure heavyweight villainy and MacDonald is charming as the youngster looking up to O'Brian as a role model, especially in the quick draw stakes.

Dialogue:
Burr to O'Brian: "You don't think I look like the type who goes 'round shootin' little kids, do you?"
O'Brian: "You're the type that'd shoot butterflies if you thought you could hit 'em."

The Broken Star

Bel-Air/United Artists; 82 minutes; Producer: Howard W. Koch; Director: Lesley Selander; Cast: Howard Duff; Bill Williams; Lita Baron; Henry Calvin; Douglas Fowley; Addison Richards; Joe Dominguez; Felipe Turich ****

A fine *noir* Western directed with panache by the reliable Lesley Selander concerning an unhinged deputy marshal (Howard Duff) who, in order to lay his hands on $8,000 gold belonging to big shot Henry Calvin, owner of the T Lazy W spread, murders rancher Felipe Turich in cold blood; Turich's been safeguarding the hoard for his boss. Duff then makes it look as though he shot in self-defense, unaware that Apache hand Joe Dominguez witnessed the killing. *The Broken Star* examines the fragile relationship between another deputy, Bill Williams, and mentally unstable Duff who once saved his life; can this be the same man, Williams wonders, who is lying his head off and prepared to shoot anyone who knows what he did? Calvin, suspicious, demands the money back from Duff; Turich's sister, Mexican singer Lita Baron (Mrs Rory Calhoun in real life), romancing Williams, is tailed by two thugs (Joel Ashley and John Pickard) who are convinced she knows where the gold is hidden, and Dominguez gets shot in the back by Duff in the Old Friar's Mine. Indian agent Douglas Fowley demands $4,000 from Duff in exchange for giving the loony lawman a safe passage out of the territory; at an abandoned mission, Duff's double-cross (rocks for gold) backfires and he flees to the mine where Williams, held captive by Duff, frees himself. Following a shoot-out with Addison Richards' posse in the old workings, Williams plugs his former pal, ending up marrying Baron in the final seconds. A thumping Paul Dunlap score and pristine photography by William Margulies (Old Tucson was the setting) add up to a little-seen oater worth ferreting out.

Dialogue:
Fowley to Williams: "Telling an Apache to do anything is like tryin' to saddle a cougar."

The Burning Hills

Warner Bros.; CinemaScope/Warnercolor; 94 minutes; Producer: Richard Whorf; Director: Stuart Heisler; Cast: Tab Hunter; Natalie Wood; Skip Homeier; Ray Teal; Claude Akins; Eduard Franz; Earl Holliman; Tyler MacDuff ****

Twenty-five-year-old pinup boy Tab Hunter and 18-year-old Hollywood hopeful Natalie Wood were teamed together in Stuart Heisler's exciting adaptation of Louis L'Amour's novel concerning rancher Hunter locking horns with Ray Teal's gunhands after his brother is shot in the back. Teal (as Sutton) runs the town of Esperanza and wants to lord it over the whole territory; following a heated confrontation, Hunter puts two slugs into Teal (but fails to finish him off) and hightails it to Mexican Wood's ranch where, wounded, he hides out in an old

Spanish mine. Needless to say, Hunter and Wood fall for each other as Teal's loose cannon son, Skip Homeier, and a dozen cowpokes converge on Wood's spread ("I gotta stop them," barks Teal). Fending off Homeier and Earl Holliman's brutal sexual overtures, the lass goes on the run with Hunter to Fort Stockwell where it is hoped the military will step in and oust Teal from Esperanza. Homeier's gang whittled down to three men following a Comanche attack, the hothead is slugged by Hunter in a vicious river fistfight, his body swept away in the rapids; Indian scout Eduard Franz lets the pair of lovers continue on their way to the fort, having no taste for further killing. David Buttolph's bulldozer of a score drives the narrative, Homeier (an underrated talent in '50s Westerns) and Holliman are suitably repellent while the two attractive leads acquit themselves with honors. "Good and lively," commented the *New York Times*.

Highlights:

Hunter and Wood, both prime examples of Hollywood '50s glamor—and they could act. And watch out for the stuntman rolling down a slope straight under the hooves of a galloping horse, unplanned but retained in the print.

Dialogue:

Franz, watching Hunter and Wood depart: "Fort Stockwell is just over the next bridge. I'll be waiting back at Esperanza, just to see the look on old man Sutton's face."

Trivia:

The Warner Bros. publicity machine went into overdrive, hinting at a romantic liaison between Hunter and Wood, even though most people in the business were aware of Hunter's preference for the male of the species; it worked, the movie raking in nearly $2,000,000 at the box-office.

Comanche

United Artists; CinemaScope/DeLuxecolor; 87 minutes; Producer: Carl Krueger; Director: George Sherman; Cast: Dana Andrews; Kent Smith; Nestor Paiva; Henry Brandon; Stacy Harris; Linda Cristal; John Litel; Lowell Gilmore ****

In 1875, the Mexicans are at war with the Comanches in a conflict stretching back to the 1660s, Stacy Harris' American scalp-hunters adding fuel to the fire. The U.S. military, led by General John Litel, are determined to parley with Kent Smith (Chief Quanah Parker), scouts Dana Andrews and wig-wearing Nestor Paiva instructed to negotiate peace terms with the Comanche chief, warmonger Henry Brandon (Black Cloud) stirring up trouble by forming his own renegade pack. Beautifully shot in Durango, Mexico (photographer: Jorge Stahl, Jr.) and presenting large-scale cavalry/Indian attacks rarely seen outside of a John Ford cavalry saga, *Comanche* is a much underrated Western directed with panache and a real eye for the wide-open landscapes by the prolific George Sherman (Herschel Burke Gilbert's noisy score throws everything into the pot). From the savage opening raid on a village bursting alive with colors to the final skirmish (featuring hundreds of extras) when Litel's regiment and Smith's braves corner Brandon and his warriors in a huge box canyon, the excitement level never lets up. Okay, Smith is about as wooden as a totem pole (but weren't all Indians supposed to be impassive?), but Paiva coping with his curly wig is a joy to behold, and even The Lancers warbling the catchy "A Man is as Good as his Word" at sporadic intervals doesn't intrude on the stirring action sequences.

Highlights:
Frequent sweeping panoramic shots of troops and Comanches tearing over the rugged Durango wilderness, spectacular fare in a B-Western of this type.

Dialogue:
Andrews: "You don't see Comanches until they're on top of you."
Trivia:
　　Brandon's ferocious performance so impressed John Ford that he promptly placed him in the part of another Comanche villain, Chief Scar, in *The Searchers*, and in the same year! Brandon also played Chief Quanah Parker in Ford's *Two Rode Together* in 1961. And married Andrews fell for Linda Cristal (her first major role) during filming, his wife flying down to Mexico and confronting the guilty pair on set.

Dakota Incident

Republic; Trucolor; 88 minutes; Producer: Michael Baird; Director: Lewis R. Foster; Cast: Linda Darnell; Dale Robertson; John Lund; Ward Bond; Regis Toomey; Whit Bissell; Skip Homeier; John Doucette ****

　　There is bags of incident in *Dakota Incident*, a little-seen gem from Republic's golden period featuring a striking mandolin-based score from R. Dale Butts and a great star turn from Dale Robertson. Bank robber Robertson, left for dead by double-dealing "pardners" Skip Homeier (his brother) and venomous John Doucette, treks on foot to the desert town of Christian's Flat where he finds a diverse bunch of characters waiting to catch the stage to Laramie: Ravishing showgirl Linda Darnell, self-righteous "give peace a chance" senator Ward Bond, shady John Lund (a bank cashier blamed for the robbery who wants Robertson alive as a witness) and prospector Whit Bissell, among others. Frederick Louis Fox's pithy script focuses on the sparky Robertson/Darnell relationship; he reckons that deep down, under that decorative red dress and haughty demeanor, the fancy dame's just longing for a good 'ole piece of rough, and he's the man to provide it. Robertson shoots Doucette dead in a white-knuckle street standoff and lets his brother go; the stage roles in, peppered with arrows, its occupants dead ("What do you think about Indians now?" spits Robertson to Bond). Robertson elects to ride the coach to Laramie, Lund on shotgun duty, Bissell, Regis Toomey, Bond and Darnell the passengers. The final third of Lewis R. Foster's riveting little oater deals with the group as they are pinned down without any water in a dry gulch by Cheyenne braves positioned in rocks high up on Red Rock Canyon's ledges. One by one they succumb, leaving Robertson and Darnell alone. Sparing a warrior's life in a tussle, the thankful Indian brings the survivors two horses as a gift ("The language of friendship.") and the pair ride off, Robertson at last having broken down Darnell's barricades by promising her a future after he has gone straight.

Highlights:
Robertson and Darnell's nonstop verbal spats; and a splendid opening sequence in the desert, Robertson, horseless, slogging through the wastes.
Dialogue:
Robertson to Homeier: "Walking 40 miles, a man can get pretty mad, Frank. How you doin' with my money?"
Trivia:
Anne Baxter pulled out at the last minute due to filming commitments on *The Ten Commandments*.

Daniel Boone, Trail Blazer

Republic; VastVision/Trucolor; 76 minutes; Producer: Albert C. Gannaway; Directors: Albert C. Gannaway and Ismael Rodriguez; Cast: Bruce Bennett; Lon Chaney, Jr.; Kem Dibbs; Faron Young; Jacqueline Evans; Nancy Rodman; Damian O'Flynn; Gordon Mills **

Set in 1775, Republic's rough and ready colonial adventure starred Bruce Bennett as the infamous frontiersman, clashing with Shawnee chief Lon Chaney, Jr. (as Blackfish) and his sidekick, evil French/Indian renegade Kem Dibbs. Up until the climactic mass attack on Fort Boonesborough, Republic's widescreen opus looks frayed around the edges, Bennett unconvincing in the title role, a couple of musical interludes thrown in and some shoddy direction from Gannaway and Rodriguez; Bennett's men are captured by the Redskins, Bennett has to run a gauntlet of tomahawks and eventually they escape back to the fort, scene of a final bloody massacre filmed with a certain degree of panache. Chaney (proving yet again that he could act outside of the horror medium) buries a tomahawk in Dibbs' chest when it is revealed the sneering traitor murdered one of the chief's two sons and the Shawnee depart the carnage, leaving Bennett and company to clear up a stockade littered with corpses. The gruesome outcome of a ferocious fort battle is well-executed and it is left for Chaney to turn in the picture's best performance as the sad-eyed Blackfish at odds with blood brother Bennett (Chaney was good at playing Indians, scoring a major success as Chingachgook in TV's popular *Hawkeye and the Last of the Mohicans*).

Dialogue:
Damian O'Flynn to Bennett, concerned he can't see any Indians: "If they're out there."
Bennett: "They're out there alright."
O'Flynn: "Well, why don't I see 'em?"
Bennett: "You don't see an arrow in your back, Andy. You only feel it."

A Day of Fury

Universal; Technicolor; 78 minutes; Producer: Robert Arthur; Director: Harmon Jones; Cast: Dale Robertson; Jock Mahoney; Mara Corday; Carl Benton Reid; Jan Merlin; John Dehner; Dee Carroll; James Bell *****

Gunslinger Dale Robertson (as Jagade) is a harbinger of death, destruction and plain old trouble, riding into West End on a Sunday after killing an outlaw wanted by Marshal Jock Mahoney and stirring up a hornet's nest of raw emotions: Former flame Mara Corday is due to marry Mahoney but Robertson has other ideas, forcing the lady to revert to her saloon-gal past; youngster Jan Merlin hero-worships the killer, strapping on a gun belt to please his new idol; Robertson guns down a man who was about to shoot him, but is let off, the act deemed one of self-defense; Preacher John Dehner is powerless to stop Robertson in his tracks; Judge Carl Benton Reid wants Mahoney replaced and Robertson kicked out of West End ("He'll turn this town into hell."); the gunman opens up the saloon (normally closed on the Sabbath) on his terms; and schoolteacher Dee Carroll, lusting after Robertson, hangs herself in self-loathing. Audie Murphy's *No Name on the Bullet* (1959) and Clint Eastwood's *High Plains Drifter* (1973) spring to mind here; both featured an unstoppable stranger hell-bent on running things *his* way, never mind the consequences. Mahoney is the only man who stands in the path of Robertson's hunger for town domination but in a saloon standoff, the cold-hearted gunslinger loses out to the marshal's fast draw, the chiming of bells (retribution from above?) distracting him for a vital second. *A Day of Fury* is a shining example of a mid-'50s Universal-International oater at its finest: Bright cinematography (Ellis W. Carter), a dynamic score (Henry Mancini and Irving Gertz), incisive screenplay (James Edmiston and Oscar Brodney) and Harmon Jones' taut direction are all top-notch, as are the performances, especially Robertson as the charismatic gunman unearthing one can

of worms after another in a town crammed full of hypocrites, for reasons never really established; a power-pressure morality Western that improves on repeated viewings.
Highlights:
Robertson, proving he was a vital, yet somewhat overlooked, leading man ingredient in the decades' run of must-see horse operas.
Dialogue:
Robertson to Mahoney on his scathing opinion of West End's yellowbellied citizens: "I turned over a rotten log. I didn't create what came crawling out from under it."

The Desperados Are in Town

Regal Films/20th Century Fox; RegalScope; 73 minutes; Produced and Directed by Kurt Neumann; Cast: Robert Arthur; Kathleen Nolan; Rhys Williams; Rhodes Reason; Dave O'Brien; Kelly Thordsen; Morris Ankrum; Mae Clark ****

Sick of plowing cotton and kowtowing to financier Rhys Williams, young Robert Arthur quits the family home, heading out West to San Antone and straight into trouble, meeting Rhodes Reason, the big guy taking the lad under his wing. But Reason is a wanted outlaw, part of the Lapman Brothers gang and soon, Arthur is participating in stage holdups. During a bank raid in Plainfield, Texas Rangers bushwhack the gang, Reason (wounded), Arthur, Dave O'Brien and Kelly Thordsen the only ones to make it out alive. Reason tells Arthur to head back to his homestead in Double Rivers and is shot in the head by O'Brien (a venomous performance from the six-foot-three B-actor). Back home, his parents dead, Arthur successfully brings the farm back to life, romances sweetheart Kathleen Nolan and befriends Williams. But his past comes back to haunt him—he's got a $500 reward on his head and, worse, O'Brien and Thordsen turn up at the ranch, demanding Arthur joins them in robbing the local bank. Arthur backs off and, in retaliation, kills the pair, taking their bodies into town, ready to confess all. But Williams, on the boy's side, covers Arthur's tracks (with help from Nolan), letting the sheriff keep the $2,000 bounty on the brothers' heads; Arthur and Nolan are now free to tie the knot. A neat, relatively obscure low-budgeter that has an evocative honky-tonk score from Paul Sawtell and Burt Shefter to help it on its way, plus likeable performances from all concerned; and O'Brien and Thordsen make as thuggish a pair of polecats you're ever likely to meet in this setup.

Dialogue:
Arthur to the Lapman boys, explaining why he won't cooperate with them on their next job: "When I got out, it was to stay out."
O'Brien: "You ain't never got out, Lonny. Remember what I told you? The only way anybody ever quits Tobe and me is to die."

The Fastest Gun Alive

MGM; 89 minutes;

Belgian poster for *The Desperados Are in Town*

Producer: Clarence Greene; Director: Russell Rouse; Cast: Glenn Ford; Jeanne Crain; Broderick Crawford; John Dehner; Noah Beery, Jr.; Russ Tamblyn; Allyn Joslyn; Christopher Olsen ****

Just who *is* the fastest gun alive? Hulking outlaw Broderick Crawford (as Vinnie Harold), seen gunning down Walter Coy at the beginning; or Glenn Ford, Cross Creek's storekeeper, who, for reasons best kept secret, keeps his shooter hidden from view. News of Crawford's bragging trickles over to Cross Creek; sick of all the gossip, and against wife Jeanne Crain's wishes, Ford straps on his gun belt and demonstrates to the astonished town citizens just how fast and accurate *he* can be with an iron. Russell Rouse (he co-scripted with Frank D. Gilroy) jumped on the psychological Western bandwagon, in full swing by 1956, constructing a volatile oater (set in 1889) centered on the formidable acting talents of Ford, an expert in *noir* drama. He's the son of a renowned square-shooting lawman who was murdered by Crawford, refusing to follow in his father's footsteps; now the outlaw boss, along with scurvy partners John Dehner and Noah Beery, Jr., is on his way to Cross Creek after robbing the bank in Yellow Fork and killing the sheriff's brother. When Crawford hears from youngster Christopher Olsen that Ford is lightning-quick on the draw, the stage is set for a classic showdown, Ford retrieving his Colt from the church to face the outlaw, who has threated to torch the town, in the open street; Dehner and Beery hightail it out and are dispatched by Sheriff Paul Birch's posse. When Birch arrives in Cross Creek, there are two graves, one for Crawford, the other for Ford. But Ford wins the standoff and is still alive, electing to stay as storekeeper, the townspeople no doubt glad to have someone like him living among them. After all, unlike them, he can handle himself. True, there's a lot of chat going on, but scowling Crawford, hands flexing over twin guns, makes a fearsome heavyweight villain and Ford, as always, is excellence personified. Crain's refined beauty is also a plus.

Highlights:

Thirteen minutes into the film, Russ Tamblyn performs a fabulous three-minute acrobatic dance routine; okay, it's somewhat out of place in this setup, more suitable for a Hollywood musical, but it's worth watching all the same.

Dialogue:

Glenn Ford and Broderick Crawford go for the draw in *The Fastest Gun Alive*.

Bank customer to Crawford, recognizing him during a holdup: "Vinne Harold! I thought it was you."
Crawford shoots him dead: "Now you can be positive!"

Flesh and the Spur

Hy Prods./American International; Pathécolor; 78 minutes; Producer: Alex Gordon; Director: Edward L. Cahn; Cast: John Agar; Mike (Touch) Connors; Marla English; Raymond Hatton; Maria Monay; Joyce Meadows; Kenne Duncan; Frank Lackteen ***

A little-seen American International oater that has farmer John Agar hunting the killer of his twin brother, callously shot by an escaped convict who also stole his brother's ivory-handled Colt. Agar possesses the other Colt and is determined to find its match, forming an uneasy alliance with likeable rogue Mike Connors after the gunman has saved Havasupai half-breed Marla English from being throttled in a lake. Traveling showman Raymond Hatton's little troupe also joins the trio, Hatton happening to be a very handy trick-shot. Kenne Duncan, boss of the Checker gang, is tracked down in Red Bud's Chisholm saloon, the incriminating fancy gun in his holster; during a ruckus, Duncan hightails it into the hills with his boys, Agar and company in pursuit. Romance rears its ugly head. Connors has a romp with stagehand Maria Monay but rebuffed by darkly attractive English who fancies Agar, while Hatton's daughter, Joyce Meadows, is strangled by Duncan in a secret liaison with him. A prolonged shoot-out in high country sees Hatton shot dead and the entire Checker gang wiped out except for Duncan; Agar dispatches him, only to be told by Connors that the outlaw was his father and that he, Connors, was the convict who murdered Agar's brother, not Duncan ("I killed your brother. You killed my father."). The two challenge each other to a border-roll showdown, twirling their pistols before firing, Agar winning the contest. Agar then rescues English from an anthill (her red brothers tied her up because she walked out on the tribe), the pair galloping away to a new life. Cheap, maybe, but the picture has a nice score from Ronald Stein, Edward L. Cahn directs with a sprightly hand on the tiller while good-looking Connors looks as though he's enjoying himself immensely, counteracting Agar's rather severe expression.

Dialogue:
Hatton to Connors, pointing a rifle at him: "Don't come any closer because I'll shoot a hole through your head big enough to plant onions in."

Trivia:
During the anthill scene, the insects kept running away, English complaining to producer Alex Gordon, who was piling on more of the creatures, "Isn't six enough?"

Frontier Gambler

AFRC; 71 minutes; Producer: Sigmund Neufeld; Director: Sam Newfield; Cast: John Bromfield; Coleen Gray; Kent Taylor; Jim Davis; Veda Ann Borg; Margia Dean; Stanley Andrews; Nadine Ashdown ***

Otto Preminger's *noir* masterpiece *Laura* (1944) revisited as Deputy Sheriff John Bromfield tries to uncover the circumstances surrounding the death of Sylvia "The Princess" Melbourne, shot in the back, her home badly burned, as is the body. Card sharp Kent Taylor relates the story in flashback. He found the little girl, victim of an Indian massacre, and brought her up as his own. But his protégée grew to be an ambitious, attractive woman (Coleen Gray) who ran the town of Fairweather and had saddle trash Jim Davis after her hand in marriage, even though he was carrying on with saloon singer Margia Dean and rancher Veda Ann Borg without his fiancée suspecting. Candidates for the crime come crawling out of the woodwork thick and fast, the denouement being that Gray isn't dead; Dean, wearing Gray's dressing gown, was shot by Taylor who, obsessed with his "creation," drives the lass out to Massacre Valley, the spot where he found her, in an effort to rekindle a love that never existed, only in his own tortured mind. Rebuffed ("I felt suffocated!" Gray cries), he goes to kill her but is brought down in a fusillade of bullets from both Bromfield and Davis. A nifty little Western detective mystery feature that is intriguing but not overly exciting.

Dialogue:
Taylor, enthusing about Gray: "My creation, Sylvia Melbourne, was a warm, breathing perfection. A living masterpiece."

Fury at Gunsight Pass

Columbia; 68 minutes; Producer: Wallace MacDonald; Director: Fred F. Sears; Cast: David Brian; Neville Brand; Richard Long; Lisa Davis; Percy Hilton; Katherine Warren; Joseph Forte; Addison Richards ***

David Brian, Neville Brand and their sidewinders are holed up outside of Gunsight Pass (the Vasquez Rocks area was the location). They're going to rob the bank of $35,000, mouse-like official Percy Hilton in on the deal to enable him to escape his harridan of a wife, Katherine Warren. But Brian has his own ideas. Riding into town with three outlaws, one hour ahead of Brand and the rest of the bunch, he plans to take the cash, kill Hilton and hightail it out, leaving Brand high and dry. But Richard Long's marriage to Lisa Davis holds matters up, resulting in a mass shoot-out. Hilton dies from a bullet in the face, Brian and his three compatriots are arrested and Brand, who comes in on the end of the action but then rides off, is left wondering where the money is, and who has it. Brian and company are set free by Brand's boys on the trail north, the entire bunch converging on Gunsight Pass in a raging windstorm to locate the loot. Warren hits the dirt trying to escape with the dollars, Brian shoots Brand, bank teller Joseph Forte finishes off Brian and the newlyweds embark on a new life elsewhere. Cheap but solid, with Brian and Brand in villainous top form, Columbia's low-budgeter is a great way to treat yourself to 68 minutes of golden B-Western thrills.

Dialogue:
Brand to Brian: "After this job, I oughta be worth more money on them wanted posters."
Brian: "What they offerin' for you now, Dirk?"
Brand: "$15,000. Offered up to 25 for Jesse James."
Brian: "You'll make it that high."
Brand: "Gonna die tryin'."

Ghost Town

Bel-Air/United Artists; 77 minutes; Producer: Howard W. Koch; Director: Allen H. Miner; Cast: John Smith; Kent Taylor; Marian Carr; Serena Sande; William "Bill" Phillips; Joel Ashley; Gilman Rankin; Gary Murray ****

On the run from Cheyenne and Arapaho Indians, a stagecoach carrying disparate passengers takes refuge in a ghost town where the former inhabitants have perished from fever ("We're holed up in a graveyard!"), each person harboring his/her own hidden agenda. Shot over six days on a $100,000 budget in Utah, Allen H. Miner's spare oater has much to recommend: Paul Dunlap's first-rate score; Joseph F. Biroc's deep monochrome photography; Jameson Brewer's witty screenplay; an eerie deserted town set; and a solid cast. John Smith and William "Bill" Phillips play two sparring gold miners; Marian Carr, Smith's pernicious fiancée, hankers after that gold, willing to throw in her lot with conniving Indian gun runner Kent Taylor who has designs on the lady; preacher Gilman Rankin rants and raves about Redskin injustice; army deserter Joel Ashley continually bullies his son, Gary Murray; and half-breed Serena

Sande cares for Chief Ted Nez, the pair hunted by Edmund Hashim's tribe. Five Indian attacks on the besieged group, who have run out of ammunition, result in the old chief returning to the tribe to try and restore peace, thus ending hostilities; Carr, spurned by all, boards the stage without Smith who elects to stay behind with Phillips and Sande, the new love of his life. An atmospheric low-budgeter that is taut and involving.

Dialogue:

Smith, preparing to parley with Hashim and his braves, to Phillips: "Cover me with that rifle, Crusty." Phillips: "What'll I do if I have to use it? Point it at them and go bang bang?"
Smith: "It looks good. They don't know it's empty."

Great Day in the Morning

RKO-Radio; SuperScope/Technicolor; 92 minutes; Producer: Edmund Grainger; Director: Jacques Tourneur; Cast: Robert Stack; Virginia Mayo; Ruth Roman; Raymond Burr; Alex Nicol; Leo Gordon; Donald MacDonald; Carleton Young **

Great Day in the Morning (from the old Southern expression)—*not* a great title for a disjointed Western overcrowded with too many subplots and a less-than-assured performance from Robert Stack. He plays a Southern gunslinger arriving in Denver, Colorado in 1861, just as the Civil War is about to blow up in his face. Denver is a Northern stronghold; Stack (first seen fending off Indians in the Rockies) isn't wanted there but manages to win the Circus Tent saloon from town bullyboy Raymond Burr in a fixed poker game. Saloon gal Ruth Roman (brunette) and fashion store keeper Virginia Mayo (blonde) vie for Stack's attentions, Rebels led by Dan White pool $2,000,000 in gold from the surrounding mines, intending to use it for the Southern cause, Burr's heavyweight sidekick, Leo Gordon, huffs, puffs and snarls, Southerner Alex Nicol is, in fact, a Union spy in love with Mayo, saloon lackey Peter Whitney scuttles around looking dim and Burr has the hots for Roman. As if all this isn't enough to be getting to grips with, screenwriter Lesser Samuels throws in the old "I'm gonna kill the man who shot my father" routine and we're off on yet another tangent. Stack drops miner George Wallace in an argument, befriends his son (Donald MacDonald), teaches the boy how to shoot and then informs him that he killed his father, going from hero to zero in a flash. The whole convoluted exercise ends with Nicol and Gordon mustering a band of makeshift troopers in the saloon (an unintentional comical scene) and Burr stabbing Roman to death; he's then flattened by dynamite as the Johnny Rebs escape in their gold-loaded wagons, Stack, acting as a decoy, driving an empty wagon into the hills. Stack's cornered in a cave by Nicol who lets him go because of their past friendship, the gunman telling him he can carry on romancing Mayo without any more interference on his part. RKO and Jacques Tourneur must have studied every Civil War Western made up until this point and decided, "We'll include a bit of this, and a bit of that," producing a hodgepodge that contains so many differing ideas that it refuses to gel. A genuine misfire and an unsatisfactory one (that title doesn't help), Roman and Mayo's glamor plus the Colorado scenery perhaps worth the price of a ticket, the movie containing one great line: "North and South are natural enemies—like husband and wife."

Dialogue:
Roman to Stack: "Owen. If there's a war, I'm North, a Yankee, you're South. What happens to us?"
Stack: "I shoot you, I guess."

Gun Brothers

Grand Prods./United Artists; 79 minutes; Producer: Edward Small; Director: Sidney Salkow; Cast: Buster Crabbe; Neville Brand; Ann Robinson; Michael Ansara; Walter Sande; James Seay; Lita Milan; Roy Barcroft ***

Wyoming, 1879: Buster Crabbe leaves the army after six years to reunite with wayward brother Neville Brand and help him run his cattle ranch. Trouble is, Brand is leader of the Nighthawks, a gang of notorious stagecoach robbers and rustlers, and hasn't the slightest intention of giving up his way of life, goading Crabbe into joining him. Crabbe (in fancy buckskins) dallies with saloon songstress Ann Robinson; Michael Ansara, Brand's second-in-command, fancies his chances with the dame; jealous squaw Lita Milan plots in the background, as does slimy tinhorn gambler James Seay, also lusting after Robinson; and slowly, Brand has a change of heart, coming to the aid of Crabbe and Robinson (now married), barricaded in at the Jackson Trading Post, under attack from Ansara and five gunslingers who are bent on grabbing the winter's haul of valuable furs. In a triple shoot-out, Crabbe gets wounded, Ansara shoots Brand dead and is then dispatched by Crabbe; the final scene has Robinson giving birth to a daughter. A tough B-oater bolstered by Irving

Gertz's decent score and Kenneth Peach's stark monochrome photography, *Gun Brothers* packs quite a punch, Crabbe and Brand both excellent as the feuding Santee siblings.
Dialogue:
Robinson to Crabbe: "Thought I'd gotten rid of him (Seay) when I took that job in Laramie."
Crabbe: "Doin' what?"
Robinson: "I'll be singing in the Sundance saloon (sees the expression on Crabbe's face). Huh, what'd you expect? I'm the new schoolmarm?"

Gun the Man Down

Batjac Prods./United Artists; 76 minutes; Producers: Robert E. Morrison, Andrew V. McLaglen (uncredited) and John Wayne (uncredited); Director: Andrew V. McLaglen; Cast: James Arness; Robert J. Wilke; Don Megowan; Angie Dickinson; Emile Meyer; Harry Carey, Jr.; Michael Emmet; Pedro Gonzalez Gonzalez *****

1885: Three men (James Arness, Robert J. Wilke and Don Megowan) rob the Palace City Bank of $40,000; back at the gang's hideout, Arness, wounded in the heist, is callously left behind, his two partners plus faithless girlfriend Angie Dickinson heading off without him. Captured, Arness spends a year in prison. On his release, he's got one almighty score to settle and tracks the trio down to the small border town of Gunther Wells run by Sheriff Emile Meyer and Deputy Harry Carey, Jr.; Wilke is now the owner of the Red Dog saloon. Once there, Arness makes his presence felt, and what follows in Andrew V. McLaglen's taut oater is a game of cat-and-mouse. Arness stalks Wilke and Megowan, rejects Dickinson and has to face gunman Michael Emmet, hired to finish him off. Arness finishes *him* off and chases his quarry into a box canyon, followed by Meyer and Carey. In an explosive shoot-out among rocks, Wilke shoots Dickinson in the back, Megowan is gunned down and Arness slugs Wilke senseless, handing him over to the lawmen for a more legal form of justice. A riveting slow-burner with *noir* overtones filmed over nine days, *Gun the Man Down* is a pared-to-the-bone Western dominated by Arness' six-foot-seven monosyllabic cowpoke on a revenge mission, Henry Vars' fine score and a splendid performance from snarling movie heavy Wilke, given more screen time than usual, and deservedly so.

Highlights:
Emmet, spurs jingling, slowly prowling the streets in search of Arness, a lengthy sequence dripping in menace.

Dialogue:
Dickinson to Wilke, realizing that Arness doesn't figure in his plans: "He wouldn't leave you." Wilke: "Maybe not, but we got our hands on a lot of money and I'm not goin' to spend it at the end of a rope."

Trivia:
McLaglen's directorial debut; on this showing, John Wayne recommended Arness for the role of Marshal Matt Dillon in TV's popular *Gunsmoke* series.

Gunslinger

ARC/Roger Corman Productions; Pathécolor (WideVision Color); 77 minutes; Produced and Directed by Roger Corman; Cast: Beverly Garland; John Ireland; Allison Hayes; Martin Kingsley; Jonathan Haze; Chris Alcaide; Margaret Campbell; William Schellert ***

Well, if Hollywood legend Joan Crawford can dress in black and wear a gun belt in *Johnny Guitar* (Republic, 1954), so can Beverly Garland in Roger Corman's cheapo gender-bender excursion out West, set in 1878. Filmed over seven days on a lower-than-low budget, the rain didn't let up for a second, Allison Hayes tumbled off her horse and broke an arm (some say to get out of the movie which she hated), and Corman later described it as "one of the worst experiences of my life." After her marshal hubbie is shot dead, Garland (Rose Hood) dons a shooting iron, becomes Oracle's new marshal and decides to clean up the town by first curtailing the opening hours of Hayes' saloon. The dame is up to her pretty neck in corruption with crooked mayor Martin Kingsley, buying property that the new railroad *might* want to run through and sell it at a profit. Gunslinger John Ireland is hired by Hayes to finish off "the chesty marshal" ("Whadd'ya know. A lady with a star!"), the black-clad hunk smooching both women while deciding which lady will receive a bullet after he's put paid to old enemy Kingsley. Hayes' lackey, "Little Man" Jonathan Haze, dashes around in a sweat, trying to keep his unrequited lust for his mistress under control and Hayes' scheme eventually collapses when it transpires that another town is earmarked for the new railway. Hayes, Ireland and Kingsley all bite the dust by the final reel, notorious lawman Sam Bass arriving on the scene to take over where Garland left off. The movie looks dingy, thanks to all that bad weather, while Ronald Stein's score belongs to one of the director's X-rated sci-fi efforts released in 1956 (*It Conquered the World* and *Day the World Ended*), not in this setup. Nevertheless, scriptwriters Charles B. Griffith and Mark Hanna take full advantage of the bizarre scenario to conjure up some amusing lines and Ireland somehow manages to keep a straight face throughout. "A startling Western," said *The Hollywood Reporter*, and on this occasion, they got it right.

Highlights:

Delectable Garland, at her husband's funeral, pumping two slugs into one of the deceased's killers.

Dialogue:

Deputy Chris Alcaide to Garland: "I don't know. I reckon some people won't think it's proper for a new widow to go around in pants, even if they are black."

Garland: "Ever see a peace officer in a corset?"

Trivia:

This was Corman's fourth and final '50s Western. In their kissing scene up a tree, shot at six-thirty in the morning, Ireland and Garland were so cold that their teeth chattered nonstop and both were covered in red ant bites after disturbing a large nest.

Hidden Guns

Republic; 66 minutes; Produced and Directed by Albert C. Gannaway; Cast: Bruce Bennett; Richard Arlen; John Carradine; Faron Young; Lloyd Corrigan; Angie Dickinson; Tom Hubbard; Lee Morgan ***

A hackneyed plot built around saloon owner Bruce Bennett's iron grip on Youngstown, surrounding himself with hired guns and weak politicians, is played out to singing hit parader Faron Young's warbling narrative, the twee lyrics contrasting wildly with some pretty violent gunplay. Bennett plugs anyone accusing him of cheating at cards while the citizens won't back Sheriff Richard Arlen. When Arlen brings in Ron

Kennedy, a witness to his own brother's shooting, in order to convict Bennett and get the villain hanged, Bennett employs two jackals to cause mischief (Tom Hubbard and Lee Morgan) plus back-shooter John Carradine, the smartly attired killer increasing his fee from one minute to the next. In a showdown with Bennett, Arlen is shot in the back by Carradine but recovers from his wounds, his right hand rendered useless. It's up to his son, double holster wearing deputy Faron Young (yep, the singer starred as well), to confront the saloon boss in the final reel, Carradine crouching behind a door with a rifle. Young empties both of his revolvers, a bullet for Bennett, who's wounded, and 11 for Carradine, expiring in a shower of splinters. A final shot of a hangman's noose signifies what's in store for Bennett. Angie Dickinson is almost unrecognizable in her small role as a doctor's daughter and if you are not distracted by the peculiar soundtrack, *Hidden Guns* personifies typical mid-'50s gritty, bullet-strewn, *noir*-ish Western thrills, probably unsuitable for a younger audience.

Dialogue:
Bennett to Carradine, as Young approaches: "Shoot for his gun hand, just like you did before with Sheriff Young."
Carradine: "Faron wears two guns. Which hand?"
Bennett: "Shoot to kill, d'you hear?"
Carradine: "That's what I had in mind."

I Killed Wild Bill Hickok

Wheeler; 63 minutes; Producer: Johnny Carpenter (aka John Forbes); Director: Richard Talmadge; Cast: Johnny Carpenter; Denver Pyle; Helen Westcott; Tom Brown; Virginia Gibson; I. Stanford Jolley; Frank "Red" Carpenter; Roy Canada *

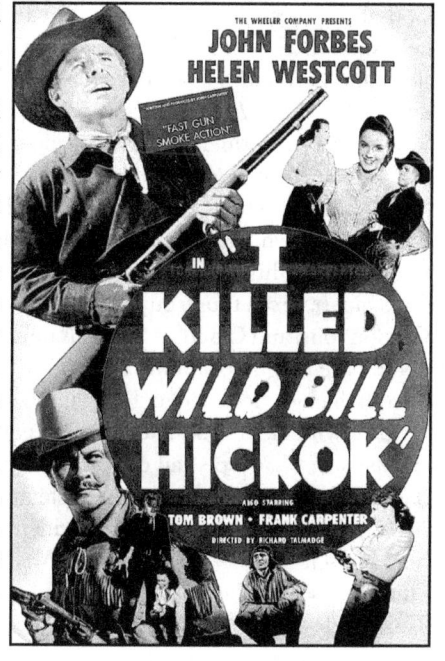

On August 2, 1876, Wild Bill Hickok met his end at a poker table in Deadwood, South Dakota, shot in the back of the head by drunken drifter Jack McCall. But not according to director Richard Talmadge and writer/producer/actor Johnny Carpenter. In their grade Z "revisionist" version of events (told in flashback), Hickok (played by Tom Brown) was a no-good horse thief, falling dead in a hail of bullets from Johnny Rebel's repeating rifle in the streets of Tri City. Carpenter was responsible for the terrible *Son of the Gunfighter* (1953); here, he's on equally shaky ground as ex-Confederate Johnny Rebel (who?), at odds with Denver Pyle about who's selling horses to the U.S. army; Brown and Pyle have piled the pressure on horse trader I. Stanford Jolley that if he doesn't fall in with them, he'll pay, even though Carpenter is acting under a government contract. At Virginia Gibson's ranch, ramrod Pyle is putting it about that cows have contracted Blackleg disease, a ruse to get ranchers to sell their properties at rock-bottom price to Jolley, alcoholic doctor/vet Harvey B. Dunn murdered when he threatens to tell all. Shifty Indian Roy Canada (Nato) hovers in the background, extensive stock footage of buckin' broncos and wild horses led by a magnificent white stallion, plus a lone Redskin on a ledge, fill the gaps, the Arizona Kid (Bron Dellar) is hired to kill Carpenter (but doesn't), Helen Westcott shines (the only one who does) as Jolley's daughter and the whole tawdry exercise finishes with Carpenter kneeling in the dirt, blasting everything in sight with his rifle, the notorious Hickok biting the dust. Resembling something knocked up in the 1930s, Talmadge's Ed Wood-style oater is depressing, cheap and not very cheerful.

Dialogue:
Brown to Pyle, amused that his partner is becoming jealous over the delights of Gibson: "Why don't you relax. She's yours as far as I'm concerned. All I'm interested in in this deal is my cut in good old U.S. currency."

Johnny Concho

United Artists; 84 minutes; Producer: Frank Sinatra; Director: Don McGuire; Cast: Frank Sinatra; William Conrad; Phyllis Kirk; Christopher Dark; Keenan Wynn; Wallace Ford; Harry Bartell; Willis Bouchey ***

In the town of Cripple Creek, Frank Sinatra (as Johnny Concho) rules the roost ("I'm number one here!"). He only has to snap his fingers and people jump: a new horse and saddle, provisions on credit and lying at the card table to rake in the winnings—all this because big brother, Red Concho, is the fiercest gunslinger in the terrritory ("His gun casts a long shadow.") and if Johnny gets upset, Red will come a-running. Only Wallace Ford's daughter, Phyllis Kirk, has any feelings for this "punk with no gun" and "little man made of nothin'." But when bad hombres William Conrad and Christopher Dark arrive in the town saloon, Sinatra's comfortable world collapses around his ears. Conrad catches Sinatra cheating at cards and announces that, two days previously, he'd killed Red Concho in a gunfight; he now plans to take over Cripple Creek lock, stock and barrel and if anyone tries to stop him, they can book a ticket to the nearest undertaker. From *High Society* to *Johnny Concho*—you have to hand it to the slightly built five-foot-seven crooner, he wasn't afraid of making sudden career changes, playing here a character so spineless that you simply cannot sympathize with anything he says or does. Shunned by the citizens, Sinatra slinks out of Cripple Creek, going to a church in a distant town to marry Kirk; she changes her mind (who can blame her?) when he refuses to give his real name to gunman-turned-preacher Keenan Wynn; Wynn then saves Sinatra from tough guys Leo Gordon ("Is that Red Concho's brother—or sister?" Gordon spits) and Claude Akins (this must be the only Western in which bruiser Gordon doesn't fire his gun or thump somebody), telling him to grow up and return to Cripple Creek which he does, facing Dark and Conrad ("Lookin' for me, chicken?") and calling on the townsfolk to strike back. Sinatra gets wounded and the two gunslingers die under a *Bonnie and Clyde*-type hail of lead from Ford and company, a violent climax; Sinatra, back in Kirk's arms, is told he can stay on in town, having slightly redeemed himself. Nelson Riddle's score is odd and strident, acting honors go to Conrad, Wynn and the man himself ("A good job," said the *New York Times*), while Don McGuire and David P. Harmon's screenplay bristles with acidic one-liners, mostly at the expense of the star's Texas-wide yellow streak.

Highlights:
Seeing Sinatra on unfamiliar ground, starring as one of the genre's biggest of all cowards and pulling it off, even though the film was a box-office flop.
Dialogue:
Sinatra to Kirk after she's given him money to get married: "Congratulations! You've just bought yourself a $300 rat."
Trivia:
Sinatra's first movie as producer; and writer McGuire only directed two other feature films before returning to TV work.

Jubal

Columbia; CinemaScope/Technicolor; 101 minutes; Producer: William Fadiman; Director: Delmer Daves; Cast: Glenn Ford; Ernest Borgnine; Rod Steiger; Valerie French; Felicia Farr; Charles Bronson; Noah Beery, Jr.; John Dierkes *****

Delmer Daves' Westerns were nearly always a pictorial feast for the eyes and *Jubal* didn't buck the trend. Wyoming's Grand Teton Range, photographed in knife-edge color by Charles Lawton, Jr., forms the magnificent pictorial backdrop to a sexually charged adult Western containing strong performances all round. Glenn Ford stars as Jubal Troop, a drifter taken in by cattle rancher Ernest Borgnine; he rapidly rises through the ranks to ranch foreman, much to the chagrin of top hand Rod Steiger, who, in the words of Borgnine, "hates your gizzard." "Let's get one thing straight, mister—as far as I'm concerned, you still stink," Steiger spits after learning that Ford used to work on a sheep farm. Steiger once had a fling with Borgnine's bored, promiscuous wife (Valerie French in her Hollywood debut); now she casts her bewitching eyes on Ford, sexual temptation raising its ugly head. Ford resists the offer ("You're the boss' wife." "So what?"); he feels he owes Borgnine a great deal and besides, has met Felicia Farr, a member of a wagon train containing religious settlers on their way to Ohio and the Promised Land ("I've never been kissed," she whispers to Ford, begging him to do the obvious). Farr's intended, Robert Knapp (she hates him), seethes with jealousy every time he sees Ford and Farr in conversation, Steiger boils at the thought of desirable French jumping into bed with Ford and Charles Bronson is recruited, performing fancy gun tricks with the new foreman. This hotbed of open lust, vice, hostility and secret flirtatious meetings can only culminate in one thing—a killing. Steiger lies to Borgnine over Ford and French's relationship, saying they spent a night together in his bed, leading to a furious Borgnine confronting Ford in a saloon, his rifle spraying bullets; Bronson tosses his Colt to Ford who shoots his benefactor dead in self-defense. Steiger, seeing himself in Borgnine's shoes as ranch boss, stirs up trouble and, brimming with fury, violates and assaults French at the ranch, killing her, but in a showdown is unmasked in front of a posse as the treacherous, lying rat he is; Daves closes up on a winch hook outside the stables, leaving the audience in no doubt as to his fate, while Ford, Farr and Bronson ride off

to a more peaceful life. A terrific, meaty Western for grown-ups that still looks mighty fine on the big wide screen; David Raksin's score is also a treat for soundtrack lovers.
Highlights:
That glorious Wyoming scenery, plus the entire cast acting with conviction.
Dialogue:
French's views on Borgnine's ranch: "His castle! 10,000 acres of nothin'! 10,000 acres of lonesomeness!"
Trivia:
For those students of film wishing to know what the term "method acting" meant, watch live wire Steiger going through his mannerisms in this movie.

The Last Hunt

MGM; CinemaScope/Eastmancolor; 108 minutes; Producer: Dore Schary; Director: Richard Brooks; Cast: Robert Taylor; Stewart Granger; Lloyd Nolan; Russ Tamblyn; Debra Paget; Constance Ford; Ed Lonehill; Ed Black ****

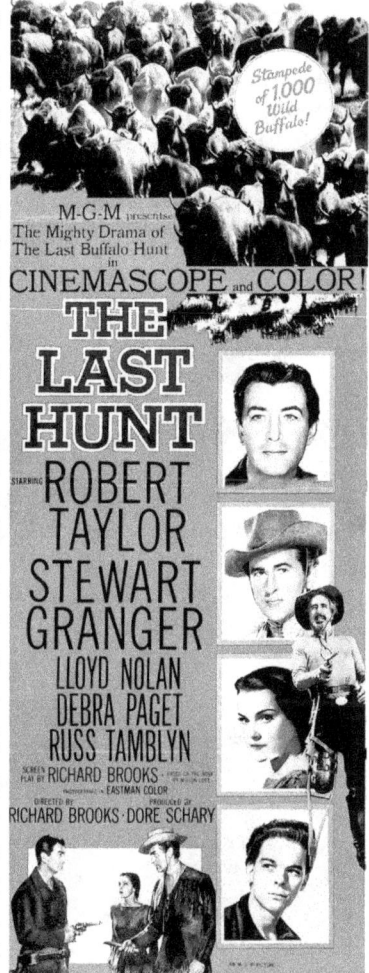

"Killin's the natural state of things." Yep, Robert Taylor played a character several light years away from his heroic figures in *Quo Vadis*, *Knights of the Round Table* and *Ivanhoe*, a Western sociopath who's personal creed is death, a buffalo hunter without a conscience. Fellow hunter Stewart Granger *has* a conscience. Lining his aim at the magnificent beasts through his rifle sight, he refuses to pull the trigger while Taylor slaughters an entire herd using rifle and six-gun, grinning as he does so. Indian-hating Taylor also murders a couple of bucks, sparing squaw Debra Paget and a toddler but molesting the girl at night, much to Stewart's disgust. Half-breed Russ Tamblyn and one-legged Lloyd Nolan attempt to keep the peace between Taylor and Stewart, Taylor going berserk when he discovers that a sacred white hide worth $2,000 has been stolen by Tamblyn and used as a burial shroud for another of Taylor's Sioux victims ("You take away our food and now you kill our religion," Paget accuses Granger). Another disturbing trait of Taylor's comes to light when Nolan asks, "How does it feel to kill so many buffalo ... like being around a woman?" "Yeah, somethin' like that," replies Taylor, ordering Stewart to stay away from Paget. "Killin' is the only real proof you're alive," he adds. "I've never known a gun to wear a man before," Granger snaps at Taylor, holding a knife to his belly, thus terminating their fragile partnership. In a chilling climax, Taylor, who has shot dead Nolan, waits in the bitter cold below a cave for Granger and Paget to emerge. Come morning, the pair find Taylor's frozen corpse wrapped in a buffalo hide, gun in hand, Nolan's discarded accordion and that precious white buffalo skin close by. As the wind gets up, Granger and Paget set off for a new life. *The Last Hunt*, although undeniably well-made, is uncomfortable to sit through and hard to stomach, especially for animal lovers and those of a delicate nature; the picture would probably never get past the censor's office in this more sensitive day and age. It's all pretty nasty and brutal, propelled by Taylor's uncompromising star turn as a complete and utter louse who only gets his kicks, sexual and otherwise, through violence; and that final shot of his ice-encrusted body, blue eyes staring into oblivion, is like something out of an X-certified 1950s horror movie.

Highlights:
Filmed in Custer State Park and Badlands National Park in South Dakota, Russell Harlan's sparkling color enhances those sweeping vistas which should be viewed in letterbox format for full impact.

Dialogue:
Nolan to Granger: "Hey, what got yer back in the butcherin' business?"
Granger: "Easy money."
Nolan: "Ah, I never knew easy money without a bad conscience."
Granger: "I already got the bad conscience. Might as well have the money."

Trivia:
In 1853, 60,000,000 bison roamed America; by 1883, the figure was 3,000, a shocking statistic. Taylor's wholesale shooting of the buffalo herd was, in fact, carried out by government marksmen in a herd-culling exercise and used in the film, something which would horrify today's animal rights activists.

The Lone Ranger

Warner Bros.; Warnercolor; 86 minutes; Producers: Willis Goldbeck and Jack Wrather; Director: Stuart Heisler; Cast: Clayton Moore; Jay Silverheels; Lyle Bettger; Robert J. Wilke; Bonita Granville; Michael Ansara; John Pickard; Frank DeKova ****

To the opening tones of Rossini's "William Tell" overture, The Lone Ranger and Tonto charge across California's Bronson Canyon country on Silver and Scout to stop Red Hawk's warriors from going on the warpath. And as soon as you see oily Lyle Bettger and sneering Robert J. Wilke, two of the slimiest villains in Western history, you know darned well who is responsible for the Indians' unrest. Bettger is after laying his greedy hands on massive silver veins found in lofty Spirit Mountain, a protected monolith overlooking the reservation; if the new governor won't shift those red buzzards north, his men, led by gun-happy Wilke, sure will, by framing every killing they undertake on the Indians, thus forcing the military to move them out. Elderly Red Hawk (Frank DeKova) wants peace; young Angry Horse (Michael Ansara) desires war. Clayton Moore (as our masked hero in blue), on the reservation to retrieve Bettger's abducted daughter, defeats Ansara in a fistfight and uses Bettger's own supply of dynamite to prevent Wilke's weasels storming a barricade in Pilgrim Crossing's deep canyon, the cavalry riding up and arresting both Wilke and Bettger. Wilke shoots his boss at point blank range, tussles with Moore on a steep rocky slope and is eventually hanged; Bonita Granville, Bettger's widow, is left to run the ranch with her daughter, glad to be rid of her corrupt bully of a husband. As for Kemosabe and his Indian pal, it's a case of "Hi-Yo Silver, away!" as the pair ride off for more adventures. Juvenile, maybe, yet hugely enjoyable, particularly to fans of the immensely popular TV series, David Buttolph's pounding music an added bonus, Silverheels mouthing some amusing lines: "Trouble find Tonto even when him not look for it."

Highlights:
Simply watching these two legendary Western heroes strutting their stuff is reason enough to watch. And that theme music has embedded itself in the psyche of a generation of Baby-Boomers.

Dialogue:
Moore to a startled settler: "Don't worry about the mask. It's on the side of the law."

Trivia:
Moore starred in 169 episodes of the most famous of all Western tele-series which ran from 1949-1957, John Hart appearing in the title role in 52 episodes during 1952/1953.

Man from Del Rio

United Artists; 82 minutes; Producer: Robert L. Jacks; Director: Harry Horner; Cast: Anthony Quinn; Peter Whitney; Katy Jurado; Douglas Fowley; Whit Bissell; Douglas Spencer; John Larch; Adrienne Marden ****

Fresh from winning an Oscar for playing painter Paul Gauguin in *Lust for Life* (1956), Anthony Quinn starred as a washed-up, too-fond-of-the-bottle Mexican gunman who arrives in the town of Mesa, drills three bad guys in the space of three hours and is promptly given the job of town sheriff at $100 a month, cowardly Douglas Spencer certainly not up to the job. But the townsfolk want greedy ambitious saloon owner Peter Whitney out of the way and Quinn, his gun hand busted in a bruising fistfight with the burly saloon boss, isn't quite sure how to handle the situation; bluff his way out of a gunfight with the bully, or leave Mesa with firebrand Katy Jurado, the two having struck up a stormy relationship based on mutual lust. A riveting if downbeat *noir* Western little remembered today, with Quinn turning in his usual edgy, highly watchable performance and fine deep-focused black-and-white photography from Stanley Cortez, dark-eyed Jurado an added treat. Whit Bissell is almost unrecognizable as a drunken lowlife and the narrative travels down the tried and tested route of a new town tamer ostracized by the community who only hired him for his guns, not his flawed personality, which gets in the way of their cosiness, a particular scenario that reached its peak in Fox's *Warlock* (1959), also featuring Quinn alongside Henry Fonda. Quinn wins the day, fooling Whitney into thinking he can still draw with his ruined right hand; the schemer backs down, hands over his gun and Quinn, sobered up, leaves with Jurado at his side to play house with her in another town.

Highlights:
Quinn dispatching two toughs who have strung up crybaby Spencer on a tree branch.

Dialogue:
Quinn to Whitney after one more standoff in the saloon: "You know, Ed, someday you're gonna make a mistake and draw on me. That's a single action gun, Ed. I hear it click, you're a dead man."

Trivia:
Unsurprisingly, Quinn and Jurado's fiery Mexican temperaments got the better of them, the two enjoying a fling throughout the entire shoot.

Massacre

Lippert Pictures; Anscocolor; 76 minutes; Producer: Robert L. Lippert, Jr.; Director: Louis King; Cast: Dane Clark; James Craig; Marta (Martha) Roth; Miguel Torruco; Jaime Fernández; José Pulido; José Muñoz; Enrique Zambrano ***

Filmed in Guatemala and around the volcanic hinterlands of Mexico, *Massacre* is an odd mix of striking landscapes (photographer: Gilbert Warrington), operatic score (Gonzalo Curiel) and over-the-top histrionics courtesy of Italian actress Marta (Martha) Roth, who specialized in Mexican dramas. She's the wife of a trader who's supplying rifles and ammunition to the Yaqui Indians, Mexican Rurales' officers Dane Clark and James Craig on Miguel Torruco's trail, accompanied by devious warrior Jaime Fernández. On the grueling trek to retrieve the firearms, Roth lies her head off, using her feminine wiles on Clark and Craig, tying both men up in knots. She secretly agrees with what Torruco is up to, seeing it as a way to escape her harsh life and live high on the hog, so tries her hardest to foil the troop detail at every step of the way. *Massacre* is one movie that contains no happy ending, the entire cast expiring when the Yaquis storm a ruined mission the whites are holed up in, enraged that dynamite has put paid to their rifles and ammunition; Roth is the last to die, screaming in agony. Only Fernández survives, back with his tribe; he was leading them a merry dance in the first place. Roth is eminently watchable as the scheming hussy flaunting her sexuality to get what she wants; her performance, plus that arid volcanic scenery, make *Massacre* a little-seen adventure that is slightly more hot, dusty and sweaty than most.

Dialogue:
Clark to Roth, explaining why he wants to continue the mission: "Because I haven't found the guns yet."
Roth: "Oh, guns, guns. What difference do a few guns make in this ugly, filthy wilderness?"
Clark: "There are a few people in this ugly, filthy wilderness and people can be hurt."

The Maverick Queen

Republic; Naturama/Trucolor; 90 minutes; Produced and Directed by Joseph Kane; Cast: Barbara Stanwyck; Barry Sullivan; Scott Brady; Mary Murphy; Howard Petrie; Wallace Ford; Jim Davis; Emile Meyer ****

HERBERT J. YATES presents **BARBARA STANWYCK · BARRY SULLIVAN · SCOTT BRADY · MARY MURPHY** in **THE MAVERICK QUEEN** — NATURAMA TRUCOLOR

with WALLACE FORD · HOWARD PETRIE · JIM DAVIS · EMILE MEYER · WALTER SANDE · GEORGE KEYMAS · JOHN DOUCETTE

Screenplay by KENNETH GAMET and DeVALLON SCOTT · Based on the novel entitled "THE MAVERICK QUEEN" by ZANE GREY · Associate Producer-Director JOE KANE · A REPUBLIC PRODUCTION

Barbara Stanwyck meets Butch Cassidy and the Sundance Kid's Wild Bunch gang! Republic's first movie shot in Naturama was a polished Western boasting two things in its favor: Stanwyck (48 at the time of filming) and a tremendous pumped-up, menacing score from Victor Young. The actress was the epitome of the tough-as-nails, hard-ridin', fast-shootin' female whom no one messed around with, here (as Kit Bannion) having climbed over a string of lovers to become owner of The Maverick Queen Hotel in Rock Springs. The dame's being romanced by Scott Brady (Sundance) but turned off by his uncouth manners. In walks smooth-talking Barry Sullivan, posing as Jeff Younger, part of the notorious Younger Brothers outfit; he's just sent the Wild Bunch packing after they tried to rustle Mary Murphy's cattle. Stanwyck takes an instant shine to the dude and makes him head dealer at the tables; Brady is not amused. The plot thickens in Kenneth Gamet and DeVallon Scott's involved screenplay (from Zane Grey's novel): Stanwyck buys Murphy's cattle but plans to steal the cash back *and* $50,000 in gold on board the next train out, Sullivan to assist the Wild Bunch in the robbery as proof of his background ("The only way you leave the Wild Bunch is feet first."); Murphy's cook, Wallace Ford, is a spy, relaying information to Stanwyck about cattle herds; and Sullivan, in fact, is a Pinkerton agent, working with Emile Meyer and Pierre Watkin to rid the territory of these bandits. Brady gets jealous every time he spots Stanwyck making eyes at Sullivan, tries to kill her in an exciting chase sequence and dies following a tussle with his rival, a knife in his back. Jim Davis turns up as the real Jeff Younger and in a climactic shoot-out, Stanwyck expires in Sullivan's arms from a bullet wound, the Wild Bunch rounded up by Sheriff Walter Sande's posse, leaving the door wide open for Murphy to make her move on Sullivan.

Highlights:

Jack A. Marta's pristine photography of the mountainous area in Durango, Colorado, plus Stanwyck at her most captivating.

Dialogue:
Stanwyck to Brady, fending off his clumsy advances: "Oh for heaven's sake. Take a bath first. You smell like a combination brewery and a horse stable."

Mohawk

National Pictures/20th Century Fox; Pathécolor; 80 minutes; Producers: Charles B. Fitzsimons and Edward L. Alperson; Director: Kurt Neumann; Cast: Scott Brady; Ted de Corsia; Allison Hayes; Rita Gam; Lori Nelson; Neville Brand; John Hoyt; John Hudson **

Taking place during the French-Iroquois-Mohawk wars of the late 17th century, Scott Brady plays a New York painter up to his neck in rampaging Indians and a triple romance: bar girl Allison *Attack of the 50 Foot Woman* Hayes, socialite Lori *Revenge of the Creature* Nelson and Mohawk beauty Rita Gam. At Fort Alden, bad guy John Hoyt, who wants the Mohawk Valley all for himself, stirs up trouble with the savages, killing Tommy Cook, Chief Ted de Corsia's son, while screen tough guy Neville Brand, in full war paint, yells, scowls and brandishes a tomahawk as Tuscarora troublemaker Rockhawah. Shot in garish color by Karl Struss and featuring a great deal of stock footage from John Ford's 1939 epic *Drums Along the Mohawk*, Kurt Neumann's frontier offering suffers from a one-dimensional performance from Brady, obvious studio sets and a lack of action until the final reel. The three girls are attractive to look at and, for a change, you have a white man opting for an Indian bride, Brady marrying Gam at a Mohawk ceremony after de Corsia declares peace. Edward L. Alperson, Jr.'s hokey title music is a regrettable turnoff.

Dialogue:
Clegg Hoyt to Lori Nelson as she applies make-up: "When a woman puts on war paint, she's more dangerous than any Mohawk!"

Naked Gun

AFRC; 69 minutes; Producer: Ron Ormond; Directors: Edward Dew and Paul Landres (uncredited); Cast: Willard Parker; Mara Corday; Barton MacLane; Tom Brown; Veda Ann Borg; Chick Chandler; Billy House; Morris Ankrum **

Insurance agent Willard Parker rides into Topaz with the Salazar treasure, a chest containing gold, jewels—and a curse! The riches were stolen from the Indians by the Mexicans and Parker's job is to return the chest to its rightful Indian owners, thereby lifting the curse. Narrated by whiskey-drinking Chick Chandler, *Naked Gun* is a wonky oater featuring a wooden Parker fending off all manner of crooks bent on laying their greedy paws on the treasure; raven-haired Mara Corday is wasted as a saloon singer who eventually winds up the heir to the fortune, her deceased mother the person Parker was going to deliver the chest to. Morris Ankrum is the town's incompetent sheriff, grumpy Billy House scuttles here, there and everywhere as the town's "Hanging Judge," owner of the Four Aces saloon Barton MacLane sells the place to Tom Brown, then has him bumped off so that he can reclaim the joint and blonde saloon tart Veda Ann Borg charges around on a horse, dressed like Zorro, until Parker unmasks her as the chief villain. There isn't a single break in Walter Greene's meandering soundtrack to relieve the tension of watching this clumsily put-together B-Western shot in five days on a $15,000 budget by ex-Western bit player Edward Dew (Paul Landres was hired to tidy up the finished product); needless to relate that Parker gets Corday to himself, Chandler about to spill the beans on more facts surrounding the cursed Salazar treasure before, thankfully, the end credits arrive to curtail the proceedings.

Dialogue:
Chandler, narrating: "Judge Cole. The Hanging Judge. He was the best thing that ever happened to the rope business. He'd given Topaz more stretched necks than a herd of giraffes."

The Naked Hills

La Salle/Allied Artists; Pathécolor; 72 minutes; Produced and Directed by Josef Shaftel; Cast: David Wayne; Denver Pyle; Keenan Wynn; James Barton; Jim Backus; Marcia Henderson; Myrna Dell; Frank Fenton ***

A poor man's *The Treasure of Sierra Madre* sums up *The Naked Hills*, set during the Californian gold rush of 1849, David Wayne the prospector full of hopes who becomes so obsessed with finding "the big strike" that he turns into a gold-hungry maniac, antagonizing all around him: Long-suffering girlfriend/wife Marcia Henderson; friend Denver Pyle (who narrates); rival-cum-partner Keenan Wynn; old-timer James Barton; and Jim Backus, claim jumper extraordinaire. Henderson has to put up with Wayne coming back to her, getting drunk, then disappearing into the hills, the lure for gold too great for him to ignore ("You've got to stop dreamin' Tracy."); even the birth of a son doesn't quench his gold fever or make him settle down (although he tries it for a short spell). But when the gold rush ends in 1869 and his latest grubstake has collapsed around his ears, he meets his boy, Steven Terrell, now grown up, and returns to Henderson resembling a bewhiskered tramp, Pyle looking on with regret; he always thought the lass far too good for the likes of his deranged, unreliable pal. An interesting oddity shot in garish color, Herschel Burke Gilbert's music ranging from folksy to near-classical and Wayne (to his acting credit) coming across as someone so loathsome you would avoid him like the plague.

Dialogue:
Wayne, inebriated, to Barton: "Am I something, or am I nothing?"
Barton, spelling it out: "You're nothin'."

The Oklahoma Woman

Sunset/ARC; SuperScope; 73 minutes; Produced and Directed by Roger Corman; Cast: Richard Denning; Peggie Castle; Cathy Downs; Mike (Touch) Connors; Martin Kingsley; Tudor Owen; Tom Dillon; Jonathan Haze **

Made for $60,000, Roger Corman's third Western canters along without stirring up too much excitement, Richard Denning starring as a man released from prison after six years, hoping to live the quiet life on his deceased grandfather's ranch and finding trouble brewing in Silver Hill, Oklahoma. Ex-flame Peggie Castle, owner of the town saloon, is in cahoots with crooked senator Tom Dillon, wanting to own large areas of the territory and ordering henchman Mike Connors to terrorize local ranchers into submission, including Tudor Owen, Denning's neighbor. Owen's daughter, Cathy Downs, can't handle a rifle, so Denning takes up the reins and has a series of confrontations with the blonde, whip-wielding, gun-toting hussy and trigger-happy Connors, who fancies his boss like crazy (as does Sheriff Martin Kingsley). Owen is beaten to death after daring to stand as a local election candidate, Denning is framed for the murder, an angry mob throws mud at Castle, Downs has a catfight with the saloon owner, Denning is saved from a lynching and following a rooftop tussle with Denning, Connors is put behind bars, Castle riding off into the distance and leaving her confession for all to read; needless to say, Denning and Downs decide to play house. So-so fare, saved by the widescreen photography, Ronald Stein's low-key but effective score and Denning, one of those personable actors who always turned in a pleasing performance whatever he appeared in.

Dialogue:
Castle to Kingsley when he appears in her room: "You're on dangerous ground, Sheriff. Downstairs, I'm a saloon keeper. Up here, I'm a woman."

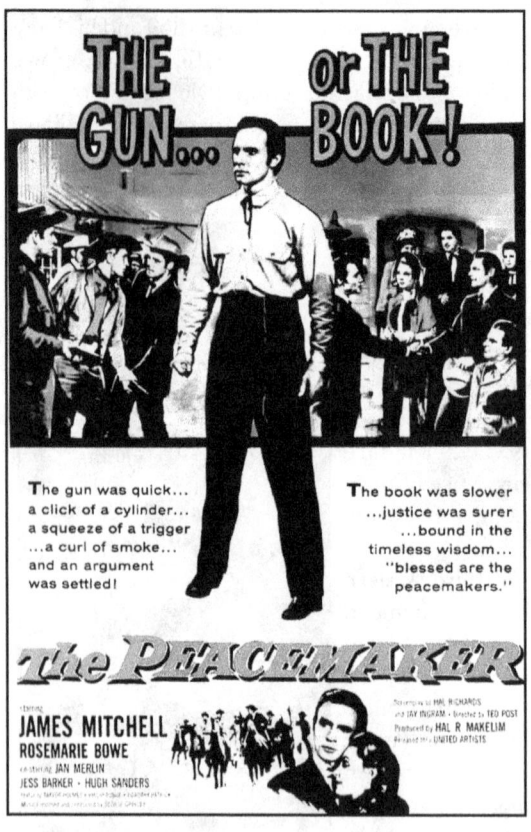

The Peacemaker

Hal R. Makelim Prods./United Artists; 82 minutes; Producer: Hal R. Makelim; Director: Ted Post; Cast: James Mitchell; Rosemarie Bowe; Jan Merlin; Jess Barker; Hugh Sanders; Herbert Patterson; Robert Armstrong; Philip Tonge ***

The town of Pembroke cautiously welcomes its new parson (James Mitchell), a reformed gunslinger ("I rode with a bad bunch.") who uses words from the Bible and his fists to sort out a war between cattle rancher Hugh Sanders, farmer Jess Barker and railroad boss Herbert Patterson; ineffective sheriff Robert Armstrong is powerless to prevent trouble brewing and the townsfolk sit on the fence. Rosemarie Bowe (Miss Montana 1951) falls for the sharp-featured newcomer while hoodlum Jan Merlin, in the pay of Patterson, stirs up trouble by burning homesteads and running off steers; Patterson wants to own both cattle and farming land, pocketing the profits, and is the "ungodly lion" behind the conflict. Hal Richards and Jay Ingram's wordy script reinforces the old good versus evil scenario in a Western setting, Mitchell triumphing (or should that be God?) by getting Barker and Sanders to settle their differences after Armstrong shoots Patterson dead—even Merlin, dying, realizes he had a friend in Mitchell. And the preacher gets delectable Bowe all to himself. Mitchell makes a good fist of the role and while there's not an over-abundance of gunplay, *The Peacemaker* still makes for intriguing viewing of a different kind.

Dialogue:
Mitchell, revealing his background to the town dignitaries: "Yes, I've been in prison, Mister Maddox."
Philip Tonge: "And you expect us to welcome a murderer as our spiritual leader?"

Pillars of the Sky aka The Tomahawk and the Cross

Universal; CinemaScope/Technicolor; 95 minutes; Producer: Robert Arthur; Director: George Marshall; Cast: Jeff Chandler; Dorothy Malone; Ward Bond; Keith Andes; Lee Marvin; Willis Bouchey; Michael Ansara; Charles Horvath ***

Fifty-six minutes into George Marshall's religious-themed cavalry versus Indians opus, Colonel Willis Bouchey's column comes under a mass attack from Palouse chief Michael Ansara's scalp-hungry savages, six minutes of stirring, bloody action as the regiment, gaining a foothold on top of a bluff, is whittled down to 32 men, one woman, four scouts, no water, no ammo, no cannons and no wagons. Before that, the pace is languid and rather dull. In Oregon territory, 1868, the U.S. army wants to cross protected Indian land; under a clause in the peace treaty, they are allowed to construct a bridge spanning the Snake River, build a road and erect a fort on the reservation. At a gathering of tribal chiefs, Ansara, angry at what he perceives is the white man's deceit, advocates war and storms out, leaving Bouchey to undertake a perilous mission through hostile territory. Along on the trip is Sergeant Jeff Chandler, romancing Dorothy Malone, wife of Captain Keith Andes, doctor-cum-missionary Ward Bond, whiskey-loving Irishman Lee Marvin and a bunch of Indian scouts all given Christian names by Bond. Religious cynic Chandler and stiff-as-a-board Andes argue over who can claim doe-eyed Malone, soldiers are picked off and massacred and after that lengthy skirmish, Malone flounces and pouts under the disapproving eyes of Bond, the picky dame deciding to stay with her wounded husband. Ascending the hill at night, the group makes it to Bond's missionary and comes under further attack from lighted arrows. Bond, acting on God's orders, rides out to confront the Redskins but is shot dead by Ansara, Chandler calling the chief a coward. As Ansara charges at him to strike, a rifle bullet from another chief finishes him off; the Indians have had enough and now desire an end to the fighting. Inside the church, Chandler addresses the congregation, stepping into Bond's footsteps by asking the Almighty to consider his calling to the faith—from tough guy to priest in one fell swoop; it's a twee scene that many Chandler fans will find hard to swallow.

Highlights:
The panoramic Oregon landscapes photographed in rich colors by Harold Lipstein, and that exciting battle, filmed like a Second World War combat out West.

Dialogue:
Floyd Simmons to Chandler after questioning Indians fighting after sunset: "But I heard that Indians wouldn't fight at night. Something about their ghosts not being able to find their heaven in the dark."
Chandler: "Those Indians don't believe in ghosts, lieutenant. Thanks to Doctor Holden (Bond), they're Christians."

Trivia:
William Lava and Heinz Roemheld's strident marching soundtrack is tremendous; what a shame that they didn't receive a credit, Universal's musical director Joseph Gershenson, as was his wont, claiming the glory.

The Proud Ones

20th Century Fox; CinemaScope/DeLuxecolor; 94 minutes; Producer: Robert L. Jacks; Director: Robert D. Webb; Cast: Robert Ryan; Jeffrey Hunter; Virginia Mayo; Robert Middleton; Walter Brennan; Ken Clark; Rodolfo Acosta; George Mathews *****

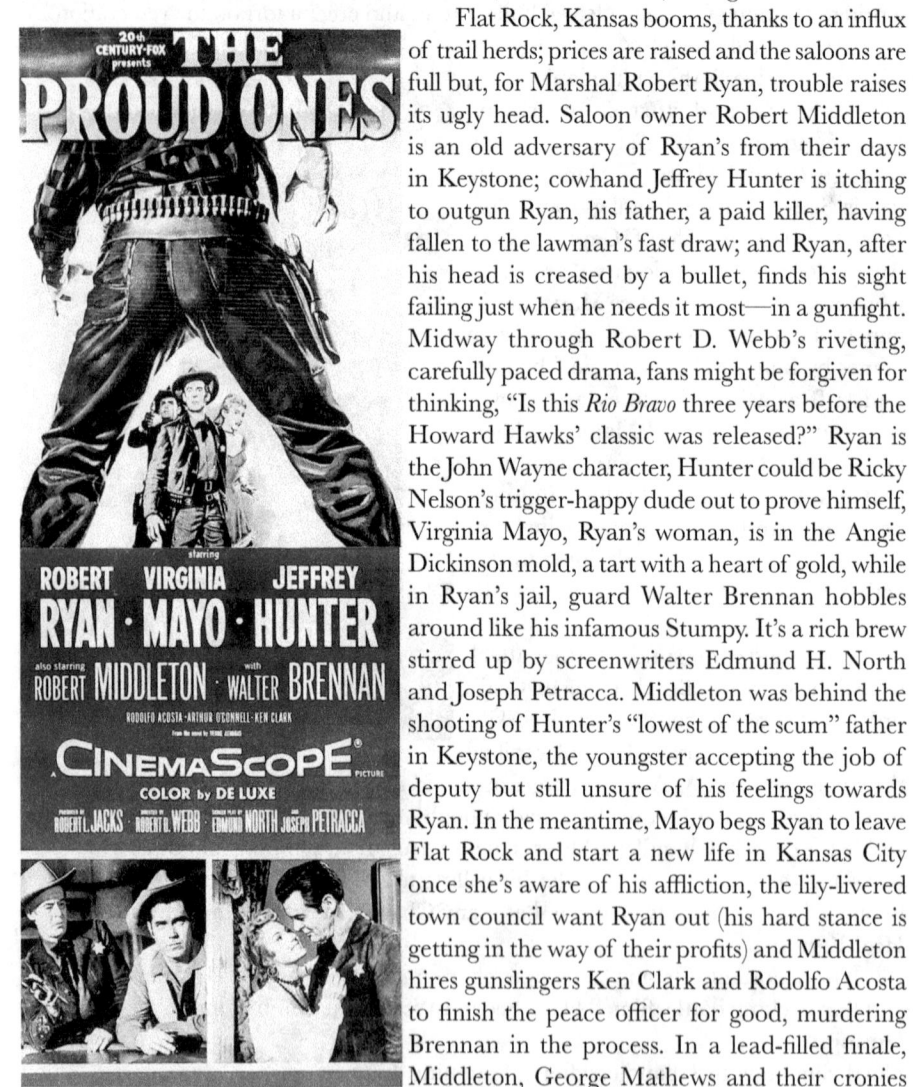

Flat Rock, Kansas booms, thanks to an influx of trail herds; prices are raised and the saloons are full but, for Marshal Robert Ryan, trouble raises its ugly head. Saloon owner Robert Middleton is an old adversary of Ryan's from their days in Keystone; cowhand Jeffrey Hunter is itching to outgun Ryan, his father, a paid killer, having fallen to the lawman's fast draw; and Ryan, after his head is creased by a bullet, finds his sight failing just when he needs it most—in a gunfight. Midway through Robert D. Webb's riveting, carefully paced drama, fans might be forgiven for thinking, "Is this *Rio Bravo* three years before the Howard Hawks' classic was released?" Ryan is the John Wayne character, Hunter could be Ricky Nelson's trigger-happy dude out to prove himself, Virginia Mayo, Ryan's woman, is in the Angie Dickinson mold, a tart with a heart of gold, while in Ryan's jail, guard Walter Brennan hobbles around like his infamous Stumpy. It's a rich brew stirred up by screenwriters Edmund H. North and Joseph Petracca. Middleton was behind the shooting of Hunter's "lowest of the scum" father in Keystone, the youngster accepting the job of deputy but still unsure of his feelings towards Ryan. In the meantime, Mayo begs Ryan to leave Flat Rock and start a new life in Kansas City once she's aware of his affliction, the lily-livered town council want Ryan out (his hard stance is getting in the way of their profits) and Middleton hires gunslingers Ken Clark and Rodolfo Acosta to finish the peace officer for good, murdering Brennan in the process. In a lead-filled finale, Middleton, George Mathews and their cronies bite the dust; Ryan rides away with Mayo, leaving Flat Rock in the capable hands of Hunter, the new town marshal. Lionel Newman's memorable whistling theme tune and vivid cinematography from Lucien Ballard highlight a great slow-burning Western of the old school, Ryan (tough and silent), Hunter (anxious to demonstrate he's quick slapping leather) and Middleton (a sneering heavyweight bully) turning in telling performances.

Highlights:

The gun-blazing finale in a barn, expending more lead than your average Western of this period.

Dialogue:
Ryan, his vision blurred, to Hunter, bullets whizzing around their heads in the climactic gunfight: "Get outta here while you can."
Hunter: "I like it here. Besides, I got no place to go."

Quincannon, Frontier Scout aka Frontier Scout

Bel-Air/United Artists; DeLuxecolor; 83 minutes; Producer: Howard W. Koch; Director: Lesley Selander; Cast: Tony Martin; Peggie Castle; John Bromfield; John Doucette; John Smith; Ron Randell; Morris Ankrum; Edmund Hashim **

Lesley Selander made some outstanding B-Westerns in his time, but in *Quincannon, Frontier Scout* he had one major obstacle on his hands—Tony Martin. Hit parade singer Martin displays all the emotions of a totem pole. First, dressed from head to toe in black, and then as a bogus Indian, his acting and vocal delivery is one-dimensional to say the least, sabotaging what could have been a half-decent horse opera concerning corrupt cavalry officers Ron Randell and John Smith exchanging guns for gold with Iron Wolf's Arapahos. However, Martin had a contender in the wooden performance stakes in Randell, as stiff as a buckboard, his face an expressionless mask. The rocky Kanab, Utah locations were dimly shot (especially in the movie's interminable second half, filmed at night), Les Baxter's music jarred, so it was left to Peggie Castle, John Bromfield and dependable John Doucette (who acts Martin off the screen) to breathe some life into a tale concerning Martin (the scout of the title) traveling to Fort Smith on a mission to find out why Castle's brother mysteriously died, and what happened to those 800 missing Henry repeating carbines plus 10,000 rounds of ammunition. Castle, convinced her brother is still alive, is offering $2,000 reward for his return, although Smith's the man behind his death. Even when all is done and dusted (Randell shoots Smith, is arrested, the guns destroyed and Iron Wolf locked away) and Martin is reinstated as a major, receiving a marriage proposal from Castle, it hardly brings a hint of any sort of feeling to those frozen features.

Dialogue:
Bromfield to Martin, confronting the elusive scout: "In the name of the United States, I hereby arrest you, using force if necessary."
Martin: "Force *is* necessary."

Rebel in Town

Bel-Air/United Artists; 78 minutes; Producer: Howard W. Koch; Director: Alfred L. Werker; Cast: John Payne; Ruth Roman; J. Carrol Naish; Ben Cooper; John Smith; Ben Johnson; James Griffith; Bobby Clark ****

A Shakespearean tragedy out West as John Payne's young cavalry-mad son, Bobby Clark, in Kittreck Wells for his birthday party, is gunned down in the street by John Smith after sneaking up behind him and letting loose with his cap guns. Smith is one of four Confederate brothers led by patriarch J. Carrol Naish, ornery Rebels who have just robbed the bank in White Springs. Accident or no accident, ex-Union officer Payne is determined to hunt down the person responsible, even at the expense of his own marriage. Ruth Roman, Payne's wife, witnessed the shooting and knows who did it, but when Naish's younger son Ben Cooper arrives at their ranch with a knife wound in his back, inflicted in an argument by his brother Smith, she doesn't let on to her husband who the boy is to avoid possible reprisals. When the truth emerges, Cooper, conscience-stricken over Clark's death, gives himself up, claiming he didn't pull the trigger, but faces an angry lynch mob, Marshal James Griffith calling on Payne to assist him which he doesn't. Naish and his three sons ride in, Smith is revealed as the man behind the shooting of Clark and, in a knife fight with Payne, falls on his own blade. Naish, a chastened man, gives himself over to the law, Payne and Roman reconciling their differences. A bleak, tough unsentimental Western, one of Payne's finest, containing a terrific star turn from grizzled Naish as the battle-hardened father trying to keep order among his mangy, quarrelsome offspring.

Highlights:
Naish stringing up Smith to a tree and thrashing him with a bullwhip, very graphic for 1956.

Dialogue:
Roman to Payne, complaining about Clark's fixation with all things military: "That's all your son ever thinks about. He doesn't play with other children. He spends all his time killing Confederates. He doesn't even have a father. He has a commanding officer."

Reprisal!

Columbia; Technicolor; 74 minutes; Producer: Lewis J. Rachmil; Director: George Sherman; Cast: Guy Madison; Felicia Farr; Kathryn Grant; Michael Pate; Edward Platt; Wayne Mallory; Otto Hulett; Phillip Breedlove ****

Half-Comanche Guy Madison rides into the racially prejudiced town of Kendall, Oklahoma, to take up the deeds of the Hammond spread and finds himself at the mercy of three Indian-hating brothers, whose land borders his property. Produced by Madison's own company, Romson, *Reprisal!* is a tough B-Western that ably illustrates, over 74 minutes, the lost art of packing it all in over a short running time. Despicable siblings Michael Pate, Edward Platt and Wayne Mallory have just been found not guilty by a one-sided jury for the hanging of two Indians they say were trespassing on their property, even though they are as guilty as sin. Pate, married, is lusting after sexy Redskin lass Kathryn Grant while taciturn Madison, nursing grievances relating to his ancestry, catches Felicia Farr's attention. David P. Harmon, Ralph Hayes and David Dortort's screenplay focuses on pro and anti-Indian issues, the three brothers, forever trying to prod Madison into action, reduced to two when Mallory is shot dead by Phillip Breedlove; his sister was one of the Indians hanged by Mallory and his siblings. Madison is blamed for the shooting, set free from the lynch mob when Grant lies about them spending the night together and, in the final reel, guns down Pate and Platt; he then confesses to the bigoted townsfolk that the old Indian servant killed in the crossfire was his grandfather ("I stand by my people."). Leaving Kendall for good, he puts his ranch up for sale and rides off with Grant to plan a better life. Colorful photography around Old Tucson, Arizona (Henry Freulich), a familiar but telling Western score (Mischa Bakaleinikoff) and no-nonsense direction (George Sherman), plus an understated performance from likeable Madison, make *Reprisal!* a well-crafted winner.

Highlights:
A tense standoff in the saloon between Mallory and Madison, actual brothers in real life.

Dialogue:
Madison to Sheriff Otto Hulett after being thumped by all three siblings: "What'd they hit me with?"
Hulett: "A big surprise—a fist."

Revolt at Fort Laramie

Bel-Air/United Artists; DeLuxecolor; 73 minutes; Producer: Howard W. Koch; Director: Lesley Selander; Cast: John Dehner; Gregg Palmer; Francis Helm; Don Gordon; Robert Keys; William Phillips; Eddie Little Sky; Robert Knapp ***

The prolific Lesley Selander racked up a total of over 30 trail busters during the decade, eight in collaboration with producer Howard W. Koch. *Revolt at Fort Laramie* epitomized the Selander '50s outdoor Western. Short, brisk, bags of action and shot in picturesque locations, Utah's Kanab region was used on this occasion. John Dehner and Gregg Palmer, so often the supporting stars in B pictures, were given a chance to shine in a tale surrounding divided loyalties at Fort Laramie. When Civil War is announced, the fort's Southern contingent cause mischief, singing songs from the south and scalping an informer. Eventually, the Southerners, including Dehner, who resigns his commission, shed their uniforms and head out to a Confederate fort, hoping to waylay a shipment of gold that forms part of a peace treaty deal with Chief Red Cloud's Sioux; the gold will come in handy for the Southern war fund. Red Cloud, however, wants the gold *before* a new treaty is signed, meaning a prolonged (and violent) clash between Redskins and ex-soldiers, ending when Palmer, promoted to major, arrives with his detail and sends the Sioux packing. Dehner is killed in the skirmish, the Southerners allowed to proceed on their trek, Palmer planning to wed Dehner's niece, Francis Helm, on his return to Fort Laramie.

Belgian *Revolt at Fort Laramie*

Highlights:
Selander orchestrates the lengthy skirmish between Dehner's men and Red Cloud's warriors with dash.
Dialogue:
Helm to fiancé Palmer: "You report to Uncle Seth and then you better rest up."
Palmer: "For the dance?"
Helm: "Yes. Or *after* the dance."
Trivia:
The film debut of Harry Dean Stanton, well known for starring in *Alien*.

Showdown at Abilene

Universal; Technicolor; 80 minutes; Producer: Howard Christie; Director: Charles F. Haas; Cast: Jock Mahoney; Martha Hyer; Lyle Bettger; Grant Williams; Ted de Corsia; David Janssen; Harry Harvey; John Maxwell ✱✱✱

Ambitious cattle baron Lyle Bettger has plenty to be sore about when ex-Confederate Jock Mahoney, returning from the war, trots into Abilene City. Bettger lost his right hand in a childhood accident involving Mahoney; Mahoney (we learn later) accidentally shot dead Bettger's brother during a skirmish in the war; and Bettger's intended, Martha Hyer, was once *Mahoney*'s intended, the girl still in love with him. In a formulaic farmers-versus-cattlemen scenario, Mahoney takes up his former position as sheriff, deputy David Janssen at his side, bad 'un Ted de Corsia relieved of his duties but still up to no good, Bettger his paymaster in crime. Trouble is, Mahoney, like Audie Murphy in *Destry* (which also starred Bettger), refuses to pack a pistol, preferring to use his fists instead, much to the amusement of gunman John Maxwell and his bunch of critters; even when young sidekick Grant Williams is whipped to death, he still won't reach for his gun belt. Long on talk, slow on action, *Showdown at Abilene* is still a serviceable oater from the Universal stable despite Mahoney, in some scenes, looking stiff and uninterested.

Oily Bettger, enraged at losing Hyer to his love rival, is killed by de Corsia who bites the dust in a sweaty climactic showdown with Mahoney, Hyer getting the tall silent lawman all to herself.

Highlights:
A rascally performance from Ted de Corsia, as the bad guy with a rotten heart; and California's parched Agoura grasslands, shot in glowing Technicolor by Irving Glassberg.

Dialogue:
One of John Maxwell's boys spotting Mahoney in the street minus a six-shooter: "What's the matter, Trask? You ain't scared, are you? We're as gentle as lambs. Baaaa!"

Trivia:
Director Haas didn't rate Mahoney as the lead player, claiming that Janssen was the better actor; on Universal's orders, Janssen was made to loiter in doorways so as not to upstage the former stuntman. Joseph Gershenson borrowed liberally from *Tarantula*'s soundtrack; and the film was remade in 1967 as *Gunfight in Abilene*, crooner Bobby Darin in Mahoney's role.

Stagecoach to Fury

Regal Films/20th Century Fox; RegalScope (CinemaScope); 75 minutes; Producer: Earle Lyon; Director: William F. Claxton; Cast: Forrest Tucker; Mari Blanchard; Rodolfo Hoyos, Jr.; Rico Alaniz; Margia Dean; Wallace Ford; Wright King; Paul Fix **

Passengers on a stagecoach are held hostage at a relay station by murderous Mexican bandit Rudolfo Hoyos, Jr. and his confederates; they're to wait for the next wagon to roll in carrying a gold shipment which the bandidos plan to rob. While everyone sits around, ex-cavalry officer Forrest Tucker schemes to escape while Mari Blanchard, Judge Wallace Ford and cocksure young gunslinger Wright King's murky past histories unfold in flashback; character case studies of a kind. Filmed in the studio apart from the opening and closing sequences (shot in Montana), *Stagecoach to Fury*

is talkative Western fare and not all that interesting, picking up in the last 10 minutes when Hoyos and his men attempt to hijack the gold in a box canyon, only to be beaten off by the wagon crew and crack shot Tucker who goes head-to-head on horses with Hoyos, flooring the bandit boss with a single bullet. Grim-faced Tucker is more dour than usual, glamorous Blanchard flaunts her considerable B-movie assets in front of grinning henchman Rico Alaniz and Paul Dunlap's curious booming score threatens to bring down the studio sets; not one of Regal's better efforts.

Dialogue:
King to Ford: "Well, I've heard of this Grazia (Hoyos) feller before. If I was you, I wouldn't even breathe wrong 'cos if he don't like it, you just likely liable to wind up part of his reputation."

Trivia:
Walter Strenge's black-and-white photography was nominated for an Oscar, one of the last to do so before the category was disbanded.

Star in the Dust

Universal; Technicolor; 80 minutes; Producer: Albert Zugsmith; Director: Charles F. Haas; Cast: John Agar; Mamie Van Doren; Coleen Gray; Richard Boone; Leif Erickson; Randy Stuart; Paul Fix; James Gleason ****

Gunslinger Richard Boone is behind bars, awaiting the noose, gallows erected in the street below (yes, this sheriff's office is upstairs for a change). Gunlock's sheriff, John Agar, anxious to live up to his father's reputation, has his hands full with a possible range war between Leif Erickson's cattlemen, led by Harry (Henry) Morgan, and local farmers stirred up by schoolteacher Robert Osterloh. A trio of dames is involved in Charles F. Haas' tense *High Noon*-type oater: Mamie Van Doren, Agar's busty fiancée and Erickson's sister; Randy Stuart, Morgan's wife; and Coleen Gray, Boone's moll. Two letters incriminate Erickson in the killing of three men; he hired Boone to shoot any farmer at $1,000 a head but claims the gunhand had orders only to frighten them. Boone is sprung from jail by Stuart but is back in his cell pronto after crusty old deputy James Gleason shoves a rifle in his back; meanwhile, Morgan organizes the cattlemen to storm Gunlock and get Boone out before he's hanged. A shoot-out between Morgan's mob and Osterloh's bunch results in the gallows burned to the ground, but it makes no difference to the outcome; after confessing all, Boone is hanged from a tree and Erickson shot by Morgan, who realizes at last what a conniving rat his boss was. As for Agar, he's back in the arms of the delicious Van Doren, whom he had unfairly ostracized for falling in with her crooked brother. A cracking minor Western from Universal whose only downside is a minstrel strumming a guitar and updating the audience on what's taking place (music: Frank Skinner.)

Highlights:

For John Agar fans, it's a treat to see our favorite wearing a gun and holster and *not* combating Universal's gill-man or giant tarantula!

Dialogue:

Boone, on refusing a blindfold before he's strung up: "The sun's setting for me. It'd be a shame to miss a minute of it."

Trivia:

Six minutes into the movie, Clint Eastwood makes a 28-second appearance and walks off camera; it was the future superstar's sixth film and first-ever Western.

Stranger at My Door

Republic; 85 minutes; Producer: Sidney Picker; Director: William Witney; Cast: Macdonald Carey; Patricia Medina; Skip Homeier; Stephen Wootton; Louis Jean Heydt; Slim Pickens; Howard Wright; Malcolm Atterbury ****

Skip Homeier is the stranger at Patricia Medina's door, a bank robber on the run from a holdup in West Bridge; his horse is lame, forcing him to stop at her homestead so that her 10-year-old son, Stephen Wootton, can tend to the animal's swollen foreleg. Medina is Macdonald Carey's wife; he's a preacher building a nearby church, and when Homeier's identity is revealed, Carey takes on the mission to "show him the light," to offer the outlaw redemption from a life of crime. Homeier ain't interested; eyeing up Medina's ample cleavage and shapely butt, he forces his attentions on the lady, creating a great deal of sexual tension between the pair. There's a terrifying sequence in which Carey, followed by Homeier, attempts to tame one of lumber mill owner Slim Pickens' wild horses, a rampaging beast that smashes everything in its path and when Sheriff Louis Jean Heydt and Homeier later engage in a gunfight, Wootton is accidently wounded in the crossfire. Homeier vows to kill Heydt for putting a bullet in the kid; in a tussle with the lawman, the bandit is shot in the chest. Returning to Carey's house, Homeier learns that Wootton has recovered;

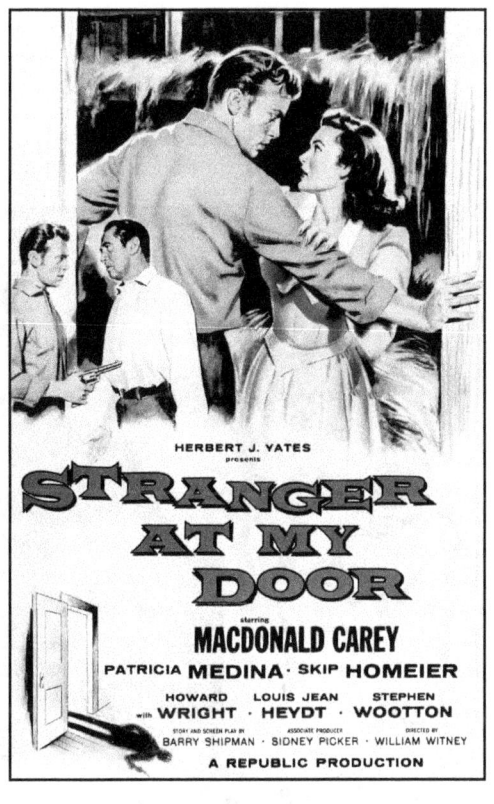

bleeding profusely, he staggers to the partly erected church and collapses, dead, the shadow of the cross falling across his body—perhaps God has forgiven him for the error of his ways after all. A tautly handled Western that verges on psychological *noir*, Homeier exhibiting his skills at playing the mean and silent loner who is perhaps a little more scared of getting close to Carey and his family, and Carey's religious beliefs, than he lets on; R. Dale Butts' lush score is straight out of a Hollywood '40s melodrama, a major plus for a B-movie of this type.

Highlights:
The opening bank raid; gunfire, panic, buildings on fire, stampeding horses and a spectacular wagon crash; and Pickens' wildest of wild horses, hooves flying on a trail of destruction.

Dialogue:
Carey to Homeier: "You don't have to threaten me. I'm glad you've decided to stay with us. It isn't everyday a preacher gets the chance to save the soul of an all-fired big sinner like Clay Anderson."

Tension at Table Rock

RKO-Radio; Technicolor; 93 minutes; Producer: Sam Wiesenthal; Director: Charles Marquis Warren; Cast: Richard Egan; Dorothy Malone; Cameron Mitchell; Billy Chapin; Royal Dano; DeForest Kelley; John Dehner; Edward Andrews *****

From the opening shots of a posse hunting outlaw Paul Richards in the rugged terrain of California's Red Rock Canyon to the sound of Dimitri Tiomkin's evocative score, fans will know they're in for a tasty Western dish, and they won't be disappointed. *Tension at Table Rock* takes in themes from *Shane* and *High Noon* in its tale of a silent gunman (Richard Egan), carrying the burden of a crime he didn't commit, idolized by a young boy (12-year-old Billy Chapin), fancied by Dorothy Malone (married to Sheriff Cameron Mitchell, nursing psychological hang-ups) and coming up against John Dehner's rowdy cattle drovers *and* hired gun DeForest Kelley, an ex-pal of his. It's a heady brew and Egan has never been better. Falsely accused of shooting dead outlaw boss Richards, a former friend (Angie Dickinson plays his wife), even though Richards went for the draw, Egan's tarnished reputation has resulted in a poisonous ballad sung about him, the loner inviting trouble wherever he goes. Taking care of Chapin (suffering from a severe case of hero-worship) following the death of the boy's father in a way station holdup (Egan drops all three assailants), Egan delivers the lad to his uncle (Mitchell) in Table Rock, finding the town under threat from Dehner's unruly cowpokes, bent on causing maximum mischief despite Dehner's warning of no gunplay and limited alcohol consumption. When farmer Joel Ashley is murdered by James Anderson, one of Dehner's men, Anderson is placed behind bars but acquitted, claiming he shot in self-defense, although he planted a gun in Ashley's dead hand. Mitchell finally recovers his guts, admitting he saw the incident; Anderson is sent back to jail and Dehner, infuriated, hires Kelley to kill Egan. In a street showdown which neither really wanted ("You're gonna have to go through me. I don't bluff," states Egan. "You and me?" says a startled Kelley, not pleased at the prospect), Egan outdraws Kelley, the gunslinger hitting the dirt. Dehner and his boys ride in to bust Anderson out of jail, but Mitchell has gained his self-respect and so has the town, covering the cowpunchers with rifles. Dehner shrugs and departs, and so does Egan, leaving behind two sorrowful figures, Malone (who loved him) and Chapin (who wanted him to be his new dad.)

Highlights:

A tense (as the title suggests), beautifully acted Western drama, especially Egan's man of few words, Kelley's charismatic gunslinger, Malone's emoting with her large glowing eyes and Chapin admirably proving that child actors *don't* always spoil a good film.

Dialogue:

Dehner to Mitchell: "I know sometimes my boys get kinda rough. After four months on the trail, I don't expect to send them to Sunday school."

Three Violent People

Paramount; VistaVision/Technicolor; 100 minutes; Producer: Hugh Brown; Director: Rudolph Maté; Cast: Charlton Heston; Anne Baxter; Tom Tryon; Gilbert Roland; Forrest Tucker; Bruce Bennett; Barton MacLane; John Harmon ***

Charlton Heston and Anne Baxter were reunited right after appearing in Cecil B. DeMille's *The Ten Commandments* in a fine-looking Western where the whole doesn't equal the sum of its parts. Heston commanded the attention, but Baxter looked uneasy with the material, and there are long stretches of lethargy. The first 20 minutes is lightweight fare, showgirl Baxter breezing into a town run by carpetbaggers and getting hitched to Southerner Heston after the quickest romance in screen history. Matters turn serious when Heston, who's been away fighting in the war for five years, returns to reclaim his ranch, the Bar S, being run by Gilbert Roland and his five sons. One-armed sibling Tom Tryon festers in the background, wanting his share of the spread, while crooked commissioner Bruce Bennett, aided by surly hombre Forrest Tucker, suffering from a severe case of itchy trigger finger, hands out exorbitant tax demands in the hope that the Union will reclaim Confederate property, by fair means or foul. James Edward Grant's talky script centers more on rivalry and hostility than action, stubborn-as-a-mule Heston kicking Baxter out with their new baby when he discovers her dubious background. It finishes in a blistering shoot-out at the ranch, Bennett and his cohorts meeting their Maker under a hail of bullets; Tryon lies dead, and Heston climbs off his high horse to make amends with the lovely Baxter and their son.

Highlights:
Baxter's voluminous gowns when Heston lifts her upside down—is that what gals *really* wore in the Old West?

Dialogue:
Heston's proposal to Baxter, short and sweet: "I'm looking for a woman who ... a wife ... and you're looking for a husband. Wait now. Miss Hunter, do you wanna get married?"

Trivia:
Heston and Tryon didn't get on; the ex-Moses star thought him wrong for the part and said so to Paramount's bosses. And the portraits of the elderly couple in the Bar S Ranch were copied from portraits of Heston's own grandparents to achieve a family resemblance.

Thunder Over Arizona

Republic; Naturama/Trucolor; 70 minutes; Produced and Directed by Joseph Kane; Cast: Skip Homeier; Kristine Miller; George Macready; Wallace Ford; Nacho Galindo; Jack Elam; George Keymas; John Doucette ***

Arizona, 1879: It's a case of mistaken identity when cowpoke Skip Homeier guns down killer Shotgun Kelly (George Keymas) at Nacho Galindo's stage relay station; riding into Tombstone armed with Keymas' shotgun, crooked town boss George Macready and slimeball lawyer Wallace Ford think the youngster *is* Kelly who has been hired to put pay to the Warren family (three brothers and a sister). They're working the McIntyre Mine, the motherlode running through Macready's property; Macready wants that mine all to himself and has already organized the killing of the Warren family's father, together with issuing them with a fake tax demand for $52,000. Homeier befriends Kristine Miller (Fay Warren), continually evades the attention of lawmen-but-baddies Jack Elam, John Doucette and Rocky Shahan and turns the tables on Macready after 50 minutes; the corrupt mayor cottons on to who the lanky cowboy really is, but Skip has figured out that he's already been rumbled! Eight charges of dynamite detonated at the mine entrance eliminate Macready and his mob, the mayor receiving a bullet for good measure, Ford confessing that he was coerced into doing what he did against his legal ethics; Homeier and Miller ride off in a cart to make plans for their future together. There's incident a-plenty in Joe Kane's solid, fast-moving timewaster, shot in Naturama, Republic's own widescreen process; Homeier makes an engaging hero, while Macready sneers, connives and bosses his way through the proceedings with ease, as he had done so in countless Westerns before this one.

Highlights:
None to speak off, but *Thunder Over Arizona* remains a decent example of a Republic Western before the company folded a couple of years later.

Dialogue:
Galindo to Homeier, after he has shot Keymas: "I bet he tried to bushwhack you."
Homeier: "He wasn't trying to shoot fish for breakfast."

Trivia:
Homeier starred in 13 Westerns in the 1950s; this was the only occasion in which he received top billing.

Tribute to a Bad Man

MGM; CinemaScope/Eastmancolor; 95 minutes; Producer: Sam Zimbalist; Director: Robert Wise; Cast: James Cagney; Irene Papas; Don Dubbins; Stephen McNally; Vic Morrow; James Bell; James Griffith; Lee Van Cleef ****

With screen legend James Cagney in the lead, Robert Wise at the helm, a semi-Biblical-type score from Miklos Rozsa, Robert Surtees' stunning photography of the

Colorado Rockies plus Michael Blankfort and Jack Schaefer's discerning screenplay, you couldn't go far wrong and you don't. The plot is narrated by Don Dubbins, playing a greenhorn from Philadelphia who goes out West in 1875 to taste the life of a wrangler on Cagney's spread, the Jeremy Rodock Ranch. Cagney lays down his own brand of justice in this remote area, stringing up anybody caught rustling his horses, much to the horror of his mistress, Irene Papas ("You've become sick! You are not the law!"). The Greek beauty (her Hollywood debut), rescued from the saloon life by Cagney, is lusted after by boss wrangler Stephen McNally, and soon, naïve Dubbins professes his love for her, the drama escalating when McNally is fired, falling in with rival rancher/ex-partner James Bell, the man behind a string of horse thefts. Bell is shot dead in a standoff, Papas promises Dubbins that she'll leave with him and the final act is grueling stuff. Dubbins and Cagney, discovering that McNally is deliberately crippling stolen mares by cutting their hooves, forces him, Vic Morrow and James Griffith to walk the 20 miles to Fort Witney jail in stockinged feet over rough terrain, eventually, after days of hard walking, sending McNally and Griffith packing and taking Morrow (Bell's son) back to his mother's ranch. In a buckboard, Papas prepares to ride off with Dubbins but, hearing of Cagney's declaration that he's had enough of all the violence and hanging, has a change of heart, electing to stay with him and get married. *Tribute to a Bad Man* was Cagney's third and final Western, not really his genre but a fine, good-looking picture anyway. "When the smoke clears, it's all 'Old Master' Cagney'," commented the *New York Times*.

Highlights:
Cagney was one of Hollywood's all-time greatest actors and watching him go through the motions in this film, you can understand why; all the customary dynamic Cagney mannerisms are on display in full force.

Dialogue:
Papas to Dubbins, telling him he should give up his dream of breaking in horses: "That's what a wrangler is. A nobody on a horse with bad teeth, broken bones, double hernia and lice."

Trivia:
Spencer Tracy turned down Cagney's role, stating he couldn't work in the Rockies' high altitude.

The White Squaw

Columbia; 75 minutes; Producer: Wallace MacDonald; Director: Ray Nazarro; Cast: David Brian; May Wynn; William Bishop; George Keymas; Frank DeKova; Nancy Hale; Paul Birch; Myron Healey **

The White Squaw begins splendidly with a ferocious shoot-out at a watering hole. Swedish settler David Brian and his three boys are poisoning the water as they don't want an Indian reservation on their land and come under fire from George Keymas' Sioux warriors. Indian agent Paul Birch rides in to calm things down, gets hit and later dies, but not before revealing that he's May Wynn's (as Etay-O-Wahnee) father; therefore, half the property in his will goes to her, the other half to second daughter Nancy Hale. After that promising start, matters get slightly tedious, half-breed Wynn trying to gain her copy of the will (and her entitlements) and being prevented from doing so by short-fused Brian and Myron Healey, his fist-happy son. Cattleman William Bishop, sympathizing with Wynn's plight, comes to her aid, the will is eventually retrieved after the safe holding it has been dynamited and in a fiery climax,

Redskin-hating Brian is burned to death; in a blind rage, he sets fire to the Sioux's wigwams and falls into flaming embers. Bishop then swears that he will help Wynn and her people build a new life and supply them with the cattle they need. Not one of Ray Nazarro's better Westerns; Wynn is darkly attractive but wooden, the movie sags in the middle and it is left to Brian to chew the scenery with relish and bring some much-needed vigor to the production.

Dialogue:
Keymas to Wynn as they ride into town to view the will: "I don't like the way the man looks at you. All over he looks."
Wynn: "You look. Same way."

The Young Guns

Allied Artists; 84 minutes; Producers: Albert Band and Richard V. Heermance; Director: Albert Band; Cast: Russ Tamblyn; Gloria Talbott; Perry Lopez; Walter Coy; Scott Marlowe; Chubby Johnson; Myron Healey; Wright King ***

Before Emilio Estevez and Kiefer Sutherland in *Young Guns* (Fox, 1988), there was Russ Tamblyn and Perry Lopez in *The Young Guns*. Juvenile delinquency was making inroads into cinema in the mid-1950s, Nicholas Ray's *Rebel Without a Cause* the frontrunner. Tamblyn (Tully Rice) plays the son of a notorious Wyoming gunfighter; the kid's on release from a detention home, working in a store in Chalmers. Bullied out of town by Sheriff Walter Coy's hothead deputy, Myron Healey, Tamblyn walks over to nearby Black Crater, an ungovernable backwater where a bunch of disaffected youths run by Perry Lopez kick their heels all day long, waiting for some much-needed action. Tamblyn soon proves he's top dog by administering a violent thrashing to Wright King and starts a romance with Gloria Talbott, her father an outlaw on the run. Short of food and the money with which to buy it, the gang pistol-whip Scott Lee for his cash won at the card table, Tamblyn refusing to join in; Talbott has warned him she doesn't want *her* offspring to have an outlaw father like she has. Rayford Barnes, the only survivor from the original Black Crater gang, turns up and intends to pocket all the cash taken in a raid on the Chalmers Bank by the *new* Black Crater gang (Lopez and King are killed in the shoot-out). Scott Marlowe, Rayford's son, refuses to hand the money over and challenges him to the draw—both die from two shots. Coy sees to it that Black Crater's women and children are housed and fed in Chalmers, Healey makes it up with Tamblyn and the youngster sets off to town to play house with Talbott. Guy Mitchell sings the plaintive title track to a watchable, slow-paced melodrama focusing on the aggravation felt by the Western younger generation to the Western older generation (proving that, in society, nothing has changed!), photographer Ellsworth Fredericks providing nice touches of *noir*-type imagery; and 21-year-old Tamblyn holds the whole thing together with an engaging performance, a rebel *with* a conscience.

Dialogue:

Coy to Tamblyn: "A gun stays young as long as it stays quiet. The minute it starts to make a noise, it gets old. The man who fires it—he gets old 'cos he don't have long to live. Keep your guns young, Tully."

Chapter 12
The James Stewart/Anthony Mann Westerns

Between 1950 and 1955, director Anthony Mann and top Hollywood star James Stewart pooled their talents, collaborating on five outstanding psychological Westerns: *Winchester '73* (Universal, 1950), *Bend of the River* (Universal, 1952), *The Naked Spur* (MGM, 1953), *The Far Country* (Universal, 1954) and *The Man from Laramie* (Columbia, 1955). Shedding his easygoing, homespun "Aw, shucks" screen image (perfected in Frank Capra's *It's a Wonderful Life*, 1946), Stewart was to play a troubled cowpoke seeking redemption in all five productions, a man not quite on the side of the law, but not quite on the side of evil, either. For his part, Mann brought a new level of sophistication, dynamism and realism to the sphere of Western filmmaking, utilizing deep-focus photography and full-on framing techniques, thus capturing those stunning landscapes to maximum effect and bringing a sense of urgency and vitality to the proceedings; these magnetic Westerns are great to look at, period. Rising above the pack, Stewart and Mann's forays out West remain classy, invigorating and timeless, mature works that entertain time and time again; needless to say, all are five-star rated.

The Stewart/Mann partnership commenced in 1950 with *Winchester '73* (the only one made in black-and-white) and in this influential, 92-minute production, the Western came of age, a gritty, utterly compelling yarn concerning cowpoke Stewart's (Lin McAdam) dual mission: to retrieve his stolen "One of a Thousand" rifle won as a prize at a July 4th celebration in Dodge City, 1876; and to kill his brute of a brother, Stephen McNally, who shot their father in the back years ago. The first 16 minutes focused on the shooting-target contest, the brothers (the audience is not made aware that they're siblings until the closing minutes) vying for the winner's slot. Stewart triumphs by blasting a hole through an Indian trinket; in anger, McNally and his two gunhands beat up Stewart, pinch the valuable weapon and hightail it out. Thus begins "the tale of a gun" in a number of suspenseful interrelated vignettes, the carbine changing hands with alacrity,

Jimmy Stewart and Anthony Mann with crew on the set of *Winchester '73*

Westerns of the 1950s: The Classic Years 331

Stewart and sidekick Millard Mitchell always one step behind. Indian trader John McIntire buys it from McNally for $300 gold; Chief Young Bull (Rock Hudson) murders McIntire (and scalps him) for the rifle; trooper Tony Curtis collects the weapon when Hudson falls in a cavalry versus Redskins skirmish, handing it to no-good coward Charles Drake; dance hall gal Shelley Winters and fiancé Drake get caught up in a gunfight between Dan Duryea's gang and the law in a boarding house, Duryea killing Drake, grabbing the high profile Winchester and heading out to McNally's hideout to plan a bank/gold shipment heist in Tascosa, Old Tucson; McNally reclaims the rifle from Duryea's clutches; there's a chaotic robbery, Duryea biting the dust as bullets fly in all directions; and in the movie's famous five-minute showdown, played out among Arizona's high cliffs and jagged rocks, Stewart shoots his near-psychotic brother, McNally's body tumbling off a precipice. Once again in possession of "The Gun that Won the West," Stewart, Winters and Mitchell ride off to pastures new.

Scripted by Borden Chase and Robert L. Richards and blessed with diamond-hard black-and-white imagery, the emphasis very much on deep-focus framing from Mann and cinematographer William H. Daniels, *Winchester '73* saw the Western format discarding its outdated '40s trappings by presenting the audience with an antihero as ruthless as the villains he's pursuing and plagued by his own inner demons to boot. The shocking scene where Stewart smashes Duryea's face into the saloon bar, a look of pure savagery contorting his features, took the actor's legion of admirers by sheer surprise, but Stewart and Mann did it on purpose; the six-foot-three leading man may have been slight in build, but he wanted to prove that he could be as mean as the rest of them (Stewart, his career in the doldrums, was anxious to show the paying public that there was another side to him, feeling he had become typecast as a family friendly persona). *Noir* overtones dominate, Mann having his characters positioned in close-up and from ground-level upwards, dragging you into the helter-skelter action, backed by a thumping score concocted by Joseph Gershenson from the output of eight composers. Performance-wise, the cast are faultless: McNally makes a repulsive, snarling unshaven bad guy; Duryea was a perfectionist at creating oddball, slightly unhinged gunfighters, which he does here ("You're about the lowest thing I've seen standing in a pair of boots," Shelley spits at him while later, McNally adds "Sometimes I think he's a little on the crazy side."); Will Geer makes an honest, if elderly, Wyatt Earp ("I don't know what you're problem was before," he says to battered and bruised Stewart after he's been roughed-up by McNally. "You can add the rifle to it now."); Mitchell provides solid support to Stewart's troubled psyche; and Winters is blonde, busty and sexy (she later complained that her role was superfluous to requirements amid all the machismo on display: "If I hadn't have been in it, would anybody have noticed?"). To round off a superlative picture, that gripping climactic shoot-out, among the hundreds of Western shoot-outs that would take place amid rocky heights over the next nine years, is undoubtedly a genre best. Regularly included in lists of the greatest westerns ever made, the first Stewart/Mann collaboration was an instant classic and a massive commercial success, boding well for things to come: "A Western masterpiece" commented Britain's *Daily Telegraph*, mirroring the overall critical acclaim. And Stewart, sensing victory, eschewed a $200,000 wage in favor of a cut of the profits, eventually pocketing $600,000, the first instance of a major Hollywood star to carry out this type of lucrative deal.

Next up on the Stewart/Mann agenda, two years later, was *Bend of the River*, filmed in Oregon under the towering snow-capped peak of Mount Hood, the majestic scenery shot in rich Technicolor by Irving Glassberg; Hans J. Salter's score was equally as rich. Stewart played a scout (Glyn McLyntock) with a shady past, leading settlers over rough terrain to a large open valley via the town of Portland. En route, he saves Arthur Kennedy from a hanging; Kennedy used to be a member of the notorious Missouri Raiders gang, as was Stewart who bears the mark of the rope around his neck. Stewart and Kennedy foil a band of Indians, Kennedy homing in on Jay C. Flippen's daughter, Julie (Julia) Adams, while in Portland, Flippen's other daughter, Lori Nelson, eyes up big handsome gambler Rock Hudson (Stewart and Hudson didn't get on during the shoot). Chartering Chubby Johnson's riverboat, they continue on the journey to their own Promised Land, leaving Kennedy and Adams (she's recovering from an arrow wound) behind. Several months later, the vital supplies the settlers have paid for haven't arrived and food is scarce. Stewart and Flippen ride to Portland to find out what's wrong and from here, *Bend of the River* changes tack, a nastier, more violent edge attaching itself to the free-flowing narrative. Gold fever rages, trader Howard Petrie upping prices and demanding more money from Flippen; Adams, meanwhile, works at the gold counter and is hitched to gunslinger Kennedy. In a bullet-strewn fracas, Stewart, Flippen, Kennedy, Hudson, Adams and Jack Lambert's cronies escape down river on Johnson's vessel with the supplies, continuing on land over the perilous mountain terrain in wagons. But Kennedy, reverting to type, wants to sell those goods to miners at a hefty $100,000 and turns vicious, ordering the wagons back under gunpoint and leaving beaten-up Stewart for dead. "I figure we're even," he says to horseless Stewart. "You'll be seein' me. You'll be seein' me," gasps Stewart. "Every time you bed down for the night, you'll look back into the darkness and wonder if I'm there, and some night, I will be. You'll be seein' me." With those words ringing in his ears, Kennedy gallops away. But Stewart follows, finishing off Lambert and his hyenas with a rifle. Encountering the river, the wagons are waylaid by a posse of trigger-happy miners who are driven off under heavy gunfire. In a tussle, Stewart drowns Kennedy and the supplies reach the settlers' new territory, Stewart cozying up to Adams, Hudson and Nelson looking to play house.

Dynamic use of deep-focus framing, taut pacing, visually arresting tracking shots and expert handling of complex characters meant that Mann's 91-minute outdoor yarn set new standards in realism for this kind of outdoor fare, the rumble of wagon wheels, the dust and stones thrown up and the spectacular backdrops almost dropping into the audience's laps. Stewart was beginning to wear his newfound "cynical tough cowpoke" persona like a glove, the perfect counterpart to Kennedy's oddly charismatic, snarling no-gooder. Stewart "handles his role with punch," stated *Variety*, Kennedy a "likeable heavy." Grossing $3,000,000 at the box-office, Mann and Stewart's second Western is as fresh today as it was when first released, a superior "settlers adventure" that places many of its competitors firmly in the shade.

Star and director moved from Universal to MGM in 1953 for their next opus, the critically acclaimed *The Naked Spur*, made on a $1,200,000 budget. "Taut outdoor drama," "Tersely produced," "A masterpiece," and "Undiluted violence" crowed the writers of an outstanding Western that narrowly escapes inclusion in the "Classics" chapter of this book. With a cast of five (discounting the Indians) and not a single interior shot, this tale of a group of disparate characters trekking over rugged mountains to Abilene, one of them to be brought to justice, was a pared-to-the-bone exercise in greed motivation, Mann having his retinue occasionally stepping right back into the camera lens to impart that "I'm really here" atmosphere so evident in *Winchester '73* and *Bend of the River*. Together with the director's bold use of deep-focus photography and that wonderful Colorado Rockies scenery, you had a high-spirited oater that dragged one by the scruff of the neck for 91 involving minutes; many state that this was Mann's finest hour out West.

Stewart, getting tougher and meaner in each successive Mann outing, played embittered ex-Civil War soldier Howard Kemp, on the trail of grinning outlaw Robert Ryan; Stewart lost his ranch during hostilities, his gal selling the spread and running off with another man. Ryan, who shot a sheriff in the back, has a $5,000 reward on his head; Stewart needs the money to finance a new ranch and Ryan's pert, blonde companion, Janet Leigh, is willing to throw in her lot with Stewart after he's saved her life in a Blackfoot raid. Grizzled old Millard Mitchell on his "flop-eared cactus-eater" mule, forever dreaming of striking gold, and discharged, unreliable trooper Ralph Meeker, greedily thinking about that reward money, make up the five as they struggle over steep cliffs, scramble along narrow trails, negotiate icy streams and torrents and shelter from a storm in an abandoned mine tunnel, Ryan intent on breaking free by ordering Leigh to flaunt her goods to the three men and thus stir up discord. Stewart, wounded in the leg in the Indian attack, finds it tough going, telling the others that their captive is "not a man, he's a sack of money." Eventually, Ryan breaks loose, callously gunning down Mitchell and using his body as bait to lure Stewart and Meeker into a trap. Positioned high above a raging river, Ryan seems to have an open field, but Stewart clambers up a rock face in front of the killer and throws a spur into his neck, Meeker firing four rifle slugs into Ryan who tumbles into the seething waters. Attempting to recover the corpse, Meeker is hit by a log and swept away; Stewart drags Ryan's body ashore, drapes it over his horse but has a fit of conscience, questioning the morality of hunting and killing a man just for financial gain. "I'm gonna sell him for money," he says ruefully to Leigh; disgusted at the thought, he gives Ryan a respectful burial, Leigh promising to marry Stewart and set off to California with him, "Beautiful Dreamer" the leitmotif played in the background. Cinematography (William C. Mellor) and score (Bronislau Kaper) complement Sam Rolfe and Harold Jack Bloom's pithy script in a Western that made big bucks for MGM and cemented the Stewart/Mann partnership as a cinematic force to be reckoned with (the two made eight films together.)

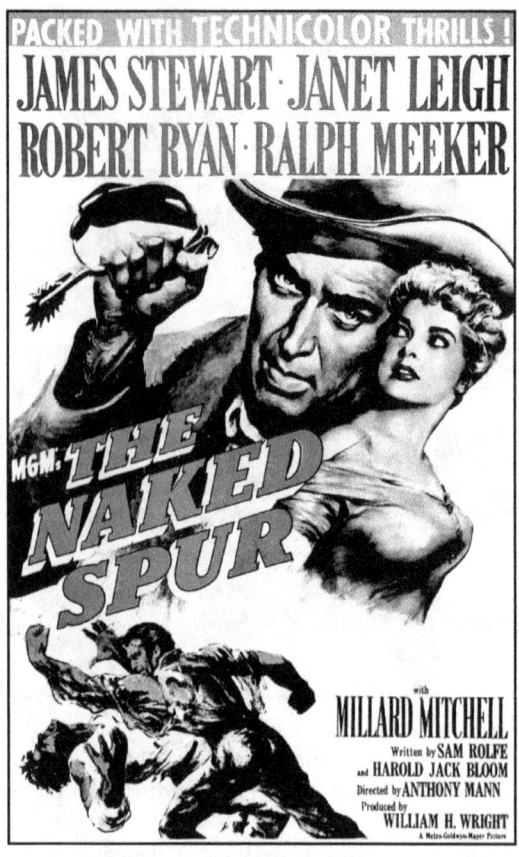

Stewart was on a roll—Mann had redefined his movie career and so had Alfred Hitchcock: 1954's *Rear Window* was the actor's second picture with The Master of Suspense and a massive hit with both critics and public alike; it's regularly voted the third greatest Hitchcock film behind *Psycho* and *Vertigo*. After that triumph came the fourth Stewart/Mann Western, *The Far Country* (made before *Rear Window* but not released in America until February 1955). Stewart starred as a Wyoming cattleman (Jeff Webster) traveling from Seattle to the Klondike with partners Walter Brennan and Jay C. Flippen during the gold rush days of 1896; he's wanted for the killing of a couple of cattle rustlers (he shot in self-defense), deceitful beauty Ruth Roman saving his neck from inquisitive officers on the riverboat to Skagway, Alaska. *The Far Country*, filmed in Jasper

National Park, Alberta, Canada, had more than its fair share of characters, more so than Mann's other four entries in the series, keeping scriptwriter Borden Chase extremely busy: arrogant bully John McIntire rules Skagway, gun in one hand, rope in the other, a self-imposed corrupt judge who gets on the wrong side of Stewart by confiscating his cattle in lieu of a prison sentence ("I'll hang you when you come back," he grins when Stewart heads out); Corinne Calvet ("Freckle Face") is a French-Canadian tomboy smitten with Stewart; Roman plays a saloon/hotel owner, also eyeing up Stewart's manly charms; garrulous Brennan yearns for the day when he and Stewart can buy their own ranch; Flippen, hitting the bottle, is unreliable but friendly enough; and among a plethora of villains including Jack Elam, Robert J. Wilke's sneering gunman stands out. Trekking to Dawson via the hazardous two-mile White Horse Pass, Stewart doubles back to Skagway one night and retrieves his cattle, McIntire and his coyotes in hot pursuit. McIntire then sets up stall in disorderly Dawson, claim-jumping and ambushing miners in a killing spree, Stewart buying his own claim for $40,000. It all leads up to a blazing after-dusk showdown between McIntire's boys and Stewart after Steve Brodie has shot Brennan in the back and wounded Stewart as the pair were preparing to reach the coast by way of a river. Stewart guns down Wilke and Elam, McIntire shoots Roman but dies after falling to Stewart's three slugs. Confronted by Dawson's citizens all sporting rifles, Brodie and his gang quit Dawson, leaving Stewart in the loving arms of Calvet. Mann ends with a closing shot of the little bell on the saddle of Stewart's horse, a gift given to him by Brennan many years ago, a poignant closing scene.

Crammed full of lively incident over 97 engrossing minutes, *The Far Country* continued the Stewart/Mann success story: breathtaking snowy mountain

Westerns of the 1950s: The Classic Years   337

scenery (cinematographer: William H. Daniels), rugged treks over rough terrain and violent gunplay, filmed in the director's "grab you by the throat" style—it also made a small fortune at the box-office. "Laconic Stewart ... is tall in the saddle and quick on the draw," said the *New York Times*, the film containing "spectacular backdrops," *Variety* stating, "Rugged action." As a side note, Stewart's favorite horse Pie made one of his 17 Western appearances with the actor; when he died in 1970, he was laid to rest on Stewart's California ranch.

"That was a spanking good Western." So said my father on emerging from Leatherhead's Crescent cinema in December 1955 after sitting through the last of the Stewart/Mann collaborations and I, a mere eight-year-old, had to agree. *The Man from Laramie*, produced by Columbia, *was* a spanking good Western, hitting all the right notes; acting, direction, script (Philip Yordan and Frank Burt), cinematography (Charles B. Lang, Jr.) and music (George Duning); in addition, the picture was in CinemaScope and Technicolor, Mann intelligently handling the widescreen process instead of flamboyancy for flamboyancy's sake. The theme song, written by Lester Lee and Ned Washington, was also very popular; Al Martino climbed to #19 in the U.K. charts in October 1955 with his version, while Jimmy Young topped the charts for four weeks in September 1955. After this production, Stewart and Mann fell out over the troubled making of *Night Passage* (Universal, 1957), Stewart's next Western co-starring Audie Murphy which Mann thought "trash," quitting as director (TV hack James Neilson took over); regrettably, the two never spoke to one another again. In a taut tale of rivalry and revenge set against a stunning New Mexico backdrop, Mann introduced moments of violence and sadism to appeal to an adult audience, hence the U.K "A" rating, the movie possessing a lean, hard edge without any semblance of fat. Some critics are of the opinion that *The Man from*

Laramie was the least distinguished of the five Stewart/Mann oaters; others say it was the best of the five. I concur with the latter viewpoint; this is the revisionist '50s Western grown to maturity, a streamlined exercise in Shakespearean-type vengeance, Stewart, as blunt as ever, at the top of his game.

Stewart (Will Lockhart) and sidekick Wallace Ford roll their three wagons packed with supplies into Coronado, unload at Cathy O'Donnell's mercantile store and, to make their trip more profitable, top up their freight with salt from a nearby salt lagoon. In rides psycho Alex Nicol and his ruffians from the Barb Ranch, claiming that Stewart and his boys are trespassing. Stewart is roped and dragged through the campfire, his wagons burned, 12 mules shot to death (a distressing scene for animal lovers). Seething with anger, Stewart vows to get even, though he's on a revenge mission anyway; someone is supplying the Apaches with brand new repeating rifles, and it was those carbines that massacred a 12-man army patrol at Dutch Creek, his brother among the victims ("I'm here to hunt a man and kill him."). The plot may become convoluted at times, but Mann keeps the narrative on an even keel, his pacing and pictorial composition spot-on. Donald Crisp, owner of the Barb, is Nicol's father, realizing his son is a wastrel, favoring ambitious foreman Arthur Kennedy who hopes to take over the ranch one day, Crisp viewing Kennedy as the son he wished he'd had; O'Donnell is going out with Kennedy but starting to like stranger Stewart a lot; Aline MacMahon, owner of the Half Moon Ranch, is in direct opposition to Crisp's ambitions, the old man steadily losing his sight;

Westerns of the 1950s: The Classic Years

and when no-good Jack Elam is knifed to death, Stewart is held responsible. Bruising fistfights in the dust, edgy clashes, Stewart hired by MacMahon ("You're just a hard, schemin' old woman," he smiles at her. "Ugly, too," is the rejoinder), Nicol, wounded in the hand, plugging Stewart's right hand (another vicious moment) and some snappy dialogue ("You're a bachelor, aren't you, Mister Lockhart?" O'Donnell says to Stewart. "Well, uh, how d'ya know that?" "Only a lonely man could find pleasure in watching a woman unpack bolts of cotton."), played out against those rugged vistas, add up to a grade A Western that pulls no punches. Nicol is the rat selling those rifles to John War Eagle's tribe, Kennedy aware of it. In a set-to amid the high hills, Kennedy shoots the hothead; Crisp goes gunning for Stewart who he thinks is Nicol's killer, fails in the attempt and winds up pushed over a precipice by Kennedy when the two go looking for that incriminating wagon carrying 200 rifles. Kennedy heads for the rocky heights (Mann makes excellent use of the dizzying, crumbling terrain) to signal the Indians that the rifles are there; Stewart follows, confronting Kennedy ("I came 1,000 miles to kill you!") and hauling the wagon over the cliff where it explodes. Stewart allows Kennedy to ride away but the enraged Apaches corner the hombre, shooting him three times, an arrow in his back the coup de grâce. MacMahon promises to wed Crisp, the rancher, having survived that fall but now blind, while Stewart *doesn't* ride off with O'Donnell, telling the lass that if she passes through Laramie someday, she might look him up. Stewart is "Heroic ... stoic," said the *New York Times*, *Variety* adding that the star carries the film with "easy assurance." A stimulating, terrific-looking oater, *The Man from Laramie* is 103 minutes of Western perfection, marking the end to one of the genre's most successful and rewarding partnerships in the form of James Stewart and Anthony Mann.

Chapter 13
1957

TIN STAR MAN OF STEEL!
The Badge of Marshal Brennan

THE PISTOL-HOT SAGA OF THE WEST'S MOST WANTED WOMAN!
The Buckskin Lady

CHALLENGE ONE BROTHER ... YOU ANSWER TO ALL!
Gun for a Coward

HE'S GOT THE SOUTHWEST ... OVER A GUN-BARREL!
The Hard Man

WHEN DEADLY KILLERS TERRORIZED THE GOLDEN WEST!
Hell Canyon Outlaws

THE FATHER WHO KILLED! THE SON WHO EXPLODED!
Outlaw's Son

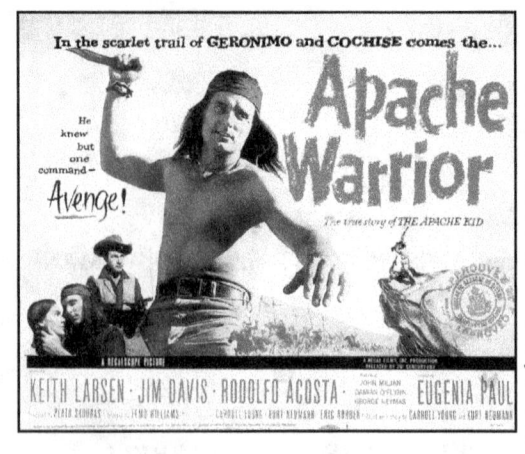

Apache Warrior

Regal Films/20th Century Fox; RegalScope; 74 minutes; Producer: Plato A. Skouras; Director: Elmo Williams; Cast: Keith Larsen; Jim Davis; Rodolfo Acosta; Eugenia Paul; Damian O'Flynn; John Miljan; George Keymas; Lane Bradford **

If it wasn't for the presence of tough, rangy six-foot-two and a half Jim Davis, *Apache Warrior* wouldn't be worth a look. Supposedly based on true events that took place in 1885, Davis plays an army scout, partnered with Keith Larsen (as Katawan, or The Apache Kid), the pair first seen tracking down three renegades led by Rodolfo Acosta who have murdered and scalped two whites. Larson, for his endeavors, is promoted to corporal but branded a traitor by some members of his tribe. He's also in love with Eugenia Paul, as is hothead brave George Keymas. When Keymas kills Larsen's brother during an argument over divided loyalties, he's stabbed to death in a fight with his love rival; Larsen is charged with manslaughter, given a seven-year sentence in Yuma prison and chained on a prison truck with Acosta and his two buddies. At a watering hole, all four overpower their guards, Davis shot in the leg. Recovered, he vows to bring Larsen to justice, The Apache Kid choosing not to throw in his lot with scalp-hungry Acosta, instead fleeing into the hills with Paul, thereby setting the scene for a showdown between them, Davis and a trio of bounty hunters who have disposed of Acosta and his warriors. The three gunslingers converge on Larsen's hideout, anxious to claim the $1,000 reward on his head; Davis joins his old friend in shooting two of the gunmen and bids farewell to Larsen as he rides away with Paul, never to be heard of again. Larsen and Paul make an impassive pair of lovers, composer Paul Dunlap tries in vain to inject some life into Elmo Williams' lackluster direction and studio sets replace exterior shots one too many times. Only the rough charms of Davis hold it together.

Dialogue:
Davis to Major Damian O'Flynn: "The only man who can catch an Apache is another Apache."

The Badge of Marshal Brennan

Allied Artists; 76 minutes; Produced and Directed by Albert C. Gannaway; Cast: Jim Davis; Arleen Whelan; Carl Smith; Harry Lauter; Marty Robbins; Lee Van Cleef; Louis Jean Heydt; Lawrence Dobkin ***

Drifter Jim Davis, on the run from the law for a killing he claims he didn't commit, comes across dying marshal Douglas Fowley, takes his badge (and his identity) and gallops into Banock, a town where the inhabitants are sick from fever caused by Louis Jean Heydt's cattle, infected with Black Spot disease. The stubborn rancher won't allow Doc Harry Lauter to take blood samples to produce an antidote for the epidemic; he's determined to take his steers on a drive for profit, whether they're diseased or not, and trigger-happy son Lee Van Cleef is there to shoot any man who disagrees. Davis sides with Sheriff Carl Smith in obtaining those vital samples after saving Lauter from a necktie party instigated by Heydt, even though Smith knows the big man's a fraud. Davis' no-nonsense attitude, fists and twin guns win the day, Heydt's wranglers blasted en masse as they attempt to drive the herd across a river; Van Cleef is knocked senseless in a fight with the bogus marshal. The townsfolk recover, Lauter's antidote a success, and, job done, Davis rides away with Arleen Whelan, the hussy having thrown herself at the black-clad hunk since casting her eyes on him in reel two. A strange low-budget oater lumbered with a curious guitar-based score from Ramey (Ramez) Idriss which, in this setup, falls far short of what Western incidental music should sound like; the ending seems rushed and, overall, the production appears underdeveloped. But the picture works, mainly due to Davis' machismo, several lively confrontations and Van Cleef at his sneering best. *Raiders of Old California* followed hot on its heels, featuring the same cast and technicians.

Dialogue:
Davis to Van Cleef: "What's your name, mister?"
Van Cleef: "Doniphan."
Davis: "I won't forget that name."
Van Cleef: "What's yours—friend?"
Davis: "I don't have any."
Van Cleef: "No name?"
Davis: "No friends."

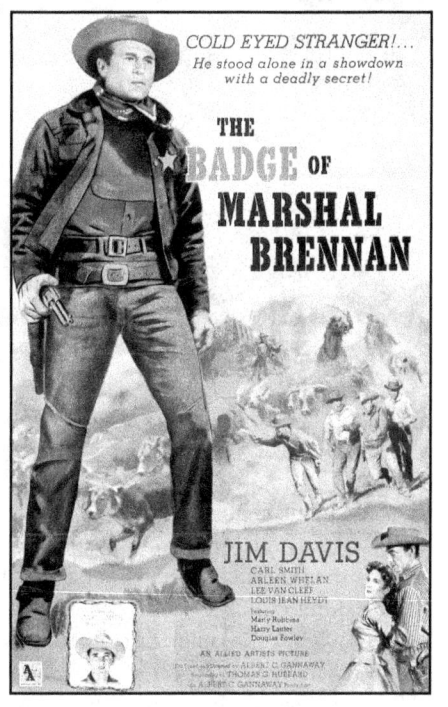

Badlands of Montana

Regal Films/20th Century Fox; RegalScope; 75 minutes; Produced and Directed by Daniel B. Ullman; Cast: Rex Reason; Beverly Garland; Emile Meyer; Keith Larsen; Margia Dean; John Pickard; Stanley Farrar; Rankin Mansfield ****

Scriptwriter Danial B. Ullman contributed to over 30 Westerns during the decade, from Whip Wilson B-oaters to Joel McCrea A-features, but only directed two movies, *Dial Red 0* (Allied Artists, 1955) and *Badlands of Montana*, a meaty outing that gave veteran tough guy Emile Meyer a chance to show his mettle playing a killer bandit befriending Rex Reason, on the run from Cascade for out-gunning corrupt mayor John Pickard. Reason was an election candidate but forced out of the contest when his rival's scheming wife Margia Dean falsely accused him of assault; Reason was savagely lashed by Pickard's thugs and then, the following morning, shot Pickard in a street showdown. With Meyer in his retreat are four outlaws, a Chinese helper and frustrated daughter Beverly Garland, the lass yearning for a man in her life and falling for Reason, young gun tough Keith Larsen as jealous as hell. Reason (not, as Meyer suspects, a bounty hunter) survives a mock trial and joins the gang, participates in a few holdups but returns to Cascade as marshal and instigates a "No Guns" policy, leaving him in a quandary; he likes Meyer, loves Garland and doesn't want to cross the bunch, and Larsen in particular, in Cascade, advising them to stay away; Meyer agrees to this condition. But during a stage robbery, Meyer's outfit is ambushed by the army, Meyer brought to Reason's jail, loose cannon Larsen at large, the other three members dead. Larsen (he tended to play brooding, disturbed characters) enters town and teams up with bitter Dean, anxious to claim the $2,000 on Reason's head. In a showdown at Meyer's homestead, Meyer (released on purpose by Reason) and Dean shoot each other dead and Reason, although slower on the draw than Larsen, is the more accurate shot, bringing him down with two bullets. Reason and Garland depart to Cascade where he plans to continue as marshal and marry the gal into the bargain. Another solid Regal horse opera written by Ullman; Reason, Meyer, Garland and Larsen all contribute telling performances to the sound of Irving Gertz's nicely judged score.

Dialogue:
Reason to Meyer and his gang as he leaves for Cascade: "Well, I hope you all die of old age."

The Big Land aka Buffalo Grass

Jaguar Productions/Warner Bros.; Warnercolor; 92 minutes; Producers: George C. Bertholon and Alan Ladd (uncredited); Director: Gordon Douglas; Cast: Alan Ladd; Edmond O'Brien; Virginia Mayo; Anthony Caruso; Don Castle; John Qualen; Julie Bishop; James Anderson ****

A slim-looking Alan Ladd starred as an ex-Confederate officer herding beef from Texas to Missouri, being offered a measly price by black-clad cattleman Anthony

Caruso and befriending alcoholic Edmond O'Brien en route, the pair stopping off at John Qualen's homestead. In Rebel-hating Kansas City, O'Brien, a former architect and now sobered up, decides to go into partnership with Ladd and railroad friend Don Castle in creating a spur from the main rail line to outlying farming areas which will enable cattle and buffalo grass wheat to be delivered to townships; the ambitious project includes the construction of a new town. Ladd's flowering romance with O'Brien's sister, Virginia Mayo, arouses jealousy in fiancé Castle while out on the prairie, smirking Caruso waits to cause mischief. The half-built town is burned to the ground by Caruso and his sidewinders, O'Brien is shot dead by Caruso in a saloon standoff, cattle are brought in but stampeded through the rebuilt town and Ladd, in a *Shane*-type saloon showdown, finally guns down the troublesome killer cattle boss and his henchman, James Anderson. Realizing that Ladd and Mayo are now a couple, Castle leaves them to it, returning to Kansas City alone. David Buttolph's resonant score adds spice to a nicely put together but leisurely moving oater shot around Sonora, California, O'Brien giving a fine performance playing the reformed drunk who had Ladd to thank for putting him on the straight and narrow before his brutal death. "Plodding," commented the *Los Angeles Times*, somewhat unfairly.

Dialogue:
Ladd to O'Brien at a river, O'Brien suffering severe pains through lack of whiskey: "Don't you wanna drink?"
O'Brien: "Water? What am I, a trout?"

The Buckskin Lady

United Artists; 66 minutes; Produced and Directed by Carl K. Hittleman; Cast: Patricia Medina; Richard Denning; Gerald Mohr; Henry Hull; Hank Worden; Robin Short; George Cisar; Louis Lettieri *

Carl K. Hittleman directed four movies, three of them Westerns; he also co-scripted *The Buckskin Lady* with David Lang, the idea being to have a femme fatale in the lead, everyone at the mercy of her whims and pleasure. Unfortunately, what you got for your buck was an overwrought exercise in female histrionics courtesy of pouting, hair-tossing Patricia Medina, the talents of Henry Hull (her drunken doctor father), Gerald Mohr (a jealous gunslinger), Richard Denning (a kindly medic) and Hank Worden (a dimwitted cowpoke) utterly wasted. Also wasted on this badly written material was Albert Glasser's score; the composer, noted for his pulsating horror soundtracks, threw everything into the pot in an unsuccessful attempt to add polish to what must count as one of the cheapest and poorest oaters issued under the United Artists banner during this decade. Medina, flaunting her wares, is desperate to leave Bitter Water with killer Mohr, that is until Denning, who has bought into Hull's practice for $250, arrives on the scene. Mohr gets angry over Medina's interest in the fair-haired newcomer, dragging her off to Butte City where he holds up a bank to finance their marriage and honeymoon. Wounded by a pursuing posse, Medina realizes what a fool she's been, especially when Mohr puts a bullet in Worden; the loony old polecat was only delivering a letter from Denning, telling her to come back to him. In a tussle with Denning, who catches up with the pair, the no-good is shot dead by his mistress who heads back to Bitter Water with her new beau. Medina overacts like there's no tomorrow, Denning looks bemused and Mohr resembles a young Humphrey Bogart in some scenes, his lines of "I want you," "You're mine," "I'll never let you go," and " I care for you," repeated ad nauseam, as are his repeated promises to Medina to give her the earth. Notwithstanding lustful scenes of Mohr slobbering all over Medina's heaving breasts, this is a tatty Western soap opera by any other name.

Dialogue:
George Cisar, alighting from a stage and not liking what he sees: "From the looks of this metropolis, a man could take three steps and be in the middle of nowhere."

Copper Sky

Regal Films/20th Century Fox; RegalScope; 77 minutes; Producer: Robert Stabler; Director: Charles Marquis Warren; Cast: Jeff Morrow; Coleen Gray; Strother Martin; Paul Brinegar; John Pickard; Jack Lomas; William Hamel; Patrick O'Moore ***

Alcoholic ex-cavalryman Jeff Morrow (as Hack Williams) lurches into the town of Occidental, tethering his horse to a rail by the stables; an Indian emerges from behind a wall, shoots another Indian and runs off after Morrow fires at him. The townsfolk materialize, Morrow is arrested for a murder he didn't commit and sentenced to be hanged; the citizens are scared of Apache reprisals and justice, however far beyond the law it may be, must be seen to be done. It's all to no avail. In storm the Apaches and the town is wiped out—all, except that is, for Morrow. Schoolteacher Coleen Gray arrives on a wagon, her driver is killed by a dying Apache and Morrow, whiskey bottle in hand, introduces himself to the horrified lass. What follows is a low-budget Western variation of *The African Queen* and *Heaven Knows, Mr. Allison* as Morrow and Gray, two opposites flung together by circumstance, trundle across Utah's rocky Kanab region, away from "them Redsticks," in search of refuge. Ice maiden Gray thaws, loner Morrow realizes he's a much nicer person without the need to continually guzzle whiskey, a massacred settlement is encountered, and Morrow eventually saves an army patrol from being slaughtered by drawing a war party away from the troops. Recovering from his wounds and looked upon as a hero of sorts, it's clear from their final kiss and embrace that this is one odd couple that will soon start planning a life together. An air of erotic tension runs through the narrative, especially when Gray cuddles up to her drunken partner at night ("I'm frightened and cold. Could I move a little closer for safety? Can I trust you?") and later, as the pair bathe in a river, both giving in to (for 1957) unbridled lust. An unusual Western offering, the two main leads turning in credible performances, Gray radiant, unshaven Morrow rough but vulnerable; these stalwarts of the B-programmer are a delight to watch as they bicker, fight and finally fall in love.

Dialogue:
Jail keeper Strother Martin to Morrow, behind bars: "I'll get you something special; supper, anything."
Morrow: "Get me a bottle."
Martin: "For supper?"
Morrow: "I'll drink my supper."

The Dalton Girls

Bel-Air/United Artists; 71 minutes; Producer: Howard W. Koch; Director: Reginald LeBorg; Cast: Merry Anders; Lisa Davis; Penny Edwards; Sue George; John Russell; Ed Hinton; Glen Dixon; Malcolm Atterbury ****

A posse closes in on two of the Dalton Brothers, gunning them down; in town, two genteel-looking ladies, the Dalton's sisters, go to view the bodies and murder the mortician with a single blow of a shovel after he tries to assault

Westerns of the 1950s: The Classic Years   347

one of them. Six years later, the four Dalton sisters are terrorizing the territory: Rose, the cold, trigger-happy one (Lisa Davis); Holly, the older, more sensible one (Merry Anders); Columbine, who's fallen for smooth gambler John Russell (Penny Edwards); and sensitive Marigold, who just wants to settle down and get married (Sue George). Changing from dresses to jeans and shirts, each sporting a hefty amount of hardware, these gun-toting dames are not to be messed with, especially Davis, who has no hesitation in dropping anyone who crosses her path. Plugging Malcolm Atterbury in Dry Creek for $6,000, the girls go on the run, Russell after not only that cash (he was owed it by the bank manager, a gambling debt) but sexy Edwards into the bargain. Also, on their trail is Detective Ed Hinton, tracking them to Tombstone where the foursome plan to rob a high-stakes card game set up by Russell. In a shoot-out, George is killed and Edwards wounded; refusing to give herself up, Davis is shot dead, leaving Anders and Edwards to surrender. Surprisingly violent in some scenes, *The Dalton Girls* has obvious male-fantasy overtones and is one of the last of the true '50s out-and-out B-Westerns: A decent score (Les Baxter), needle-sharp photography of Utah's Kanab region (Carl E. Guthrie) and four very attractive female leads make for an enjoyably different women-out-West yarn directed with vigor by Reginald LeBorg.

Dialogue:
Edwards to Davis: "You kill like other women love."

Dragoon Wells Massacre

Allied Artists; CinemaScope/DeLuxecolor; 88 minutes; Producer: Lindsley Parsons; Director: Harold D. Schuster; Cast: Barry Sullivan; Dennis O'Keefe; Mona Freeman; Katy Jurado; Sebastian Cabot; Max Showalter (Casey Adams); Trevor Bardette; Jack Elam *****

Take the occupants and guards of a prison wagon, a stagecoach and its passengers and a wagon containing rifles and whiskey for Indians, throw them all together in Apache-infested country and you have a splendid Allied Artists' Western of some note, containing a great Paul Dunlap score, glowing photography from William H. Clothier (Kanab, Utah was the location), a canny Warren Douglas script and solid performances all round. The film is also very violent, showing the graphic aftermath of three separate massacres. The principal characters are Barry Sullivan and Jack Elam, two outlaws Marshal Trevor Bardette is bringing to justice; Mona Freeman, a spoiled bitch, engaged to dull Max Showalter; Katy Jurado as her usual sexually charged self; evil gun runner Sebastian Cabot; and Captain Dennis O'Keefe, trying to negotiate everyone through hostile territory towards Fort Dragoon Wells. Despite their differences, the group bonds in the face of adversity; Jurado makes a play for O'Keefe ("I want to be loved by a man like you."), haughty Freeman falls for the rough, macho charms of Sullivan, Elam gets attached to a small girl found at the scene of a massacre (and dies protecting her), the two women engage in a catfight ("You don't love anyone but yourself. You don't know what you want," Jurado spits at Freeman) while Bardette finds himself rather liking Sullivan, the two engaged in playing umpteen rounds of cards. Edgy nighttime scenes, the contingent picked off by the ever-watchful Apaches, are complemented in rousing action set pieces, Sullivan trying to get help from Fort Buchanan after Fort Dragoon Wells is found full of corpses, only to be caught by Chief Yellow Claw (John War Eagle); he's exchanged for Cabot, the toad getting a well-deserved slug in the back from Sullivan, the survivors slaughtering the Redskins in a carefully planned ambush and making it to Fort Buchanan where Bardette does the right thing and allows Sullivan to ride off; hot on his heels is Freeman, looking for a far more exciting life than the one she would have led with Showalter. As for O'Keefe, he has the fiery delights of Jurado to look forward to. "Pointless," moaned the *New York Times*; "Exciting," enthused Britain's *MFB*, perfectly highlighting the differences found in film critique. "Pointless" this movie is not; it's a

Belgian popster for *Dragoon Wells Massacre*

gripping, atmospheric yarn shot amid spectacular scenery, strong on characterization and perfectly timed pace, the '50s Western at its very best.
Highlights:
Kanab's striking rock formations and a likeable performance from Sullivan as the rogue with a conscience of sorts, if not a heart of gold.
Dialogue:
Sullivan to Freeman after one of her rants: "You've got the disposition of a sick Apache."

Drango

United Artists; 92 minutes; Produced and Directed by Jules Bricken and Hall Bartlett; Cast: Jeff Chandler; Joanne Dru; Ronald Howard; Donald Crisp; Julie London; John Lupton; Milburn Stone; Morris Ankrum ***

In the period following the end of the Civil War, Major Clint Drango (Jeff Chandler, who dabbled in the production end) and Captain John Lupton ride into the ruined Confederate town of Kennesaw Pass, Georgia with orders to install a military governorship, meeting resentful opposition from everyone except Doc Walter Sande. Union sympathizer Morris Ankrum, confessing to the killing of one of his pursuers, is hanged by an angry mob after a farcical trial, Rebel Ronald Howard plotting to overthrow Chandler and murder Lupton, who's carrying on with Southern belle Julie London behind his back. Chandler nurses a secret. In the days of the war and under orders from General Sherman, he was responsible for sacking the town and now wants to make amends by adopting a softer approach to that dictated by Colonel Milburn Stone, who prefers to use brute force if necessary to "whip them into line." With Oscar-winning composer Elmer Bernstein and double Oscar-winner cinematographer James Wong Howe on board, you might expect great things, but they fail to materialize, the end result rather talkative, stodgy and dour, just like Chandler's unchanging expression. Even when Lupton's beaten-up corpse is found and the Union-biased newspaper office burned to the ground, it fails to ignite any real passion, the townsfolk, whipped up into a frenzy by Howard, on the point of storming Fort Dalton for supplies until Chandler confronts them minus his pistol; Howard fires at Chandler, wounding him, and is shot dead by his father, Judge Donald Crisp ("There can be no new war."). The citizens down weapons and, led by Chandler, ride off to the fort for those much-needed provisions, Ankrum's daughter, Joanne Dru, promising herself to the upright Union officer on his return. For lovers of Civil War Western dramas only.

Dialogue:
Milburn to Chandler, noticing that he wishes to govern without firearms: "Without your guns? Who's your next of kin? I'd like to know where to send the body."

Duel at Apache Wells

Republic; Naturama; 70 minutes; Produced and Directed by Joseph Kane; Cast: Ben Cooper; Jim Davis; Anna Maria Alberghetti; Bob Steele; Harry Shannon; Frank Puglia; Francis McDonald; John Dierkes ***

After spending four years across the Mexican border, young Ben Cooper arrives at his father's (Harry Shannon) Lodgepole Ranch in the middle of a range war. Jim Davis (as Dean Cannary), owner of the Circle C, once worked for Shannon but was fired; in retribution, he refuses to allow his rival use of the Apache Wells' watering hole, meaning long delays and detours for Shannon if he is to get his 300 head of cattle through to market; Davis also harasses Shannon's attempts to water his steers from two wagons carrying mobile water tanks. Cooper strikes up a relationship with Anna Maria Alberghetti, who Davis lusts after, and comes up against Davis' trigger-happy thugs, led by Bob Steele. But the fresh-faced youngster is more than Davis bargained for; he can handle himself in a fight and is lightning fast on the draw, a fact which Davis finds out at the end. In a standoff, Cooper reveals himself to be the notorious Durango Kid, wanted in Mexico, and guns Davis down; their boss dead, Steele and the others turn tail and run like rats on a sinking ship, leaving Cooper and Alberghetti to tie the knot, and for Shannon and other ranchers to water their cattle. Smug Davis, wolf's grin to the fore, bulldozes his hefty bulk through the picture and Italian-born Alberghetti resembles Audrey Hepburn at times; the movie's slightly flat in the middle, but ends on a high note with that tense Cooper/Davis showdown.

Dialogue:
Steele to cohorts after his boss bites the dust, displaying a complete lack of loyalty: "Cannary's dead. That ends our payroll. Well, I ain't fightin' for free."

Escape from Red Rock

Regal Films/20th Century Fox; RegalScope; 75 minutes; Producer: Bernard Glasser; Director: Edward Bernds; Cast: Brian Donlevy; Gary Murray; Eilene Janssen; Jay C. Flippen; Myron Healey; William Phipps; Natividad Vacio; Rick Vallin ***

Westerns of the 1950s: The Classic Years   351

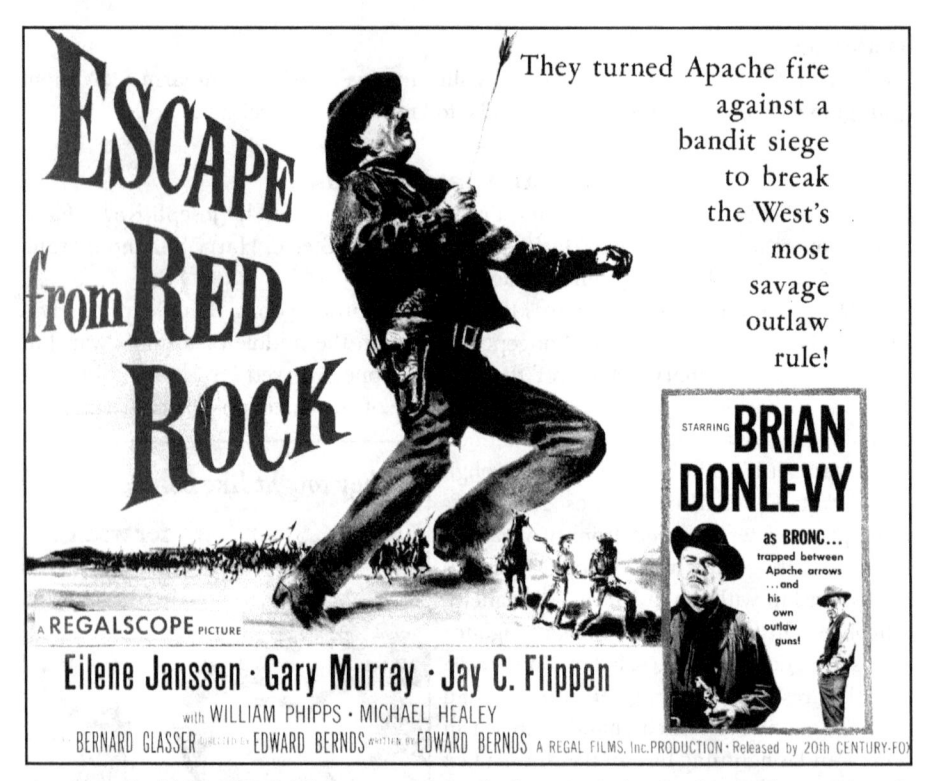

Regal's $100,000 B-Western packs a hefty punch in the beginning and end, becoming a tad too sentimental mid-section. In Red Rock, Sheriff Jay C. Flippen orders young hothead Gary Murray outta town for causing yet another saloon fracas, while Murray's gal, Eilene Janssen, asks Flippen to sort out her abusive stepfather. At Murray's ranch, outlaw Brian Donlevy and his three coyotes have moved in; Murray's brother, a wanted man, lies sick on his bed from a gunshot wound, Donlevy telling Murray he can call a doctor *if* he scouts out Red Rock's express office for a possible holdup. Murray does as he's told, Donlevy and his boys steal the cash, shoot a woman and bystander during the robbery and ride off, one of their number brought down. Blamed for the killing of the old lady, Murray leaves Red Rock with Janssen and, after that gritty start, the movie changes gear. The pair end up in Natividad Vacio's hacienda, get wed ("You wanna marry now? Good!") and stumble across a homestead raided by Apaches. A baby girl is the only survivor, Murray and Janssen playing father and mother until, on the 50th minute, Donlevy, Myron Healey and William Phipps turn up seeking shelter, food and, in the case of Phipps, a woman—Murray's woman. Donlevy, keeping his two snarling compadres at bay, sides with the newlyweds and the baby, Phipps shoots Healey and the Apaches attack; Donlevy expires from an arrow in his barrel chest, Phipps rides off on an Indian pony and is later found cut to pieces, and Flippen arrives with his posse; after some deliberation, he allows Murray, Janssen plus the baby to carry on to California and locate the infant's kinfolk. Brydon Baker's stark black-and-white photography and mean performances from screen toughs Donlevy, Healey and Phipps give *Escape from Red Rock* a grimy, authentic Western feel; if the picture hadn't sagged a bit in the middle, this could well have been regarded as a little-seen minor classic.

Dialogue:
Donlevy to Murray: "Who's the girl?"
Murray: "She's my wife."
Donlevy: "Your wife!"
Murray: "That's right."
Donlevy: "Looks like you've been pretty busy since we saw you last."

Forty Guns

20th Century Fox; CinemaScope; 80 minutes; Produced and Directed by Samuel Fuller; Cast: Barbara Stanwyck; Barry Sullivan; John Ericson; Dean Jagger; Gene Barry; Robert Dix; Eve Brent; Hank Worden *******

As brothers Barry Sullivan, Gene Barry and Robert Dix ride their rig towards Tombstone, rancher Barbara Stanwyck (black outfit, white steed) and her 40 hired guns come thundering down the trail, a striking pre-credit opener to Samuel Fuller's uneven Western, heavy on symbolism and violence, overly plotted, stylistically great in parts, melodramatic and hysterical in others. Gunman Sullivan knows his era is coming to a close, but he's intent on bringing down the curtains on the Baroness of Tombstone Territory's iron-fisted reign; Stanwyck's brother, loose cannon John Ericson, has tormented and murdered partially sighted Sheriff Hank Worden in cold blood but was let off with a $50 fine by spineless lawman Dean Jagger, in Stanwyck's pocket, as are most of the town's serving officials. Barry falls for gunsmith Eve Brent; younger sibling Dix wants to become a gunfighter like Sullivan; Ericson romps in the hills with a dark-haired lass (this storyline is rapidly discarded); Dix saves Sullivan from being shot in an alleyway ambush; Sullivan and Stanwyck bond when they're caught in a desert tornado and Barry is gunned down on his wedding day by unhinged Ericson. "I'll do everything I can to see him live," states Stanwyck, knowing that Sullivan, whom she now loves, is determined to bring her crazy killer brother to justice. Jagger hangs himself in Stanwyck's mansion after his declared feelings for her are rebuffed, Ericson is busted out of jail and in a street shoot-out, Sullivan empties the chamber of his fancy Colt .45 Peacemaker; one bullet wounds Stanwyck, the remaining five leave Ericson sprawled in the dust. Dix is now the new marshal in Tombstone; as Sullivan rides off in his buggy to California and a new life, Stanwyck, having lost everything, runs after him in a white fluffy dress and joins him on his journey. Fuller, who also wrote the script, crams everything in, including a warbler singing about "The High Ridin' Woman With a Whip," resulting in an operatic, *noir*-type mishmash of divergent techniques and wild emotion that somehow doesn't quite gel, despite Stanwyck's barnstorming performance and superb widescreen photography from Joseph F. Biroc.

Dialogue:
Barry, smooching with Brent: "I never kissed a gunsmith before."
Brent: "Any recoil?"

Trivia:
The lengthy tracking shot showing Sullivan approaching Ericson in the street during the opening few minutes, Fuller's lens closing in on his eyes, is said to have influenced Sergio Leone in his *Dollar* Westerns; when Stanwyck is dragged through the desert on her horse, the actress, 49 at the time, did her own stuntwork, escaping with a few minor scratches and bruises.

Fury at Showdown

United Artists; 75 minutes; Producer: John Beck; Director: Gerd Oswald; Cast: John Derek; Nick Adams; John Smith; Carolyn Craig; Gage Clark; Robert Griffin; Sydney Smith; Ken Christy ****

Produced in five days on a $100,000 budget, German director Gerd Oswald's spare little *noir* Western is a knockout, both in overall performances, direction, music (Harry Sukman), script (Jason James) and cinematography (Joseph LaShelle). John Derek is released from prison after serving a year for the killing of a man; he claims he was provoked, but no one believes him. Brother Nick Adams, who has the job of keeping his excitable sibling in line, collects him from jail, the pair riding over to their hometown of Showdown Creek, where lawyer Gage Clark, brother of the man Derek shot, has ensured that his presence isn't welcomed, not by the citizens or girlfriend Carolyn Craig, daughter of Sheriff Robert Griffin. Derek and Adams strike a deal with two ranchers to provide services to the new railhead but their loan note is due to be paid in three days, banker Sydney Smith warning the brothers that Clark, a director, is all for purchasing it to enable him to lay his grubby hands on their ranch; Smith needs a signed contract pronto from rail boss Ken Christy to have the loan extended. Not only has the toad-like lawyer prevented Christy traveling from Gunstock to Showdown Creek to give Derek that important promissory note and contract but he's hired smooth-faced gunslinger John

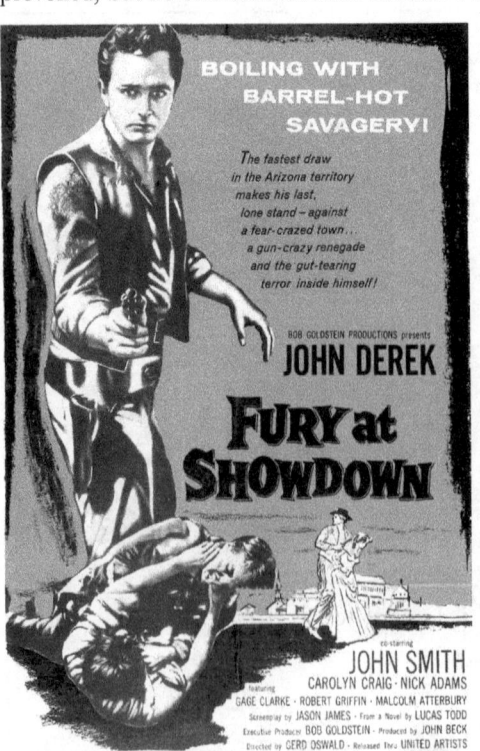

Smith to protect him *and* goad Derek into drawing his gun; Derek's fast, but maybe Smith's faster. Oswald composes his characters full frame to impart that edgy *noir* feeling, James' dialogue short and snappy, while Sukman's music is a menacing, low-key aural backdrop, keeping the tension on the boil. Heaping insult upon insult on Derek, who has left his gun in Griffin's office ("Look Ma, no guns! The gunless, gutless wonder!"), Smith (a venomous performance) engages in a bruising three-minute fistfight with Derek, one of the B-Western's most ferocious, and ends up killing Adams, who is returning from Gunstock with those vitally needed papers that will let Derek off the hook. In a suspenseful showdown, Smith grabs Craig as a shield but is shot three times by Derek, leaving Clark crawling in the dirt and begging for mercy before he's arrested. Needless to say, Craig goes off in Derek's arms. A riveting minor Western mood piece, very rarely seen but worth seeking out.

Highlights:
Derek and Smith's saloon/street brawl, a real cracker.

Dialogue:
Smith, noticing that Derek isn't wearing a gun: "I'll meet you with anything you call. Even feather pillows at 10 paces."

Gun for a Coward

Universal; CinemaScope/Eastmancolor; 88 minutes; Producer: William Alland; Director: Abner Biberman; Cast: Fred MacMurray; Jeffrey Hunter; Dean Stockwell; Janice Rule; Chill Wills; Josephine Hutchinson; John Larch; Paul Birch ***

Universal's medium-budget psychological Western focused on three ranching brothers: elder statesman Fred MacMurray, nervy Jeffrey Hunter and young hothead Dean Stockwell. Ever since Hunter as a seven-year-old saw his pa die from a rattlesnake bite, he's retreated into a shell, unable to draw a gun or stand up for himself in a fight. Ma Josephine Hutchinson doesn't help, babying the lad to the point of suffocation, a severe case (in modern vernacular) of the Jocasta complex ("Let him grow up," says MacMurray to her). MacMurray's been dating Paul Birch's daughter, Janice Rule, for four years, reckoning on marrying the lass when his cattle drive reaches Abilene. Trouble is, the gal loves Hunter and admires his non-fighting qualities, even if those around him jeer and make jokes. The first half of Abner Biberman's horse opera drags, the fact that Hunter simply cannot raise a fist in anger or cock a pistol rammed home to the point of exhaustion. The movie gains pace when nesters move in on private land, causing a nuisance, and MacMurray's cattle drive gets underway, Hunter free of his mother's shackles (she dies of old age), a tense saloon standoff raising the tempo, cocky, argumentative Stockwell gunning down two toughs. Troublemaker John Larch stirs things up between Hunter and Stockwell when rustlers steal the herd, Stockwell shot dead during a stampede; Hunter and his cowhands forlornly canter into Abilene with Stockwell's body and no beef, MacMurray (who's gone on ahead to propose to Rule) incensed that his intended loves his weakling sibling. But Hunter proves his mettle in a barroom showdown with Larch, challenging him to the draw; MacMurray fires first ("I don't want to see another brother die.") and then finds himself on the end of Hunter's lethal fists. Finally, Hunter is recognized as a real man, leading his drovers to chase down the rustlers, who are making for Texas, and retrieve the herd. MacMurray, knowing he has lost Rule, decides to travel the West where the wind takes him. An uneven mix, MacMurray accused of being too old (at 48) for the part against Hunter, 30 and Stockwell, 20; Hutchinson, playing MacMurray's mother, was just under five years older than him. Chill Wills shines, playing, as usual, a hard-bitten, yarn-telling veteran cow puncher.

Dialogue:
Larch to the saloon clientele as Hunter enters: "Here comes the rabbit going hoppity hoppity hop."

Trivia:
This was former child actor Dean Stockwell's first picture playing an adult after a screen hiatus of six years.

Gun Glory

MGM; CinemaScope/Metrocolor; 89 minutes; Producer: Nicholas Nayfack; Director: Roy Rowland; Cast: Stewart Granger; Rhonda Fleming; Chill Wills; Steve Rowland; James Gregory; Jacques Aubuchon; Arch Johnson; Rayford Barnes ***

Gunfighter Stewart Granger rides into a Wyoming town, visits his ranch which he left years back and resumes an uneasy relationship with sullen son Steve Rowland, Granger's wife having died in his absence. When cattle baron James Gregory, aided by thug Arch Johnson, makes it clear that he wants to drive 20,000 head of cattle over Granger's land *and* through the town, preacher Chill Wills decides to call on Granger's help in stopping Gregory in his tracks, despite town opposition. Meanwhile, Rhonda Fleming has escaped the predatory clutches of lecherous storekeeper Jacques Aubuchon by taking on the role of Granger's housekeeper; soon, young Rowland is kissing her, even though Fleming only has eyes for his father. Shades of *The Gunfighter* and *Shane* crop up in William Ludwig and Ben Maddow's intelligent screenplay, Englishman Granger a pleasure to watch, as is Fleming. Dynamiting a pass drives Gregory's steers to pastures new; in a tense showdown, wounded Rowland plugs villainous Johnson and realizes at last that his dad is going to have a future with their sexy housekeeper, not himself. An easy-on-the-eye oater that passes the time in decent-enough style.

Highlights:
Oft-used Bronson Canyon, beautifully photographed by Harold J. Marzorati, plus Granger and Fleming in top form.

Dialogue:
Aubuchon to Granger: "You live by the gun, you die by it."
Granger: "Depends on what kind of shot you are."

Trivia:
Granger, well known for his general distaste for all things Hollywood, claimed he was completely wrong for the part, that MGM bamboozled him into making the movie and that Steve Rowland, the director's 25-year-old son, had no acting experience, dismissing the picture as "average."

Gunfight at Indian Gap

Ventura/Republic; Naturama; 70 minutes; Producer: Rudy Ralston; Director: Joseph Kane; Cast: Anthony George; Vera Ralston; George Macready; Barry Kelley; John Doucette; George Keymas; Chubby Johnson; Sarah Selby *

In what was possibly Joseph Kane's worst-ever Western, a trio of stagecoach robbers led by George Macready, together with Mexican Anthony George and Vera Ralston, leave the Eldorado relay station and head across country with the stolen takings, the whiff of double-cross in the air. Sheriff Barry Kelley is hot on their trail, determined to nail George whom he believes to be one of the outlaws; he isn't, George a victim of circumstances, picked up by the stage after his horse had become lame and quickly falling in lust with bored, frustrated Ralston at the station. With 10 minutes to go, Macready shoots Keymas, John Doucette wounds Macready and drools over Ralston, Macready kills Doucette and George puts a slug into Macready, not wanting to share in a 50/50 cut of the cash; Kelley catches up with the remaining "two fugitives from the law" and lets them go, content to have recovered the money. Not even the scenic splendor of Lone Pine's Alabama Hills can save Republic's lame

Westerns of the 1950s: The Classic Years   357

oater, shot in their own widescreen format, Naturama, from being a dull trek out West, Ralston, the company's oft-promoted Czech star (married to studio head Herbert J. Yates), emoting like crazy, George wooden, Macready less evil than usual and Doucette unconvincing in his role of a leering lech.

Dialogue:

Doucette during a night storm, hovering over Ralston: "You must be cold, honey. Why don't ya take your wet things off and let them dry by the fire, huh? Or, you can take 'em off under a blanket and hand 'em out to me."

Gunfight at the O.K. Corral

Paramount; VistaVision/Technicolor; 122 minutes; Producer: Hal B. Wallis; Director: John Sturges; Cast: Burt Lancaster; Kirk Douglas; Jo Van Fleet; Rhonda Fleming; John Ireland; Lyle Bettger; Frank Faylen; DeForest Kelley *****

Grossing $11,000,000 on a budget of $2,000,000, John Sturges' version of the famous gunfight which took place in Tombstone, Arizona on October 26, 1881 boasted two of Hollywood's big hitters in key roles: Burt Lancaster as Marshal Wyatt Earp, and Kirk Douglas as gambling dentist-cum-gunfighter Doc Holliday. With the combined star power of these two legends in full flight, it was easy to overlook the historical inaccuracies and concentrate on how the Earp Brothers and Holliday cleaned up the Clanton gang: from preparations for the showdown to the final dispatch of youngest Clanton sibling Dennis Hopper, Sturges used up 11 minutes of screen time on the infamous shoot-out and a classic 11 minutes it turned out to be. From the onset, the film concentrated mainly on Douglas' corrosive relationship with Jo Van Fleet (as Kate: "You are dirt—just like me," she spits at him) and hesitant friendship with taciturn Lancaster; it's not until the 43rd minute that the first slice of action takes place, Lancaster and Douglas dropping three bank robbers. The narrative switches from Dodge City to Tombstone and its cemetery, Boot Hill, Douglas, suffering from tuberculosis, coughing constantly and rejecting Van Fleet who turns to killer John Ireland (Johnny Ringo) for solace. In a leisurely paced Western, Lancaster cuts a fine, stoical figure, Douglas acts his socks off and although gambling dame Rhonda Fleming looks gorgeous playing Lancaster's love interest, you can't help wondering whether the flame-haired lass was included for decorative purposes only; she doesn't do a great deal. Vivid color photography from Charles B. Lang, Jr. is rounded off by Dimitri Tiomkin and Ned Washington's stirring title song, sung by Frankie Lane, a melody which latches onto the brain and won't let go; the Oscar-winning composers almost topped it with "Follow the River" which featured in the Audie Murphy oater *Night Passage*, released by Universal the same year. *Variety* stated, "An absorbing yarn ... leading to a gory gunfight," *Films and Filming*'s John Cutts cautiously adding "Carefully and lavishly mounted, but overlong and overwrought."

Highlights:
The actual gunfight itself, one of the genre's finest, even though the original skirmish lasted a mere 30 seconds!

Dialogue:
Douglas to Lancaster: "You want a gunhand?"
Lancaster: "You? No thanks."
Douglas: "I do handle 'em pretty well. The only trouble is, those best able to testify to my aim aren't around to comment."

Trivia:
Humphrey Bogart and Richard Widmark were considered for the Doc Holliday role; and the Old Tucson site used for the climactic showdown was featured in Howard Hawks' *Rio Bravo* as the location for *that* movie's climactic showdown.

The Halliday Brand

United Artists; 79 minutes; Producer: Collier Young; Director: Joseph H. Lewis; Cast: Joseph Cotten; Ward Bond; Bill Williams; Viveca Lindfors; Betsy Blair; Christopher Dark; Jeanette Nolan; Jay C. Flippen ***

The intensity never lets up in Joseph H. Lewis' minimalistic, psychological *noir* Western in which estranged son Joseph Cotten, a fugitive from justice, is brought back to the family ranch by sibling Bill Williams for a conciliatory meeting with their dying father, lawman Ward Bond. But is it that easy to forgive or forget? In flashback, we see for ourselves just what a tyrannical bigot the patriarch was (and still is), destroying everything around him: He objects to Betsy Blair's involvement with half breed Christopher Dark, getting him jailed on a trumped-up charge of rustling and stampeding 3,000 head of cattle, the wrangler lynched by a mob; Cotten's growing attachment to half-Indian Viveca Lindfors is also shouted down and to cap it all, Bond kills Dark's father in a showdown. Cotten, alienated by Bond's unrelieved vitriol and pure hatred, becomes an outlaw in an attempt to get his father to throw in his badge, Bond forced to hunt down his own son; it culminates in a fistfight between the pair, Bond suffering a stroke. Back to the present, and Cotten, Williams and Blair walk away from their monster of a father when he drags himself out of bed and pulls a gun on Cotten but refuses to fire; cruel to the very end, he collapses dead on the bedroom floor as they depart the home with Lindfors. It's not a comfortable movie to watch, Stanley Wilson's operatic score pumping up the characters' angst, ensuring that you are left as emotionally drained as they are after 80 minutes-worth of Bond's ranting and raving, but the performances, as you would expect from this cast, are exceptional, as is Ray Rennahan's pristine black-and-white photography.

Dialogue:
Cotten to Bond, having well and truly run out of patience: "You can spew your poison on yourself. You're gonna die alone … we're all leaving."

Trivia:
Bond, playing Cotten's father, was only two years older than his fellow actor.

The Hard Man

Columbia; Technicolor; 80 minutes; Producer: Helen Ainsworth; Director: George Sherman; Cast: Guy Madison; Lorne Greene; Valerie French; Robert Burton; Barry Atwater; Rudy Bond; Frank Richards; Rickie Sorensen ***

Ex-Texas Ranger Guy Madison *doesn't* bring 'em in alive, preferring to shoot first and face an inquiry later ("They all died resisting arrest," is his explanation). Assigned as deputy sheriff to keep law and order in El Solito alongside Robert Burton, Madison finds his patience (and itchy trigger finger) tested to extreme limits by Lorne Greene, an ambitious cattle baron who wants to control the territory, bringing in gunslingers to sort out the opposition. But Madison is a former gunslinger himself, dispatching henchman Rudy Bond with ease; Greene stomps around his ranch fuming, his promiscuous wife, Valerie French, throwing herself at Madison and weakling Barry Atwater in an effort to escape her bullying husband's clutches. French was also behind the frame-up of Myron Healey, shot dead by Madison for a murder he didn't commit, and is being investigated for the crime behind her back. In a rather lame showdown, Madison takes care of hired gunfighter John Cason and French puts three slugs into Greene for good measure, leaving Madison to ride off with young Rickie Sorensen whose father was murdered by Greene's jackals. Madison is solid, Greene puffs and bellows and French plays her "cold-hearted wife of tyrannical rancher" role to perfection, but the picture runs out of steam in the last 20 minutes and should have ended on a higher note.

Dialogue:
Burton to Madison who's going to face gunman Bond in the hotel saloon: "Steve. This is Rodman. You don't stand a chance."
Madison: "That's something I'm gonna find out."

Hell Canyon Outlaws

Republic; 72 minutes; Producer: Thomas F. Woods; Director: Paul Landres; Cast: Dale Robertson; Brian Keith; Don Megowan; Mike Lane; Buddy Baer; Charles Fredericks; Dick Kallman; Rossana Rory *****

Relieved of his job as sheriff of Goldridge ("You're fired. You've had your day. Times change."), fast draw Dale Robertson, with partner Charles Fredericks, sits back in the sun and watches as smirking outlaw Brian Keith and his three compatriots (Don Megowan, Mike Lane and Buddy Baer) ride into town, bent on causing maximum chaos ("We wait three years for somethin' to do and they show up after we get fired," says Robertson ruefully to Fredericks). With the horrified townsfolk powerless to act, horses and saddles are stolen, occupied hotel rooms commandeered and wrecked, citizens intimidated and beaten up, shots fired, card tables taken over and whiskey and clothes purloined without payment. Makeshift sheriff Alexander Lockwood balks at the task of facing up to these four hard cases, regretting the day when the town council dispensed with Robertson's services, and quick gun. Young punk Dick Kallman, anxious to be a deputy, is shot dead by Keith in a standoff while blonde Rossana Rory pleads with Robertson not to take action, which he ignores; someone has to sort this problem out, besides which Keith's constant needling has got under his skin. A lengthy nighttime climax sees Robertson, with Fredericks' help, dispatch Lane, Baer and Megowan in the hotel saloon bar; lamps are lit and Robertson challenges Keith. Two shots are fired; Keith lies dead, Robertson is wounded, walking off with Fredericks and Rory and reinstated as Goldridge's law officer. A volatile actioner from Republic, laconic, slow-drawl Robertson proving a likeable Western star, whether he was playing good guys or bad guys; Paul Landres' spare direction, Irving Gertz's moody score and a witty script all contribute to a terrific B-oater where every single second counts.

Highlights:

Six-foot-seven Baer, six-foot-six Megowan, six-foot-five Lane and six-foot Keith swaggering down the street, hands hovering over gun butts—no wonder Goldridge's citizens fled indoors!

Dialogue:

Robertson to Keith: "I ain't sheriff no more."
Keith: "You got a new sheriff here in town?"
Robertson: "Yep."
Keith: "He ain't anybody famous, is he, like Pat Garrett or somthin'?"
Robertson: "He ain't no Pat Garrett, that's for sure."

Trivia:

"Introducing Dick Kallman," said the credits, but the actor was to die in shocking circumstances; at the age of 46, he and his business partner were shot to death during a robbery at their Manhattan apartment on February 22, 1980.

Hell's Crossroads

Republic; Naturama; 73 minutes; Producer: Rudy Ralston; Director: Franklin Adreon; Cast: Stephen McNally; Peggie Castle; Henry Brandon; Barton MacLane; Robert Vaughn; Harry Shannon; Grant Withers; Myron Healey ****

Over 40 movies have been made featuring the life and times of outlaw Jesse James; *Hell's Crossroads*, directed by Franklin Adreon (he spent most of his career in television) is one of the better of the low-budget efforts, containing pristine widescreen photography from John L. Russell, Jr., one of Orson Welles' favorite cinematographers, and a grim stock score to match the somber mood. Commencing with a tense raid on Muncie's express office by the James and Younger boys, gang member Stephen McNally is wounded in the leg, recuperating at Jesse's (Henry Brandon) house. But McNally (he rode with Quantrill's Raiders) isn't welcome when he turns up at ex-girlfriend Peggie Castle's homestead with her brother, Bob Ford (Robert Vaughn). Dad Harry Shannon wants nothing to do with McNally romancing his daughter and from thereon in, John K. Butler and Barry Shipman's involved screenplay focuses on attempts to bring Jesse James to justice, Sheriff Grant Withers and Pinkerton detective Barton MacLane on the outlaw's trail, McNally and Vaughn promised clemency by the governor of Missouri if James is brought in alive or dead. Shannon looks more kindly on McNally when the

The Romantic Story of the Fabulous Outlaw JESSE JAMES!

Hell's Crossroads

REPUBLIC PICTURES presents a **NATURAMA** Picture starring
STEPHEN McNALLY · PEGGIE CASTLE · ROBERT VAUGHN
with BARTON MacLANE · HARRY SHANNON · HENRY BRANDON · DOUGLAS KENNEDY · GRANT WITHERS · MYRON HEALEY
Screenplay by JOHN K. BUTLER & BARRY SHIPMAN · Story by JOHN K. BUTLER · Produced by RUDY RALSTON · Directed by FRANKLIN ADREON

James and Younger gang save Vaughn from a lynch mob in Rayville, Vaughn ("The dirty little coward.") repaying the debt by shooting the notorious outlaw in the back as he's erecting a Christmas tree in his parlor. Following another shoot-out, the Youngers are wiped out, Frank James (Douglas Kennedy) is pardoned as part of an amnesty bill and McNally recovers in bed from a wound, taking up where he left off with Castle. A terrific cast turns in telling performances in a strong, adult-themed oater from Republic that packs quite a gritty punch.

Dialogue:
Brandon to McNally: "A man runnin' around with a bullet hole in his leg can wind up at the bottom end of a rope."

Joe Dakota

Universal; Eastmancolor; 79 minutes; Producer: Howard Christie; Director: Richard H. Bartlett; Cast: Jock Mahoney; Luana Patten; Charles McGraw; Claude Akins; Lee Van Cleef; Barbara Lawrence; Paul Birch; Anthony Caruso ***

Jock Mahoney, minus a revolver, canters into the one-horse town of Arborville, chats to Luana Patten, the only person around, rides over to where Charles McGraw and his gang are drilling for oil and begins firing off questions—lots of questions. Upended into a pool of oil, the taciturn stranger cleans up in town by washing in a water trough and stirs the seeds of unrest when the men and their women return. Who are you, demands McGraw, and what are you here for? Mahoney's there because an old Indian that once resided on his property, a scout he befriended in his army days, used Mahoney's real name of Joe Dakota as he was unable to write and signed over the deeds to McGraw with what amounted to be forged papers; the land, and the oil well, belongs to Mahoney, and no one else ("He sold you land he had no right to sell."). McGraw and the townsfolk lynched the Indian for apparently molesting Patten, but this was fabricated by McGraw to enable him to claim the property as his own, although he states that he never knew oil existed there. In the final reel, the well erupts, everyone is plastered in oil, Mahoney slugs McGraw and a match is put to the gusher, setting the well ablaze. The contrite citizens, now aware of their faults, view Mahoney in a different light, the tall stranger visiting the old Indian's grave with Patten (who thinks he's "nice.") to ensure that he will never be forgotten. Ex-stuntman Mahoney, in Gary Cooper mode, does a good job in a variation of John Sturges' *Bad Day at Black Rock*, the picture played out on comedic lines at first and featuring an infuriatingly catchy score. Even screen bad guys Claude Akins and Lee Van Cleef are reasonably funny, especially in their "knock each other off the stool" scene.

Highlights:

Mahoney returning to town coated in black, glistening oil, looking as though he has just escaped from a Universal horror movie.

Dialogue:

McGraw to Mahoney: "What's an Indian against an oil well?"

Trivia:

The two sequences involving oil used real oil and were shot in tandem over three days; Mahoney claimed it took him a full two weeks scrubbing to clear his body of the mess.

Last Stagecoach West

Ventura/Republic; Naturama; 67 minutes; Producer: Rudy Ralston; Director: Joseph Kane; Cast: Jim Davis; Mary Castle; Victor Jory; Lee Van Cleef; Roy Barcroft; Grant Withers; Glenn Strange; Willis Bouchey ***

Shark-faced Victor Jory, made up to look twice his age, played the embittered leader of a gang terrorizing railroad property, their activities forcing the Railroad Protection Association to enlist the aid of investigator Jim Davis; he's ordered to travel to Cedar City and unravel the brains behind the crimes which include cattle rustling, bank and express office holdups and the wrecking of rail tracks. Jory is aggrieved that he lost his stage line franchise to the railroad and found himself up to his eyes in debt, employing ex-Quantrill Raider Roy Barcroft and Lee Van Cleef as his right-hand men. Van Cleef hankers after Jory's daughter, Mary Castle, but when hunk Davis appears on the scene, the snake-eyed one is rudely shunted to one side by Castle who sets her sights on the tall, deep-voiced stranger. In a raid on a rival rancher's cattle arranged by Jory, Barcroft is shot dead; Davis, convinced that Jory is the gang's ringleader *and* the mysterious man in black who keeps turning up at shoot-outs, plans a trap in the form of a train holdup. During the robbery, Glenn Strange's posse arrives and, following a gunfight, Jory and Van Cleef are both wounded, fleeing to Jory's ranch. "I organized the gang. The gold will pay off our bank debts," confesses Jory to Castle before expiring. Van Cleef's wedding proposal rejected by Castle, the rat goes to run off with the stolen loot but falls to Davis' bullet. Mission accomplished, Davis weds Castle without any further preliminaries. Produced on a $150,000 budget, Joseph Kane's actioner is lively Western fodder, Davis, Jory, Van Cleef and Barcroft all in fine fettle, California's Towsley Canyon region making for an attractive backdrop.

Dialogue:
Davis to agency chief Willis Bouchey: "I've got a new boss ... come in, dear. Mister Bryceson, I want you to have the pleasure of meeting the person who'll be giving me all my orders from now on. Mrs. Bill Cameron."

The Lonely Man

Paramount; VistaVision; 88 minutes; Producer: Pat Duggan; Director: Henry Levin; Cast: Jack Palance; Anthony Perkins; Neville Brand; Robert Middleton; Elaine Aiken; Claude Akins; Lee Van Cleef; Elisha Cook, Jr. ****

Reformed killer Jack Palance has earned himself a big reputation, but not with his estranged son, resentful Anthony Perkins. He walked out on Perkins and his mother years back, his wife jumping to her death into a ravine five years ago ("A killer's wife doesn't have friends."). Palance wishes to mend broken fences but sulky Perkins doesn't want to know and neither do the citizens of Red Bluff, booting Palance out of town ("We don't want no gunfighters here."). Meanwhile, in a cabin up in the hills, surly Neville Brand polishes the slug from Palance's gun that maimed him, thirsting for retribution. Henry Levin's taut oater focuses on the fractured Palance/Perkins relationship, rancher Elaine Aiken Palance's woman, the blonde attracting the attention of gauche Perkins, ranch hand Robert Middleton trying to keep the peace between all three. A chance meeting with Claude Akins and his horse thieves shows Perkins just how quick on the draw his father is, the lad finally growing up fast in a showdown at Brand's old King Fisher Bonanza saloon when he helps Palance, slowly going blind, to gun down coyotes Brand, Lee Van Cleef, Elisha Cook, Jr. and Adam Williams. The picture ends on a sudden bleak, sad note, Perkins grieving over Palance's body, Aiken looking on in despair. Handsomely shot in pristine black-and-white around Lone Pine's Alabama Hill region in VistaVision (Oscar-winner Lionel Lindon) and boosted by Van Cleave's noisy score, *The Lonely Man* is a mood piece strong on acting performances: Palance is terrific, as is Perkins and Aiken, while Brand, Akins and Van Cleef demonstrate what being a bad guy in a Western was all about.

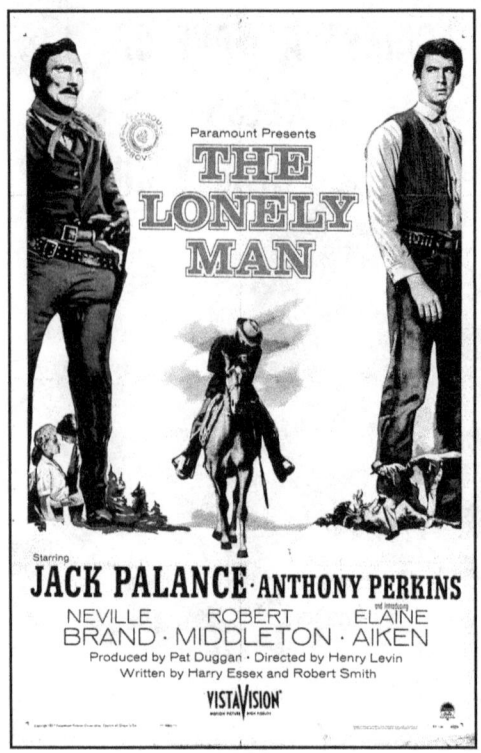

Highlights:
A tense human drama taking place beneath the towering snow-capped Sierra Mountains.

Dialogue:
Palance to Perkins, in town: "Where you goin'?"
Perkins: "Feed myself."
Palance: "Man feeds his horse first."
Perkins: "I gotta lot to learn—not from you."

Trivia:
This was Spanish-born Aiken's film debut; she only starred in another four movies.

Oregon Passage

Allied Artists; CinemaScope/DeLuxecolor; 80 minutes; Producer: Lindsley Parsons; Director: Paul Landres; Cast: John Ericson; Lola Albright; Toni Gerry; Edward Platt; Rachel Ames; Paul Fierro; H.M. Wynant; Jon Shepodd ****

Vivid widescreen location shooting around Oregon's Deschutes National Forest (photographer: Ellis W. Carter) and a stirring Paul Dunlap soundtrack ensure that *Oregon Passage* is a cut above the average cavalry versus Indians yarn. In 1871, renegade Shoshone

Black Eagle (H.M. Wynant) is the only Indian in the area refusing to make peace. Lieutenant John Ericson, leading a raiding detail, brings Wynant's virgin bride Little Deer (Toni Gerry) back to the fort and finds himself up against a strict new commanding officer, Edward Platt. Platt, a stubborn martinet, plays it by the book ("The army doesn't rescue Indians. It destroys them."); when he discovers that, five years back, his wife (Lola Albright) had a fling with Ericson, he does his best to make life as uncomfortable as possible for the young officer. Former commander Harvey Stephens is escorted out of the fort to face a court martial for being drunk on duty and returns on his horse, butchered, but Platt still refuses to listen to common sense, resulting in another troop massacre in which he's wounded. Scout Paul Fierro reports that much-needed reinforcements are not forthcoming from Fort Rock and dishy Albright's overtures to Ericson concerning deserting the army to live abroad with her, plus a $20,000 incentive, are turned down flat ("You only care about one person—yourself."). Albright, out riding, is captured by Wynant's braves, Platt staggering over to their camp and shooting his wife dead before a Shoshone knife does its worst; he's then hacked to pieces by a screaming mob of Redskins. In a climactic showdown outside the fort, the Indians are annihilated in a trap devised by Ericson, the lieutenant engaging in a fierce struggle with the chief, suffocating him in the dirt. The utterly delectable Gerry hitches herself to Ericson and fellow officer Jon Shepodd hitches himself to Rachel Ames, the end to a sturdy, picturesque actioner that looks good on a big screen, even today.

Highlights:
Oregon's forested Bend region forms a glorious backdrop to the well-filmed action set pieces.

Dialogue:
Ericson to Albright: "I'm a professional soldier, Sylvia."
Albright: "I like you better when you act like a professional lover."

Outlaw's Son

Bel-Air/United Artists; 88 minutes; Producer: Howard W. Koch; Director: Lesley Selander; Cast: Dane Clark; Ben Cooper; Joseph Stafford; Ellen Drew; Lori Nelson; Charles Watts; Cecile Rogers; Les Mitchel ****

Wanted bad man Dane Clark rides into Plainsville to see his 12-year-old son (Joseph Stafford), brought up by his aunt, Ellen Drew. He abandoned the boy when he was four months old, but Drew resents his visit, not wishing the lad to rub shoulders with a criminal ("He doesn't need you," she says to Clark). "You're not my father!" shouts Stafford, but his feelings soon change to hero-worship when Clark teaches him how to use his Colt .44. "Call me a vindictive old maid" fumes Drew, living up to that description by maliciously blaming the murder of a bank official on Clark when his old bunch robs the joint; Clark, who had nothing to do with the job, is placed behind bars but escapes. Ten years later, Clark is a fugitive on the run south of the border, his son (now Ben Cooper) a hotheaded deputy, mistreating those he apprehends, much to Sheriff Charles Watts' dismay. The young punk is romancing demure store girl Cecile Rogers *and* feisty cattle rancher Lori Nelson; when he learns of Drew's lies about his father ("I did it for you," she sobs), he chucks in his badge and hits the outlaw trail with Les Mitchel and his gang, prompting Clark to return to Plainsville in an attempt to steer Cooper back on the straight and narrow. During the Silver City payroll holdup that goes wrong, Mitchel fatally wounds Clark before getting a knife in the back; Clark dies in bed, Drew (now forgiven for her deceit) promising to look out for Cooper who decides to take up with man-hungry Nelson. A solid oater intelligently scripted by Richard Alan Simmons, *Outlaw's Son* demonstrates, yet again, that Lesley Selander certainly knew how to string a decent Western together.

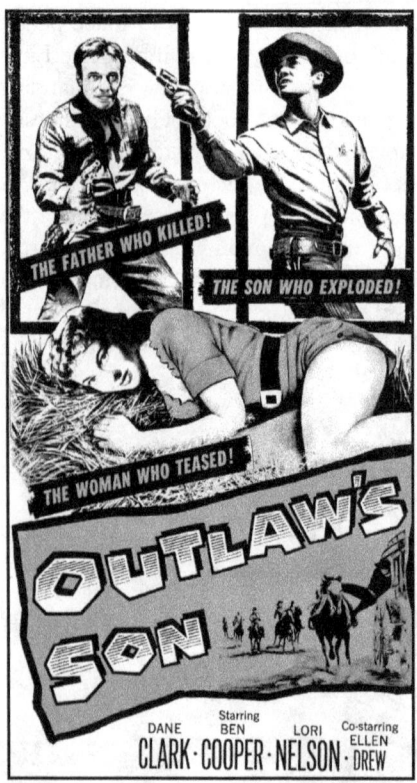

Dialogue:
Clark, sneering at Cooper: "A man with a gun!"
Cooper, spitting back: "You slung one long enough."

Quantez

Universal; CinemaScope/Eastmancolor; 81 minutes; Producer: Gordon Kay; Director: Harry Keller; Cast: Fred MacMurray; Dorothy Malone; John Gavin; John Larch; Michael Ansara; Sydney Chaplin; James Barton; Tony Urchal ***

Filmed in Arizona's arid Sonoita territory (photography: Carl E. Guthrie) and featuring a strident Herman Stein score, *Quantez* has a terrific beginning and end—what comes in the middle lacks a certain amount of passion and is too talkative, R. Wright Campbell's script dragging the action to a standstill. En route to Mexico, four robbers and a girl enter the deserted ghost town of Quantez, a splendid atmospheric opener; unknown to them, the place is surrounded by Apaches, led by Delgadito (Michael Ansara), and only untrustworthy Sydney Chaplin, raised by Cochise's tribe ("A man without people."), knows how to deal with them. Inside the derelict saloon, distraught Dorothy Malone, John Larch's moll, sobs and screams her head off every five minutes, throwing herself at Fred MacMurray and then young John Gavin in an attempt to get one of the men to take her out of the godforsaken place; angry, punch-happy Larch, forever on the prod, antagonizes MacMurray and Gavin and wandering minstrel/painter James Barton turns up to dampen the histrionics, only to leave 10 minutes later. Treacherous Chaplin is finished off by the Indians when they break into town, MacMurray, a once-famous gunslinger, outdrawing Larch and riding out with Malone and Gavin, Ansara and his braves in pursuit. In a lively finale, Gavin and Malone clamber down a rickety broken bridge into the depths of a ravine while MacMurray, wounded in the leg and picking off the marauding Redskins, desperately cuts the bridge's rope supports to save his companions; he succeeds, but pays with his life. Those glorious opening and closing sequences, plus six-foot Larch's towering performance as the unhinged thug with a gun, make *Quantez* far better than the *New York Time*'s savage put-down: "Static, turgid, claptrap … bites the dust long before Indians converge." No, Western fans, it ain't as bad as all that.

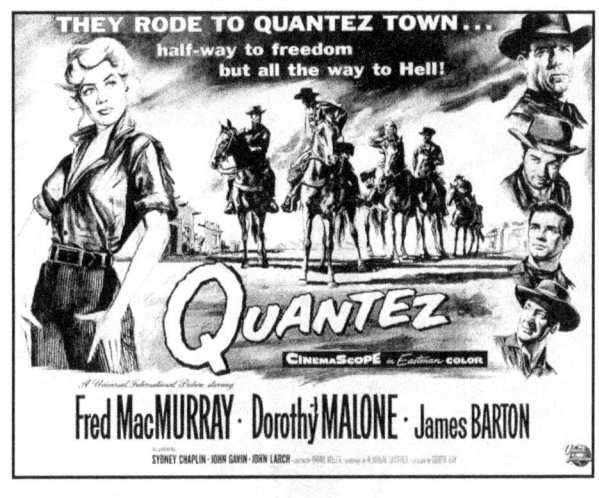

Highlights:
Guthrie's bleached-out color tones mirroring Sonoita's dusty, rocky, sun-blasted terrain, in eye-catching CinemaScope.

Dialogue:
Chaplin to MacMurray, about their chances of making it out of the ghost town alive: "All things are clearer in the sun."
MacMurray: "I'm hopin' we get to see it."

Trivia:
MacMurray didn't particularly like being around horses, finding the scene where he bathed his steed's legs in soothing water uncomfortable to shoot.

The Quiet Gun

Regal Films/20th Century Fox; RegalScope; 77 minutes; Producer: Earle Lyon; Director: William F. Claxton; Cast: Forrest Tucker; Jim Davis; Lee Van Cleef; Mara Corday; Hank Worden; Tom Brown; Lewis Martin; Kathleen Crowley *****

Sneering Lee Van Cleef rides into Rock River, demands that Hank Worden tends to his horse and roughs the old boy up until Sheriff Forrest Tucker arrives on the scene; Van Cleef backs off, Tucker's mean expression speaking volumes. Saloon owner Tom Brown has brought Van Cleef into town, the pair planning to oust Tucker's friend Jim Davis from his ranch and use it for cattle rustling by instructing attorney Lewis Martin to issue the rancher with a lawsuit for indecency and immoral conduct. An Indian

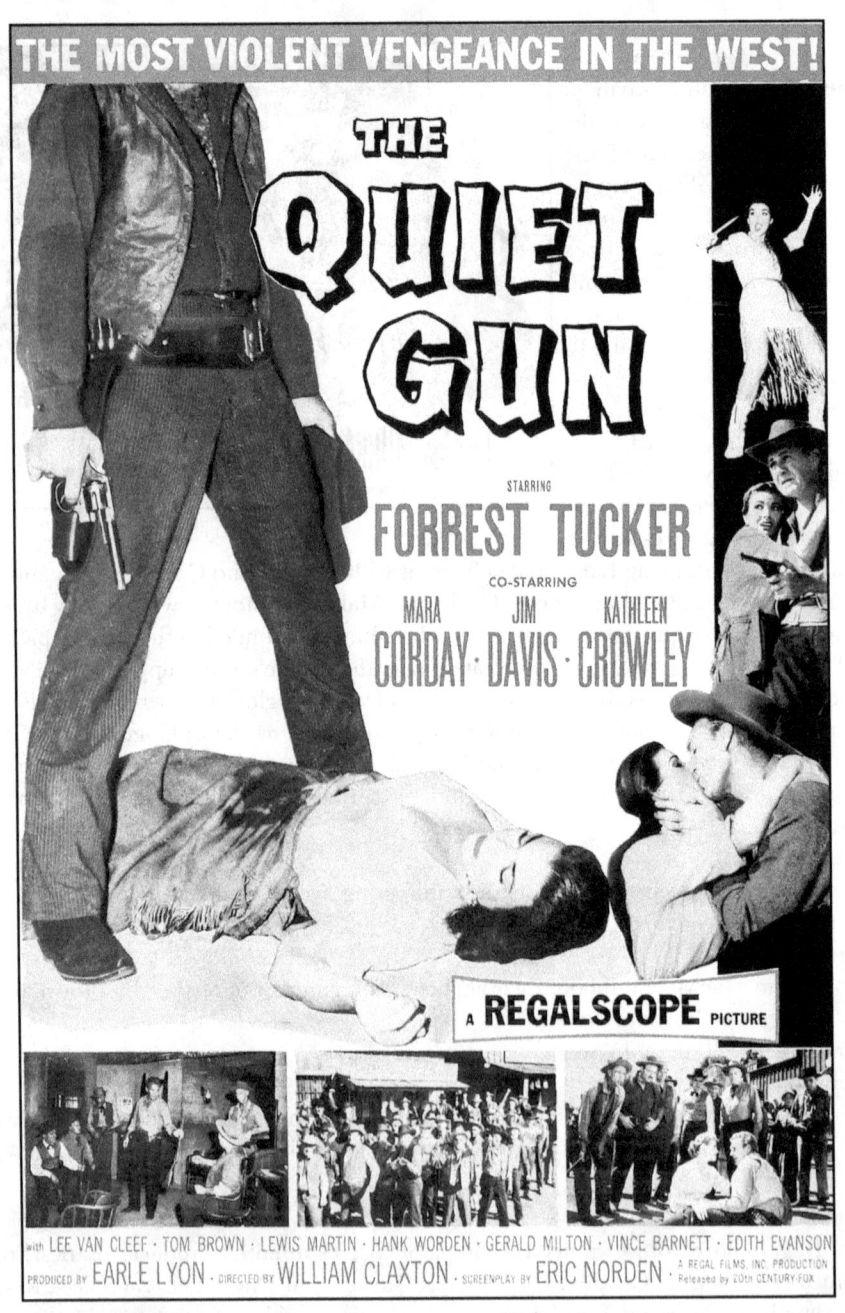

woman, Mara Corday, is living with Davis and loves him ("It looks bad. People are talking," states Martin), his wife (Kathleen Crowley) having temporarily walked out, and the town is in an uproar. But volatile Davis is handy with a gun, Tucker warning the lawyer to tread carefully. In a meeting at the ranch, Martin stupidly reaches for a rifle; Davis plugs him and the indignant citizens are outraged, particularly when Tucker lays the blame at their door, not Davis'. Matters worsen when Tucker is slugged by a mob and Davis hanged; Tucker arrests two men involved, shoots a third and sticks another three behind bars, deputizing Worden. Crowley returns to Red Rock (she once romanced Tucker), Tucker calls for a circuit judge and blacksmith Gerald Milton demands that the prisoners be released, but Tucker turns the table on troublemaker Milton and his righteous council members—he pins a star on each one of them, thus ensuring they obey the law (his law) and keep the simmering tension under control. At Davis' ranch, Van Cleef assaults Corday, the lass turning a gun on herself and receiving a fatal wound; she tells Crowley about Brown and Van Cleef's scheming before dying. At their trial, all five prisoners receive three years in the pen, the judge accusing the townsfolk of being just as guilty ("A bleak and black town on the map."). In the street, Tucker calls out Brown and Van Cleef ("I want you for murder."): Van Cleef runs out from the right, Brown on a horse from the left; Tucker gets them both, two bullets each, but is wounded, the grateful (at last) townsfolk gathering round their fallen sheriff. A terrific, low-budget, slow burning Western from Regal, shot in their RegalScope format: Tucker, looking as though he has the weight of the world on his shoulders.

Highlights:
Forrest Tucker at his world-weary best, and that's saying something.

Dialogue:
Milton to Tucker in the jailhouse: "Carl. If you don't let them men out, I'll take the keys and do it myself."
Tucker: "Yeah. You do that, Harold. You gotta choice. You can get yourself killed, join 'em or back down. What'll it be?"

Raiders of Old California

Republic; 72 minutes; Produced and Directed by Albert C. Gannaway; Cast: Jim Davis; Arleen Whelan; Lee Van Cleef; Faron Young; Marty Robbins; Louis Jean Heydt; Harry Lauter; Laurence Dobkin ***

Following a fierce skirmish between Mexican and American troops in 1847, cavalry officer Jim Davis spares Mexican supremo Laurence Dobkin's life and releases the fort commander on one condition—he signs his land deeds over to him. The war ended and now a civilian, Davis, as the new land owner, tramples all over Mexican farmers in the territories of Arizona and California, throwing them off their land, and if they put up any kind of resistance, psycho gunman Lee Van Cleef will ensure that they never see another sunset. In rides circuit judge Louis Jean Heydt and his son, Marshal Faron Young, to expose Davis as a cheat, bring him to justice and ensure the Mexicans are given back their properties. Rough around the edges, historically inaccurate and boasting an ear-splitting stock soundtrack by Hugo Friedhofer and Geordie Hormel, *Raiders of Old California* just about scrapes through in a basic kinda way thanks to Jim Davis' towering presence, a sadistic turn from Van Cleef and Country and Western singer Faron Young's sharpshooting, smartly dressed lawman. Davis, having been charged with high treason and unlawfully obtaining land grants among other things, is trampled to death in a climactic stampede he organized, his men vanishing from the scene once they hear of his death. The Mexicans are now able to move back into their former homesteads.

Dialogue:
Davis to Harry Lauter who is unsure about the legality of grabbing Dobkin's land title papers: "Now you either sign this deed or you're gonna be listed as one of our casualties."

Trivia:
Young, nicknamed "The Singing Sheriff," had a number of C&W hits during the 1950s and a sporadic film career, committing suicide on December 9, 1996 through depression.

The Restless Breed

Renown Pictures; Eastmancolor; 86 minutes; Producer: Edward L. Alperson; Director: Allan Dwan; Cast: Scott Brady; Anne Bancroft; Leo Gordon; Jay C. Flippen; Jim Davis; Rhys Williams; Scott Marlowe; Myron Healey **

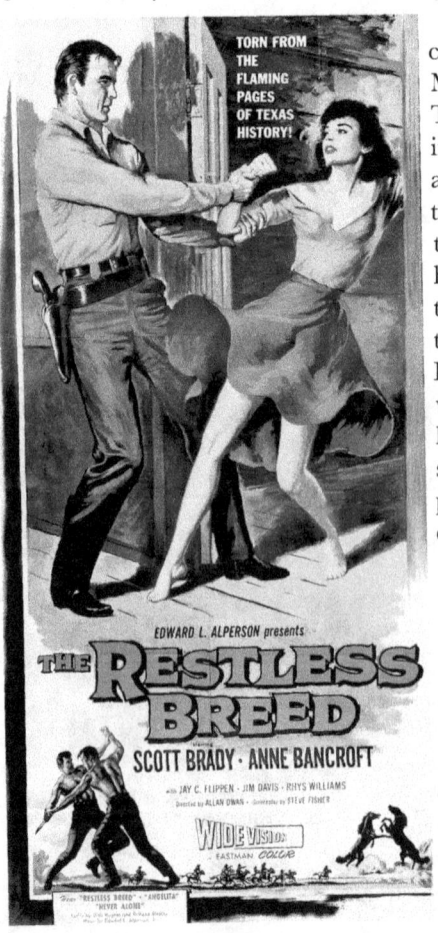

1865: Newton's Raiders, a bunch of cold-blooded killers, are supplying Emperor Maximilian's army with guns across the Texas/Mexico border and have murdered an investigating secret service agent. The dead agent's son, Scott Brady, is assigned to travel to the lawless town of Mission and bring in the leader of the gang, Jim Davis. Once there, he falls for dancing lass Anne Bancroft, under the care of Reverend Rhys Williams, and has to deal with Davis' thugs, headed by snarling Leo Gordon, before facing Davis, the man who killed his father. Allan Dwan's strange little oater is virtually confined to a town stage set and, the theme music (written by the producer's son) is catchy but overplayed to death throughout the entire picture. Bancroft, at 25, is too mature to star as a virginal teenager with an almighty crush on broad-shouldered 32-year-old Brady (Williams deeply disapproves of the relationship), the agent going off the rails, hitting the bottle and acting like one of Newton's Raiders himself, gunning down anyone who stands in his way. Good support comes in the shape of Myron Healey, another Mission sheriff to last all of one day, Jay C. Flippen, a lawman who also bites the dust, Gordon, a bruising bully throwing his considerable weight around and Davis, the sneering outlaw boss who meets his end in a saloon shoot-out with Brady. Scott Marlowe, Davis' furtive resident spy, is irritating as a would-be gunslinger lurking behind doors and peering through windows, while expressionless Brady, the main star, has just about enough charisma to hold it all together. The twitchy gunfights are worth a look, though.

Dialogue:
Brady to Bancroft: "Anyone would think I was a professional gunman."
Bancroft: "Aren't you?"
Brady: "No. Disappointed?"

The Ride Back

Associates and Aldrich Company/United Artists; 79 minutes; Producer: William Conrad; Directors: Allen H. Miner and Oscar Rudolph (uncredited); Cast: Anthony Quinn; William Conrad; Lita Milan; Victor Millan; Ellen Hope Monroe; Jorge Treviño; Louis Towers; Joe Dominguez ****

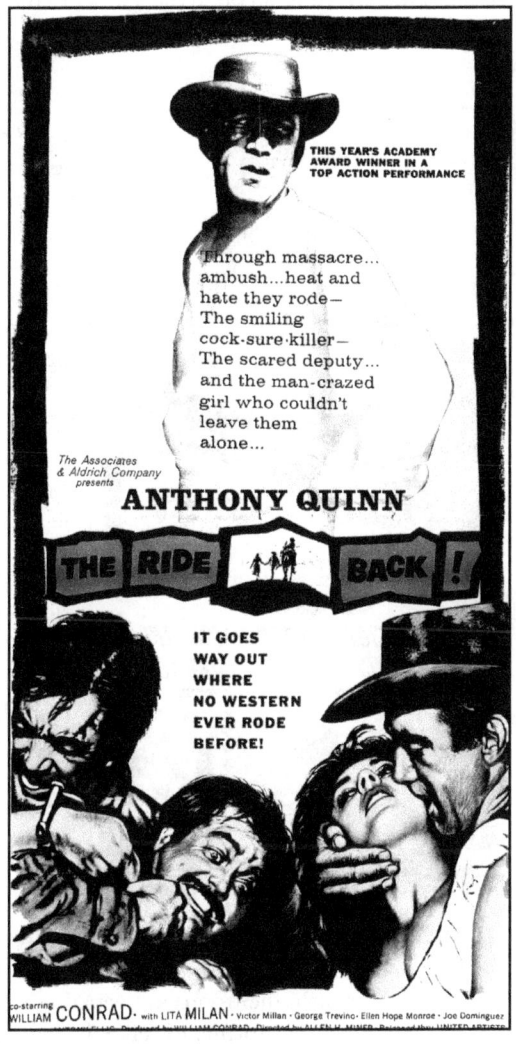

Allen H. Miner's psychological mood piece is similar to his work on George Montgomery's *Black Patch* (WB, 1957), a dark, *noir*-type Western a world away from the usual colorful blood-and-thunder oaters of the day. Anthony Quinn, toning down his usual larger-than-life performances, is a killer on the lam in Mexico, trailed by Sheriff William Conrad, a man who hasn't done a thing right in his miserable life, failed marriage, failed jobs, failed relationships. Bringing back Quinn alive over the Texas border for a fair trial will, he hopes, redeem himself and his personal esteem (Quinn claims he shot his victim in self-defense). Captured and cuffed, Quinn is escorted across hostile country, niggling at Conrad all the way and questioning his bravery, the pair menaced by a group of drunken Apaches. Rescuing a young girl from a family massacre, Conrad is wounded and reluctantly hands his gun to Quinn who dispatches the Indians and decides to ride into Scottsville with the lawman to take his medicine, both men having formed a bond of sorts. Surreal black-and-white photography (Joseph F. Biroc) and taut handling of the spare material make for an offbeat Western gem—just get past that irritating opening ballad over the credits and you're in for a treat.

Highlights:
Biroc's striking monochrome photography and Quinn in full flight, always worth the price of a ticket.

Dialogue:
Conrad: "You afraid of Indians, Kallen?"
Quinn: "No more than you're afraid of me."

Trivia:
Conrad starred in the radio program *Gunsmoke* from 1952 to 1961 but was considered too short to play Matt Dillon in the TV series that ran from 1955-1975—James Arness made the role his own.

Run of the Arrow

RKO-Radio; RKO-Scope/Technicolor; 86 minutes; Produced and Directed by Samuel Fuller; Cast: Rod Steiger; Brian Keith; Sara Montiel; Ralph Meeker; Charles Bronson; Jay C. Flippen; H.M. Wynant; Tim McCoy ***

Palm Sunday, 1865: Graycoat Rod Steiger fires the last shot on the final day of the Civil War at Union officer Ralph Meeker, saving the bullet plucked from his unconscious body. Depressed at losing the war, Steiger, a rebel without a cause, heads off into the West, joining Charles Bronson's Sioux tribe after undergoing the run of the arrow ritual with aging Indian scout Jay C. Flippen and surviving the ordeal. Wed to squaw Sara Montiel, the Irishman is given the job of scouting for the U.S. cavalry; General Tim McCoy wants a fort built further West, Steiger ensuring that the blockade doesn't encroach on Sioux land and specifically their buffalo hunting grounds. But hothead Meeker is still around, an Indian-hating bigot who begins to erect a post deep in Sioux nation territory following the death of engineer Brian Keith (providing the picture's moral stance); he also wants Steiger hanged. In a bloody skirmish, the troops are wiped out, the fort destroyed. Screaming as he's skinned alive, Meeker's torment is ended when Steiger uses the bullet dug out of him to put him out of his misery; realizing that he's not really a Sioux at heart, Steiger rides off with Montiel, their adopted son and the wounded survivors. Typical violent

Samuel Fuller fare (he wrote the script) which, in Europe, ran into censorship problems; many countries passed it with an adult certificate while in Britain, it was unaccountably released as a "U" (suitable for all) after several minor cuts. Filmed in Arizona and Utah, the movie, an early precursor to *Dances With Wolves*, possessed a stark reality and the Sioux raid on Fort Lincoln was extremely bloody for its time (the scene of the sergeant falling into a quicksand after rescuing the Indian boy was equally harrowing). But for many, it remained oddly unpleasant, method actor Steiger overemphasizing everything he did and said to the nth degree, his faux Irish accent downright peculiar (but that was the man's style). RKO sold the rights to Universal-International which is why, in the United Kingdom, this bullish Western could often be found sharing the bill with one of Universal's X-rated horror features of the period; I caught it in 1964, double billed with *Revenge of the Creature*.

Highlights:
The exciting, though gory, Sioux assault on Fort Lincoln plus Bronson's incredible pumped-up physique, oiled muscles glistening in the sun.

Dialogue:
McCoy to Steiger: "Well, I must say it's the first time I've ever met an Irish Indian."

Trivia:
A stand-in was used for close-ups of Steiger's torn feet during the arrow run sequence; the actor had sprained an ankle prior to filming.

The Storm Rider

Regal Films/20th Century Fox; RegalScope; 72 minutes; Producer: Bernard Glasser; Director: Edward Bernds; Cast: Scott Brady; Mala Powers; Bill Williams; John Goddard; George Keymas; Roy Engel; William Fawcett; Hank Patterson ****

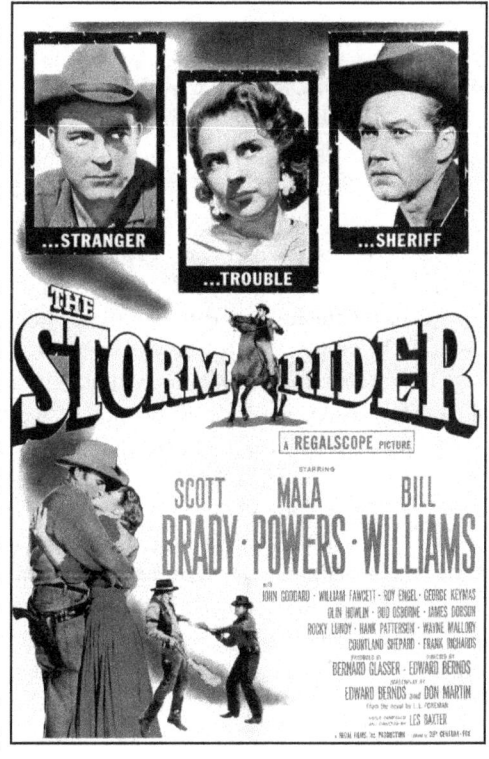

Another fine example of a Regal Films' horse opera shot in their widescreen format RegalScope, scriptwriters Edwards Bernds and Don Martin concocting an involved screenplay, the narrative carried out to perfection by a solid cast. *The Storm Rider* had fast gun Scott Brady riding into town in a howling gale, only to be ordered by Sheriff Bill Williams to head on out at sunup. Brady killed local hero rancher Red Jim (in a fair fight, so it happens) a while back and will only cause more trouble if he hangs around. Next morning, in the OK saloon, Brady demonstrates his toughness by ejecting a gang of roughnecks. William Fawcett, head of a small-ranchers consortium, likes what he sees and promptly takes on Brady for his gun skills, the ranchers under threat from cattle baron Roy Engel, the bully refusing to allow them to graze their steers in peace on open range. Brady buys the nearby Easy Ace Ranch for a dollar, organizes the cutting down of Engel's fences and falls for Mala Powers, which creates its own problems. Williams loves the lass, so does Red Jim's brother, volatile John Goddard and Powers was married to Red Jim, unaware that Brady, whom she fancies like mad, was the man behind her husband's death ("A loudmouth with no guts," Brady calls him). When Hank Patterson is shot dead by one of Engel's men, Brady and Fawcett declare war; Engel reacts by hiring cattle association gunslinger George Keymas (The Apache Kid) to put a stop to the small ranchers' activities. Keymas, on the prod and thirsting for action, guns down James Dobson in the street; Engel, horrified, fires him and joins forces with Fawcett; and Brady, enraged at the senseless killing, has a showdown with Keymas, letting him have it with two slugs. Range hostilities over with, Brady rides off in the end, gritting his teeth and, with difficulty, rejecting Powers' pleading looks, leaving the girl to carry on her faltering romance with Williams. Composer Les Baxter uses the plaintive refrains of "Greensleeves" as a leitmotif throughout (it works) while Brady's quiet, understated role-playing works wonders in this minor league setup, his scenes with Powers containing quite a bit of sexual chemistry to set the pulses racing.

Highlights:

Keymas must have studied Jack Palance's performance in *Shane*; his Apache Kid is a dead ringer for Palance's Jack Wilson, an object lesson in how to play a villain one step away from the Devil himself.

Dialogue:

Brady to Keymas, facing each other in the street, hands poised over gun butts: "End of the line, kid. This is where you get off."

3:10 to Yuma

Columbia; 92 minutes; Producer: David Heilweil; Director: Delmer Daves; Cast: Glenn Ford; Van Heflin; Felicia Farr; Leora Dana; Robert Emhardt; Richard Jaeckel; Henry Jones; Ford Rainey ****

Broke cattle farmer Van Heflin, needing the $200 offered for the job (and maybe to prove he's a man to his wife and kids), elects to escort stagecoach robber Glenn Ford to Contention City and put him on the train to Yuma at 3:10 precisely; alcoholic Henry Jones is his disreputable companion, and Heflin has to run the gauntlet of Ford's gang, led by Richard Jaeckel, before the outlaw boards the locomotive. Mentioned in the same hallowed breath as *High Noon* and *Rio Bravo*, *3:10 to Yuma* hasn't aged quite as well as those two undisputed '50s Western classics, coming across now as a psychological *noir*-type drama rather than a straightforward shoot-'em-up, very talky (script: Halsted Welles) and slow-paced; many reckon that James Mangold's 2007 remake, with Russell Crowe and Christian Bale in the leads, beats it by a whisker. What Delmer Daves' oater has in its favor is great needle-sharp monochrome photography from Charles Lawton, Jr. (he utilized red filters to achieve that knife-edge effect) and two tremendous performances in the shape of Ford and Heflin, the latter almost reprising his down-to-earth character in *Shane*. The two play cat-and-mouse mind games in the hotel room they share as the minutes tick by, Ford's thousand-dollar bribes falling on stony ground; he eventually accompanies Heflin on the train without causing further trouble as thanks to the farmer for saving his life earlier. Atmospheric and tautly directed, this is a Western for adults, Britain's *Guardian* stating "A vivid, tense intelligent story … supremely efficient direction and playing."

Highlights:
Watching Ford and Heflin in their hotel room scenes, two consummate Hollywood legends showing an audience what understated acting was all about—less *is* more!

Dialogue:
Ford to Heflin: "I mean, I don't go round just shootin' people down. I work quiet, like you."
Heflin: "All right, so you're quiet like me. Well then, shut up like me."

Trivia:
Ford was offered Heflin's role but rejected it, preferring to be cast as the bad guy for a change.

The Tin Star

Paramount; VistaVision; 93 minutes; Producers: William Perlberg and George Seaton; Director: Anthony Mann; Cast: Henry Fonda; Anthony Perkins; Betsy Palmer; Michel Ray; Neville Brand; John McIntire; Mary Webster; James Bell ****

Tenderfoot sheriff Anthony Perkins needs all the help he can get in a town unofficially run by troublesome bully Neville Brand and his jackals; in canters bounty hunter Henry Fonda with a body, claims the $500 reward and reluctantly helps the youngster to

Westerns of the 1950s: The Classic Years   377

find his feet, even though the community resents his presence. Anthony Mann's taut, wordy psychological Western is rarely seen these days, filmed in deep black-and-white by Loyal Griggs (he won an Oscar for *Shane*) and containing a spare Elmer Bernstein score. Perkins not only has Brand to contend with but Lee Van Cleef and his brother who have just robbed a stage and shot Doc John McIntire in the back on the eve of his 70th birthday celebrations. Brand and his boys want the reward on the brothers' heads, forming a necktie party after the pair, holed up in a canyon, are captured by Perkins and Fonda, but in a tense standoff, Perkins' double guns outdraw Brand's double guns and the smarmy killer bites the dust. Steely-eyed Fonda rides away with widow Betsy Palmer and her son, Michel Ray, with whom he has formed a close bond, while Mary Webster makes plans to wed Perkins; the capable new lawman now has the town firmly under *his* control. "Quality Western," said *Variety* but then, did the mighty Fonda appear in anything else?

Highlights:
Perkins' lengthy climactic night showdown with Brand, as suspenseful as they come.
Dialogue:
Fonda's blunt advice to rookie Perkins: "You better take off that tin star and stay alive."
Trivia:
James Stewart was originally earmarked for Fonda's role of Morg Hickman, but bowed out at the last minute. And, as we all know, Perkins and McIntire both turned up three years later at the Bates Motel in Alfred Hitchcock's *Psycho*.

Tomahawk Trail aka Mark of the Apache

Bel-Air/United Artists; 60 minutes; Producer: Howard W. Koch; Director: Lesley Selander; Cast: Chuck Connors; John Smith; George Neise; Susan Cummings; Robert Knapp; Harry Dean Stanton; Lisa Montell; Eddie Little Sky ****

Following the death of their lieutenant, a weary platoon is lead through Apache-infested territory by replacement officer George Neise to hoped-for safety at Fort Bowie. The unhinged officer is at loggerheads with tough sergeant Chuck Connors; although a West Pointer, Neise is totally unfit for command, an incompetent, ranting and raving, unable to get to grips with the encroaching Redskins, the harsh climate, the tired, disgruntled men and the grueling trek. Connors, threatened with insubordination, relieves Neise of his command when he passes out through fatigue; the fort is reached, the detail discovering the stockade littered with corpses, the commanding officer pinned to the wall by a lance, Neise screaming at the body about Connors' possible board of enquiry and court martial. En route, they have picked up Susan Cummings, sole survivor of the Fort Defiance massacre, and Lisa Montell, daughter of Chief Victorio. During a climactic bloody attack, Neise is killed; Montell goes back to her people who depart and Connors kisses Cummings. Only an hour long, maybe, but Lesley Selander's vivid, economical Western (shot in Kanab, Utah) is low-budget filmmaking at its best: cinematography (William Margulies), music (Les Baxter), script (Gerald Drayson Adams and David Chandler) and performances all hit the right note; if only it had been just a little longer…

Dialogue:
Chuck Connors, narrating after the credits and setting the savage tone: "Lieutenant Merriman was dead, the brains cooked out of his skull over an Apache torture fire."

The True Story of Jesse James
20th Century Fox; CinemaScope/DeLuxecolor; 92 minutes; Producer: Herbert B. Swope, Jr.; Director: Nicholas Ray; Cast: Robert Wagner; Jeffrey Hunter; Hope Lange; Alan Hale, Jr.; Agnes Moorehead; Rachel Stephens; Carl Thayler; Chubby Johnson ***

Fox's glossy remake of their 1939 classic, *Jesse James* (Tyrone Power was the lead), commences with the James gang's demise during the Northfield Minnesota Bank raid on September 7, 1876 and revisits the holdup an hour later; the Jesse/Frank James story, starting with the Remington Detective Agency's pursuit of the brothers who are hiding out in a cave, is related in three lengthy flashback sequences, culminating in the outlaw's death at the hands of Robert Ford. Fox's executives had the bright idea of casting two of the '50s popular pinup boys in the main roles, Robert Wagner as Jesse, Jeffrey Hunter his brother Frank and, on the whole, it worked, Hunter probably coming out the better of the two. Nicholas Ray's flashback narrative (frowned upon by Fox) tends to confuse the action, of which there is plenty, Jesse portrayed as a Western Robin Hood-type figure with a love of killing; the Northfield Bank raid, occurring in full in the 70th minute, is a five-minute thrilling set piece, the James and Cole Younger outfits shot to pieces in crossfire. The movie climaxes with Carl Thayler (the coward, Robert Ford) running out of the outlaw's house yelling, "I've just killed Jesse James," wife Hope Lange, Ma Agnes Moorehead, Hunter and his wife, Rachel Stephens, grieving over his body. It's not bad, but one is left with the feeling that in the hands of a director with more Western movie knowledge and nous (for example, Henry Hathaway), it could have been that much more interesting.

Dialogue:
Wagner to Hunter: "Jesse James. That name means something. And when those Yankee bankers hear it, they start shakin'."

Trivia:
Elvis Presley was mooted as a possible for the Jesse James role but was dropped through lack of acting experience.

War Drums
Bel-Air/United Artists; Technicolor; 75 minutes; Producer: Howard W. Koch; Director: Reginald LeBorg; Cast: Lex Barker; Joan Taylor; Ben Johnson; Larry Chance;

Richard H. Cutting; John Pickard; Jil Jarmyn; James Parnell ***

UA's cut-price version of Fox's *Broken Arrow* (1950) had dark-haired, hot tempered Mexican lass Joan Taylor kidnapped by Lex Barker's Apaches while Barker's pal, trader Ben Johnson, tries to keep the peace between the whites and the Redskins: Like Barker, he's fallen for Taylor's feisty charms and who could blame him; Taylor in Indian garb was a darned sight more alluring than playing a doctor in her two Columbia/Ray Harryhausen classics, *Earth vs. the Flying Saucers* (1956) and *20 Million Miles to Earth* (1957). The ex-Tarzan star wants Taylor as his warrior wife so marries her against the tribe's wishes, both attired in fetching white buckskins, the saucy lass showing her new Apache husband how to make love Mexican style! Pesky gold miners hit pay dirt on Apache land, sparking an uprising (a federal judge is killed) that ends with Barker, seriously wounded, operated on by a cavalry surgeon in a captured fort; eternally grateful, the Apache chief (Taylor by his side) and his braves head off deep into the mountains, promising to stick to the peace treaty if no more trouble is met from miners or the meddlesome bigwigs in Washington. Reginald LeBorg's serviceable, quick-paced oater boasts striking location filming in Utah's rugged Johnson Canyon territory, with bright photography courtesy of William Margulies, and a couple of violent encounters between Injuns and the boys in blue, plus the opening graphic flogging of Barker which ranks as number 71 in Alvin Easter's *Lash! The Hundred Great Scenes of Men Being Whipped in the Movies* (Barker also comes in at number 22 for being whipped half to death in the 1960 Italian peplum opus *Terror of the Red Mask*). All in all, a colorful, entertaining time-passer.

Highlights:
Taylor, semi-nude, bathing in a river, plus attractive location work in Utah's Kanab region.

Dialogue:
Johnson in a tepee, a barbed arrow sticking out of his chest, to Taylor: "You have to push it clear through and out my back."
Taylor, handing him a cloth: "Bite hard, Senor!"

Trivia:
The shoot was beset by problems: Lightning wrecked a generator and the wardrobe trailer was destroyed by fire.

Chapter 14
1958

A TREASURE TO STEAL ... A WOMAN TO WIN ... A PAST TO FORGET!
The Badlanders

DON'T BE ASHAMED TO SCREAM! EVERYONE IN THE THEATER WILL BE SCREAMING WITH YOU!
The Fiend Who Walked the West

GOLD FEVER ... WOMAN FEVER ... AND NOW ... MASSACRE FEVER ... WAS RAGING ACROSS THE LENGTH AND BREADTH OF THE WEST!
Gun Fever

THE SCREEN'S FIRST REAL STORY OF THE STRANGE TEENAGE DESPERADO!
The Left Handed Gun

MAN OF THE SOFT WORD AND SLOW WALK ... MAN OF THE NOTCHED GUN AND FAST DRAW ... MAN OF THE LEAN JAW AND HARD FIST!
Man of the West

A TOUGH FRONTIER KILLER SETS A MURDEROUS MANTRAP ... BUT INSTEAD CATCHES THE GIRL HE LOVES!
Man or Gun

THEY RODE LIKE HELLIONS, HID LIKE GHOSTS, KILLED LIKE WARRIORS!
Quantrill's Raiders

A GHOST TOWN HID THE SECRET OF THE WEST'S MOST BRUTAL KILLERS!"
Seven Guns to Mesa

Ambush at Cimarron Pass

Regal Films/20th Century Fox; RegalScope; 73 minutes; Producer: Herbert E. Mendelson; Director: Jodie Copelan; Cast: Scott Brady; Margia Dean; Clint Eastwood; Irving Bacon; Frank Gerstle; Ray Boyle; Baynes Barron; William Vaughn **

"A career low point which almost made me want to quit the film industry." So spoke Clint Eastwood of Regal's cut-price tale of a Union cavalry troop teaming up with a group of Johnny Rebs in 1867 to negotiate themselves through hostile Apache territory to Fort Waverly; they're carrying a prisoner (Baynes Barron), who has been selling repeating carbines to the Redskins, a cowardly judge (Irving Bacon) and a sexy woman (Margia Dean) left behind from a massacre. Forming an edgy relationship, the disparate bunch have to foot it when their horses are stolen by the Indians; ex-Confederate Eastwood, indignant at having to be ordered around by officer Scott Brady, gets the hots for Dean, but she fancies Brady, the Yankee forcing everyone to drink water polluted from the butchered corpse of their scout. Bacon is all for handing over the rifles for horses, releasing Barron who stabs him to death, the gun runner receiving a spear in the chest for his troubles. Managing to run the horses off from the Apaches, Brady kills their chief after a shoot-out in Cimarron Pass, the 36 rifles burned, deemed too heavy to carry; finally, the fort is reached, the last word going to the future Man With No Name: "Sometimes you got to lose before you finally win." The end is abrupt, the acting so-so and Jodie Copelan never directed another feature film (this was his first). But it isn't all *that* bad, if only to see Clint (billed third) trying his hardest to bring some life to his rather gauche character; there were a heap more Westerns made in the 1950s that were inferior to this one.

Dialogue:
Brady to Ray Boyle, elected as the new scout: "Here, I'll take your pack. Better hold on to your gun, you might run across some jackrabbits."
Boyle: "The kind with feathers?"

Trivia:
Eastwood, in one of his first major film roles (he was 27 at the time), denounced the movie as the lousiest Western ever made, but that didn't stop the producers from giving him top billing when it was reissued in the 1960s to cash in on the actor's *Dollar* successes; against Brady's salary of $25,000, he was paid a measly $750, small change even by Hollywood standards of the day.

The Badlanders

MGM; CinemaScope/Metrocolor; 85 minutes; Producer: Aaron Rosenberg; Director: Delmer Daves; Cast: Alan Ladd; Ernest Borgnine; Katy Jurado; Claire Kelly; Kent Smith; Robert Emhardt; Nehemiah Persoff; Adam Williams
*****

Delmer Daves' $1,400,000 tough, gritty rehash of 1950's *The Asphalt Jungle* had Alan Ladd and Ernest Borgnine released from Arizona Territorial Prison, Yuma, in 1898 and making their separate ways to the mining town of Prescott on the Mexican border. Warned by the sheriff to quit town the next day, Ladd, who was swindled over his share of a rich gold mine and imprisoned an innocent man, sets about getting his revenge. Enlisting the help of Borgnine and Mexican Nehemiah Persoff, he plans a daring heist, to haul $200,000 worth of ore out of the old Lisbon Mine, taking a 50/50 cut with crooks Kent Smith and Robert Emhardt, $10,000 going to his ex-convict buddy. In Richard Collins' involving screenplay, Borgnine forms a touching relationship with troubled Katy Jurado, creepy deputy Adam Williams, in cahoots with Smith and Emhardt, has orders to kill Ladd and his partners in crime when the gold is handed over for the cash and the final part of the movie is staged in the claustrophobic interior of the mine itself, the ore loaded into sacks, the workings collapsing and, at Smith's ranch, Borgnine blasting the lawman after he goes for his guns. A riotous climax sees the Mexicans, a fiesta in full swing, assisting Ladd and Borgnine in defeating Smith's jackals who are shot dead, Smith and Emhardt herded up in the dust like cattle. Borgnine and Jurado leave to start a new life in Durango while Ladd boards the stage with Smith's gal, decorative Claire Kelly, promising to join Borgnine in June after he's played house with the sexy dame. From its brutal prison opening scenes to the uplifting ending, *The Badlanders* is a terrific vintage actioner, shot around Tucson and the abandoned Tennessee Mine at Kingman, featuring Ladd in fine fettle and sizzling chemistry between Borgnine (in a sympathetic role for a change) and Jurado—the two were married a year after the film's release.

Highlights:

Tucson's stark mine workings form an unusual backdrop to a riveting Western drama.

Dialogue:
Emhardt to Ladd, worried about him enlisting a Mexican as a powder monkey: "Personally, I don't trust Mexis."
Ladd: "Personally, I do. I've even forgotten the Alamo."
Trivia:
The sinister-sounding stock soundtrack comprising the works of six composers was used extensively in American TV shows of the period, and in MGM's *The Law and Jake Wade*, released the same year as *The Badlanders*.

The Big Country

United Artists; Technirama/Technicolor; 166 minutes; Producers: William Wyler and Greogory Peck; Director: William Wyler; Cast: Gregory Peck; Carroll Baker; Charlton Heston; Jean Simmons; Charles Bickford; Burl Ives; Chuck Connors; Alfonso Bedoya ****

Big in scope, big on budget ($2,000,000), big on length, stars and director; but it could be said that the likes of John Ford, Anthony Mann and John Sturges had the knowhow to have brought in *The Big Country* on lesser finances *and* at under two hours; someone like Lesley Selander or Ray Nazarro, at 90 minutes, maybe. The saga of the Terrills, led by Major Charles Bickford, head of the Ladder Ranch, and the Hannasseys, lorded over by Burl Ives in Blanco Canyon, both ranchers feuding over water rights, was the mainstay storyline in countless Westerns of this period. Add to that cultured Easterner Gregory Peck's arrival in the town of San Rafael to marry Bickford's fickle daughter Carroll Baker, whose foreman Charlton Heston fancies, pacifist Peck, a former sea captain, having to prove he's a man in a roughhouse Western macho society ("It's dog eat dog," Bickford levels at him) and you had a very conventional storyline indeed. What made *The Big Country* so different was the sweeping Californian grasslands, beautifully composed by William Wyler and shot in bright colors by Franz F. Planer and, of course, Jerome Moross' Oscar-nominated score, as lush as those panoramic prairies. Ives won the Best Supporting Actor Oscar, chewing the scenery as embittered Hannassey, holed up in his canyon retreat (filmed in California's Red Rock State Park), son Chuck Connors lusting after and wanting to wed schoolteacher Jean Simmons, who has sold her property, the Big Muddy, to Peck—and that land contains those much-sought-after water rights. Peck and Heston go head-to-head in a marathon, five-minute fistfight (neither comes out on top: "What did we prove?" says Peck to Heston), Peck jettisons Baker on realizing what a little bitch she is (the actress disappears from the last part of the movie) and in a superb canyon showdown, Ives shoots Connors after the coward loses out to a duel with Peck, the grizzled old warrior and Bickford blazing away at each other with rifles, both expiring on the canyon floor; Peck rides away with Simmons and ranch hand Alfonso Bedoya to start their own spread. Many complained about the epic length, a lot of scenes stretched out to boost the running time, as in Peck trying to tame wild horse Old Thunder ("Overblown" was one word used by the critics), but it's all very watchable, although a tad rambling and loose around the edges—and no one in the film looks particularly happy, Simmons most of all. "War and Peace on the range," said the *New York Times*; "Story dwarfed by scenic outpourings," commented *Variety*.

Highlights:
Those marvelous wide-open landscapes augmented by Moross' famous score; and Ives as Hannassey, worthy of the Oscar.

Dialogue:
Bickford to Peck: "Here in the West, Jim, a man is still expected to defend himself. If he allows people to think he won't, he's in trouble. Bad trouble."

Trivia:
Peck, Bickford and especially Simmons disliked working with perfectionist Wyler, who demanded repeated takes and umpteen script rewrites, Simmons later stating she was traumatized for years after her time spent on the production; Bedoya died of alcoholism soon after completion on the film, aged 53; the picture was the second biggest box-office hit in Britain in 1959.

Blood Arrow

Regal Films/20th Century Fox; RegalScope; 76 minutes; Producer: Robert Stabler; Director: Charles Marquis Warren; Cast: Scott Brady; Paul Richards; Phyllis Coates; Don Haggerty; Rocky Shahan; John Dierkes; Richard Gilden; Patrick O'Moore ***

Mormon lass Phyllis Coates enlists the aid of taciturn gunman Scott Brady, grizzled trapper Don Haggerty, ambitious gambler Paul Richards and dumb Indian Rocky Shahan (his tongue was torn out) to escort her to the Mormon settlement through dangerous Blackfoot territory. Vital medicine is needed to prevent an outbreak of smallpox in the valley, Chief Little Otter (Richard Gilden) and his braves making life difficult at every turn of the trail. A sturdy B-oater from Regal whose efforts were marginally a cut above the rest of the low-budget pack, blessed with the added bonus of sparkling widescreen photography. There's one horrifying sequence when unkempt hunter John Dierkes is found wandering like a madman in the bush in hysterics, both eyes burned to blackened cinders by the Blackfoot, but in 1958, disturbing scenes such as these were beginning to creep into the Western genre to appease a more adult audience. Richards is itching to lay his greedy hands on the supposed gold mine in Coates' valley, dismayed when she informs him that the Mormon gold originates from Tombstone, Arizona. Shahan receives an arrow in the chest and in a smoke-filled finale, Dierkes and Haggerty are shot dead, Brady finishing off the Blackfoot chief; Richards then decides to challenge Brady to the draw, losing out. Granite-faced Brady has now sufficiently thawed to accompany Coates into her valley and maybe set up home with the gal.

Dialogue:
Brady to Richards: "Do you wanna be on your way? Or do you wanna try me?"
Richards: "Well, I been wantin' to try you for a long time. (Pauses). I think I'll try."

The Bravados

20th Century Fox; CinemaScope/DeLuxecolor; 98 minutes; Producer: Herbert B. Swope, Jr.; Director: Henry King; Cast: Gregory Peck; Joan Collins; Stephen Boyd; Henry Silva; Lee Van Cleef; Albert Salmi; Herbert Rudley; Gene Evans *****

A high-voltage Super Western from Henry King, filmed in Mexico, in which tight-lipped hombre Gregory Peck rides into the border town of Rio Arriba to witness the hanging of four outlaws: Stephen Boyd, Henry Silva, Lee Van Cleef and Albert Salmi. But why has the stranger ridden 100 miles to watch the event? When, during a church service, the hangman, an imposter, springs the coyotes from Herbert Rudley's jail, the truth emerges via Padre Andrew Duggan to Peck's ex-girlfriend, Joan Collins: Peck is on a revenge mission for the rape and murder of his wife by the men who have just escaped, taking Kathleen Gallant as a hostage, and no one's gonna stop him from finishing off each and every one of them. A posse is formed, Peck leading it but doing his own thing. First to die is Van Cleef, groveling for mercy in the prairie grass and claiming not to recognize the photo of Peck's wife in a watch; he's brutally stamped on and blasted to oblivion. Salmi is next, strung up on a tree branch by the feet and denying that he had anything to do with the crime before shot dead. Boyd and Silva make it to Gene Evans' homestead, a gold miner and neighbor of Peck. Boyd attacks and molests Gallant, shooting Evans in the back, Silva grabbing a pouch full of gold coins found beside Evans' body. Peck refuses to give up when the posse reaches the border, crossing the river and gunning down Boyd in a

Mexican adobe town, even though Boyd, on seeing the photo in the watch, says he hasn't a clue what Peck is talking about. The manhunt ends at Silva's smallholding where Peck confronts the last member of the gang. Silva, anxious to protect his wife and child ("Why do you hunt me?"), states that they had no knowledge of Peck's farm or his wife; after carrying out a robbery, they crossed the border to Rio Arriba, bypassing Peck's spread. Peck spots the small sack of coins on a shelf, knowing it to be the family life savings, but when Silva insists that he stole it from Evans, the terrible truth dawns on him: Evans, after robbing his ranch, violated and killed his wife; Peck has murdered three men for a crime they never committed. Back in Rio Arriba, Peck confesses all to Duggan but hailed as a hero by the townsfolk ("You merely carried out a legal execution," says the priest). Chastened by the experience, Peck, Collins and Peck's small daughter exit the church to start a new life together. Great acting (Peck commands the attention), great score (Lionel Newman), great scenery, great action—a great Western! "Glossy ... Peck on top form," enthused *Variety*.

Highlights:

Mexico's rocky, volcano-strewn hinterland split by ravines, defiles and gorges, shot in deep colors by Leon Shamroy.

Dialogue:

Peck to Duggan: "I set myself up as the judge, the jury and the executioner ... I killed them for something they didn't do."

Trivia:

Peck admitted in a later interview that he found playing such a mean, dislikeable character extremely difficult to pull off.

Bullwhip

Allied Artists; CinemaScope/DeLuxecolor; 80 minutes; Producer: Helen Ainsworth; Director: Harmon Jones; Cast: Guy Madison; Rhonda Fleming; James Griffith; Don Beddoe; Peter Adams; Dan Sheridan; Burt Nelson; Hank Worden **

William Shakespeare's *The Taming of the Shrew* out West as Guy Madison, framed for a killing, is released from prison on condition he weds, on paper, a mysterious woman (Rhonda Fleming) but *doesn't* consummate the sham marriage; her dead father's will stipulated that in order to manage the O'Malley Fur Trading Company as boss, she should have a husband. Once out, bemused Madison decides to bring the half-Comanche dame to heel and in doing so comes up against rival businessman Peter Adams, after Fleming's lucrative outfit himself and desiring a partnership. Lurking among the trees and boardwalks is blank-faced gunslinger James Griffith, willing to hire his lethal Colt to the highest bidder. *Bullwhip* is neither one thing nor another, Fleming (she's an Indian princess called White Deer) dressed in an array of outrageous fluffy dresses and enjoying Madison's roughhousing love technique but not daring to show it, her Indian pal, Burt Nelson (Pine Hawk), nothing more than a wooden stooge; meanwhile, Madison's friend, Dan Sheridan, growls, threatens and does very little else. There's virtually no action apart from repeated scenes of freighter wagons trundling past the same old wooded scenery and the limp closing sequence has Madison slugging Adams and retrieving vital documents everyone has been chasing after for 80 minutes; the papers confirm he married the vixen, legal proof that he now owns part of the company. Ordering Fleming to "Come here, you," Madison grabs his wife, the prelude to another romp between the sheets. All forced style and no substance, *Bullwhip* is a chore to sit through, despite the presence of glamorous Fleming and beefcake Madison.

Dialogue:

Madison, on learning that marriage will prevent him from being hanged: "Well, a wedding ring is better than a noose."

Cole Younger, Gunfighter

Allied Artists; CinemaScope/DeLuxecolor; 78 minutes; Producer: Ben Schwalb; Director: R.G. Springsteen; Cast: Frank Lovejoy; James Best; Abby Dalton; Jan Merlin; Ainslie Pryor; Myron Healey; George Keymas; Douglas Spencer ***

A remake of Allied Artists' *The Desperado*, made four years earlier. Daniel Mainwaring's script was a scene-for-scene copy of the earlier picture, James Best teaming up with outlaw Frank Lovejoy (as Cole Younger) and going on the run after being falsely accused of murdering Blue Bellies Ainslie Pryor and George Keymas during the Texas carpetbaggers troubles of 1873; two-timing pal Jan Merlin is the culprit, anxious to get his greasy paws on Best's lass, perky blonde Abby Dalton, and claim the $10,000 reward money on the outlaw's head. Although shot in CinemaScope and color, it's inferior to *The Desperado* in many ways, failing to capitalize on the Best/Lovejoy relationship so successfully put across by Jimmy Lydon and Wayne Morris (who starred as Sam Garrett) in the Thomas Carr version, the narrative not as tightly knitted and the courtroom climax a damp squib. Myron Healey, playing the part of twin trigger-happy brothers, is the best thing in the picture.

Dialogue:
Best to Lovejoy, on a cattle drive and sick of the dusty conditions: "How long do we have to take this?"
Lovejoy: "Don't start squawkin'. It's better than chokin' to death at the end of a rope."

Trivia:
Lovejoy's last feature film; he carried on in various TV shows, dying from a heart attack in October 1962 at the age of 50. And Pryor was only 37 when he died of cancer on May 27, 1958.

Cowboy

Columbia; Technicolor; 92 minutes; Producer: Julian Blaustein; Director: Delmer Daves; Cast: Glenn Ford; Jack Lemmon; Anna Kashfi; Brian Donlevy; Dick York; Victor Manuel Mendoza; Richard Jaeckel; Eugene Iglesias ***

Hotel desk clerk Jack Lemmon yearns for the outdoor life, paying hardened Longhorn cattle boss Glenn Ford his life savings of $3,800 to join his crew as a partner on a trip down Mexico way; as well as the experience of herding, his love interest, Anna Kashfi, has moved there and Lemmon wants to be reunited with her, unaware that, on the orders of her father, she's married pompous Eugene Iglesias. Based on Frank Harris' 1930 novel *My Reminiscences as a Cowboy*, tenderfoot Lemmon gradually turns into an unfeeling bully during the return journey ("You haven't got tough—you've just got miserable," barks Ford at him), ordering the drovers about and driving them hard when Ford is laid low with a Redskin bullet in his knee. The pair wind up in twin bathtubs at the end, looking forward to the next job, Ford having resigned himself to quite liking the man he initially thought wasn't up to the task of trail buster. A hit-or-miss affair: Saul Bass' trademark quirky title graphics combined with George Duning's twee score didn't bode well for more serious Western buffs, *Variety* saying the film was "too short," the *New York Times* calling Lemmon's performance "extremely ineffectual." Shot in Oklahoma's wide-open spaces, relaxed-paced *Cowboy* supposedly represented life on the open range as it actually was but suffered from a lengthy prologue set in Lemmon's plush hotel, Lemmon appearing slightly uncomfortable dressed as a cowhand. Ford, though, is his usual

sardonic self, a terrific star turn, while Brian Donlevy brings a measure of gravitas as a retired Wichita lawman sick of killing for a living.
Dialogue:
Dick York to Strother Martin: "Women like the smell of a horse on a man. Makes 'em giggle."

Day of the Bad Man

Universal; CinemaScope/Eastmancolor; 81 minutes; Producer: Gordon Kay; Director: Harry Keller; Cast: Fred MacMurray; John Ericson; Joan Weldon; Edgar Buchanan; Marie Windsor; Robert Middleton; Skip Homeier; Lee Van Cleef
****

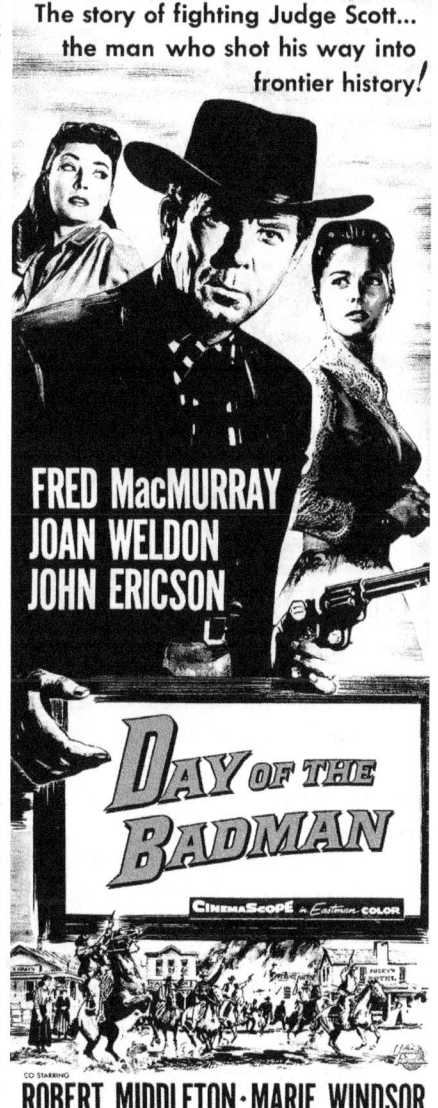

Killer Christopher Dark is due to be tried at 11 o'clock and sentenced to death by hanging, but stern-faced judge Fred MacMurray has a lot to contend with as the minutes tick by. Dark's vicious relatives, the Hayes bunch (Robert Middleton, Skip Homeier, Lee Van Cleef, Chris Alcaide) are intimidating the townsfolk by violence, demanding banishment as punishment instead of the noose; anyone who dares to disagree will find themselves in deep trouble if Dark is strung up. Sheriff John Ericson is no help, a spineless coward who has somehow attracted the attention of MacMurray's intended wife, Joan Weldon. When the judge's ex-love Marie Windsor (also a Hayes) sees the pair kissing in an alleyway, she spills the beans to her former beau who has recently purchased not only a wedding ring but a sheep ranch to settle down on. MacMurray's only ally in a town crammed full of gutless yellowbellies is Edgar Buchanan, his old sidekick. Similar in content to both Allied Artists' *At Gunpoint* and Columbia's *Good Day for a Hanging* which also starred MacMurray, Harry Keller's tense Western boasts a strong cast plus a great Hans J. Salter score, the leading man, along with Middleton as the chief villain, commanding the attention throughout. At the trial, MacMurray doesn't bow to public pressure, sentencing the rat to death *but* to be hanged in another town; incensed at the verdict, Middleton and company follow MacMurray out to his ranch (Ericson refuses to assist the judge, sweating in fear) where, following a shoot-out and the tossing of firebombs into the ranch house, the Hayes boys bite the dust with help from Buchanan, the only reliable soul to back the judge up. As for Weldon, she's back in MacMurray's arms after realizing what a weakling Ericson is.

Dialogue:
Ericson, backing down to Homeier's gun barrel: "What'd you think you're gonna do?" Homeier: "Do? Why nothin'. Maybe blow your nose off. Make you extra pretty for the girls."

Escort West

Romina/Batjac/United Artists; CinemaScope; 75 minutes; Producers: Nate H. Edwards, Robert E. Morrison and John Wayne (uncredited); Director: Francis D. Lyon; Cast: Victor Mature; Faith Domergue; Elaine Stewart; Reba Waters; Leo Gordon; William Ching; Rex Ingram; Noah Beery, Jr. **

Made by John Wayne's own production company, *Escort West* is another in a long line of '50s "stragglers working their way through Indian country" sagas. In this case, widower Victor Mature, daughter Reba Waters and sisters Faith Domergue and Elaine Stewart, among others, are on their way from Nevada to Oregon in 1865, hoping to rendezvous with Captain William Ching and his detachment. Ching is holed up in hill country, pinned down by Modoc renegades; Mature has to cope with Domergue, a Confederate-hating harpy, Gordon (he co-wrote the script), who's intent on knocking off the army payroll they're carrying, and Stewart, betrothed to Ching but falling for Mature's manly charms. It's a fairly slow-moving trek, concentrating mainly on Mature trying to protect Waters from the Modocs and coping with Domergue's tantrums. Ching and his depleted detachment of eight troopers are reached, Domergue sacrificing herself to enable safe passage for Mature, Stewart and Waters. During a tussle in a cave, the Modoc chief has a rattler flung into his face by Mature and then shot; minus their leader, the warriors melt into the rocks. Ching is resigned to the fact that Stewart has changed her affections, the remnants of both parties making their way towards Fort Clement. A good cast includes Harry Carey, Jr., Ken Curtis, Slim Pickens, Noah Beery, Jr. and Rex Ingram but, overall, this cheaply produced movie is okay fare without any singular redeeming features.

Dialogue:
Proprietress Claire Du Brey to Mature, commenting on Domergue's bad manners: "Funny thing about running a place like this, Reb. You get the damndest assortment of critturs comin' through."

The Fiend Who Walked the West

20th Century Fox; CinemaScope; 101 minutes; Producer: Herbert B. Swope, Jr.; Director: Gordon Douglas; Cast: Hugh O'Brian; Robert Evans; Linda Cristal; Dolores Michaels; Stephen McNally; Emile Meyer; Ron Ely; Ken Scott *****

1876: During 4th of July celebrations, Hugh O'Brian is shut in a vault when taking part in the Aureate City Bank robbery, his fellow outlaws, led by Ken Scott, escaping. O'Brian reckons the judge will go lenient on him, this being his first offence. Wrong. He's handed a stiff 10-year sentence and incarcerated in Fort Smith Prison, presided over by brutal guard Emile Meyer, finding himself sharing a cell with Robert Evans (Felix Griffin) who's in the middle of a six-week spell for selling whiskey to Indians. Evans, however, is no ordinary young cowpoke. He's a sadistic, mentally unstable, splinter-chewing psychopath with a troubled past, and when O'Brian lets slip information about the robbery, Evans, on his release, makes it his business to hunt down and grab the stolen cash, murdering anyone who stands in his way—and enjoying it. Scott's crippled mother gets an arrow in her chest, Scott is blasted in the back and their ranch set on fire, deputy Ron Ely is shot to pieces after slapping Evans, O'Brian's pregnant wife, Linda Cristal, miscarries when Evans terrorizes her in her bed and Dolores Michaels is repeatedly beaten by her unhinged boyfriend who eventually breaks her neck. To stop the madman in his tracks, O'Brian (called Sad Man by Evans) is allowed to bust out of prison as he's the only man ever to get close to him; taking the law into his own hands and after a series of tense confrontations, he ends up emptying all six revolver bullets into the loony during a saloon standoff. Marshal Stephen McNally and the authorities allow O'Brian and Cristal to get on with their lives, glad to be rid of Griffin. X-rated in England and banned in some parts of Europe, the psychological 1950s Western reached its peak in Gordon Douglas' grim, dialogue-driven "Gothic-style Western version of *Psycho*," 28-year-old Evans, shortly to become boss of Paramount Pictures, playing it to the hilt, a career-best performance. Harry Brown and Philip Yordan's screenplay, adapted from Ben Hecht and Charles Lederer's 1947 script for *Kiss of Death*

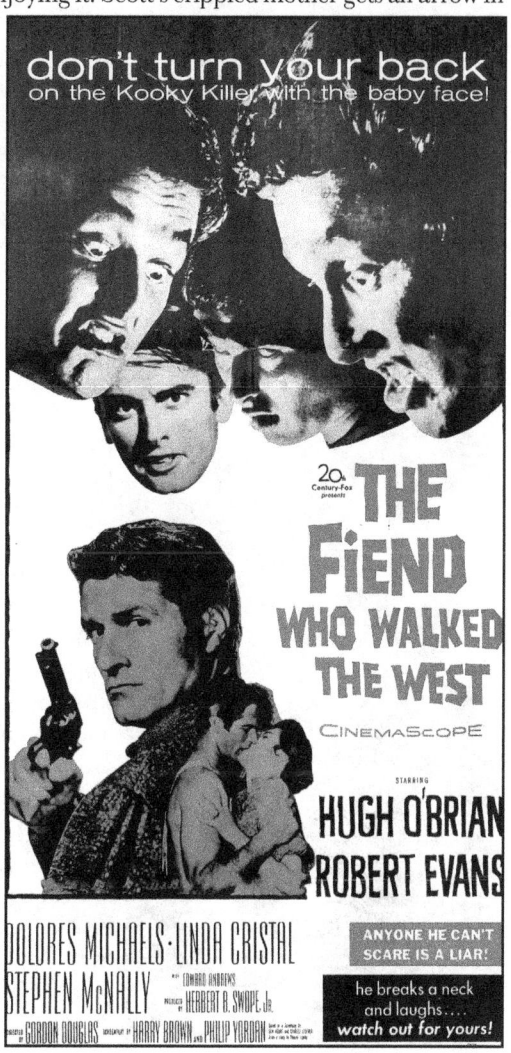

(Richard Widmark starred as the deranged killer), bristles with biting one-liners, especially in the lengthy scenes of Evans and O'Brian matching verbal blows across the table, while Joseph MacDonald's sharp black-and-white widescreen photography adds mood to a radically different Western. Critics may have scoffed at the time, but there's no getting away from it—Evans' Felix Griffin is on a par with any psycho ever portrayed on the silver screen; you cannot take your eyes off him for a single second.

Highlights:
Stammering, sneering, blank-eyed, volatile, cunning, slack-jawed, poised like a rattlesnake to strike, a misogynist *and* a good-looker; Evans is the complete movie psychopath.

Dialogue:
Evans' chilling words of introduction to new cellmate O'Brian: "I ain't asleep. No man can sleep in a cage. I don't like nobody to grab hold of me so I, I won't shake hands. My name's Griffin. Felix Griffin. After my pa."

Trivia:
In his autobiography *The Kid Stays in the Picture*, Evans relates how he got so much into his character of "The Kooky Killer" that it scared off all his numerous girlfriends, distressing for a man married seven times! In the United Kingdom, distributors hooked up on the movie's splendid title and horror strengths, frequently pairing the picture with Fox's *She Devil*, Regal's *Kronos* and Toho's *Rodan*. And Bernard Herrmann was outraged at discovering snippets of his soundtrack for *The Day the Earth Stood Still* tagged onto Leon Klatzkin's title/incidental music, letting his views be known to studio executives.

Flaming Frontier

Regal Films of Canada/20th Century Fox; RegalScope; 70 minutes; Produced and Directed by Sam Newfield; Cast: Bruce Bennett; Jim Davis; Paisley Maxwell; Larry Solway; Cec Lindar; Ben Lennick; Don Garrard; Shane Rimmer ***

During filming of the TV series *Hawkeye and the Last of the Mohicans* in 1957, Sam Newfield drummed up this cavalry versus Redskins yarn in a matter of weeks; if anything else, *Flaming Frontier* looks unusual because of its Canadian location work. Otherwise, we have the old commonplace story of Captain Bruce Bennett (half-Danish, half-Sioux), trying to keep peace with the Sioux so that food can reach Union troops caught up in the Civil War; meanwhile, Indian (and wife)-hating Colonel Jim Davis, commander of Fort Ridgley, does his best to thwart Bennett's plans and prevent the Indians from obtaining provisions. Bennett is Chief Little Crow's (Larry Solway) childhood friend and blood brother (although he looks years older); Davis' brother, Cec Lindar, and Indian Agent Ben Lennick, are the coyotes stirring up unrest, Davis' abused wife, Paisley Maxwell (she's part Blackfoot), turning to Bennett after one punch in the face too many. Although Bennett is a trifle morose and stiff in his part, Davis makes up for it in a brutish performance and the Sioux assaults on the fort are moderately exciting, as is a gun-smoked clash between Injuns and traders at a post. Davis dies from a bullet wound, Lindar and Lennick's corpses, peppered with arrows, are found tied to a tree, Solway agrees to a peace treaty and Bennett gets Maxwell, the officer smiling the only time in 70 minutes. Not memorable, perhaps, but efficiently cobbled together by Newfield and directed with pace.

Dialogue:
Bennett to Davis: "Little Crow and I were boys together, Colonel."
Davis: "And now he's a man."
Bennett: "So am I. Half Danish and half Sioux Indian."

Fort Bowie

Bel-Air/United Artists; 80 minutes; Producer: Aubrey Schenck; Director: Howard W. Koch; Cast: Ben Johnson; Jan Harrison; Kent Taylor; J. Ian Douglas; Maureen Hingert (Jana Davi); Larry Chance; Peter Mamakos; Jerry Frank ***

Major J. Ian Douglas, an unsentimental West Pointer with little experience of how to handle delicate Indian affairs, orders the massacre of a party of Apaches who have come to talk peace under a flag of truce. Enraged Chief Victorio (Larry Chance) jumps the reservation and declares war on the whites, so Colonel Kent Taylor, after instructing Ben Johnson (he wears a tomahawk strapped to his waist) to collect his wife (Jan Harrison) from Tucson, tells him to meet the Apache chief and try and calm things down; Taylor and Johnson are all for negotiating, Douglas all for extermination. Howard W. Koch introduces a bit of romance midway through; Harrison hates the West but loves Johnson, while beautiful Indian lass Chanzana (Maureen Hingert) declares herself to be Johnson's woman. We finally get a thrilling 13-minute slice of smoke-filled, noisy action, the Apaches refusing to listen to Johnson's friendly overtures and wiping out Douglas' regiment to a man before storming Fort Bowie. Taylor shoots Chance dead as the Redskin boss fights Johnson with a knife and the Indians retreat, Harrison falling back into her husband's arms, Hingert kissing Johnson. A solid oater from United Artists, indicative of a lot of their Western fodder from this productive period in the genre's history.

Highlights:
A lengthy, fantastic Apaches versus cavalry climax, brilliantly orchestrated by director Koch.

Dialogue:
Harrison to Peter Mamakos, on seeing a body strung up near a burning homestead: "Is, is that man dead?"
Mamakos: "Oh yeah. Deader than a doornail. Had his brains cooked over a slow fire. It's a favorite pastime with Indians."

Trivia:
Stunning Hingert quit the movie business only a year after *Fort Bowie* was released; and Douglas vanished off the face of the earth, this his one and only screen appearance.

Fort Dobbs

Warner Bros.; WarnerScope; 93 minutes; Producer: Martin Rackin; Director: Gordon Douglas; Cast: Clint Walker; Virginia Mayo; Richard Eyer; Brian Keith; Russ Conway; Michael Dante; John Cliff; Bud Osborne ****

Taciturn, six-foot-six inch Clint Walker, sporting shoulders "rivaling King Kong" (as one critic wrote) escorts Virginia Mayo and her young son, Richard Eyer (the genie in *The 7th Voyage of Sinbad*), through dangerous Comanche territory towards Fort Dobbs. Walker's on the run from Lago after shooting his wife's lover, but Mayo is convinced that the tall stranger murdered *her* husband after finding his bloodied jacket among Walker's possessions; Walker, in fact, stole the dead man's jacket (he was killed by Comanches) to elude Russ Conway's posse. On the trail, they meet gun runner Brian Keith, busy selling rifles to the Indians, the smirking ruffian making a play for "fine lookin' woman" Mayo. After a slow-paced first half, Gordon Douglas increases the tempo. The trio reaches the fort to the pulsating sound of Max Steiner's music, finding its garrison wiped out, a total massacre. Conway rides up with wagons packed with Lago's citizens (the town has been overrun), thus setting the scene for a vigorous-whites versus Redskins clash, the Indians eventually driven off by Keith's Henry repeating rifles, the weapons taken off Keith by Walker following a fatal shoot-out. Conway lets Walker off the hook, knowing he shot in self-defense, leaving him to escort Mayo (whose eyes have lit up at the sight of her savior's mighty hairy chest) and Eyer to Santa Fe. And for the first time in the picture, Walker gets to smile!

Highlights:
Walker, a giant of a man, slowly riding through Utah's splendid rocky Kanab region, on the lookout for marauding Indians.

Dialogue:
Mayo: "Thinkin' of leaving us, Mister Davis?"
Walker: "I've thought about it. Can't. Keep thinkin' how you'd look after the Comanches get through with you."

Trivia:
The film would have benefited from color, but Warner Bros. was unwilling to risk extra finances on Walker's debut star role, even though he had made himself a household name as Cheyenne Bodie in the immensely popular television series *Cheyenne*, which ran from 1955 to 1962.

From Hell to Texas aka Manhunt

20th Century Fox; CinemaScope/DeLuxecolor; 100 minutes; Producer: Robert Buckner; Director: Henry Hathaway; Cast: Don Murray; Diane Varsi; Chill Wills; R.G. Armstrong; Dennis Hopper; Jay C. Flippen; John Larch; Rodolfo Acosta *****

Henry Hathaway is up alongside John Ford as one of the great Hollywood Western directors, and no further proof is needed of his talents than *From Hell to Texas*, a veritable blueprint of how a Western should be constructed. Frame by frame and in pictorial composition, Hathaway's cultured, insightful saga of an innocent man pursued by a vengeful gang is a vivid reminder that, during the 1950s, the genre achieved an absolute pinnacle of excellence. Don Murray is the subject of obsessed R.G. Armstrong's manhunt; during a fight with Murray over a girl, the rancher's younger son fell on his own knife and died. Armstrong blames Murray for the boy's death; in the opening minutes, Murray, stalked by Dennis Hopper and his hands, causes a horse stampede in which another of Armstrong's sons is injured, later dying. Not wearing a gun but a deadly shot with a rifle, Murray, pursued by Armstrong, Hopper, John Larch and three others, makes his way on foot over a scorching desert (Hopper has shot his horse), meets Chill Wills and his daughter, Diane Varsi, at a river, falls for the tomboy, guns down Larch who tries to ambush him and is guided through Comanche territory by trader Jay

C. Flippen; he finally reaches Socorro where he finds his father's grave at a mission. The action comes thick and fast, Wills seriously wounded in a shooting, Mexican Rodolfo Acosta the culprit; Murray wounds him in turn and, during a gunfight with Armstrong and Hopper, the hotel is set ablaze. Hopper runs screaming from the inferno, his clothes on fire, and Murray, instead of killing him, smothers the flames. "You saved my last son," says grateful Armstrong to the cowboy in the morning and rides away, the vendetta over with; Murray gallops off to Wills' home (the rancher has recovered) to greet delighted Varsi who has only one thing on *her* mind—marriage! "Solid Western," stated the normally over-critical *New York Times*.

Highlights:

California's Lone Pine, Death Valley and Hot Creek vistas, stunningly photographed by Wilfrid M. Cline.

Dialogue:

Varsi's unsuccessful pleas to get Murray to take an urgently required wash in the river: "You smell like a goat. Well, go on, I wanna bathe too."

Murray: "I always thought it was ladies first."

Varsi: "No ladies here. I can rope and brand and I don't ride sidesaddle."

Murray: "Well maybe you can do all them things, but you can't watch me take no bath."

Varsi: "Then stink! But sleep 100 feet away from us."

Trivia:

Hathaway fumed that it took Hopper 85 takes to complete one particular scene and vowed to kick him out of Hollywood, although Murray later disputed this.

Frontier Gun

Regal Films/20th Century Fox; RegalScope; 70 minutes; Producer: Richard E. Lyons; Director: Paul Landres; Cast: John Agar; Joyce Meadows; Barton MacLane; Morris Ankrum; Robert Strauss; James Griffith; Sammy Ogg; Lyn Thomas ***

Following the murder of yet another marshal, the town of Honcho hires John Agar to clean the place up, but Agar nurses a secret: a gun exploded in his right hand years back, and although he's a dead shot, he's not that quick on the draw. His gunfighter father, Barton MacLane, a feared town tamer (18 notches on his six-gun), is and rides into Honcho to advise his son to give up the job, but Agar digs his spurs in; he's always wanted to be a lawman, and now is his big chance to shine. The story, by 1958, was very familiar but *Frontier Gun*, bolstered from a fine Paul Dunlap score, managed to remain refreshing thanks to Agar's easygoing charm and decent backup from the support players: Joyce Meadows is a delight, sizing Agar up after *he's* sized up the town, lowering her dress top just a little when in Agar's presence; beefy Robert Strauss rolls his eyes and throws his weight around as Yubo, the resident half-breed bad man treating brassy saloon hussy Lyn Thomas like dirt; James Griffith turns in a telling performance as a drinking, no-good gambler, the butt of Strauss' horseplay ("I'm Yubo's court jester," he moans to anyone who cares to listen); Morris Ankrum, Meadows' father, is his usual crusty self; and MacLane cuts a menacing figure, ready to back Agar at the first hint of trouble. The tense climax sees Strauss and six toughs in the street, calling Agar out after MacLane has been killed. Although Strauss draws first, Agar, wounded, gets the drop with two slugs, one in Strauss' chest, another in his forehead. The townsfolk stream out of church in a show of strength and the six gunmen turn tail and ride away; Agar is carried off to be tended to by the doctor and lovely Meadows who has fallen in love with him after a couple of days.

Highlights:
The 1950s perfected the Western street showdown; *Frontier Gun*'s example is a showcase in how to pull it off, notwithstanding the picture's low budget.
Dialogue:
MacLane, spelling it out to Agar: "Either you're gonna be a big man, Jim—or a dead one."

Gun Fever

United Artists; 83 minutes; Producer: Harry Jackson; Director: Mark Stevens; Cast: Mark Stevens; John Lupton; Maureen Hingert (Jana Davi); Aaron Saxon; Larry Storch; Dean Fredericks; Clegg Hoyt; Robert Stevenson ***

Star Mark Stevens had a hand in the script of a murkily shot *noir* Western heavy on violence (the picture was banned in some parts of Europe and might well have received a British "X" certificate) and atmosphere, the entire scenario filmed either in a hurricane or by liberal use of a wind machine. In 1871, psycho outlaw Aaron Saxon and his thugs are murdering settlers (men, women and children) for their goods, assisted by the Sioux. Stevens, a gold prospector, is tailing the maniac, his family slaughtered by Saxon for their valuable furs; partner John Lupton, sick from a hacking cough, is Saxon's son (he walked out on the gang six years back) but wants to put an end to his father's trail of carnage. Almost outdoing Saxon in the loony stakes is Larry Storch, a grimy, sweaty Mexican who likes nothing better than to rub strangers up the wrong way, then shoot them—he gets a bullet in the guts from Lupton following a particularly vicious saloon brawl. The accent is on sheer nastiness, Stevens and Lupton gunning down three inquisitive cowpokes at their campfire for no other reason than one of them going for his iron; the incident seems added for shock value only. Assisted by Indian Maureen Hingert (her husband was murdered by Storch), Saxon and his two coyotes (one's a young insane punk kid) are cornered at Yellow Rock; Saxon stabs Lupton in the back, Stevens puts paid to the henchmen, grapples with knife-wielding Saxon, stumbles and, as Saxon is about to administer the death thrust, the outlaw boss is blasted by his wounded son. Paul Dunlap's minimal score underlines a film that, at times, threatens to derail (the opening 10 minutes is just plain confusing) but deserves to be noticed because of its unrelenting grim, sadistic tone; a *very* adult Western, *not* suitable for kids.

Highlights:
A savage, over-the-top, leering performance from ex-wrestler Saxon in perhaps his only major film role.
Dialogue:
Lupton to Saxon: "I'm not ridin' with you, Trench."
Saxon: "Not ridin' with me? You didn't come all this way to talk, did yer?"

Lupton: "No, I didn't."
Saxon: "Oh, what then?"
Lupton: "I came to kill you."

Gunman's Walk

Columbia; CinemaScope/Technicolor; 97 minutes; Producer: Fred Kohlmar; Director: Phil Karlson; Cast: Van Heflin; Tab Hunter; James Darren; Kathryn Grant; Mickey Shaughnessy; Robert F. Simon; Ray Teal; Paul Birch *****

Racial tensions, bigotry and father/sibling rivalry rear their ugly heads in Phil Karlson's powerful psychological horse opera centering on bully-boy rancher Van Heflin's (as Lee Hackett) tempestuous relationship with his two sons: sensible, upright James Darren and gun-crazy, short-fused Tab Hunter, whose main aim in life is to better his Indian-hating father, including which of them is quicker on the draw. Argumentative Hunter's like a bomb about to explode, his kinship with Heflin built on a mutual loathing; during a cattle drive, he purposely pushes half-breed Bert Convy off a cliff to his death in a chase for a white mare, thus precipitating a series of confrontations in Jackson City, a gun-free zone where the only hombres allowed to carry firearms are the Hackett clan. Loose cannon Hunter sneers at any kind of authority and is jailed for Convy's murder but set free when horse trader Ray Teal lies in court on condition Heflin gives him 10 mustangs, including Hunter's prized white mare; on his release, Hunter guns down Teal for "stealing" his treasured horse and is locked up again. Breaking out of his cell, the hothead kills deputy Mickey Shaughnessy and heads for the hills, Heflin plus a posse on his trail. It culminates in the inevitable tragic showdown between father and son, Hunter biting the dust as Heflin clears leather first. Contrite, the rancher, now a broken man, brings his son's body into town, bestowing his blessing on Darren's romance with Kathryn Grant who he has previously referred to as "part stinking Sioux." Frank Nugent's lucid script and telling interplay between Heflin and Hunter contribute to an "excellent adult Western with emotional power," as the critics described the film, Hunter belying his teen idol blond surfer-boy looks with a performance of sheer ferocity, probably, for him, a screen best.

Highlights:
Tab Hunter's sensational performance: From the opening shot of him whistling the tuneful "I'm a Runaway" on the open range to his standoff with Heflin, he gives his psychotic Ed Hackett a deranged presence all of its own.

Dialogue:
Heflin, bemoaning his lot: "One son in jail. The other one moonin' over a half-breed. I don't know which shames me more."

Trivia:
Confidential magazine published reports on both Hunter and Rory Calhoun's past criminal misdemeanors as part of a deal with agent Henry Willson not to disclose, in an exposé, the fact that Rock Hudson was gay. And Hunter's fictitious romance with Natalie Wood was concocted by Willson to divert attention from the truth that Hunter was gay!

Gunsmoke in Tucson

Allied Artists; CinemaScope/DeLuxecolor; 80 minutes; Producer: William D. Coates; Director: Thomas Carr; Cast: Mark Stevens; Forrest Tucker; Gale Robbins; Vaughn Taylor; John Ward; John Cliff; George Keymas; Kevin Hagen ***

Two boys witness their father being hanged for horse theft; years later, one's a marshal (Forrest Tucker), the other (Mark Stevens) head honcho of the Blue Chip gang, terrorizing the local communities. From a frantic opening, Thomas Carr quickly changes tack. Cattle baron Vaughn Taylor, head of the Turkey Ranch, is buying up all available land at public auction to force farmers, led by Kevin Hagen, off the property, using gunslingers to carry out his dirty work. In gallops Stevens, wanting at least 1,000 acres of prime land in the Santa Cruz basin all for himself. Old flame saloon gal Gale Robbins has married Taylor to better herself, while Tucker is pursuing his brother for gunning down George Keymas in a bar standoff, even though the shooting was in self-defense. Carr's solid oater is boosted by the heavyweight presence of Keymas, John Cliff and Richard Reeves, but the director confuses the narrative by introducing, halfway through and without any real explanation, Gail Kobe, another of Steven's old girlfriends, who looks so much like Robbins that you could be forgiven for thinking that both dames were one and the same. Stevens resurrects his old gang to combat Taylor's underhand tactics, using the help of pal John Ward, lightning quick on the trigger, Taylor fabricates a "Blue Chip" imposter to throw inquisitive Tucker off the scent and the whole shebang ends in a satisfactory shoot-out in Tucson between the "sodbusters" and Taylor's mob. The bad guys bite the dust and Robbins is wounded, Stevens carrying her off as she declares her undying love, while Robbins look-alike Kobe, standing on the sidewalk, says she loves him as well.

Highlights:
A lengthy, well-staged climactic street shoot-out.
Dialogue:
Reeves to Cliff, who has a shotgun trained on defenseless Tucker: "Start counting."
Cliff: "One. Two…"
Gunman Ward suddenly walks up behind Cliff, who gets nervous.
Reeves: "Go on, Cass, count."
Cliff, shaking in his boots, aware of Ward's presence: "Three."
Reeves: "Keep countin' Cass."
Cliff, sweating: "Three."
Reeves: "You said three. It's four!"
Trivia:
Stevens' slick dark hair was, in fact, a curly red: Warner Bros. ordered his hair dyed and straightened when they first signed him up.

The Last of the Fast Guns

Universal; CinemaScope/Eastmancolor; 82 minutes; Producer: Howard Christie; Director: George Sherman; Cast: Jock Mahoney; Gilbert Roland; Eduard Franz; Lorne Greene; Linda Cristal; Carl Benton Reid; Edward Platt; Lee Morgan *****

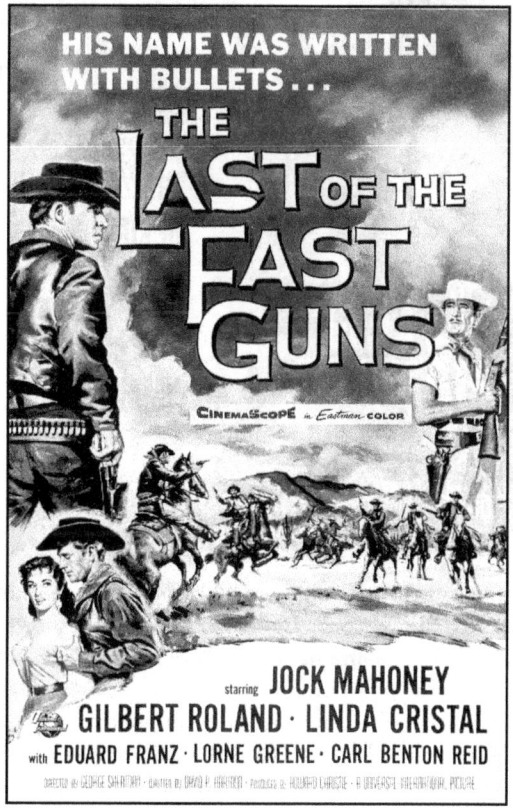

Into a shanty town rides a lone gunslinger, a freshly dug grave waiting for a corpse. In the street, a man waits. Three shots ring out. Next time we see the grave, it's filled in. Jock Mahoney has finished the job he came to this backwater to do, but before he departs, the loner's offered a lucrative job by wheelchair-bound Easterner Carl Benton Reid. For the sum of $25,000, locate his brother, last seen 30 years ago, and either bring him back or return with proof of his death; Reid wants to leave his lucrative holdings to his sibling, not to his crooked ex-partner. Mahoney heads towards Mexico and Lorne Greene's hacienda at San Vicente, where he teams up with Spaniard Gilbert Roland to find Reid's elusive brother, spotted in the hills 10 years back and now believed dead. But who is this mysterious brother, and why have previous investigators into his whereabouts met with violent ends? Splendidly shot in CinemaScope in rocky Mexican locations, David P. Harmon's pithy screenplay piles on both twists and turns and short one-liners spat out by Mahoney, his top Western performance: "If he's alive, I'll find him," says Mahoney to Roland. "And if he's dead?" "I'll bring back the man who killed him." Furthermore, George Sherman's oater plays on the bald truth that Mahoney's profession as a hired gun is coming to an end, as when three former outlaws bemoan the demise of Jesse James and his kind. Roland is also after laying his hands on the brother for $150,000, the sum that Reid's ex-partner has promised to pay him. Eduard Franz turns out to be the long-lost brother, a padre afforded the protection of the local populace. When Roland attempts to kill him, the villagers arrive en masse to prevent the murder; Roland is chased up a cliff by Mahoney who tosses a bolas at his rival's legs. Roland tumbles over the precipice to his death, and Franz decides to return to his brother across the border, Mahoney (hanging up his guns) following to collect his $25,000 and play pat-a-cake with Greene's daughter, delectable Linda Cristal; the gal's been flashing her eyes at the big man since the second reel.

Highlights:
A great Hans J. Salter/Herman Stein score, pristine photography from Alex Phillips, George Sherman's incisive direction and taciturn Mahoney riding tall in the saddle; this is one of Universal's most telling Westerns of the late 1950s.

Dialogue:
Cristal to Mahoney after he's watched her bathing nude in a river: "I've been swimming there since I was a little girl."
Mahoney: "Yes, ma'am. But you're a big girl now."

The Left Handed Gun

Warner Bros.; 102 minutes; Producer: Fred Coe; Director: Arthur Penn; Cast: Paul Newman; John Dehner; Lita Milan; James Best; James Congdon; Hurd Hatfield; Colin Keith-Johnston; Robert Foulk ***

Arthur Penn's directorial debut was a revisionist, psychological slant on the troubled youth that was Billy the Kid, taken from Gore Vidal's play. In this scenario, the Kid guns down the four men who murdered kindly cattleman Colin Keith-Johnston, slays a couple more on his escape from jail and eventually gets a bullet from onetime friend Pat Garrett. Originally, James Dean was earmarked to have been cast as Billy, Penn choosing 33-year-old method actor Paul Newman on the strength of his performance in MGM's *Somebody Up There Likes Me* (1956). Many thought Newman miscast in the role, being too mature to play an 18-to-20-year-old hotshot and guilty of overstating his part to the point of cheesiness on occasions (as does James Best and James Congdon, his partners-in-crime); his constant mugging, grinning and emoting seems at odds with a typical '50s Western, though quite commonplace in the 1960s when tomfoolery took over from serious plot. Vidal disliked the picture and critics were divided: "A lame oater," griped the *New York Times*, *Variety* counteracting with "smart and exciting." John Dehner (over 260 movies to his credit) stands out as the tall, stern Pat Garrett, Lita Milan is the unwilling subject of Newman's sexual appetite and J. Peverell Marley's diamond-hard black-and-white photography brings a glossy sheen to the proceedings. *The Left Handed Gun* appears out-of-context with the average 1950s horse opera and may have worked better with an unknown in the lead, or even someone like Robert Evans who did such a marvelous job in *The Fiend Who Walked the West*. In the main, it's interesting to watch as one further rung up the ladder to Newman's eventual standing as a Hollywood icon.

Dialogue:
Dehner's warning to Newman on his wedding day: "It's my wedding, Billy. You start something, I'll take it hard."

The Lone Ranger and the Lost City of Gold

United Artists; Eastmancolor; 81 minutes; Producer: Sherman A. Harris; Director: Lesley Selander; Cast: Clayton Moore; Jay Silverheels; Noreen Nash; Douglas Kennedy; Lisa Montell; Ralph Moody; Dean Fredericks; John Miljan ****

The last outing for Clayton Moore and Jay Silverheels as The Lone Ranger and Tonto saw the crusading duo hunting down the Hooded Raiders gang who have killed two Indians in a series of holdups—but for what purpose? Each man wore a necklace that contained part of a five-piece medallion; when all the pieces are joined together, they depict a map that points the way to a fabled Spanish city constructed of pure gold. Rancher Noreen Nash and would-be lover Douglas Kennedy are behind the raids in the Redskin-hating town of Sandorio, and Doctor Dean Fredericks possesses one of the medallions; he's also an Indian, but the bigoted townsfolk are unaware of this. Moore disguises himself as a Southern gentleman bounty hunter to worm the truth out of unsuspecting Nash ("You and I can become *permanent* partners," she coos), arousing Kennedy's jealousy, and Fredericks ends up with Indian lass Paviva (Lisa Montell) in Chief John Miljan's deserted village, at the mercy of Kennedy and his gunmen, the tribe performing a ceremony at the Lake of Fire. Moore and Silverheels finish the gang off; wounded, Kennedy returns to Nash with the final segment of the map, the lass showing her gratitude by hurling a Spanish war axe into his back, just as Moore rides up and, in his Southern accent, informs her that she's going to spend an awful long time behind bars. Back at Miljan's camp, the Lost City is discovered at the end of a network of passages inside a cliff, enough gold for Fredericks to build his own mission hospital and marry Montell. The Lone Ranger and Tonto ride off, leaving behind them a tribe of happy contented Indians. Expertly directed by Lesley Selander and boasting picturesque location shooting around Arizona's cactus-strewn Old Tucson and Sonoran Desert regions (photography: Kenneth Peach), the final adventure featuring the "Zorro of the West," his faithful Indian companion and, of course, trusty steed Silver, is a nostalgia trip for men and boys of all ages, pure and simple, but a well-made, thoroughly enjoyable one nevertheless.

Dialogue:
Padre Ralph Moody to Fredericks and Montell, after stumbling across the golden city: "Our people have a new and shining hope, Paviva. A new life stands before us. None of this would be possible were it not for Tonto and The Lone Ranger."

A Lust to Kill

Barjul International Pictures; 74 minutes; Producers: Pat Betz and A.R. Milton; Director: Oliver Drake; Cast: Jim Davis; Don Megowan; Allison Hayes; Gerald Milton; Tom Hubbard; Claire Carleton; John Holland; James Maloney ***

A violent little sagebrush saga distributed by cheapo outfit Barjul Productions, whose only other two features were *Attack of the Jungle Women* (1959) and *The Beatniks* (1960). Lawman Jim Davis is on the trail of ex-buddy-turned-outlaw Don Megowan, who in turn is hell-bent on killing Gerald Milton, the gang's boss. During a posse chase, Milton left Megowan's wounded brother to fend for himself; Megowan went back to rescue him, was put behind bars and his sibling died. The townsfolk, headed by Mayor John Holland, object to a no-gooder being buried in their midst, so following a makeshift funeral, burly Megowan is busted out of his cell by girlfriend Allison Hayes and goes on the warpath, Milton and those sniveling citizens his prime targets. Shoot-outs, fistfights, beatings with a rifle butt and the distasteful sight of a near-naked, roly-poly Milton, laughing like a maniac and cavorting in a pond with a couple of women, add up to a low-budget erratic mix, Megowan given a chance to shine as the psycho gunman but proving he didn't really possess the ability to carry a picture on his broad shoulders, as in the sequence where Holland and his retinue are held hostage in Claire Carleton's store; he shouts and intimidates but fails to convince.

Surrounded by Milton's men, Holland and company grab weapons and open fire, Hayes unlocking Davis' cuffs; Megowan is slugged and cuffed and Milton wounded, his men retreating; Davis, tussling with Megowan, drowns him face-down in a muddy pool. Pages of the Bible superimposed over the end credits signify a religious moral message of some kind, but it probably went right over the audience's head; no doubt they were pondering on whether lanky Davis would now hitch up with the adorable Hayes.

Dialogue:
Megowan to Deputy Tom Hubbard who was responsible for shooting his brother: "I'm gonna count to 10. If you haven't drawn, I'm gonna spread what little guts you have all over the floor."

Man of the West

United Artists; CinemaScope/DeLuxecolor; 100 minutes; Producer: Walter Mirisch; Director: Anthony Mann; Cast: Gary Cooper; Julie London; Lee J. Cobb; Arthur O'Connell; Jack Lord; Robert J. Wilke; John Dehner; Royal Dano *****

Reformed outlaw Gary Cooper (Link Jones), on the lookout to finance a schoolteacher for the community of Good Hope, boards a train from Crosscut to Fort Worth; the locomotive is held up by Lee J. Cobb's gang, Cooper, singer Julie London and conman Arthur O'Connell left stranded 100 miles from the nearest town. Coming across a dilapidated ranch, Cooper enters the place to discover his past has returned to haunt him; Cobb and his boys are in residence—and Cobb (as Dock Tobin) was his former boss and mentor. What follows in Anthony Mann's fraught psychological drama is a battle of wills. Cobb wants Cooper back in the gang to perform one last job, the bank in Lassoo ("You were my right arm. I trained you. You ran off and left me!"); loose cannon Jack Lord, dumb Royal Dano and leering Robert J. Wilke don't want him—they want London's charms instead, Lord forcing her to strip at gunpoint ("She's my woman!" warns Cooper). Reginald Rose's articulate screenplay has London falling for Cooper, even though he's married, the man of few words plotting to extricate himself and London from Cobb's clutches, more so when John Dehner turns up, the lanky gunman deciding that Cooper is better off dead. On the way to Lassoo in three wagons, Cooper and Lord indulge in a violent slugging match, Cooper ripping Lord's clothes off; in the ensuing fracas, O'Connell is shot dead by Lord who gets his from Cobb. The landscape switches from open grasslands to lofty rock formations (California's Red Rock Canyon) and we're in arid, sun-bleached Spaghetti Western territory six years before the Italians muscled in on the action. Lassoo is a ghost town only occupied by a Mexican woman and her husband; twitchy Dano kills the woman without flinching. Cooper plugs Dano, strapping on the man's gun belt, prompting Wilke and Dehner to investigate, Cooper disposing of both. Back at camp, sobbing London has been assaulted and raped by Cobb, the maniac on a cliff top, calling Cooper out. Cooper, face set grim, eyes narrowed ("Lassoo's a ghost town. And that's what you are, Dock. A ghost!") shoots the desperado, Cobb's body tumbling down a rock slide, and rides away with London; the girl loves him but realizes they have no future together, a touching fadeout in a brutal, slow-burning oater heavy on sadism and sexual desire, one of Mann's finest genre achievements, as it was 56-year-old Cooper's—but it's not for the kids!

Highlights:
Ernest Haller's color photography plus Mann's careful orchestration of events set amid Red Rock Canyon's fluted rock columns.

Dialogue:
Dehner: "Link! I wanna see yer, cousin!"
Cooper: "Over here—cousin!"

Trivia:
James Stewart approached United Artists for the lead role but Mann refused to work with the actor following the *Night Passage* debacle (see Chapter 12), leaving Stewart feeling "betrayed"; Stewart Granger was also considered at one stage.

Man or Gun

Republic; Naturama; 79 minutes; Producer: Vince Skarstedt; Director: Albert C. Gannaway; Cast: Macdonald Carey; Audrey Totter; James Craig; Warren Stevens; Harry Shannon; James Gleason; Ken Lynch; Jil Jarmyn ****

"Was it the gun, or maybe it was the man." That's the burning question sung out at the end after Macdonald Carey has wandered into Dutch Flat from the desert and gunned down five men in the space of 10 minutes, all members of Harry Shannon's clan ("Five men dead and nobody's bothered," says Carey to Sheriff James Gleason). Is Carey's deadly Colt Wesson .44 [sic] blessed with supernatural powers? After all, he did find it in a grave ("I got the gun from a corpse," Carey tells Audrey Totter). Saloon boss Totter flirts outrageously with Carey, urging him to shoot those getting in the way of her own ambitions to run the town, including Shannon, shoving aside lovesick boyfriend Warren Stevens who also eyes that "charmed" pistol greedily; with the fancy weapon in *his* hand, he can rule the roost and get Totter back ("The gun that can't be beat."). "I want you to be the law in this town. Gun them all down," is Gleason's offer to Carey, which he rejects; a rancher's life is what he's after, not a gunslinger's life. Backed by a spare, creepy score from Gene Garf and Ramey Idriss, sharpshooter Carey seems like the avenging angel of death, events culminating in a well-staged street gunfight; James Craig and Carey face each other, guns and rifles explode in smoke and bullets, Craig lies dead, Totter shoots Stevens, Shannon bites the dust and Jil Jarmyn, Craig's Indian wife, sells the fabled six-gun to Gleason for a dollar—he's head honcho now! As for Gregory Peck look-alike Carey, he goes off with the delicious Totter to play house,

the climax to an unusual oater that threatens to drift into the uncanny at times without straying too far from its Western roots.
Highlights:
Carey's initial saloon standoff with leering Ken Lynch is a beauty, and a beauty is what Totter is. The blonde exuded oodles of sex appeal and could act, but she spent most of her long career in B-movies such as this one.
Dialogue:
Gleason to Carey, seeing him bringing in another body: "Witness?"
Carey: "Just the horse."

Money, Women and Guns

Universal; Eastmancolor; 80 minutes; Producer: Howie Horwitz; Director: Richard H. Bartlett; Cast: Jock Mahoney; Kim Hunter; Jeffrey Stone; Gene Evans; Tim Hovey; James Gleason; Lon Chaney, Jr.; William Campbell ****

Gold prospector Edwin Jerome is attacked by three masked bandits and fatally wounded; he kills two, the third rides off and he has just enough time to scribble his last will and testament on a board before expiring. Detective Jock Mahoney ("Silver" Ward Hogan) is assigned the task of tracking down the legitimate heirs to the will, each of whom will receive $50,000, plus finding out who the mysterious "Judas" is among the list *and* bring to justice the third man involved in the miner's death. Played out like a Western murder mystery, Richard H. Bartlett's engaging horse opera is episodic in design, Mahoney locating one name after another in a series of well-constructed vignettes, bounty hunter Jeffrey Stone in on the action and willing to share the whopping

$50,000 fee with his reluctant partner. The twist in a very absorbing tale is that Stone's mule is called Judas and he is the third bushwhacker connected in Jerome's murder: Stone tells Mahoney that he was against the killing and didn't fire a shot, only wanting some of the riches the prospector unearthed in a claim that the old-timer bought from him; he reckons he was due *something* from the strike. Mahoney believes him, stating that he will testify on his behalf at Stone's trial. Tired of a life on the detective trail, Mahoney then decides to set up home with widow Kim Hunter and young son Tim Hovey (a recipient in Jerome's will) at the new ranch they have purchased. Lean, rangy, six-foot-four Mahoney, in the last Western he would appear in before he embarked on his *Tarzan* adventures, ambles through the proceedings with tough, good-natured aplomb, another very pleasing cowboy role; there's not a great deal of gunplay, but the various character studies and plot intrigues, plus some decent acting, make for a very tasty Western dish.

Highlights:

Mahoney, long and lean in the saddle, featured in a series of great mid-budget Westerns in the '50s, of which *Money, Women and Guns* is a prime example; he's often overlooked in favor of other stars of the genre and deserves more recognition.

Dialogue:

Mahoney to Hunter: "I'm leavin' before sunup."

Hunter: "You gettin' that hemmed in feeling again, Mr. Hogan?"

Mahoney: "Well, with a ranch like that, a kid like Davy, a woman like you, you've got to admit that you dangle some pretty nice bait."

Quantrill's Raiders

Allied Artists; CinemaScope/DeLuxecolor; 68 minutes; Producer: Ben Schwalb; Director: Edward Bernds; Cast: Steve Cochran; Leo Gordon; Diane Brewster; Gale Robbins; Myron Healey; Will Wright; Lane Chandler; Dan White ★★★★

Confederate officer Steve Cochran rides into Lawrence, Kansas in 1863, pretends he's a horse trader dealing with the Union and gains vital information about the Union arsenal for William Quantrill, played with psychotic relish by screen bruiser Leo Gordon; Gordon's after that ammunition and wants to wipe Lawrence off the face of the map into the bargain. Gordon's mistress, redhead Gale Robbins, throws herself at Cochran, the good-looking hunk also catching the attention of decorative Diane

Brewster, owner of a boarding house; meanwhile, Judge Will Wright, head of the vigilance committee, grows increasingly suspicious of Cochran's comings and goings, especially when a group of Cherokee are slaughtered by Quantrill's men following an exchange of horseflesh. Edward Bernds' colorful actioner (a great score from Marlin Skiles) never eases up in the excitement stakes, climaxing in a terrific town versus Quantrill's Raiders shoot-out in which Cochran, his conscience pricked over a possible Lawrence massacre ("He's out to kill everyone in this town."), sides with the citizens, ending up pumping three slugs into the guerrilla boss (*not how Quantrill met his demise!*). He's sentenced to jail but promises to return to Brewster and her young son on his release. "Rousing yarn," commented *Variety* of one of the best of the many films to be based on Quantrill and his infamous exploits.

Highlights:
Gordon with his foot on the gas pedal; no one could sneer, bellow and throw his burly weight around like the legendary screen heavy in his heyday, six-foot-two inches of mean attitude.

Dialogue:
Robbins to Gordon: "He (Cochran) said no looting."
Gordon: "No looting? I'll take everything I can lay my hands on. Kill every Yankee that crosses my path. Lawrence! Take a good look at it, Kate, while it's still on the map."

The Rawhide Trail

Allied Artists; 67 minutes; Producer: Earle Lyon; Director: Robert Gordon; Cast: Rex Reason; Nancy Gates; Richard Erdman; Ann Doran; Robert Knapp; Sam Buffington; Rusty Lane; Maureen Hingert (Jana Davi) **

All the action in *The Rawhide Trail* occurs during the first 14 minutes. Comanches attack the Texas town of Gunsight, intent on laying their hands on scouts Rex Reason and Richard Erdman, behind bars awaiting the noose, the pair accused of leading a wagon train into an Indian ambush. They reckon they're innocent and that the Redskins are after them and no one else. In the meantime, a stage leaves Winthorst en route for Gunsight, carrying Indian agent Robert Knapp, his unhappy fiancée Nancy Gates, newspaperman Sam Buffington and Ann Doran. Reason, Erdman, Erdman's Indian wife Maureen Hingert and a platoon of soldiers headed by Captain Rusty Lane leave

Gunsight and both stagecoach passengers and Lane's group meet up at a stage depot. From thereon in, after that lively beginning, the movie becomes slightly bogged down. Lane is seriously wounded and tended to by Doran, it transpires that oily Knapp withheld supplies from the Comanches and supplied them with mismatched rifles and ammunition, and Gates casts her eyes over Reason's manly physique. Reason (he's half Kiowa) and Erdman are entrusted with leading the bunch to safety through hazardous territory which they do after Reason uses a Winchester repeating rifle to pick off the Indians and detonate an ammunition crate, causing a deadly landslide; Knapp gets a well-deserved arrow in the back. In the end, Reason, Gates, Erdman and Hingert gallop away to start a new life, well away from Gunsight and those troublesome Comanches. The opening noisy assault on Gunsight, plus personable Reason's solid performance, are the two main reasons for catching this strictly routine oater.

Dialogue:
Knapp to Reason, grumbling that he's having to lug a box of ammunition across country: "You'll live to regret this."
Reason: "Chances are we won't."

Trivia:
If for nothing else, Reason is best-remembered for starring in two classic Universal sci-fi/horror flicks of the 1950s, *This Island Earth* (1955) and *The Creature Walks Among Us* (1956).

Return to Warbow

Columbia; Technicolor; 67 minutes; Producer: Wallace MacDonald; Director: Ray Nazarro; Cast: Philip Carey; Andrew Duggan; Catherine McLeod; Robert J. Wilke; William Leslie; James Griffith; Jay Silverheels; Christopher Olsen ****

Incarcerated for 11 long years in Arizona Territorial Prison, hardened bank robber Philip Carey, along with Robert J. Wilke and William Leslie, busts free from the chain gang and heads towards Warbow. His brother, gambler James Griffith, knows the whereabouts of the $30,000 Carey stole, and Carey wants that loot as compensation for his years spent in captivity. Carey's ex, Catherine McLeod, is now married to Andrew Duggan, but her son (Christopher Olsen) isn't Duggan's—he's Carey's. Carey threatens to tell the boy the truth if Duggan doesn't go into Warbow and collect whiskey-sodden Griffith; all the while, Wilke and Leslie plot to get rid of Carey and divide the cash two ways, *if* it can be located. Carey and Wilke accompany Duggan into town and Griffith is dragged off after a shoot-out, only to reveal that the money is located in an abandoned mine. The final 15 minutes takes place in the dangerous mine tunnels. Griffith confesses the cash was blown on booze and gambling debts ("11 dirty rotten lousy years when you lived on my money!" roars Carey), Wilke puts the waster out of his misery, the gallery roof begins to collapse, Leslie is crushed under tons of falling rock, Carey plugs Wilke and, fatally wounded, is helped out of a side entrance by blind Indian Jay Silverheels, electing not to tell Olsen his true identity before dying. Over a hard-driving 67 minutes, Ray Nazarro manufactures a taut oater lit by Henry Freulich's vivid Technicolor photography, the whole cast on top of their game, especially heavies Carey and Wilke; if only they could make tough-as-nails, riveting little Westerns like this these days…

Highlights:
Freulich's rich photography and both Carey and screen hard guy Wilke in sweaty, in-your-face form.

Dialogue:
Leslie to Wilke: "You know, splittin' that money up there three ways, it makes less, don't it?"
Wilke: "You're forgettin' Johnny, we're just gonna split it up two ways."

Saddle the Wind

MGM; CinemaScope/Metrocolor; 84 minutes; Producer: Armand Deutsch; Director: Robert Parrish; Cast: Robert Taylor; John Cassavetes; Julie London; Donald Crisp; Royal Dano; Ray Teal; Charles McGraw; Richard Erdman ****

Saloon dame Julie London rues the day she ever allowed John Cassavetes to bring her to his brother's Double S Ranch on the promise of a new life; Cassavetes is an immature, trigger-obsessed hothead, one step away from being a fully-fledged psycho, liking rough love-making (she doesn't) and needing to prove he's quicker than anyone with a gun, including elder sibling Robert Taylor, a reformed gun hawk-turned-rancher (he rode with Quantrill's Raiders) who rents land owned by Donald Crisp of the Deneen Ranch. London sees Cassavetes' dark side surface when, drunk, he plugs Charles McGraw in a saloon, reveling in the experience; McGraw was in town to shoot Taylor but Cassavetes does his brother's job for him ("A gun-happy loco kid. That's what people think."). Trouble escalates when embittered ex-Union major Royal Dano arrives on Crisp's property with a party of settlers, claiming his father's land rights: Crisp allows him to stay, but Cassavetes, having no truck with squatters, wrecks their camp and kills Dano in a street standoff, Crisp, calling Cassavetes a "dirty little trigger-happy jackal," telling Taylor he's going to erect fences all over his land and ordering him to quit the Double S Ranch. Cassavetes, wounding Crisp in another showdown, flees to the hills, winged in the stomach; Taylor confronts him in the climax, his brother taking the coward's way out by shooting himself to prevent Taylor from finishing him off. Crisp, hearing the news, says Taylor can stay—and London elects to stay with him! An intelligent, unusual Western filmed in Colorado, featuring fine photography from George J. Folsey, a spare Elmer Bernstein score and highly watchable contrasting performances from stern-faced Taylor and edgy Cassavetes; and singer London looks ravishing.

Highlights:
Colorado's magnificent panoramic scenery, plus Taylor and Cassavetes sparking off one another, two performers from two very different schools of training.

Dialogue:
Ray Teal: "I don't think Tony (Cassavetes) ever did git born. I think that someone just found him wedged into a gun cylinder and shot him onto the world by pressing the trigger."

Trivia:
Cassavetes and Parrish didn't see eye-to-eye during filming, the highly strung Brooklyn-born method player demanding everything be done *his* way and acting difficult on set, even if it meant shooting 20 takes on one scene; *Newsweek*'s comment on Cassavetes read like this: "Cassavetes talks and looks about as Western as a member of the switchblade set."

Seven Guns to Mesa

Allied Artists; 69 minutes; Producer: William F. Broidy; Director: Edward Dein; Cast: Charles Quinlivan; Lola Albright; James Griffith; Jay Adler; John Cliff; Burt Nelson; Charles Keane; Neil Grant **

Stopping over in the ghost town of Mesa, a San Francisco-bound coach is waylaid by James Griffith and his six partners-in-crime, the passengers held hostage in the saloon. Griffith plans to relieve an army-escorted wagon train of its load of gold and his captives are insurance if the scheme backfires. In rides ex-circus performer Charles Quinlivan to stir up trouble, but his wooden presence does little to enliven a static oater where an inordinate amount of time is spent in the cast sitting around in saloon chairs discussing how to escape the gang's clutches. Humor is provided by whiskey-loving Jay Adler (he gives all his bottles a name), glamor by Lola Albright and menace in the shape of Griffith's evil gang boss; in a shoot-out with the troop detail guarding the gold, the outlaws are wiped out, Quinlivan finishing off the last of the bunch (John Cliff) in a barn before setting off to 'Frisco with vivacious Albright.

Dialogue:
Adler, picking up a whiskey bottle: "Nothing ugly or useless as an empty bottle. Just look at it. While ago it was a living thing."

Trivia:
Cliff, pursued by Quinlivan, lets off 13 continuous shots from a gun that holds six bullets.

The Sheepman

MGM; CinemaScope/Metrocolor; 85 minutes; Producer: Edmund Grainger; Director: George Marshall; Cast: Glenn Ford; Shirley MacLaine; Leslie Nielsen; Mickey Shaughnessy; Edgar Buchanan; Pernell Roberts; Pedro Gonzalez Gonzalez; Willis Bouchey ****

Partly serious, partly comedic, always easy on the eye, *The Sheepman* was a big commercial success for MGM, its combination of Glenn Ford, Shirley MacLaine, lush color and sweeping Colorado location work going down a bomb with audiences. It's the old cattle versus sheep scenario. Smooth-talking Ford wants to set up a sheep ranch in Powder Valley; cattle baron Leslie Nielsen is dead set against the idea, trying every trick in the book to get rid of his stubborn rival, who happens to be lightning quick on the draw, as his glass/poker counter shooting trick in the saloon proves. But in spite of Nielsen's repeated efforts to drive him out of town, Ford keeps coming back, threatening to expose Nielsen as a criminal living under an alias, forcing the crook to hire three gunslingers to eliminate the sheep farmer. Ford steals MacLaine from under Nielsen's nose, guns down baddie Pernell Roberts in a tense street showdown, puts paid to Nielsen and even gets to tame tough hombre Mickey Shaughnessy, the big beefy guy helping Ford with his sheep when he eventually settles in Powder Valley; Ford then sells the lot to buy cattle, much to MacLaine's amusement—here is a man who likes to surprise people by not letting the grass grow under his feet, and she likes it!

Highlights:
Shirley MacLaine, 24 and looking delicious, plus Ford proving he was one of Hollywood's finest, most dependable actors.

Dialogue:
Ford to MacLaine, after she has pulled a gun on one of Nielsen's bushwhackers, ready to shoot Ford in the back: "Thanks, lady!"
MacLaine: "Anytime, mister!"

Showdown at Boot Hill

Regal Films/20th Century Fox; RegalScope; 71 minutes; Producer: Harold E. Knox; Director: Gene Fowler, Jr.: Cast: Charles Bronson; Robert Hutton; John Carradine; Carole Mathews; Fintan Meyler; Thomas B. Henry; Mike Mason; Paul Maxey ***

In his first movie as top billing, Charles Bronson played a United States deputy marshal-cum-bounty hunter who rides into Mountain City, walks into the hotel lobby and beats triple-killer Thomas B. Henry to the draw. But he's unable to collect the $200 reward money because the citizens refuse to acknowledge that Henry was who Bronson claimed him to be; Henry took on the mantle of town benefactor, Bronson viewed as trouble with a six-gun. Bronson strikes up a relationship with shy waitress Fintan Meyler, the two lonely souls finding solace in each other's company, Bronson buying cream for his new girl's rough hands. In the saloon, Bronson puts two bullets into cocksure pretty-boy Mike Mason, wounding him on purpose; the outraged townsfolk, headed by Judge Paul Maxey, have had enough of this interloper prying into their shady affairs, forming a mob to oust the poker-faced stranger. In a frenetic climax, Mason staggers from his bed and shoots Meyler's mother, Carole Mathews, by mistake; she dies, and at Henry's funeral on Boot Hill, Bronson is beaten to the ground by the deceased's brother wielding a pole, the mourners filing past him in derision. Sick of Mountain City and the people who live there, Bronson and Meyler decide to leave and set up house elsewhere. Louis Vittes' screenplay introduces a plethora of characters but fails to fully explain Henry's importance to the town, or the motives behind those trying to protect his reputation, if in fact he had one. Bronson is the main attraction and it's easy to see, in the opening sequence, why Sergio Leone considered him for the role of the Man With No Name in *A Fistful of Dollars*; a long tracking shot of Bronson slowly ambling down the street, everyone avoiding eye-contact, has "Spaghetti Western" written all over it.

Dialogue:
Bronson to Robert Hutton, after gunning down Henry: "You better have an inquest pretty quick. Weather like this, he won't keep."

Trivia:
Great play is made throughout the picture of Bronson being short: He was of average height, five-foot-eight and a half, but appeared smaller against Hutton's six-foot-two and John Carradine's six-foot; director Gene Fowler, Jr. was responsible for the start of the '50s craze in teenage horror films in the 1957 classic *I Was a Teenage Werewolf*.

Sierra Baron

20th Century Fox; CinemaScope/DeLuxecolor; 80 minutes; Producer: Plato A. Skouras; Director: James B. Clark; Cast: Brian Keith; Rick Jason; Rita Gam; Mala Powers; Steve Brodie; Lee Morgan; Lewis Allan; Carlos Múzquiz **

A lush score provided by Paul Sawtell and Bert Shefter and stunning widescreen photography courtesy of Alex Phillips do their utmost to enhance a dull tale set in 1848 concerning Spaniard Rick Jason and his sister, Rita Gam, protecting their Mexican property from crooked real estate dealer Steve Brodie. Their land was part of the Princessa Grant treaty of 1761, but Brodie, busy building a nearby town, is having none of it, and neither are miners looking for gold. Gringo pistolero Brian Keith, offered $1,000 to kill Jason, visits the hacienda, falls for glamorous Gam and offers his revolver for hire to the Spanish baron—at $6.00 per month. Midway through, a wagon train appears on Jason's ranch; he allows them to stay, latching onto recently widowed Mala Powers after just one dance and proposing marriage. In a standoff between Brodie's thugs and Jason and his settlers, news comes through that the Senate in Washington has honored those ancient land rights. Brodie, defeated, gallops off, returns to the hacienda and is shot by Jason, but not before Keith has taken a bullet; he dies in Gam's arms, Powers finding solace in Jason's embrace. The canvas could have been much broader in this underdeveloped actioner that is pleasing on the eye and ear but has little else to offer in the way of full-blooded drama.

Dialogue:
Gam, at the dining table: "I hope the message Senor McCracken (Keith) brought us was a welcome one."
Jason: "What message? You brought a message for me?"
Keith: "Yeah, in a way ... it is kinda personal. See, I come out here to kill you."

Wild Heritage

Universal; CinemaScope/Eastmancolor; 78 minutes; Producer: John E. Horton; Director: Charles F. Haas; Cast: Will Rogers, Jr.; Maureen O'Sullivan; Paul Birch; Rod McKuen; George Winslow; Gary Gray; Gigi Perreau; Jeanette Nolan ***

Paul Birch, his wife (Maureen O'Sullivan), three sons (Rod McKuen, George Winslow, Gary Gray) and daughter (Gigi Perreau) move out West to set up a homestead at Topknot; in the rough, tough settlement town, Birch is gunned down by cattle rustling no-goods John Beradino and Phil Harvey, leaving his wife and children to fend for themselves and try to make a living, first by building a home on the prairie and growing vegetables. *Almost* a family-type yarn with violent undercurrents describes Universal's underproduced

Western, nicely photographed by Philip H. Lathrop but lacking a certain degree of bite. O'Sullivan's brood have recently widowed Jeanette Nolan's family living nearby, moody Troy Donahue not hitting it off with McKuen and his siblings, tomboy Judi Meredith casting her eyes over McKuen as possible husband material; town judge Will Rogers, Jr., meanwhile, decides to romance O'Sullivan when the time is right. The best part of the film occurs in the middle section, cattle boss Casey Tibbs instructing McKuen and Gray how to draw and fire a six-gun after his herd has been stampeded and run off by Beradino and Harvey's bunch, leaving only 100 head which is shared between the two ranches. The much-anticipated showdown in the town's street, greenhorns McKuen, Gray and Donahue facing up to old pros Beradino and Harvey, packs a punch, young Winslow handing McKuen a gun after his has been shot out of his hand; the two killers are brought down in a storm of lead. The final frame has McKuen and Meredith acting like man and wife, Donahue putting his arm around Perreau and Rogers nestling up to O'Sullivan, a cozy family portrait to round things off.

Dialogue:
Tibbs to novices McKuen and Gray: "Point is, there's no use tryin' to draw fast until you hit a target. And the hardest targets to hit are the ones that move and shoot back at you."

Chapter 15

Hope Out West: *Fancy Pants,*
Son of Paleface and *Alias Jesse James*

Throughout the 1940s, Bob Hope and Bing Crosby were consistently Hollywood's biggest box-office draws, either when acting as a pair, as in the *Road* movies, or on their own, top flight celebrities who reigned supreme during the movie industry's golden period. Hope's first major success sans Crosby was Paramount's *The Paleface* (1948) in which he played "Painless" Peter Potter, a heavy-handed dentist who unwittingly becomes involved with Calamity Jane (Jane Russell) in rounding up a gang of outlaws. Eventually grossing a whopping $6,000,000, *The Paleface* is generally regarded as the all-time greatest joke Western, but, never one to be content to rest on his laurels, the comedian followed it up in the 1950s with three other essential genre mickey-takes, *Fancy Pants* (Paramount, 1950), *Son of Paleface* (Paramount, 1952) and *Alias Jesse James* (Hope Enterprises/United Artists, 1959). I've purposely steered clear of comedy Westerns in this book but, to lighten the tone after all that gunfire and villainy, let's have a look at this trio of classic comedy horse operas highlighting Hope in his prime; it goes without saying that all three merit five-star ratings.

"No popcorn during my performance—peasants!" Thus spoke Mr. Robert (formerly Bob) Hope to the audience, snootily adjusting his monocle in *Fancy Pants*, Paramount's uproarious remake of their own *Ruggles of Red Gap* (1935), Charles Laughton in Hope's role. It's 1912: Bob plays actor Arthur Tyler who in turn is playing Humphrey the

Butler in a none-too-successful English stage comedy attended by Americans Lucille Ball and her Ma, Lea Penman. They're on the lookout for an Englishman to bring a bit of refinery to their life out in the Wild West in Big Squaw, New Mexico. Would-be aristocrat Hugh French seizes on the bright idea of using his friend's mansion and the repertory company to impress Ball whom he's fallen for, even though she's not the slightest bit interested. The first 23 minutes contains more strangulated English vowels than you can throw a stick at (especially from bumbling Eric Blore), but it's Calamity Hope (Hope was an actual Englishman himself, born in Eltham, London) who catches Penman's beady eye, even though Ball says, after watching the bogus butler spill one tray of drinks too many over hapless Norma Varden, "How often do you have to wind him up?" "Take that home with us? Ma, have you got bats in your belfry?" she adds, but Ma thinks he's just what Big Squaw (and her husband) needs to smooth out its uncouth edges; Hope travels to the dusty, noisy town ("I hope he jumps all the way back to England," complains Ball when the butler hops off the train), immediately arousing the jealousy of burly Bruce Cabot who wants to marry Ball but reckons she's in love with old "Fancy Pants."

Once out West, Hope's on overdrive, running like a scared rabbit from a bunch of Indian kids ("Indians! Midget Indians!"), getting into scrapes with Cabot's fists and guns, running foul of Ball's cantankerous Pa (Jack Kirkwood), leading the townsfolk into believing that he's the Earl of Brinstead, hero of various fictitious African adventures, and involving himself in a fox hunt with President Teddy Roosevelt (John Alexander)—this lengthy farcical episode (one of the funniest in any Bob Hope movie) sees the pack of dogs chasing Hope (coated in gravy) here, there and everywhere, not the fox! Throw in two great songs ("Hey, Fancy Pants" and "Home Cookin'"), Hope forced to ride buckin' bronco Peaceful ("That's a horse? Peaceful? Nickname, huh?") and plenty of witty banter between the two leading stars (Ball: "First time I saw you, I said to myself—there's a lowdown lily-livered coyote. Then, as I got to know you better, I figured you for a filthy, sneaking rat." Hope: "I grow on people like that.") and you have a Western comedy all dressed up in glowing Technicolor hues (photographer: Charles B. Lang) that never dates, directed with zeal by George Marshall over 92 very entertaining minutes, an old-school Hollywood romp at its best; and, naturally, Hope and highly decorative Ball (they made four films together) end up a lovin' couple. A big hit in 1950, *Fancy Pants*

amassed $3,000,000 in rentals in America alone. "A cunningly comical job as the phony butler," enthused the *New York Times* on Hope, adding, "Ball is gorgeously brazen."

Frank Tashlin directed *Son of Paleface*, the follow-up to the phenomenally successful *The Paleface* (Tashlin was one of three scriptwriters on that picture, and one of three here). Tashlin had been dissatisfied with Norman Z. McLeod's handling of the 1948 movie and wanted to direct *Son of* himself, to make it even stupider and more side-splitting, if that was at all possible. Many are of the opinion that *Son of Paleface* is as good as, if not better, than the original; it's certainly more manic and absurd in approach. Either way, the production featured Hope at the very top of his game, 95 minutes of pure Hollywood screwball entertainment, one of, if not the, most hilarious Western parodies ever committed to celluloid. You have to concentrate for the whole of the running time; verbal and sight gags come so thick and fast that if you blink, you'll miss a choice tidbit—and Hope puts more energy into this zany opus than any one of today's comics would manage to do in half-a-dozen. Kicking off at Harvard University campus, Hope (as Peter "Junior" Potter) informs girlfriend Jean Willes (Penelope) that he's off to the Wild West to cash in on his inheritance. A brief clip of Bing Crosby driving a car, Hope adding, "An old character actor on the Paramount lot we like to keep working ... but I guarantee you this feller will *not* be in the picture tonight" done and dusted with (yep, it's that kinda show!), we next see a mysterious gunman in black named The Torch and his/her outlaw gang hold up a stage, using a secret tunnel under a bridge to gain access into their mine hideout. Federal Agent Roy Rogers on Trigger, the "Smartest Horse in the Movies," and sidekick Lloyd Corrigan are on their way to Sawbuck Pass to nail the outfit, Singing Cowboy Roy crooning "A Four Legged Friend" in the town square (the film includes seven songs). Into the street roars Bob in his clapped-out automobile (the action takes place around 1900), creating chaos, the wheels spraying mud over half the town's population who are baying for his blood; Potter Senior ran up a whole load of debts and the irate citizens demand payment pronto, out of Hope's inheritance money. The will is read, stating that Hope's father "didn't leave anything to my wife because she presented me with an idiot for a son." But the inheritance chest is empty, leaving Hope to pretend there's gold in there to stave off a necktie party: "I got gold stones! I got gallstones! Gold gallstones!" Iron Eyes Cody (Chief Yellow Cloud) is also after Hope's scalp as he came on the wrong end of his father's shady dealings. Hope, desperate and disguised as an Indian, wires Willes: "Penelope. No money. You send." The reply is suitably blunt: "You get lost. Heap Big Penelope."

From thereon in, the scatty plot hinges on Rogers (he carries a rifle in his guitar) and "Doc" Corrigan tailing Hope who, they reckon, will lead them to The Torch, none other than the owner of the Dirty Shame saloon, Jane Russell (Hope wanted Maureen O'Hara in the role, but she turned it down for personal reasons); the dame wishes to lay her manicured hands on that inheritance gold, having been swindled, like so many others, by Potter Senior. Hope homes in on Russell's voluptuous curves, much to gunman Bill Williams' annoyance, Rogers tries unsuccessfully to romance her, Hope and curmudgeonly prospector pal Paul E. Burns search for clues to the whereabouts of the gold coins (they're inside a moose head in the ghost town of Sterling City), Russell dopes Hope and uses the sap as an alibi in a holdup and frisky Trigger causes the funny man no end of hassles. Among a barrage of rat-a-tat-tat verbal exchanges and visual shenanigans, standouts are: Hope's comment on seeing Russell flaunt her figure on stage in a skimpy outfit: "If we could bottle it, we'd make a fortune"; Hope to Rogers at the bar: "What's the matter? Don't you like women?" "I'll stick to horses, mister." "Horses. Horses? Huh, horses! That's ridiculous," Hope sidling away in disgust; Russell asking Hope what he would like: "What would I like? Can't we discuss it in the cellar of my hotel?"; "Give me back my yellow liver. Matches my spine," he blurts to Williams, a gun planted in

Westerns of the 1950s: The Classic Years

his back; Hope emerging from his tub in red long johns to find a camera crew setting up their equipment: "Who do you think you are? Cecil B. DeMille?" DeMille himself, emerging from behind camera: "Somebody call me?"; Hope attired in giant Stetson, double gun and holster, furry chaps and huge spurs; Hope in bed with Trigger, vying for which of them gets the sheets ("Want me to steal your teeth?"); and Russell stroking Hope's face the next morning: "They been abusing my baby?" "I hate to tell you who I slept with last night. Those cold hoofs on my back." And I haven't even mentioned those two buzzards Martin and Lewis (Hope: "Beat it or you're gonna make the whole thing unbelievable."), Trigger rescuing tied-up Rogers and Hope ("When Trigger sees the spot we're in, he'll get us out. He's got horse sense." Hope: "If he had any sense, he wouldn't be a horse."), the Indians' steeds sliding on banana skins to the sound of screeching brakes, Hope's car floating over a deep ravine, held up by an umbrella, to the sound of a jet engine, Hope confronting his Dad's ghost that's accompanied by an attractive Red Devil ("It's me. Your own flesh and idiot!"), a dozen arrows festooning Hope's hat...

Yes, it is literally a laugh/gag/jape a minute, breathless lunacy of the kind only Hope could pull off all those years ago. Following a thrill-a-second "Redskins chasing car" ride (all to the sound of Civil War music), Hope gets his inheritance and marries Russell, the gal having to spend time behind bars in the state prison. On release date, she comes through the prison gate and embraces her four children, much to Rogers' surprise. "Yours?" he asks Hope who grins at the camera. "Let's see them top that on television." The picture ends with Rogers on Trigger who rears up on his hind quarters, outlined against the setting sun; Hope's "horseless carriage" performs the same stunt! "Cutting looks and knife-edged gags," said *Variety*, the picture a huge grosser at the time. Comedy Westerns in all shapes and guises have come and gone over the intervening 60-odd years, but none can equal *Son of Paleface* for undiluted craziness combined with inventiveness, propelled by one of Tinseltown's legendary comedians in full flight. Silliness with a capital S—the funniest spoof Western of them all? It's gotta be! The *New York Times* wrote "Freewheelin' and hilarious," *The Hollywood Reporter* chipping in with, "Stupidly funny."

Ol' Ski Nose was slightly less ebullient (and not all that much of a scaredy-cat) and just a tiny bit more subdued in Norman Z. McLeod's *Alias Jesse James*, playing bungling insurance salesman Milford Farnsworth, but after all, he was 55 so entitled to cut down on all those frenetic antics that highlighted the *Road* movies and the two *Paleface* outings. Will Wright (Titus Queasley), elderly boss of New York firm Plymouth Rock Insurance, wants nothing better than to fire hopeless Hope, pointing out his numerous deficiencies: "What do you expect to achieve with such crass ineptitude, such utter incompetence, such colossal stupidity?" "Well, I was hoping to become your assistant," smiles the loser, the first of many such gags littering the script (writers: Robert S. Aubrey, Bert Lawrence, Daniel B. Beauchamps, William Bowers). But the man who palmed off a 30-year endowment policy on a 98-year-old woman is in for the chop ("Well, she lied about her age."). In a bar drowning his sorrows, he bumps into Wendell Corey (Jesse James) and, to his amazement, succeeds in selling him a $100,000 policy based on a $33,000 premium, the money of which is delivered to Wright in a bag (the takings from a bank robbery). A certain Cora Lee Collins (Rhonda Fleming) is the beneficiary if Corey dies; Hope is then ordered to travel West by his boss to protect their prime asset ("I'm likely to get killed." "Stop trying to cheer me up."), Corey having departed the city in a hurry, the law on his tail. Hope boards a train heading into the Wild West and the fun begins, starting with him trying to sell a policy to two Redskin agents of the Aetna Insurance Company, one of whom is Sam Hiawatha! (Aetna is one of America's oldest and wealthiest Healthcare Insurance companies, hence the in-joke.)

In the town of Angel's Rest, Hope soon finds himself up to his neck in all kinds of trouble, as one might expect. After downing two whiskies in the Dirty Dog saloon,

BOB HOPE RHONDA FLEMING **ALIAS JESSE JAMES** WENDELL COREY

which sends his Boss of the Plains hat into a steaming spin, Hope is reunited with Corey who hatches a plan to have the salesman impersonate him and then bumped off, the outlaw to collect the $100,000 and marry reluctant fiancée Fleming, the dame setting her sights on Hope and his bright red long johns! The storyline veers all over the place, highlights including Hope triumphing at the card table and having his winning deck eaten by a goat; Jim Davis (Frank James) breathing down his neck, Hope drawing a gun and spluttering, "Don't anybody move or I'll blow my brains out"; Hope meeting Indian Princess Gloria Talbott ("Do I curtsy or tip my scalp?"); Hope and Fleming warbling the delightful "Ain't-a-Hankerin'" (Guy Mitchell sings the title song over the credits); Hope dispatching a Gila monster ("The mice sure grow big around here.") with a rattlesnake; Hope dressed as Jesse James, wounding Jack Lambert in a street showdown using a trick shot, prompting Fleming to ask the question of her new beau: "You're a gunslinger?" "Yep. Yep—nope!"; Hope caught with lipstick on his face by a furious Corey after necking with Fleming: "What's that?" "Well, I shaved this morning and I'm a slow bleeder; better get outta here before I become a faster one"; and Hope leading the James gang in a train holdup in which he robs Wright, his old boss, of the $33,000 he's returning to Corey. Hope is fired at by Corey's outfit to finish him off but survives the fusillade by donning a suit of chest armor, cantering into the outlaw's homestead on a cow, much to the glee of Fleming, who, by the way, is as radiantly attractive as ever.

It's time for the picture's riotous climax, Hope and Talbott waylaying a Justice of the Peace en route to Corey and Fleming's wedding: "We gotta figure out a way to stop that," says Hope to the lovely Injun when he hears news of the nuptials. "How?" "This is no time for Indian talk. Let's get movin'." Disguised as the JP, Hope laces the party punch with magic mushrooms, leading to a fistfight in slow-motion among the hallucinating guests, then hightails it back in a buggy to Angel's Rest with Fleming in her wedding dress ("First time the preacher's ever eloped with the bride."), Corey and his boys in hot pursuit. In town, Hope tools up with artillery, hides behind a barrel and the shoot-out commences, the James gang dropping one by one to Hope's deadly accurate aim—but is it Hope's aim that's actually doing the job? No folks, it's cameo appearances by sharpshooters Hugh O'Brian (Wyatt Earp), Ward Bond, James Arness (Matt Dillon), Roy Rogers, Gary Cooper, Fess Parker (Davy Crockett), Gail Davis (Annie Oakley), Jay Silverheels (Tonto; he lets loose with an arrow) and Hope's old sparring partner, Bing Crosby ("This feller needs all the help he can get."); Gene Autrey and James Garner's spots were omitted due to royalty hassles. Hope is now the hero of the day, a statue to be erected in his honor. The movie finishes with Hope at his plush desk in New York, now President of the Plymouth Rock Insurance Company, being informed by wife Fleming that there is going to be a new addition to their brood of six. "Hope plays it tongue-in-cheek," commented the *New York Times*; how else could he have done it?

McLeod (he directed *Road to Rio* and *The Paleface*) orchestrates a fun-packed 92 minutes produced in glossy DeLuxecolor which will appeal to the comedian's legion of admirers. *Alias Jesse James* made a lot of money (practically all of Hope's films did) and, while not up to the sky-high standards set by previous Hope features, most notably the classic evergreen *Road* series, still remains a rib-tickling exercise in Western goofiness, the third funniest oater of the 1950s behind *Fancy Pants* and *Son of Paleface*; and Hope's renowned genius at comic timing and rapid wise-cracking asides, even by 1959, showed no signs of letting up. If you want a mirth-packed night in, disengage the brain, grab the popcorn (even though Mr. Robert Hope told you not to in *Fancy Pants*!) and Coke, stick these three classic 1950s Western farces on and prepare to have your funny bone assaulted, big time!

Looks like Trigger got the girl!

Westerns of the 1950s: The Classic Years

Chapter 16
1959

HIS BODY IS AN EMPTY SHELL THAT HIDES A LUSTFUL FIEND!
Curse of the Undead

**JUST TIME ENOUGH ... TO CHANGE HIS CLOTHES ...
HIS GIRL AND HIS NAME!**
Face of a Fugitive

VIOLENCE EXPLODES FROM HIS EYES!
Good Day for a Hanging

**HE WAS A U.S. MARSHAL BUT THE NAME
THEY CALLED HIM WAS ... THE HANGMAN!**
The Hangman

THESE WERE THE WILD-RIDING VIKINGS OF THE GREAT PLAINS!
The Jayhawkers!

**CLINT'S BACK! AND KOOKIE IS WITH HIM! THE YEAR'S BIG NEW
THRILL ON THE BIG THEATER SCREEN!**
Yellowstone Kelly

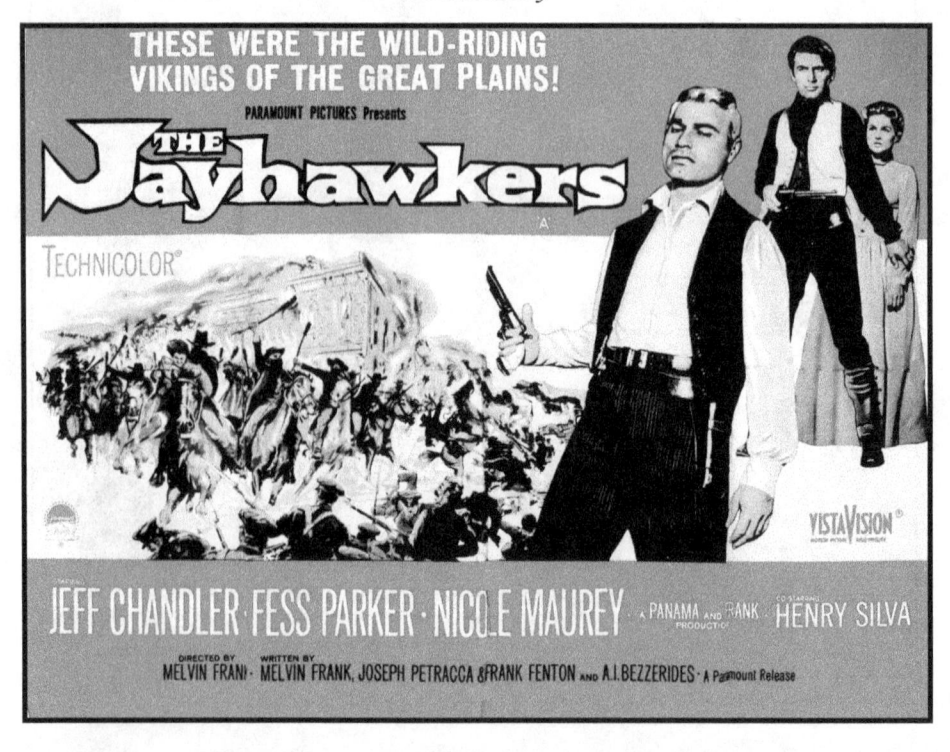

Curse of the Undead

Universal; 79 minutes; Producer: Joseph Gershenson; Director: Edward Dein; Cast: Michael Pate; Eric Fleming; Kathleen Crowley; John Hoyt; Bruce Gordon; Edward Binns; Jimmy Murphy; Helen Kleeb ****

Universal Horror meets the Universal Western in Edward Dein's imaginative merging of the vampire myth with Old West values, the result now regarded as something of a mini-classic. A mysterious epidemic is hitting town, young girls expiring through loss of blood. Preacher Eric Fleming notices puncture wounds on the deceaseds' necks and at this juncture, Dein changes tack to bring in the Western angle: Land baron Bruce Gordon and his thugs are furtively stealing John Hoyt's property; when Hoyt is killed, young Jimmy Murphy suspects Gordon, challenging him to the draw and losing. Her brother and father dead, Kathleen Crowley puts up posters offering $100 to the man who will put pay to Gordon or anyone else connected with her father's murder. In rides black-clad Michael Pate (on a black horse, naturally), a menacing gunslinger who's slow on the draw but impervious to bullets, confessing to sunlight hurting his eyes and recoiling from the shadow of the cross. Very soon, he's sucking Crowley's delicious neck and retreating into his coffin housed in a mausoleum, Fleming (Crowley's boyfriend) unearthing some disturbing facts about the stranger from a diary dated 1860. In fact, Pate (as Drake Robey) is Don Drago Robles, a Spaniard who stabbed himself to death in 1859 after knifing his brother, found in a compromising embrace with his intended, in a jealous rage; cursed with vampirism, he wanders the West, satisfying his bloodlust on nubile females. It was Pate who murdered Hoyt and Pate who bites Sheriff Edward Binns to death (a harrowing moment), the undead one also shooting down Gordon after it has been ascertained that ancient Spanish deeds point to 500 acres of the land-grabber's property actually belonging to Crowley. In a street standoff, Fleming ("Your force is the Devil!") fires a bullet containing part of a crucifix into the monster; he hits the dirt and dissolves in the dust, the curse lifted. An eerie score from Irving Gertz, combined with Ellis W. Carter's artful lighting, Dein's assured direction and a leprous performance from Pate, no stranger to a gunslinger role, add up to a vampire B-movie with a difference; X-rated in the United Kingdom, it could be found sharing the bill with Universal's *The Thing that Couldn't Die* in the mid-1960s.

Highlights:
Several creepy, shadowy scenes showing Pate going about his dirty business are commendable in their acknowledgement of the vampire legend portrayed in other more notable Universal films, and even the Hammer productions of the day.

Dialogue:
Pate to Crowley: "The dead don't bother me. It's the living who give me trouble."

Trivia:
Dein and wife Mildred originally sketched a short story entitled *Eat Me Gently*, about a gay bloodsucker eating little boys out West, until producer Gershenson persuaded them to rehash the story on more serious lines; the film was shot in 18 days on a $300,000 budget.

Day of the Outlaw

Security/United Artists; 92 minutes; Producer: Sidney Harmon; Director: André De Toth; Cast: Robert Ryan; Burl Ives; Tina Louise; Venetia Stevenson; Alan Marshal; Nehemiah Persoff; Jack Lambert; Frank DeKova ***

Cattleman Robert Ryan and pal Nehemiah Persoff arrive in the Wyoming frontier town of Bitters, hemmed in by snowdrifts; Ryan objects to farmer Alan Marshal erecting fences over what he sees as open range for his steers and wants to sort matters out, with pistols if necessary. Marshal's wife, Tina Louise, is Ryan's old flame and still loves him, ready to throw herself at her surly ex-lover if he will refrain from killing her husband. Ten minutes into the scenario, we change direction. Burl Ives and his six hard-bitten gunmen barge in, on the run from the cavalry, carrying thousands of dollars in stolen gold; they want food and service, Ives, a strict disciplinarian, laying down the law to his unruly followers: "No whiskey and no woman. That's an order." Philip Yordan's screenplay then focuses on Ryan leading Ives and his coyotes on a lengthy, grueling trek through the snow-laden wastes to freedom via a supposed secret mountain pass, away from the posse on their trail and, just as importantly, away from causing further trouble in town. One by one, the men perish, Ives from an old gunshot wound, the others from treacherous bullets and, in Lance Fuller's case, frozen to death. Only youngster David Nelson makes it back with Ryan, into the welcoming arms of Venetia Stevenson. Alexander Courage musters up a gloomy score to match the harsh surroundings, artfully shot by Russell Harlan, but repeated scenes of horses floundering in the deep drifts, obviously in distress, plus a lame animal shot, will upset many horse lovers. André De Toth directs with a firm hand on the tiller and Ryan is excellent, but this bleak, downbeat movie falls into too many different categories, part psychological, part soap opera, part goodies versus baddies, leaving you wondering about the point of it all.

Dialogue:
Ives to the gathered townsfolk: "My men won't molest your women unless I give them permission."

Trivia:
Director De Toth's final Western.

Face of a Fugitive

Columbia; Eastmancolor; 81 minutes; Producer: David Heilweil; Director: Paul Wendkos; Cast: Fred MacMurray; Lin McCarthy; Dorothy Green; Alan Baxter; Myrna Fahey; James Coburn; Ron Hayes; Francis De Sales *****

Six-foot-three Fred MacMurray brought his considerable acting expertise and screen presence to bear in Paul Wendkos' taut oater, playing a bank robber who comes to the aid of tinhorn sheriff Lin McCarthy, at odds with land-grabber Alan Baxter and his hyenas. Baxter is erecting fences over public property; McCarthy is tearing them down, so Baxter wants the lawman dead, pronto, lanky James Coburn (in his second Western) his top honcho. MacMurray, who has thrown the body of his dead brother (Ron Hayes) from a train after a shoot-out, will soon be known to every law officer in the territory, including McCarthy, as his wanted poster is about to be distributed, but this doesn't stop him adopting an alias, being deputized, helping McCarthy in his struggle *and* falling for the sheriff's widowed sister, red-haired Dorothy Green (and her charming daughter, seven-year-old Gina Gillespie). David T. Chantler and Daniel B. Ullman's pithy script allows MacMurray to fire off blunt one-liners as quick as he can draw leather, Wendkos rounding off the tense incident and action by staging his finale in a ghost town, MacMurray dropping Baxter, Coburn and the rest before getting wounded and returning to town for what hopefully will be a fair trial, and marriage to the delectable Green. Jerry Goldsmith's thunderous score is another highlight in a tough, adult-oriented Western that's dripping with menace and in-your-face standoffs.

Highlights:
A tremendous cat-and-mouse showdown in a deserted desert ghost town.

Dialogue:
Baxter to MacMurray: "Mister, you're buttin' in on something that doesn't concern you. Either you're extra good with that gun or you're bluffing."
MacMurray: "All you gotta do is figure out which it is."

Trivia:
MacMurray never had an acting lesson in his life, was an accomplished musician and was the inspiration behind DC Comics' Captain Marvel. He also wasn't overkeen on the Western genre, although this was his second of three cowboy flicks in 1959.

Four Fast Guns

Phoenix Film Studios Prods./Universal Pictures; 72 minutes; Produced and Directed by William J. Hole, Jr.; Cast: James Craig; Martha Vickers; Paul Richards; Edgar Buchanan; Brett Halsey; Richard Martin; Blu Wright; John Swift ★★★

1873: The town of Purgatory ("When you ride into Purgatory—say goodbye to God.") is run by crippled former gunfighter Paul Richards, owner of the Babylon saloon where he plays piano all day; the townsfolk demand that a town tamer is appointed and in trots outlaw James Craig who's just gunned down James Hurley on the way in—and he was the real law officer marked for the job. With cantankerous old Edgar Buchanan by his side, Craig quickly dispatches a gunman paid by Richards to finish him off; Richards then sends letters to the four fastest guns in the territory, offering $1,000 to get rid of Craig. One is killed on the trail, Mexican Richard Martin (Tim Holt's former sidekick) is outgunned, Blu Wright ends up in a grave and it's left to black-clad Brett Halsey to challenge Craig—but he's Craig's brother! Richards ups the money to $3,000, Halsey scares off cocksure would-be gunslinger John Swift, the little guy throwing out the gauntlet to every gunfighter he meets but backing off at the vital moment, and Craig refuses to draw against his own brother. In spite, Halsey blasts Richards at point-blank range ("I cut you free from the cripple," he tells Richards' wife, Martha Vickers) and, in a standoff, Craig has no other option but to plug Halsey. "The town's yours now," say the grateful citizens, but Craig ain't interested, giving Buchanan the marshal's badge and riding off to Tombstone, Vickers promising to meet him

there ("Tom. I love you," she says. "I'm no marshal," replies Craig. "I'm no wife," she responds). A dour minor league Western with mean attitude, Halsey coming off best as a grinning, charismatic gun tough only interested in two things; money and women.
Dialogue:
Vickers to Craig: "I'll tell you something about a man who lives by the gun. He'll never have a happy woman."
Trivia:
This was to be Vickers' last feature film; a fine-looking actress who promised much, she died of cancer in November 1971, aged only 46.

Good Day for a Hanging

Columbia; Columbiacolor; 85 minutes; Producer: Charles H. Schneer; Director: Nathan Juran; Cast: Fred MacMurray; Robert Vaughn; James Drury; Margaret Hayes; Joan Blackman; Wendell Holmes; Edmon Ryan; Emile Meyer *****

"On June the 20th, 1878, you will be hanged by the neck until dead." Thus, intones the court judge to a sobbing Robert Vaughn, found guilty of killing Marshal Emile Meyer who, with a posse that included stage line owner Fred MacMurray, chased Vaughn and his gang into the hills after they had robbed the Springdale National Bank. But did he pull the trigger? MacMurray, a former lawman, is elected new town marshal and about the only person to think so. Most of the spineless local citizens have doubts, as does Vaughn's former girlfriend, Joan Blackman, and even MacMurray's intended, Margaret Hayes. Medic James Drury, dating Blackman, is jealous of her rekindled emotions for the outlaw, defense lawyer Edmon Ryan doing his level best to stir up trouble, convinced he will get Vaughn off; he doesn't, prosecution lawyer Wendell Holmes winning the case. Gallows are erected ("Takes a lot of work to hang a man.") and MacMurray, as he was in *At Gunpoint*, is treated like a leper, a petition drawn up by the town committee ("See, 212 signatures!") with the aim of commuting the death sentence to life imprisonment in Lincoln County Prison, Nebraska; that works, MacMurray riding into Springdale with the news and turning in his badge just as Vaughn is sprung from his cell by the two surviving gang members, the young renegade finally showing his true nature by callously shoving Blackburn aside and engaging in a cat-and-mouse shooting match with MacMurray; Vaughn loses, his body, ironically, sprawled on the very gallows built to hang him. Again, as in *At Gunpoint*, MacMurray stays on as marshal in a town that doesn't deserve a man of his guts and iron resolve. A meaty, adult Western from Columbia and producer Schneer who would henceforth find themselves up to their necks in the fantasy works of one Ray Harryhausen.

Highlights:

MacMurray's nine 1950s Westerns were always a bit more unconventional than most, due to the man himself and benefiting from decent scripts (Daniel B. Ullman and Maurice Zimm on this occasion); *Good Day for a Hanging* is no exception.

Dialogue:

Drury, hitting back at Blackman over her feelings for Vaughn: "It's hard being the only doctor in town. But the job has its compensations. When they hang him, I'll be the one to pronounce him officially dead."

Gunfighters of Abilene

United Artists; 66 minutes; Producer: Robert E. Kent; Director: Edward L. Cahn; Cast: Buster Crabbe; Barton MacLane; Rachel Ames; Russell Thorson; Lee Farr; Eugenia Paul; Kenneth MacDonald; Richard H. Cutting **

Buster Crabbe played professional gunfighter Kip Tanner in Edward L. Cahn's so-so oater, not one of the director's better efforts, mainly down to Crabbe's wooden, unconvincing performance. On his way to Abilene, Crabbe is ambushed and almost strung up by three of rancher Barton MacLane's boys, a revenge attack: MacLane claims that Crabbe's brother Gene (an uncredited Boyd "Red" Morgan) swindled him out of $64,000 obtained in a stolen cattle scam. Crabbe is rescued by Marshal Russell Thorson and rides into town, determined to find out what happened to his brother and why the townsfolk are so hostile towards him. Turns out that MacLane's daughter, Rachel Ames, wanted to marry Morgan but MacLane's son, Lee Farr, was dead set against the match. Morgan was also organizing the local ranchers to stand up to MacLane who was trampling all over their property; that stolen money, in fact, came from a stage holdup, Morgan framed for the job. Because of his involvement with the ranchers, Morgan was lynched on MacLane's orders. In a gunfight at Morgan's ranch, MacLane shoots Farr by accident and gets a bullet in a showdown with Crabbe, collapsing and dying at his ranch. Crabbe then decides to hang up his guns for good and settle down—with Ames? Yep, there's plenty of incident and double-dealing, but the pace drags; not even the likes of Paul Dunlap's boisterous score and Maury Gertsman's deep monochrome photography can lift the movie out of the "dull" category, an end-of-the-decade minor Western (it was released in January 1960) that very few fans remember today.

Dialogue:

Ames to MacLane: "Dad? Were you deliberately going to lynch him?"

MacLane: "Quick justice. It's what built this country, and that what it's gonna be to keep it the way it is."

Westerns of the 1950s: The Classic Years

Gunmen from Laredo

Columbia; Columbiacolor; 67 minutes; Produced and Directed by Wallace MacDonald; Cast: Robert Knapp; Maureen Hingert (Jana Davi); Walter Coy; Paul Birch; Charles Horvath; Don C. Harvey; Jean Moorhead; Clarence Straight
**

En route from Mexico to San Antonio, cattle boss Robert Knapp's wife is callously murdered by Walter Coy and his confederates, Knapp's herd also rustled. Saloon boss Coy (he's crossed Knapp before), has Laredo in a stranglehold; Knapp walks into his saloon, guns down one of Coy's sidewinders and is arrested for murder, even though he shot in self-defense. New marshal Paul Birch knows Knapp is innocent but needs proof; Knapp is handed a 10-to-25-year prison sentence but breaks out of New Mexico Territorial prison to mete out his own brand of justice in Laredo. Attractive Apache lass Maureen Hingert, pursued by Chiricahua Indians led by Charles Horvath, joins Knapp on his quest and is soon throwing herself at him in lust, although he blows hot and cold. Birch and his deputies catch up with Knapp, allow him to bury a hatchet in Horvath's face during a hand-to-hand contest with the chief and also let him steal the marshal's rifle. Thus armed, he rides into Laredo and, in a showdown, kills Coy and his two sons, much to Birch's delight—Laredo is now free of the controlling rat and he couldn't be happier. In fact, he's so pleased that he lets Knapp and Hingert ride away together to start a new life. Rattled off in a fortnight by Wallace MacDonald, *Gunmen from Laredo* is cheap-looking and routine, the climax a damp squib as far as Western showdowns go; only Birch stands out as the heavyweight lawman putting up with no nonsense from smirking Coy and his boys.

Dialogue:
Birch in court, spelling out his intentions: "Mister Keefer (Coy). Everybody. When there's trouble, I don't keep out of it. I get in it. With both feet."

The Hanging Tree

Warner Bros.; WarnerScope/Technicolor; 107 minutes; Producers: Martin Jurow and Richard Shepherd; Directors: Delmer Daves and Karl Malden; Cast: Gary Cooper; Karl Malden; Maria Schell; Ben Piazza; Karl Swenson; Virginia Gregg; George C. Scott; King Donovan ****

Into the Montana gold mining shanty town of Skull Creek strides black-clad doctor Gary Cooper, enigmatic, tight-lipped and nursing a boatload of problems; he can also deal a mean card, slap leather faster than most *and* is handy with his fists. Rescuing sluice-robber Ben Piazza from prospector Karl Malden and his heavies, he takes on the boy as a servant, controlling his every move. When Maria Schell is rescued after surviving a stage crash, Cooper tends her injuries, the "Lost Lady" acting as a catalyst for Skull Creek's deep-seated psychological hang-ups and bigotry. Cooper admires Schell, keeping her all to himself, while Piazza has a crush on her and Malden seethes with lust. Delmer Daves' adult Western lays the emphasis very much on character study as opposed to action, coming across like an Old West Shakespearean tragedy; Cooper's secret involves his dead wife and brother and a burned-out house. We still don't learn the whole story, but coming from Coop, the master of the terse delivery, that's not surprising. Following the discovery of a glory hole rich in nuggets, worked by Malden, Schell and Piazza, the townsfolk lose their senses to drink and set fire to Skull Creek. Malden, after attempting to rape Schell, receives four slugs courtesy of Cooper's six-gun and the doc is saved from a lynch mob led by bible-thumper George C. Scott after Schell hands them the claims to her riches, said to be worth a million dollars; she also gets Cooper, a slight smile (long overdue) playing across those craggy features. Full marks also go to Max Steiner for a magnificent score.

Highlights:

Gary Cooper in his final Western: The man was a screen legend, and his understated performance in *The Hanging Tree* proved it.

Dialogue:

Schell to frustrated Malden: "Must you always look at a woman like that?"

Malden: "Well, don't a partner have some rights, eh? Don't even get a free look. I suppose you gotta be a doctor to get that, huh, I suppose if you were a, a doctor, then you could get an eyeful."

Trivia:

The debut of George C. Scott; Cooper had a complete facelift two months prior to filming; and Malden took over the director's reigns when Daves fell ill halfway into the shoot.

The Hangman

Paramount; 87 minutes; Producer: Frank Freeman, Jr.; Director: Michael Curtiz; Cast: Robert Taylor; Tina Louise; Fess Parker; Jack Lord; Gene Evans; Mickey Shaughnessy; James Westerfield; Shirley Harmer ***

A leisurely paced psychological Western short on action starring Robert Taylor in the title role, the "toughest lawman in the territory" who always gets his man hanged after being caught. The U.S. deputy marshal offers Tina Louise $500 to identify Jack Lord, wanted for armed robbery and murder; she lived with him for a while and the only other witness to the crime is behind bars, due to be strung up in a week. In North Creek, Taylor awaits the arrival of Louise, befriends amiable sheriff Fess Parker and has a couple of ladies lusting after his good-looking charms, despite his reputation ("Mr. Bovard. Do you really hang people?"). Parker works for James Westerfield's freight company and is very popular around town, thus posing a dilemma for Taylor when Louise eventually turns up; should he carry out his job, or let the reformed outlaw go free with his wife, Shirley Harmer? Taylor and frosty Louise unexpectedly bond, Parker falls for the dame and, after being busted out of jail by Mickey Shaughnessy, Lord, in a street showdown, gallops off to a new life, Taylor firing two shots over his head on purpose; Louise has refused to name him as the man Taylor is after. Taylor also plans to start a new life in California and, to his (and our) surprise, Louise rejects Parker's marriage proposal, hitching her skirts to Taylor who, on looks alone, still had what it took to make women's hearts flutter. Loyal Griggs' deep-focus photography is a treat in a thoughtful drama well-acted by the entire cast—and Taylor, a true Hollywood great, is as watchable as ever.

Dialogue:

Taylor to Parker: "I seem to be in a minority of one."

Parker: "You ain't popular!"

The Horse Soldiers

United Artists; DeLuxecolor; 120 minutes; Producers: John Lee Mahin and Martin Rackin; Director: John Ford; Cast: John Wayne; William Holden; Constance Towers; Ken Curtis; Judson Pratt; Bing Russell; Willis Bouchey; Althea Gibson ***

John Ford's Civil War drama, set in 1863, was an unhappy shoot: John Wayne and William Holden fell out over their differing political views; Ford was in a perpetual foul temper, dogged by drink problems, having little regard for the project; Wayne's mind was preoccupied on his own forthcoming project, *The Alamo*, busy raising finances from backers; and a stuntmen fell from a horse and was killed, virtually causing Ford to call it a day. Colonel Wayne's Union troops head out on a 300-mile mission to blow up the Confederate railhead at Newton Station and escape south via Baton Rouge, Major Holden the detail's surgeon. En route, they pick up flighty Southern belle Constance Towers and her maid (played by ex-tennis champion Althea Gibson) from their Greenbriar mansion; Towers (in Scarlett O'Hara mode) provides the romantic spark, vying for both Wayne and Holden's attention, even though she hates Yankees: "You nameless, fatherless scum," she screams after eavesdropping on Wayne's battle tactics and caught out. Ford whips up a frenetic clash at Newton Station, Rebel soldiers decimated in a street skirmish, the railroad and Confederate supplies blown sky high and totally destroyed; Wayne also comes under attack from a regiment of Southern cadets fresh from military academy, refusing to open fire on the boys. The finale, taking place at a Rebel-held bridge, is equally exciting, Wayne (who professes his love for Towers) and his men riding away following the demolition of the bridge, leaving the lass and Holden to fend for themselves when a Confederate detachment arrives on the scene. That climax, however, has a rushed feel, pointing to Ford wanting to quit after the death of the stuntman, and the animosity between the two leading men is only too evident in their frequent spats and arguments. As a Civil War actioner, it's not that bad. As a John Ford film, it's way below the director's usual impeccably high standards; in the words of *Variety*, "uneven."

Highlights;

The Ford magic is still noticeable in his use of longshots showing lines of soldiers on the march, set against a wide-open backdrop.

Dialogue:

Towers to Wayne at the dinner table, exposing her cleavage as she presents him with a roast chicken: "What is your preference? The leg or the breast?"

Trivia:

Wayne and Holden each received a bank-busting salary of $775,000 plus 20% of the profits, their combined contracts twice the size of the film script, but the movie wasn't a great success with both public and critics.

The Jayhawkers!

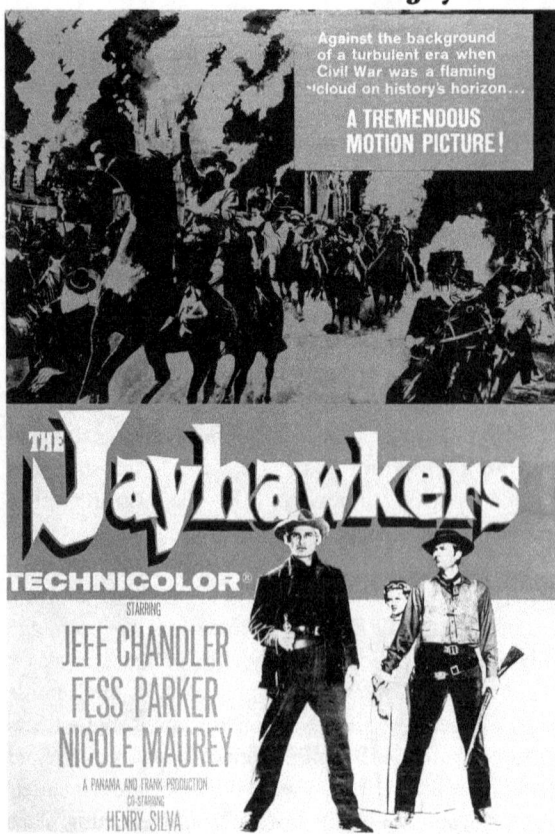

Paramount; VistaVision/Technicolor; 100 minutes; Producers: Melvin Frank and Norman Panama; Director: Melvin Frank; Cast: Fess Parker; Jeff Chandler; Nicole Maurey; Henry Silva; Leo Gordon; Herbert Rudley; Don Megowan; Frank DeKova *****

Prior to the outbreak of the American Civil War, Jeff Chandler and his Jayhawkers are ousting the Missouri Redlegs pro-slavery mob from towns all across the Republic of Kansas, then forcing themselves on the citizens as their true saviors. In fact, it's a clever ruse by megalomaniac Chandler, the "backwoods Napoleon," to control Kansas for his own egotistical benefit. Fess Parker, having escaped from the Kansas Territorial Prison, returns to his ranch to find his wife dead and buried, Frenchwoman Nicole

Maurey having bought the lease from the government. Promised a pardon by Governor Herbert Rudley if he can infiltrate the Jayhawkers' secret hideout and bring Chandler in alive to be hanged, Parker worms his way into the gang by saving gunman Leo Gordon from the noose; he's also got another agenda on his plate, to kill Chandler. The man, he learns, had an affair with his wife and caused her death while he was locked behind bars. Jerome Moross' vibrant music is just one plus factor in a brilliant Western crammed with great performances. Chandler a cold-hearted control freak, discarding women he has used (and abused) like "empty wine bottles"; Parker falling under the tyrant's overpowering charisma, almost forming a brotherly bond with him and loath to see Chandler dangle "like a clown" on the end of a rope ("I've tried to hate him but I don't."); widow Maurey hoping that Parker will forget all about revenge and settle down with her; and dead-eyed Henry Silva lurking in the background, forever on the prod. Chandler and the Jayhawkers are foiled in the end by an elaborate plan involving a train carrying not only an enticing $500,000 in gold to cattle-rich Abilene but hundreds of government troops. Following a shoot-out, Chandler knows his time is up but almost begs Parker to gun him down (after he's disposed of Silva and Gordon) rather than face the already-erected gallows, Parker obliging by beating him to the draw ("I couldn't let him hang," he says to Rudley). Parker gets his freedom, riding off to his old ranch with Maurey and her two delightful children.

Highlights;
Six-foot-five Parker's verbal spats with six-foot-four Chandler, six-foot-six Don Megowan and six-foot-two Gordon adding to the picture's "big men" quota.

Dialogue:
Chandler to Parker, who has just stunned Silva by throwing a bottle at his head: "You've humiliated him. Someday, he'll have to kill you. But not until I say so."

Trivia:
Jerome Moross' stirring score was used in TV's *Wagon Train* series.

Last Train from Gun Hill

Paramount; VistaVision/Technicolor; 95 minutes; Producers: Hal B. Wallis and Kirk Douglas (uncredited); Director: John Sturges; Cast: Kirk Douglas; Anthony Quinn; Carolyn Jones; Earl Holliman; Brian G. Hutton; Brad Dexter; Walter Sande; Ziva Rodann *****

Action director John Sturges' run of superlative '50s Westerns (*Gunfight at the O.K. Corral*; *The Law and Jake Wade*) continued with *Last Train from Gun Hill*. The combined star power of Kirk Douglas and Anthony Quinn, plus James Poe's biting script, Dimitri Tiomkin's busy score and Charles Lang, Jr.'s sharp photography ensured maximum Western thrills, and you got it, in spades. Douglas (as usual, in blistering form) is the marshal of Pawlee, whose Cherokee wife (Ziva Rodann) is raped and murdered by cowpokes Earl Holliman and Brian G. Hutton. Incriminating evidence is left behind; an ornate saddle and a telltale lash mark on Holliman's right cheek. The saddle belongs to cattle rancher Quinn, an old acquaintance of Douglas—and Holliman just happens to be his son. Douglas takes the train to Gun Hill and rides out to Quinn's spread, determined to get even by bringing Holliman and Hutton to justice, whether the cattle baron, who has the entire town in his pocket, including the sheriff, objects or not ("I got two warrants and I'm gonna serve them … and the long view is this. Don't try and stop me."). The scene

An Italian poster for *Last Train from Gun Hill*

is thus set for a nail-biting showdown, Douglas holed up in an hotel room with handcuffed Holliman, the clock ticking, waiting for the train to arrive, while outside, Quinn and his 20 men prowl the streets, waiting to finish the marshal off and rescue Holliman from a probable hanging. Quinn's much abused on/off love, fancy dame Carolyn Jones, comes to Douglas' aid, smuggling him a shotgun; the gripping climax has Douglas escorting Holliman on a rig to the station, the loaded shotgun pressed to his throat. As the train arrives, Hutton leaps from the shadows, shoots Holliman by mistake and is blasted by Douglas. Enraged, Quinn challenges his former friend to the draw and loses, biting the dust, leaving Douglas to board the locomotive in sorrow; Jones watches him depart with tears in her eyes. "Graphic drama," enthused the *New York Times* of a tough revenge Western that ranks among the decade's finest.

Highlights:
Douglas forcibly telling sniveling Holliman in no uncertain terms what will happen to him when he's jailed, from spending months festering in a cell to choking to death on the end of the hangman's noose, a wonderful piece of acting from one of Hollywood's greats.

Dialogue:
Tony Russel (Rodann's father) to Douglas: "Kill him. Real slow. The Indian way."
Douglas: "I'll kill him. In my own way."

Lone Texan

Regal Films/20th Century Fox; RegalScope; 71 minutes; Producer: Jack Leewood; Director: Paul Landres; Cast: Willard Parker; Grant Williams; Audrey Dalton; Douglas Kennedy; Dabbs Greer; Lee Farr; Jimmy Murphy; Richard Monahan ****

Arroyo, Texas 1865: It's brother versus brother as former Union officer Willard Parker rides into a bigoted town crammed full of Confederate sympathizers, to find sibling Grant Williams, who once rode with Quantrill's Raiders, the resident peace officer— trouble is, Williams ("I hate Yankees.") and his four unkempt cronies act as judge, jury and executioner, stringing up Indians and traders without a fair trial and ruling Arroyo *their* bullying, intimidating way. Targeted a turncoat, Blue Belly and carpetbagger, Parker is soon clashing with Williams and crazy henchman Lee Farr, a vile specimen who has the hots for Audrey Dalton, Parker's former flame. Vaguely reminiscent at times of Edward Dmytryk's *Warlock*, Jack W. Thomas and James Landis' smart script takes in sibling rivalry and town cowardice, Parker having a hard time convincing the council (except Doc Dabbs Greer) that law of the variety that his unhinged brother lays down, a law built on hatred, has had its day. One-armed attorney Douglas Kennedy (Dalton's father) is gunned down in the street by Farr while trying to prevent a hanging; in a struggle, Dalton accidentally shoots Deputy Jimmy Murphy and now *she's* shoved behind bars, awaiting a mock trial. Assaulted in her cell by Farr (a vicious scene), she runs outside. Enraged at Dalton's treatment (she lies sobbing in the street), Parker gets the drop on Farr, the rat sprawled lifeless in the dust; these cumulative incidents force the town council to at last listen to what Parker has to say. The inevitable showdown is a cracker, Parker walking towards Williams, surviving deputy Richard Monahan lurking in an alley, ready for the back shot. Williams spots him and fires, Monahan dropping dead, but by going for his gun, Parker is forced to draw, killing his brother. Peace is restored to Arroyo, Parker and Dalton arm-in-arm as the final credits roll.

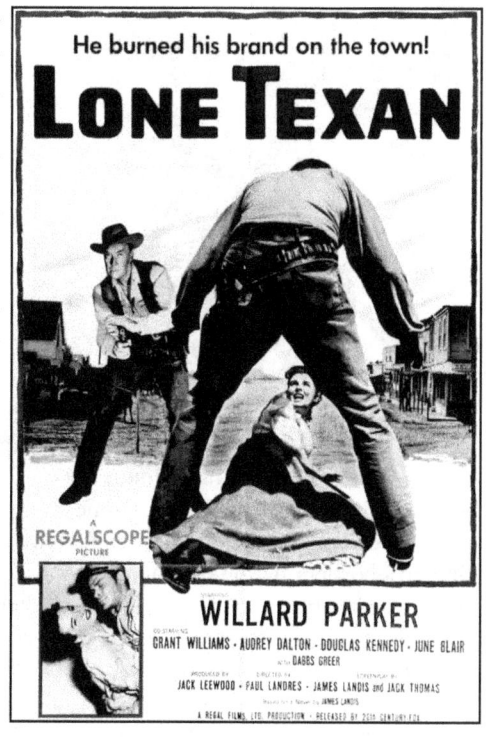

Dialogue:
Williams to Parker, demonstrating not-so-brotherly love: "Remember this. I'm not the same boy that used to lick your boots."

Trivia:
In the 48th minute, a large Gothic baroque house is seen at the top of a hill, resembling the infamous Bates' residence in *Psycho*—it isn't.

The Oregon Trail

20th Century Fox; CinemaScope/DeLuxecolor; 86 minutes; Producer: Richard Einfeld; Director: Gene Fowler, Jr.; Cast: Fred MacMurray; William Bishop; Nina Shipman; Gloria Talbott; John Carradine; Henry Hull; Tex Terry; Addison Richards *

A "B" production masquerading as an A movie sums up *The Oregon Trail*, a clumsily put together settlers versus Injuns yarn firmly rooted within the confines of stage sets and painted backgrounds. Yes, there are a few inserted views of Oregon's wild natural wonders, but this is footage plundered from other movies, much of the cavalry/Indian action sequences towards the end filched from Allied Artists' *Oregon Passage*, a far superior Western in every respect. In what undoubtedly counts as his lamest trip out West, *New York Herald* investigative reporter Fred MacMurray, looking distinctly out of his comfort zone, is instructed to join a wagon train in 1846 bound from Westport to Fort Laramie. It's all to do with British interests in Oregon and the fact that President Addison Richards has troops disguised as pioneers to take Oregon's borders by force; MacMurray's secret mission is to ferret the soldiers out. Veering awkwardly from folksy pseudo-comedy to scenes of massacred, arrow-riddled corpses, and to the booming vocals of Will Miller warbling "Ballad of the Oregon Trail" throughout, the wagons finally get rolling in the 25th minute, trundling past the same old studio painted backdrops time and time again. Loopy John Carradine tends to his plants, scout Henry Hull tries to keep order, sadistic whip-wielding thug Tex Terry has a couple of fights with MacMurray, William Bishop, an army captain in disguise, romances an anonymous Nina Shipman and there's too much reminiscing. Even when Fort Laramie is reached, practically the last couple of reels are taken up by stock footage of Redskins on the warpath, Gloria Talbott appearing as half-breed Shona who takes one look at bumbling MacMurray and smothers him in kisses. "I denounce my people," storms the lass as the fort's complement is nearly wiped out (even a small boy is killed by an arrow); a wagon detonates, all and sundry open fire with brand new Colt six-shooters, the Indians retreat, news comes through of a war with Mexico, Bishop kisses Shipman and MacMurray resigns his position, preferring Talbott's delights to sitting behind a desk in New York. If *The Oregon Trail* had been concocted by a smaller outfit other than Fox on minimal funds in black-and-white, then you would say "so be it." But there was no excuse for the giant studio to come up with this ramshackle effort on the finances they possessed, and in 'scope and color to boot. A poor presentation all round; never have 86 minutes seemed as long as they do in this picture.

Dialogue:
MacMurray to Hull after being shown how to saddle a horse: "Well, thanks very much, Mr. Seton."
Hull: "Ain't you ever rid a horse before?"
MacMurray: "Oh yes, quite a while ago, though I remember it had rockers under it."

Trivia:
This was MacMurray's final '50s Western before embarking on a career with the Disney studios; and, for very different reasons, it was Bishop's last picture, the actor dying from cancer in October 1959 aged only 41.

Plunderers of Painted Flats

Republic; Naturama; 77 minutes; Produced and Directed by Albert C. Gannaway; Cast: John Carroll; Skip Homeier; George Macready; Corinne Calvet; Edmund Lowe; Joe Besser; Madge Kennedy; Bea Benaderet ***

Republic Pictures' swansong commenced in grim fashion, land-grabber George Macready (even more vile than usual) and his sidewinders setting fire to Skip Homeier's ranch, his father dying in the inferno. Macready hates squatters in "my town and my valley," conducting a war of extermination, even terrorizing those attending the funeral of Homeier's parent. In Painted Flats, former fast gun Edmund Lowe shoots one of Macready's goons in the street, prompting the tyrant to hire professional gunshot John Carroll to get rid of Lowe and anyone else opposing him. Carroll just happens to be on the stage carrying Corinne Calvet, Madge Kennedy and Bea Benaderet to town, a trio of mail order brides; three of Macready's boys hold up the stage and Carroll plugs all three, making a play for Calvet who doesn't want to know. The narrative then goes through a "happy families" stage: Lowe marries Kennedy, Joe Besser weds Benaderet and Homeier gets hitched to Calvet, a woman who has had ten times the experience with men that her gauche new husband has had with the opposite sex, even though she's useless in the kitchen ("I'll make you some biscuits," she tells Homeier after serving him burned meat). Carroll creeps into Calvet's bedroom one night ("Where's your husband?" "In the barn."), is slugged by Homeier and, back in town, ordered to kill Lowe which he does in a street showdown. But Carroll doesn't enjoy the experience, drinking himself into a stupor. In a climactic standoff between Macready (his mob have been wiped out) and Homeier's settlers outside a church, the gunslinger shoots Macready for slapping Calvet, whom he desires; it's left to nine-year-old Ricky Allen to squeeze the trigger of a six-gun and send Carroll toppling into an open grave. The conflict over, Homeier can now look forward to nights of uninterrupted love with sexy French lass Calvet, whether she can cook or not!

Dialogue:
Carroll to Macready, ready to face Lowe but seeing Allen close by: "What about the boy?"
Macready: "He'll have something to remember—if he grows up."

Thunder in the Sun

Paramount; Technicolor; 81 minutes; Producer: Clarence Greene; Director: Russell Rouse; Cast: Jeff Chandler; Susan Hayward; Jacques Bergerac; Carl Esmond; Blanche Yurka; Felix Locher; Veda Ann Borg; Albert Carrier **

In 1847, Basque immigrants enlist the aid of disreputable Indian scout Jeff Chandler to escort them from Missouri to California in one of the '50s weirdest, most tiresome, wagon train yarns. Chandler only agrees to go along because he lusts after Susan Hayward, engaged to Carl Esmond. When Esmond is accidentally shot dead, his closest relative, Jacques Bergerac, is next in line for the nuptials, but not if the burly scout has anything to do with it. A drums-and-pipes score from Cyril J. Mockridge, nerve-shredding Pyrenean Mountain cries from the Basques, syrupy moments of teaching kids how to speak English, precious water spent on keeping vines, not people, alive, and a slower-than-slow pace equates to a bumpy, incident-free ride for the viewer; both Chandler and Hayward appear uncomfortable among all the French blather, and a climactic Redskins versus Basques clash is rendered almost comical by those irritating mountain ululations. Chandler gets his woman at the end (after all, he's slobbered all over her for most of the running time), California is reached and, in the words of the *New York Times*, this "sluggish, mediocre little picture" for which you will earn an "Oscar for plain endurance," draws to a close; definitely a strong contender for one of Chandler's (and Hayward's) dullest movies; there's little in the way of "Thunder" in *this* production.

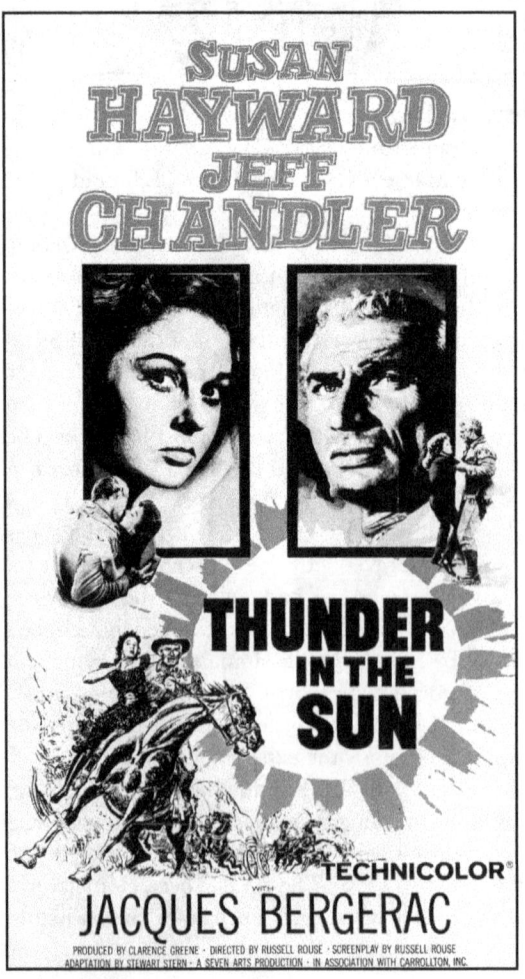

Dialogue:
Carl Esmond to Veda Ann Borg, watching a saloon tart draping herself all over Chandler: "Madame, is he to be trusted?"
Borg: "With wagons, yes."

The Wonderful Country

United Artists; Technicolor; 98 minutes; Producer: Chester Erskine; Director: Robert Parrish; Cast: Robert Mitchum; Julie London; Gary Merrill; Albert Dekker; Charles McGraw; Pedro Armendáriz; Victor Manuel Mendoza; Jay Novello ***

On the run for killing his father's murderer, Robert Mitchum plies his gun running trade between the Castro Brothers on the Mexican border and the U.S. military on the Texas side, eventually helping General Gary Merrill's cavalry fight the Apaches, busy raiding Mexican homesteads. Mitchum took over as executive producer in a "down Old Mexico way" yarn that slowly unravels in the first hour, finally coming to life in the final third. Very little action, bags of talk, Mitchum and Merrill's wife, Julie London, making eyes at each other, fiestas, Albert Dekker trying to get Mitchum to join the Texas Rangers—it frankly goes nowhere, Parrish content to include a plethora of close-ups of the main attraction's sleepy-eyed features and lazy drawl, the Robert Mitchum show in all but name only. Things pick up when Mitchum (speaking in an odd American/Mexican accent) crosses the border, involving himself in the double-crossing of brothers Victor Manuel Mendoza and Pedro Armendáriz, the latter assassinated by Mendoza who becomes governor. Fleeing Mendoza's troops after being accused of losing a quantity of guns, Mitchum gets caught up in a clash with Apaches, Merrill fatally wounded in a skirmish, Mitchum promising to return to London after he has sorted out unfinished business. Shot in Mexico, the Durango scenery is sweeping and Mitchum is Mitchum, exuding laconic star quality in an erratic, clumsily plotted Western that is as slow-moving as its leading man's infamous acting style, an atmospheric, nice-to-look-at but slightly ponderous period piece that won't appeal to fans looking for something a bit more impassioned on their menu. "The plot is as snarled as a ball of tumbleweed," stated *Time*.

Highlights:
The Mexican locations and Mitchum's legendary presence.

Dialogue:
London to Mitchum, abhorring the sight of his gun: "You're not complete without your machinery for killing."

Trivia:
Henry Fonda and Gregory Peck both turned down the project before Mitchum took up the reins.

Clint's back!... and 'Kookie' is with him!
He's bigger than ever!
Clint Walker
Kookie's first starring role!
Edward Byrnes
...and 'Lawman', too!
John Russell
"Yellowstone Kelly"
A WARNER BROS. PICTURE
TECHNICOLOR®
with
RAY DANTON · CLAUDE AKINS · RHODES REASON · ANDRA MARTIN
Screenplay by BURT KENNEDY · Directed by GORDON DOUGLAS

Yellowstone Kelly

Warner Bros.; Technicolor; 91 minutes; Producer: Burt Kennedy; Director: Gordon Douglas; Cast: Clint Walker; Edward Byrnes; John Russell; Ray Danton; Andra Martin; Rhodes Reason; Claude Akins; Gary Vinson *****

Once mooted as a possible vehicle for John Ford and John Wayne, Gordon Douglas' gem of a Western opens and closes with a shot of six-foot-six trapper/scout/surveyor Clint Walker firing three shots from a wooded rise, his message to a riverboat that he's got pelts to offload. The difference is that in the final shot, Arapaho squaw Andra Martin (Wahleeah) is at his side. How she got there makes for an engrossing outdoor adventure, beautifully photographed around Arizona's Sedona and Coconino Forest regions by Carl E. Guthrie. It's the 1870s: Walker's a loner, spending the last seven years trapping up Missouri's Snake River, Indian pal John Russell content to let him alone as the big man once saved his life. When Walker heads back into the wilds with greenhorn sidekick Edward Byrnes (Kookie in TV's *77 Sunset Strip* series) and the cavalry, led by Major Rhodes Reason (he's bitter over Custer's death at the Little Bighorn), sets out from Fort Buford to drive the Sioux from their lands, trouble comes in double-doses: Reason's stubbornness and Arapaho lass Martin, desired by Russell, hothead brave Ray Danton, Byrnes and, although he wouldn't care to admit it, Walker himself. Walker digs a bullet out of her spine, and she recuperates in his cabin, Byrnes getting hot under the collar at the sight of Martin's blazing green eyes and naked back. Douglas piles on the incident and action as Reason's regiment is decimated by the Sioux in a canyon surprise attack, Byrnes receives a fatal arrow from Danton who is later is shot dead by Walker and hundreds of savages led by Russell converge on the beleaguered soldiers under the shadow of a mighty red mesa. "Take your warriors and go. This land no longer smiles on your people," Walker says to the chief and they depart, the battle over, Walker free to take the delectable Martin as his woman—he will never be alone again!

Highlights:

Walker knocking half-a-dozen troopers senseless in a fistfight; the climactic confrontation; Walker's sheer bulk and terse delivery; and Martin's hypnotic eyes plus semi-nude dip in the river.

Dialogue:

Walker to Reason, advising him not to cross the river where 1,000 head of Sioux await: "On this side, you're in trouble. Over there, you're dead."

Trivia:

Most cast members caught a bout of flu on the shoot except for Walker, a health-food fanatic; 120 Navajo Indians were hired to swell the Sioux ranks; and Howard Jackson's score contains snatches of Max Steiner's music used in *The Searchers*.

The Young Land

Columbia; Technicolor; 89 minutes; Producers: Patrick Ford and C.V. Whitney (uncredited); Director: Ted Tetzlaff; Cast: Patrick Wayne; Yvonne Craig; Dennis Hopper; Dan O'Herlihy; Roberto De La Madrid; Ken Curtis; Cliff Ketchum; Pedro Gonzalez Gonzalez **

Two killings bookend *The Young Land*. In the opening minute, Dennis Hopper puts three slugs into a Mexican for kicks; in the closing minutes, Sheriff Patrick Wayne, useless with a pistol but handy with a rifle, shoots Hopper dead. What happens in between can best be described as colorful tedium, the screen filled with laughing, dancing, singing, merrymaking Mexicans all enjoying themselves at the audience's expense, the background to a woeful performance from the Duke's son. Wayne, Jr. looks, in many of his scenes, to be in urgent need of acting lessons, hindered by a flat, one-note vocal delivery and expressionless features. As for Wayne's love interest Yvonne Craig, all she does is ride into San Bartolo, pout, toss her mane of dark hair, flounce and ride out again. Judge Dan O'Herlihy is assigned to try Hopper for murder but somehow pass a sentence agreeable to both Roberto De La Madrid's glowering vaqueros and a gringo contingent itching for trouble; the jury finds Hopper guilty, the judge giving him a 25-year prison term, suspended on condition he never handles or carries a gun. Hopper promptly ignores O'Herlihy's verdict, grabbing Deputy Cliff Ketchum's revolver and challenging Wayne to a street showdown, leading to the killer's death. Ted Tetzlaff's pace is leaden (the cinematographer's final directorial effort), Ken Curtis staggers around as an unruly cowpoke and the whole shebang reminds one of a low-grade *Rio Bravo*, due to Dimitri Tiomkin's overactive soundtrack (he scored *Rio Bravo*, one of his most memorable pieces of work). The talents of one of Hollywood's most notable of all composers are utterly wasted here, all those much-loved Tiomkin leitmotifs, themes and codas falling like dust on the dry Mexican street. The movie's watchable if only for Tiomkin's contribution and for seeing Wayne ambling through the non-action as though he was desperately trying to be somewhere else.

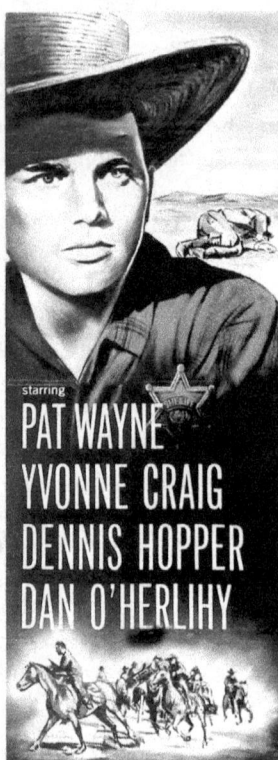

Dialogue:
O'Herlihy to Wayne: "Why are you saluting me? I'm not an officer."
Wayne: "No sir, but you sound like one."

Chapter 17
Whip Wilson at Monogram

Born Roland Charles Meyers in Granite City, Illinois on June 16, 1911 and one of eight children, Meyers had a moderately successful career as a singer during the late 1930s before Monogram executive producer Scott R. Dunlap spotted him in a club and thought he bore a strong resemblance to cowboy star Buck Jones. Jones, who had been signed to Monogram, died in Boston's Cocoanut Grove Nightclub fire of November 28, 1942, aged 50, and the company was searching for a new Western leading man. Given the stage name of Whip Wilson, his character based unashamedly on Lash LaRue, the popular whip-wielding cowboy hero of the day, his personal details greatly exaggerated to make him appear more bankable to the public (it was even claimed he was a direct descendant of General George Custer), Wilson was handed an uncredited role in Action Pictures' *God's Country* (1946) and then cast as Whip Wilson in Monogram's *Silver Trails* (1948), 12th on the cast list. He went on to star in a further 22 Westerns, ending his career with uncredited cameos in Fox's *The Silver Whip* (1953) and United Artists' *The Kentuckian* (1955). Aged only 53, he died from a heart attack on October 22, 1964. Unlike many of the serial/series-type Western heroes of the '30s and '40s, Wilson had no cowboy or ranching background to fall back on, making him appear clumsy and somewhat awkward in many of his hour-long oaters. He also came in on the tail end of this kind of low-budget actioner which, by and large, had run their course by 1953. Wilson's pictures from 1950 to 1953 now seem archaic and forced compared to, say, the Tim Holt, Wild Bill Elliott and Allan "Rocky" Lane series, and he never did make much of an impact as a bona fide Western star; nevertheless his output serves as a reminder that, over 60 years ago, customers, especially the kids, could, and were, entertained by fodder of a very basic, no-frills Western kind. All films are listed in order of release.

1950
Fence Riders

Monogram; 57 minutes; Produced and Directed by Wallace W. Fox; Cast: Whip Wilson; Andy Clyde; Reno Browne; Myron Healey; Riley Hill; Ed Cassidy; Mike Ragan; Buck Bailey **

The first outing of the 1950s for our six-foot-one inch, barrel-chested, whip-wielding sagebrush savior on his large white horse Bullet (formerly Silver Bullet, later changed to

Rocket) and wearing a big white Stetson was a play-it-by-numbers affair that teetered on the edge of being just a tad boring. Whip Wilson and garrulous sidekick Andy Clyde (Winks McGee) are hired by ranch cowgirl Reno Browne (resembling a '30s starlet) to stop her cattle being rustled. When she boots out foreman Riley Hill in favor of Wilson, Hill joins forces with town crook Myron Healey, keen to get his hands on Browne's ranch and herd; the two-timer is shot by Healey, the killing pinned on Wilson. Whip escapes from behind bars to find that Mike Ragan, Healey's chief henchman, is Browne's new foreman; slugged by Wilson, he confesses that it was his boss who murdered Hill. Sheriff Ed Cassidy and his posse arrive on the scene to round up the rustlers, Wilson's trademark single blow felling Healey after the coyote's upended by that lashing whip. There are a couple of stilted moments between Wilson and Browne where you suspect acting lessons needed to be the order of the day, Wilson sings "Sweet Genevieve" to the lass on her piano and veteran comic Clyde's dopey impersonation of the likes of Fuzzy Knight and Eddy Waller gets tiresome at times. After this tame, old-fashioned looking oater, things, surely, could only get better.

Dialogue:
Browne to Wilson, observing Clyde's silly antics: "He's fun. He'll put some life into this place."
Wilson: "Yes, if he doesn't eat you out of house and home and oversleep every morning."

Gunslingers

Monogram; 55 minutes; Produced and Directed by Wallace W. Fox; Cast: Whip Wilson; Andy Clyde; Reno Browne; Bill Kennedy; Sarah Padden; Dennis Moore; George Chesebro; Steve Clark *

Bill Kennedy is foreclosing on ranchers' properties, having taken over their mortgages, to obtain profitable water rights for a new railway being built through their land at Rockhill, employing a bogus marshal (actually a wanted outlaw) to carry out his dirty work and framing various people, including Whip Wilson, George Chesebro and owner of the Lazy "C" Ranch Steve Clark, for crimes they didn't commit. Adele Buffington's convoluted script doesn't work well in this low-budget 55-minute setup, only confusing the issue as the narrative lurches from one scene to another without any cohesion. Old coot Andy Clyde (Winks) plays a judge, blonde Reno Browne still maintains that '30s look (as does the entire picture) and Reed Howes finally turns up as a bona fide

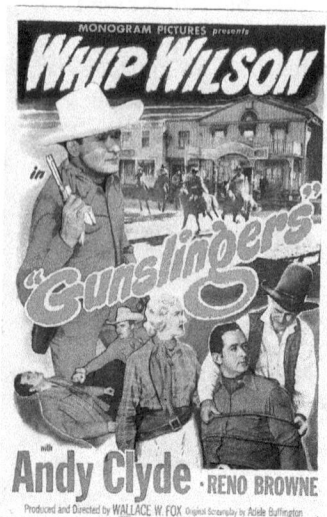

lawman, arresting Dennis Moore, the imposter. Poorly acted in parts (apart from Sarah Padden's spirited "Rawhide Rosie"), this is one Whip Wilson quickie to forget.
Dialogue:
Moore to Wilson who's wearing a mask: "Say. Who are you?"
Wilson: "Keep your mouth shut and those hands up or I'll give you the answer in lead."

Arizona Territory

Monogram; 56 minutes; Producer: Vincent M. Fennelly; Director: Wallace W. Fox; Cast: Whip Wilson; Andy Clyde; Nancy Saunders; Dennis Moore; John Merton; Carol Henry; Carl Mathews; Frank Austin ***

Prospector Whip Wilson (as Jeff Malloy) comes to the rescue of Nancy Saunders when she's wounded by her own uncle, John Merton, while ferrying a shipment of Indian pottery loaded on her wagon; the pots contain counterfeit notes in their false bases and Merton, in cahoots with Saunders' intended, smarmy Indian agent Dennis Moore, is trying to scare her from snooping into his activities. Whip cashes in some gold in exchange for $500, plugs henchman Carl Mathews, ordered by Merton to kill the Stetson-headed big guy on the magnificent white horse (Bullet, Wilson's preferred mount), and unearths Merton's scam at the reservation with the assistance of old-timer marshal Andy Clyde. A thumping stock score concocted by Edward J. Kay and Wilson using his lash to bring down the baddies adds up to a fast-paced matinée B-yarn, even though the main man, carrying a bit too much weight, looks as though he has just stepped out of a 1930s oater; but it's a vast improvement on the dire *Gunslingers*.
Dialogue:
Wilson, finding Saunders lying injured in the back of her wagon: "Steady there, young fella—why, you're a girl!"

Silver Raiders

Monogram; 55 minutes; Producer: Vincent M. Fennelly; Director: Wallace W. Fox; Cast: Whip Wilson; Andy Clyde; Leonard Penn; Virginia Herrick; Dennis Moore; Patricia Rios; Reed Howes; Riley Hill ***

Screenwriter Daniel B. Ullman was hired to bring some much-needed polish to the series, and it worked. Less frenetic scenario, tighter editing, stronger story and the leading man at last acting the part. He's Arizona Ranger Larry Grant, posing as a wanted outlaw in order to infiltrate Dennis Moore and Leonard Penn's gang, dressed as Mexicans and stealing silver from across the Mexican border but claiming it was mined in a derelict silver working. Wilson causes trouble with his whip in Silver Springs, gets himself arrested on purpose, catches the eye of Sheriff Andy Clyde's granddaughter Virginia Herrick, is sprung from jail by two masked men and recruited into the outlaw gang while buddies Reed Howes and Riley Hill observe the hideout from a deserted shack, Clyde and his men waiting in the wings to back Wilson up. Things go wrong for the outfit when they kidnap Mexican Patricia Rios (her only film appearance) and hold her for ransom. The money is paid but Wilson steals the flirtatious lady from under Moore's nose, eventually flooring him with one hefty punch after a smoke-filled shoot-out; Penn attempts to escape on a buggy but is brought down by Whip's lariat and his handy right fist. A decent stock score from Edward J. Kay and sharp black-and-white photography (Harry Neumann) of California's Santa Clarita hilly terrain go towards making *Silver Raiders* one of the better of the series.

Dialogue:
Herrick as Wilson mounts Bullet to escort Rios back home: "'Bye Larry."
Wilson: "So long, Patricia. I'll be seeing you."
Herrick: "Will you Larry?"
Wilson: "I sure will."
Rios, tossing her head: "Ha! That's what you think!"

Cherokee Uprising

Monogram; 57 minutes; Producer: Vincent M. Fennelly; Director: Lewis D. Collins; Cast: Whip Wilson; Andy Clyde; Lois Hall; Sam Flint; Forrest Taylor; Marshall Reed; Iron Eyes Cody; Chief Yowlachie **

Not so much an uprising as a bunch of Redskins robbing wagons, killing settlers and handing their stolen property over to a gang who, in return, supplies them with hooch whiskey. By and large, Indians on the warpath didn't figure in these hour-long cheapo Westerns (too expensive), so the promising title doesn't deliver: What we have is Whip Wilson (Marshal Bob Foster) and Marshal Andy Clyde traveling to Canyon City, their mission to uncover the gang and stop the slaughtering—and that's just about it. Chief Yowlachie is friendly Injun Gray Eagle, helping out on Lois Hall's ranch; he receives an arrow in the back from bad Injun Iron Eyes Cody (Long Knife), while Clyde is eyed up as a possible husband by plump squaw Edith Mills (Strongbow). Indian agent Forrest Taylor is the brains behind the operation, Marshall Reed the corrupt sheriff helping him out and getting hammered by Wilson's lethal right fist and lash. In places, the deafening score threatens to overwhelm the few action sequences in a tired-looking oater, the series in urgent need of fresh impetus to keep it on the move.

Dialogue:

Clyde, staring at the bandits' homemade whiskey distillery: "There's enough of that stuff to take a bath in."

Wilson: "When did you start bathing?"

Outlaws of Texas

Monogram; 56 minutes; Producer: Vincent M. Fennelly; Director: Thomas Carr; Cast: Whip Wilson; Andy Clyde; Phyllis Coates; Terry Frost; Stephen Carr; Tommy Farrell; George DeNormand; Zon Murray ****

B-Western specialist Thomas Carr took over the driving seat in 1950's sixth entrant, coming up with one of Whip Wilson's more fully-rounded, cohesive efforts. Daniel B. Ullman's taut and very amusing script sticks to basics. U.S. Marshal Wilson (Tom Yeager) and U.S. Marshal Andy Clyde (Hungry) are on the trail of outlaws who are robbing stagecoaches of government bonds and cashing the notes in over the Mexican border; feisty cowgirl Phyllis Coates plays the gang leader, taking over the criminal life from her father, although it turns out that the real boss isn't her dad (he's been dead for three years) but bad guy Stanley Price. In order to infiltrate the gang, Wilson is "arrested" by Sheriff Stephen Carr (the director's brother) and "sprung" by Clyde; once in with the bunch, Wilson finds himself at odds with bruiser Zon Murray ("If you think you're tough, swing on me," growls Wilson) and sympathizing with "punk-kid" Tommy Farrell, picked on by Murray. There's a running gag concerning Clyde's voracious appetite ("When do you git to eat around here?") and Wilson more or less falls for Coates' stunning blonde charms ("We ain't got no time for romancin'," moans Clyde). Following an excitingly staged holdup at the Braxton Bank, Clyde shoots Murray, just about to gun down Wilson, and the whole bunch are eventually put behind bars after chief henchman Terry Frost has come off worse in a tussle with Whip. "We gotta fence to finish," says Wilson to Clyde who's just stuffed himself full of food, the outlaws herded onto a prison wagon to the sound of Edward J. Kay's mournful score, Wilson feeling regret at Coates and Farrell's wasted lives, hoping that they will eventually be reformed. A solid, entertaining Whip Wilson Western, nicely paced and decently acted; even the star of the show seems relaxed, spitting out one-liners of the Randolph Scott variety with ease.

Dialogue:
Wilson to Clyde: "Ah, Hungry, don't you ever get tired of eatin'?"
Clyde: "Ain't never have yet. If I ever do, I know I'm dead."

1951
Abilene Trail

Monogram; 54 minutes; Producer: Vincent M. Fennelly; Director: Lewis D. Collins; Cast: Whip Wilson; Andy Clyde; Tommy Farrell; Steve Clark; Dennis Moore; Marshall Reed; Lee Roberts; Noel Neill ****

Whip Wilson, as Dave Hill alias The Kansas Kid, and Andy "Sagebrush Charlie" Clyde are on the run from the law for a horse rustling crime they didn't commit. Tommy Farrell shows them a shortcut to avoid a posse, is badly wounded and taken into town by the wanted duo, to be patched up by the doctor. In gratitude, the lad points them in the direction of his father's ranch where the jobs of cattle hands are on offer; Steve Clark is trying to drive his herd to Abilene, but rival cattleman Bill Kennedy is employing roughhouse tactics to prevent Clark's beef from reaching Abilene ahead of his own, thus putting him out of business; this includes forcing the sheriff to jail Clark's wranglers on a trumped-up charge of rowdy behavior (the men are bailed out by Clyde using illegal Confederate money). In the bunkhouse, snarling foreman Lee Roberts faces up to Wilson, is knocked to the ground and defects to Kennedy's outfit after being sacked by Clark's tomboy daughter Noel Neill, Wilson now promoted to head trail ramrod. Roberts, Marshall Reed and Dennis Moore then harass the Clark herd, including starting a stampede, crafty Clyde (while Wilson's asleep) using Bullet to lead off Kennedy's horses—and unfortunately their own! Law officer Stanley Price and his boys ride up, Wilson and Clyde cleared of horse theft following a near-lynching by the Kennedy mob; they're arrested en masse, Roberts floored by Whip's fists and stinging lash. An amusing script from Harry L. Fraser (Clyde to Wilson: "I love stampedes. Could handle one every night and ride drag every day."), sparkling monochrome photography courtesy of Gilbert Warrenton and Edward J. Kay's thumping score make for an enjoyable Whip Wilson package still capable of thrilling cowboy-mad kids today.

Dialogue:
Roberts, coming to blows with Wilson: "I thought he was crawlin' out of the argument." Clyde: "He ain't be crawlin' since he cut his choppers with a six-gun."

Wanted: Dead or Alive

Monogram; 58 minutes; Producer: Vincent M. Fennelly; Director: Thomas Carr; Cast: Whip Wilson; Fuzzy Knight; Jim Bannon; Christine McIntyre; Leonard Penn; Lane Bradford; Zon Murray; Marshall Reed ****

Leonard Penn, leader of the Taggart gang operating out of Copper City, is arranging for high-ranking desperadoes to be broken out of jail, then ordering his henchmen to murder them and collect the bounty, amounting to thousands of dollars. To bust the racket, Whip Wilson poses as wanted outlaw Alan Mason and, together with Jim Bannon and Fuzzy "Texas" Knight, throws out a series of red herrings to bring Penn, hulking Lane Bradford and their outfit to justice. Gold Ace saloon owner Christine McIntyre

(Spangles Calhoun), girlfriend of the wanted man, cooperates with Whip as Penn is all for buying her out on the money, while Knight takes on the guise of a horse trader to gain the gang's trust. After Penn and his coyotes have been caught in a gunfight, McIntyre is reunited with her paroled feller. There's no dialogue (or Whip Wilson) in the movie's first five minutes which, together with Ernest Miller's dark photography, imparts a *noir* feeling to one of the better of the latter-day Whip oaters, Bradford in suitably menacing form.

Dialogue:
Knight's horse-selling banter to Bradford and company: "Yes, sir, gentlemen, every one of them is of genuine Arabian stock, the fastest horses that ever outran a posse, I, I mean the fastest horses that ever outran *anything*."

Trivia:
This particular scenario appeared in George Montgomery's *Last of the Badmen* (Allied Artists, 1957) and Audie Murphy's *Gunfight at Comanche Creek* (Allied Artists, 1963).

Canyon Raiders

Monogram; 54 minutes; Producer: Vincent M. Fennelly; Director: Lewis D. Collins; Cast: Whip Wilson; Fuzzy Knight; Phyllis Coates; I. Stanford Jolley; Marshall Reed; Riley Hill; Barbara Woodell; Jim Bannon **

A trio of crooks (I. Stanford Jolley, Marshall Reed and Riley Hall) is organizing the theft of ranchers' horses to enable their own herds plus those stolen to be sold to the army at a profit. Whip Wilson (he played himself for the remainder of the series) is an army agent sent to deal with the matter, settlers Fuzzy Knight and wife Barbara Woodell taking up residence in an abandoned homestead near Baxter Canyon but bullied off the property by Jolley and his varmints. Phyllis Coates is a very attractive sheriff, standing in for her father, Wilson aiding rancher Jim Bannon to retrieve his horses out of Baxter Canyon where they're corralled by the thieves as the army urgently needs remounts. A promising start bogs down in the last 25 minutes, the action almost grinding to a halt when Coates is kidnapped, leading to murky-looking scenes of Wilson trying to rescue the lass from a cabin and bring the criminals to justice. In the final few minutes, Wilson addresses the townsfolk, informing them that their horses will be returned and the army contracts with them honored. As for Knight, he can be allowed back to his homestead. Coates is lovely, Wilson sprightly but Knight's shenanigans at the card table aren't at all funny and Jay Gilgore's script fails to sizzle.

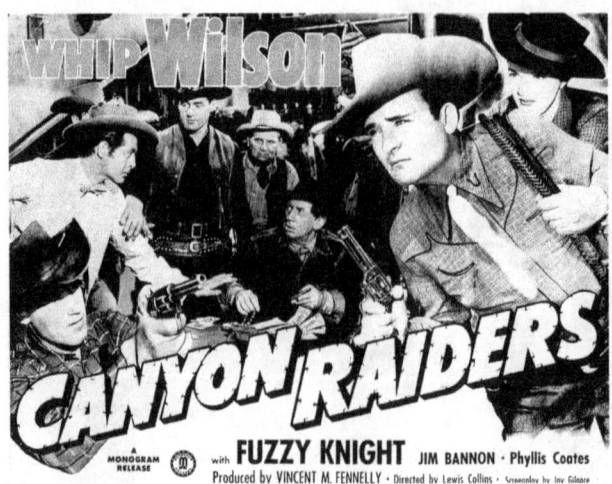

Dialogue:
Wilson to sexy sheriff Phyllis Coates: "By the way, it's a good thing there aren't too many law officers like you. I'd be in deep trouble *all* the time!"

Nevada Badmen

Monogram; 58 minutes; Producer: Vincent M. Fennelly; Director: Lewis D. Collins; Cast: Whip Wilson; Fuzzy Knight; I. Stanford Jolley; Jim Bannon; Phyllis Coates; Bill Kennedy; Marshall Reed; Lee Roberts ***

Cowhands Whip Wilson and Fuzzy Knight (Texas) plan to go off to California, but when boss Jim Bannon states that gold has been found on his brother's ranch at Opal Springs but no claim has yet been filed, the pair change their minds, pronto. Corrupt banker Bill Kennedy learns of the discovery via crooked express office agent I. Stanford Jolley; Bannon's brother is murdered, and Kennedy gives Bannon and niece Phyllis Coates 15 days to settle the ranch's debts, otherwise he will foreclose on the property and grab the gold strike for himself. To flush out Kennedy, Jolley and polecats Marshall Reed, Lee Roberts and Riley Hill, the ranch is put up for auction—the highest bidder obviously knows about the gold mine. Bannon bids the highest on purpose, Wilson letting slip to Kennedy that the $21,000 due will be on the Wild Oaks' stage; the stage is held up by Kennedy's bunch, the money found to consist of two-dollar notes and a quantity old ripped-up paper! Knowing their game is up, Kennedy, Jolley, Reed, Roberts and Hill attempt to light out but are arrested by Pierce Lyden and his posse. Coates receives $25,000 from the mint in exchange for gold nuggets, Knight (less of a buffoon than usual) painting "CWJT MINING CO." on a sign—Carol, Whip, Jim and Texas! Joseph O'Donnell's concise script and expert pacing contributes to an okay Wilson oater let down somewhat by a hurried ending—a shoot-out would have made all the difference.

Dialogue:
Knight, on hearing about the grubstake. "California? Sunshine? After we get the gold!"

Stagecoach Driver

Monogram; 56 minutes; Producer: Vincent M. Fennelly; Director: Lewis D. Collins; Cast: Whip Wilson; Fuzzy Knight; Jim Bannon; Sam Flint; Pierce Lyden; Leonard Penn; Gloria Winters; John Hart ***

Monogram's 56-minute version of the nascent Pony Express versus stagecoach lines is a fast-moving B-programmer, Whip and John Hart (both in buckskins), the

Pony Express riders, in friendly rivalry with Sam Flint's Prescott Stage Company. Elsewhere, crooked partners Leonard Penn and Pierce Lyden aren't so friendly, organizing the murder of Flint, pinning the crime on Jim Bannon, Flint's partner, plus running off Hart's supply of horses, to enable them to set up their own business at the expense of everyone else. A plethora of slugging matches between Whip and Lane Bradford, a protracted trial in which Bannon is acquitted of the killing of Flint and some hammy acting from all concerned, especially Gloria Winters, make for a decent Whip oater, the leading man only using his lash once. *Stagecoach Driver* moves briskly enough, but the suspect performances in many scenes lets it down on occasions.

Dialogue:

Fuzzy Knight (as Texas McGillicudy, blacksmith, lawyer and doctor) to Hart who wants his horse shod: "Why, all the old-timers around here knows that when Texas McGillicudy puts a shoe on a horse, the shoe never comes off."

Hart: "Didn't you shoe him the last time?"

Lawless Cowboys

Monogram; 58 minutes; Producer: Vincent M. Fennelly; Director: Lewis D. Collins; Cast: Whip Wilson; Fuzzy Knight; Jim Bannon; Pamela Duncan; Lee Roberts; I. Stanford Jolley; Bruce Edwards; Richard Emory ***

Whip Wilson is assigned to go undercover and find out those responsible for fixing events at the Central City Rodeo, whereby riders are bribed not to compete too hard, gamblers placing bets on the victors and raking in a profit. Lee Roberts employs rodeo cheat Marshall Reed, gunman Richard Emory and gambler Richard Avonde to deal with those crossing his route to riches, ace rider Jim Bannon aiding Whip to bust the scam wide open. Pamela Duncan, boss of the Bar Circle Ranch, also helps in bringing Roberts to heel, particularly as her banker boyfriend, Bruce Edwards, is in Robert's clutches, up to his eyes in debt to Roberts; she offers huge amounts of prize money to pull in the punters and thereby boost Roberts' saloon business. *Lawless Cowboys* is lively Western confection but dated in appearance, Wilson looking uncomfortably overweight and acting with a complete lack of charisma. It's left to Emory to carry the day as a cold-blooded killer and for Fuzzy Knight to clown around in 1930s-style as a newspaper editor forever on the hunt for a good story.

Dialogue:
Wilson to Bannon, on seeing Reed (Bannon's rival) ride out of town: "That's Paul Maxwell, isn't it?" Bannon: "Yuh. Good thing he didn't see me. A little hot for fightin' at high noon."

Stage to Blue River

Monogram; 56 minutes; Producer: Vincent M. Fennelly; Director: Lewis D. Collins; Cast: Whip Wilson; Fuzzy Knight; Phyllis Coates; Lee Roberts; Lane Bradford; John Hart; Pierce Lyden; I. Stanford Jolley ****

Masked raiders are attacking I. Stanford Jolley's stagecoaches on a regular basis in an effort by someone to prevent him from being issued with a lucrative U.S. mail contract. When Jolley is found murdered in a mining shack at Twin Rocks, undercover marshal Whip Wilson, Fuzzy Knight and Lee Roberts help Jolley's daughter, Phyllis Coates, to run the Blue River Stage Line on time in order to fulfill the franchise and root out the men responsible for her father's death. A postal inspector is due at any moment, Wilson needing to ensure that he makes it in one piece before the miscreants get up to any more tricks. Devious lawyer John Hart is one of the crooks behind the attacks, the others being Lane Bradford and Sheriff Pierce Lyden, the "Mister Big" of the operation; they're determined to grab the stage route as a means to rob it of gold shipments from the surrounding mines. The three no-goods are arrested at the end with their gang of coyotes after Wilson has laid a trap using a coded letter, used his whip, fists and six-shooters and driven a stage himself to prevent trouble; Coates is awarded her contract and gets doting Roberts into the bargain. Plenty of inventive action and gunfights plus Raoul Kraushaar's pumping score equate to a jaunty Wilson outing, surprising when you consider there were only four more to go in the series before Monogram pulled the plug.

Dialogue:
Lyden to Wilson and Knight following a saloon brawl: "I ought to jail you for disturbin' the peace." Knight: "Why, sheriff? Did we break up your afternoon nap?"

Westerns of the 1950s: The Classic Years 461

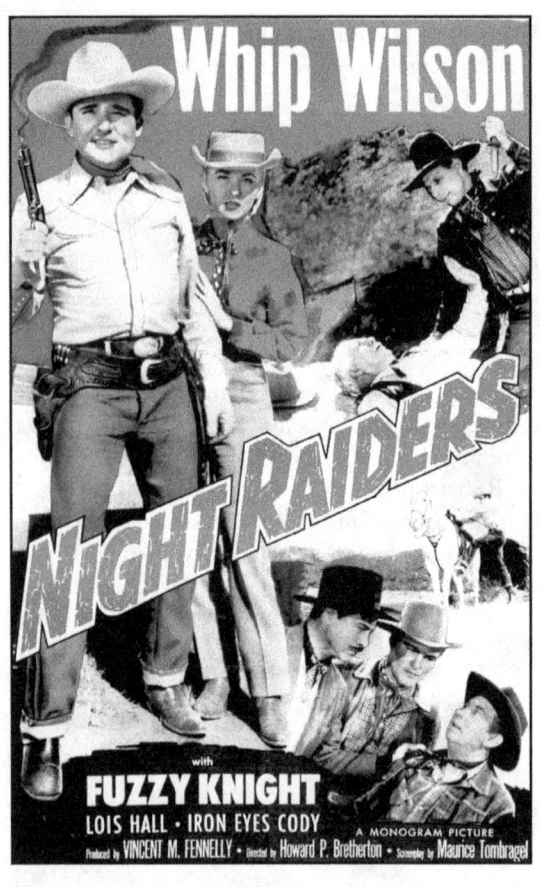

1952
Night Raiders

Monogram; 52 minutes; Producer: Vincent M. Fennelly; Director: Howard P. Bretherton; Cast: Whip Wilson; Fuzzy Knight; Lois Hall; Tommy Farrell; Terry Frost; Lane Bradford; Marshall Reed; Iron Eyes Cody **

Ranches are being ransacked by a group of masked raiders at night, but for what? Somewhere among the homesteads lies $10,000 stolen from a train holdup years back; Terry Frost, owner of the saloon in Bitter Springs, served four years for the robbery, one accomplice getting away, and he wants that loot plus the man who knows where it is. Enter Marshal Whip Wilson, Fuzzy Knight and Marshal Tommy Farrell who, following a series of so-so gunfights, unmask Frost as the criminal and Sheriff Marshall Reed his ex-accomplice, the cash buried in the vicinity of the Davis Ranch run by Lois Hall and Steve Clark. Not one of Wilson's finest hours, even by these cheapskate standards, the action static and bogged down by too much aimless chat; Raoul Kraushaar's noisy stock score fails to lift the picture out of its serial-type rut, and Whip only uses his deadly lash once.

Dialogue:
Frost to sidekick Lane Bradford, knowing that Wilson and Farrell are on his trail: "What's the latest way of getting rid of bloodhounds?"
Bradford: "The old way is still the best. Winchesters at 25 feet."

Trivia:
Howard P. Bretherton's final movie; he then concentrated on TV work before quitting the business in 1958.

The Gunman

Monogram; 52 minutes; Producer: Vincent M. Fennelly; Director: Lewis D. Collins; Cast: Whip Wilson; Rand Brooks; Fuzzy Knight; Phyllis Coates; Terry Frost; Lane Bradford; I. Stanford Jolley; Russ Whiteman ***

Outlaws rule the roost in Eagle Pass. Sheriff Russ Whiteman is powerless to do anything, being in protection racket boss Terry Frost's pocket, while newspaperman I. Stanford Jolley is under constant threat from Frost's prairie dogs, led by hulking

Lane Bradford, for daring to print inflammatory news. In rides Marshal Whip Wilson and buddy Rand Brooks from Texas, their mission to take Bradford across the border to stand trial for murder. When Whip learns about the town's lawlessness, Whiteman's ineptitude and the murder of homesteader Robert Bray, a possible replacement for the sheriff's job, he decides to nail Frost who's also a wanted man living under an alias, clean the place up and complete the job he came to Eagle Pass for in the first place. Fuzzy Knight plays Jolley's blabbermouthed assistant, unwittingly passing on information to Frost and his toughs, while ladies' man Brooks homes in on Jolley's daughter, pretty Phyllis Coates. There are a couple of vicious Wilson/Bradford saloon fistfights and a few shoot-outs before Whiteman realizes he's got a duty to perform as a peace officer and arrests Frost; Whip and Brooks escort Bradford over the border, Brooks promising to return to Coates' loving arms as soon as possible. A competently made B-Western, Wilson using his lash a bit more than usual and snarling heavy Bradford displaying a nice turn in Western villainy.

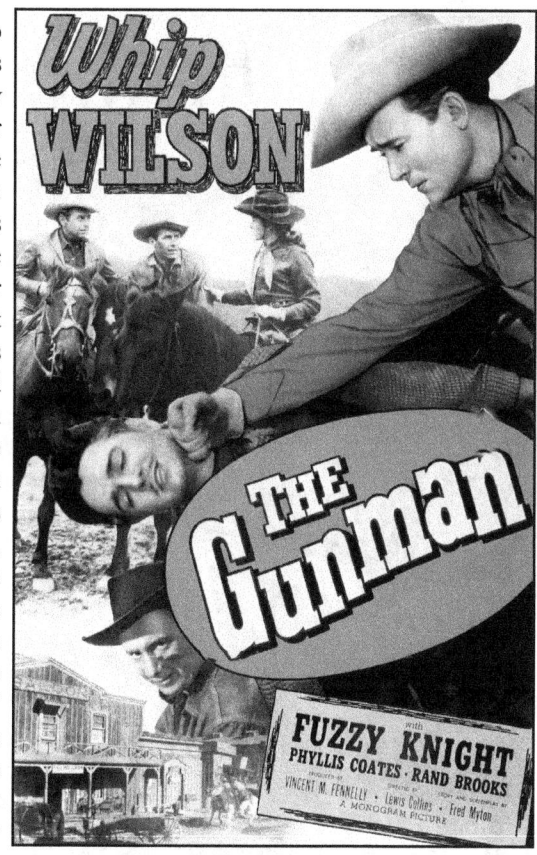

Dialogue:
Knight to Coates: "I think I'll, er, mosey out and get me a little fresh air."
Coates: "Be careful and don't get too much fresh air."
Knight: "Why Miss Anita, fresh air never hurt nobody."
Coates: "Well it does when it's 100 proof!"

Montana Incident

Monogram; 54 minutes; Producer: Vincent M. Fennelly; Director: Lewis D. Collins; Cast: Whip Wilson; Rand Brooks; Noel Neill; Peggy Stewart; William Fawcett; Hugh Prosser; Bruce Edwards; Lyle Talbot *****

Experienced Western writer Daniel B. Ullman was brought in to script what can be classed as a classic Whip Wilson oater concerning Whip and skirt-chasing buddy Rand Brooks (no Fuzzy Knight around) playing surveyors for the Central Valley Railroad Company. The company wishes to build a railroad through a cattle-rich valley and Martinsville, but landowner Hugh Prosser is against the idea; he owns the town lock, stock and barrel, viewing the railway as a threat to him monopolizing the area.

Daughter Noel Neill sides with Whip and especially Brooks, as does crusty homesteader William Fawcett; however, Neill's older sister, ambitious Peggy Stewart, decides to run things her way, first trying to bribe Wilson to reroute the rail line 80 miles south through Cactus City (it fails) and then sending out masked thugs to upset the surveyors' plans and schedules, and wreck their surveying instruments. Stewart verges on the psychotic, eventually going against Prosser's wishes (and the government project) by planning the wholesale massacre of Whip, Brooks and their guards; two of her assassins are brought down in a shoot-out and the rest surrender, leaving the dark-haired devil riding off to rendezvous with banker boyfriend Bruce Edwards who has stolen the bank's cash in order for the pair to start a new life together. But the dame has other plans, plugging Edwards; as she rummages in his saddlebags for the money, he summons up enough strength to blast her in the back before expiring, both corpses sprawled in the dust. The end sees a locomotive steaming through the valley; Prosser is a happy man and so is Brooks, having bagged Neill. Ullman's intelligent script is topped off by Raoul Kraushaar's low-key score, Ernest Miller's deep monochrome photography and Lewis D. Collins' taut, carefully orchestrated direction—even Whip, at this late stage in his career, is in commanding form, while Brooks makes a great sidekick, amusing but never silly. As stated, a Whip Wilson classic!

Dialogue:
Wilson to Brooks, seeing his pal swivel the surveying telescope in the direction of Neill: "I don't want to disturb you or anything, but your 'scope is pointed the wrong way."
Brooks: "Uh uh, that's what you think. Come here, take a look."

Wyoming Roundup

Monogram; 53 minutes; Producer: Vincent M. Fennelly; Director: Thomas Carr; Cast: Whip Wilson; Tommy Farrell; Phyllis Coates; Robert J. Wilke; Richard Emory; I. Stanford Jolley; Henry Rowland; House Peters, Jr. ****

The end of the trail for Whip Wilson and not a bad picture to go out on. Touches of imagination from director Thomas Carr, a standard Raoul Kraushaar ear-blasting musical background, decent photography from Ernest Miller and Charles Van Enger and the addition to the cast of Robert J. Wilke, one of the genre's classiest of all Western baddies. He's a killer hired by merchant House Peters, Jr. who wants to put small ranchers out of business and stir up a range war between Henry Rowland, boss of the "B" Bar H Ranch, and fellow rancher I. Stanford Jolley to enable him to get his hands on Rowland's spread. To complicate matters, Jolley's son, Richard Emory, is romancing Rowland's daughter, Phyllis Coates. Wilson and Tommy Farrell are hired as town marshals when Wilke murders the sheriff in the opening scene, Wilson laying down a "No Guns" policy and becoming suspicious of Peters and saloon owner Lyle Talbot. Peters organizes the rustling of Rowland's beef which are skinned for their hides, prompting Rowland and Jolley to join forces and write a letter to the governor explaining the trouble they're experiencing; the mail bag containing the vital letter is taken in a stage holdup; it shows Peters that his game is up. In a tense climax, Peters and his boys, using Farrell as hostage, storm Rowland's ranch; in a prolonged gunfight, Peters shoots Wilke by mistake, Emory wounds the merchant and the whole gang surrenders. The film finishes with Wilson laughing his head off, unable to drag Farrell, who's lost his pants, out from under the ranch house.

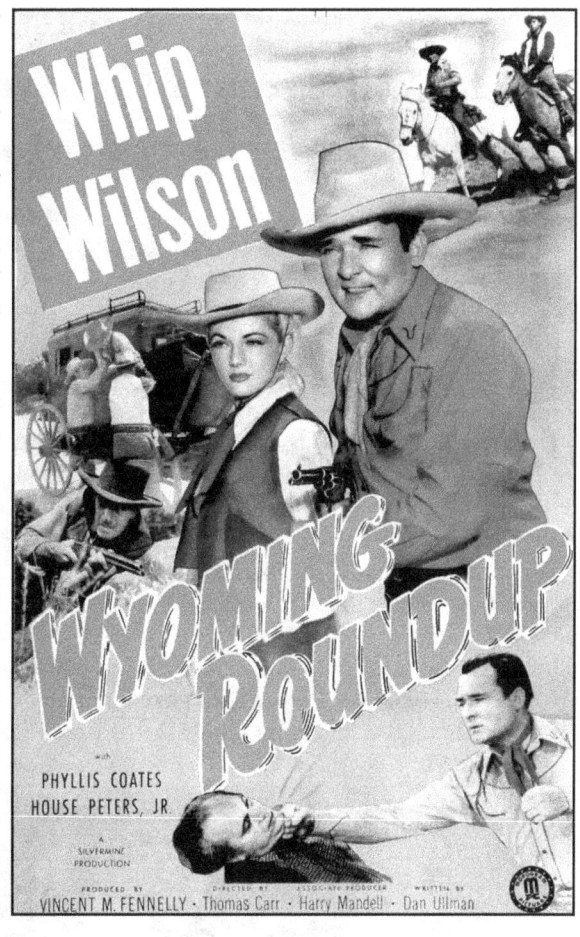

Dialogue:
Farrell to Wilson, about to fetch grub for imprisoned Wilke: "You mean we're gonna feed *that*? What for?"
Wilson: "Ah, we gotta keep him strong enough to walk to the scaffold."

Trivia:
Wilson was minus his trademark whip, Farrell later joking that Monogram sold it to finance the production.

Chapter 18
The Classics: *High Noon, Shane, The Searchers* and *Rio Bravo*

The cinematic hothouse atmosphere of the 1950s was responsible for giving birth to four definitive Westerns that were not only classics of the genre but transcended their chosen genre, becoming classics of cinema per se: *High Noon* (United Artists, 1952), *Shane* (Paramount, 1953), *The Searchers* (Warner Bros., 1956) and *Rio Bravo* (Warner Bros., 1959). Other Westerns have come close to achieving that status, but none have figured in the Hollywood Hall of Fame to such a degree as these four illustrious examples of moviemaking. Although embodying very recognizable Western tropes (the honest lawman up against town cowardice and bigotry; the mysterious gunman coming to the aid of homesteaders under a tyrannical cattleman's thumb; a revenge mission triggered by Indian atrocities), these renowned titles, by sheer professionalism and star power alone, elevated the sagebrush saga to new heights, directors Fred Zinnemann, George Stevens, John Ford and Howard Hawks each producing a cinematic work of art that, in their own individual way, have survived the decades and have *never* been bettered for breadth of vision, templates of how any motion picture should be put together for maximum and everlasting impact; a quartet of out-and-out five-star durable masterpieces that Western lovers and filmgoers visit time and time again.

High Noon, produced by Carl Foreman and Stanley Kramer on a budget of $730,000, eventually grossed $18,000,000 worldwide and won four Oscars: Gary Cooper

(Best Actor); Elmo Williams and Harry W. Gerstad (Editing); Dimitri Tiomkin (Score); Dimitri Tiomkin and Ned Washington (Best Song); it narrowly missed out on Best Picture to Cecil B. DeMille's colorful but empty *The Greatest Show on Earth*. Cooper was 50 at the time of filming, suffering from hip trouble and stomach ulcer problems, hence the grim, sweaty lines etched on his face (Coop eschewed the use of make-up in the movie in the name of realism). He was also 29 years older than leading lady Grace Kelly but the two formed a satisfactory, if somewhat passionless, match. Fred Zinnemann and writer Foreman created a pressure-cooker atmosphere by setting the chain of events in "real time" over the space of 85 minutes (slightly adrift overall, but who noticed?), the pared-to-the-bone production

Belgian poster for *High Noon*

shot in cut-glass black-and-white by Floyd Crosby with not a single second wasted. On his wedding day, Marshal Will Kane, having handed in his badge, is informed that killer Frank Miller (Ian MacDonald) has been released from prison and is on the train to Hadleyville, set to pull in at noon. At the station, cohorts Lee Van Cleef, Robert J. Wilke and Sheb Wooley lounge and grumble in the blistering heat, awaiting the arrival of their revenge-driven boss, all four bent on getting rid of Cooper. After the marriage ceremony, Cooper (officially no longer town marshal) and new bride Kelly ride off in their buggy, but the lawman has a fit of conscience, turning back ("I've got to go back. I've never runned!"), pinning on his badge, strapping on his gun belt and asking Hadleyville's morally bankrupt citizens to help him combat the four gunslingers, to no avail ("I'm not tryin' to be a hero. I've got to stay," Cooper explains to his anxious wife). In a screenplay packed with spineless characters putting self-preservation before civic duty, Deputy Lloyd Bridges, romancing Cooper's ex, fiery Katy Jurado, quits his job; Judge Otto Kruger, responsible for placing MacDonald behind bars, races out of town like a scared rabbit; many are of the opinion that Hadleyville was a boom town when MacDonald was around anyway; an appeal to the church congregation for deputies falls on deaf ears; ex-marshal Lon Chaney's hands are riddled with arthritis, so he can't help ("Get outta town, Will. It's all for nothin'."); Mayor Thomas Mitchell tells Cooper to leave, stating that a gunfight would spoil the town's image ("It's our problem, Will. I think you better go."); the one person deputized, James Millican, throws in the towel on realization that nobody else has volunteered; and, to cap it all, Kelly, a Quaker, decides to board the noonday train to escape the turmoil, much to Jurado's disgust ("If he was my man, I would get a gun."). Coop, a worried, vulnerable man, prowls the emptying sidewalks to the haunting refrains of Tex Ritter singing "Do Not Forsake Me, Oh My Darlin'" (the song is thought to have contributed to *High Noon*'s enormous commercial success and critical high standing), while Zinnemann includes, at frequent intervals, close-ups of clock faces, their second hands ticking away towards the fateful 12 o'clock; he also uses ground-level and full frame shots and rapid crosscut editing to maximize the mounting tension. Town drunk William Newell and 14-year-old Ralph Reed are the only two with guts enough to assist Cooper, but their requests are turned down. As noon approaches, Tiomkin's evocative music rises to a crescendo, abruptly broken by the blast of the locomotive's whistle as it pulls in at the station where Kelly and Jurado are waiting. MacDonald alights and joins his companions, Zinnemann's famous overhead crane shot highlighting Cooper utterly alone in a deserted street, a truly moving moment. What follows is a suspenseful nine-minute cat-and-mouse showdown, Cooper dropping Wooley first, then Van Cleef; Kelly leaves the train, running to her husband's aid and blasting Wilke in the back from a shop window. In a standoff, MacDonald grabs Kelly; she struggles, and Cooper puts two slugs into his foe. As the townsfolk come out of hiding and converge on Cooper and Kelly, the marshal looks at them with disdain; throwing his badge into the dirt, he turns on his boot heels and rides out of Hadleyville with his bride, well away from the town and its self-righteous townsfolk.

It's well documented that John Wayne hated *High Noon* and its occasionally *noir*-style look, labeling it "Un-American" by "not showing Americans promoting patriotic values"; they should have "got behind their town peace officer," he argued, not ignored him. The film was also seen as a dig at Hollywood refusing to stand up to Senator Joseph McCarthy's Communist witch-hunts of the period, scriptwriter Foreman blamed and blacklisted for several years. Gregory Peck also bemoaned the fact that he turned down the role of Will Kane, calling it the biggest career mistake of his life, later admitting that, "I couldn't have done a better job than Cooper anyway." In 2008, *High Noon* was voted the second greatest Western of all time, one place behind *The Searchers*; above all else, it serves as a reminder of Hollywood icon Gary Cooper's exceptional easygoing talents and screen magnetism. One-tone delivery, a pained expression throughout, a masterclass in how to create something immortal in an understated, effortless manner; Coop didn't have to act the part of Will Kane, he *was* Will Kane, everyone's heart going out to him (yes, men, boys *and* women) as his six-foot-three lean frame patrolled those friendless streets to "do what a man's gotta do," backed by that insidious tune. Cooper earned his Oscar by being himself—how many of today's performers could pull *that* off? *High Noon* is grounded in the man's legendary performance. Trivia: In his movie debut, Van Cleef was rejected for Bridges' part because of his crooked nose but, as compensation, managed to appear in the opening scene, standing beside a tree, waiting for Wilke and Wooley to turn up. And in that bruising stable fight with Bridges, Cooper refused a stunt double, ending up slightly worse for wear. "The Western grown up," crowed the critics, heaping well-deserved praise on *High Noon*, the *New York Times* adding "A Western to challenge *Stagecoach* for the all-time championship."

Alan Ladd may well have stood at five-foot-six, but his stature filled those boots nicely and made him appear twice the size in George Stevens' *Shane*, an inspirational forerunner to the Spaghetti Man With No Name sagas that would surface from Europe a dozen years later (plus a few of Clint Eastwood's movies, *Pale Rider* being a prime example). Ladd starred as a lone gunfighter, materializing out of the wilderness (location filming took place in Wyoming's lofty Grand Teton Range) and befriending homesteader Van Heflin, wife Jean Arthur and 10-year-old Brandon De Wilde. Heflin and the surrounding settlers (sneeringly referred to as sodbusters) are being terrorized by ruthless cattleman Emile Meyer and his sidewinders; Meyer wants the "squatters" off what he terms *his* open range and employs satanic gun hawk Jack Palance to do his dirty work (screen heavy Jack Elam rejected the role, a decision he lived to regret). When Palance shoots dead ex-Confederate Elisha Cook, Jr. in the muddy town street, Ladd reverts to his old ways, preventing Heflin from tackling Palance and getting killed by carrying out the deed himself in one of the genre's finest saloon showdowns. Realizing his past won't let him settle down, Ladd rides off into the hills, De Wilde's "Come back Shane!" echoing across the plains (and the auditorium) as his hero disappears into the night.

Budgeted at $3,000,000 and grossing $20,000,000, Stevens' Technicolored masterpiece won a single Oscar for Loyal Griggs' cinematography; how Victor Young's glorious score, one of the most instantly recognizable Western title themes ever composed, didn't receive an award is a mystery. Among other things, *Shane* is all about the hero-worship of a young boy towards a man of unknown background and few words who has been kicking around far more than his father, scriptwriters A.B. Guthrie, Jr. and Jack Sher emphasizing this point throughout the 118-minute running time. From the moment De Wilde sets eyes on the buckskin-clad stranger, he idolizes him, following him around, eyeing his revolver and fancy studded belt, sensing that here is a person who can look after himself in every situation. Arthur also eyes Ladd with more than passing interest, especially when he strips to the waist and tackles a stubborn tree stump with Heflin. But Ladd gives nothing away about his past. "It's a long story, Joey," he tells the boy, saying to Arthur, "A gun is as good or as bad as the man using it" when she objects to her son being taught how to shoot. Ladd, perhaps, is the man De Wilde would like as a father; to Arthur, he's the man she would take as a lover,

Italian photobusta for *Shane*

something Heflin senses when the two dance at a July 4th celebration party and get a tad too close for his liking.

Scenically, the movie scores heavily, the drama played out under a vast sky and those mighty, mist-wreathed mountain peaks filmed in bright sunlight; even the animal shots fall far short of Disney family cuteness. Highlights include a seven-minute mass saloon brawl to end them all, Ben Johnson realizing he has picked on the wrong person, Ladd, to call "sody pop"; Ladd, sipping water and circling Palance at Heflin's homestead like a rattlesnake about to strike; a moving funeral sequence, a dog whining when his master's coffin is lowered into the ground; little Elisha Cook facing up to Palance without a chance in hell of outdrawing him, thunder rolling ominously over the mountains; Ladd and Heflin's set-to, the pair tussling under the hooves of panicking horses; and the lengthy finale, Ladd dressed in his buckskins and riding out to confront Palance, De Wilde and his dog hot on his heels. "We'll never see you again?" says Arthur to Ladd before he departs. "Never is a long time, Marian," he answers. "Take care of yourself," she replies, tears in her eyes, a touching few minutes in a film strong on varying emotions. As stated, the showdown between Ladd and Palance is a beauty. Entering Grafton's saloon (Young's music lowers to a menacing drone), Ladd sidles up to the bar, two customers quickly walk out, and he challenges Meyer about the homesteaders' rights, putting him straight; he then turns to Palance, sat in a corner drinking coffee. Palance slowly rises, hands hovering over twin gun butts, a cowed dog slinking off, aware of the killer's evil presence.

Palance: "I wouldn't push too far if I was you."
Ladd: "So you're Jack Wilson."
Palance: "What's that mean to you, Shane?"
Ladd: "I've heard about you."
Palance: "What have you heard, Shane?"
Ladd, staring the gunslinger out: "I've heard that you're a lowdown Yankee liar."
Palance, smirking: "Prove it."

Ladd does, emphatically; in an explosion of gunfire, Palance, Meyer and John Dierkes lie dead amid saloon wreckage. "I gotta be going," Ladd tells De Wilde. "We want you Shane," cries the distraught youngster. "There's no goin' back," replies the loner before riding away, De Wilde's shouts receding in the distance as he canters into the heights.

Belgian poster for *Shane*

Westerns of the 1950s: The Classic Years 471

Voted number three in the 2008 "Greatest Westerns of All Time" list, *Shane* also pleased the critics, *Variety* enthusing "socko drama of the early West," the *New York Times* chipping in with "another great Western. Magnificent." Yes, magnificent is the appropriate word, Stevens' simple drama of frontier life elevated to classic immortality by Ladd's quiet, charismatic gunfighter, De Wilde's charming hero-struck kid, Palance's "devil incarnate" gunslinger, eye-catching landscapes and a beautiful, elegiac score; a film that you never tire of watching as the years go by.

Acknowledged as the genre's number one Western; voted the seventh best film of all time in 2014; lauded by illuminati such as David Lean, Steven Spielberg and Martin Scorsese; John Wayne's personal favorite; raking in $19,000,000 at the box-office on a budget of $3,750,000; and not a single Oscar to its name: John Ford's *The Searchers* has had volumes written about it, from the awesome Monument Valley scenery (both in Arizona and Utah) shot in VistaVision (photographer: Winton C. Hoch), to Ford's artistic framing of dim interiors contrasting with harshly lit exteriors (used throughout), to Frank S. Nugent's insightful script (from Alan Le May's novel) and to Wayne's key performance, as towering as those mighty sandstone cliffs that dwarf the action taking place. Put into context beside the 400 plus Westerns contained within this volume, why is Ford's masterpiece so revered? After all, it tackles the same ground and themes that a lot of other cowboys versus Indians sagas cover. The answer lies in Ford's undisputed expertise and knowledge of the genre, his use of light and shade, of the way in which he places his characters in vast empty panoramic settings over the course of 119 minutes, of once-in-a-lifetime roles from all concerned, in Max Steiner's fabulous score and in the way the movie is constructed for maximum effect, especially the first enthralling 45 minutes.

Steiner's music blasts out over the main title before seguing into the Sons of the Pioneers singing "The Ballad of the Searchers." It's 1868 and Civil War veteran Wayne (as Ethan Edwards) returns to the family homestead after eight years where, in a series of near-silent vignettes, we are made aware of a past relationship between him and Dorothy Jordan, his brother's (Walter Coy) wife; their mutual glances, her stroking his army greatcoat with undisguised fondness, gentle touches and a kiss on the brow; all point to an unspoken love. Wayne is one mean hombre with a dubious past, again conveyed by few words when Texas Ranger/reverend Ward Bond arrives, worried about

Indians spotted in the area ("You wanted for a crime, Ethan?" he asks. "You fit a lot of descriptions."); he also loathes Redskins ("Well, I could mistake you for a half-breed," Wayne barks to Jeffry Hunter at the meal table, glowering at the youngster who's eighth Cherokee). When Wayne and company are lured away from their homesteads by the slaughter of John Qualen's prize bulls, the former Confederate spells it out straight: "This is a murder raid." Wayne's family (Coy, Jordan and nephew Robert Lyden) are massacred, nieces Debbie (Lana Wood; she *could* be Wayne's daughter) and Lucy (Pippa Scott) abducted, kicking off the initial hunt for Chief Scar (Henry Brandon) and his Nawyecka Comanches. For this next section, Ford piles on the dramatics, manufacturing a series of pulsating mini-climaxes, akin to operettas, punctuated by Steiner's forceful music: the discovery of the buried Indian (the moment when Wayne shoots out the corpse's eyes was in recent years excised from prints shown on British television); Wayne reporting on his reconnaissance mission, grudgingly bowing to Bond's order ("If you're wrong, don't ever give me another!"); the pursuers finding a burned-out Indian campfire, leading to the picture's (and Western cinema's) most famous line from Wayne of "That'll be the day" in response to Bond's questioning, "You wanna quit, Ethan?"; the Comanche attack by the river (including that wonderful shot of the Redskin patrol filing past a gigantic mesa); Wayne, Hunter and Harry Carey, Jr. forging on ahead; Carey challenging Wayne to a fight if he mentions Lucy and Debbie as being possibly not alive; Wayne's discovery of Lucy's violated body in a remote canyon; Carey, learning of Lucy's gruesome death, riding into Scar's camp and getting killed; and a reflective scene in the snow, Hunter turning to Wayne: "Well, why don't you say it. We're beat and you know it," the reluctant partners having lost the scent.

Yes, that opening, breathless 45 minutes is, from a film student's point of view, nigh on faultless, an exercise in powerhouse Western dynamics that knows no equals, orchestrated for in-your-face impact by a master craftsman at the peak of his powers. The narrative then settles down (and needed to, audiences of the time in a state of high tension), becoming episodic as Wayne and Hunter begin their relentless search for Debbie, spread over five years; in Wayne's case, the hunt is one of almost inhuman persistence. Ford chucks in a few amusing interludes to lighten the mood (Hunter taking a

Belgian poster for *The Searchers*

bath, sweetheart Vera Miles fussing over him; Hunter's sham marriage to Comanche squaw Beulah Archuletta; doddery Hank Worden yearning for a rocking chair; and Hunter and Ken Curtis scuffling in the dust at Miles' wedding ceremony—to Curtis). But the tone still remains serious: Wayne shooting three men in the back, out to steal his gold; Hunter realizing that Wayne is a driven man, bent on killing Debbie after she's found because, in Wayne's eyes, the girl is tainted goods; and a harrowing sequence in an army camp, Wayne viewing with open disgust women driven crazy by "living with bucks." ("They ain't white anymore. They're Comanch," he spits). The absolute highlight of this second half occurs after 78 minutes, Wayne and Hunter entering Scar's camp in New Mexico territory to the sound of

Italian poster for *The Searchers*

low, pounding drums, an edgy sequence oozing in intimidation; prey entering the lion's den ("Medicine country, huh?" Wayne says). The drums cease, Ford's camera pans back, then zooms in, Brandon emerging from his wigwam, face impassive; Wayne glares and Hunter looks overawed. Brandon is introduced to the pair as Cicatriz; six-foot-four Wayne sidles up to his six-foot-five enemy and eyeballs him, one of filmdom's greatest standoffs. "Scar, eh? Plain to see how you got yer name." Brandon, visibly rattled, bites back: "You, Big Shoulders. Young One—He Who Follows." Wayne sneers: "You speak good American—for a Comanch. Someone teach ya?" Debbie (Natalie Wood) makes her appearance inside the wigwam, later warning Hunter off, Hunter having to warn *Wayne* off as "Big Shoulders," gun in hand, goes to shoot Wood. Eventually, in a climactic skirmish with the Comanches led by Bond ("How many do you figure?" Bond says to Wayne. "About a dozen each. Enough to go around," is the terse response), Hunter rescues Wood from Brandon's tepee, firing three slugs into the chief. For good measure, Wayne scalps Brandon after Bond's detachment has stormed the savages' camp and, in the touching ending, returns Wood to Qualen's family home, Hunter at long last hitching up with Miles. In one of the most moving of all cinema fadeouts, Wayne stands outside the door in bright sunshine, alone and rootless; slowly turning, his job done, he ambles off with that distinctive gait, the door closing behind him, leaving the screen in darkness.

Ford's "Homeric Odyssey," as expected, drew favorable critical response. Wayne's performance was "uncommonly commanding" wrote the *New York Times*, *Variety* stating "A Western on the grand scale ... handsomely mounted in the tradition of *Shane*." "Distinguished," commented the *New York Herald Tribune*, while *Newsweek* added "remarkable." Visually arresting to the level of cinematic poetry, *The Searchers* is a vivid reminder of Old West times and values and of John "Duke" Wayne's star turn: His Ethan Edwards represents an embittered, tough, friendless figure of heroic solitude tempered with fleeting glimpses of humanity; a deeply rewarding study of racial hatred and obsession. Wayne, in this as in other pictures, was Wayne; never was the Hollywood cowboy legend more imposing in the saddle than in this enduring Western.

Spanish poster for *Rio Bravo*

John Wayne's fourth Western outing of the 1950s was Howard Hawks' leisurely *Rio Bravo*, a direct counter-response to the black-and-white realism of *High Noon* in that it portrayed the "lone sheriff against outlaws" scenario in a more positive *American* light, according to Wayne (Gary Cooper found the movie "phoney and unbelievable," a barbed riposte to Wayne's acid comments on *High Noon*). Budgeted at over $2,000,000, the picture, shot in arid Old Tucson, went on to gross around $15,000,000 worldwide; it was particularly popular on the Continent, especially in Italy, Spain and Greece, also playing continuously in the United Kingdom years after release (the picture was reissued in London in 1974). Initially thought too long at 141 minutes by many film writers and generally misunderstood, the length didn't deter the paying public who were totally entranced by the five colorful main characters involved: Wayne's stalwart Sheriff John T. Chance; Dean Martin's reformed drunk, Dude; Ricky Nelson's

> In his younger days as a *Cahiers du Cinema* critic, Jean-Luc Godard wrote, "How can I hate John Wayne ... and yet love him tenderly ... in the last reel of *The Searchers*?"—referring to the scene when Wayne scoops Wood up in his arms and says: "Let's go home Debbie..."
>
> Godard would later list *The Searchers* as his fourth favorite American sound film.

Westerns of the 1950s: The Classic Years

| JOHN WAYNE | DEAN MARTIN | RICKY NELSON | RIO BRAVO | ANGIE DICKINSON · WALTER BRENNAN WARD BOND · JOHN RUSSELL TECHNICOLOR® from WARNER BROS. |

cocksure young gunfighter, Colorado; Angie Dickinson's slinky, sexy Feathers; and, most of all, Walter Brennan's marvelous, forever complaining deputy, Stumpy. Jules Furthman and Leigh Brackett's script gave garrulous, curmudgeonly Brennan some of the picture's best lines, an Oscar-worthy performance if ever there was one, in strong contrast to the sometimes awkward Wayne/Dickinson relationship which the Duke, at 51, felt uncomfortable with (Dickinson was 27). Many fans thought the pair's romantic tussles held up the excitement (although there was plenty of it at the end), but *Rio Bravo* wasn't really about all-out action, concentrating more on character study and mood, and in this respect, Hawks' unhurried-paced horse opera scored highly; you became so wrapped up in what these people were doing and how everything was going to pan out to such an extent that the overall lack of gunplay didn't matter that much.

Hawks begins with a three-minute silent sequence, Wayne tracking down Claude Akins who has cold-bloodedly shot a man in a saloon for butting in when he's just hit Martin, suffering from drink pangs. Akins is slugged and put behind bars, prompting brother John Russell and his men to make life difficult for Wayne and deputies Martin and Brennan, holed up in jail awaiting the arrival of the U.S. marshal. Dickinson, a card-playing beauty, turns up on the stage, adding pressure on Wayne who's got enough on his plate without finding those flashing, come-on eyes and shapely legs totally irresistible; this leads to a series of typical Hawks male/female sparring sessions. When old pal Ward Bond is murdered by one of Russell's paid killers, self-assured gunman Nelson (Wayne and Hawks rejected Elvis Presley for the role, Hawks going on to state that Nelson's teen appeal added $2,000,000 to box-office takings) is eventually deputized; Martin conquers his craving for booze, Brennan, limping around on set, huffs and puffs and the whole entertaining shebang ends in a famously explosive eight-minute set piece, Wayne, Nelson and Martin, aided by Brennan's lethal shotgun, going head-to-head with Russell's gang on the outskirts of town. Their hideout is dynamited after a prolonged shooting match, leaving Wayne to take up with Dickinson while Martin and Nelson patrol the streets.

Dimitri Tiomkin's atmospheric title theme and score (Wayne cited the composer as one of his favorites), including snatches of music the composer would use in *The Alamo* a year later, contains two catchy tunes, "Cindy" and "My Rifle, My Pony and Me," engagingly sung in the jailhouse by Nelson, Martin and Brennan. Great snatches of dialogue include Bond talking to Wayne: "A game-legged old man and a drunk. That's all you got?" Wayne: "That's *what* I got!" Later, Martin goes to have a drink, then pushes the bottle away, Brennan griping bitterly: "Bring it out. Put it back. Nobody ever ask me if I needed a drink. Well, I ain't gonna wait for 'em to ask me 'cos I do. You two's enough to drive a man to it." "Old cripples ain't wanted," he grumbles when Wayne tells him he isn't to take part in the final shoot-out (but he does), and Wayne gets a few sharp lines for himself: "You want that gun, pick it up. I wish you would," he snarls to a cowpoke after Martin has brought down Bond's murderer. "Alright Joe. You can start walking very slow. And stop if I say stop. Or I'll stop you," Wayne growls to Akins as the outlaw prepares to be swapped for captive Martin. "A Big, Brawling Western," commented *Variety*, the *New York Times* stating, "a celebration of taking it easy." Now cited as one of the most important American motion pictures ever made (it frequently appears in that 2008 top Western list), *Rio Bravo* sucks you into its border town world with its acutely observed conflicting dramas; like a good book, the film can be viewed and treasured for what it is, a carefully paced, timeless classic of Hollywood old-school cinema containing a truly unforgettable star turn from 64-year-old Walter Brennan; and big John Wayne is at his most iconic. (On a personal note, I caught *Rio Bravo* in September 1965 in Piraeus, Greece, double billed with, of all things, Jesús Franco's *The Awful Doctor Orloff*, the most bizarre pairing of movies I have ever encountered in a lifetime of going to the cinema.)

German poster for *Rio Bravo*

Film Titles

Johnny Mack Brown—**JMB**
Wild Bill Elliott—**WBE**
Tim Holt—**TH**
Allan Lane—**AL**
Whip Wilson—**WW**

Abilene Trail 1951 (**WW**)
Across the Wide Missouri 1951
Al Jennings of Oklahoma 1951
Alias Jesse James 1959 (**Bob Hope**)
Along the Great Divide 1951
Ambush 1950
Ambush at Cimarron Pass 1958
Ambush at Tomahawk Gap 1953
Apache 1954
Apache Ambush 1955
Apache Drums 1951
Apache War Smoke 1952
Apache Warrior 1957
Apache Woman 1955
Arizona Manhunt 1951
Arizona Territory 1950 (**WW**)
Arrowhead 1953
At Gunpoint 1955
The Badge of Marshal Brennan 1957
The Badlanders 1958
Badlands of Montana 1957
Badman's Gold 1951
Bandit Queen 1950
Bandits of the West 1953 (**AL**)
Barricade 1950
The Battle at Apache Pass 1952
The Battles of Chief Pontiac 1952
Bend of the River 1952 (**James Stewart/Anthony Mann**)
Best of the Badmen 1951
The Big Country 1958

The Big Land 1957
The Big Sky 1952
The Big Trees 1952
Bitter Creek 1954 (**WBE**)
The Black Dakotas 1954
Black Hills Ambush 1952 (**AL**)
The Black Lash 1952
Blackjack Ketchum, Desperado 1956
Blazing Bullets 1951 (**JMB**)
Blood Arrow 1958
Bonanza Town 1951
Border Fence 1951
Border Outlaws 1950
Border Rangers 1950
Border Treasure 1950 (**TH**)
Born to the Saddle 1953
Branded 1950
The Brass Legend 1956
The Bravados 1958
Broken Arrow 1950
The Broken Star 1956
Buckaroo Sheriff of Texas 1951
The Buckskin Lady 1957
Buffalo Bill in Tomahawk Territory 1952
Bugles in the Afternoon 1952
Bullwhip 1958
The Burning Hills 1956
The Bushwhackers 1951
California Conquest 1952
California Passage 1950
Canyon Ambush 1952 (**JMB**)
Canyon Raiders 1951 (**WW**)
Captive of Billy the Kid 1952 (**AL**)
Cattle Queen 1951
Cattle Queen of Montana 1954
Cattle Town 1952

Cave of Outlaws 1951
The Charge at Feather River 1953
Cherokee Uprising 1950 (WW)
Chief Crazy Horse 1955
City of Bad Men 1953
Code of the Silver Sage 1950 (AL)
Cole Younger, Gunfighter 1958
Colorado Ambush 1951 (JMB)
Colorado Ranger 1950
Comanche 1956
Comanche Territory 1950
The Command 1954
Conquest of Cochise 1953
Copper Canyon 1950
Copper Sky 1957
Covered Wagon Raid 1950 (AL)
Cow Country 1953
Cowboy 1958
Crooked River 1950
Curse of the Undead 1959
Dakota Incident 1956
Dallas 1950
The Dalton Girls 1957
The Daltons' Women 1950
Daniel Boone, Trail Blazer 1956
A Day of Fury 1956
Day of the Bad Man 1958
Day of the Outlaw 1959
Dead Man's Trail 1952 (JMB)
Desert of Lost Men 1951 (AL)
Desert Passage 1952 (TH)
Desert Pursuit 1952
The Desperado 1954
Desperadoes' Outpost 1952 (AL)
The Desperados Are in Town 1956
Devil's Canyon 1953
Devil's Doorway 1950
Distant Drums 1951
Dragoon Wells Massacre 1957
Drango 1957

Drum Beat 1954
Drums in the Deep South 1951
Duel at Apache Wells 1957
Dynamite Pass 1950 (TH)
The Eagle and the Hawk 1950
El Paso Stampede 1953 (AL)
Escape from Fort Bravo 1953
Escape from Red Rock 1957
Escort West 1958
Face of a Fugitive 1959
Fancy Pants 1950 (Bob Hope)
The Far Country 1954 (James Stewart/Anthony Mann)
The Far Horizons 1955
Fargo 1952 (WBE)
Fast on the Draw 1950
The Fastest Gun Alive 1956
Fence Riders 1950 (WW)
The Fiend Who Walked the West 1958
The Fighting Lawman 1953
Five Guns West 1955
Flaming Frontier 1958
Flesh and the Spur 1956
Fort Bowie 1958
Fort Defiance 1951
Fort Dobbs 1958
Fort Dodge Stampede 1951 (AL)
Fort Vengeance 1953
Fort Yuma 1955
Forty Guns 1957
The Forty-Niners 1954 (WBE)
Four Fast Guns 1959
Frisco Tornado 1950 (AL)
From Hell to Texas 1958
Frontier Gambler 1956
Frontier Gun 1958
The Frontier Phantom 1952
The Furies 1950
Fury at Gunsight Pass 1956

Westerns of the 1950s: The Classic Years   **479**

Fury at Showdown 1957
Ghost Town 1956
Gold Fever 1952
Good Day for a Hanging 1959
Great Day in the Morning 1956
The Great Jesse James Raid 1953
The Great Missouri Raid 1951
The Great Sioux Uprising 1953
Gun Brothers 1956
Gun Fever 1958
Gun for a Coward 1957
Gun Fury 1953
Gun Glory 1957
The Gun that Won the West 1955
Gun the Man Down 1956
Gunfight at Indian Gap 1957
Gunfight at the O.K. Corral 1957
The Gunfighter 1950
Gunfighters of Abilene 1959
Gunfire 1950
The Gunman 1952 (**WW**)
Gunman's Walk 1958
Gunmen from Laredo 1959
Gunmen of Abilene 1950 (**AL**)
Gunplay 1951 (**TH**)
Gunslinger 1956
Gunslingers 1950 (**WW**)
Gunsmoke in Tucson 1958
The Half-Breed 1952
The Halliday Brand 1957
The Hanging Tree 1959
The Hangman 1959
The Hard Man 1957
Hell Canyon Outlaws 1957
Hell's Crossroads 1957
Hiawatha 1952
Hidden Guns 1956
High Lonesome 1950
High Noon 1952 (**The Classics**)
The Homesteaders 1953 (**WBE**)

Hondo 1953
Horizons West 1952
The Horse Soldiers 1959
Hostile Country 1950
Hot Lead 1951 (**TH**)
I Killed Geronimo 1950
I Killed Wild Bill Hickok 1956
I Shot Billy the Kid 1950
The Indian Fighter 1955
Jack Slade 1953
The Jayhawkers! 1959
Jesse James vs. the Daltons 1954
Jesse James' Women 1954
Joe Dakota 1957
Johnny Concho 1956
Jubal 1956
Jubilee Trail 1954
Kansas Territory 1952 (**WBE**)
The Kentuckian 1955
Kentucky Rifle 1955
The Kid from Broken Gun 1952
King of the Bullwhip 1950
The Last Frontier 1955
The Last Hunt 1956
Last of the Comanches 1953
Last of the Desperados 1955
The Last of the Fast Guns 1958
The Last Outpost 1951
The Last Posse 1953
Last Stagecoach West 1957
Last Train from Gun Hill 1959
Law and Order 1953
Law of the Badlands 1951 (**TH**)
Law of the Panhandle 1950 (**JMB**)
The Law vs. Billy the Kid 1954
The Lawless Breed 1952
Lawless Cowboys 1951 (**WW**)
Leadville Gunslinger 1952 (**AL**)
The Left Handed Gun 1958
Little Big Horn 1951

The Lone Ranger 1956
The Lone Ranger and the Lost City of Gold 1958
Lone Star 1952
Lone Texan 1959
The Lonely Man 1957
The Lonesome Trail 1955
The Longhorn 1951 (**WBE**)
A Lust to Kill 1958
A Man Alone 1955
The Man from Bitter Ridge 1955
Man from Del Rio 1956
The Man from Laramie 1955 (**James Stewart/Anthony Mann**)
Man from Sonora 1951 (**JMB**)
The Man from the Alamo 1953
Man from the Black Hills 1952 (**JMB**)
Man of the West 1958
Man or Gun 1958
Man with the Gun 1955
Man Without a Star 1955
The Marksman 1953
The Marshal of Cedar Rock 1953 (**AL**)
Marshal of Heldorado 1950
The Marshal's Daughter 1953
The Marauders 1955
Massacre 1956
Massacre Canyon 1954
The Maverick 1952 (**WBE**)
The Maverick Queen 1956
The Missourians 1950
Mohawk 1956
Money, Women and Guns 1958
Montana 1950
Montana Belle 1952
Montana Desperado 1951 (**JMB**)
Montana Incident 1952 (**WW**)

Montana Territory 1952
The Moonlighter 1953
My Outlaw Brother 1951
The Naked Dawn 1955
Naked Gun 1956
The Naked Hills 1956
The Naked Spur 1953 (**James Stewart/Anthony Mann**)
The Nebraskan 1953
Nevada Badmen 1951 (**WW**)
New Mexico 1951
Night Raiders 1952 (**WW**)
Night Riders of Montana 1951 (**AL**)
Northwest Territory 1951
Oklahoma Justice 1951 (**JMB**)
The Oklahoma Woman 1956
The Old Frontier 1950
Only the Valiant 1951
Oregon Passage 1957
The Oregon Trail 1959
The Outcast 1954
The Outcasts of Poker Flat 1952
Outlaw Gold 1950 (**JMB**)
Outlaw Women 1952
The Outlaw's Daughter 1954
Outlaw's Son 1957
Outlaws of Texas 1950 (**WW**)
Over the Border 1950 (**JMB**)
Overland Pacific 1954
Overland Telegraph 1951 (**TH**)
Passage West 1951
The Peacemaker 1956
Pillars of the Sky 1956
Pistol Harvest 1951 (**TH**)
Plunderers of Painted Flats 1959
Pony Express 1953
Pony Soldier 1952
The Proud Ones 1956
Quantez 1957
Quantrill's Raiders 1958

The Quiet Gun 1957
Quincannon, Frontier Scout 1956
The Raid 1954
Raiders of Old California 1957
Rails into Laramie 1954
Rancho Notorious 1952
Raton Pass 1951
Rawhide 1951
The Rawhide Trail 1958
The Rawhide Years 1955
Rebel City 1953 (**WBE**)
Rebel in Town 1956
Red Mountain 1951
The Redhead and the Cowboy 1951
The Redhead from Wyoming 1953
Reprisal! 1956
The Restless Breed 1957
The Return of Jack Slade 1955
Return to Warbow 1958
Revolt at Fort Laramie 1956
The Ride Back 1957
Ride, Vaquero! 1953
Rider from Tucson 1950 (**TH**)
Riders of the Range 1950 (**TH**)
Riders of Vengeance 1952
Rio Bravo 1959 (**The Classics**)
Rio Grande 1950
Rio Grande Patrol 1950 (**TH**)
Road Agent 1952 (**TH**)
The Road to Denver 1955
Rock Island Trail 1950
Rocky Mountain 1950
Rose of Cimarron 1952
Rough Riders of Durango 1951 (**AL**)
The Rough, Tough West 1952
Run for Cover 1955
Run of the Arrow 1957
Rustlers on Horseback 1950 (**AL**)
Saddle Legion 1951 (**TH**)

Saddle the Wind 1958
Salt Lake Raiders 1950 (**AL**)
Saskatchewan 1954
The Savage 1952
Savage Frontier 1953 (**AL**)
The Savage Horde 1950 (**WBE**)
The Searchers 1956 (**The Classics**)
The Secret of Convict Lake 1951
Seminole 1953
Seven Guns to Mesa 1958
Shane 1953 (**The Classics**)
Shark River 1953
The Sheepman 1958
The Showdown 1950 (**WBE**)
Showdown at Abilene 1956
Showdown at Boot Hill 1958
Siege at Red River 1954
Sierra Baron 1958
Sierra Passage 1950
Silver Lode 1954
Silver Raiders 1950 (**WW**)
The Silver Star 1955
Singing Guns 1950
Sitting Bull 1954
Six Gun Mesa 1950 (**JMB**)
Smoke Signal 1955
Smoky Canyon 1952
Son of Belle Starr 1953
Son of Paleface 1952 (**Bob Hope**)
Son of the Renegade 1953
Springfield Rifle 1952
Stage to Blue River 1951 (**WW**)
Stagecoach Driver 1951 (**WW**)
Stagecoach to Fury 1956
The Stand at Apache River 1953
Star in the Dust 1956
Storm Over Wyoming 1950 (**TH**)
The Storm Rider 1957
Stranger at My Door 1956
Streets of Ghost Town 1950

The Sundowners 1950
The Tall Men 1955
The Tall Texan 1953
Target 1952 (**TH**)
Taza, Son of Cochise 1954
Tennessee's Partner 1955
Tension at Table Rock 1956
Texas City 1952 (**JMB**)
Texas Lawmen 1951 (**JMB**)
They Rode West 1954
Three Desperate Men 1951
Three Hours to Kill 1954
3:10 to Yuma 1957
Three Violent People 1956
Thunder in the Sun 1959
Thunder Over Arizona 1956
Thunder Pass 1954
Thundering Caravans 1952 (**AL**)
The Thundering Trail 1951
The Tin Star 1957
Tomahawk 1951
Tomahawk Trail 1957
Topeka 1953 (**WBE**)
Track of the Cat 1954
Trail Guide 1952 (**TH**)
Trail of the Rustlers 1950
Treasure of Ruby Hills 1955
Tribute to a Bad Man 1956
The True Story of Jesse James 1957
Two Flags West 1950
Two-Gun Lady 1955
Two Guns and a Badge 1954
Untamed Frontier 1952
The Vanishing Outpost 1951
The Vanishing Westerner 1950
The Vanquished 1953
Vengeance Valley 1951
Vera Cruz 1954
Vigilante Hideout 1950 (**AL**)
Vigilante Terror 1953 (**WBE**)

The Violent Men 1955
Waco 1952 (**WBE**)
Wagon Master 1950
Wanted: Dead or Alive 1951 (**WW**)
War Arrow 1953
War Drums 1957
War Paint 1953
Wells Fargo Gunmaster 1951 (**AL**)
West of the Brazos 1950
West of Wyoming 1950 (**JMB**)
Westward the Women 1951
Whistling Hills 1951 (**JMB**)
White Feather 1955
The White Squaw 1956
Wild Heritage 1958
Wild Stallion 1952
Winchester '73 1950 (**James Stewart/Anthony Mann**)
Woman They Almost Lynched 1953
The Wonderful Country 1959
Wyoming Mail 1950
Wyoming Renegades 1955
Wyoming Roundup 1952 (**WW**)
The Yellow Mountain 1954
Yellowneck 1955
Yellowstone Kelly 1959
Young Daniel Boone 1950
The Young Guns 1956
The Young Land 1959
Yukon Vengeance 1954